THE LETTERS OF
THOMAS MOORE

THE LETTERS OF
THOMAS MOORE

EDITED BY
WILFRED S. DOWDEN

VOLUME II

1818–1847

OXFORD
AT THE CLARENDON PRESS
1964

Oxford University Press, Amen House, London E.C.4

GLASGOW NEW YORK TORONTO MELBOURNE WELLINGTON
BOMBAY CALCUTTA MADRAS KARACHI LAHORE DACCA
CAPE TOWN SALISBURY NAIROBI IBADAN ACCRA
KUALA LUMPUR HONG KONG

PRINTED IN GREAT BRITAIN

PR
5056
.A58
2

CONTENTS

Boden Taylor 1977

†

LIST OF PLATES

LIST OF REFERENCES

THIS list includes the principal works used in the preparation of this edition. Other references are cited in the notes with an abbreviated title or by the name of the author or editor.

Allgemeine Deutsche Biographie, Leipzig, 1875–1912.

Biographie Universelle, Paris, 1854–8.

Burke's Peerage, Baronetage and Knightage, London, 1956.

Cambridge Bibliography of English Literature, Cambridge, 1941.

Coleridge, Ernest Hartley, ed., *The Works of Lord Byron: Poetry*, London, 1898–1904. 7 vols. (Cited in the notes as Byron, *Poetry*.)

Collins's Peerage of England, edited by Sir Egerton Brydges, London, 1812.

Dictionary of American Biography, New York, 1928–58.

Dictionary of National Biography, London, 1917–59.

Halévy, Élie, *A History of the English People in the Nineteenth Century*, London, 1949–52. 6 vols.

Jones, Frederick L., ed., *The Letters of Mary W. Shelley*, Norman, 1946. 2 vols.

Jones, Howard Mumford, *The Harp that Once—: a Chronicle of the Life of Thomas Moore*, New York, 1937.

Lavisse, Ernest, *Histoire de France Contemporaine: depuis la Révolution jusqu'à la Paix de 1919*, Paris, 1921. 10 vols.

Lecky, W. E. H., *A History of England in the Eighteenth Century*, London, 1919–25. 7 vols.

Lippincott's Pronouncing Biographical Dictionary, New York, 1930. 5th edition.

Macmanus, M. J., *A Biographical Hand-List of the First Editions of Thomas Moore*, Dublin, 1934.

Marchand, Leslie, *Byron: a Biography*, New York, 1957. 3 vols.

Moore, Doris Langley, *The Late Lord Byron*, London and New York, 1961.

Moore, Thomas, *Letters and Journals of Lord Byron: with Notices of His Life*, London, 1830. 2 vols.

Moore, Thomas, *The Poetical Works*, edited by A. D. Godley, Oxford, 1924. (Cited in the notes as *Poetry*.)

Moore, Thomas, *The Poetical Works, Collected by Himself*, London, 1841–2. 10 vols.

Moore, Thomas, *The Works of Lord Byron: with His Letters and Journals, and His Life*, London, 1834. 17 vols.

Neue Deutsche Biographie, Leipzig, 1953.

Nouvelle Biographie Generale, Paris, 1860.

Prothero, Rowland E. (Lord Ernle), ed., *The Works of Lord Byron: Letters and Journals*, London, 1898–1901. 6 vols. (Cited in the notes as *LJ*.)

List of References

Russell, Lord John, ed., *The Memoirs, Journal and Correspondence of Thomas Moore*, London, 1853–6. 8 vols.

Strong, L. A. G., *The Ministrel Boy: a Portrait of Tom Moore*, London, 1937.

Webster's Biographical Dictionary, Springfield, Mass., 1943.

LIST OF LETTERS

(ix)

List of Letters

List of Letters

List of Letters

(xiii)

List of Letters

List of Letters

Letter	Date	Recipient	Page
928	10 May	Lord Dudley	692
929	14 June	Unknown	694
930	17 June	Mary Shelley	694
931	June	Unknown	695
932	6 August	John Murray	695
933	6 September	C. Fitzsimon	696
934	20 September	Sir Charles Morgan	697
935	5 October	John Murray III	698
936	10 October	John Murray III	698
937	15 October	Sir John Doyle, Bt.	699
938	21 October	John Murray III	700
939	27 October	John Murray	701
940	27 October	James Power	702
941	October	Samuel Rogers	703
942	24 November	Lord John Russell	703
943	1 December	John Murray	704
944	3 December	John Murray	705
945	7 December	Marquess of Lansdowne	705
946	8 December	John Murray	708
947	12 December	John Murray	708
948	12 December	Unknown	708
949	19 December	John Murray	709
950	22 December	Lady Morgan	709
951	31 December	John Murray	711
952	1830	John Murray	711

1831

Letter	Date	Recipient	Page
953	13 January	Unknown	712
954	31 January	John Murray	712
955	6 February	John Murray	713
956	9 February	W. M. Robinson	714
957	10 March	Arthur O'Connor	714
958	21 March	Arthur O'Connor	716
959	25 March	Mary Shelley	718
960	15 April	Arthur O'Connor	719
961	19 April	Colonel Houlton	719
962	21 April	John Murray III	720
963	2 May	Unknown	720
964	8 May	James Crissy	721
965	19 May	John Murray	721
966	20 May	John Murray	723
967	27 May	John Murray	723
968	May	John Murray III	724
969	25 June	Mary Shelley	725
970	8 July	D. F. Ryan	725
971	19 July	Lord Brougham	726
972	20 July	Lord Brougham	727
973	25 July	D. F. Ryan	727
974	19 August	Macvey Napier	728
975	1 September	Macvey Napier	728

(xvii)

List of Letters

List of Letters

List of Letters

List of Letters

List of Letters

Undatable Letters

List of Letters

Appendix

563. *To Leigh Hunt*

B.M. Add. MS. 37210, f. 176

Sloperton Cottage, Devizes
October 10, 1818

My dear Hunt— I intended that a letter from me should accompany your Copy of the 7ᵗʰ Number of my Melodies; but I rather think, from your paper of Sunday last,[1] that Power has had the start of me, and I only write now in order to get a little credit from you for my *intentions,*—which in general, indeed, are the best thing about me, but which unfortunately the matter-of-fact people of the world are never satisfied with—as *you* have imagination, however, as well as heart, I shall leave you to fancy all the kind things I have felt towards you, during the long, long time I have passed in saying nothing whatever about them—and, I am the more inclined just now to trust a good deal to your imaginative power as I am disabled from writing much by a slight strain in shoulder, which I received the night before last—when the world was near being a bad part out of pocket by the upsetting of the carriage in which I was return-ing from Bowood—

Shall you be in London about the latter end of November? I hope to be there at that time and we *must* meet for I have much to say to you—much to *give & receive* sympathy about. I suppose you have heard of the calamity that has befallen me, through the defalcation of my deputy at Bermuda, who has made free with the proceeds of two or three ships & cargoes deposited in his hands,[2] & I am likely to be made responsible for the amount—you will, it is most probable, have an opportunity of returning my *prison visits;* as, if it comes to the worst, the Rules must be my residence— However (as I have just written to Lord Byron) *unity* of *Place* is one of Aristotle's *Rules*, and, as a Poet, I must learn to conform to it— By the bye, he has made many enquiries about you in his two last letters to me, and I should be glad to hear from you, before I write to him again— I hope you will like my Irish Melodies better than you did Lalla Rookh—

You were right about the verses to H. Lowe.[3]

Yours, my dear Hunt, very truly
Thomas Moore

---

[1] 'A *seventh* number of the *Irish Melodies* has just appeared,—the more delightful from it's [*sic*] being unexpected.' The *Examiner*, 4 Oct. 1818, p. 631.

[2] See letter No. 535 to Lady Donegal, 2 Apr. 1818. The usual assumption is that Moore's deputy sold one ship and cargo, the total amounting to about £6,000.

[3] On 6 Sept. 1818 Moore recorded in his diary, 'The "Examiner" quoted

564. *To Mary Godfrey*

Russell, ii. 140, no. 398

Sloperton Cottage
Sunday, Oct. 11. 1818.

I have only time to write you a few words, in order to take advantage of a parcel I am sending to Power; but you shall have more anon. The tone of your letter has saddened me not a little,—Lady Donegal in bad health, and *you* evidently not at all in spirits; this is sad work, and I wish from my soul I could do anything to mend it. As for myself, it is not true that there has occurred anything to darken the gloom of my Bermuda prospects: on the contrary, since I received your letter, I have had one from Bermuda of rather a comfortable nature, as, in the first place, it assures me of my having a man of respectability there (to whom I applied), ready and willing to look after my interests; in the next place, it gives me intelligence that my deputy has not absconded from the island, which I rather feared; and, in the third place, it informs me that he has some property, which I much doubted.

Rogers is expected here soon. I have not time for another word. Ever yours,

T. Moore.

565. *To Mary Godfrey*

Russell, ii. 141, no. 399

Saturday, Oct. 24. 1818.

My dear Mary,

All's safe and well; our darling Bessy is, at this moment, lying snug and smiling, with a little *boy* in her arms![1]

I have not time for a word more, as I am writing dispatches in all directions. God bless you, my dearest Mary. Ever yours,

T. Moore.

some lines to "Sir Hudson Lowe," which I had sent to Perry, and added, "We think we can recognize whose easy and sparkling hand it is." I wonder he found me out.' (Russell, ii. 183.) Sir Hudson Lowe (1769–1844) was Governor of St. Helena from 1815–21. See *Poetry*, p. 567.

[1] Thomas Lansdowne Parr, Moore's first son.

PLATE 4

THOMAS MOORE at Forty by Thomas Phillips

566. *To James Power*

Yale

Thursday Night Oct^r [31] 1818*

My dear Sir— Many thanks for your congratulations—[1] We are getting on as well as we could expect, though Bessy is not quite so stout to-day and yesterday as she has been— I want to trouble you to send me some good butter-biscuits, and some rusks, when you are making up another parcel, which, I dare say, will be next week—

I have been kept in such a state of anxiety lately that I have not been able to do any thing—but I hope, as soon as Bessy is quite recovered, to return to my operations.

Best regards to Mrs Power & Jane from Bessy.

Yours ever
Thomas Moore.

I find that Wilkie & Murray are coming down to me about my Sheridan Work— If *you* & the Longmans were to join the party, I should be finely beset!

567. *To William Lisle Bowles*

Rice University

Saturday [*c.* October 1818]

My dear Bowles— If you have not made up your mind to go to Houlton's on Tuesday, it will be just as well for me (in the way of *business*, though certainly not of pleasure) to defer leaving home till Wednesday, when, if you can take me to Bath, 'have with you.' If you have, however, screwed your courage up for Tuesday, I should be the last to balk such a noble inclination, & am equally ready to hold myself at your service for Houlton's. Only let me know, *either* way & believe me

Ever yours.
T. Moore

568. *To Mary Godfrey*

Russell, ii. 141, no. 400

Sunday, Nov. 8. 1818.

My dear Mary,

I address you thus familiarly, because I am about to do a very familiar and (I am afraid, you will think) *too* friendly thing by you; and that is, to make you godmother to our little Johnny Newcome. It is Bessy's wish; and as it makes no *additional* tie between us (for I am sure you feel quite as much interested about me and mine as

[1] On the birth of his son. See letter No. 565, to Mary Godfrey, 24 Oct. 1818.

if you 'were ten times our (god) mother'), why, I don't see any great objection you can have to the ceremony. Your *compères* are Lord Lansdowne and Dr. Parr, so that, as far as Greek and nobility go, you will be in good company.

I am glad you are returning to your own *couleur-de-rose* state of mind again, and hope our dear Lady D. will continue well enough to *keep* you in it. Poor Bess is not so stout as she was at first; her efforts to suckle the little hero do not well agree with her, and I am afraid she must give it up. God bless you ever. Your gossip,

T. M.

569. *To Alicia Lefanu*

Russell, viii. 251

Sloperton Cottage, Devizes
Dec. 21. 1818.

Dear Miss Lefanu,

It was a little unlucky that I did not receive your letter in London, from which I am but just returned, as I could then have requested you to send your manuscript up instantly, and presented it myself in Paternoster Row. As it is, I think the surest as well as speediest way will be for you to forward it immediately by the coach, directed to Messrs. Longman, and I shall lose no time in preparing them to receive it.[1] As they must be your ultimate judges (at least before publication), it would be, perhaps, but a waste of time to let *me* have the previous perusal of the manuscript, however gratifying and flattering such a reference to my judgment might be. In all this, however, I shall be guided entirely by your wishes, and if it be your desire that I should look over the work before it is submitted to them, you have but to forward it to me by the coach, as you did the papers relative to your uncle. But I must repeat that as the booksellers are to be your grand jury, either to find the bill or throw it out, you had perhaps better, in the first instance, send the manuscript to them, and you may depend upon my backing it with all the recommendations which my opinion of your talents, as well as my warm interest in yourself, incline me to give it. I am sorry to tell you that the interference of Burgess and the creditors has produced such a hitch in our *Sheridan* affairs as I fear will be fatal to their further progress.

With best regards to Mr. and Mrs. L., believe me,

Faithfully yours,
Thomas Moore.

[1] See letter No. 560, to Mrs. Lefanu, 16 Sept. 1818.

570. *To Leigh Hunt*

B.M. Add. MS. 37210, f. 174

Sloperton Cottage, Devizes
Janu^r 21st 181[9][1]

My dear Hunt— Having the opportunity of a frank, I must write you a line or two to thank you for your very kind notices of me, and still more to express regret that, in my short & busy visit to town I had not the happiness, to which I looked forward, of passing at least one day with you & your family. I am always so thrown 'in medias res' when I go to London, that I have never a minute left for any thing agreeable—but my next visit will, I hope, be one of pleasure, and then you are *sure* to be brought in among the ingredients. For the cordiality with which you have praised & defended me I am, I assure you, most deeply grateful, and, though less alive, I am sorry to say, both to praise & blame than I used to be, yet coming from a heart and a taste like yours, they cannot fail to touch me very sensibly. You are quite right about the conceits that disfigure my poetry; but you (& others) are quite wrong in supposing that I *hunt* after them—my greatest difficulty is to *hunt them* away— If you had ever been in the habit of hearing Curran converse—tho I by no means intend to compare myself with him in the ready coin of wit—yet from the tricks which his imagination played him while he talked, you might have some idea of the phantasmagoria that mine passes before me while I write— In short St. Antony's temptations were nothing to what an Irish fancy has to undergo from all its own brood of will-o-th'-wisps and hobgoblins.[2]

I was sorry to see that Cobbet found such a sturdy defender in your correspondent of last week—[3] indeed I am grieved to the heart

---

[1] Moore made an understandable mistake in dating this letter, writing '1818' instead of '1819'. The text obviously refers to the article cited in note No. 2 below.

[2] A review of the Seventh Number of the *Irish Melodies* was begun in the *Examiner*, no. 575 (3 Jan. 1819), p. 11, and concluded in no. 577 (17 Jan. 1819), pp. 43–44. The article is on the whole favourable, and the only critical note struck is that which Moore cited: 'The faults of these, like the rest of all Mr. Moore's writings, are a tendency to repeat the same images, and now and then (arising perhaps from a consciousness of this) an elaborate hunting after others.' Hunt also defends Moore against the charge of licentiousness.

[3] The defence of Cobbett is a lengthy letter in the *Examiner*, no. 577, pp. 34–39. The writer, who signs himself 'No Partisan', defends Cobbett in an affair involving a debt to Sir Francis Burdett. An exchange of letters between the two was published in the *Examiner*, no. 575, pp. 3–6, indicating that Cobbett, though willing to pay the debt, thought he should be considered an 'insolvent debtor'. Hunt sided with Burdett and indicated that Cobbett's actions toward Sir Francis were vindictive. The writer of the letter in defence of Cobbett objects to the publication of private correspondence and notes six matters on which Cobbett's actions were misconstrued in the *Examiner*.

at many things I see among the friends of Liberty, and begin to fear much more harm from the advocates of the cause than from its enemies— You, however, are always right in *politics*— &, if you would but keep your theories of religion & morality a little more to yourself (the mania on these subjects being so universal & *congenital*, that he who thinks of curing it, is as mad as his patients) you would gain influence over many minds that you now unnecessarily shock & alienate. I would not say this of you in public (for *I* cannot review my friends) but I say it to you thus privately with all the anxious sincerity of a well-wisher both to yourself & the cause you so spiritedly advocate. I intended to have written you a long letter, but the post-*belle* (an old woman whom I employ for that purpose) is ringing her alarum below & I must finish.

My best regards to Mrs Hunt.

Yours very faithfully
Thomas Moore

571. *To Thomas Wilkie*

B.M. Add. MS. 29764, f. 32

March 4th 1819

My dear Sir— I have been in some anxiety about Mrs Moore's health for these two or three days past, in consequence of a mistake made by her servant in giving a wrong medicine, or I should have answered your letter sooner— It gives me, I assure you, much pain to be obliged to disappoint, in some degree, the impatience you feel for the appearance of our work— But, in addition to the more enlarged scale & more serious responsibility which our new plan of a quarto has brought with it, I have found it necessary to re-model, if not wholly re-write, all the early part of the life, in consequence of a new view I have had reason to take of Sheridan's motives in some of the transactions related— All this, together with the necessity, that is continually occurring, of making enquiries and ascertaining dates & circumstances, will make it a much more tedious business than even I had, myself, foreseen, and I very much doubt whether it will be possible to put it to Press before the latter end of Autumn— You may be sure that my finances are by no means such as not to render the receipt of so many hundreds as I am to have for this work a sufficient stimulus to my hastening its completion— But I wish to make it as good & authentic as all the talents & industry I am capable of can effect, & this, I assure you, cannot be done in a hurry—as I think it possible the advance of £100, which you have made me, may somewhat inconvenience you, it is my intention as soon as possible to send you a draft for the sum, with my best thanks at the same time for the accommodation.

Yours, my dear Sir, very truly
Thomas Moore

572. *To William Lisle Bowles*

Harvard

March 9th 1819*

My dear Bowles— Do you mean to be at the Harmonic on the 19th?—if you do, and can take me, I shall be most happy to accompany you—[1] Let me know

Yours most truly
Thomas Moore

573. *To John Murray*

Sir John Murray

Post Office, Devizes
Thursday March 25 1819

My dear Sir—

I find the Bank here will not give me cash for a Bill at three months; I have, therefore, for the present, drawn for £100 at two months, which I hope will not be inconvenient to you—

When you talk of sending up the MS. that is ready, you frighten me—for I shall not have a sheet fit to venture to Press till the middle of Autumn, *at the soonest*. I must have two or three weeks rummaging in London, among those who knew Sheridan—such as Peter Moore, Lord J. Townshend &c. &c. & for this purpose shall be up in May.

C[rib][2] is certainly 'd——d low'— As for myself, I have cut all that kind of thing, and mean (seriously) never to attempt another line of humour or satire in my life—for to have such ricketty things laid at one's door is too bad—

Ever yours
T. Moore.

[1] See the diary for 19 Mar. 1819 (Russell, ii. 279). Moore and Bowles attended the 'Harmonic'.
[2] Probably a reference to *Tom Crib's Memorial to Congress*, which appeared in March 1819.

574. *To William Linley*[1]

Robert H. Taylor

Sloperton Cottage
April 8th 1819.

My dear Sir— I do not know that I have ever been more flattered than I am by the anxiety which you express for my opinion of your music, and humility is such a rare virtue in this world that I am afraid you will hardly believe me when I say that I should, long ere this, have told you how much your compositions had delighted me, could I have persuaded myself that my praises were of much value to you— But I am well aware, whatever your partiality may have attributed to me, that my real *knowledge* of music is very limited, and though I *feel* it deeply, I am by no means entitled to take a critic's station by either praising or blaming, or, at least, giving *reasons* why I like or dislike. It was this consciousness, I assure you, that made me rest satisfied with *enjoying* the compositions you sent me, without running the risk of exposing my own ignorance to you, by any remarks upon the peculiarity of their style or merits. I can only say that 'Ariel's Adieu' is now not my *only* favourite, and that many of your melodies (such as 'Fair Leila, gentle, young & fair') are among the first that come to my lips, when I sing to please *myself*. I hope, when we meet in the summer, to convince you that (though I own I am too much given to the *sensual* part of music, and that its intellectual graces too often escape me) such good music as yours is not wholly thrown away upon me.

The 'Life'[2] is in full progress again, & I have promised to let Murray have it in the course of the Autumn— It is my intention to go to town next month, & make a complete & final search among all the surviving friends of *Sheridan* for any remaining *memorabilia* I may be able to glean—a task, in which I trust I may look for your kind assistance.

Believe me, my dear Sir, very truly yours,
Thomas Moore.

[1] Although the name of the addressee does not appear on the letter, he is obviously William Linley, as is shown by the following entry in Moore's diary for 6 and 7 Apr. 1819: 'Received a letter from Linley, expressing great impatience at not hearing my opinion of his music; in other words, dying to be praised. Must do it for the poor man. Some of his things are, indeed, very pretty; particularly the "Ariel's Adieu" to Bowles's words, and a particularly sweet melody, "Fair Leila, gentle," &c.: but his style, in general, is too old-fashioned for my taste.' (Russell, ii. 287.)

[2] The *Life of Sheridan*.

575. *To William Lisle Bowles*[1]

Rice University

Wednesday [April 1819].

My dear Bowles—

Many thanks for the offer of the Blackwood, but I am quite satisfied with knowing that they don't abuse me, and, still more, with your kindness in hastening to tell me so. You don't forget, I hope, that we are to go together to the Anacreontic (that vile epithet, as you call it, for us elderly gentlemen). I shall be at Buckhill at whatever hour you appoint in the morning of that day, & Bessy considers herself as invited to go too. I have written to Sir John Stevenson, who is in London, to ask him to come down.

Yours ever
T. Moore.

Your pamphlet is unanswerable, but I fear the public *will not* read.[2] Corn Laws & the Currency will beat you out of the field.

576. *To Captain Macdonald*

Rice University

Among the many reconcilements that puzzle people is that of the Regent with Lord Hutchinson—

Friday July 2nd 1819

My dear Macdonald— I have ordered Crokin Spirit for you, and, as I think it will *keep cool* till I return, myself, I shall not send it down by Coach— Bessy sailed on Tuesday, so that I may expect her now every day; though the wind has been, I believe, too southerly to expect a very short passage for her—

I took the field in gaieties immediately on my arrival—Lady Grey's Ball on Tuesday night & Almack's on Wednesday—and, at this moment, if it had not been so wet, I should be at the Countess St. Antonio's breakfast— 'So merrily we live, that vagrants be!' As to Politics, I see nothing of Phipps's projected Coalition yet— but I dine at Holland House to-day, and may possibly return wiser on the subject— I mean to call at 84 Sloane St. on my way back in the morning—

---

[1] This letter was published in Greever, *A Wiltshire Parson*, p. 84.
[2] Probably *The Sentiments of a True Patriot. Tom Paine's 'Rights of Man'* (1819). Bowles also published another pamphlet in 1819, entitled *The Invariable Principles of Poetry, in a Letter Addressed to Thomas Campbell*.

I think it very possible that Bessy will be at the Cottage before me—for I have business that will keep me here near a week yet.

Remember me to the Phipps, & tell Hughes that Sr James Mackintosh has been very good-natured about the letters.

With best regards to Mrs Macdonald, believe me

very truly yours,

Thomas Moore

577. *To John Murray*

Sir John Murray

Thursday [July 1819]

My dear Sir— I have been prevented from calling upon you by some country commissions I have had to execute, but, as I have much to talk with you about, I hope we may find a quiet hour in the course of tomorrow for that purpose— I had hopes that I should not be obliged to trouble you for the remainder of my *half*, but Mrs Moore's journey to Scotland,[1] and some other unforeseen exigencies will oblige me to draw upon you for it—and as soon as I return to Sloperton, I shall (in order that you may have some *set-off* for your advance) send you the MS. as far as it is finished—

The remaining five hundred guineas I mean to leave for you to lay out, at your own time, in some advantageous way for my little boy, to whom I mean to make it over—

Yours very truly

Thomas Moore

I have brought up a copy of the Irish Edition of the School for Scandal, which I have compared with the original MS. and which (you will perceive by my marks) differs but very triflingly from it.

578. *To Sir Charles Morgan*

Lady Morgan, *Memoirs* (Leipzig, 1863), ii. 220

Sunday Night, October [1819][2]

My dear Morgan,

This leg of mine seems inclined to turn out rather a serious concern, and the sooner I avail myself of your skill, the better. Can you make it convenient to call upon me soon after breakfast to-morrow morning?

Yours very faithfully,

Thomas Moore.

---

[1] Bessy Moore visited Edinburgh in June and July 1819 (see Russell, ii. 334).

[2] See letter No. 580, to Sir Charles Morgan, 7 Nov. 1819.

579. *To Thomas Wilkie*

B.M. Add. MS. 29764, f. 37

11 Duke Street, St. James's
Monday, Novr 3rd 1819*

Sir—

Having given your proposal all the consideration which its importance both to you & myself requires, I fear very much that the result I have come to is not such as will meet your wishes satisfactorily— From some other engagements which will occupy my time for a few months to come, it would be impossible for me to have the Essay written (*in the manner I should wish to write it*) before the ensuing autumn—so as to be ready for publication early in the winter— This, I fear, will be in limine an insurmountable objection with you—but, if it should not, the terms upon which I agree to furnish you with the Essay by that time, and to have my name announced as Editor of the Volumes will be five hundred pounds—[1]

Whatever conclusion you may come to upon the subject, I beg to return you my best thanks for the very flattering tribute you have paid my talents by selecting me for such a task—and to assure you that I am

Sincerely your obliged servant
Thomas Moore

580. *To Sir Charles Morgan*

Lady Morgan, *Memoirs* (Leipzig, 1863), ii. 250

Rome
November 7th, 1819.

My Dear Morgan,

I have only time for a line; but a line from Rome is worth a hundred from anywhere else. This place does not disappoint. There are some old brick walls to be sure, before which people stand with a delight and veneration in which I cannot sympathize; but the Coliseum is the very poetry of ruins. My leg, thanks to you and Goulard, arrived quite sound and well, and has never troubled me since.

I think of being off from here the latter end of this week. It was my intention at first to go to Naples, but Cannæ was by no means

---

[1] Moore is referring to the two-volume *Works of the Right Honourable Richard Brinsley Sheridan* (1821). Moore misdated the letter. See letter No. 571.

tempting, and then there is such talk of escort, &c., &c., that, what with the Colonel and the guards, I thought it much too dilatory a proceeding, and gave it up.

Love to Lady Morgan

From hers and yours truly,
Thomas Moore.

581. *To Samuel Rogers*

Russell, viii. 252

Paris
Dec. 23. 1819.

My dear Rogers,

There is but little use now in mentioning (though it is very true) that I began a letter to you from Rome, the first fragment of which is now before my eyes, and is as follows, 'One line from Rome is worth at least two of even yours from Venice; and it is lucky it should be so, as I have not at this moment time for much more.' There I stopped; and if you had ever travelled on the wing as I have done, flying about from morning till night, and from sight to sight, you would know how hard it is to find time to write, and you would forgive me. Taking for granted that you *do* forgive me, I hasten to write you now some very valueless lines indeed, as they must be chiefly about myself. I found a letter here on my arrival, from the Longmans, telling me that I must not venture to cross the water (as was my intention, for the purpose of reaching Holyrood House) till they had consulted you and some others of my friends with respect to the expediency of such a step.[1] I have heard nothing more from them on the subject, and therefore I suppose I must make up my mind to having Mrs. Moore and the little ones over, and remaining here. This is disappointing to me in many respects, and in few more than its depriving me of all chance of seeing *you*, my dear Rogers, and of comparing notes with you on the subject of the many wonders I have witnessed since we parted. Lord John has, I suppose, told you of the precious gift Lord Byron made me at Venice—his own memoirs, written up to the time of his arrival in Italy.[2] I have many things to tell you about him, which at this moment neither time nor inclination will let me tell; when I say

[1] Moore was forced to live on the Continent from late 1819 until 1821 as the result of the defalcation of his deputy in Bermuda. See letter No. 535, to Lady Donegal, 2 Apr. 1818.

[2] This is the first mention in Moore's letters of the now-famous Memoirs, which were burned in Murray's drawing room on 17 May 1824. See letter No. 583 to John Murray, 7 Jan. 1820.

'inclination,' I mean that spirits are not equal to the effort. I have indeed seldom felt much more low and comfortless than since I arrived in Paris; and though if I had you at this moment *à quattr' occhi*, I know I should find wherewith to talk whole hours, it is with difficulty I have brought myself to write even these few lines. Would I *were* with you! I have no one here that I care one pin for, and begin to feel, for the first time, like a banished man. Therefore, pray, write to me, and tell me that you forgive my laziness, and that you think I *may* look to our meeting before very long. If it were possible to get to Holyrood House, I should infinitely prefer it.

Lord John, in a letter I have just received from him, says you have not been well; but I trust, my dear Rogers, you are by this time quite yourself again.

> Ever yours most truly,
> Thomas Moore.

582. *To Thomas Sheridan*

National Library of Ireland

> Wednesday Night* [*c*. 1819]

Dear Tom— As I am leaving town tomorrow for a week, I devoted to-day to my *notitiae Gymnasticae* for you, and here is my morning's work just as my pen transplanted it— Though I have not read it over, I think I can answer for the references being correct, and you shall have many more from me if you wish them—

> Ever yours.
> T. Moore

I hope you'll be able to read my scribble-scribble.

583. *To John Murray*

B.M. Add. MS. 29764, f. 38

> Paris, 30, Rue Chantereine
> January 7th 1820

My dear Sir—

I meant to have written to you long before now but the very uncertain state I have been kept in, and latterly, the bustle of settling my family here, have prevented me— You know, of course, that I passed some time with Lord Byron at Venice & that he made me the very precious gift of his memoirs, continued up to his arrival in Italy— If I had been lucky enough to be allowed to reach England, you should have read this 'curious paper' (as Lord Burghersh diplomatically called it), and, as it is, if any thing should bring you to Paris, you shall have your wicked will of it in every way but publishing— *That* must be reserved for the [middle *deleted*] end of the nineteenth century— What shall I say about Sheridan ? It was chiefly for the purpose of finishing my task that I have made every effort in my power to be suffered to go to Holyrood House—but my friends would not hear of it,[1] and what I am to do at this distance, without access to English books or English evidences, I know not— I had the precaution to pack up all the papers, and as many books on the subject as would be portable before I came away, and, if you know of any one coming that would take charge of them, it would be perhaps the best way to send them, and let me endeavour to dispatch the work in the best way I can— They lie at Longmans's in a trunk & a packing-case, the former of which I brought up, myself, from Wiltshire, & the latter was left there by Mrs Moore— If there appeared any chance of a speedy termination to my Bermuda affairs, it would be better to wait till I could reach England—but as all is, at present, uncertain, it is as well perhaps that I should proceed with the Life as soon as possible.

I shall be most happy to hear from you and am, my dear Sir
Truly yours
Thomas Moore

584. *To the Marquess of Lansdowne*

Bowood

30, Rue Chantereine
January 14, 1820

My dear Lord Lansdowne— I should have written to you long before now, but that, as I was in rather a croaking mood on my arrival here, I did not like to inflict a specimen of my plaintive style on *you*—particularly as my chief grievance, that of being obliged to remain in Paris, was one of the few in which I knew you would not sympathize with me— It is, however, not the less a grievance, in many ways. Mrs Moore's economical powers are all nullified here by her ignorance of French, which throws, too, a good deal of minor details of our little ménage upon me, in consequence of all which we shall manage, I fear, to be very uncomfortable at a very great expence— The distractions of society here I mean to get rid of in a very summary way, by not going into any at all, but there are quite enough other distractions in our new mode of living to prevent me, I fear, from doing much good while I remain here—

[1] Lord Lansdowne had investigated the possibility of Moore's going to Holyrood House, Edinburgh, until his Bermuda troubles were over.

When the weather gets a little more rural, I shall try whether the country may not be better for my purpose—

I have read with much interest, both of a public & private nature, the speeches in which you & some others have fought such a good fight during this session— It has been a noble stand, and doubly valuable as showing how much spirit may be combined with moderation, and what a strong guard is still left on the frontiers of the Constitution against the inroads of Ultras of every kind—Lord John's success I was particularly delighted with;[1] because, I think, he *wanted* it to encourage him in the path which every thing has marked out for him— You, I am told, never spoke so well, and one cannot better express how well you must have spoken.

Pray, tell Lady Lansdowne that I thought of her enthusiasm about Italy very often—particularly when I wanted something to excite my own, which, I am ashamed to say, not infrequently happened— I heard of her instruction to all travellers (though she did not favour *me* with it) to be sure to go on the top of the Temple of Peace (not forgetting the caution about the *hole*); and I made many efforts to lead my leaders thither, till at last the weather became so bad that it was impracticable— They say, however, it is only when the flowers are out that it is beautiful—

I shall send by this post a letter which Scroope gave me for our friend Bowles, & which it would have made me happier than I shall venture to say (for fear of croaking you) to have been the bearer of. Pray tell him I have also a bit of Rosso Antico for him from Scroope, which I shall send by the first safe hands I can find.

Mrs Moore regretted very much she did not see you before her departure—but the only day (of those you were good enough to call) that she was at home, she was engaged in nursing a sick friend that was with her.

Ever, my dear Lord, yours most gratefully
& faithfully

Thomas Moore

---

[1] Moore is alluding to the session of Parliament which followed the Peterloo Massacre, 16 Aug. 1819. On 29 Nov. Castlereagh introduced the 'Seditious Meetings Prevention Bill', designed, as he put it, 'for the more effectually preventing Seditious Meetings and Assemblies'. Debate on this Bill (and its corollary Parliamentary Reform) continued through November and December. The Whigs considered the Bill oppressive and tyrannical, and, led by the Marquess of Lansdowne, Lord Holland, and Lord John Russell, they spoke eloquently against it. Nevertheless, it passed the House of Lords on 21 Dec. 1819. See Hansard, *Parliamentary Debates*, xli. 378 and *passim*.

585. *To Thomas Wilkie*

B.M. Add. MS. 29764, f. 40

Paris
Jan^r 25 1820

My dear Sir, I have only time (lest I should lose the Post) to tell you that all the papers & books contained in those boxes are necessary to me; but if you think they could be packed more conveniently, I shall most willingly entrust to *you* the task of opening & re-arranging them— I should not like the memorandum books, which lie about among them, to be seen by any one else, as with you I am quite sure they are sacred.[1]

I shall, I fear, also want an Annual Register *from* the year 80, (but this we must leave till another time) and, if there is not a Copy of Mills's India[2] in the boxes, I must trouble you to put one up for me— I had one at my Cottage, but Mrs Moore, I fear, forgot to put it up.

If these boxes should be too much for your friend to bring, there is a young gentleman gone to London, who returns here soon, & will bring one of them— His name is Rawlins & you will find him at No. 4 Cleveland Court, St. James's—

With best regards to all your family
I am, my dear Sir
Very faithfully y^{rs}

Thomas Moore

I shall now lose no time in completing the long-delayed Life.

586. *To Thomas Wilkie*

B.M. Add. MS. 29764, f. 42

[January 1820]

My dear Sir— I have but just time to return you my best thanks for your kindness in sending me the book & letter— I have also to ask your forgiveness for not having acknowledged a former letter with which you favoured me— It was not at all fair of my friend, Mr. Rees, to send you that scrap in which I applied such an uncourtly & undeserved epithet to you—but it gave you an opportunity of showing your good temper & good sense, which is always a triumph to him who knows how to display them so seasonably—

---

[1] The following note, not in Moore's hand, appears at the top of the manuscript: 'Delivered the Trunk & Box which I recd from Mr. Rees—to Mr. Rawlins at his Lodgings No. 4—Cleveland Court for him to take charge of conveying them to Mr. Moore.'

[2] James Mill, *The History of British India* (London, 1817), 3 vols.

I shall proceed with the Life,[1] and though slow, hope to be *sure*, in the execution of it— To dash through it, as the poor fellow himself did, would be as little profitable to you as it was to him— I wish you could send me Mills's History of India,[2] as I want it very much.

[*Signature effaced*]

587. *To Lady Morgan*

Yale

11 Allée des Veuves
[Postmark March 17, 1820]

I thought to have reached you to-day, but was detained at home too late—Pray, fix either Friday or Saturday to dine with us— The former day would, perhaps, be better, as I find Mad[e] de Flahaut expects us all on that evening, and, her house being near this, we could go together—only, let me know as soon as you can—

Yours most truly
Thomas Moore

588. *To John Murray*

Sir John Murray

April 14th 1820

My dear Sir— M[r] Wilkie tells me that it is your wish as well as his own, to have some prefatory remarks from me upon the *Rivals*, which you are about to publish separately—[3] This I confess I do not understand—neither with respect to the wisdom of publishing in such a manner, nor the policy of gutting the life of some pages for the purpose of forming a garnish to this Play as a single dish— You will, however, explain it to me, I have no doubt, in your answer. With respect to the Life, I fear it must be, after all, no more than was originally intended—an Essay; in which case you will at least have the pleasure of receiving what remains of the work without any further paying. But of this more in my next. I write now chiefly at the request of Madame de Souza to put the following questions to you on the subject of her Romance.[4] How

---

[1] The *Life of Sheridan*.

[2] See letter No. 585, to Thomas Wilkie, 25 Jan. 1820.

[3] Murray did not publish *The Rivals* as a separate work. Sheridan's *Complete Works*, with a preface by Moore, appeared in two volumes in 1821.

[4] Moore is probably referring to Adele de Souza's *Madamoiselle de Tournon* (Paris, 1820), 2 vols.

many copies do you think you can sell, and how many shall she send you? Can you insure her against piracy in England? How much can she sell the work for, consisting as it does of two volumes, 250 pages each, printed upon excellent paper by Didot? and how much do you require for commission?— As I live very near Mad^e de Souza, and can expect but little peace from a Frenchwoman, so far gone with a Romance, till her queries are satisfied, in mercy to *me* do not delay your answer.

You see I announced a Fudge Family in Italy,[1] but I have not been able to make it what I wished, and accordingly, for the present, it is laid up in ordinary. I shall, however, publish a few detached trifles in May, merely as a fly-catcher in the warm weather— I have been for some time so unsettled here that I could do nothing but curse the French & Doctors' Commons all day long—but I am growing philosophical enough about *both* these grievances.

Yours very truly
Thomas Moore

589. *To Viscount Percy Strangford*

De Fonblanque, *Lives of the Lords Strangford* (London, 1877), p. 125

Paris
April, 1820.

My Dear Strangford,

Douglas has just offered me an opportunity of writing a few lines to you, and I hasten to say what all my life will not be long enough to feel as much, and as strongly as I ought to do, the deep, hearty, genuine gratitude with which my heart is full towards you for the letter you wrote me. I should have preferred waiting till we met, rather than attempt through the cold medium of a letter to tell you half how much I thank you, had not Douglas hinted that you were displeased at my silence. My dear friend, how delightful to have the companion of one's young days taking the part you have done in the moment of need, and showing that, even scapegraces as we were, there was stuff in us for better things.[2] Don't mind my grammar, I

---

[1] Moore published *The Fudge Family in Paris* in 1818 but never took the famous family to Italy. A manuscript dealing with their travels in Italy was forwarded to the Longmans in May, but the publishers pointed out to Moore that an attack on Castlereagh and other government officials would not help in the settlement of his Bermuda troubles. Much of the material in this poem was later included in the *Fables for the Holy Alliance* (1823).

[2] Strangford had evidently helped Moore out of his financial difficulties. For a reference to Strangford's attitude toward Moore's 'silence' see Russell, iii. 117.

am in too great a hurry, and feel too much to write intelligibly; as my friend Sir T. says, 'Don't mind what I say, mind what I think.'

590. *To Samuel Rogers*

Russell, viii. 254

La Butte
July 17. 1820.

My dear Rogers,

As I have just been answering a letter of Sir J. Mackintosh, and thereby got my hand back into some notion of letter-writing, I shall slip in a hasty line or two to you. As you have *never* written to me, and I have only written *once* to you, the difference of virtue between us is so small that I shall not crow over you upon the strength of it; besides, the solitary letter I *did* write was of so dreary and croaking a nature (at a time, too, when you might have expected me to return with all the sunbeams of Italy fresh about me), that I do not wonder at your having waited for some pleasanter tones to send an echo to. I afterwards got into a much happier mood, having exchanged my wretched *entre-sol* in Paris for a very pretty cottage in the Allée des Veuves, where I contrived to get on very comfortably indeed. Often and often did I think of communicating my bright side to you, as I had done the dark one; but I had no time for letters; scribbling of another kind came so hard upon me. The necessity of doing some jobs for Power, and my anxiety to finish the work I had promised to the Longmans altogether absorbed every instant of my time; and, having got into arrears of letter-writing with every friend I have in the world, I had not the courage to begin discharging the amount, but thought a declaration of insolvency at once to all was the only decent and honest mode to pursue. You have heard, I dare say, that the Longmans have suppressed my book, at which I am not at all sorry, for I can make a much better thing out of its materials at another time, and I have availed myself of their readiness to withhold the publication, though with very different views from those upon which they recommended it.[1] Nothing can be more liberal, considerate, and kind than the conduct of those men to me. It is really friendship, assuming the form of business, and making itself actively useful, upon a fair debtor and creditor account of obligations.

We are now passing the summer months at a place which *you* would delight in. It is the house (forming part of Belle-Vue) which hangs over Sêvres, and faces you as you cross the bridge.

[1] See letter No. 588, to John Murray, 14 Apr. 1820.

The view from it of woods and palaces is superb, and the grounds (about fifty or sixty acres in pleasure-ground) include every variety one could wish. It was bought by a friend of ours, a Spaniard, with whose wife we were very intimate in England;[1] and he has given us a beautiful little *pavillon* near his house, where I pass my mornings quietly and independently, and then join the rest at a dinner as good as one of the best artists from the Rocher de Cancale can make it. The walks about us, through the Woods of Meudon and St. Cloud, are of the true kind for study ; and, in short, I enjoy myself so thoroughly here, that if the sun would but go on shining this way all the year, and the flowers blooming and the nightingales singing, I should begin to care very little about the Treasury or Doctors' Commons, and sigh for nothing in England but the never-to-be-forgotten friends I left behind me there. But, then, winter *will* come, and then Paris is the devil.

Pray write soon, my dearest Rogers, and add to my sunshine by showing that I am remembered by you as kindly as ever, in spite of my *one* letter in eight months, and your —*none*.

Bessy sends her kindest regards. Anastasia is quite well, and is pronounced here to have a *Grecque* face, and little Tom, in spite of his teeth, flourishes.

Remember me most kindly to Miss Rogers.

Yours ever,
T. Moore.

591. *Addressee unknown*

Morgan Library

11, Allée des Veuves
Novr 16th 1820

My dear Sir— I forwarded your letter to Lord Byron, but I fear that your hopes about his tragedy will be disappointed, for it has been some time in Murray's hands, &, from what I can understand, is neither fit nor indeed intended for representation—[2] As to myself, I feel much flattered by your anxiety to have something from me, but, until a task or two which I have now upon my hands are finished I must not think of any thing else.

Kenny [*sic*], whom I see very frequently here, bids me say that he has long been in expectation of hearing from you on the subject of his tragedy,[3] and that, as it is nearly finished, he should be glad to

---

[1] The Villamil family.

[2] Byron's *Marino Faliero* was published in 1821.

[3] The only play on which James Kenney was apparently working at this time was *Sweethearts and Wives*, which was produced at the Haymarket on 7 July 1823.

know your intentions before he takes any further step respecting
it— He has promised to let me see it, when it is done—

Believe me, my dear Sir, very truly yours
Thomas Moore—

I sent a copy of the 'Voitures Venice' by a gentleman who left this
the day after your letter arrived and hope you received it, —though
I rather think it had got into some dramatizing hand here before
you thought of turning it to account—

592. *To James Power*

National Library of Ireland

11 Allée des Veuves
December 11, 1820

My dear Sir— I have very sincere pleasure in congratulating you
upon the event, which has just taken place in your family— I
should have taken for granted, even without knowing the husband,
that neither you nor your daughter had been much *out* in your
choice, but, having had the pleasure of making Crawford's acquaintance, I can judge for myself, and I do really & sincerely congratulate both you & her upon this alliance with a person so sensible,
manly & amiable—as to the felicitations that are to be offered to
him, I do not so well know what to say, for I rather fear that, much
as I like him, I cannot help *grudging* her to him—but this must be a
secret.

May I beg of you, if the Longmans send you (as I have long
wished they should) some verses of mine to Lord John Russell, to
change the last stanza into the following form:—

Like the boughs of that laurel, by Delphi's decree
Set apart for the Fane and its service divine,
All the branches, that spring from the old R—— tree,
Are by Liberty *claim'd* for the use of her shrine.[1]

You may sign my name to it either thus—T——s M——e, or put
it and his name in full, just as you think best, and pray date the
poem at the top 'Padua, October 1819.'

Now, after giving you this trouble I must reward you by a most
amusing little Epigram, written by Lord B. for the next anniversary (being the sixth) of his marriage—Jan^r 2nd 1821.

To Penelope.
This day, of all our days, has done
The worst for me and you,
Tis now six years since we were *one*,
And five since we were *two*.[2]

[1] *Poetry*, p. 530.   [2] Byron, *Poetry*, vii. 71.

You may show this as much as you please, but do not print it.

I often sigh to be back again among you, near as you are all to the embraces of Old Nick—but when that is destined to happen, Old Nick alone knows—

> Yours, my dear friend, very faithfully
> Thomas Moore.

The paragraph in the Courier about my proposals for a Dinner here was a lie—I had not the least concern in that 24 franc business, but on the contrary gave up a little private dinner a few of us were going to have on the occasion, lest we should be confounded with those other diners, who, I believe, were not of the most respectable order. I did not, however, chuse to contradict the statement, lest it should be thought I disapproved of the *principle* of the plan.

I need not tell you to see that the Lines to Lord J. are correctly printed.

593. *To Thomas Phillips*

New York Public

> Allée des Veuves, No. 11*
> [December 1820]

My dear Sir— We shall be most delighted to see Mrs Phillips & you on Friday, and pray, let it be as soon after twelve as you can, as we have an appointment with Lady Davy at two in Paris.

The engravings (which I had already seen at Denon's) are admirable and almost do justice to the pictures—which is saying much for them.

> Yours very truly
> Thomas Moore

594. *To the Marquess of Lansdowne*

Bowood

> Wednesday* [*c.* 1820]

I send back the Pamphlet, which is certainly clever and often eloquent, though such passages as the whole paragraph, beginning 'There is a broad & visible line &c.' (page 21) make one tremble a little for the future displays of the author. His description of the Protestant clergy-man and the relation in which he stands to the people is admirable—but I confess the perusal of the pamphlet has rather added to the hopelessness which I feel about Ireland—the remedies proposed are so remote, speculative, & almost visionary, while the evils described are so real, rooted, &, I fear, essential to the anomalous condition of Ireland. It is easy to say 'educate'—but until Mr Driscol can persuade (as he benevolently flatters himself he can) the Protestant Rector to go & preach *general* morality in the peasant's cabbin—until he can get the Baptists to instruct without attempting to proselytize—until he can promise some better success to such liberal plans as that of 'the London Hibernian Soc.', whose liberality & wisdom have had no other effect than that of bringing them into heavy arrears to their treasurer—and, finally (supposing him to have conquered all those difficulties) until he can bring the Irish Peasant to *listen*, without distrust, to instructions from those whom he considers as, both temporally & spiritually, his enemies—until he can effect all those wonders (which it is more benevolent than wise of him to consider so feasible) I must be allowed to despair of better instruction for my countrymen than what their own low, miracle-working, whisky-drinking priests afford.[1]

It is well, however, that others do not despair, and I only wish, for my own comfort, that I could share any part of their hope. So ill-assorted a marriage as that of England & Ireland can never, to the world's end, be productive of any thing but unhappiness—at least to the weaker party.

But I am becoming a sort of *Bennet upon paper*, and must stop. You should have the work upon Greece in a day or two.

Yours faithfully
Thomas Moore

595. *To William Lisle Bowles*

Greever, p. 87

Sloperton
Friday [c. 1820][2]

My dear Bowles—

In consequence of my having consented to become arbiter between Sir J. Stevenson and his publisher, (in order to prevent *them* too from going to logger-heads) I last night received an immense packet of the Knight's Music to sit in judgment upon, which will make it impossible, I fear, for me to go to Bremhill

---

[1] J. O'Driscoll, *Thoughts and Suggestions on the Education of the Peasantry of Ireland* (London, 1820).

[2] Date supplied by the editor. This letter must have been written about the time of Moore's difficulties with the Power brothers over the publication of the eighth number of the Irish Melodies (1821), for which James Power had retained Henry R. Bishop to arrange the music. See Jones, *The Harp that Once—*, pp. 159–60.

before the Sothebys leave you. I regret this most heartily, but so it is, and I cannot help it. Give my best regards to Mr. Sotheby.

If it should be fine on Monday, and my task is entirely got through, I may perhaps walk over to you and stay the night.

Ever yours,
T. Moore.

596. *To Longman & Company*

Rice University

11, Allée des Veuves*
Jan^r 27, 1821*

Gentlemen—

This will be delivered to you by a person who goes to London for the purpose of giving instructions in Dancing, and for whom my interest has been solicited— He belongs to the French Opera & has taught the Royal Family of Wirtenberg— Any recommendations or services you can afford him will much oblige

Yours &c
Thomas Moore.

597. *Addressee unknown*

Rice University

Sloperton Cottage, Devizes
April 27th 1821[1]

Dear Sir— I regret extremely that the necessity I was under of leaving London suddenly, on account of the illness of Mrs Moore, prevented me from having the pleasure of calling upon you, as I intended. It is my intention, however, to return to London, as soon as I have seen her safely through her confinement, and I shall then not lose a moment in atoning to myself for the disappointment I have now experienced.

Yours very truly
Thomas Moore.

---

[1] The date of this letter and that of No. 600, to Locke, Hughes & Company, 21 July 1821, are confusing. Both letters give Sloperton Cottage as a return address, yet Moore's diary and other letters written in April and July 1821 prove that he was in Paris at this time. Moreover, he does not mention Bessy's illness elsewhere during this period.

598. *Addressee unknown*

Rice University

Wednesday Night Twelve o'clock
[April 28 1821]

Notwithstanding the rain to-day, the night is so clear that we think it not improbable tomorrow may be fine enough to go to Malmaison; and what we propose is that you should come *here* as early as you can manage it in the morning, and then we may either proceed to Malmaison together, or make ourselves as happy (in case the day should prove too bad) as song, laugh & champagne can enable us to be— If you can lay hold of Irving, bring him with you—[1]

Did I leave my spectacles at your house? Bring the Royal *clock*, if you have got it.

Yours ever
T. M.

599. *To Washington Irving*

Pennsylvania Historical Society

[June 1821]

My dear Irving—

Mind, you come dine with me on Wednesday next at *five*— Lord Rancliff has fixed that day for our dinner & we are to be treated with the *father-in-law* into the bargain— In *importe* however— come at MS. time, and let me have the rest of the authors.[2]

Y^{rs}
T. Moore

---

[1] Moore planned to go to Malmaison on 29 Apr., but the weather was bad, and the visit was postponed until 10 May 1821. This letter was evidently written on the day before the proposed trip on 29 Apr. See the diary for that date, Russell, iii. 226.

[2] A note, evidently in Irving's hand, on the reverse side of the page reads: 'This scrawled from Moore the poet is the only autograph of note that I have by me at present. I am generally pretty well drained of every thing of the kind.' David Bonnell Green, who first published this letter and No. 1005, to Washington Irving, 14 June 1832, in *Notes and Queries* (July–August 1959), pp. 288–9, identified the 'father-in-law' as George Forbes, sixth Earl of Granard. See the Glossary of Proper Names.

600. *To Locke, Hughes & Company*

Rice University

Sloperton Cottage*
July 21st 1821*1

You will have the goodness to send me thirty pounds in Bank of England notes or Sovereigns, and the remainder in your own notes—

Yrs &c
Thomas Moore.

601. *To Leigh Hunt*

B.M. Add. MS. 37210, f. 178

Paris
August 20 1821

My dear Hunt— I take the opportunity of a frank to send you a hasty line of acknowledgement for your kind remembrance of me. I was indeed most happy to see the announcement of your recovery, for public as well as private reasons—for, though you have right good auxiliaries, there is but one Richmond in the field after all.[2]

This is a very delightful place to live in, &, if I were not *obliged* to stay in it, I should find the time pass happily enough—but

> 'Were ev'n Paradise itself my prison
> Still should I long to leap the crystal walls.'[3]

Your friend Mr Bowring & I were rather unlucky in our attempts to meet, but we *did* meet at last, and I liked him exceedingly. [*Remainder of the letter and signature missing.*]

602. *To James Kenney*

Harvard

[Postmark August 27, 1821]

My dear Kenny [*sic*]—
I cannot dispatch the inclosed without one word to thank you for your most lively & welcome letter, dated 'Thieves Inn'—a place I am sorry you have quitted, as your vein seemed to be excellent there— I saw Mrs Kenny yesterday—she & little ones all well,

---

1 See letter No. 597, addressee unknown, 27 Apr. 1821.
2 *Richard III*, v. iv. 9.
3 Not identified.

PLATE 5

BOWOOD, seat of the Marquess of Lansdowne. From an old print

You cannot think how I have missed you here— Lord John has been domesticated with me almost ever since, and our little dinners wanted *you* most egregiously.

Tell Irving, when you see him, with my best regards, that in one of Lord Byron's late letters to me his name is thus introduced 'Your friend Irving (whose works are my delight) &c. &c.'[1]

You will see Bessy, I trust, in [*sic*] her way back.

Yours ever
T. Moore.

603. *To Douglas*[2]

Rice University

Monday* [August 1821]

My dear Douglas— As our well-beloved Bill has been (with the help of the Bishops) sent to the Devil, we must now have our dinner, and I propose Saturday next at the Two Swans.[3] I am going to write to Lord Rancliffe, Mildmay &c and do you take care to secure Lord Miltown— All private, you know, & select. Let me know if Saturday will suit.

I am sorry to perceive that you have given up the idea of being our neighbour.

Yours ever
Thomas Moore

604. *To William Perry*

Rice University

Saturday [12 September 1821]

My dear Sir— We expect you & Mr Hill to dinner here tomorrow— it is not yet decided whether we shall dine before or after the waters, but if you are with us at a quarter before three, you will be in time for either plan— I tremble a little about the weather, but, if there is no Fête for us at St. Cloud, we must only make one at home, and I can promise you some very good singing from Mrs Villamil.[4]

Yours very truly
Thomas Moore.

1 See the letter from Byron, 5 July 1821 (*LJ*, v. 318).

2 During the summer and fall of 1821, Moore was associated in Paris with Douglas, an 'old college friend', and the others mentioned in the text of the letter (Russell, iii. 105 and *passim*). In his index Russell mistakenly identifies Moore's friend as Frederick Sylvester North Douglas, the son of Lord Glenbervie. The son died in 1819.

3 On 30 Aug. 1821 Moore recorded in his diary that he had dinner at the Two Swans with Miltown, Sir Henry Mildmay, and Douglas. He did not mention Rancliffe as being one of the party. (Russell, iii. 142.)

4 See the diary for 12 Sept. 1821 (Russell, iii. 277), where Moore recorded his visit to the fête at St. Cloud.

605. *To John Murray*

Sir John Murray

Paris
Monday Septr 17th 1821

My dear Sir— I have received Lord Byron's answer, which I thought it right to wait for— He gives his full sanction to every arrangement which I may make with you on the subject of his Memoirs—[1] and it is my intention, therefore, to proceed immediately to London, not only for this purpose, but in order to make myself acquainted with the real state of the negotiation which the Longmans undertook with the agent of the American claimants, and which (between you & me) they have managed, as far as I can understand, rather inefficiently. I must, of course, be *incog.* while I stay, and as it will be only for a very few days, I hope you will be able to be in London at the time. I shall want your advice, as well as your money. The greater part of the sum (15 or 16 hundred) shall remain in your hands till the compromise with the agent is effected—the remainder I shall have occasion for more speedily, and have begun upon it already by drawing on you here for one hundred pounds at three months from Saturday last, the 15th—[2] Whether the *Sheridan* advance is to be deducted, you must decide when we meet— but my being enabled to live again in England will give you a *chance* of seeing that work finished.

You will, of course, not mention to *any one* my projected visit. I have waited some days for Lord John Russell, with whom I was to have gone, but he is delayed for want of permission to send his *mares* back to England, and, whether he is ready or not, I shall, myself start on *Wednesday*.

Yours very faithfully
Thomas Moore.

606. *To Lord Byron*

Moore, *Byron*, v. 318

September 30. 1821.

Since writing the above, I have read Foscari and Cain. The former does not please me so highly as Sardanapalus.[3] It has the fault of all

[1] See letter No. 581, to Samuel Rogers, 23 Dec. 1819, and No. 583, to John Murray, 7 Jan. 1820.

[2] Murray offered Moore 2,000 guineas for the Memoirs, on condition that, if he survived Byron, Moore should be the editor. For further details of the transaction see letter No. 631, to John Murray, 13 Feb. 1823. See also Marchand, *Byron*, pp. 884–5, and Doris Langley Moore, 'The Burning of the Memoirs', *The Late Lord Byron* (New York, 1961) pp. 12–45.

[3] *The Two Foscari, Cain,* and *Sardanapalus* were published together on 19 Dec. 1821. Murray had evidently shown the manuscript to Moore.

those violent Venetian stories, being unnatural and improbable, and therefore, in spite of all your fine management of them, appealing but remotely to one's sympathies. But Cain is wonderful—terrible—never to be forgotten. If I am not mistaken, it will sink deep into the world's heart; and while many will shudder at its blasphemy, all must fall prostrate before its grandeur. Talk of Æschylus and his Prometheus!—here is the true spirit both of the Poet—and the Devil.

607. *To James Power*

University of Texas

[September 1821]

My dear Sir— I wrote to you by the common post yesterday to beg you would announce my intention of delaying my departure for a few days to Rogers's house-keeper & Murray— I hope that letter will reach you on Saturday—on which day I mean to start, and hope to be in London about Tuesday or Wednesday.— *I shall have another National Melody ready for you* on my arrival— What a nice selection we may make now for the 3rd Number!

If we cannot make out those missing Songs in the Assignment, I must only write you two others to the same title.

Yours ever
T. Moore

Keep my coming as secret as you can.—too many here know it.

608. *To John Murray*

Sir John Murray

Sunday Night [1 October 1821]

My dear Sir— I don't like to teaze you, but it is as well for you as for me that there should be some *regular* agreement about this business— I must be off to Woburn, on my way to Ireland, on Tuesday evening, therefore pray let me see you tomorrow between 12 & five.[1]

I have enquired into the state of the negotiation and find that there will be abundance of time granted for the payment of the £1000— As to the £400 I shall draw for it as accommodatingly as I can— Yours very truly
Thomas Moore

I am delighted with Sardanapalus—for interest and originality it is far beyond the Doge of Venice.[2]

---

[1] Moore visited Woburn *en route* to Ireland on 3–8 Oct. 1821.
[2] See letter No. 606, to Lord Byron, 30 Sept. 1821.

609. *Addressee unknown*

Rice University

Tuesday [18 October 1821][1]

Sir—

I regret that it was not convenient for you to call upon me yesterday morning—as, this evening, I am obliged to sail for Holyhead— I take your manuscripts with me, and as soon as I learn the determination of the booksellers, I shall let you know through Mr Power of Westmoreland St—[2]

I have not had a moment to look over the last Poem which you did me the favour to send me.

Your very obliged S.
Thomas Moore

610. *To Mrs. Belcher*

Rice University

London, 22 St. James's Place
October 27th 1821*

My dear Mrs Belcher— The girls, I suppose, had informed you of my fly-by-night excursion over to Ireland to see my Father & Mother— I was on my way back again as secretly as I came, when, on arriving in London I found that the Agent of the Americans had accepted the terms proposed to him for the settlement of my debt, and I am accordingly now as free as such an amateur of Liberty ought to be—[3] I hasten (though having scarcely a minute) to communicate this intelligence to you, well knowing that there is no one who will rejoice at it more sincerely.

Fanny has been ill, since I left home, but by the last accounts, was well & walking in the garden again— I start from this for Paris on Sunday, so send anything you may have for the girls before then.

Ever yours faithfully
Thomas Moore.

[1] Moore was in Ireland in October 1821, and recorded in his diary that he sailed for Holyhead on 18 Oct.

[2] Neither the addressee nor the manuscripts have been identified.

[3] Lord Lansdowne had arranged for the settlement to be made. See letter No. 535, to Lady Donegal, 2 Apr. 1818.

611. *To Lady Holland*

The Earl of Ilchester[1]

22 St. James's Place
Wednesday [October 1821]

Your Ladyship well deserves to be one of the first of those friends
to whom I communicate the intelligence of my emersion from my
long eclipse.[2] Since yesterday I am a free man again, and may walk
in the full sunshine of London (if such a thing could be found) with
impunity. I mean to start in a day or two for Paris, but shall have
the pleasure of calling at Holland House before I go.

Ever yours faithfully,
Thomas Moore.

612. *To Lord Holland*

The Earl of Ilchester[3]

Monday, November 5 1821.

Dear Lord Holland— What you said yesterday about the sale of
Lord B's Memoirs[4] made so strong an impression upon me, that my
thoughts have been, ever since, occupied upon the subject, and it
was my resolution if, after an honest consideration of the transaction, it appeared to me that I could be fairly thought to have
done anything wrong or unworthy in thus disposing of these
papers—to prevail upon Murray (which I could easily have done)
to cancel the deed between us and take back the money he had paid,
having it in my power from the kindness of Lord Lansdowne & Lord
John Russel [*sic*][5] to refund nearly the whole of the sum without
much inconvenience to me. After the most anxious consideration,
however, I so little change affected in the original state of the case
by my late arrangement with Murray, that I cannot perceive any
necessity for retracing the steps I have taken. In the first place my
depositing the M.S. in Murray's hands neither increases the
certainty of publication, nor hastens the time of it, and in the next
place I had already pledged myself to Lord Byron to be the Editor
in case I should survive, of these papers leaving a part of them in
their present state & exercising my discretion over the rest. With
respect to the portion of them that is to remain unaltered—except

---

[1] Transcript provided by the Earl of Ilchester.
[2] See letter No. 610, to Mrs. Belcher, 27 Oct. 1821.
[3] Transcript provided by the Earl of Ilchester.
[4] See letter No. 605, to John Murray, 17 Sept. 1821.
[5] Lords Lansdowne and Russell had offered to lend Moore the money
necessary to redeem the Memoirs.

the passage about Madame de Staël and an indecent circumstance
alluded to in his last interview with Lady Byron (which, however,
interpreting my pledge to extend to facts rather than phrases I shall
feel no hesitation whatever in softening down) I know but little in
the responsibility which I have incurred to shrink from. The alleged
misstatement of Sir S. Romilly's conduct may be easily remedied by
furnishing me with the means of contradicting it,[1] and with respect
to any charge against Mr Brougham (though I do not remember
that any exists in the work) I can answer for his seeing all that is
said about him & thereby having an opportunity of correcting any
misrepresentation.[2] What Lady Holland remarked yesterday about
Mrs L. is, I find upon recollection, founded entirely on her own
suspicions, as Lord B. merely mentions a nameless person whom he
calls 'love of loves' & I never met with but one individual, besides
Lady H. who supposed it to allude to the Lady in question.[3] The
slighting passage about Rogers's Human Life[4] is in the part over
which I have discretionary power, and, at all events, is fully atoned
for by the estimation which Lord B. on all other occasions, shows
for his works, ranking him indeed, at the very head of all the poets
of the present day. The allusion to Lady Holland herself deserves
no further notice than her own excellent sense bestows upon it, and
would from the present state of his feelings to her be most easily
relinquished! Altogether indeed as far as concerns those I care for,

[1] Byron's dislike of Sir Samuel Romilly began during the separation settlement with Lady Byron. Lady Noel told Romilly of her daughter's complaints
against Byron and sought his advice. Romilly sided with her in the preparation
of the settlement agreement. On 12 Feb. 1816, however, Byron wrote to
Hanson, his lawyer, to ask if Romilly had been retained for him. Hanson
replied that Romilly had a general retainer for Byron; but he did not know
that Sir Samuel had been counselling Lady Byron, and Byron did not learn
this until 16 Mar. When Hobhouse reminded him that he was obligated to
Byron, Romilly admitted that 'he had done a very incorrect thing in being
consulted by Lady Byron, but that in the multiplicity of retainers, it was
sometimes the case that names were overlooked'. Even though Romilly then
refused to arbitrate the separation, Byron never forgave him. See Marchand,
Byron, pp. 568, 571, and 571 n.

[2] Byron's dislike of Henry Brougham, Lady Byron's lawyer, was as great
as his contempt for Romilly. On one occasion Brougham accused Byron of
cheating the Duchess of Devonshire out of £500, and Hobhouse promptly
called him a liar. Brougham also gossiped about the separation, saying that
the cause of it was something 'too horrid to mention'; and when Byron guessed
that it was he who wrote the caustic review of *Hours of Idleness* in the *Edinburgh
Review* for January 1808, his hatred for 'that blackguard Brougham' increased
tenfold. See Marchand, *Byron*, p. 614 n.

[3] 'Mrs L.' is evidently Augusta Leigh, Byron's half sister. If so, this is the
only time in Moore's references to the Memoirs that he alludes to Byron's
relations with Augusta.

[4] Samuel Rogers published *Human Life* in 1819.

or who, I think, *ought* to be cared for, there is nothing besides the
usual difficulties attending all such responsibilities to make her
regret or wish to alter the arrangement I have made.

There is one suggestion, however, which I owe to my conversation with your Lordship, and that is the necessity of exercising the
discretion given me as soon as possible & not leaving the passages
which I think ought to be omitted to the chances of a future time
or the taste of a less scrupulous Editor.

May I ask you to show this letter to Lord Lansdowne on his
arrival?— To him, above most of the persons of this world, I should
wish my conduct on every occasion to appear free from suspicion
and reproach.[1]

Ever, my dear Lord, yours most faithfully
Thomas Moore

613. *To Lady Holland*

The Earl of Ilchester[2]

St. James's Place
Tuesday Night [6 November 1821]

I ought to have added yesterday, in my letter to Lord Holland, that
not only Brougham shall see whatever has been said of him (though
I scarcely think his name is mentioned) but that—what is much
more important—he shall on my return if he chooses, have the
perusal of all that is said of Lady Byron (who has herself you know,
already refused to read the work) in order that he may thus have an
opportunity of refuting or correcting whatever has been mis-
stated or mis-represented.[3]

Whatever may be thought of the propriety of publishing Private
Memoirs *at all*, it certainly appears to me infinitely fairer thus to
proclaim & lay them open to all eyes, while the persons interested
are still alive to put the refutation upon record with the charge,
than (according to the usual mode) to keep them as a fire in reserve
till those who are attacked have passed away and no longer possess
the means either of retorting or justifying.

I am off for Paris in the morning. I have often entreated your
Ladyship to employ me in some of your Paris commissions, but I am
afraid you think I have too *Paddy* a head to be trusted with them.
Pray try me however.

Ever your faithful & obliged Servt
Thomas Moore

---

[1] See letter No. 614, to Lord Lansdowne, 6 Nov. 1821.
[2] Transcript provided by the Earl of Ilchester.
[3] See letter No. 612, to Lord Holland, 5 Nov. 1821.

614. *To the Marquess of Lansdowne*

Bowood

St. James's Place
Tuesday Night Nov[r] 6th 1821

Dear Lord Lansdowne— I wish I could thank you as I ought—though it seems like profaning what I feel to attempt anything *but* feeling it, and endeavouring, as well as I can to deserve such friendship— I am enabled to discharge the *pecuniary* part of the obligation so soon by that present which, you no doubt have heard, Lord Byron made me of his Memoirs at Venice, and which Murray has purchased (under the same condition of not publishing them till after Lord B[s] death) for two thousand guineas—[1] whether it was prudent of me to promise to be the Editor of those papers may well admit of a doubt, but having done so, the sale of them to Murray neither increases the certainty of their appearance nor hastens the period of it. I am most anxious you should see a letter which I wrote to Lord Holland, upon some scruples with which he not a little alarmed me on this subject.[2]

I have waited till my last moment in the hopes of your arrival, but to-morrow morning I must be off for Paris— In Spring I hope for the happiness of seeing you, and, in the mean time, must trust that you, who do generous actions so unostentatiously, can give credit to those who feel them in the same silent manner.

Ever faithfully & gratefully
yours
Thomas Moore

Inclosed is a draft for £740.

615. *To John Murray*

Nottingham Public Libraries

Rue d'Angor, 17*
Decr 21st 1821*

A thousand thanks, my dear Sir, for your beautiful present to Mrs Moore, which has just come in time to put all her other Étrennes to the blush— She shall thank you, herself, for it in Spring.

---

[1] See letter No. 605, to John Murray, 17 Sept. 1821. Moore means that his negotiations with Murray will enable him to repay Lord Lansdowne for the latter's financial assistance in settling Moore's Bermuda difficulties. See letter No. 535, to Lady Donegal, 2 Apr. 1818, and No. 610, to Mrs. Belcher, 27 Oct. 1821.

[2] See letter No. 612, to Lord Holland, 5 Nov. 1821.

You will be glad to hear that I have had a letter from Lord Byron, giving *me* full power to alter or omit whatever I please in the whole of the Memoirs— This is a vast relief to us both and as soon as I arrive in London, I shall lose no time in exercising the enlarged discretion he has given me, taking care at the same time not to do his case injustice by any over-scrupulous deference to the feelings of others.

Ever yours very truly
Thomas Moore

616. *To John Murray*

Sir John Murray

[Postmark December 27, 1821]

My dear Sir— Galignani gives a hundred pounds—but *not* upon the condition you annexed, which would be indeed impossible—for nothing could give him the right of first publication here but the actual copy-right, it being necessary that that should exist somewhere in Paris in order to give a power of preventing others from printing— If Lord Byron himself were here, or you (upon going through the necessary forms) or if you had invested me with the Copy-right (which is a thing, unfortunately, I never thought of till this moment) there would have been a power of limiting Galignani's hold over the work, but as it *is*, to have any thing worth paying you sixpence for he must have the whole—so that between a hundred pounds & nothing, I thought there was no room for hesitation—particularly as he received his copy about 12 hours after yours reached me, and therefore had no inducement on the score of dispatch to make him open his purse-strings— *My* copy arrived with me on the evening of the 20th (Wilson having forwarded it from Calais by the Mail) and on my taking it, which I did instantly, to Galignani, he told me that he expected his by express next morning, & accordingly it arrived on the 21st at ½ past ten—how is this managed?[1]

On the other side I shall copy out, at Galignani's request (who is very anxious to stand well with you, & who, I believe, means

[1] Moore is probably referring to the five-volume edition of Byron's collected works, Paris, 1821. Byron refused to give Galignani copyrights on his works and referred two requests from the French publisher to Murray. Byron manifestly stated that he would 'have no bargain but with English publishers', and desired 'no interest out of that country' (*LJ*, v. 235). For further details of Galignani's efforts to secure copyrights on Byron's works see *LJ*, v. 216, 223, 224, and 233.

fairly) a letter, which Manning, the most respectable attorney here, has addressed to him on the subject of his affair with Belzoni—[1]

Rue St. Honoré, 337,
Decr 19th 1820

Gentlemen—

I have no difficulty in saying that I think, under all the circumstances the arrangement concluded between yourselves & Mr Belzoni is creditable alike to you & him.

Having been called upon by him to advise him on the subject of his agreement, I have sufficient reason to believe that his complaints against you for an infringement of that Contract were not founded in fact & arose from his unacquaintedness with the usages of publishers in this country, & I endeavoured to convince him that the advantages you are likely to derive from the work are much less considerable than he seemed to imagine.

I am, Gentlemen &c—
J. E. Manning

617. *To Lord Byron*

Moore, *Byron*, v. 317

[January 1822]

I heard some days ago that Leigh Hunt was on his way to you with all his family; and the idea seems to be, that you and Shelley and he are to *conspire* together in the Examiner. I cannot believe this, —and deprecate such a plan with all my might. *Alone* you may do any thing; but partnerships in fame, like those in trade, make the strongest party answerable for the deficiencies or deliquencies of the rest, and I tremble even for *you* with such a bankrupt Co. —* * * *. They are both clever fellows, and Shelley I look upon as a man of real genius; but I must again say, that you could not give your enemies (the * * *'s, 'et hoc genus omne') a greater triumph than by forming such an unequal and unholy alliance. You are, single-handed, a match for the world, —which is saying a good deal, the world being, like Briareus,[2] a very many-handed gentleman,— but, to be so, *you must stand alone*. Recollect that the scurvy buildings about St. Peter's almost seem to overtop itself.[3]

---

[1] In 1820 Murray published Giovanni Battista Belzoni's *Narrative of the Operations and Recent Discoveries within the Pyramids, Temples, Tombs, and Excavations in Egypt and Nubia*. Moore is referring to a French version of the work, which Galignani published.

[2] In Greek mythology a giant with a hundred hands.

[3] Writing to Moore on 19 Feb. 1822 (not on 24 Jan., as Moore states in his *Life of Byron*), Byron said in answer to this letter: 'Be assured that there is no such coalition as you apprehend' (*LJ*, vi. 22).

618. *To Lord Byron*

Moore, *Byron*, v. 318

February 9. 1822.

Do *not* take it into your head, my dear B. that the tide is at all turning against you in England. Till I see some symptoms of people *forgetting* you a little, I will not believe that you lose ground. As it is, 'te veniente die, te, decedente,'—nothing is hardly talked of but you; and though good people sometimes bless themselves when they mention you, it is plain that even *they* think much more about you than, for the good of their souls, they ought. Cain, to be sure, *has* made a sensation; and, grand as it is, I regret, for many reasons, you ever wrote it. * * For myself, I would not give up the *poetry* of religion for all the wisest results that *philosophy* will ever arrive at. Particular sects and creeds are fair game enough for those who are anxious enough about their neighbours to meddle with them; but our faith in the Future is a treasure not so lightly to be parted with; and the dream of immortality (if philosophers *will* have it a dream) is one that, let us hope, we shall carry into our last sleep with us.*

* It is to this sentence Lord Byron refers at the conclusion of his letter, March 4.[1] [*Moore's note*]

619. *To Lord Byron*

Moore, *Byron*, v. 319

February 19. 1822.

I have written to the Longmans to try the ground, for I do *not* think Galignani the man for you. The only thing he can do is what we can do, ourselves, without him,—and that is, employ an English bookseller. Paris, indeed, might be convenient for such refugee works as are set down in the *Index Expurgatorius* of London; and if you have any political catamarans to explode, this is your place. But, *pray*, let them be only political ones. Boldness, and even licence, in politics, does good,—actual, present good; but, in religion, it profits neither here nor hereafter; and, for myself, such a horror have I of both extremes on this subject, that I know not *which* I hate most, the bold, damning bigot, or the bold, annihilating infidel. 'Furiosa res est in tenebris impetus;'—and much as we are in the dark, even the wisest of us, upon these matters, a little modesty, in unbelief as well as belief, best becomes us. You will

[1] See the letter from Byron, 4 Mar. 1821 (*LJ*, vi. 30–33).

To Lord Byron

easily guess that, in all this, I am thinking not so much of you, as of a friend and, at present, companion of yours, whose influence over your mind (knowing you as I do, and knowing what Lady B. *ought* to have found out, that you are a person the most tractable to those who live with you that, perhaps, ever existed) I own I dread and deprecate most earnestly.*

* This passage having been shown by Lord Byron to Mr. Shelley, the latter wrote, in consequence, a letter to a gentleman with whom I was then in habits of intimacy, of which the following is an extract. The zeal and openness with which Shelley always professed his unbelief render any scruple that might otherwise be felt in giving publicity to such avowals unnecessary; besides which, the testimony of so near and clear an observer to the state of Lord Byron's mind upon religious subjects is of far too much importance to my object to be, from any over-fastidiousness, suppressed. We have here, too strikingly exemplified,—and in strong contrast, I must say, to the line taken by Mr. Hunt in similar circumstances,—the good breeding, gentle temper, and modesty for which Shelley was so remarkable, and of the latter of which qualities in particular the undeserved compliment to myself affords a strong illustration, as showing how little this true poet had yet learned to know his own place.

'Lord Byron has read me one or two letters of Moore to him, in which Moore speaks with great kindness of me; and of course I cannot but feel flattered by the approbation of a man, my inferiority to whom I am proud to acknowledge. Amongst other things, however, Moore, after giving Lord B. much good advice about public opinion, &c. seems to deprecate *my* influence on his mind on the subject of religion, and to attribute the tone assumed in Cain to my suggestions. Moore cautions him against any influence on this particular with the most friendly zeal, and it is plain that his motive springs from a desire of benefiting Lord B. without degrading me. I think you know Moore. Pray assure him that I have not the smallest influence over Lord Byron in this particular; if I had, I certainly should employ it to eradicate from his great mind the delusions of Christianity, which, in spite of his reason, seem perpetually to recur, and to lay in ambush for the hours of sickness and distress. Cain was *conceived* many years ago, and begun before I saw him last year at Ravenna. How happy should I not be to attribute to myself, however indirectly, any participation in that immortal work!' [*Moore's note*]

620. *To Lord Byron*

Moore, *Byron*, v. 321

March 16. 1822.

With repect to our Religious Polemics, I must try to set you right upon one or two points. In the first place, I do *not* identify you with the blasphemies of Cain no more than I do myself with the impieties of my Mokanna,[1]—all I wish and implore is that you, who are such a powerful manufacturer of these thunderbolts, would not *choose* subjects that make it necessary to launch them. In the next

[1] The 'Veiled Prophet of Khorassan' in Moore's *Lalla Rookh*.

place, were you even a decided atheist, I could not (except, perhaps, for the *decision* which is always unwise) blame you. I could only pity,—knowing from experience how dreary are the doubts with which even the bright, poetic view I am myself inclined to take of mankind and their destiny is now and then clouded. I look upon Cuvier's book[1] to be a most desolating one in the conclusions to which it may lead some minds. But the young, the simple, —all those whose hearts one would like to keep unwithered, trouble their heads but little about Cuvier. *You*, however, have embodied him in poetry which every one reads; and, like the wind, blowing 'where you list,' carry this deadly chill, mixed up with your own fragrance, into hearts that should be visited only by the latter. This is what I regret, and what with all my influence I would deprecate a repetition of. *Now*, do you understand me?

As to your solemn peroration, 'the truth is, my dear Moore, &c. &c.'[2] meaning neither more nor less than that I give into the cant of the world, it only proves, alas! the melancholy fact, that you and I are hundreds of miles asunder. Could you hear me speak my opinions instead of coldly reading them, I flatter myself there is still enough of honesty and fun in this face to remind you that your friend Tom Moore—whatever else he may be,—is no Canter.

621. *To the Marquess of Lansdowne*

Bowood

[May or June 1822]

My dear Lord Lansdowne— It is very good of you still to have such neighbourly feelings towards us, long as we have been separated, and I assure you Sloperton has lost none of its charms for either Mrs Moore or myself, but that we still think it (to use a phrase of our Wiltshire maid, when she last saw it) the most 'natural' place for us to be in. The Longmans promise me a speedy release, but Rees, who is my chief negotiator, has been for some weeks past, on his annual tour of business 'spargere voces' (or rather *in*voices) through Scotland & Ireland, and I suppose I shall hear no more of *my* business till his return— I have been employed since I came to Passy in writing a poem upon a subject which many years since occurred to me, but which was again thrown by in the lumber-room

---

[1] Georges Cuvier, *Discours sur les révolutions de la surface du globe*, translated by Robert Kerr in 1813. In a note to the preface to *Cain*, Byron had written, 'The reader will perceive that the author has partly adopted . . . the notion of Cuvier, that the world had been destroyed several times before the creation of man' (*LJ*, v. 367 n.).

[2] See *LJ*, vi. 33.

of my memory, till (in consequence of Lord Byron's intention of producing something on the same theme) I have again rummaged it out, & mean to publish as soon as the Longmans think it prudent to announce me.[1] Their opinion being, that, untill this last claim is settled, the appearance of any new work from me might tend to raise the demands of the claimants, and so embarrass the negotiation. My larger Poem has been, of course, in the mean time suspended.

You know, I dare say, all the news of Paris. The most important thing (next to the establishment of a new Restaurateur on the Boulevard) is the trial of the Conspirators, and if you are in the way of reading the details, you must be disgusted by the total want of anything like judicial fairness in the proceedings—[2] The President is completely formed on the model of Lord Norbury's judge with a wen on his cheek, having 'his *jaw* all on one side', and that side never by any chance the prisoner's—[3] It makes one wretched to read it—but neither in Law nor in Politics does the 'Grande Nation' seem at all *at home*— What Montaigne calls 'La Police des Sauces' (with a strong seasoning of gendarmerie) is the only thing they are formed to appreciate or enjoy.

What I feel most worth thinking about here is Madame Pasta. She is perfection. Her Romeo & Tancredi are the most touching exhibitions altogether I ever saw on the stage. For countenance, for acting, for pathos of voice, she has in my opinion, no equal. Mrs Moore, who does not know a word of Italian, cried as much at Romeo the other night as ever she did at Miss O'Neil's best character.

I do not know Parson Croly personally, but, from what I hear of him, he must be rather a disagreeable person, though certainly a

---

[1] *The Loves of the Angels.* Byron's poem was *Heaven and Earth.*

[2] In December 1821 some youths of the military school at Saumur were arrested for conspiring in favour of Napoleon II, their 'conspiracy' being nothing more than a single demonstration. Several officers on regular duty were arrested merely on suspicion; a few men under a General Breton attempted to seize Saumur and Thouars in Vendée; and a near mutiny occurred at La Rochelle.

Throughout 1822 the civil and military courts of France vied with one another in giving death sentences to the conspirators, and nine men, who had been arrested as leaders, were executed. The result of the conspiracies was that Parliament enacted restrictive legislation. For a good account of this phase of French history see Émile Bourgeois, *Modern France, 1815–1913*, in the *Cambridge Historical Series* (Cambridge, 1919), pp. 43–46.

[3] John Toler, first Earl of Norbury (1745–1831), was made Chief Justice of the Court of Common Pleas in 1800. He concealed his ignorance of law, callousness, and partiality behind a broad show of humour, which often kept his courtroom in an uproar. Moore is obviously referring to one of the numerous *bon mots* attributed to him.

very clever one. Not that I am however qualified to judge him impartially, for I have reason to know that wherever there has been an opportunity of 'roasting' me publicly, he has been one of those that with true Irish good-nature, 'turned the spit'. I suppose Bowles's Holy Alliance with Blackwood's magazine has been the origin of this league between him & Parson Croly.

As soon as I hear anything definitive about my business, I shall acquaint you with it. And ask the kindness of your mediation between me & my Landlord about the Cottage.

Pray, give my best remembrances to Lady Lansdowne, & believe me, with the deepest feeling of your goodness towards me, ever faithfully yours

Thomas Moore

622. *To Samuel Rogers*

Russell, viii. 283

19. Rue Basse, à Passy, près Paris.
July 16 [1822][1]

My dear Rogers,

I find that, though you do not write to me, you are still thoughtful as usual about everything that may tend to either my profit or reputation, and I think it must be with a view to gratifying me on the latter score that you recommended the application from 'The Times' that Brougham has just forwarded to me. It does indeed flatter me very much to have it thought that I could wield such a powerful political engine as 'The Times' with either that strength or promptitude which such a task requires, and it flatters me the more from my being conscious that I do not deserve it. Putting my ability, however, out of the question, it is impossible that I should now undertake such an office; for, in the first place, I cannot come to England, and, in the next, if I could, there are so many tasks before me (from the long spell of idleness I have indulged in), that every minute of my time will hardly be sufficient to accomplish them. So, pray take some means of letting Mr. Barnes know that, with every acknowledgment of the honour which he has done me by the application, I feel myself obliged to decline his proposal for the present.[2] I write in haste and by the common

---

[1] Russell added a note to this letter, saying that Moore dated it 1842 instead of 1822.

[2] On 17 July 1822 Moore recorded in his diary: 'Received to-day a letter from Brougham, inclosing one from Barnes (the editor of *The Times*), proposing that, as he is ill, I shall take his place for some time in writing the leading

post, because I have understood that an immediate answer was necessary, and I would not have troubled you, my dear Rogers, with this letter, had not Brougham desired me to make you the medium of my reply.

I am afraid there is no chance of our meeting here very soon, for you must have had a sufficient dose of the Continent for some time; but, about the beginning of winter, if the Fates and the Yankees[1] are propitious, we may stand a chance of shaking hands with each other in St. James's Place.

Ever yours,
Thomas Moore.

623. *To John Hunt*

University of Bergen

Sloperton Cottage, Devizes, Wilts*
Decr 24th 1822

Dear Sir—

I called upon you before I left town & regret very much that I was not lucky enough to see you. There are two or three subjects upon which I wished much to have half an hour's conversation with you, and, on my return to London, I shall have the pleasure of calling upon you for that purpose. In the mean time, there is one point, more urgent than the rest, as it regards the Second Number of the Liberal, which I see announced for immediate publication. I have, from time to time, in my letters to Lord Byron inserted some hasty verses, chiefly satirical, which it has struck me he might, from thoughtlessness or *fun*, let, some time or other, escape among the minor pieces of the Liberal, and I have often intended to give him a little caution on the subject, but have always forgot it. One of the purposes, therefore, of my visit to you the other day was to request, in *perfect confidence*, that if any such trifles should occur among the contributions to this or any succeeding Number, you will not insert them, without, at least, consulting my wishes on the subject.[2]

Believe me, Dear Sir, with much
esteem, yours very truly
Thomas Moore.

articles of that paper; the pay to be 100£ a-month.' On the 18th he noted: 'Wrote to decline the proposal of *The Times*' (Russell, iii. 362).

¹ An allusion to his difficulties with the Bermuda post. See letter No. 535, to Lady Donegal, 2 Apr. 1818.

² None of Moore's poems were published in the *Liberal*.

624. *Addressee unknown*

National Library of Ireland

Sloperton Cottage, Devizes
Decr 27th 1822*

Sir—

I have received an anonymous letter from your neighbourhood, which (in consequence of my absence from home, did not reach me till within these two days) informing me of the distressed situation of a person, who is represented to be a near relative of my father, and requiring of me some aid toward his relief & support— Having never heard before even the name of the person in question, I have thought it right to apply to my father, in order to know if the statement is correct, and, in the mean time, I trust I do not take too great a liberty in requesting of *you*, Sir (to whom I have been referred for the particulars of this case) to afford whatever immediate supplies may be necessary for the comforts of this person, if he should appear to have those claims upon my relationship & humanity which are set forth in the letter I have received, and to favour me with a line or two upon the subject as soon as is convenient— I never was, myself, in a situation less capable of affording assistance to others than at present, but hold myself bound to make every effort in my power (however trifling even *that* must be) to assist a person so nearly connected with my dear father as Mr Mahony is represented to be— You will have the goodness not to exceed five pounds in your *immediate* disbursements, and your draft upon me for that sum directed to Mr Power 34, Strand, London, will be paid upon being presented—or, if that be inconvenient, I can, as soon as I hear from you, give orders for its being paid in Dublin— When I am in possession of all the particulars of the case, I shall see what further it may be in my power to do.[1]

With many apologies for the trouble which I thus unwillingly give you, I remain, Sir,

Your very obliged &c.
Thomas Moore.

[1] No more is known of this matter than is contained in this letter. Moore did not mention it in his diary nor have other clarifying letters been found.

625. *To James Carpenter*

Harvard College Library

[c. 1822]

Dear Carpenter— I will not for one instant suppose (though unluckily your letter might to some minds convey such a notion)
that you could harbour the least intention of publishing, in its
present form, a really *juvenile* production, which was so many
years ago suppressed, at my wish, and with your consent, as not
likely to be at all creditable either to the author or the publisher.
To think, for an instant, I repeat, that your letter was meant to
convey any unworthy threat of this kind would be to do you gross
injustice, and I shall at once dismiss it from my mind.

That you should wish to be repaid, in some manner, the expence
which this suppressed work has brought upon you is of course all
fair and in the regular course of trade, and I shall be most ready
to enter into any such arrangement with you (whether by taking
the work entirely off you hands or by endeavouring to shape it
into a form fit for publication) as may be most likely to relieve
you from the *only* loss, I flatter myself, which your being my first
publisher has ever entailed upon you.[1]

Yours very truly
Thomas Moore.

626. *To Colonel Houlton*

B.M. Add. MS. 27425BC, f. 4

Bowood
Wednesday [c. 1822]

My dear Houlton— Notwithstanding Mrs Moore's note, I had some
hope of being able to join you at Grittleton, but having promised
to meet Lord Cawdor, whenever he should come here, I have been
nailed for these two days. What I write to say is that Newton is
here on his way to Farley, and leaves this on Friday, so that, unless
you can receive him at Grittleton, he will *be on the parish*— If you
can, write a line directed to him here immediately to say so—&
should my engagements of business permit, I will follow him either
to Grittleton or to Farley.

Yours most illegibly (I fear)
T. Moore

Post just going out.

[1] The tone of this letter suggests that it dealt with 'The Sketches of Pious
Women', a youthful production which was never published. The date of the
letter is conjecturally 1822.

PLATE 6

JOHN MURRAY'S DRAWING ROOM. From a painting by C. Werner

627. *To Wadham Locke*

Rice University

[Watermark 1822]

My dear Locke— We have this instant received a letter from a particular friend of ours to say that he is on his way to us, & hopes to arrive here to-day— Our first impulse was to send you an excuse, but it occurred to me that I might perhaps trespass so far upon your hospitality, as (*if* he comes) to take *him* with us to dinner— It will, of course, depend upon whether he has either the mind or the *toilette* for such a step, but I shall presume so far upon your good-nature as, at all events, to *ask* him, in case he should arrive before we set off.— I am just despatching a note, upon the chance of its stopping him at Devizes—

Ever yours truly
Thomas Moore

628. *To John Murray*

Sir John Murray
Confidential

Sloperton Cottage
January 11th 1823

Dear Murray— I am anxious to hear what you are doing *for* me, or *against* me, in the Quarterly— Whatever may be said of the *talent* of the thing (which I give up, to be dealt with as you please) I only hope & trust that there will be no giving in to the cry of 'impiety' 'blasphemy' &c. which, I see, is endeavoured to be raised in John Bull & other quarters, & which (if such a leading journal as yours should take it up) would leave me to be carried away down the current of Cant without redemption— This is all I deprecate—the charge is unjust, *certainly* with regard to the *intention*, and, as far as I can judge, with respect to the *execution*, also— Within the circle of my own friends, I have found (with only one exception) unmixed praises—at Bowood the Poem is preferred, without hesitation, to Lalla Rookh— I have had similar good accounts from Middleton, Holland House &c. &c.—but all this is nothing if the d——d sturdy Saints of the middle class should take it into their heads not to buy me—for, *you* know well, how they can send one to Coventry—so, pray, take care of me on this point—this one point—and I'll forgive every thing else *printed* that even Croker can produce—if Croker has *indeed* had the good-nature to

undertake me, as he half promised the other day at Kensing-
ton—[1] At all events, let me hear something comfortable from you
& believe me

> Very faithfully yours
> Thomas Moore

629. *To Miss Lavinia Forster*

Yale

[January 1823]

I know you will all be glad to hear that my Book is succeeding
beyond my best hopes—near 5000 have been sold in a week.

I hope the copies I sent (both of the Angels & the Nat[1] Melodies)
arrived safe.

> Love to all.
> T. M.

630. *To John Murray*

Sir John Murray

> Sloperton Cottage, Devizes*
> Feb[r] 11. 1823*

My dear *Sir*—(You see, as you wouldn't answer me, I have returned
to formalities)— I inclose a Bill upon Power, which you will perhaps, if not inconvenient, cash for me & if I do not receive a 'no'
from you by return of post, I shall draw upon you for some of the
amount accordingly—

What keeps your Quarterly so long? I am rather in trepidation
about it, and shall be not at all sorry to find myself left out—
particularly as my angels will be all turned into good Mohametans
in the forth-coming Edition,[2] which metamorphosis would be a

---

[1] Moore's *Loves of the Angels* was published on 23 Dec. 1822. The reviews in
the leading journals attacked the poem on religious grounds, and Moore
promptly changed his angels into Turks (i.e. into Moslem angels) and God into
Allah. The poem was reviewed in *Blackwood's*, iii. 63–71; *London Magazine*,
vii. 212–15; and the *British Critic*, xix, 2nd Series, 236–46. Moore found some
consolation in the admiration of the *European Magazine*, lxiii. 256–9. The most
severe attack came from the Tory organ *John Bull* on 5 Jan. 1823. The attack
was directed both at Moore and his poem, saying, 'There is a convivial good
nature and perpetual pleasantry about little MOORE' which wins favour
among his acquaintances, but indicating that he was, nevertheless, a shallow
dilettante. Many details of *The Loves of the Angels*, the reviewer maintained,
'were not fit for the public'. The poem was not reviewed in the *Quarterly*.

[2] See letter No. 628, to John Murray, 11 Jan. 1823.

most edifying subject for the succeeding number to dilate upon.
I am going to publish another slight matter in the course of March
(from the pen of Tom Brown)[1] and, after that, shall set seriously
to my Sheridan task for the rest of the year, so as to have it ready
before Christmas.

Croker was very kind upon the subject of my former letter to
you, and would, I am sure, have been very well inclined to give me
a lift if he could.

Yours very faithfully
Thomas Moore.

631. *To John Murray*

Sir John Murray

Thursday Night, Feb^r 13th 1823

My dear Sir— I feel much obliged by your kindness in discounting
my Bill upon Power—but, as I fear, from what you say, that it has
not been convenient to you, I shall not again encroach so far upon
your good-nature.[2]

I send, inclosed, a scrap which I have cut out of your letter (not
having time to copy it) and, without alluding to the old woman's
appeal to Philip *Sober*, I ask you, as a matter of curiosity, whether
you *remember* having written it? I certainly do not recognize your
style in it, at least such as you have hitherto favoured me with.

I shall most readily make the alteration in our agreement which
you propose; it not being my wish to do any thing which could for
a moment be stigmatized as 'unfair'—but as I do not think it would
be quite a regular way of proceeding to 'send you back that part
of the engagement' (by which you can only mean tearing off the
portion of the deed which contains it) I trust you will consider it
time enough to make the alteration when I shall arrive in town
towards the latter end of next month—at which time I shall also
consider whether it may not be in my power to pay back the whole
of what I owe you upon this account, and receive the MS. again
into my own hands.[3]

[1] The volume containing *Fables for the Holy Alliance, Rhymes on the Road*,
and a few miscellaneous poems by 'Thomas Brown, the Younger' did not
appear until 7 May 1823.

[2] See letter No. 630, to John Murray, 11 Feb. 1823.

[3] The agreement was that if Moore would repay, during Byron's lifetime,
the 2,000 guineas which Murray had originally given him for it, the manuscript
of Byron's Memoirs would be returned to Moore. Had Moore acted upon this
agreement immediately (instead of after Byron's death, when he did borrow
the money from the Longmans) he would have succeeded in preserving all or
part of the Memoirs. (See letter No. 605, to John Murray, 17 Sept. 1821.)

Many thanks for the extract from the Review, which will be of great service, I think, to Power.

Yours truly
Thomas Moore

As to what you call Mr Kinnaird's 'ungentlemanly' conduct (mine, luckily, having been *only* 'unfair') you must address yourself to *him* upon that subject.

632. *To Lord Byron*

Moore, *Byron*, vi. 7

[February 1823]

I am most anxious to know that you mean to emerge out of the Liberal. It grieves me to urge any thing so much against Hunt's interest; but I should not hesitate to use the same language to himself, were I near him. I would, if I were you, serve him in every possible way but this—I would give him (if he would accept of it) the profits of the same works, published separately—but I would *not* mix myself up in this way with others. I would *not* become a partner in this sort of miscellaneous '*pot au feu*,' where the bad flavour of one ingredient is sure to taint all the rest. I would be, if I were *you*, alone, single-handed, and, as such, invincible.[1]

633. *To John Murray*

Sir John Murray

Sloperton Cottage*
March 5th 1823.*

Dear Sir

I have drawn upon you to-day for twenty pounds, which with the two former drafts (one of thirty & the other of fifty) makes the amount of the hundred pound Bill upon Power, which you have been so good as to cash for me— As I do not know how much the discount is, I have not, as you perceive, allowed for it, but must give you the trouble of putting it to my account.

Your very obliged &c.
Thomas Moore

[1] Byron replied to this letter on 20 Feb. 1823, assuring Moore that he did not intend to become involved with Hunt, but asking 'You would not have had me leave him in the street with his family, would you?' (*LJ*, vi. 167).

634. *To John Wilson Croker*

Princeton

Sloperton
March 23rd 1823

My dear Croker— I am quite sorry that *you* have been troubled
with this nonsense— It reached me some time ago, with this difference, that it was about something I had written in 'the Tickler'
(whatever that may be) you and I had quarrelled— I am afraid it
originated with my friend little Power, whose imagination, like that
of his Poet, is always at work (though in a different way) and, upon
this occasion, I believe, it was put into increased activity by the
terms in which your message was conveyed to him— I wrote to
him immediately that he might be quite sure there was no incivility
intended either to him or to me—for that, on the contrary, you
were, every two or three days, forwarding large packets to me—
but that his might have been *too* large, or that he had, on this
occasion, put my French newspapers in, or that something else
might have been the reason, and that, at all events, he had better
not send any more, as I knew (though very kind to me) you were
rather particular about your covers.[1] There was a similar rumor
about me & Lord Byron two or three months ago (which reached
me at the same moment both from France & from Ireland) stating,
with all the usual 'Art de verifier les Lates', that we had had an
irremediable & inextinguishable blow-up—a day or two after, however, I received a letter from him, beginning 'My *dear Tom*', which
(not looking very bloody-minded) set all my apprehensions to rest.

You have had a respite from my Longman Packets lately, as my
corrected Edition is finished—but, as there still remain on hands
some copies of the 4th Edition (which, when sold, completes the
sixth thousand since publication) they mean to keep the 5th, I
believe, for their Trade Sale in April.[2]

I am sorry I am so like you in being lame, but my lameness has
prevented me from taking any exercise these four or five weeks.

Yours very truly
Thomas Moore

Pray, send the inclosed to Murray.

[1] 'Little Power' is James Power and 'his Poet' is Moore himself. The *Tickler*
was a journal published from 1818 to 1824, but Moore was not a contributor.
Power often sent Moore letters and packets franked through Croker's office.
Evidently Croker had objected to the type or amount of material Power had
sent, and the publisher's imagination was 'put into increased activity' by
Croker's objection.
[2] The significant change in *The Loves of the Angels* was made in the fifth
edition of the work. See letter No. 630, to John Murray, 11 Feb. 1823.

635. *To John Murray*

Sir John Murray

March 27ᵗʰ 1823*

My dear Sir— I had great pleasure in receiving your letter yesterday— It has been my good fortune to have passed so far through
life, without having had, in either friendship or business, a serious
misunderstanding with any one—and it would have given me great
pain to begin with *you*, whose real & friendly kindness to me, on all
occasions, I have always acknowledged more warmly to others than
to yourself— But not less new to me than quarrelling, was the having the word 'unfairness' coupled with any transaction in which I
was concerned, and I own it startled me into something like indignation— Your explanation, however, is perfectly satisfactory—only
I suspect you are mistaken as to the persons under whose advice
you think I acted— The friend, who suggested the clause to which
you allude, is as little what is called a man of business as myself,
and quite as incapable, I believe, of producing two thousand
guineas, at a minute's warning, as I am— I shall have no objection
to tell you who it was when I see you in town, which, I expect, will
be in the course of next week—[1] Poor Mʳ Taafe!— Bore as he is,
I can't help pitying him—[2]

Yours very faithfully
Thomas Moore

636. *To Lady Holland*

The Earl of Ilchester[3]

Tuesday morning* [April 1823]

Dear Lady Holland,

There is a great friend of Mrs Moore's come from Paris to pass
only this week with Mrs Henry Ogle, and it has occured [*sic*] to me
that, as you are going out of town, you might possibly have no

---

[1] Moore made the following entry in his diary for the period 12 Feb. through
15 Mar.: 'Received a letter from Murray about my bond to him for the Byron
Memoirs; far from civil: returned an answer in kind and have received no
reply.' Later in the same entry he says, 'Received a letter from Murray,
explaining away most anxiously any appearance of offence there might have
been in his former one . . .' (Russell, iv. 44). See also letter No. 631, to John
Murray, 13 Feb. 1823.

[2] In 1822 Murray published anonymously the first volume of John Taaffe's
Comment on the Divine Comedy of Dante. The work was not successful and was
never completed.

[3] Transcript provided by the Earl of Ilchester.

objection to lend me your box for them some night in the week—
either tomorrow, Thursday or Friday— Don't be angry with me,
if I ask too much— I know it is like asking for the loan of one's
house or one's lodgings, but I have a great wish to oblige them, and
as I know you would not refuse me without good reasons for doing
so, I thought I might as well try the chance of asking.

If you have not seen the Engravings of the Costumes worn at the
Court of Berlin in *Lalla Rookh*, I'll send you my Copy to look at.[1]

Very faithfully your obliged
Thomas Moore

637. *To Samuel Rogers*

Russell, viii. 257

Friday, May 23. 1823.

My dear Rogers,

I have to ask a great favour of you, which is that you will take
an opportunity (as soon as you can conveniently) of putting my
name down to the Greek subscription for five pounds, and paying
that sum for me.[2] I would not give you this trouble, but that Power
is in Ireland, and that I do not like employing the Longmans any
further in this way till I have settled my account with them. As
soon as I return to town, I shall pay you with many thanks, and
you will, I know, recollect that I wish the thing to be done *before*
any new list of subscribers is printed.

It was very kind of you to write to me so encouragingly about
the 'Fables';[3] but I fear (from not seeing any announcement of
a second edition) that the sale begins already to 'drag its wounded
length along.'[4] To be sure, the first edition was 3000, and (as you
say sometimes) one *used* to be satisfied with such things.

I am beginning very *seriously* to turn my attention again to
Sheridan, and shall not be, this time, diverted from it by *anything*.

I see 'Italy' quoted everywhere.[5] Bessy hopes you do not forget
her old claim (like that of the Universities), that a copy of every
work of yours should be duly deposited with her. She is still of the
dual number.

Ever yours, faithfully,
Thomas Moore.

[1] See Russell, iii. 217, and letter No. 1245, to Andrew Doyle, 15 June 1846.
Moore first learned of the fête in April 1821.

[2] Moore is referring to the subscription for the relief of Greece, which was
raised at this time by the Greek Committee in England.

[3] *Fables for the Holy Alliance* (1823).

[4] *Essay on Criticism*, l. 350.

[5] Rogers published *Italy, a Poem*, Part I, in 1822.

638. *To James Power*

Yale

[June 30th 1823, *not in Moore's hand*]

My dear Sir—

I send you the Song I promised—the words for the last verse of 'Poor wounded heart'[1] did not please me as I wrote them down, so I must have a little more work at them.

Yours ever

T. M.

639. *To Lord Byron*

Maggs Brothers Catalogue   473, Spring 1926

Devizes

17th July, 1823

Why don't you answer my letter? It was written just before the publication of my last catch-penny,[2] and gave you various particulars thereof, such as its being dedicated to you, the Longman's alarm at its contents, Denman's opinion, etc.

The fact is, the Public expected personality, as usual, and were disappointed not to find it, and, though I touched five hundred pounds as my share of the first edition, the thing is 'gone dead' already.

This public tires of us all, good and bad, and I rather think (if I can find some other more gentlemanly trade) I shall cut the connexion entirely. How you, who are not obliged, can go on writing for it, has long you know been my astonishment. To be sure, you have all Europe and America at your back, which is a consolation we poor insula wits . . . have not to support us in our reverses.

I have not yet seen your new Cantos,[3] but Christian[4] seems to have shone out most prosperously, and the truth is that yours are the only 'few fine flashes' of the 'departing day' of Poesy on which the Public can now be induced to fix their gaze. My 'Angels'[5] I consider a failure—I mean in the impression they made—for I agree with a 'select few' that I never wrote anything better.

---

[1] *Poetry*, p. 309.
[2] *Fables for the Holy Alliance* (1823).
[3] *Don Juan*, cantos VI, VII, and VIII, appeared in 1823.
[4] *The Island, or Christian and His Comrades* (1823).
[5] *Loves of the Angels* (1823).

640. *To John Murray*

Sir John Murray

Sloperton Cottage
August 31st 1823

My dear Sir—

I hold myself bound, as a matter of business (putting friendship out of the question) to report myself to you, as returned alive out of the hands of Captain Rock's Kerry boys.[1] I arrived here on Thursday Evening, after a most interesting & delightful tour, and do not mean to stir again from my writing-desk for six or eight months.

Your account-keeper will tell you that I have drawn (upon my Bill on Power) all but fifty pounds—which fifty pounds must follow the rest in the course of this next week.

I wish you would send for me to Power's a copy of Watkins's Life of Sheridan, as mine has been lost in transporting my books from France.

Yours very truly
Thomas Moore

641. *To John Murray*

Sir John Murray

[6 December 1823]

My dear Sir— I take the opportunity of writing you a line by Power, who has been with me here on a short visit of business.[2] There was an announcement about the *Life* in the Chronicle the other day, which makes me rather fear that you expect the Work sooner than it can possibly be ready, & I therefore think it but fair to put you in possession of the real & bona-fide state of the case. I have not the least doubt of being able to take the MS. up to you in the course of May, but there will still be points upon which I shall find it necessary to make enquiries, and for which I have adopted the plan of *leaving blanks*, instead of stopping at them till fully informed, as I have hitherto done. I should also like, at that time, to have the Work *set up* (which I shall willingly go to the expense of myself) in order that I might submit it to the perusal of those persons best acquainted with Sheridan & so have the

---

[1] Captain Rock was an imaginary leader in the battle for Irish independence. Moore made use of the character in his *Memoirs of Captain Rock* (1824).

[2] Moore recorded Power's visit in his diary, noting that the publisher left at half-past five on 6 Dec. 1823 (Russell, iv. 151).

advantage of their suggestions & corrections. All this, you see, would make it impossible for the publication to take place during the season, but, by devoting the summer to re-touching & printing, it might be out as early as you pleased in the winter. I am afraid you will be much disappointed at this delay & to me (who have imposed upon myself the abstinence of not touching any more of your money till I have, at least, *virtually* finished) it is even more inconvenient than to you. But my fruit will not 'fall without shaking.'

I shall have to trouble you for some books soon.

Pray, give my best regards to Mrs Murray & believe me yours very truly

Thomas Moore

Lord Byron seems inclined to cut *me* as well as you & others. I have not heard from him for some months.

I wrote a pamphlet on my return from Ireland,[1] to get rid of the bile that was (in Lord Melville's phrase) 'rolling on my stomach'. It will not, however, be printed (if at all) till the meeting of Parliament.

642. *To Frederick (?) Byng*

New York Public

Bowood
Decr 17 1823

Thanks, my dear Byng, for your amusing news which (though the *villain* is too busy otherwise to turn it to account) produced some good fun at the dinner-table yesterday. Mrs Moore (Strangways says) is a very pretty woman & daughter of a Dragoman.

I shall be obliged to run up to town on Sunday for two days, & hope to have a glimpse of you.

Poor Kerry has been very ill, but is better this morning.

Y^rs ever
T. Moore.

Pray send the inclosed to my lodgings for me.—2^d Post will do, but as *early* as possible.

643. *To John Murray*

Sir John Murray

Decr 26th 1823

My dear Sir— I have just had a letter from Charles Sheridan inclosing me the copy of a note he had received from you, by which I see that there is likely to be another hitch in our Sheridan business.

---

[1] *Memoirs of Captain Rock* appeared on 17 Apr. 1824.

I certainly was not aware (no more than you seem to be yourself by this note) that there was any claim meant to be brought forward for a share of the profits of the Life, and I mean to tell Sheridan as much in my answer.[1] I see you mention that you have advanced me £500 on the task, which is true (within a few pounds) as far as regards what I actually drew upon that account—but I trust you have not forgotten (what was made clear between us when I was last in town) that the £200 I left undrawn of the £500 bond I had of you, is, *pro tanto* a set-off against my debt on the Sheridan account & reduces it to £300— This is of the more importance to me now, as from the readiness you express in the note to Sheridan to break off the contract with me, & from the embarrassments I see likely to attend the whole concern, I think it is not improbable I shall have to pay you back this £300—for I have half made up my mind to send the papers back to Sheridan & give up the task of writing the Life entirely. I shall however ask Lord L^s advice, & be a good deal guided by what he recommends me.

Yours, my dear Sir, very faithfully
Thomas Moore

I shall be able, I hope, to run up to town in about three or four weeks hence, when we can consult on this & other matters.

644. *To Samuel Rogers*

Russell, viii. 258

Sloperton Cottage
Jan. 18. 1824.

My dear Rogers,

On my return from Ireland the latter end of last week, I found my table and drawers heaped with letters and manuscripts (among the latter a Tragedy, a Poem, and the rough copy of the Memoirs of a Rebel Chief, sent to me from America), and your precious little letter lay so modestly lurking under all this mass, that it was but the night before last I fished it up, like a pearl, from among them. Thank you, many, many times, for the encouraging things you say about my book. It certainly succeeds with the public, which ought to be a consolation to me for the heart-burning it produces in various quarters.[2] Radicals hate me for my praise of the aristocracy, Whigs

---

[1] See letters Nos. 546 and 558, to Thomas Wilkie, 19 June and 25 Aug. 1818.

[2] Representative reviews of the *Fables for the Holy Alliance* may be found in the *Westminster Review*, i. 18–26; the *Literary Gazette*, 10 May 1823, pp. 289 ff.; and *Blackwood's*, xiii. 574–9. The article in the *Westminster* was generally favourable, although it pointed out that Moore seemed 'ignorant of the fact

hate me for my candour to the Tories, and Tories hate me for all possible reasons. The cannonade from the Royal battery which you mention is, I suppose, only reserved, and may perhaps be dealt out to me in small shot th[r]ough the 'Representative,' or kept to give *éclat* to the commencement of the Lockhart dynasty. Should there be anything worth answering (which as yet there has not been, the statement in the 'Westminster,' as to the gift of the four thousand pounds, being, I am pretty sure, false), I must take the field in a pamphlet, like Bowles. In the mean time, during all this my private affairs go on most dishearteningly—'*en attendant l'amant périt.*' You have heard of my refusal of Lord Wellesley's offer,[1] and think, perhaps, with others (who have a different standard for a poor man from that which they go by themselves) that I *ought* to have accepted it. But if you knew all the circumstances, and heard my own view of it, you would not think so. Such a favour from the other side at this moment, coming in coincidence with the impression on some minds that I have *courted* the Tories in my book, would have left a vulnerable point in my character through life; and as character is my only property (though a damned bad property I find it), I must only endeavour to make the best of my bargain.

Bessy is better than I have known her some time; she and Anastasia enjoyed the Twelfth Night at Bowood without me. God bless you, my dear Rogers: it will be a good while before we meet, as I mean to work without intermission, if I can, for the next six months. You will ask—at what? and that's the question, for I have not even yet decided; but it must be at something little short of *coining*, or I'm ruined.

Yours ever,
T. Moore.

645. *To James Power*

New York Public

Friday *Feb^r 20^h 1824*

My dear Sir— Bessy sends you up the promised Pork by this day's Coach— You are to send the small joint & the jar to Mrs Dyke.

I feel, I assure you, very guilty for the great obstructions thrown

that not individuals, but *systems* were at fault, and that vices will remain as long as the system does'. The *Literary Gazette* found the work 'discreditable and degrading'.

¹ Moore learned through Philip Crampton that Lord Wellesley, the Lord Lieutenant of Ireland, meant to continue his father's half-pay (see letter No. 486, to Lady Donegal, 12 Jan. 1817) in the form of a pension to Moore's sister. Moore refused to accept such an arrangement and later found that the plan had been instigated by Crampton himself.

in your way with respect to your publications, but I do not think I am *yet* to blame for any of them— It was your own wish that I should attend first to the Sacred Songs, and *my* part of them is so far ready that there is but one (that I recollect) without a second verse; and that is very [soon] made out—so that there is nothing on my side to produce the delay in the work & [I] really think if Stevenson does not answer satisfactorily very soon, you ha[d] much better give him up & have them done by Bishop— With respect to the Irish Melodies, you shall have the second verse of Desmond's Song[1] next week (and of 'Where's the Star'[2] if I am obliged to keep it) and there will be thus very nearly the whole number compleat—but I own I should like to put some spirited, martial air in, if I can find one.

I am, in another respect, much annoyed at not having been able to get my Irish pamphlet out before the discussion of the affairs of Ireland in the House— I send part of the MS. to the Longmans to-day & It [*sic*] will take me my first week in town to copy the remainder of it—[3]

I am afraid you sometimes think me not attentive enough to your interests; and it is true that my literary labours take also a good deal of my attention—but what am I to do? My great delight would be, if I could afford it, to confine myself wholly to Songs & Music, but there are so many calls on me besides, that I am obliged to labour a little at every thing— At this moment my hand is so weary with transcribing, that I doubt whether you will be able to make out this scrawl.

Ever yours faithfully
Thomas Moore

646. *To John Murray*

Pforzheimer Misc. MS. 1336

March 17th 1824*

My dear Sir—

Sheridan promised to be with me at ½ past eleven; therefore I suppose some time between that & one you may expect to see us.

Yrs truly
Thomas Moore

---

[1] *Poetry*, p. 225.

[2] 'Where is the Star' was not included in the 1841 edition of Moore's works.

[3] *The Memoirs of Captain Rock* (1824). The first clause of this sentence is an interlineation, which accounts for the capital 'It'.

647. *To Lady Holland*

Rice University

Thursday Evg* [2 April 1824]

I am off to Wiltshire the day after tomorrow, and, what is worse, fear I shall not be able to come up again this season. Never had I a visit here of more bustle & less amusement.

I have bid the Longmans send you an early copy of my Bandit—[1] though I *know* you won't read it. However if you always continue so kind to my*self*, I shall not care much what you do with my *books*.

> Ever your Ladyship's
> obliged S
> Thomas Moore.

648. *To John Murray*

Sir John Murray

Albemarle Street*
May 14ᵗʰ 1824*

Dear Sir— I have called in consequence of this melancholy intelligence to know when it will be convenient to you to complete the arrangement with respect to the Memoirs which we agreed upon when I was last in London—[2] Your answer, as soon as possible, will very much oblige

> Yours truly
> Thomas Moore.

649. *To William Lisle Bowles*

Greever, p. 85

Wednesday [*May*, 1824].[3]

My dear Bowles—

My only reason for taking my book to you was that I thought (of the two) you had better read *me, myself,* than the misrepresentations of me in John Bull and Blackwood—and if I had stayed

---

[1] Moore is probably referring to *The Memoirs of Captain Rock*. On 9 Apr. 1824 he recorded in his diary that he received copies of the book, 'which is published to-day'. On the 11th he received a letter from Lady Holland, 'full of the warmest praise of "Captain Rock"'. It is reasonable to assume that he would refer to the fictitious rebel chieftain as a 'bandit'. Since Moore left London on 4 Apr. this letter must have been written on the 2nd. (See Russell, iv. 177–8.)

[2] Moore had just learned of Byron's death. For an account of the events which followed see Doris Langley Moore, 'The Burning of the Memoirs', *The Late Lord Byron* (New York, 1961), pp. 12–45. See also letter No. 631, to John Murray, 13 Feb. 1823.   [3] Greever's date.

a little longer with you, I think I should have forced you to swallow at least a chapter or two, as physic.[1] Not that I believe you to *want* physic of any sort or kind, as you will confess yourself before you are a week in London.

I mean to start on Saturday and shall be on the watch for you next week.

Yours ever most truly,
Thomas Moore.

650. *To the Marquise de Dolomieu*

British Museum[2]

Sloperton Cottage, Devizes
June 23rd 1824

I know not how I can sufficiently apologize for my most ungallant delay in answering your letter, but I trust that the precious scrap which I inclose will make my peace with you. You have by this time, I dare say, seen my statement in the newspapers with respect to Lord Byron's memoirs, but as the facts are very few and simple, I shall repeat them here:

Finding that his lordship's family felt such anxiety on the subject of these memoirs, I placed them at the disposal of the person whom I knew he loved best among them (his sister), and only suggested that the papers should not be entirely destroyed, but that such parts as, upon perusal, should be found unobjectionable might be preserved and published. It was the wish of his sister, however, that they should be utterly & without previous perusal destroyed, which was accordingly done, & I paid back to the bookseller the 2,000 guineas which he had advanced to me on the manuscript. The family have since been very anxious to be allowed to reimburse me this money, but I have declined their offer. I ought to mention that the motive which determined me to give up the memoirs was the knowledge that Lord Byron himself had lately expressed some regret at having written them.

As soon as I have time to look over my Sheridan papers I shall send you the promised fragment of his handwriting; and have the

[1] Moore recorded a visit to Bowles in his diary for 1 May 1823, at which time he left a copy of *The Memoirs of Captain Rock* with the Vicar of Bremhill, who refused to read it. He told Moore that his paper, the *St. James Chronicle*, abused it, and the poet noted that Bowles 'will read the abuse readily enough, though he won't the book' (Russell, iv. 181–2).

[2] The text of this letter was taken from Alfred Morrison's *Catalogue of the Collection of Autograph Letters and Historical Documents Formed between 1865 and 1882* (London, 1890), vol. iv. 311 (4).

honour to be, my dear Mᵉ la Marquise, your very obliged and faithful servant.

651. *To John Cam Hobhouse*

Sir John Murray

Sloperton Cottage, Devizes
July 4ᵗʰ 1824*

Dear Hobhouse— I trust to your kindness for communicating to me any particulars respecting our lost friend, which you think I ought to know.[1] The account of the will in Saturday's Chronicle was, I suppose, correct, but it would be a great relief to me to know that there were no injunctions in it with respect to the Memoirs.[2] I should also like to be informed of the time & manner in which the Funeral is to take place, as, of course, it would be right that I should join his other friends in attending it. If you can find a moment to dispatch me a few words on these points, you will much oblige me.[3]

I have been told that Mʳ Hanson means to write a Life of Byron —*can* this be true? I have much to consult with you on this subject, but shall not trouble you about it till you have got through your present melancholy task.

Yours very truly
Thomas Moore

652. *To Lupton Relfe*

Rice University

Sloperton Cottage*
August 1ˢᵗ 1824*

Sir— I feel much obliged by your kindness in sending me a Copy of your very elegant little work, and it would give me great pleasure to contribute to it, but that my time is already *bespoke* by more tasks than I fear it will be equal to.[4] With many thanks for the kind terms in which you express yourself towards me, I am

Your obliged &c
Thomas Moore.

[1] Byron died on 19 Apr. 1824.

[2] Hobhouse and John Hanson were named co-executors of the will which Byron made in 1815, leaving the bulk of his estate to Augusta and her children (see Marchand, *Byron*, p. 1253). Since the will was dated August 1815, there was, of course, no mention of the Memoirs.

[3] Hobhouse replied, writing on the back of Moore's letter, on 6 July, saying that the plans had not been fixed. He hoped for Westminster Abbey, but there were complications. He promised to let Moore know of further plans but made no mention of the will or Memoirs.

[4] Lupton Relfe was a hymnologist who published *Hymns, Composed for the Use of the Chapel of the Royal Seamen at Greenwich* (London, 1789). The work to which he wanted Moore to contribute has not been identified.

653. *To Washington Irving*

Yale

[August 1824]

My dear Irving— I take the opportunity of a packet to Paris to tell you that your Book is delightful—[1] I never can answer for what the Public will like, but if they do not devour this with their best appetite, then is good writing, good fun, good sense & all other goods of authorship thrown away upon them— I had to listen to Lord Lansdowne the other evening reading over whole pages of Buckthorne[2] which I already knew by heart, but which he seemed so pleased with that it would have been a sin to stop him— Luttrell also has been warm in your praises, and altogether, your Muse, I think, treads upon velvet.

We have had Bowood swarming with Aristocracy & wit, and I have been gallanting the fair Genoese, Mad^e Durazzo to Mass (at Wardour) and other gaieties— Lord Bath's also has been among my visiting-places, and upon the whole I have been quite as idle as I ought *not* to have been.

Your lively letter from Brighton was far too sprightly to be kept under cork, and accordingly it effervesced out at Bowood, much to poor Kerry's exposure & the delight of every one— I *never* read any thing so good even in your books. That 'infidus scurra', Kerry, (as I could collect from Rogers) showed me up for the dinner I made my good-natured friend in Cleveland Row give you all. It *was* an officious trick of me, I own.[3]

We had little Russell christened while Lord John was here, and I am afraid he will be a chip of the old Rock, for he was laughing at the Parson all the time of the operation.

God bless you, my dear Irving—

Ever heartily yours
Thomas Moore.

Bessy likes you rather too well to make her praise of your book worth much—but she is enchanted.

[1] *Tales of a Traveller* (1824).
[2] 'Buckthorne and His Friends', one of the sections in the *Tales* having a European setting.
[3] Moore attended mass at Wardour with the Durazzos and Bowles on 23 Aug. and produced the letter from Irving, which he had received on the 16th, on the evening of 24 Aug. (see Russell, iv. 232–7).

654. *To T. Phillips, R.A.*[1]

Rice University

Sloperton Cottage, Devizes
September 15th 1824

My dear Sir— In compliance with the request of a particular friend I write to you, among other R. As with whom I have the pleasure of being acquainted, to express my wishes in favour of Mr William Allan,[2] as a candidate for a place among your body at the next election. I am well aware that *interest* can have nothing to do with the matter, and therefore cannot well understand what object can be gained by my application—particularly as the talents of Mr Allan himself are such as to render him independent of, at least, such humble recommendations as mine—but, having been requested by my friend to make this application, I could not well refuse—and being well assured that you will forgive any irregularity I may be guilty of in doing so, I am, my dear Sir,[3]

Very truly yours
Thomas Moore

655. *To Hannah Bloomfield*[4]

B.M. Add. MS. 30809, f. 65

Sloperton Cottage, Devizes
October 3rd 1824

Dear Madam— When Mr Rogers was down in this neighbourhood he kindly undertook to transmit a letter of thanks to you from me, for the very great favour you conferred upon me in sending me your brother's Poems—but, by some mistake, he left this without taking the letter with him, and I have since deferred my acknowledgements till I am heartily ashamed of myself— Not knowing your address, I shall take my chance of this letter reaching you through the publisher of the Poems,[5] and trust you will believe, notwithstanding my long silence, that I have duly felt the distinction with which you honoured me, and that I am, Dear Madam

Your obliged & faithful Servt
Thomas Moore

[1] Probably Thomas Phillips, the painter.

[2] Probably Sir William Allan, a Scottish painter.

[3] See letter No. 656, to John Murray, 11 Oct. 1824.

[4] Note by Hannah Bloomfield: 'This was written to me, eldest *Daughter, not Sister* of Robt Bloomfield. Hannah Bloomfield. October 1824.'

[5] Moore is probably referring to Bloomfield's *May Day with the Muses,* which was published in 1822.

656. *To William Murray*

Huntington Library

Sloperton Cottage*
October 11th 1824.*

Dear Murray— Soon after I received your letter, I wrote to Shee
& Philipps (the only academicians with whom I am intimate,
besides Chauntrey, who, you told me, was already secured) and I
feel ashamed of having so long delayed letting you know their
answers. I luckily took the precaution, in applying to them, to say
that I was well aware how little *interest* had to do with such elec-
tions as theirs, which, it was evident from looking over the list of
their Members, were influenced by considerations of merit alone.
But even this did not save me from a pretty smart trimming from
both the R As, who, though very civil & kind in their replies, contrived to let me know that both myself & the friend that set me on
had (even by the remotest thought that such an application [could]
be useful) offended their sense of purity in no trifling degree. The
main point, however—their voting for Mr Allan—had been decided
on by both before they heard from me, and Philipps bid me say
that it was not from want of good will to Mr A. that he has not
hitherto given him his suffrage, but from thinking that the general
interests of the Institution demanded the previous choice of others.
He now, however, thinks the way open to him. From all this I conclude that your friend is pretty sure of his election, & nobody, you
may tell him, will rejoice at it more sincerely than I.[1]

I had intended to advert to the other subject mentioned in your
letter, but I wish to have another consultation with Bessy concerning it, and you shall hear all the particulars of our arrangement
in a few days.

With best love to Anne from both, believe me, dear Murray
(you see I tout you in the *family* way, & expect the same
compliment in return from you)

Yours very faithfully
Thomas Moore

657. *Addressee unknown*

Rice University

Sloperton Cottage, Devizes
October 11th 1824.

My dear Sir— Your letter arrived here, during my absence from
home on a visit to a neighbour, and it was but yesterday, on my

---

[1] See letter No. 654, to Thomas Phillips, 15 Sept. 1824.

return that I received it. I cannot tell you what pain it gives me to refuse a request, which, in many respects, it would be most gratifying to myself to comply with—but I have long made up my mind as to the impossibility of my doing justice to such a task. Two or three times I have tried it, but as often failed, and with the certainty of another failure before my eyes, I should do as little justice to you as to myself in making the attempt. I think I told you what real remorse I felt in declining the request of Kemble (to whom I was bound by feelings of friendship as well as of admiration) that I should write the address to be spoken at his dinner, which Campbell afterwards undertook—but I thought it better even to do this violence both to my own feelings and his, than to wrong and disappoint both by a failure in such a task. The power of writing dramatic addresses is, I think, a talent by itself, which no one has possessed since Garrick, the elder Colman & Sheridan. Even Lord Byron fell far below himself in attempting it.

I trust (even if you do not feel the weight of my reasons in refusing) you will, at least, acquit me of any want of zeal in such a cause as yours—combining the interests, as it does, of the Drama, of Ireland, and of a person so perfectly entitled to esteem as yourself— You have also lately established a claim on my gratitude by your kindness to my dear family in Dublin, which I feel, I assure you, more than ten times the same amount of kindness to myself— All these considerations would, of course, most forcibly incline me to oblige you—but my Muse is paralyzed at the very thought of an address, and I *must* refuse you.

I hope to be in Ireland in the course of the summer, and—in spite of all this—to have an *Irish* meeting with you—, though not such as your 'asking for my *address*' might seem to imply.

Yours very truly
Thomas Moore.

658. *To Colonel Francis Doyle*

Rice University

Sloperton Cottage, Devizes
November 5th 1824.

Dear Doyle.— As you & I are old friends, & you understand me better than I can expect mere strangers to do, I am about to select you (if you will allow me that privilege) to be the medium of a communication to Lord Byron's family, which I feel it due both to them & to myself to make.

It is my intention, in the course of the following year, to give a Life of Lord Byron to the world, as authentic as the kindness of his friends will enable me to make it; and I wish you to say, both to Lady Byron & Mrs Leigh, that any materials for that purpose which they may do me the honour of entrusting to me, shall be employed in such a manner as will not, I trust, leave them to regret their confidence in me. I find, from one of the Journals of Lord Byron in my possession, that he also kept a journal during his stay in Switzerland, which he gave to Mrs Leigh—any extracts from this, which she may think worthy of publication, I shall feel most happy & most honoured in being allowed to make use of.

It was always Lord Byron's wish that, if I survived him, I should write something about his Life & Character, and it appears to me that it must be equally the desire of his friends, that some hand, on whose delicacy they can rely, should undertake the task, instead of leaving it to persons, who have no object but to make money by his memory, & who dishonour alike the living & the dead.

Knowing that you will make this communication in the manner most likely to meet the feelings of all parties, I shall offer no apology for giving you the trouble, but merely assure you, my dear Doyle, how much I am

Yours truly
Thomas Moore

659. *To John Wilson Croker*

American Art Association, Sale Catalogue, 6 December 1928

Nov. 11. 1824

I am glad to see that Murray has so triumphantly set down the Captain (Medwin).[1] In a less important way, this Conversationalist has equally misrepresented me—the whole account of my first acquaintance with Lord Byron being incorrect.[2] Indeed, his entire book is a series of lies 'at random strung' upon a slender thread of truth.

---

[1] Thomas Medwin's *Conversations of Lord Byron* appeared in 1824, and John Murray published a pamphlet entitled *Notes on Captain Medwin's Conversations of Lord Byron*, in which the publisher contradicted some of Medwin's statements.

[2] Medwin gives a highly condensed, but otherwise fairly accurate account of Moore's writing to Byron concerning the reference in *English Bards* to Moore's duel with Jeffrey (see letters Nos. 168 and 197, to Lord Byron, 1 Jan. 1810 and 22 Oct. 1811). Some of the details are inaccurate, however, such as the statement that Moore's first letter was sent to Hanson instead of Hodgson, and that 'One of the balls fell out [of the pistol] in the carriage, and was lost; and the seconds, not having a further supply, drew the remaining one' (Medwin, *Conversations*, p. 218).

660. *To William Murray*

Rice University

Sloperton Cottage
Novr 13th 1824.

My dear Murray— I trust you received my letter respecting your
friend Mr Allan safe, though Anne has not mentioned it in any of
hers to Bessy. I have to accuse my laziness in not sooner following
it up with the promised communication on the subject of Mrs D.[1]—
though, indeed, a great part of the interval has been employed in
endeavouring to bring Bessy into my views of the matter. She still
continues full of apprehension, lest the [discov]ery, at any time, of
your contributing your share to the support of M^rs [D] should drive
her into the desperate resolution of shaking off ours also. [I] have
however prevailed so far as to have the arrangement left entirely to
me, without any references to Bessy whatever, by which means she
will have it in her power to deny any concern in the transaction
should she ever be reproached with it— I am the more desirous of
your doing something in conjunction with me, from the state of
infirmity to which Mrs D. is evidently hastening—her eyes are
become so bad that she can no longer work, & of late she has been
sometimes ten or twelve weeks, at a time, without being able to
leave her room— This being the case, and the chance of her ever
discovering your interference being (from the silence which I know
you will preserve on the subject) very small, I think it would be
foolish to let such an apprehension stand in the way of her receiving
that great addition to her comfort which might be thus stolen upon
her, by your putting at my disposal the sum we agreed upon. What
I pay her regularly is two pounds every four weeks, in addition to
which I have this last year given her, at intervals, at least fifteen
pounds—five of which, by the bye, was a present to our Anastasia
on her birth-day from her god-father, which we devoted to this
purpose. These occasional advances, you see, are a good preparation
for the introduction of your contribution, which shall be bestowed
in the same irregular & chance way, so as to avoid suspicion. It is,
to be sure, whimsical enough to be obliged to take all these pre-
cautions in increasing a woman's comforts, but you know her well
enough to understand the necessity of it.

What I think, therefore, is that ten shillings a week from you, in
addition to mine, will be abundantly sufficient, and you may remit
me the sum at intervals, or in whatever way is most convenient to

---

[1] Mrs. Dyke, Moore's mother-in-law. William Murray married Bessy Moore's
sister.

you. I will, *myself*, (as Bessy will have nothing to do) keep an account of the times & manner of the disbursements of your money & acquaint you with it accordingly.

It is a long time since I have written such a *lengthy* ([as] the Yankees would call it) Epistle, & I have scribbled [*MS. damaged*] But I doubt whether you will be able to make it out. We a[re *MS. damaged* de]lighted at the improvements that affairs to have taken place [*sic*] in [*MS. damaged*] I wish she could transmit the secret to Sloperton, where it is mu[ch needed].

Yours, my dear Murray, very truly
Thomas Moore.

661. *Addressee unknown*

Rice University

Bowood*
Decr 31st 1824*

My dear Sir— I inclose you the Greek Air & beg you will give my best thanks to Mr Serdin for his kindness in lending it to me.

I have not forgot your Greek verses, but was puzzled by a word which turns out to be an error of the Press, and which Hallam assisted me in detecting—You shall have the translation the next time I write.

Y^rs ever
Thomas Moore

662. *To Wadham Locke*

Rice University

Saturday* [watermark 1824]

My dear Locke. I found your note on my return from Gloucester yesterday evening. We shall be most happy to dine with you on Tuesday, but must, I am sorry to say, leave you on Wednesday morning, as there are some friends of mine coming to Bowood for whom I must reserve that day.

Yours very truly
Thomas Moore

663. *To James Power*

Pennsylvania Historical Society

[Feb^r 8th 1825, *not in Moore's hand*]

My dear Sir

I merely make use of you as a Cat's-Paw this time through which to forward the inclosed letters which you must frank for me.

Thanks for the money, which I hope will come to-morrow, as we are obliged to go to Bath on Wednesday morning.

Y^{rs} ever
T. M.

664. *To James Power*

Rice University

Want, when you are sending down a parcel two copies of the 2nd No. of Sacred Songs & one of the 9th of Irish Melodies—also the song of 'my heart with love is beating'.

March 29th 1825.

My dear Sir. I send you the Proof corrected, and a National Melody. It is very unlucky that Bishop should have delayed the Great Work so long, as I am now going to press with Sheridan, & shall be hunted by the Devils for the next two months— I think you had better make sure, at all events, of the National Melodies.

I have made use of the Longmans' names for a supply & shall send you the £20 as soon as I can get into Devizes—though I don't think I shall leave it very long in your pocket.

This Life of Sheridan has been a heavy mill-stone round my neck, & even now, I doubt whether I shall be able to have it out before the season dies away.

Many, many thanks for the excellent dish of fish, which we enjoyed with double relish both from its own merits & those of the sender.

Best regards to Mrs Power & girls—
Ever yours.
T. Moore.

665. *To James Power*

Pennsylvania Historical Society

[Rec^d 25th April 1825, *not in Moore's hand*]

My dear Sir— I have been at work for the Press since ten this morning & it is now dinner-time, when I hope I may make up to myself by a hearty repast upon your excellent mackerel, for which a thousand thanks— You will of course send me copies of Bishop's arrangements that I may see how he has done them—

You must not be surprised if I am later this next week with my musical communication, as I expect Woolriche here to consult with him about Bessy's health (which is far from what it ought to be)

& he may distract me a little from business. But I have got a subject for another Glee, & shall compleat it as soon as possible.

My hand is too tired to write any more.

666. *To James Power*

Pennsylvania Historical Society

Mrs Branigan, who is with us, bids me say that she has taken the liberty of sending to your care a portmanteau & bag.

April 28th 1825

My dear Sir— As Woolriche is with me at this moment, I have time for little more than to acknowledge the receipt of the Nationals, which I shall try over immediately, & dispatch for you without any loss of time—

I was going, indeed, to write to you upon the old subject of Finance—being brought to what I told you I should, when I sent up the twenty pounds—but I have not time now to enter at large into the Ways & Means measure I meant to propose. My great object is *not* to press upon you more than is absolutely necessary, but by a sort of *kite-flying process* between you & the Longmans to keep myself afloat till better prospects open upon me—As there is plenty of *capital* amongst us—on your side in credit & character, on that of the Longmans in *money*, & on mine in *head*, it cannot be called mere *paper* work among us, and, without borrowing from friends (which is the last thing I shall ever be driven to) or sinking myself deeper with you & the Longmans than I should wish, I have no *other* mode of getting on for this year.

I doubt whether I have written as you will understand & have not time to look over what I have said—but more, when I write again—

Ever yours

T. Moore

667. *To Lord Holland*

The Earl of Ilchester[1]

Saturday* [April or May 1825]

Dear Lord Holland

You mentioned yesterday some notes that were at Bennet's service, and as there are some friends of mine very anxious about him, perhaps you will have no objection to telling me, for their information, where these notes are to be found.

I should like much to have a few minutes more conversation with

---

[1] Transcript provided by the Earl of Ilchester.

you about Sheridan before you leave Bowood, as I find you are the only person who can tell me the things I want. Perhaps on Monday morning, if I come to breakfast, you will be at leisure to talk to me a little.

Your Lordship's ever obliged

Thomas Moore

I shall collect Mr Fox's letters on Monday.

668. *To Lord Holland*

The Earl of Ilchester[1]

Sloperton Cottage, Devizes

May 7. 1825.

Dear Lord Holland— I hope you will forgive my pestering you for the Copy of Sheridan's letter to the King (for the Prince) after the first Regency which you were so kind as to promise me.[2] I have, indeed, deferred troubling you on the subject to the last moment, as I am now 'sous la Presse' (as the French very feelingly call the process of printing) and shall soon come to the niche I left for the document. I have, as I mentioned to you, the note that accompanied the statement, but it would be like giving the shell without the kernel, to publish one without the other, & I trust to your often-proved good nature for letting me have the copy as soon as possible.

I find my work of revision much more tedious than I expected. I had left a number of important & difficult points untouched, as Napoleon used to leave towns untaken in his rear—but I don't find them fall so easily under my hands as he did. The consequence of all this is that I shall be most unseasonably late in coming out. Indeed, if the Houses are to break up as soon as they say, I shall be the 'vox clamantis in deserto.'[3]

I was sincerely glad to hear from Woolriche (who was exercising his kind skill here the other day for Mrs Moore) that Lady Holland is so much better. Pray, give my best remembrances to her, & believe me, my dear Lord Holland,

Ever faithfully yours,

Thomas Moore.

[1] Transcript provided by the Earl of Ilchester.

[2] In 1789 Sheridan was given the task of drawing up several state papers for the Prince of Wales. Moore refers here to a letter addressed to the King, written after the latter's recovery from his second attack of mental illness. The Prince announced his intention of submitting 'to His Majesty a Memorial, in vindication of his own conduct and that of his Royal brother the Duke of York throughout the whole proceedings consequent upon His Majesty's indisposition'. For the quotation and text of the letter see Moore's *Life of Sheridan* (London, 1827), 5th edition, vol. ii, p. 67.

[3] Isaiah xl. 3 (*Vulg. Es.* 40. 3).

669. *To Mrs. Cockle*

B.M. Add. MS. 18204, f. 138

Sloperton Cottage
May 8th 1825

Mr Moore has been much flattered by the honour which Mrs Cockle has conferred upon him in sending for his perusal her verses upon Lord Byron, which he has read with much pleasure & admiration, & which he will take the liberty of keeping, to add to the other interesting tributes of the same nature, which he has in his possession.[1]

670. *To Dr. Bain*[2]

John Rylands Library

Wednesday [May 1825]

My dear Dr

I inclose you Croften Croker's letter which, you will see, *adjourns* his information on the subject. I did not, of course, mention your name.

I send you also, to look at, a scrap in our *theological* line, which has more knowledge & good sense in it than often comes from Ireland—or, at least, than often *stays* there. I don't know who the man is—his signature being fictitious, but I collect from other things of his, that he stops at that half-way house, *Unitarianism*.

Ever yours
T. Moore

Take care of Wm Saxon for me.

671. *To Sir Walter Scott*

University of Edinburgh

Sloperton Cottage, Devizes
July 24th 1825

My dear Sir Walter— I wish most heartily that I had been in my own green land to welcome you.[3] It delights me, however, to see (what I could not have doubted) that the warm hearts of my

---

[1] 'Lines Addressed to Lady Byron' and 'Reply to Lord Byron's "Fare Thee Well" ', attributed to Mrs. Cockle, appeared in 1817. She had probably sent Moore the latter poem.

[2] This letter was probably written to Dr. Bain, and the reference to Crofton Croker indicates that Moore had applied to him for information for his *Life of Sheridan*. The basis for this conjecture is that Moore was associated with Croker and Bain at this time (see Russell, iv. 279–80).

[3] Scott visited Ireland in July and August 1825. See Lockhart, *Life of Scott*, iv. 280–308.

countrymen have shown that they know how to value you. How I envy those who will have the glory of showing you & Killarney to each other!— No two of nature's productions, I *will* say, were ever more worthy of meeting. If the Kenmares should be your Ciceroni, pray, tell them what I say of their Paradise, with my best regards & greetings— I received your kind message, through Newton,[1] last year that 'if I did not come & see you, before you died, you would appear to me afterwards'— Be assured that, as I am all for living apparitions, I shall take care & have the start of you, and would have done it this very year, I rather think, only for your Irish movements.[2]

Present my best regards to your son-in-law, & believe me, my dear Sir Walter (though we have met, I am sorry to say, but once in our lives)

Yours cordially & sincerely
Thomas Moore.

672. *Addressee unknown*

National Library of Ireland

Sloperton Cottage, Devizes
September 28. 1825.

Sir.

I have but just had the pleasure of receiving your letter, on my return home after a long absence.

It will gratify me very much to be able to be of any service to you, and my name is quite at your service for your list of Subscribers.

I am, Sir, your very obliged &c.
Thomas Moore

673. *To Charles Brinsley Sheridan*

National Library of Ireland

October 7th 1825.*

My dear Sheridan— Having but a few minutes to catch the Post, I can only say that your letter has given me the most real & heartfelt pleasure.[3] I assure you I was more anxious about your opinion

---

[1] A note in an unknown hand identifies this man as the artist Gilbert Stewart Newton.

[2] For an account of Moore's visit to Abbotsford see Lockhart, *Life of Scott*, iv. 321–5. See also letter No. 681, to Sir Walter Scott, 6 Dec. 1825.

[3] On 7 Oct. 1825 Moore made the following entry in his diary: 'Received a letter from Charles Sheridan full of the warmest admiration and gratitude; a most seasonable relief to my mind, as I have been even more anxious about his opinion than that of the public' (Russell, iv. 322). Moore's *Memoirs of the Life of Richard Brinsley Sheridan* appeared in 1825.

than that of the Public, & that *you* should be pleased with what I have done is to me the sincerest delight. My wish was to leave the same impression on my readers as your father did on those who knew him—namely, a feeling of love towards him in spite of all his irregularities & faults, and this I most anxiously hope I have effected. I had two female hearers crying over the last pages to-day, as if it were a Novel. I hardly know what I write, but as this is the last post-day till Sunday, I did not like defer [*sic*] so long acknowledging the great gratification you have given me.

Yours, my dear Sheridan, very truly
Thomas Moore.

674. *To William Lisle Bowles*

Huntington Library

October 11ᵗʰ 1825

My dear Bowles. What Hughes tells me of your delight at the success of my Books is quite heart-warming to me. Your remarks upon the faults of my style are quite just—but I cannot help letting the *potatoe* show itself now & then, & the fact is, I should not produce the things that people admire, if I did not run the risk also of falling into what they condemn. The same dash produces both the hits & the misses.

I have written up to have the word 'Masters' substituted for 'scholars', which is all the correction there is time for—as they have put two sets of printers on, so as to print the two octavo volumes *together*,[1] and I doubt whether even [the] correction of the Scholars will not be too late.

Yours ever very affectionately
& gratefully
Thomas Moore

675. *To William Lisle Bowles*[2]

Rice University

Saturday Night [October or November 1825]
My dear Bowles—
I should have answered your note sooner, but that I expected to meet you at McDonald's dance the other night, where I am sorry you & Mrs. Bowles did not attend. How are we to come together?

[1] The *Life of Sheridan*, 2 vols., 1825.
[2] This letter was published in Greever, *A Wiltshire Parson*, p. 86.

I have been in town since I saw you, and want to tell you about the pangs of Rogers's parturition, which I witnessed. As to the Quarterly Review, it does you honour—as it shows you are not *partizan* enough to suit the tastes of those *ultra* gentlemen—[1]

Yours very truly,
Thomas Moore

676. *To Henry Mackenzie*[2]

Bodleian MS. Eng. Letters e. 1, f. 159

November 10th 1825

My dear Sir. I was much gratified by the perusal of your lines, which are as great a 'psychological curiosity' as those of Coleridge written under the same circumstances. If the ancients had an *Apollo* Somnialis (as we know they had a Jupiter with that title) it would be worthwhile invoking him, after such specimens of his inspiration.[3]

I have been prevented from starting to-day by rather a brisk attack of illness but hope to be well enough to leave Edinburgh tomorrow.

Be assured that I shall remember with much pleasure the few moments that it has been my good fortune to pass in your society & that I am,

Dear Sir, very truly yours
Thomas Moore

677. *To Mr. Fletcher*

Rice University

Edinburgh
Novr 10th 1825

Dear Sir— The letter with which you have favoured me has given me the sincerest pleasure. To be praised for my principles by a person who has, himself, been so consistent a friend to all that is right & independent, is no ordinary gratification. I had already known of your intimacy with Sheridan & found a very interesting letter of yours among his papers, which I was at one time anxious to have your leave to publish, and (encouraged by the character which my friend, Sir James Macintosh gave me of you) was about to address

[1] Bowles was attacked for his strictures on Pope in the *Quarterly Review*, xxiii (July 1820), 400–34, and again in vol. xxxii (October 1825), 271–311. This letter was evidently written in 1825, after the appearance of the latter, rather than in 1820, as Greever suggests. Moore was in Paris in 1820 and hence would not have been attending a dance at which he would expect to meet Bowles.

[2] This letter is endorsed in pencil on the back 'to Henry Mackenzie'.

[3] The allusion is not clear. It may be that the addressee had sent Moore a poem which was never published.

you a letter on the subject. But considerations, which I shall mention to you, if ever I am lucky enough to have the opportunity, induced me to give up the idea of making your letter public.

As all I have seen since my arrival in this place gives me a strong wish to renew the pleasures of my visit, there is but little doubt that I shall soon come again to Scotland, and I assure you the gratification of meeting with you will not be among the least of my inducements to do so.[1]

I am, Dear Sir, very truly yours,

Thomas Moore.

I shall leave the MSS. you were kind as to entrust to me in the care of Mr Constable.

678. *To Sir Walter Scott*

James C. Corson[2]

Friday [11 November 1825]

The inclosed was written under the impression that I was about to start yesterday morning—but rather a brisk attack of illness has laid me by the heels, and I shall not be off now, I think, till Sunday morning so that there is a chance of my having one more shake of the hand from you.

Yrs. ever

T. Moore

679. *To Owen Rees*

American Art Association, Sale Catalogue, 6 December 1928

Nov. 18th 1825

Here I am at home again, having given up my visits in Derbyshire. I had rather a brisk attack of Cholera Morbis in Edinburgh, which not only detained me there two or three days longer than I intended, but made me think it prudent to get home to the Nurse as soon as possible. I would not have lost this visit to Scotland for any consideration. Great as *Scott* is to the world, one must see him closely and at home to appreciate him properly, and the words with which he parted from me: 'My Dear Moore, we are now friends for life,' are worth going round the world for.[3] I found Jeffrey, too, all

---

[1] On 8 Nov. 1825, Moore recorded in his diary: 'Letters from Mrs. Dugald Stewart and old Mr. Fletcher (a friend of Mackintosh's), full of the most flattering kindness. . . . Mr. Fletcher, with many praises of my writings, expresses his regret that his infirmities would not allow him to [meet me]' (Russell, v. 11).

[2] Transcript provided by Dr. James C. Corson, University of Edinburgh Library.

[3] Moore visited Abbotsford on 29 Oct., staying until 2 Nov. 1825. See his diary for this period (Russell, iv. 330–43; v. 3–5) and Lockhart, *Life of Scott*, iv. 321–5. See also letter No. 681, to Sir Walter Scott, 6 Dec. 1825.

kindness.[1] It was, indeed, altogether, the most gratifying fortnight I ever spent, and has sent me home with a sunshine on my spirits that nothing else could have given.

I now mean to write to Hobhouse and Mrs. Leigh about the '*Life*.'[2] Sir Walter is of opinion that they cannot, in honour and good-feeling, do otherwise than atone to me for the sacrifice I have made by giving me every assistance in their power, and he advises that I should get Lord Lansdowne to be my mediator with them, which suggestion, perhaps, deserves some consideration.[3] My visit to Scott was, in this respect, particularly lucky, as I have reason to think that Murray had some hope of persuading him to undertake the '*Life*,' himself, which, after our confidential intercourse on the subject, is, of course, out of the question. This between ourselves. I think I gave you commission for two copies of the '*Sheridan*' before I went, one to Mademoiselle Drew . . .; the other to *Sir Arthur Falkner*. . . . I hope these two copies are forwarded. I have now another to trouble you with: 'From the Author' also—'Lady Virginia Murray' . . . I wish you could borrow or procure for me '*Guy's Greece*,' and '*Douglas on the Festivals of the Greeks*.' Send them to Power, who will forward them. I rather believe I told you Scott's words before—but, no matter—they bear repeating, at least to a friend like you. Black, I find, has stopped my Morning Chronicle, which will be such a sad privation to my mother (to whom I have sent it now for so many years) that I must beg of you to get me a second-hand Chronicle (I mean one that has gone the rounds in the morning and is sent off at half price) in order to continue this comfort to her. I suppose what you did about the Times (added to circumstances that occurred in the summer, which I shall tell you of sometime) was what produced this ill-tempered action of Black's. You will, of course, order the newsman to address the Chronicle to me.

680. *To George Agar Ellis*

Devonshire Papers: Sixth Duke's Series no. 1234[4]

Sloperton Cottage
Novr 24, 1825.

Dear Ellis, your letter (though it certainly did not, like Madeira, want travelling to increase its value) has had a long excursion

[1] Moore visited Jeffrey and other friends in Edinburgh after he left Abbotsford (see the diary, Russell, v. 5–15).

[2] The *Life of Byron*, which he conceived at this time. See letter No. 682, to John Cam Hobhouse, 21 Dec. 1825.

[3] The 'sacrifice' was his insistence on returning to Murray 2,000 guineas which the publisher had paid him for Byron's Memoirs. See letters Nos. 631 and 648, to John Murray, 13 Feb. 1823, and 14 May 1824.

[4] Transcript provided by Mr. T. S. Wragg, Keeper, Devonshire Papers.

before it reached me, having been sent after me to the North & from thence followed me here. I cannot tell you how delighted I am by what you say of my book—for, though it has succeeded with the public far better than I expected, one individualized opinion, such as yours, is ten times more satisfactory & flattering than the best success *en masse*.[1] I shall not, however, I fear, find all my political friends in such a laudatory vein as you are—you are just of that standing to be able to view the events of which I treat historically; but some of those, who were themselves actors in the scene will, I fear (for I have no other reason to say so than my fears) take rather a less favourable view of my impartiality.

You may be sure that the few days I passed with you & Lady Georgiana at Bowood have left in me a desire for more, which, whenever I have an opportunity, I shall be but too ready to gratify. Best remembrances to her, & believe me

Very truly yours,
Thomas Moore

I had already heard, with much pleasure, from Lady Donegall, Lord Clifden's favourable opinion of the book.

681. *To Sir Walter Scott*

N.L.S. MS. 3901, f. 191

Sloperton Cottage, Devizes
Decr 6th 1825*

My dear Scott— As you seemed to be somewhat puzzled about the name of my Cottage (which, when spelled with two *ps*, gives but too true an idea of its present state) I think it right to put you in possession of the true reading, lest I should lose Miss Scott's promised Song from any want of Cottage orthography— Though I left Edinburgh (thanks to the 'praesidium et dulce deus' which you afforded me) so covered with glory as to serve, I thought, as quite a sufficient surtout against cold, the Shap Fells would not let me escape, and I came home with as bad a cough as could well be imported from the north. I am now however quite well and there remains nothing of my journey but the most pleasant & heartwarming recollections—such as, I am convinced, no other journey

---

[1] The *Life of Sheridan*, 2 vols., 1825.

could have given me.[1] I remember going, one summer's day, with William Spencer to a Panorama of Naples, & the effect it had upon him was such that he could talk nothing but Italian for the rest of the day.— In the same way, since I have been to the Yarrow, I find myself singing nothing but Scotch music, and that air of Miss Scott's haunts me so much more than any other, that (if I was as gay a young fellow as our friend Crampton) I should say she herself had something to do with the charm. I lost no time, you may be sure, in communicating your kind invitation to Mrs Moore, and she already raves and romances in anticipation of Abbotsford almost as much as I do from recollection of it.

Mind you do not think yourself bound to answer this hasty note— I shall take the opportunity of my frank through Croker to trouble you with two inclosures for Jeffrey & M^r McKenzie, the latter of whom I ought to have answered some weeks since.

With best remembrances to Lady Scott and *both* your daughters, believe me

Very faithfully yours
Thomas Moore

682. *To John Cam Hobhouse*

Sir John Murray
Private   Dublin
                                                December 21, 1825

Dear Hobhouse— You have heard, I dare say, that I am at last about to occupy myself seriously with some Memorial of our friend Byron. Whether, however, it is to be a regular biographical Memoir, or merely such a sketch as my own knowledge & materials afford must depend entirely upon the assistance I receive from his family & executors. The object of this letter, therefore, is to ask you, without reserve, how far your approval of my undertaking, or your duty as an Executor,[2] will allow you to sanction, assist, or cooperate with me.

And, now that the word 'cooperate' has escaped me, allow me to ask, my dear Hobhouse, whether it be wholly impossible that we should undertake such a work *jointly?* We are both equally interested in the memory of our common friend, & can each bring such materials & authority to the task as no other person possesses. This sort of Beaumont & Fletcher partnership in Biography is, I believe,

---

[1] See letter No. 679, to Owen Rees, 18 Nov. 1825.
[2] Hobhouse and Hanson were co-executors of Byron's will.

new; but with a good understanding between us, it might be easily managed, & so the work is but well executed, I shall be well satisfied with a share of the glory of it. I know you do not think much of my Life of Sheridan; but I may improve as I go on, & the present subject, perhaps, would be more in my line—though this, I confess, is by no means my own opinion. However, pray, think over what I have here proposed, with attention, &, above all, with the heartiness which should subsist between the friends of Byron. Your answer will be time enough on my return from Ireland, whither I have come upon a no less melancholy mission than that of paying the last duties to a most kind & excellent father,[1] and—still more painful—trying to comfort a mother, who notwithstanding his age, was *still* but ill prepared to lose him. I shall apprize you of my return.[2]

Give my best regards to Burdett when you see him & believe me

Very truly yours

Thomas Moore.

683. *To William Charles Macready*

Huntington Library

Sloperton
Dec[r] 26th 1825

Many thanks, my dear M[r] Macready, for your kind recollection of so secluded a country-gentleman as myself— It is indeed tantalyzing to think how little I shall be able to avail myself of the privilege.

Still, one great privilege—that of calling such a man as you are my friend—I can even at this distance enjoy.

Wishing you every success, I am,
dear Macready, very truly yours
Thomas Moore

684. *To William Lisle Bowles*[3]

Rice University

Tuesday [*c.* 1825]*

My dear Bowles—

I forgot when Hughes gave me your note yesterday that the day was to be so soon. I am sorry to say I can not go with you. I hate to

---

[1] On 6 Dec. Moore received word from his sister Ellen that their father was seriously ill. He died on 17 Dec. (see Russell, v. 16 and 22).

[2] See letter No. 688, to John Cam Hobhouse, 15 Jan. 1826.

[3] This letter was published in Greever, *A Wiltshire Parson*, p. 89.

be made sing at such a large party as the Anacreontic, and refusing is both disagreeable & troublesome.

I am delighted that Methuen & you have made up. He showed me your answer which was sensible & good-humoured, and *firm* at the same time.

Y^{rs} ever
T. Moore

685. *Addressee unkown*

N.L.S. MS. 3907, f. 323

19 Bury Street, St. James's
[*c.* 1825]

I have been all in alarm lest you should be off before I came— Is there any chance of seeing you before you go to Brighton ?— I was told at Murray's that you were going to Brighton tomorrow, & I meant to have offered myself as your companion on the road, but I now find Tuesday is your day, and I am engaged for that day to my *partners* in the Row. Let me know something about you.

Ever yours
T. M.

686. *To William Lisle Bowles*[1]

Rice University

Friday, four o'clock [*c.* 1825]
My dear Bowles—

In coming home I read the article more attentively, and feel that I was perhaps a little unjust, as well as ungrateful, in the way I spoke of it. There are, I find, passages of a serious kind, that show considerable powers of writing, and the author is no doubt a very clever fellow ; but he is one of those '*creatures moving along Fancy's enchanted floor*' (to quote a strange phrase of his own) that cut rather awkward capers on said 'floor,' both in the way of *ground & lofty* tumbling—both in declamation and in humour; and I still think his fun of the very worst quality possible. The article, however, is a good article, and a friendly article, and, if it will but help the sale of *my* article, I shall be most exceedingly obliged to it.[2]

Yours ever
T. M.

---

[1] This letter was published in Greever, *A Wiltshire Parson*, p. 90.
[2] Bowles expressed considerable interest in Moore's *Life of Sheridan*. Moore is probably referring to an article which concerned that book.

687. *To Charles Brinsley Sheridan*

Yale

Sloperton Cottage
Friday Jan^r 1826 [postmark January 14, 1826]

My dear Sheridan— I returned here from Ireland only last night, having been detained in Dublin four or five days by the Easterly winds or rather storms, which would not let any Packets get out. The letters of Dr Parr are, I believe, all in that promiscuous heap which I left with you, but they are not very many, and an eye, accustomed to the hand-writing of him & his scribe would soon single them out. I meant long ago to have told you that there still remain in my hands some of the Manuscript Books of the School for Scandal &c. which I did not pack up when collecting the rest of the Papers—you shall, however, have them when I next come to town.

I have raised a storm against me in various quarters by this Work—[1] but as the Public seems to be at my back, I have but little doubt of weathering it. The story of the £4000 is, I am convinced, an imposture as to the main fact, that of the Prince's *giving* it to your father— I knew (as well as those Messrs Cocker, Fortlanger &c.) that four thousand pounds was the price to be given for the Seat; but I also knew that your father said to Lord Holland (who mentioned it to me as characteristic of him) that, though he never would come into Parliament by the purchase of a seat for him by the Prince, yet he would be most happy if the Prince would *lend* him the four thousand pounds to enable him to purchase a seat with it himself—for 'then (said he) I should *only* owe the Prince £4000.' This anecdote (coupled with the certainty that there was no more important or urgent use to which your father would have been impatient to devote such a sum (if he had it) than that of placing himself in Parliament—satisfies me that the *sequel* of the story, which is the only part of it that is new, is *not* true.[2]

Yours, my dear Sheridan, very truly
Thomas Moore.

[1] Actually the reviews of the *Life of Sheridan* were about what Moore could have expected, the Tory press being unfavourable and the Whig generally favourable. The *British Critic*, New Series, i. 436–52, and the *Quarterly Review*, xxxiii. 561–93, were the most severe. The *Monthly Review*, cviii. 149–62, and *Blackwood's Magazine*, xix. 113–30, were surprisingly gentle in their treatment of Moore. The *Edinburgh Review*, xlv. 1–48, was enthusiastic, and the *European Magazine*, New Series, i. 295–300, indicated that there was no attempt in the book to violate truth or to make Sheridan seem other than he was.

[2] Moore stated that in Sheridan's later years the Prince had offered to bring him into Parliament but that Sheridan had declined. The *Westminster*

688. *To John Cam Hobhouse*

Sir John Murray

Sloperton Cottage
Friday Jan^r [15] 1826.

Just returned from Ireland, my dear Hobhouse, & shall be most happy to recieve your answer to my letter.[1]

The Catholic Cause is going to the dogs in Ireland— O'Connel's popularity is 'Tumbling all precipitate down-dashed'[2] and nothing less than another miracle of his friend Hohenlohe[3] can save him.

Yours very truly
Thomas Moore[4]

and *Quarterly* claimed that Moore ought to have known the 'sequel to the transaction', which was that the Prince had then presented Sheridan the sum of £4,000 intended for the purchase of a seat.

In the preface to the fifth edition of his *Life of Sheridan*, Moore at first denied this claim, maintaining that sufficient proof had not been given that such a gift was made. An appended statement, written after this denial, partially corrected his first contention, however. In this he noted that his own position and that of the reviewer could be reconciled, and he corrected his initial denial in the following manner:

'The sum in question (3000£ or 4000£, my informant is uncertain which,) was, it seems, transmitted, for the purpose of purchasing a seat for Sheridan. ... When Sheridan, as I have stated, declined accepting a seat on such terms, the Prince generously ordered that the money intended for the purchase should be given to him; but the person to whom it was confided, having ... "under unwarrantable pretenses" detained it in his hands, the benevolent intentions of the Royal donor were frustrated' (Moore, *Life of Sheridan*, 5th edition, 1827, pp. xv–xvii). See also letter No. 713, to Charles Sheridan, 7 Feb. 1827.

[1] See letter No. 682, to John Cam Hobhouse, 21 Dec. 1825.

[2] Dyer, *The Ruins of Rome*, l. 41. The beginning quote was added by the editor.

[3] Alexander Leopold, Prince of Hohenlohe-Waldenburg-Schillingfurst, was a German Roman Catholic priest who gained a reputation as a miracle-worker. See the Glossary of Proper Names.

[4] Hobhouse's reply, the original of which is in Sir John Murray's possession, is quoted below:

Whilton Park, Hounslow
Jan. 16, 1826

Dear Moore

I should have answered your first letter immediately on the receipt of it had it not been that I did not like to add to the annoyance of your late melancholy visit to Dublin by giving a reply which, I was afraid, would not be satisfactory to you— But I now send you, very shortly, and as you desire me, without reserve, my opinion of your meditated undertaking.

I do not see what good end can be answered by writing a life of our late friend—and I do see a great many objections to it.

So long as I look at the subject in this point of view, and I do not at present

689. *To John Cam Hobhouse*

Sir John Murray

Sloperton Cottage
Jan^r 17 1826

Dear Hobhouse— I lose not a moment in thanking you for the frankness of your answer & for the consideration which led you not to forward it to me to Ireland.[1] Though the purport of it was very much what I had reason to expect, it would most probably have annoyed me, & I had quite enough of annoyance & difficulty there without it.

However flattering it might be to my vanity to find a person like you entertaining the same partial opinion of my talents that others do, be assured that you cannot think much more humbly of them than I do myself, and that nothing but the want of means from any other source could have induced me so long to avail myself of even that 'saleable' quality (as you describe it) which, however undeservedly, my writings have hitherto possessed.[2]

You make me doubt whether I have any right to impose such a confidence on you; but I will nevertheless confess that my opinion as to the objections against writing a Life of Lord Byron at present is very much the same as your own; and, if I can possibly avoid the task, it has all along been my desire to do so. But, untill I can discharge, in some other way, the heavy obligations I am under, I must at least seem to entertain the intention. This avowal I leave to your own feelings towards me to conceal or not, just as they may dictate.

It will give me great pleasure to have my name & services joined with yours in the project which you mention for a monument to our friend.

Yours very truly
Thomas Moore.

think that I am likely to look at it in any other, I shall not be able to bring myself to be a party to your project—

You will write, there can be no doubt, a very clever and a very saleable book. But I shall be most agreeably surprised if you accomplish those higher objects which you must propose to yourself by becoming the Biographer of such a man as Lord Byron—

Before I conclude this note I beg to mention that several persons here have applied to me, & one has sent me a large sum of money, to take measures for erecting a monument to Lord Byron— If any steps should be taken for such a purpose I hope you will allow your name to be put down as a member of the committee for carrying it into effect—

I am very truly yours
J. C. Hobhouse

[1] See letter No. 688, to John Cam Hobhouse, 15 Jan. 1826.
[2] See letter No. 690, to John Cam Hobhouse, 26 Jan. 1826.

690. *To John Cam Hobhouse*

Sir John Murray

Bowood
Thursday Jan[r] 26th 1826

Dear Hobhouse— I felt, I assure you, sincerely gratified by the tone of your last letter.[1] I have no exact idea of the time when I shall be able to come to town, but whenever I do, you shall be immediately apprized of it.

Your mention of the American's tirade[2] suggests to me what I have long been intending to request of you—namely, the fulfill-ment of the promise which you made to put into some written shape what you told me as to the feelings of Lord Byron respecting the Memoirs. It was, as nearly as I can recollect, as follows—that he either told you, or gave you to understand, that he felt regret at having put such a document out of his own power, and was only restrained by delicacy towards me from recalling the gift. It would be most satisfactory to me to have your promise on this subject performed. You may recollect you added that so strong was your impression of this being the feeling of Lord Byron that you should not be surprized if the will contained some equivalent to my sacri-fice of the Memoirs.[3]

Lord Lansdowne has just mentioned to me the substance of his letter to you on the subject of the Monument, and I very much agree with the view which he has taken of it.

Yours, my dear Hobhouse, very truly
Thomas Moore.

[1] On 22 Jan. Hobhouse replied to Moore's letter of 17 Jan. (No. 689), thanking him for his name on the subscription list for the monument to Byron. He remarked that 'as we both agree about the biography I do think something might be done to enable you to abandon your scheme if you pleased to do so'. He suggested that Moore substitute the word 'popular' for 'saleable' in his last letter (dated 16 Jan., quoted in the note to letter No. 688), and all would be well. (Original in Sir John Murray's possession.)

[2] Hobhouse had told Moore about J. W. Simmons, *An Inquiry into the Moral Character of Lord Byron* (New York, 1824), which ended with a tirade against Moore for burning the Memoirs. Hobhouse, to whom Simmons had submitted the work for approval and suggestions, returned it to the author, saying that since Simmons knew nothing about the matter he had better cancel the last pages.

[3] Hobhouse replied to this letter in one dated simply 'January'. He noted that Moore need only explain to his accusers that he could not help the burning of the Memoirs and added, 'Murray over and over again protested that whether the MS were his or yours, he would not give them [*sic*] up except with the understanding that they should be put into hands which he knew would destroy them— He said this in my room before you and Luttrel, and added he did not care for consequences.' (Original in Sir John Murray's possession.)

691. *To Miss Crumpe*

Rice University

Monday Night 12 o'clock [January 1826]

My dear Miss Crumpe. I have been in the *most cruel state of fidget* about you ever since I came to town— Called up by business un-expectedly, I was unable, before I left home, to find the letter that contained your address, & have in vain asked every one I met here (that was at all *Irish* or *poetical*) to 'testify your hidden residence'. It was but to-day (a little before your note from George St. arrived) that your letter to Sloperton was forwarded to me & acquainted me with your 'whereabouts', and you may guess my dismay when I tell you that I had already made all my arrangements for leaving town tomorrow morning, and am just now in the agonies of packing for that purpose. It is impossible for me to write *satisfactorily* to you at this moment, but you shall hear from me immediately on my arrival at Sloperton and, in the mean time, I have prepared Murray for a visit from you should you like to call upon him before you receive my letter.[1]

Excuse this hasty note, which I write by a candle nearly burnt out & believe me

Most truly yours
T. Moore

I would by all means accept the offer from Paris.

692. *To Sir Walter Scott*

N.L.S. MS. 3902, f. 87

Sloperton Cottage, Devizes
[February 1826]

My dear Scott— I have been doubting for these some weeks past whether I should write to you—and yet, I don't see why I should have doubted—for the hearty sympathy of a friend can never come amiss, and mine, I assure you, goes along with you most thoroughly & sincerely. Indeed, I sometimes now almost regret my visit to you—as if I had not seen, so closely and intimately, all you were worth, I should but have shared in the general concern at what has happened, & been spared the real pain with which my *knowledge* of you makes me view what has befallen you.— That you bear it well

---

[1] Moore recorded several visits to Miss Crumpe in his diary. She read part of a novel (probably *Geraldine of Desmond*, c. 1829) to him in January 1826 and he may have interceded with Murray on her behalf. (See Russell, v. 34 and 36.)

I have no doubt— There is a rebounding power, on such occasions, even in ordinary spirits, which makes the blow seem lighter to those who suffer than to those who feel for them—and then for *you*, who spin gold from your entrails, there is, to be sure, every hope of a speedy retrieval. But, still, the calamity is a severe one, and to any one, but yourself, I would croak over it for hours.[1]

My hesitation about writing to you was put an end to some days since by the receipt of a most splendid present from you & Constable, which, I felt, gave me a right to break in upon your time, and to make you listen at once both to my gratitude & my regrets. This valuable gift had lain in the Longmans [*sic*] hands for some time, & it was only last week that I received it. To yourself I must trust for imagining all I feel at the possession of such a treasure from your own hands, and to Constable I cannot do better than send my thanks through *you*, with the addition of whatever you think most likely to convey to him my deep concern for his late calamity.[2]

Pray, give my best remembrances to Miss Scott (who, I hope, received through Shaw the Song I sent her) & believe me, my dear Scott, with a heart full of more than I venture to express to you,

Yours very faithfully
T. Moore

693. *To William Lisle Bowles*[3]

Rice University

[February 1826][4]

My dear Bowles—

I quite forgot in the midst of our gaieties yesterday to propose to you & Linley to come & dine here on Friday next, which I most anxiously hope you may be able to do; as it would be contrary to all the rules of Anacreontic brotherhood that Linley should again leave this neighbourhood without tasting *my* Port. *If* you can come, pray send the inclosed to Sir Guy Campbell, who perhaps will consent to meet you.

Yours, my dear Bowles, very faithfully
Thomas Moore

You will understand that the note is not to go to Sir Guy, unless

[1] Early in 1826 Scott was involved in the financial failure of James Ballantyne, his partner in a printing business, and found himself liable for about £130,000. He assumed the debt, which was finally paid off from proceeds of copyrights to his books.

[2] Constable was Scott's publisher.

[3] This letter was published in Greever, *A Wiltshire Parson*, p. 90.

[4] Moore attended an 'Anacreontic dinner' with Bowles on 15 Feb. 1826 (see Russell, v. 47–48). It is probable that this letter was written at that time.

you can come. If you prefer Saturday, it will be all the same to me
—only let me have an answer by bearer. We shall dine at 5.

694. *To Colonel Houlton*

B.M. Add. MS. 27425BC, f. 6

Sloperton Cottage*
March 19th 1826*[1]

My dear Houlton— I dare say you would have decided for me as I
shall myself— I was once before asked to lecture at the Institution,[2]
but I had the same objection then that I have now—namely, that
the thing would give much more trouble than it is worth. Some of
my friends, at that time, thought also that it would be *infra dig.*—
but in this I did not agree with them, though I cannot say that I
was *quite* uninfluenced by their opinion. One likes to think well of
one's dignity at all times. At present, it is out of the question—I
am too busy about other matters. I shall have no objections, however, to come & give a few lectures on *Music* at Farley, when the
fine weather arrives. Best regards to all around you.

Ev. y^{rs}
T. Moore

695. *To Mrs. Read*

John Rylands Library

Sloperton Cottage
March 24 1826.

Madam.

You do me but justice in supposing that I feel deeply interested
in the cause for which you are so laudably exerting yourself; & it
gives me great pain to be obliged, from the peculiar circumstances
in which I am placed, to withhold the sort of assistance which you
do me the honour to think I could afford you. Being exposed to
a variety of applications of this kind (though for far less interesting
purposes) I have been obliged to adopt a general resolution not to
contribute to any work of the nature of yours, *whatever*. In pursuance of this determination I was compelled, some time ago, to refuse
the request of Mr Montgomery that I would write something for his

---

[1] A note signed by Arthur Houlton on the original of this letter gives the
date as 1825, which is an obvious misreading of 1826, written in Moore's hand.
[2] Houlton identifies this as the Royal Literary and Scientific Institution at
Bath.

work in aid of the Chimney Sweepers—a work, which both from my admiration of the Editor's genius, and my interest in the benevolent object he had in view, I should have been most happy to assist to the utmost of my power.[1] This will, I trust, be a sufficient apology for the necessity which I feel myself under of adopting the same conduct with respect to *you.*

I have the honour to be your most obliged Servant

Thomas Moore

696. *Addressee unknown*

Rice University

Sloperton Cottage
March 27th 1826

My dear Sir. Though I can not *decidedly* answer for myself at so distant a time, yet I do not at present know of any business that is likely to deprive me of the very great pleasure you offer me and which (subject to the aforesaid casualty) I have much gratification in accepting.

Yours very faithfully,
Thomas Moore

697. *To Charles Brinsley Sheridan*

Yale

April 16, 1826

My dear Sheridan— The Quarterly, you see, has fired its shot, which is both more noisy & less effective than I expected.[2] I think it would be right, however, to take notice of it in a few paragraphs (in the form of a letter from myself in the newspaper) which should be quiet & decisive enough to preclude all further controversy. Have you ascertained any thing further about the £4000 ? Let me know, if you have, and, if not, what are your own impressions with respect to the view I took of the matter in my last.[3]

They have, you see, disputed the accuracy of the account I have given of the £200 through Vaughan, & as I had the authority of

---

[1] James Montgomery, ed., *The Chimney Sweeper's Friend* (1824). With poems by Montgomery.

[2] Moore's *Life of Sheridan* was reviewed in the *Quarterly*, xxxiii (1826), 561–93.

[3] See letters Nos. 687 and 713, to Charles Sheridan, 14 Jan. 1826, and 7 Feb. 1827. A note in an unknown hand on the original of this letter mistakenly states that the reference to £4,000 is to the amount offered by Murray for the *Life of Sheridan*. It also gives a brief account of the incident explained in note 1, p. 555.

Dr Bain for all this (besides that of Vaughan) a simple line or two from him would be invaluable, as it would throw the fellows on their backs at once.[1] I was going to write to Bain on the subject, but as possibly he would rather address the required testimony to *you* than to *me*, I think you had better take the application to him on yourself & lose no time about it.[2] If he has an objection to any signed statement (though all that we should require would be 'Mr Moore's account of these circumstances is correct') he will of course, at least, allow me to quote him, as authority, in my answer, which shall be, you may tell him, perfectly candid & conciliatory, and in which, while defending the accuracy of my statements, I shall disclaim all intention of questioning the general generosity of the King, in pecuniary matters. Indeed, Bain shall see what I say before it appears. Now, pray, attend to all this without delay, & believe me

Yours very truly
Thomas Moore.

Mr Ogle, I think, must know all these circumstances, if you do not yourself.

698. *To Dr. Bain*

Russell, viii. 263

Sloperton Cottage, Devizes
April 17. 1826.

My dear Friend,

I wrote to Charles Sheridan yesterday, begging him to apply to you upon a subject in which we are all pretty equally concerned; but, upon second thoughts, I feel that I ought not to have taken this *roundabout* way, but to have written to you decidedly myself. You see the 'Quarterly Review' has fired its long-threatened cannonade, and though it is more noisy than mischievous, yet some of my friends (Lord Lansdowne among many others) think I ought to take notice of it.[3] My intention therefore is, in the preface to the next edition, to put two or three paragraphs, as good-tempered and

---

[1] Moore claimed that a gift of £200, transmitted from the Prince through a Mr. Vaughan to Sheridan, when the latter was on his death-bed, was respectfully declined by the family. The *Quarterly* (p. 590) maintained that Moore was incorrect, that the sum was £500, and that the gift was accepted, used, and afterwards, 'on suspicions and pride being awakened', repaid. The statement in the *Quarterly* was refuted in the preface to the fifth edition of Moore's biography, where the author quoted a letter from Dr. Bain, who confirmed Moore's stand on the question.

[2] Moore wrote to Bain himself, however. See letters Nos. 698 and 699, to Dr. Bain, 17 and 18 Apr. 1826.

[3] See letter No. 697, to Charles Sheridan, 16 Apr. 1826.

conciliatory as possible, disclaiming all idea of imputing a general want of generosity, in pecuniary matters, to the illustrious personage concerned in these transactions, but at the same time defending the accuracy of my own statements. It is odd enough, that the only points of importance which they affect to disprove, is the account of the £200 sent through Vaughan, for which I had the authority of the two persons concerned in it, Vaughan and yourself. They say the sum was £500, and that it was accepted, made use of, and afterwards repaid. Now, what I want of you is (and indeed you could not render me a more signal service, to say nothing of what is due to the family and yourself), to let me put two or three lines, as follows, with your signature:—

'My dear Sir,
    'The statement which you have made in your Life of my friend Mr. Sheridan, that £200 was the sum proffered to me by Mr. Vaughan, and that it was respectfully declined, is perfectly correct.
                                                           'Yours, &c.'[1]

If you prefer having the words addressed to Charles Sheridan:—

'My dear Charles,
    'The statement which Mr. Moore, &c., &c.,'

it would do equally well, and perhaps better. I know it is far from pleasant for you, and God knows I heartily hate it myself, much as I am used to it, to have your name brought before the public in any way; yet, if honest men did not stand by each other on a pinch, this world would not be worth living in; besides, as your authority is already pledged on the face of my statement, this would be only the repetition of it in a more formal way, and would be, indeed, the only mode of settling all controversy on this point at rest for ever. You may depend upon my answer being such as will tend very much to remove any impression there may have been of my wishing to attack the King unfairly; and your assistance in the way I ask will materially assist me towards that object, as, in enabling me to show that I am correct in my statements, it will give me the power of being more candid and conciliatory in my admissions; in short, it will carry us triumphantly through. Though I had no answer to my last letter to you on my return from Ireland, I know from Charles Sheridan that it was received and *acted upon*. My best remembrances to your daughters, and believe me,
                                                    Ever very truly yours,
                                                         Thomas Moore.

---

[1] Bain wrote the letter as requested, and Moore published it in the preface to the fifth edition of his *Life of Sheridan* (p. xi).

699. *To Dr. Bain*

Russell, viii. 265

April 18. 1826.

My dear Sir,

I wrote to you to Heffleton yesterday, feeling that I had taken a more roundabout way than was necessary, in applying to you through Sheridan; and being anxious to explain to you more fully than I had done to him the great importance of your testimony on this occasion.[1] I am sorry that my letter of yesterday will be so long in reaching you, as I felt sure, in writing it, that you would not hesitate at granting the request it contains. I have just had a letter from my excellent and honourable friend Lord John Russell, who also thinks (this between ourselves) that something ought to be said in my answer to the 'Quarterly.'[2] The three main points on which I am charged with omission and inaccuracy, are, with respect to the 4000£. for the seat,[3] the liberation of Sheridan from the prison,[4] and the 200£. through Vaughan.[5] On the two former I am prepared with an answer; and *you* can render a triumphant one on the last. I hope they will forward to you my letter from Heffleton: at all events, do not answer this till you receive it.

I do not forget my promise for summer, and trust that my stars will be propitious enough to allow me to keep it.

Yours most truly,
Thomas Moore.

[1] See letter No. 698, to Dr. Bain, 17 Apr. 1826.
[2] See letter No. 697, to Charles Sheridan, 16 Apr. 1826.
[3] See letter No. 687, to Charles Sheridan, 14 Jan. 1826.
[4] Sheridan was arrested for debt in 1813, and Moore claimed that it was Whitbread who arranged for his release from prison. The *Quarterly Review* (xxxiii. 585–6) maintained that Whitbread went to the prison immediately after he had received a letter from Sheridan, only to find that the Prince had interceded and secured Sheridan's release. In the preface to the fifth edition of his biography (pp. vii–xi) Moore denied the accuracy of this argument by quoting a letter from Sheridan to Whitbread, which proves that the latter visited the prison and that a day or two elapsed between the visit and the dramatist's dismissal. Whitbread was aware of Sheridan's plight before he received the letter, therefore, and needed the two intervening days in order to make the necessary arrangements.
[5] See letter No. 697, to Charles Sheridan, 16 Apr. 1826, and No. 698, to Dr. Bain, 17 Apr. 1826.

700. *To Francis Jeffrey*

Rice University

Sloperton Cottage
April 29th 1826

My dear Jeffrey— I was most hugely disappointed at not [finishing] the promised article; for it would have come seasonably to my [*MS. damaged*] have saved me the trouble of a Manifesto which I must now issue, [*MS. damaged*] subject. In answering my assailants (which I shall do very [*MS. damaged*] the opinions of others rather than my own—a man, who [*MS. damaged*]s he sees) the weakness of his adversary's attack (from know- [*MS. damaged*] bearings of the question), is not likely to think an answer so [*MS. damaged*]s others do. I mean to put what I have to say in the Times [*MS. damaged*] paper, & in the form of an extract from the intended Preface to the [*MS. damaged*] Edition of the Life. You will, however, still have an opportunity of doing me a signal service, by following up my defence with your comments, & thus making it tell doubly on the enemy. I believe there is little doubt that it was that 'infidus scurra', Lockhart, who wrote the article in the Quarterly.[1] What a pity that Scott should have such a dark spot on his disk as this fellow is!

As to my journeymanship for you, I am setting off to town on Tuesday, to stay two or three weeks, during which interval I can do nothing but eat the Whigs' dinners—that is, if Whigs will *give* me dinners any longer. But, on my return I shall immediately set about an article, so as to have it ready at the beginning of June, which I rather think will be time enough for you. Let me have a line, though, to town, under cover to John Benett Esqr M.P. 19 Albemarle St.— I am going to stay at the Benett's house.

Best & most cordial greetings to Mrs J. & daughter from yours & theirs most truly

Thomas Moore.

701. *To John Cam Hobhouse*

Sir John Murray

Sloperton Cottage
May 1st 1826

Dear Hobhouse— I mean to be in town on Wednesday or Thursday next and should like to have some talk with you before you 'melt,

---

[1] Moore is referring to the review of his life of Sheridan, *Quarterly Review*, xxxiii. 561–93. See letter No. 697, to Charles Sheridan, 16 Apr. 1826.

thaw & resolve yourself'¹ into Westminster again. I mean to take
up my quarters at Benett's, 19 Albemarle St. and if you write me
a line, will come to you whenever you are most at leisure.

Yours very truly
Thomas Moore

Thank you for the truths you told the other night.

702. *To Edward Moore*

Rice University

Sloperton Cottage
June 11ᵗʰ 1826.

My dear Moore— In consequence of my being from home on a visit
to a neighbour, your letter did not reach me till Friday evening,
too late for the Post. I trust this will find you still in Cleveland
Row.

Your splendid present has already taken its station on the shelves
of my Library, and shall soon be joined by the remainder of its
brethren. Bon voyage!

Yours ever
Thomas Moore

703. *To Dr. Bain*

Russell, viii. 266

July 8. 1826.

My dear Friend,

I made a most egregious blunder in writing to you the other day.
According to your desire, I dispatched my letter on the Wednesday,
in order that it should catch you before your departure from town
on the Friday, and, as an Irish way of gaining this object, I directed
the letter, in a strange fit of absence, to Heffleton. As this, however,
cannot now be helped, I should not have thought it worth while
troubling you with a new despatch about it, if I had not another
object. You may remember, on my last visit to you, I mentioned
that my friend Bowles had expressed a longing desire to accompany
me, and that you said you would have been very glad to see him.
Now he has been with me to-day, expressing the very same wish,
and it has occurred to me that you would at least like to know the
circumstance, in order that if it suited your arrangements, you
might have an opportunity of asking him. If you have any difficulty
about lodging-rooms, you know you may put me in your worst

¹ *Hamlet*, I. ii. 129.

Poet's corner, and let Bowles have the *gîte* intended for me. His address is 'Rev. W. L. Bowles, Bremhill, near Calne,' and if you *should* write and ask him, let me have a line at the same time to say so.

Yours, in a furious hurry,
Thomas Moore.

704. *To William Lisle Bowles*

Greever, p. 84

Thursday Eve. [8 July 1826][1]

My dear Bowles,—

I have written to Doctor Bain to say that you are coming.[2] He gave me full powers last time (you know) to take advantage of any 'mollia tempora' I might see in you towards visiting him. He will therefore expect you, and you must not leave me in the lurch. As to his having *room*, he expects Mrs. Moore and all the little ones, and therefore you can easily be stowed away in their place. Besides I have bid him put me in his *worst* Poet's Corner.

We must set off Tuesday or Wednesday at the very farthest. Let me have a line.

Yours, &c.,
T. Moore.

705. *To Henry Angelo*

Harvard College Library

Sloperton Cottage*
July 10th 1826.*

Sir.

You must have thought me most culpably negligent in leaving the letter, with which you favoured me near two months since, so long unanswered—but it came here while I was away from home, and it was but a few days since, on my return, that I received it.

I am ready & happy to bear testimony to your presence, as an invited guest, at the dinner in 1806, where the Duke of Sussex presided and where his present Majesty was also one of the guests— I have also to thank you for bringing the circumstances of that very agreeable day back to my recollection & beg you to

believe me your faithful Servant
Thomas Moore.

---

[1] Date supplied by the editor.
[2] See letter No. 703, to Dr. Bain, 8 July 1826.

706. *To Colonel Houlton*

B.M. Add. MS. 27425BC, f. 8

Sloperton Cottage
October 14ᵗʰ 1826

My dear Houlton— Nothing would give me greater pleasure than to go with you *any where*—but I have been idling so desperately of late, that I *must* stay at home. Not that I shall be allowed to be a *guarda casa* very long, for business, I fear, will soon take me up to town again for a day or two— Can I do any thing for you there?
 Best regards to all at Farley from

Ever truly yours,
Thomas Moore

Mʳˢ Moore sends her love to the 'dear rogues' (as the Historiographer of Wiltshire calls them)[1] in which I join most heartily.

707. *To James Power*

Rice University

[Rec'd 10ᵗʰ Novʳ 1826]

My dear Sir— I send you more of the MSS.— You will see what I have remarked upon the Glee of 'What shall we dance?'—[2] in this way we shall be able, I hope, to preserve it at full length.
 I have not time for more.

Yours ever
T. M.

708. *To Anne Scott*

B.M. Add. MS. 33964, f. 353

Sloperton Cottage, Devizes
Nov 15, 1826

My dear Miss Scott. I was in hopes, from the beginning of your letter, that you were going to put my zeal in your service to a much more trying test. As to autographs, I'll furnish you enough for all the Offs & Owskis of your acquaintance, too happy that they don't extend their ambition (like our friend W. Gordon) to a lock of my hair,[3] in which case I should want all the oil of their own

---

[1] 'John Britton, Historiographer of Wilts.' [*A. Houlton's note.*]
[2] *Poetry*, p. 307.
[3] Mr. Gordon, a Presbyterian clergyman, came to Moore's room while the poet was at Abbotsford and requested a lock of his hair. Moore told him to 'be careful how he cut it, as Mrs. Moore would be sure to detect the "rape"' (Russell, v. 5).

Mochrikowsky to enable me to supply them. I have been thinking of you, I assure you, every day of the time that you have been
away, and wishing myself Jackal to the 'Lion' in his progress. Give
my most cordial regards to him, & with kind remembrances to
your sister & Mr Lockhart, believe me ever most truly yours

                                                Thomas Moore

I don't know whether the Princess wished more than my mere
name—if she did, only tell me, and I'll write out some lines of
somebody's for her with pleasure.

709. *To Sir Walter Scott*

N.L.S. MS. 3903, f. 194

                                Sloperton Cottage, Devizes
                                        Novr 23rd 1826*

My dear Scott— If you had not happened to be leaving London so
soon, I think I should have had a chance of seeing you there.
Indeed, Rogers promised to make out some *pretext* of business for
me, in order to justify my running up to meet you. But Murray
(with whom he is my negociator respecting Byron's Life) is too
much of a gentleman, I fear, to give us even a pretext of business.
And this reminds me of a request which I have long been intending
to make of you, my dear Scott. If Murray can be brought to any
thing definitive on this subject, I shall not be long in dispatching
the Work, as our materials, when united, will be ample, and will
enable me I think to make Byron *tell* his *own* story, which is not
only the pleasantest sort of biography to the reader but by far the
easiest to the writer. Now putting your *greatness* out of the question
(which, to talk Irishly, is the *smallest* part of you) your friendship
with poor Byron and, I think I may add, with myself, points you
out as the person, of all others, to whom my book should be dedicated—will you allow me to do so?[1]

   Murray always reminds me of an Irish story of a fellow who,
being rated by the Priest for having shirked his Easter dues (as he
had often done before) gave, as an excuse, that he had been very
near dying—so near that he had been obliged to get Father Murphy
to *oil him* (i.e. to give him extreme unction.) 'Oh, he oiled you, did
he?' says the other—'faith and there was no occasion, for you're
slippery enough without it.' Murray appears to me to be equally
well provided with this quality, but I trust Sam's *grippe* will be
able to lay hold of him for me at last.
   Thank you for Gallois' letter—he is an excellent fellow, and I

---

[1] Moore's *Life of Byron* was dedicated to Scott.

would back him for knowledge of English Parliamentary History against any Englishman extant.[1]

You have set Mrs Moore & me all agog for the north, and we shall, at least, dream of your proposal.[2] Best regards to all around you

from ever truly your
Thomas Moore

710. *To Henry R. Bishop*

Rice University

Sloperton Cottage*
Monday Morning* [November 1826]

My dear Sir— I sent a sort of a Skeleton of a Glee the other day for you to clothe with flesh, or rather 'create a soul under its ribs of death.' If I were near you, I could play it all perfect, in *my* way— but I cannot write it out—particularly the symphonies—however, I give you a carte blanche for its improvement, and, as I told Power will acknowledge your share in it most thankfully— I should not like you however to depart too much from my melody, & if I should be up in town before you do any thing to it you shall hear my symphonies & judge whether they are good enough to *pass muster*.

I am much disappointed at being kept so long in the country, and fear it will be some weeks yet before I am able to come up.

I rather think I wrote the Duett part of the Spirits wrongly on the MS. I sent you. It should be thus.

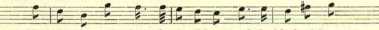

We bring her smiles from the April bow, and the blush of flowers

I forget whether these ought to be crotchets or quavers,—indeed I rather fear that I made some blunders as to the quantity of the notes in writing the Glee out, I was in such a hurry at the time. In the Bass part particularly, ('What have you brought for my lady dear?) it strikes me that I made the mistake of writing crotchets instead of quavers—but you will easily see through these blunders.[3]

It is my doom always to write in a hurry & I scribble this while the friend who takes it to town is keeping the carriage door open to receive it. So good bye.

Yours very truly
Thomas Moore

[1] Scott had forwarded a letter from Gallois to Moore (Russell, v. 132).

[2] Scott renewed his invitation for the Moore's to visit Abbotsford.

[3] The song has not been identified. It may have been one written (but not used) for *A Set of Glees* (*Poetry*, pp. 306–8), which Power published in 1827. The letter was dated by comparing its content with that of the diary (Russell, v. 132–3).

711. *To John Murray*

Sir John Murray

Sloperton Cottage
Jan^r 20 1827

Dear Sir. Some business, connected with the new Edition of my Sheridan, has for some time past required my presence in town— but in the hope of hearing from you (as you promised, many weeks since) on the subject of Lord Byron's Life, I have deferred my journey—in order to include, if possible, *both* businesses in the one visit. I now propose being in town about the 29th or 30th of this month, and trust you will be able by that time at least, to arrange definitely the matter between us.

I regretted very much not being in town to attend Mr Gifford's funeral—[1] I liked much what I knew of him, as a companion, and it is only lately that I have been made to feel what a kind and gentlemanly friend I lost in him, as a critic.

Yours very truly
Thomas Moore.

712. *To William Lisle Bowles*

Greever, p. 86

Saturday Night [January 1827][2]

My dear Sir—

I said that, if you did not hear from me to the contrary, you might depend upon us for Monday next, but I think it is as well to let you know that we are perfectly at your dispoasl [*sic*] for that day, if you are able to send the carriage for us. I find Crabbe is to be at Bowood this next week, and I wish our meeting there (as, of course, we shall all be asked 'poetis nos laetamur *tribus*') could be arranged for one of the days we meant to pass with you.—Jeffrey has been very kind to me in the Review just come out—indeed most generously so, considering all he had said before.[3]

Yours, my dear Bowles (may I say so?) very truly,
Thomas Moore.

---

[1] William Gifford died on 31 Dec. 1826.
[2] Date supplied by the editor.
[3] Jeffrey's favourable review of Moore's *Life of Sheridan* appeared in the *Edinburgh Review*, xlv (December 1826), 1–48. Moore recorded in his diary for 9 Jan. 1827 that he had read the article, and on 10 Jan. that he had written to Jeffrey to thank him (Russell, v. 142).

713. *To Charles Brinsley Sheridan*

National Library of Ireland

Feb^r 7th 1827.*

My dear Sheridan— I can tell the Public no more than I know myself. The Nobleman I *conjecture* to be Lord Moira, but have not the slightest idea who the Attorney was. Burgess was the authority to me & (through me) to the Edinburgh.[1] If you think you have any chance of ascertaining the particulars, my great object is the truth—the whole truth—and you had better set about it without delay. My correction of the rest of the Preface can go on in the mean time. You must be quick in your movements, however, as the mere chance of further information turning up is not worth waiting for.

I shall be delighted to read your Niece's Poem, & still more delighted if she will read it to me, herself.[2]

Ever yours.
T. Moore.

714. *To Owen Rees*

University of Edinburgh

Sloperton Cottage
Feb^r 14, 1827

My dear Sir— I take advantage of a frank to Lord Lansdowne to slip this note in, and announce myself as likely to be forthcoming

---

[1] Moore acquired some 'curious papers' relating to Sheridan from Burgess (see Russell, iv. 301), and it was probably Burgess who told him what he considered to be the truth about the Prince's gift of £4,000 to Sheridan (see letter No. 687, to Charles Sheridan, 14 Jan. 1826). The gift of £4,000 and that of £200 (see Letter No. 697, to Charles Sheridan, 16 Apr. 1826) are discussed in the *Edinburgh*'s review of Moore's *Life of Sheridan*. Of the former the writer says: 'With regard to the alleged gift of £4000 by his Majesty, we have the most sincere pleasure in saying, that we have every reason to believe, that the Illustrious Person is fully entitled to the credit of that act of munificence. . . . The sum which we have heard was about 3000£ was by his Royal Highness's order, placed by a distinguished nobleman in the hands of an attorney for Sheridan's benefit; but was there either attached by his creditors, or otherwise dissipated in such a manner, that very little of it actually reached its destination—a result, however, which certainly takes nothing from the merits of his princely benefactor' (*Edinburgh Review*, xlv, December 1826, p. 46).

Moore was incorrect in his conjecture about Lord Moira, as shown in the preface to the fifth edition of his biography: 'The sum in question . . . was . . . transmitted . . . through the hands of Lord Hastings, and was by him entrusted to Mr. Cockrell, an attorney, who professed to have the means of effecting the object desired' (*Life of Sheridan*, pp. xv–xvii).

[2] Probably Alicia Lefanu, who wrote light verse. See, for example, letter No. 1012, to Alicia Lefanu, 7 Aug. 1832, in which Moore thanks her for a verse tribute to him.

in Paternoster Row about this day week. I have unluckily a weakness in my eyes (from a cold caught on one of these frosty days) which prevents me from transcribing as I could wish, but I hope to be able to copy out enough to set you going while I am in town.

Yours, my dear Sir, very truly
Thomas Moore.

715. *To John Cam Hobhouse*

Sir John Murray

Athenaeum
Feb^r 28 1827

My dear Hobhouse— As I know you are up to your eyes in business, & there is but little chance of our meeting during the few days I remain in town, I think it is as well to communicate to you, by letter, the termination that has just taken place of my negociation with Murray. It was begun under your auspices, & it is right that you should know the result.

You have been, I believe, acquainted with his resolution (though I did not know it till the day before yesterday) *not* to publish any of the papers in his possession, but to leave them as a legacy to his children. This resolution of his—disconcerting as it is to me—I do not blame him for. I should have possibly adopted the same, had I been in his place. He has followed up the communication of this intention to me, by offering, for a Life written by me upon my own materials, two thousand five hundred pounds—a very liberal price, but which I have declined for the following reason. As my only motive or plea for transferring the work from the Longmans to him was the power it gave me of combining the contributions of all parties towards the work, this object being now frustrated by his resolution, I revert, of course, to the Longmans, as my own original and (if nature has any thing to do with the Row) *natural* publishers.

I must now only make out as good and harmless a book of it as I can. The Public will, of course, be disappointed, but better so than wrongly gratified. Any assistance you can give me, consistent with your own view of the undertaking, will be appreciated, I need not tell you, as it deserves ; and of your kind offer to look over the work before publication I shall most thankfully avail myself.

Yours very truly
Thomas Moore

716. *To Mrs. Houlton*

B.M. Add. MS. 27425BC, f. 11

Sloperton Cottage*
March 7th 1827*

My dear Mrs Houlton— We have been all this time 'waiting Tea', and it is not yet come. I meant to have enquired of you, before I went to town, where I should be likely to hear of it; but was so busy, both here & there, that I could not find a minute for the purpose. Will you have the goodness to let me know what we had better do about it? Bessy threatens every day to lay in her stock & we shall be soon 'steeped to the lips' in bad tea again.

Only think of my not being able to snatch a moment for a visit to Chelsea, notwithstanding all my good resolutions on the subject! My stay, however, was little more than a week & I had the business of a month to crowd into it.

My best regards to all yours & believe me, my dear Mrs Houlton, your ever obliged & faithful

T. Moore

717. *To Mrs. Houlton*

B.M. Add. MS. 27425A, f. 3

Sloperton Cottage
March 10th 1827

My dear Mrs Houlton— The Tea has arrived since I wrote, & we are at this moment in the act of trying its goodness. As Bessy has disposed of a part of it to one or two of our neighbours, she is anxious to know the price of it *per pound*, and would be much obliged by your putting us in the way of finding out, as no Bill has accompanied it.

Pray, forgive all this trouble we inflict upon you, & believe me, my dear Mrs Houlton,

Most truly yours
Thomas Moore

718. *To Mrs. Houlton*

B.M. Add. MS. 27425A, f. 1

Sunday Morning [March 1827]

My dear Mrs Houlton— Bessy would have written to you, herself, to thank you for your thoughtfulness in sending the tea, but she is (and has been, for a week past) entirely occupied with poor Russell, who is suffering from the progress of a gathering under his ear. You will, perhaps, to-day receive my letter informing you of the arrival of our Tea, and you can, at your convenience, answer the question which it contains.

I *swear* I shall run over to you before long.

Ever yours

T. Moore

Love to the Donzelle & Donze*lette*

719. *To Colonel Houlton*

B.M. Add. MS. 27425BC, f. 13

Sloperton Cottage

April 7th 1827

My dear Houlton— I have deferred discharging my debt to you under the expectation that I should be able to do it, in person, at Farley—but as this has not yet been in my power, I think it as well to inclose you a cheque for the sum, which you will find negociable at Tufnell's (the correspondent of Locke & Hughes) in Bath. Many, many thanks for all the trouble you have had about it.

I should like to know whether you are likely to be at home, (and in receipt of customers) about Friday or Saturday next, as I think of going about that time for my little girl, and would, if possible, make Farley my way.

Best regards to all your Ladies from

Ever yours

Thomas Moore

720. *To Colonel Houlton*

B.M. Add. MS. 27425A, f. 5

April 12th 1827

My dear Houlton— I received my letter yesterday too late to answer you by return of post— For Monday I am invited to Simpson's, but would much rather give the day I have to spare to you; therefore hope this may reach you in time to prevent your sending on Saturday. It was very kind of M[rs] Houlton to think of fetching my poor little girl to-day, but she will have found that she is not yet able even to come home,[1] and this circumstance, indeed, as well as my present pressure of business would *almost* induce me to postpone my visit to you till some more favourable time.

---

[1] Moore's oldest surviving child, Anastasia, was ill and had been taken to Bath for treatment.

My plan would be, if I came to you on Monday, to go into Bath
next day to see my little girl, and either start from thence hither
(to save you the trouble of sending her home again) or return with
you to Farley and come home early next day.

Yours very truly
T. M.

I shall be, at all events, ready for you (if you will have me) on
Monday.

721. *To A. Spottiswode, M.P.*

Rice University

May 30th 1827.*

My dear Sir— Without any offence to your *printing* Establishment,
I should infinitely prefer your *dining* one. But the devils have their
claws in me still, & I shall not be able, I fear, to get loose before
Tuesday next. I hope, however, you will give me another chance,
when I come up to town.

With best remembrances to Mrs Spottiswode,

Believe me very truly yours
Thomas Moore.

722. *To Dr. Adams*

Bodleian MS. Montagu d. 5, f. 105

Sloperton Cottage
June 1st 1827

Mr Moore presents his compliments to Doctor Adams, with many
apologies for the long delay of his answer to the letter with which
Doctor Adams favoured him. Not having been sooner able to gain
access to the box, in which the few papers of Mr Sheridan's, that
still remain in his hands, are deposited, it was not in his power to
comply with the request of Doctor Adams till the present moment,
when he has great pleasure in inclosing to him the specimen of
Sheridan's handwriting which he desired.

723. *To Mary Shelley*

Abinger Collection

Thursday [postmark July 5, 1827]

I am so sorry to find that the party with whom I engaged myself to
go to the Charlemonts tomorrow mean to start at ½ past one, which
will altogether frustrate our Linwood plan.[1] I tried to get off the

---

[2] Moore went with the Ruthvens to pass the day with the Charlemonts
(see Russell, v. 188).

engagement, but they will not let me, so that it will be impossible for us to meet, I fear, before Sunday. This is very provoking.

> Ever yours most truly
> Thomas Moore

724. *To Mary Shelley*

Abinger Collection

> July 11, 1827.*

Good by—a thousand thanks for the sweets of all kinds. I am off in an hour hence.

> Yours very truly
> T. M.

725. *To Lord Auckland*

B.M. Add. MS. 29475, f. 74

> July 16, 1827

My dear Lord Auckland— A thousand thanks for the anecdote, which is excellent & made me laugh 'most consumedly.' I shall try my hand at versifying it, which is all you have left me to do—but it will not be easy to manage such a *clinical* scene, without shocking people a little— Should Lord L recover sufficiently to stand a joke, there will then be no harm in it.[1]

I hope something good will come out of all this delay;—but I have my fears. The elements of dissension are too numerous to allow one to feel quite comfortable upon the subject.

I take advantage of your cover to slip in a little bit of music, knowing your tendencies that way— Pray, send it to the twopenny Post for me.

> Ever yours
> Thomas Moore

Your first contribution is so very good that I shall count most anxiously upon more.

[1] Lord Liverpool suffered a stroke in February 1827 and died on 4 Dec. 1828. There is no way of knowing what anecdote Lord Auckland sent Moore since, as Lord Liverpool did not recover, the poet did not 'try [his] hand at versifying it'.

726. *To J. R. Planché*

Rice University

Sloperton Cottage
July 23rd 1827

Dear Sir. I beg you to accept my best thanks for the two beautiful Volumes which I have just received. I had already known & admired the First, though I was not lucky enough to possess it, & I feel very grateful to you for adding such a valuable ornament to my Musical Library. Allow me to hope that, in my next visit to town, I may be fortunate enough to make your acqaintance and believe me

Your much obliged & faithful
Servt

Thomas Moore.

727. *Addressee Unknown*

Rice University

Sloperton Cottage
July 30th 1827

Sir— I feel very sensibly the honour which you have done me in sending me your compositions, which, though in many passages requiring a much quicker finger than mine to do justice to them, give me, even in my own performance of them, a very high idea of your powers as a musician. I grieve to find that your success hitherto has not been equal to your expectations, and shall feel happy in any opportunity that may occur for being of service to you.

I am, Sir, your obliged &
faithful Servt

Thomas Moore.

728. *To Mary Shelley*

Abinger Collection

Sloperton Cottage, Devizes
August 3rd 1827.

I was beginning to fear you had forgot me a little—but your letter convinced me very agreeably that you had not. I am busily employed in transcribing (which is an odious task) all of B's letters & journals that I think *presentable* to the Public, and there will be more, I think, of this description than I had supposed. Pray, remember hard & fast for me—the more the better. Talking of memory, your Spanish verses (which, by the bye, a Spanish scholar told me the other day, he thought were written by a foreigner) suggested to me some lines for music, which you have a right to see, as you were accessory to their *enfantement*—but which you must not give to any one, or Power will have you in Chancery. Here they are—as near as I can recollect them.

> Hope comes again,—to this heart long a stranger,
>   Hope comes, to soothe me once more with her strain;
> But hush, gentle syren,—for ah there's less danger
>   In still suffering on, than in hoping again.
>
> Long, long in sorrow, too deep for repining,
>   Gloomy, but tranquil, this bosom hath lain;
> And joy, coming now, like the summer light shining
>   O'er eyelids long darken'd, would bring me but pain.
>
> Fly, then, ye visions, that Hope would shed o'er me—
>   Lost to the future, my sole chance of rest
> Now lies not in dreaming of bliss that's before me,
>   But, ah, in forgetting that once I was blest.[1]

Many, many thanks for your kind offer about my little girl—but she is now sufficiently recovered from her lameness to be able to dance quadrilles.

Should your memorabilia extend (as I hope they will) to many sheets, you can send them for me under cover to our County Member, John Benett Esqr M.P. Pyt-house, Salisbury. The marriage, of which I half trusted you with the secret, is now declared, and Benett's pretty daughter, Ethel, is to be in a month or two Lady Charles Churchill. We are going to pass a few days at Pyt-house this month.[2]

Yours most truly
T. Moore

729. *To Lord John Russell*

Early Correspondence of Lord John Russell, i. 256

August 3, 1827.

My dear Lord John,—I shall pray for rain if it always produces such a nice crop under your pen as the last. It gave me great pleasure to find that you had not given up the Memoirs of the Affairs, etc., etc.[3] These are the *gros morceaux* for the table of

---

[1] *Poetry*, p. 251.
[2] See letter No. 730, to Mary Shelley, 17 Aug. 1827.
[3] *Memoirs of the Affairs of Europe from the Peace of Utrecht* (1824–9).

posterity. By the bye, did you happen to see over a year ago, a little note in the *Edinburgh Review*, alluding to this work? Answer me this.

I hope the enclosed will catch Rogers before he moves off, like the sun, on his annual visit to the 'celestial *Houses*.' I have asked him to write down for me all he remembers about Lord Byron, and it would be the kindest thing of you, too, to ransack your memory a little, and give me notes of what you recollect of the memories, but putting it out of your head that I remember anything of them, and telling all that occurs to you.[1] This will be very, very kind of you. I would enlist Lady Holland too in the same service, if I might, and if you would but excite each other's memories for me (as people rub amber to make it catch) there is no knowing how much of the past you may draw back. Pray give her my very kindest regards. There is no one (little as it is my doom to see of her) from whom I carry home recollections of such *real* kindness as from her. Her inquiries after the wife and babes in the summer-house (I mean one of those little wooden things in which I sat with her the first day I called) have not been untold at Sloperton.

Ever, my dear Lord John, faithfully yours,

Thomas Moore.

730. *To Mary Shelley*

Abinger Collection

Pyt-house
August 17th 1827

We got here late to dinner yesterday, & I found your two most welcome packets, which I have but just time to acknowledge the receipt of, as we are setting off to see Sir R. Moore's place, Stour-head.[2] I heard of the arrival of your letters, before I came; for Benett wrote to me to say that there were two packets for me so enormously above weight ('so much the better,' thought I) that he would not forward them, but keep them till I should arrive. You must, you see, divide your next under different covers, and I shall look for them with anxiety. No matter whether they contain much or not, the very thought that you consider me worth taking such trouble for is encouraging & delightful to me—that is, if it does not take you too much away from the task you said you would

---

[1] Russell wrote to Moore on 23 Oct. 1829 sending his recollections of Byron. See *The Early Correspondence of Lord John Russell, 1805–40*, edited by Rollo Russell (London, 1913), i. 265–7.

[2] Moore recorded his visit to Stourhead in his diary for 17 Aug. 1827 (Russell, v. 195).

undertake, and which I shall feel doubly interested in from your flattering me with the idea that I had, in some degree, revived your zeal for it.[1] Your notes are the only part of the contents of the packets that I have yet read. I am glad you liked my verses, though the suspicion you seem to have that I wrote them merely as an artist, without any feeling of the sadness that is in them, provokes me a little. The fact is that the two extremes—very merry things or very melancholy—are the only sort of subjects I write upon *con amore*.

Pray, urge the Guiccioli for me.[2] I have already experienced the good effects of your application to her, for Mr Barry of Genoa writes to me that he thinks she is much inclined to contribute materials to my work.

The carriages are at the door, and I must have done. Good bye.

Ever yours

T. M.

You shall have the verses in my next, and the Work itself, when I am in town to send my name with it.[3]

731. *To Mary Shelley*

Abinger Collection

August 31st 1827*

You must not mind the shortness and shabbiness of my epistles— I'll make it up all [*sic*] when we meet. You ought to have known my reputation in this way; for a very lively little friend of yours could have told you of it. 'If any one were to ask me (she said, one day) what sort of man Mr Moore is, I would answer "as little like a note I have of his as possible".'[4] She was not thinking of course of the *shortness* (which is as paralell [*sic*] a case with me as it was with Horace) but of the coldness & shabbiness of my epistolary communications, to which I am afraid, from all I hear, I must plead guilty. Another packet has arrived, and it is as interesting and *useful* as the former. 'That strain again'[5] and again is all I have time to say at this moment.

Ever most truly y^rs

T. M.

[1] Moore may be referring to Mary's novel *Perkin Warbeck*, on which she was working at this time.

[2] Teresa Guiccioli furnished Moore with an 'Istoria' of her liaison with Byron (see letters Nos. 779 and 791, to Mary Shelley, 15 Apr. and 25 July 1828).

[3] Probably *Evenings in Greece* (1825).

[4] The double quotes were supplied by the editor.

[5] *Twelfth Night*, I. i. 4.

I wish you could get from the Guiccioli the exact words written by him in 'Corinne'.[1] Lady Davy had before told me of them.

732. *To Mary Shelley*

Abinger Collection

Sloperton Cottage*
September 4th 1827.*

I am all consternation at your not having received my last two letters. I wrote immediately after each of the packets, that succeeded those I found at Pyt-house, and cannot account for their miscarriage, as I think I had acknowledgements of some that went under the same cover. My *entre-pôt* was Spottiswode, of the Longman establishment, and with him the fault must lie. My letters, though short & scrambling (as my letters always are) expressed as strongly as time would permit, not only my gratitude for all the trouble you were taking for me, but my admiration of the interest & brilliancy which you contrived to throw over every part of these details—particularly your account of the time you passed at Geneva. I assure you, the new light you have let in on my task (aided by my fresh perusal of poor Byron's letters) have [*sic*] given me a zest and courage for my undertaking which I never expected to feel. The prospect, too, of the promised Istoria from the Guiccioli (which I shall also owe to your kindness) opens another source of life to my work, which was equally unexpected.[2] In my last I begged of you to get from her, if you could, the exact words which B. wrote in the Corinne, and which Lady Davy had before told me of.[3] I also requested you would tell me in which of Shelley's works those metaphysical doctrines of his to which you allude are most developed & dwelt upon.

It grieves me sincerely to find such a tone of sorrow & hopelessness as pervades your last letter, and I would ask—if I might—what new cause has arisen to sadden you? Trusting that your next will breathe a happier spirit, I am

Ever most truly & cordially yrs
Thomas Moore.

---

[1] For the note which Byron wrote in Teresa's copy of Madame de Staël's *Corinne* see Marchand, *Byron*, p. 811.
[2] See letters Nos. 779 and 791, to Mary Shelley, 15 Apr. and 25 July 1828.
[3] See letter No. 731, to Mary Shelley, 31 Aug. 1827.

733. *To Mary Shelley*

Abinger Collection

Bowood
September 13th 1827

Your last packet found me here, where I had come with my little girl for a few days, —Mrs Moore, I am sorry to say, not being well enough to accompany us. You talk of my being 'tiresome'—and what, pray, does a lady deserve to be called to whom one has written three or four letters, and who won't say whether she has received any one of them. Have you got those two that were missing?[1] This is a point that I ought to have ascertained, before I discharged my volley of scolding against the whole House of L. R. O. B. G.[2] on the subject—but, no matter—do tell me in your next.

Provoking as was Kentish Town, in the way of a longinquity, I wish you were there now—as I have some thoughts of making London my starting-post for Derbyshire, and then I should have had a glimpse of you.

I have been singing here a good deal to a very, very pretty face, of which Newton is, at this moment making a sketch, and means to put under it 'Listening to Moore'.[3] *Is* there any chance of your being in town? I believe I have already told you that my excursion northward is for the purpose of seeing Newstead.[4]

I have not opened your last precious packet yet, and for a reason which I don't know whether you will understand. It makes me *nervous* reading them, and, as I can't afford to be that in company, I shall wait till I go home.

'More! More.'

Ever yours
T. M.

Here are the words—which are like a body without its soul, thus parted from the music.

I return home tomorrow.

[1] See letter No. 732, to Mary Shelley, 4 Sept. 1827.
[2] Evidently the initials of the names of people who franked mail for him.
[3] On 13 Sept. Moore recorded in his diary: 'N. tried to make a sketch of Anastasia, but did not succeed' (Russell, v. 205).
[4] See letter No. 739, to Mary Shelley, 9 Oct. 1827.

734. *To A. A. Renouard*

Morgan Library

Sloperton Cottage, Devizes
September 14th 1827

Dear Sir—

Your letter having been directed to my lodgings in town (which I had for some time left) was delayed so long on its way that I had not the pleasure of receiving it till yesterday. I am delighted to find that you did not give up your intention of translating my little work, and have only to regret that this delay should occur, to produce any postponement of your publication.[1] With respect to the passages of which you require an explanation, the sense of the first is— 'How bright and happy this world (meaning, *the earth*) ought to be, if, as your Egyptian sages assert, yon pure & beautiful luminary (Sothis) was *the star that shone upon its birth*'— it being the opinion of some Egyptian philosophers that this star was shining, as a sort of tutelary light, at the time when our earth was created.[2]

With regard to the 'henna' pag. 27, Sonnini, I think (indeed, I am sure) calls it 'henné'.[3]

'Bananier', for plaintain-tree, is right.[4] 'Out of the pale of the Greek alphabet' is merely a playful allusion to our phrase 'out of the pale' (or *giron*, as I believe you call it) of the Church—the Nicosians having had some superstitious notions of the efficacy of the Greek alphabet towards salvation.[5]

The 'bean-tree' is perhaps best described as *Fève d'Égypte*, or *Fève Égyptienne*.

I have secured a scrap of Lord Byron's hand-writing for you, and would have inclosed it in this, but that I know postage is rather a serious matter in France. I shall therefore give it to our friend Rees to forward to you.

---

[1] *The Epicurean* was translated into French by A. A. Renouard, Paris, 1827.

[2] ' "How bright and happy," said I,—pointing up to Sothis, . . . "if—as your Egyptian Sages assert—yon pure and beautiful luminary was its birth-star!" ' *The Epicurean* (London, 1827), p. 160.

[3] 'The north wind . . . freshened the air, while on the banks . . . sent forth, from groves of orange and henna, the most delicious odours' (p. 27).

[4] 'A plantain—that favourite tree of the genii of Death—stood behind the statue . . .' (p. 98).

[5] 'And while, on one side, her Ophite professor was seen kneeling down gravely before his serpent, on the other, a Nicosian was, as gravely, contending that there was no chance of salvation out of the pale of the Greek alphabet' (p. 24).

Hoping to learn that my explanations have arrived in time to prevent any material derangement of your plans, I am,

my dear Sir, very truly your obliged &
faithful Servant

Thomas Moore.

735. *To Mr. Billing*

Maine Historical Society

Sloperton Cottage, Devizes
September 18th 1827

Dear Sir.

Our friend B[*erased*] (whose letter I have but just received) has communicated to me the very flattering wish expressed by some gentleman of your acquaintance to translate my last work 'The Epicurean'. From the terms in which B[*erased*] speaks of the person who intends me this honour, I have no doubt of his being every way qualified to do justice to the work, and I beg you will say for me how much I feel the distinction he is about to confer upon me.

I have heard of no one likely to undertake a translation of the book, except M. Raynouard [*sic*], the French publisher, who, when I saw him in London, expressed some intentions to that effect— but whether he has thought any thing more about it since I know not.

Believe me, dear Sir, yours very truly
Thomas Moore.

P. S. Since I wrote the above, I have had a letter from M. Raynouard [*sic*] to say that he is actually engaged in translating my work.[1]

736. *To Mary Shelley*

Abinger Collection

Sloperton Cottage
September 23, 1827

Ever since the receipt of your last packets (which I grieve to find so near their 'swan-like end') I have been expecting every day to be able to tell you something certain with respect to my movements —but there are so many various impelling forces acting upon me at this moment, that I cannot, even yet, say in what direction they will project me, or whether they will not still keep me fixedly & philosophically in *equilibrio*. The opinion of the Doctor to-day with respect to my little girl will very much decide me, and, *if* I go

---

[1] See letter No. 734, to A. A. Renouard, 14 Sept. 1827.

town [*sic*], it will be on Wednesday, and to stay only Thursday & Friday. Otherwise, I mean to start from hence on the same day for Cheltenham, and from thence find my way to Lord Rancliffe's, who lives in the neighbourhood of Newstead, & with whom I intend to fix my head quarters during my visit.[1]

I am idled here beyond endurance—somebody says 'one's friends are the greatest thieves of one's time,' and mine are certainly the most larcenous friends going.

I will write again tomorrow and let you know all, though I can hardly now hope that (even in the event of my going to town) the gods will allow us to meet.

Ever very truly y[rs]
Thomas Moore

737. *To Colonel Houlton*

B.M. Add. MS. 27425BC, f. 2

Wednesday Morning* [September 1827][2]

My dear Houlton— I grieve that you have had the trouble of sending the gig & grieve still more to let it return without its freight. But the truth is, supposing that you returned to Farley on Sunday (as you told me you would) I have kept myself ready to obey your summons these two days past, which were the only disposeable ones I have in the whole week. To-day I am engaged at home, tomorrow at Locke's, Friday at Laycock, Saturday at Bowood, and either on Sunday or Monday I am off to Nottinghamshire—'So runs the world away'[3] and so run I.

Most sorry for my disappointment, I am, my dear Houlton, with best good wishes to all the gay party,

Faithfully y[rs]
T. Moore

The inclosed is for Newton. Tell him, if he will make a sketch of Isabella at the *guitar* for *me*, I will forgive him all his contempt for my connoisseurship.

[1] See letter No. 739, to Mary Shelley, 9 Oct. 1827.
[2] Arthur Houlton's note on the original of this letter gives the date as 1822, but it must have been written in September 1827, since Moore made his trip to Nottinghamshire at that time.
[3] *Hamlet*, III. ii. 285.

738. *To Mary Shelley*

Abinger Collection

London
Oc^t 1st [postmark October 2, 1827]

Arrived here, by a su[*MS. damaged*] determination, on Friday last, & as I intended to be off again on Sunday morning, did not think it of any avail to write— Mrs Moore came with me (our dear girl being pronounced quite well) and yesterday I devoted with her to visiting the grave of another dear girl, at Hornsey,—a little one we lost ten years ago.[1] Tomorrow morning I am off for Notts.— You shall hear from me on my way, & I hope to return by London.

Yours ever most truly
T. Moore.

739. *To Mary Shelley*

Abinger Collection

Bunny Park
October 9th 1827.

I saw Newstead yesterday—and, you may believe me when I say that, *next* to Byron, I thought of *you* during my visit there. It was all deeply interesting to me—the beauty of the place—its profound tranquility (such a contrast to the perturbed spirit that once inhabited it)—the pride of ancestry that speaks from its walls & almost justifies the weakness of Byron on this subject—all touched me, as much as *any thing* could touch, before witnesses & those witnesses, strangers. I would have given worlds to be alone—or, at least with some one, like yourself, that could enter into the *past*, as well as the *present*, of the scene with me. The Wildmans (its present proprietors) were most earnest in their entreaties that I should pass some days with them, & I should have been delighted, for every reason, to have done so—but, most unluckily for my object, they and my noble Host[2] have had a quarrel, and, as I saw plainly he had set his heart on my not going to them, I have been obliged to refuse their invitation & only promise to come again— which I must do, before I publish. Mrs Chaworth expressed a strong wish to see me during my stay, and Lord Rancliffe has invited her & her husband to come & dine here tomorrow—but, by another piece of ill-luck, she is, it seems, ill, and whether I am to see her or not is very doubtful.[3]

[1] Anne Jane Barbara Moore died on 18 Sept. 1817.
[2] Lord Rancliffe (see letter No. 736, to Mary Shelley, 23 Sept. 1827).
[3] Moore left a detailed account of his visit to Newstead in his diary (Russell, v. 212–13).

On my way here, I paid another very interesting visit to Donington Park (Lord Hastings's seat) where a great part of my own youthful days was passed. I found everything so exactly in the same state as it was then, that, at every step, I expected to see the same people coming out of the same rooms—but alas!

Mrs Moore inclosed me your last—every way, your last—packet about Byron, and I received it here yesterday. How *can* I thank you enough?

I shall wait my chance of seeing Mrs Chaworth, and, if it should appear hopeless, will leave this on Thursday for Ashbourne, to visit some quondam neighbours & still kind friends who are expecting me there.

I hope you got my hasty scribble from town. It is some consolation to me to find that you *could not* have come up, even had I been able to wait for you.

Yours ever most truly
Thomas Moore

740. *To John Cam Hobhouse*

Sir John Murray

Bowood
October 24th 1827

My dear Hobhouse— Before I set out on my late excursion to Nottinghamshire I had heard of your being at Buxton, and was in some hopes that our friend Rancliffe might have been able to persuade you to meet me at Bunny. But the next account dispelled all this hope, by representing you as returned to your father's. I should have been delighted to have a quiet opportunity of talking with you over the subject that now occupies all my thoughts—my book about Byron. After my conversation with you at Boyle Farm,[1] I wrote to Barry telling him of your kindness in consenting to waive any claim his promise might have given you on those papers in his possession, and the readiness which you had expressed to let *me* have the free use of them. His answer, which I shall show you when we meet, shows that he had misunderstood what you told me you had written to him—for, instead of supposing that you consented freely to having the papers forwarded to me, he understood you as being rather piqued at his having shown a disposition to send the papers to me rather than to you, and his intention was accordingly,

---

[1] Moore attended a fête at Boyle Farm on 30 June and probably talked with Hobhouse at that time (see Russell, v. 180–1).

he said, to let *you* have them in pursuance of his promise. They are, therefore, I suppose, at present in your hands.[1]

I had also, in my letter to Barry, made some enquiries after that part of the correspondence with Lord Byron, which took place while he was in Italy, and which (from my not finding any portion of it in the packet of my own letters you were so kind as to give me) I concluded might have been left in the care of Barry. But he tells me that among the letters he sealed up & forwarded to the Executors were those of mine, and you will do me, my dear Hobhouse, the greatest favour by making another search among the papers, and putting me in possession (according to what I know was your intention) of the *whole* of my letters.

The sooner too you can collect for me the materials, which in our conversation at Boyle Farm, you said you thought you could furnish me with towards the work, the more I shall feel grateful to you. As I am now in for the task, the more I am armed at all points with information & materials, the less will my natural inadequacy to the enterprize be felt. I find every one, indeed, most prompt & anxious to assist me, and you, who can do more than any one, will not, I am convinced, be backward. If there was any place where we could meet & talk before your parliamentary troubles begin, let me know & I shall be with you at a minute's notice.

Yours very faithfully
Thomas Moore

From the list Barry sent me of the papers in his possession, I fear there are but few of them that could be made use of—but it is of great importance that I should see & judge for myself of their contents—as if but a line or two, creditable to his memory could be selected, it would be of value. This remark applies, too, to the Letters of Lady Melbourne, in which it is impossible but that there must be passages, independent of all that is personal or confidential, on which the mark of his genius is stamped, & which would be precious to a reader.[2] Pray, think of all this for me, and you will have my thanks for ever.

---

[1] Byron gave Charles F. Barry, the Genoa partner of Webb & Company, with whom he banked, some valuable autographs, including letters from Scott, Moore, and Rogers. Moore was trying to gain access to these and to recover his own letters (see Marchand, *Byron*, pp. 1046 and 1090). This letter furnishes an idea of Barry's reply, which was evidently recorded in the diary but omitted by the editor (see Russell, v. 196). Moore received the letters (see letter No. 749, to John Cam Hobhouse, 12 Dec. 1827).

[2] On 28 Nov. 1827 Hobhouse replied, saying that he could not send the letters which Byron wrote to Lady Melbourne because some of them were not suitable for the work and were unintelligible to anyone not familiar with the

741. *To Mary Shelley*

Abinger Collection

My little girl is doing very well & Mrs Moore is better. Thank you a thousand times for thinking of them so kindly.

Sloperton
October 29th 1827

You will see by the inclosed frank, which I got at Bowood yesterday morning, that I was preparing a missive to you for to-day *before* I received yours from 34, Strand. Your other from Arundel came at the same time with one from Miss Wright,[1] and the latter I answered immediately. Pray, tell her that the books she was so kind to send me did not arrive till long after I had received her letter, and that I am now reading them with the utmost interest and admiration.

I am sorry, very sorry, to hear of your idleness, and feel some little compunction at the thought that *I* may have been, in some degree, the cause of it. After leaving the neighbourhood of Newstead, I went to visit some old friends in Derbyshire, and was *made much* of by them, which I am not ashamed to say I liked prodigiously.[2] The Duke of Devonshire dispatched a courier for me to Ashbourne, but having declined going to Mrs Robert Arkwright on the plea of wanting time, I should have blushed for myself & my taste for ever after, if I had yielded to the Duke. As it was I had two or three days of her singing at a friend's house near Ashbourne and it was delicious. Her setting of Mrs Hemans's pretty words 'Far from my own bright land' is (as she herself sings it) most touching, and the sound of her voice is at this moment in my ears.

Is there any chance, do you think, of the 'Istoria' from the Guiccioli? and would you advise me to write to her, myself?[3] My coming up to town depends so entirely on chance, that I can say nothing about it with certainty—but I think I am sure to come before very long.

Ever faithfully y^rs
Thomas Moore

I take for granted Power knows your address

particulars. He also declared that he did not publicly endorse Moore's book (original in Sir John Murray's possession).

[1] Probably Frances Darusmont, who was better known by her maiden name, Frances Wright. See the Glossary of Proper Names.

[2] On 11 Oct. Moore visited William Strutt of Derby, who took him to Ashbourne the following day. The visits are described fully in the diary (Russell, v. 214–15).

[3] See letters Nos. 779 and 791, to Mary Shelley, 15 Apr. and 25 July 1828.

742. *To Lord John Russell*

Early Correspondence of Lord John Russell, i. 268

Sloperton
October 31, 1827.

My dear Lord John,—It was very good-natured of you to take the trouble of writing out those recollections of Byron, and I shall be most thankful for anything more you can contrive to remember. . . .[1] I feel a little curious to know exactly the colour of your politics just now, as from the rumour I hear of some of your brother 'watchmen,' Althorp, Milton, &c., I begin sometimes to apprehend that you, too, may be among the fallers-off. Lord Lansdowne tells me, however, that you are quite staunch, and for his sake I hope so. I should be much better pleased, I own, if you were all turned to the *right* about, and my great wish is that Lord L. may either *make or find* some good public grounds for retiring before the 'ebbing neptune' of liberalism in the Cabinet leaves him quite aground.

. . . I had a glimpse of your book the other day at Bowood, but as it was in request, I could not get hold of it but for a few minutes before breakfast, so that I do not as yet know how far you have brought the very interesting information, which I see it contains, to bear upon the present state of the Turkish question.[2] How close you have been about this book, telling it to no one (Rogers) says but the *Literary Gazette!* Sam has been at Bowood, alternately amusing and disagreeable, flowery and thorny, smile and bile, as usual. . . .

Bessy sends her very best regards, and believe me, my dear Lord John,

Ever faithfully yours,
Thomas Moore.

743. *Addressee unknown*

Bodleian MS. Eng. misc. d. 279, f. 15

Nov[r] 4th 1827*

Sir. I have much pleasure in accepting the honour which you propose to bestow upon me, and shall be happy if my name would prove in the least degree conducive [to] the success of your work.

May I venture to suggest the substitution of the word 'region' for 'bosom' in the similie which you have used in your Dedication?

The Song which you have done me the honour to send as a specimen of your Poetry is full of the true feeling of an Irishman—

Your very obliged Serv[t]
Thomas Moore

[1] See letter No. 729, to Lord John Russell, 3 Aug. 1827.
[2] *The Establishment of the Turks in Europe: An Historical Discourse* (1828).

744. *Addressee unknown*

B.M. C. 44 f, vol. xxxi (an extra illustrated copy of Moore's *Notices of the Life of Lord Byron*)

Sloperton Cottage, Devizes
Novr 4th 1827

Sir— I feel much obliged by the communication which I had yester-day the honour of receiving from you. You will do me a very great service by procuring from Doctor Lee Mann whatever information or documents he may be able to furnish me with on the subject of my present pursuit.[1] It is not my intention to enter into the *particulars* of Lord B^s married life, but the sight of such papers as you say Dr Mann has in his possession could not fail to be of use to me, as contributing to my *general* knowledge of the subject on which I am employed.

I am, Sir, with many thanks,
Your faithful Servant
Thomas Moore

745. *To James Power*

Huntington Library

Tuesday— Novr 6th 1827*

My dear Sir.

I send you an experiment of three Voices to a Waltz Air, for Bishop to see & say whether he thinks any thing can be made of it, in which case I shall send another verse.

I am likely now to be left a little more to myself, and shall send you things oftener. Rogers has given me something for the Mis-cellany, and my neighbour Paul Methuen has written (wonderful to say) a very pretty & poetical thing for it. I have much to say with regard to our plan, which I think *must* be altered— *Annuals* have become so common.[2]

Y^{rs} ever
T. Moore.

Did you see there was an East India Ship called the Lalla Rookh arrived. The owners of it, I find, meditated giving me and Bessy a party on board, had we not left town so soon.

---

[1] Moore applied to Dr. Mann for some letters that were exchanged between Lord and Lady Byron, whom the doctor attended at the time of their separa-tion (see Russell, v. 271). There is no indication that Moore was successful in his attempt to secure them.

[2] Moore and Power evidently contemplated publishing some type of an-thology. Their plan was never completed.

746. *To James Power*

Huntington Library

Novr 26th 1827.*

My dear Sir—

Here is a Duett that has cost me some trouble, both from the number of the Verses & their Meter. But the air is very pretty as well as odd, and I think it will be liked.

Pray send a Copy of the Evenings in Greece to Mrs Shelley No 51, George's St. Portman Square, with the inclosed note.

Ever y^{rs}
T. Moore

747. *To Mary Shelley*[1]

Abinger Collection

Sloperton
Novr 26th 1827

I have bid Power send you the 'Evenings in Greece'[2]—(merely to show I have not forgot)—and when I come to town, which I think may possibly be at the end of December, you shall have my name inscribed.

Do you know that you are now living within 7 doors of the first house I ever inhabited in London (No. 44)—where I began with a single room on the 2nd floor at 7:6 a week, but was, in process of time, promoted down stairs, and where some adventures befell me that would tell not badly in a confessional. I often take a solitary walk through the neighbourhood, and endeavour to fancy myself what it once saw me. But, alas, Fancy is like one of those robbers' lanthorns—one can throw light with it upon every thing but one-self.

I have ventured to write to the Guiccioli, and have sent my letter through Barry of Genoa.

Yours ever
T. Moore.

Pray look up two pair of stairs (at 44,) when you pass, for *my* sake, and imagine me there between 19 & 20, correcting the first sheets of my Anacreon.

[1] Address: Mrs. Shelley / 51 George Street / Portman Square.
[2] See letter No. 746, to James Power, 26 Nov. 1827. *Evenings in Greece* appeared in 1825.

748. *To John Cam Hobhouse*

Sir John Murray

Sloperton Cottage, Devizes
November 30th 1827

Dear Hobhouse— I was, I confess, a little puzzled by your long silence, but your letter,[1] by explaining the cause, has released me from my wonderment.

If (as I fear very much) in my anxiety on the subject which occupies me, I have been at all importunate or troublesome to you, forgive me and I shall plague you no further. It is very possible that some expressions of mine relative to your kindness &c. may have been construed by Mr Barry and others into a boast of your sanction & cooperation. But be assured that I did not mean them to be so taken & that I shall do my utmost to remove the impression. Indeed, the simple fact that my book is likely to appear without a single contribution of either paper or anecdote from any one of Lord Byron's immediate friends or family will sufficiently absolve them all from any share of responsibility attached to it.

One consequence of my thus being thrown on my own resources *you*, at least, will not regret (nor do I know that I shall)—namely, that I must give up all idea of a 'Life', and merely publish such parts of the Letters and Journals as are publishable, with a running accompaniment of biographical notices, relating chiefly to what came under my own personal knowledge. This change of plan you will have the goodness not to mention. The title I think of is 'Letters and Journals of Lord Byron, with Biographical Illustrations by &c. &c.'—

The only favour I have now to ask is that you will procure for me those letters addressed to Lord B. in Italy.[2] This I shall consider a real service, and with many thanks for all your kind intentions towards me, I am, dear Hobhouse,

Truly yours
Thomas Moore

[1] Hobhouse's letter of 28 Nov. (see letter No. 740, to John Cam Hobhouse, 24 Oct. 1827).

[2] Moore is referring to the letters which he wrote to Lord Byron while the latter was in Italy.

749. *To John Cam Hobhouse*

Sir John Murray

Sloperton Cottage
Decr 12th 1827

Dear Hobhouse— Many, many thanks for the trouble you have
taken about the letters,[1] which reached me safely under (I think)
twelve or thirteen covers,—much to the astonishment of the new
Post-office which I have just succeeded in establishing near us.

It is odd enough, but I felt quite sure, when I read that passage
in Gambi's [*sic*] book, that there had been something softened
down—for what I wrote to Byron was (as I learned afterwards to
my great regret) exactly the thing most likely to put him in a rage
at that moment. It was very kind of you to suppress the passage
and I may *now* tell you that I had occasion to perform the same
service towards *you* (for which of his dear friends did he not sometimes make free with ?) in the castigated transcription of his letters
which I made some time since. It was relative to some advice or
opinion you had given him about 'Cain', a subject, on which we all
made him angry, as I fear Hunt will but too plainly tell the world.[2]

It delights me to find you alluding to my unlucky 'slap' at you
(as you call it) so good-humouredly. Indeed, I have sometimes a
little wondered you ever took it otherwise—for (if I recollect right
the guilty passage) I *avowed* myself in a minority of one by allowing
that every one else gave you the highest character, and the letter
was, besides, written after a conversation with you, in which you
had said things that (possibly from their being, in a great degree,
just) gave me more pain than I should ever like to feel again. I am
sorry to hear that that letter is in any one's hands but my own;
but rather hope I shall be able to persuade Barry to exchange it for
one that I shall feel less ashamed of.

All this brings to mind a little Volume of yours (your early
poems) which I have made many efforts to find, but without success.
My chief reason for wishing to see it is that Byron in some of his
letters mentions that there were some things of his in the collec-

---

[1] Moore's letters to Byron. See letter No. 748, to John Cam Hobhouse,
30 Nov. 1827.

[2] In Nov. 1821 Hobhouse wrote to Byron, expressing his apprehension of
the effect *Cain* would have on the public. Byron was at first angry at the presumption of his friend but controlled himself sufficiently to write a dignified
reply, in which he pretended to be interested only in the money received from
the publication. See Murray, *Byron's Correspondence*, ii. 204, and *LJ*, v. 483.

tion.[1] I saw it many years ago and it is *almost* malicious of me to mention the only thing I remember of it—

> 'For me, who am too proud or poor
> to hire a Bellington or praise a Moore.'[2]

Aren't there such lines in it? and can you tell me where I may find the book?

As we now have, I trust, settled our account of mutual injuries (and I wish that some very dear friends had nothing worse to accuse each other of) I shall feel very well disposed to open an account of a pleasanter kind, whenever you give me the opportunity.

Yours very truly
Thos Moore

750. *To John Cam Hobhouse*

Sir John Murray

Sloperton Cottage
Decr 16th 1827

Dear Hobhouse— You are, I perceive, a *matter-of-fact* creditor, to say no worse of you. When I said that I hoped we had 'settled our accounts'.[3] I had no idea of meaning, in sober *seriousness*, that the circumstance I mentioned was a set-off in my favour—the two cases being (as you have wasted a great deal of good prose in proving) not at all parallel, further than in the feeling of goodwill by which they were, on both sides (at least I can answer for myself) actuated.[4] I merely meant, in what I said, to show my wish to *be friends* with you, and, as the saying has it, 'where there is a will, there is a way'—but I suppose *my* way was a bad one, and so—we will, if you please, say no more about the matter.

---

[1] For the texts of the nine poems Byron contributed to Hobhouse's *Imitations and Translations . . . together with Original Poems never before Published* (London, 1809) see Byron, *Poetry*, i. 264–85, where they are arranged in chronological order.

[2] The poem 'To ********** A Water Drinker', imitation of Horace, *Epistle*, xix, book i, in Hobhouse's *Imitations and Translations*, contains a lengthy passage on Moore and 'scribblers' like him. The theme of the passage is that the writer is too proud to stoop to this kind of rhyme. There is no mention of Bellington, and the lines dealing with Moore are far from complimentary:

> Thus every Julia finds some poet—Moore
> And greasy ballads greet each graceless whore.
> (*Imitations and Translations*, p. 71)

[3] See letter No. 749, to John Cam Hobhouse, 12 Dec. 1827.

[4] Moore is probably referring to the suppression of Hobhouse's strictures on Byron's *Cain*. See letter No. 749.

I am *equally* innocent, I assure you, of a wish to deprecate the value (or length) of your metre.[1] But I have known half a line, and even three quarters, (which, I believe, is what I have been guilty of) quoted, without offending, I should think, the sense of proprietorship in even the most touchy of the 'genus'.

Many thanks for your verses upon Bowles.[2] Though he is my neighbour, I could not help enjoying their point of cleverness. Poor Bowles and you would never have been likely to get on very well together; for though an excellent fellow in his way, he requires, I own, large and lubricating doses of tolerance & *laisser-aller* to wash him down. Our friend Luttrel, for instance, can't stand Bowles.

A merry Christmas to you!— Mine, I fear, will be any thing but merry, as I expect to have the house full of measles—my eldest brat (happy Coelebs that you are to know nothing of such things) being now in the thick of them.

Truly yours
Thomas Moore

751. *To Colonel Houlton*

B.M. Add. MS. 27425BC, f. 15

Sloperton Cottage
Decr 20th 1827

My dear Houlton— Our Anastasia has just had the measles, and we expect our two other young ones to follow her example. It is therefore more than probable that Mrs Moore will be too much

---

[1] Hobhouse evidently objected to Moore's quotation from his *Imitations and Translations* in letter No. 749.

[2] The manuscript of the following poem, probably in Hobhouse's hand, is now in Sir John Murray's possession:

To the Tune
of
'Should Dennis publish you had stabb'd your brother'

> Should drunken Bowles yourself or friend compare
> To some French cut-throat if you will Santarre
> Or heaps malignant on your living head
> The smut & trash he pours on poets dead,
> Say, what revenge, or how with him to deal
> Sot without sense and fool that cannot feel?
> You would not parley with a printer's hack
> You cannot cane him for his coat is black
> Reproof and chastisement were idly spent
> On one who calls a kick a compliment—
> Unwhipt then leave him to lampoon & lie
> Safe in his parson's gown and infamy.

A slightly different version of these lines is quoted in *LJ*, v. 299 n.

occupied at home to admit of her joining your Christmas party, which she will lament, I assure you, heartily, for she has often fancied that yours must be the very *beau ideal* of a House for Christmas fun. It is possible I might be able to run to you for a day myself, & the Napiers I dare say could take me—or, if you are not afraid to admit Anastasia, I should like to give her 'a taste of your quality'[1] for a day or two. Let me know how you wish it to be & believe me ever

Faithfully y^{rs}
Thomas Moore

752. *To Alicia Lefanu*

Pennsylvania Historical Society

Sloperton Cottage
Jan^r 5th 1828.

My dear Miss Lefanu. If I had any shame left in me on the subject of letter-answering I should blush all over at having so long deferred my answer to yours. But, knowing your good-nature, I shall say no more about it. You have been long *due* in the literary world, and I rejoice to hear that you are about to re-appear. It will give me the greatest pleasure to be made useful to you, and any thing I can do with publishers or printers for you you may command.

Pray tell Mrs Lefanu how delighted I am by her praises of the Epicurean, and say also that, if Charles Sheridan should be in town when I next go up (about the middle of this month, I think) there will be little doubt of my being able to recover her letters for her.

Do not fail to let me know what progress you make in your work & believe me ever

truly y^{rs}
Thomas Moore

753. *To Colonel Houlton*

B.M. Add. MS. 27425BC, f. 18

Jan^r 8th 1828*

My dear Houlton— I hardly know whether I ought to write to you, but since the alarming news we heard about Mrs Shirley[2] through the Lockes, Mrs Moore feels so deeply anxious about you all that I cannot resist her desire (nor indeed, my own) to know something more certain, and I trust far more favourable, as to the state in

---

[1] *Hamlet*, ii. ii. 452.
[2] Houlton's daughter, Dorotea, married Henry Shirley.

which Mrs Houlton found her daughter when she reached her. Pray, do not think it necessary to answer this letter, but only, if you have *good* news to communicate, let us have it.

Ever faithfully y^rs
Thomas Moore

754. *To R. A. Smith*

Huntington Library

Sloperton Cottage
Jan^r 13 1828.

Sir.

I have just had the pleasure of receiving the very interesting Volume which you have done me the honour of presenting to me— I am particularly pleased with one of the airs that you have yourself composed, and both the words and music of 'Oh mournfully &c.' are beautiful.[1]

I beg you to accept my best thanks for the pretty Savoyard air you have sent me, and to believe that

I am very truly your obliged Servt
Thomas Moore.

755. *To Mary Shelley*

Abinger Collection

Sloperton
Jan^r 14th 1828

I take the opportunity of a parcel to Power to say two or three words, into which if I could throw but half the kind things I wish to say to you, they would be the most pregnant words ever known. I have been obliged to change all my plans in consequence of the illness of my young ones, and various other perplexities, and am now about to start for Derbyshire (instead of London) hoping, however, to be able to take town in my way back, when, if I forget you— 'Forget thee! no.'

Ever y^rs
T. Moore

756. *To James Power*

American Art Association, Sale Catalogue, 6 December 1928

Jan. 24, 1828

Thinking that you may want the '*Rose of the Desert*'[2] I send it up . . . and shall inclose the '*Legends*'[3] as I finish them, through the

---

[1] R. A. Smith published *The Scottish Minstrel*, 6 vols., 1824.
[2] *Poetry*, p. 319.
[3] *Legendary Ballads* (1830), *Poetry*, pp. 296–302.

Right Honorable Croker. You will have the goodness to frank the letter to Genoa for me and put the other in the 2nd [*sic*; *obviously 2ᵈ*] or send it, if you can, as there is an original letter of Byron's inclosed.

757. *To Mrs. Fellows*

Nottingham Public Libraries

Stoke
Monday [27 January 1828]

My dear Mʳˢ Fellows— I am just setting off for Newstead, and shall be in Nottingham tomorrow— Pray, let Lord Rancliffe know, if you can, & tell him how disappointed I shall be if we do not meet either at your house or at Bunny— I should infinitely prefer the former, as I must start for Derby by one of the early coaches on Wednesday.

Yours most truly
Thomas Moore.

758. *To Mrs. Musters*[1]

Nottingham Public Libraires

Derby
Friday [29 January 1828]

Dear Mʳˢ Musters. It was, I assure you, with the greatest reluctance & regret I found myself obliged to leave that message at Colwick the other day, declining the very great pleasure I had promised myself in dining with you.[2] But to you, who (to judge by what I saw) have a daughter so well worth loving, I need only say that I had just then received the intelligence of Mʳˢ Moore's having been obliged to take our little girl to London for advice in a case of lameness, which had got so much worse since I left home that she felt considerably alarmed about it. I have since had much more comfortable tidings on the subject, and as I cannot reconcile myself to the thought of leaving this neighbourhood without seeing again a person in whom, every way I feel so deeply interested, I will, if you are still disposed to receive me on Sunday, be most happy to wait upon you, and a note in answer to this will find me at Mʳˢ Fellows's in the course [of] tomorrow. I want most particularly to

[1] Mary Chaworth, who married John Musters.
[2] Moore visited Mr. and Mrs. Musters on 23 Jan. and recorded in his diary that he 'Fixed to dine with them on Sunday the 4th'. On 29 Jan. he noted: 'Resolved to give up my dinner with the Musterses' (Russell, v. 250 and 255).

receive your instructions as to the manner in which you wish to be
mentioned in the work I am preparing. On the point to which I
allude, you *cannot*, you know, escape immortality, if you would;
and the peculiar charm there is in the connection of your name with
that of my poor friend is that it is (unluckily) the only instance in
which the romance that ought to hang about such a memory as his
is kept pure & perfect, and unalloyed by any of those circumstances
which in after life, though they might have contributed to form the
poet, but too much tended to discredit the *man*. My [friend *deleted*]
neighbour *Joy* (I think it was) told me that you had either read or
shown to him some lines addressed to you by Byron with a volume
of Mad^e de Sevigné's Works.[1] If I might hope for a copy of this, or
of any other MS. you have of his, I need not tell you [how] precious
it would be to me. I have, indeed, been most lucky during my
researches in your neighbourhood, and if I could succeed in interesting you as much as I have done others, in the effort I am making
to throw all possible light round the character of my [late] friend,
I shall consider myself most fortunate.

   Believe me, dear Mrs Musters, your obliged & faithful Servant
                                                   Thomas Moore.

759. *To John Cam Hobhouse*

Modern Language Notes, lv (1940), 42[2]

                                               Newstead Abbey
                                               Jany 29^h 1828.

My dear Hobhouse. Being here alone I cannot help—with the
thoughts which the place inspires—writing to you. I returned here
for the purpose of making some further inquiries of Rushton and
old Nanny Smith,[3] whom I dare say you remember, as she does
you. How often I wish you were with me, or that I could bring
some voice out of these walls to tell me all that happened in those
joyous days when they were inhabited, I will say, by as brilliant
a knot of young fellows as ever began the career of life together. I
have been passing some days with Hodgson at Mrs Robt Arkwright's,
and found far more fun, as well as feeling, under that parsonic

---

   [1] Byron addressed several poems to Mary Chaworth, but there is no indication which of these was presented to her with a volume of Madame de Sevigné's
works.

   [2] This letter was contributed to *MLN* by Bradford A. Booth. The original is
in the William Andrews Clark Memorial Library, an adjunct of the University
of California at Los Angeles.

   [3] Robert Rushton was the son of one of Byron's tenants; Nanny Smith
was an old servant at Newstead Abbey.

japan of his than I gave him the least credit for. He not only told me many pleasant things, but gave me some letters & extracts of letters, which place poor Byron in all that amiable light, which it is my great wish & object to surround him with. I have indeed, been lucky beyond my most sanguine expectations in this neighbourhood, having found a family at Southwell[1] among whom he passed a considerable part of his early days, and who have given me letters & unpublished poems of his, written at a period which is now the most interesting of his life, as being the least known. I have got, too, a curious draft of the Will he made in 1811, with his instructions in the margin, and it is of course no new information to you that, in that Will, he left all his personal property to be divided between you, Hodgson, S. Davies &, I believe, the Revd Mr Beecher [*sic*]. I am to dine with the Musters's next Sunday, and expect to get from her two or three little unpublished things which they tell me she possesses.

By the bye, ought not you or I to give this beast Hunt a dressing in the Ed. Review? It is the only way—beyond a contemptuous sentence or two—in which one can condescend to notice him, and I really thing [*sic*] a good sousing of ridicule, 'without mitigation or remorse' is a thing that either you or I ought to inflict upon him.[2]

You mentioned, in one of your late letters, B's. translation of the Francesca,[3] and said that you took for granted I had it. I have not, nor have ever seen it, and I should have told you this before, but that, in the humour I was then in, I was afraid it would look like asking for it. This humour, however, is now gone by, and I not only mention it, but will most cheerfully ask for the manuscript, if there is any chance of your being able to give it to me.

I have been interrupted in my letter by a conversation with Nanny Smith, in which she frequently referred me to 'Hobhouse' and 'Claridge,'[4] his Lordship's 'Fadge,' for whatever she herself was unable to tell me. She has also been playing the 'anus fatidica' about Lady B.

I have time for no more—Ever
Yours
T. Moore.

---

[1] The Pigot family. See Pratt, *Byron at Southwell* (Austin, 1948).

[2] Moore is referring to Hunt's *Lord Byron and Some of His Contemporaries* (1828).

[3] A 46-line fragment entitled 'Francesca of Rimini,' *LJ*, ii. 309–11.

[4] John Claridge (afterward Sir John) was one of Byron's 'juniors and favourites' at Harrow (see *LJ*, i. 267). For accounts of others mentioned in the text see the Glossary of Proper Names.

If you cannot give me the Francesca, it is no matter—only do not *write* me about it, and receive me kindly when we meet, which I hope will be in about ten days.

Nottingham
3^d flat

I have just received a letter here from Murray, which has been delayed by my absence— It is about Byron, & I have but a minute to answer it.

760. *To Viscount Percy Strangford*

De Fonblanque, *Lives of the Lords Strangford* (London, 1877), p. 161

[January or February 1828]

Nobody (as you must know without my telling you) can differ from you more decidedly than I do in the line of politics which you have taken since you entered the House of Lords, but, at the same time, nobody can have more hearty good wishes for your welfare.[1] Our old friendship supersedes all new differences (which is *beaucoup dire*), and I am now, as ever, very cordially yours, T. M.

761. *Addressee unknown*

Rice University

Derby
Feb^r 1st 1828

My dear Sir.

On second thoughts I feel that it would be wrong to lose the chance of some further information which my visit to Cotswich promises, and have therefore written to Mrs Musters to say that I *will* dine there on Sunday. It is probable, therefore, that you will not see me in town before Tuesday or Wednesday, but I trust this delay will be no inconvenience.

Yours very truly
Thomas Moore.

[1] 'Lord Strangford . . . had attached himself to the extreme anti-Reform party, and on the formation of the Duke of Wellington's administration in 1828 . . . he seconded the address in the House of Lords at the opening of the session, and looked forward confidently to a seat in the cabinet.' He sought a post in the Foreign Office but was refused by the Duke of Wellington. 'To soothe his disappointment', however, he was 'invited to proceed on a special mission', i.e. as Ambassador Extraordinary to the Brazils (De Fonblanque, pp. 160–1). Strangford seconded the Earl of Chichester's speech at the opening of Parliament on 29 Jan. 1828 (Hansard, *Parliamentary Debates*, xviii. 8–11).

762. *To Mr. Higginson*

University of Edinburgh

Nottingham
Monday [3 February 1828]

My dear H.

I sent you a packet to-day from Colwich & have now only time to say that I think, to *enliven* your Report, you had better put in my last words.

In rising to bid the Company farewell, Mr Moore said, 'Whether eating and drinking be a *good* way of advancing the cause of education, I know not, but I am sure it is a very *pleasant* one. We must only take care that our conviviality does not injure our erudition as it did poor Skirmish's, according to his own account of it in the Farce—"if I had handled my *pen* as well as I have handled my *bottle*, what a charming hand I should have written by this time!" I shall, therefore, Gentlemen, bid you all heartily good night.'[1]

763. *To Benjamin Robert Haydon*

Willard B. Pope

19 Bury St., St. James's*
Wednesday Morning [postmark February 27, 1828]

My dear Sir— I have just been favoured with your note & feel much flattered by your confidence in me. I should, indeed, like very much to peruse the curious pamphlet of which you speak, & shall be obliged by your sending it for me to Mr Power's 34, Strand. If it should arrive any time before night, I shall have it for my travelling companion as I mean to start for Wiltshire early in the morning.[2]

Y^rs very truly
Thomas Moore

---

[1] This is evidently the letter about his 'speeches', which Moore mentioned in his diary (Russell, v. 258). For an account of the dinner at Derby (at which he made ten or twelve speeches) see Russell, v. 256.

[2] This letter is a reply to one from Haydon, who sent Moore the manuscript of his pamphlet entitled 'Leigh Hunt and some of His Companions; being an appendix to "Lord Byron and some of his Contemporaries"'. Haydon became conscience-stricken at the thought of wounding Hunt and managed to withdraw the paper from publication, in spite of the fact that Lockhart was bent on having it printed. For details see Willard B. Pope, ' "Leigh Hunt & His Companions" ', *Keats-Shelley Journal*, viii (autumn, 1959), 89–91. See also letter No. 773, to Benjamin Robert Haydon, 19 Mar. 1828. The originals of the Moore–Haydon correspondence are owned by Professor Pope, who made photostatic copies available to the editor.

764. *To Douglas Kinnaird*

B.M. Add. MS. 36464, f. 259 (copy)

Athenaeum
Wednesday [February 1828]

My dear Kinnaird/

As I am obliged to leave town in the evening, I find I cannot call upon you, as I expected, at four. I merely wished to ask (though I confess with little hope) whether I might look to you for any assistance towards the work, in which I am now fairly embarked, on the subject of our friend, Lord Byron. I say 'with little hope', because I am inclined to believe you take the same view of my undertaking that Hobhouse does; and from him (though always ready to allow his kind attention to me in other respects) I have long despaired of any thing like assistance in this humble effort to do justice to the memory of our common friend. If we could get all the world to preserve silence on the subject of Byron's private character, I agree with Hobhouse that it would be better to let him in future live only in his works; but if every rascal that ever broke bread with him is to be suffered to depreciate and vilify his character, while his friends stand by in (what they think) dignified silence, this, I do not hesitate to say, is to surrender tamely, if not faithlessly, the memory of the man we all loved, undefended, into the hands of his enemies. *You*, I know, have great means of helping me—whether you will do so or not must, of course, remain with yourself— Excuse the hurry in which I have written these few lines and believe me, my dear Kinnaird,

Yours very truly
(Signed) Thomas Moore.[1]

[1] Kinnaird's reply, a copy of which is in the British Museum (Add. MS. 36464, f. 260), is quoted below:

Pall Mall East
February 28th 1828

Dear Moore,

I really am not aware that I could in any manner render you service in your undertaking— You have correctly divin'd the view I take of what is call'd for on the part of Byron's friends in consequence of the use to which all sorts of persons have turn'd the intercourse they may have had with him.

His own example during the many years, when he was much more the topic of general misrepresentation should I think be the guide for them— I am not disposed to regard Mr L. Hunt's book as any grounds for a departure from the course hitherto pursued.

If on the one hand Mr Hunt's evident motives disqualify him from being a competent authority to judge of Lord B's character, the pen of a friend must be supposed to lie under an equal disqualification for fixing public opinion—

Your's [*sic*] truly
Douglas Kinnaird

765. *To Dr. Thomas Hume*

Harvard College Library

Sloperton Cottage, Devizes
Feb^r 29 1828

My dear Hume— I am just returned here, having been hurried out of town much sooner than I expected, and my short stay there so worryingly occupied, (between the illness of my little girl, whom I was obliged to have up for medical advice and some other affairs of a more prosperous nature, but not less occupying) that I had not a moment to offer myself for a snug day at Hanwell as I intended. It will not be long, however, before I shall be obliged to come up again, and then—*shall* we not have a bumper to the times past & gone?

I found my little girl (though doomed to the sofa for, I fear, months to come) as well otherwise & as cheerful as I could possibly have expected. You have learned, no doubt, from the newspapers some particulars of the late agreement I have made with Murray, and will be glad to hear that it promises fair to set me 'high & dry' out of the difficulties through which I have been so long wading.

Yours ever truly
Thomas Moore

766. *To Lord John Russell*

Rice University

Sloperton
[February or March 1828][1]

My dear Lord John— The gentleman (Doctor Brabant) who will have the pleasure of sending or presenting to you this note has already been mentioned by me to the Duke of Sussex when I last had the honour of seeing his Royal Highness. He has a great wish to be allowed to visit the Duke's noble Library, and I know nobody that is more capable of appreciating its treasures. Being the personal friend of Von Bohlen, Doctor Paulus, Gesenius and others of the great German theologians, his studies have lain very much in the same line which I know his Royal Highness has so successfully pursued.

Yours, my dear Lord John, very truly
Thomas Moore.

[1] Moore was given access to the Duke of Sussex's library in February 1828 (Russell, v. 264). This letter was probably written shortly afterwards, since it is unlikely that Moore would have presumed to gain admittance for Brabant without having himself been granted the privilege.

If it would be possible for my friend to have the honour of an interview with the Duke, during his short stay in London, I should esteem it as an especial favour to myself.

767. *To Mary Shelley*

Abinger Collection

Saturday 5 o'clock [February or March 1828]

I am very much afraid about Murray— He said he would consider it, but in no very promising way. *This,* I fear, will be a sad disappointment to you, but there is a hope still remaining, and perhaps on Monday he will be more favourable.[1]

I shall have barely time to breakfast tomorrow morning, as I have business before twelve in a totally opposite direction—

Ever yrs.

T. M.

768. *To Mary Shelley*

Abinger Collection

Berkely Square
[February or March 1828]

I am stopped on my way to you—(not, like Napoleon & Brummel, 'by the elements' though they are bad enough) but by business calls, cards &—the d—l knows what. I shall, however, force my way to you, if possible, in the course of tomorrow, and, at all events, shall be at your disposal on Friday, at whatever hour you may name, for the visit to Murray. Only let me know.

Yours ever

T. M.

19 Bury St.
St. James's

---

[1] On 19 Feb. 1828 Mary wrote to Murray, thanking him for the loan of £100 and asking him to undertake the publication of her novel *Perkin Warbeck*. Although Murray sent her books and helped her in other ways (possibly because of the assistance she gave Moore in his work on the *Life of Byron*), the publisher did not purchase a line of her writing (see F. L. Jones, *Mary Shelley's Letters*, i. 371 n.). *Perkin Warbeck* was published in March 1830 by Henry Colburn and Richard Bentley.

769. *To Mary Shelley*

Abinger Collection

[February or March 1828]

I am too quizzical a figure to come out & you too pretty a figure to come in—but you shall see me soon. The moment I can make my sortie to-day, I mean to call upon Murray on your business.

I send you two of four apples I have just received from Sloperton.

T. M.

770. *To Mary Shelley*

Abinger Collection

Albemarle St.
Thursday [February or March 1828]

I shall not be able to come to breakfast, but you shall find me at home at $\frac{1}{2}$ past 11, and I have strong hopes (from the disposition of the great man here) that you will not be disappointed in your object.

Yours ever
T. M.

771. *To Mary Shelley*

Abinger Collection

[February or March 1828]

I am such a figure & this house so full of gazers that I cannot come out. On *Monday* I shall *certainly* call upon you & then we shall settle about Thursday—

I have not yet got Murray to talk with me on the subject you mentioned, but mean to *enforce* something to day.

Believe me, as ever, yours most truly
T. M.

772. *To John Murray*

Sir John Murray

Sloperton Cottage
March 7th 1828

My dear Sir— Will you have the goodness to give the inclosed list of memorandums to your son, on whose leisure and industry I can better lay such a task than on yours.

I have read all you gave me, which is most precious & quite as interesting, on the whole, as what I have of my own. But, pray, be active for me. Have you applied to Lord Clare yet?

Yours very truly
Thomas Moore

I bid Power get the books you have for me, & dispatch them by his next parcel. What have you done with Fletcher about the Poem?

773. *To Benjamin Robert Haydon*

Willard B. Pope

Sloperton Cottage
March 19th 1828

My dear Sir—
    I waited an opportunity of sending your MS. to town to tell you how very thankful I felt for your kindness in lending it to me. This very day I have dispatched it to Mr Power, who will either keep it till your arrival in town or forward it to your house. It was lucky for that poor devil Hunt that you changed your mind as to publishing this exposure, though I doubt whether, armed as he is in impenetrable self-conceit, even this would have touched him.[1]

Yrs very truly
Thomas Moore

774. *To John Murray III*

Sir John Murray

Sloperton Cottage
March 25th 1828

My dear *John Junior*— I have been waiting & wondering—not a line from you in answer to my various queries! I want particularly the anecdotes of L. B. published by Knight & Lacy & beg you will send it to Power's immediately for me.[2]
    Tell your father that Lord Clare has answered very kindly to my application through Lord Lansdowne,[3] but says that he has not kept more than two or three of Lord Bs letters, & those not of any importance. He promises, however, to communicate whatever he can recall to his memory. Where is the Monthly Review with the Article on Gill's Argolis? Where is the explanation I asked about

---

[1] See letter No. 763, to Benjamin Robert Haydon, 27 Feb. 1828.
[2] Alexander Kilgour, *Anecdotes of Lord Byron, from Authentic Sources* (London: Knight & Lacey, 1825).
[3] See letter No. 772, to John Murray, 7 Mar. 1828.

the Monthly Review you sent me? Where is &c. &c. &c. &c. &c. without end?

Y^{rs}

T. M.

775. *To Lord John Russell*

University of Texas

Sloperton Cottage

March 27:1828.

My dear Lord John— In writing the other day to one of my Derby friends—one of the worthy and very dissenting Dissenters of that place—I said 'I am still prouder than ever of having pitted my friend Lord John against the Jeremiads since his late memorable [achievement]'.[1]

Notwithstanding all this, however, I am a little anxious to know that your glory has done you no harm in the way of health, as I see you are a pretty constant attendant in the House, and there is nothing, I fear, worse for a man's own constitution than to trouble himself too much about the Constitution of Church & State. So pray, let me have *one* line to say how you are.

My little girl goes on very well as far as regards general health, but she has a long, long confinement, I fear, to look forward to.

You will see a very vulgar article in the Quarterly on Leigh Hunt's book—almost as vulgar as the book itself.[2] Murray, too, has been foolish enough to drop some of the most precious things out of his Byron papers into this mess.

Yours most truly

Thomas Moore.

Will you let the inclosed go into the Post for me?

776. *To Mary Shelley*

Abinger Collection

Sloperton

April 1st 1828

[My dear M^{rs} *deleted*]

This letter was begun to somebody else, so 'my dear M^{rs}' goes for nothing. It was very wrong of me—not only towards you but

---

[1] This word is illegible and has been supplied from the context by the editor.

On 26 Feb. 1828 Lord John moved for the repeal of the Test and Corporation Acts, a motion which, as he said, had not been made since Fox moved it in 1790. His motion carried in spite of powerful opposition. Lord Holland put it through the House of Lords, and it became law on 28 Apr.

[2] Leigh Hunt's *Lord Byron and Some of His Contemporaries* (1828) was reviewed in the *Quarterly Review*, xxxvii (January and March 1828), 402–26.

myself—not to answer your last letter sooner. But, if you knew how letter-writing runs away with all my time, and how glad I am to take advantage of the good-nature, now & then, of such dear, kind, allowance-making correspondents as yourself, it would explain all without any 'further questions asked'. *Do* write to the Guiccioli, & try & get all you can from her—put whatever queries your woman's hand can devise most likely to set a woman's pen going, and say that, at all events, the unpublished things she has of Bˢ will be most welcome.[1] Seize Bowring, too, the moment he arrives & make him disgorge all his letters— Waylay every one you can for me and I will—what will I *not* do for you when we meet again?

I rejoice to hear that you have consented to send your son to school, because I know it is the best thing both for him & you— but do not stay too long in Paris— I shall be up in town toward the end of May.

My little girl's general health continues good, which is the utmost I can hope for months to come.

Ever yʳˢ
T. M.

Mille choses tendres to Isabel.

777. *To Elizabeth Pigot*

Morgan Library

Sloperton Cottage
April 12ᵗʰ 1828

My dear *Miss Pigot*—

Your fresh batch of information was a most delightful surprise to me, as I thought I had got to the end of your treasures— Pray, tell Dʳ Pigot how much obliged I am by his communication, and how happy I shall be to receive any thing further that may occur to him. I forget whether I told you that, in a list which poor Byron sent to Murray of the persons likely to have letters of his, your name was particularly mentioned, so that you are *not only* obliging me by all this kindness, but (what I know will give you pleasure to hear) complying with an express request of your lost friend.

I did not forget my *promise* to Miss Becher, but I own I *did* forget which song it was I promised, and was waiting in the hope that some hint of it might be given in your letters— As you have not, however, helped me out of my difficulty, I have transcribed & shall inclose in this the words I think she wished for, though always hating that any one should *read* poetry of mine which was only made to be *sung* and is only passable through that medium.

---

[1] See letters Nos. 779 and 791, to Mary Shelley, 15 Apr. and 25 July 1828.

We have got a very good Committee together for the monument to Lord Byron (a statue of him in Westminster Abbey) and hope soon to be able to put the commission in Chauntrey's hands. The Committee consists solely of the personal friends & acquaintances of Lord B. and if ladies were ever enlisted on such occasions, you & Mrs Pigot have every right to be in our foremost rank.

Pray let me hear from you whenever a recollection comes across you, & believe me

Most truly y^rs
Thomas Moore.

My kindest regards to Mrs Pigot, and a kiss (of which at this distance I may venture to make you the entre-pôt) to my little friend that christened the pebble so poetically— Mrs Moore is *enchanted* with this anecdote.[1]

778. *To John Cam Hobhouse*

Sir John Murray

Sloperton Cottage
April 13th 1828

My dear Hobhouse— Oddly enough, on my return home from Corsham the other day, I found a letter from the Reverend person we had been speaking of, which showed that my hint as to 'open confession being good for the soul' was not lost on his Reverence. The note he has now sent me to insert is a full & ample acknowledgement not only of the favour confirmed but of the actual amount of the sum. This is as it should be.

Having occasion to write to Beecher [*sic*] of Southwell (Lord B^s early friend) it occurred to me that he comes within the description of the persons that ought to be on the Committee, and I accordingly asked him whether he should like to join us. You shall know his answer.

Murray, I understand, is to pay the Longmans tomorrow, which is very handsome of him. I thought our day at Corsham particularly agreeable.

Yours very truly
Thomas Moore

---

[1] Elizabeth Pigot added the following note to this letter: 'The P. S. requires a note of *explanation*,— When Moore was at Southwell, my little niece Caroline Warners Pigot staid away from school on purpose to see him— & the next day came running into us, exclaiming "Oh, Grandmamma! I have found such a *beautiful* Pebble, there is a *sparkle* in it, like *MOORE'S Eye*"— It was a clear Quartz & a little fracture in it made a ray of brightness flash out— We told Moore of it, & he used to call her his "Nymph of the Eye"—'

779. *To Mary Shelley*

Abinger Collection

Sloperton Cottage
April 15th 1828

It is really very handsome of Bowring, and of *you*—beautiful. His letters will be of great importance to me, so stick like a leech till you get the rest.[1] As soon as I come to town I shall call upon him to express my thankfulness, and perhaps in the meantime, I had better *write*—what do you think? The Post has brought a shower of God-sends this morning—for the Guiccioli too has sent me the beginning of her sketch, with his translations of the Francesca, —translated, however, back again into her Italian English and hardly to be made out.[2] Her sketch, however, is perfection, & you will do me a great service by writing to her to say I *think* so—it is all told with such a beautiful unconsciousness of there being any thing at all wrong in any part of the proceeding. I should delight in printing it exactly as it is—but, I suppose, must not.

Don't go to Paris—they don't want you there & we do.

Ever yrs
T. M.

On looking at the date of your note, I see it was written so far back as the 5th and only answered this morning!

There is no coolness that I know of between Kinnaird & me. He refused to do any thing for me in the most friendly manner possible. The truth is, he sides with Hobhouse—takes the dignified line of silence, delicacy &c. &c.[3]

780. *To William Lisle Bowles*

Huntington Library

April 19th 1828*

My dear Bowles— I have just had a letter from Hobhouse in which he suggests to me that it is possible you might like to be in our Committee for a Monument to Lord Byron, and I really think you *ought*. The tribute to him is professedly on the score of his poetical talents

---

[1] Bowring agreed to furnish Moore with copies of his correspondence with Byron, in spite of the fact that Moore had attacked him in 'The Ghost of Miltiades' for his handling of the Greek Bonds (see Russell, v. 282 and 294). For the outcome of the negotiations with Bowring see letter No. 924, to Mary Shelley, 3 Apr. 1830.

[2] On 3 Mar. 1820 Byron sent to Murray a translation of the *Francesca da Rimini* episode in canto v of Dante's *Inferno* (*LJ*, iv. 313–22). It was first published in 1830 in Moore's *Letters and Journals of Lord Byron*, ii. 309–11.

[3] See letter No. 764, to Douglas Kinnaird, February 1828.

alone, which would, entirely, I think, preclude any objection you might have to sanctioning his fame *politically* or *religiously*. There are, indeed, several high Tories on our list, while in the other way we abound in sterling names, Lord Lansdowne, Duke of Devonshire, Lord Jersey &c.— In the poetical line we have Sir W. Scott, Campbell, Rogers, *Goethe* &c. Let me know as soon as you decide. The numbers are confined to those who either were his correspondents, his personal acquaintances, or personal friends.[1]

I shall not be able to go to the Concert with you on Tuesday. The weather is disagreeable & the Anacreontic diners would take it ill of me coming away. Tell me how your cough is.

Ever y^{rs}
T. Moore

781. *To Sir Walter Scott*

N.L.S. MS. 3906, f. 218

Sloperton Cottage, Devizes
April 20th 1828

My dear Scott. I have just heard from Hobhouse of your being in town, and as I would not for the world lose seeing you, I entreat of you to let me know (through Murray, if you have not time to write yourself) how long, at the very longest, you mean to stay. I am delighted to find that you do not reject my proffered Dedication,[2] though between two such names as yours & Byron's I shall but realize the description in the old couplet of

' Wisdom and Wit
' With Folly at full length between.'[3]

However, never mind—in cordial feeling & good fellowship I flatter myself I am a match for either of you.

Ever yours faithfully
Thomas Moore.

---

[1] Bowles was not a member of the preliminary committee established in an unsuccessful attempt to place a Byron memorial in Westminster Abbey; but he was on a larger committee formed in 1844, although he was not listed as one of the subscribers.

[2] The dedication of his *Life of Byron*. See letter No. 709, to Sir Walter Scott, 23 Nov. 1826.

[3] Attributed to Jane Brereton and Lord Chesterfield. See letter No. 355, to Samuel Rogers, 13 Jan. 1814. The end quotation mark supplied by the editor.

782. *To Samuel Rogers*

Russell, viii. 267

April 21. 1828.

My dear Rogers,

I have just heard that you are not very well. Pray let me have *one* line to satisfy me on the subject.

I have been getting on pretty well with Byron, though not so rapidly as I expected. Biography is like dot engraving, made up of little minute points, which must all be attended to, or the effect is lost. At every step some small subject of inquiry starts up which costs me half-a-dozen letters, to say nothing of being obliged to wait for the answers.

Our Anastasia is going on as comfortably as we could expect. *How is your sister?* I had determined never to ask *you* this question again; but feeling gets the better of pique; and so there it is. Answer it.

> Ever yours faithfully,
> Thomas Moore.

783. *Addressee unknown*

N.L.S. MS. 3813, f. 124

Sloperton Cottage*
April 29th 1828*

My dear Sir. I am most happy to be able to show, in *any* way, how agreeable to me are all the recollections connected with our first acquaintance. I inclose the letter you wish for to Jeffrey, and have no doubt that, if an opportunity occurs, he will notice your friend's useful & able pamphlet as it deserves.

> Yours very truly
> Thomas Moore.

I should be very glad of any particulars you could collect for me relative to Lord Byron's mother or her Castle.

784. *To Mary Shelley*

Abinger Collection

Murray's, Albemarle St.
[April 1828]

I have only time to say Good bye & God bless you! I inclose a formal note, which you may show or send to Bowring.

I am not, you know, a man of many words—at least, in prose—but you may believe me when I say that I am

Cordially & truly yours
T. Moore

I shall inclose the letters you sent me, when I get home.[1]

785. *Addressee unknown*

Rice University

Sloperton Cottage
May 12th 1828

Dear Sir. I was almost certain that it would have been in my power to accept the invitation with which the Noble President &c. &c. of the Literary Fund have honoured me. But, unluckily, the illness of one of my family detains me at home some days longer than I intended. May I beg of you, therefore, to express my sincerest regrets to the Noblemen & Gentlemen of the Society, & to believe me, with many thanks for the kind terms in which you conveyed their invitation to me,

Very truly yours
Thomas Moore.

786. *To Richard Sharpe*

National Library of Ireland

19 Bury St., St. James's*
Monday 19 May 28

My dear *Sir*. (*I* should not have been so formal, if you had not set me the example) Unluckily I am engaged for Friday. A card from Lord Lansdowne for that day was the first thing that met me on my arrival, and, though one could hardly be better off, I cannot help regretting the loss of the treat you offer me.

Ever truly yours
Thomas Moore.

787. *To Mary Shelley*

Abinger Collection

Sloperton Cottage
June 18th 1828

Just arrived at home, after a visit of more than usual racket in London, I find shoals of letters, all gaping for answers, on my table, but am determined not to mind *one* of them till I have despatched

---

[1] See letter No. 779, to Mary Shelley, 15 Apr. 1828.

a line to you—you, who deserve to be remembered 'first, last, midst & without end'. I have, however, but a moment, & it would take hours to tell how much I have thought about you, grieved about you, &, at last sincerely rejoiced at the account I received just before my departure of your return & recovery. I have been kept in a state of great uneasiness by the changes, chiefly for the worse, through which my poor little girl has gone since you last heard of her. She is now, however, much better & I feel far more comfortable about her. The good work you began for me with Bowring has been so far ripened by my own assiduities that he & I are now, I flatter myself, on the most friendly terms & he has done everything for me I could desire.[1] This is all I can say at present, but pray let me hear from you & tell me all you have said, done, thought, written &c. &c. &c. since we parted.

Ever yours faithfully
Thomas Moore

788. *To Henry Crabb Robinson*

Dr. Williams's Library[2]

Sloperton Cottage, Devizes
June 20th 1828

Dear Sir,

I was hurried away from here without having an opportunity of thanking you for your very great kindness in taking so much trouble on my account. The extracts you have sent me are very curious, and any further communications you may have the goodness to furnish me with will be most thankfully received, under the above address. If you should find any difficulty in procuring franks you may send the packet through the medium of John Benett Esq. M. P. 19 Albemarle St or (if it should be above Member's privilege) through the hands of Mr Croker, Admiralty.

Very truly y^{rs}
Thomas Moore.

H. C. Robinson Esqr
K. B. Walk
Temple
3.

---

[1] See, however, letter No. 924, to Mary Shelley, 3 Apr. 1830.
[2] Transcript provided by Professor John Jordan, University of California.

789. *To Dr. Brabant*

Bodleian Autograph c. 24, f. 353

Sloperton
Wednesday [June 1828]

My dear Dᵣ Brabant— I will explain, when we meet, why I did not
put myself *in evidence*, immediately in Devizes, and I should have
written to you before, but that my intelligence from Southampton
does [*sic*] not come later down than the morning but one after I left
it, when there was no change whatever from the favourable state
of things I reported to you on our arrival there.[1] Will you let me
come & have a family dinner with you some day—either at your
own house or at Mᵣ Hughes's? Phipps told me you seemed *displeased* at not having heard from me, but I *know better*.

Ever faithfully yours,
T. M.

790. *To the Countess of Blessington*

Lady Blessington, *Memoirs*, ii. 271

Sloperton Cottage, Devizes
July 4th, 1828.

My dear Lady Blessington,—Having been some days away from
home, I did not receive your kind letter till yesterday; and I am
just now so surrounded with shoals of letters, all gaping for answers,
that I have not a minute to spare for more than just to say, How
charmed I was to hear from you; how comforted I feel in the thought
that you are *even so* much nearer to me, and how delighted I should
be (if such a dream was but within the sphere of possibility just
now) to run over to you for a week or two. However, who knows?
as the old woman said who expected a prize in the lottery, though
she had no ticket, 'Sure nothing's *un*possible to God.' I will therefore hope; and, in the mean time, pray send me the promised packet,
directing, under cover, to the Honorable Frederick Byng (our
dearly beloved Poodle), Foreign Office, Downing Street.

I am so glad you like my verses! I repeat them over and over to
myself continually.

Lord Blessington's packet arrived safe, and the sooner he sends
me another, tell him (with my most cordial regards), the better.

Ever most faithfully yours,
Thomas Moore.

[1] See Russell, v. 310–11. Moore took Anastasia to Southampton on 13 June
1828.

791. *To Mary Shelley*

Abinger Collection

July 25th 1828

Why have I not written to you before? Let the swarms of little devilish cares & businesses that are buzzing about me, sleeping and waking (and against which there is no shield, like *mosquito curtains*) answer the question—all *I* have time for is to satisfy your most kind anxiety about my dear girl. She is,—thanks to all the powers that watch over precious things like her,—doing far, far better than we could have expected. We had made up our minds to at least a year of succumbency for her, and she has now been, for the last week, sitting up two or three hours every day, and with every sign of gradual & sure amendment. Isn't this delightful?

The Guiccioli has sent me her 'Istoria' entire, and, if you would write to her, & say how grateful I am, you would do (what I *will* believe you delight in doing) a great kindness by me.[1]

Ever yours faithfully
Thomas Moore

792. *To Mary Shelley*

Abinger Collection

July 30th 1828

There is no quarrelling with sensitiveness, otherwise I should scold you for making me sit down to write a comment on my own 'absolute' *will*.

'I *will* believe.'[2] The author in this passage evidently meant to imply that, notwithstanding his usual *modest* scepticism in matters relating to himself (a quality inherent in all Irishmen) he yet *could* not resist the pleasure of giving *full* evidence to the kind interest expressed by his correspondent in all that related to him. Some *perverse* commentators are inclined to take the passage in a different sense, but it must be manifest to all readers (except 'Gentle' ones) that &c. &c. &c.

There! I hope you are satisfied with that luminous exposition, and I wish I could add that it was likely I should be able to give you a still more satisfactory one, in person—but there is no chance of my coming to town for ages. Sterne talks of commentators 'hanging out lights',[3] but the *quattr' occhi* are the best lights for such

---

[1] See letter No. 792, to Mary Shelley, 30 July 1828.
[2] See letter No. 791, to Mary Shelley, 25 July 1828.
[3] Not identified.

illustrations as ours. Pray, remember me to your fair companion, and *believe* me (whether with '*will*' or '*shall*', I am not particular) most faithfully & cordially yours

T. M.

793. *To Philip Crampton*

Russell, viii. 268

Sloperton Cottage, Devizes
July 31. 1828.

My dear Crampton,

I have ventured to introduce to you by letter our great gun of the press here (Barnes, the editor of 'The Times'), who is about to take a trip to the lakes of Killarney, and means to stop a day or two in Dublin on his way. The chief service you will have to render him, is to keep him out of the hands of the Catholic Association, who are in a state of deadly ire against him (and with justice) on account of his late views of our Irish Question, which I disagree with him on, *toto cœlo*, or rather *totis inferis*, myself. He is, however, a good fellow, as well as a devilish clever one, and has done more for the Catholic cause here than ever O'Connell could *undo*, let him try ever so hard. This I say merely as relates to England, for Dan's *Irish* career has, of late, my entire approbation. Be kind to Barnes, if he gives you the opportunity. He takes also a letter from Lord Lansdowne to his agent at Kenmure. You will be glad, I know, to hear that my little girl is going on better than we could possibly have expected. She has been sitting up for some hours every day this week past, and there seems no danger of any return of inflammation in the hip.

God bless you, my dear Crampton. Ever affectionately yours,

Thomas Moore.

I did so lament leaving London before *your* reign there was over.

794. *To John Murray*

Sir John Murray

Sloperton Cottage
August 1st 1828

My dear Sir—

The parcel with your letter was delayed by some accident & did not reach me till yesterday evening too late for the Post. You *can* be of the greatest service to me at Aberdeen, and are, indeed, just the sort of envoy I could have wished— *But* for the time it would have taken, I should have gone myself to visit those Byronian regions. You must, however, extend your researches a little beyond Aberdeen for me. I want you to go up Dee side as far as Ballater, about 40 miles I believe, from Aberdeen, and to give me a full description of the farm-house where Byron lived during his residence in that neighbourhood & where, I am told, they still show his bed.[1] The scenery on approaching this place is, it appears, very beautiful, and you must therefore exert your descriptive powers in giving me as clear a notion of it as possible. At Aberdeen, find out the house where Mrs Byron lived, and, if you are a sketcher, bring back a drawing of it—also of the above farm-house at Ballater. Dr Ewing of Aberdeen, to whom you may introduce yourself with my best remembrances, will give you the *renseignements* necessary toward the ascertainment of these particulars for me, and pray, enquire of him whether the drawing he sent to me arrived safe to his hands again. Let me have some notion of your 'whereabout' in Scotland & if any thing more occurs to me I will write to you there.

Yours very truly
Thomas Moore

795. *To F. Mansel Reynolds*

Public Records Office, Lord John Russell Papers (copy)

Sloperton Cottage
Augt 2. 1828

My dear Sir. Though I am afraid that in addition to the pains you have taken in singing Iago's advice into my ears—'Put money in thy purse,'[2] you will also apply to me his words 'These Moors are changeable in their wills.'[3] I must even stand the brunt of your accusation & do—what I fear is being more obstinate than changeable—refuse your magnificent offer—[4] I told you all along it would come to this, & though £500 is a sum which deserved that I sh^d put on my *considering* cap for it, I felt that all the consideration in the world would have but this one result. Do not be angry with me for not pocketing your money—it is a fault, at least, that few poor

---

[1] Byron was taken by his mother to a farm near Ballaterich, about forty miles from Aberdeen, in the summer of 1795 or 1796. The purpose of the visit was to provide Byron with a suitable place in which to convalesce from an attack of scarlet fever (see Marchand, *Byron*, p. 42).

[2] *Othello*, I. iii. 345.

[3] *Ibid.*, 353.

[4] Heath first asked Moore to edit *The Keepsake* (see Russell, v. 272), and when the poet refused suggested that he contribute to it. This letter, sent through Reynolds, is Moore's refusal. (See also Russell, v. 315.)

poets w^d be guilty of, and even for the oddity of the thing deserve
to be forgiven—with best compliments & thanks to Mr Heath I am
my dear Sir

Very truly yours
(signed) Thomas Moore

F. Mansel Reynolds Esqr pub^r
48 Warren St.
Fitzroy Sq^r
London

796. *Addressee unknown*

N.L.S. MS. 2255, f. 79

Septr 3rd 1828

My dear Sir— The title I think of is as follows.

Odes upon Cash, Corn, Catholics & other matters, selected from
the columns of the Times Journal & revised & corrected by the
author.[1]

Thank Murray for his *fringe* to the Proof— Tell him I have been
trying the effect of some of his stories on my neighbour's gout.

Yours ever
T. Moore.

I want you to get for me a respectable publication called 'Private
Life & Amours of Lord Byron' at Duncombe's in Fleet Market.[2]

797. *To Colonel Houlton*

B.M. Add. MS. 27425BC, f. 20

Sloperton Cottage
September 25 [1828]

My dear Houlton— I am here in a state of bachelorship (having
left my family at Southampton with the hope that my poor little
girl may profit by the hot salt-water baths) and if you are disposed
to have me for a day (any time either at this side or the other of

[1] A collection of his satires published in 1828. Since Longmans published
the work, this letter was evidently addressed to someone connected with that
company.

[2] The only title resembling that cited by Moore is John Mitford's *Private
Life of Lord Byron: comprising his Voluptuous Amours, Secret Intrigues, and
close Connections with various Ladies of Rank and Fame in Scotland and London.*
. . . S. C. Chew, *Byron in England*, pp. 387–8, tentatively gives the publication
date of this book as 1837. It was translated into French in 1837 and could,
therefore, have been published in English much earlier.

Tuesday next, when I dine with Scott[1] at Devizes) I shall be most happy to come to you.

I had a very clever agreeable letter from Wilson[2] the other day.

Ever y^rs^
T. Moore

798. *To John Murray III*

Sir John Murray

Sloperton Cottage
Septr 29th 1828

Dear Murray *Junr*— I write this hasty note to take the chance of a frank & to thank you most heartily for your attention to my wishes. Nothing can be more satisfactory than the result of your researches, and you must not be surprised to see some of your well-turned sentences *cribbed* (in the way of us original writers) for the Life. I have now much distraction & anxiety about my children, but am here now working alone, my whole family being (for the health of my little girl) at Southampton.

I have not seen any of the Literary Gazettes on the subject of Byron since those you last sent me— Let me have all you think will be of use. My best remembrances to your Papa.

Ever y^rs^ truly
T. Moore

799. *To the Countess of Blessington*

Lady Blessington, *Memoirs*, ii. 272

Sloperton Cottage, Devizes
October 18th, 1828.

My Dear Lady Blessington,—. . . . I have been kept, as I told you in my last, in a state of great anxiety about our little girl, who has been for months confined with an obstinate lameness, which is only just now yielding to the remedies we have employed. Since I wrote, too, I have had an alarm about our eldest boy, who was brought home from school in consequence of a fever having made its appearance there, and who, for some time after his return, showed symptoms of having caught it. He is now, however, quite well, and is with his mamma and my daughter at Southampton.

I see, by the newspapers, that there is some chance of your

[1] Thomas Scott was a magistrate in the county.

[2] Probably Colonel Sir John Wilson of Chelsea Hospital, who was evidently a friend of both Moore and Houlton.

coming to England, and trust that there is more truth in the intelligence than newspapers in general contain. Best regards to Lord Blessington, and believe me ever most truly yours,

Thomas Moore.

800. *To F. Mansell Reynolds*

B.M. Add. MS. 27925, f. 120

Sloperton Cottage
October 21st 1828*

Dear Sir. I *was*, I own, a good deal surprized to see the announcement, not only in the Literary Gazette, but in the St. James's Chronicle of Friday last.[1] However, there is no resisting the assurances you now give me & I shall look with anxiety for the contradiction you promise in the next Literary Gazette.

Yours truly
Thomas Moore

801. *To Colonel Houlton*

B.M. Add. MS. 27425BC, f. 23

Sloperton
October 28th 1828

My dear Houlton. I send you my Squibs, which can now, I fear, boast but a *spent fire*. I inclose, too, the Spanish airs for La Bella.[2]

Mrs Houlton will be glad, I know, to hear that our little Tom is again well—the feverish symptoms having gone off. [*The remainder of the letter, including the signature, is missing.*]

802. *To Mary Shelley*

Abinger Collection

Sloperton
Novr 5 1828

I am afraid you will think me a sad fellow, and a *sad* fellow I *have* been in the literal sense of the word, almost ever since I last wrote to you. The continued infirmity of my little girl & the effect that

---

[1] The *St. James Chronicle* ran an advertisement from 14–16 Oct. 1828, announcing the publication of the *Keepsake*, edited by F. Mansell Reynolds. The journal was to appear in November, and Moore was listed, with Scott, as one of the contributors.

[2] i.e. Isabella, Houlton's daughter.

nursing & anxiety begin to produce upon Mrs Moore are sufficient to vanquish even *my* animal vivacity— I don't know whether I told you that the whole party has been for some time to Southampton to try the effects of the hot salt-water bathing— The very day I got your last I set off to join them, taking your letter with me for the purpose of answering it from thence, but—it is hardly necessary to tell you I did *not* do so. We have but just returned, and the physician here says that Anastasia is all the better for the trip, with which opinion I must be satisfied, though her delicate looks & the little progress she has made in moving, even on crutches, speak a different language to me.

I am delighted to hear you get on so prosperously in your work, and trust I shall find you on my arrival in town (which will be, for a *very* short visit, before the end of this month) not only advanced with the Muses but *restored* to the Graces—which is, I flatter myself, as pretty a cut-and-dry speech as an elderly gentleman could make you. My Byron has gone on but slowly in the midst of my distractions, but I mean to invest it vigorously from this out, and shall master it, I suppose, about the same time that the Russians will Shumla.[1]

From what you before told me of Trelawney (or rather, I believe, from what somebody else told me) I fear I should have but little chance with him. However, do what you can for me, and be always sure of my heartiest thanks for all your kindness. What an enormous Epistle!

> Ever yours most truly
> Thomas Moore

803. *To Mary Shelley*

Abinger Collection

> Middleton
> Novr 23rd 1828

Though I am afraid my last letter to you, directed 'Park Cottage,' has gone astray, yet, as I know not where else to direct, this note must take its chance of doing the same. I expect to be in town (for two days only) on Wednesday, so pray lose no time in furnishing me with all possible *renseignement* about yourself, directed, as usual, to 19 Bury St.

> Y^rs ever
> T.M.

---

[1] 'Shumla' is a common incorrect spelling of Shumen, a town in Bulgaria, 50 miles west of Varna. It was taken in the eighteenth century by the Turks and unsuccessfully attacked by the Russian armies in 1774, 1810, and 1828.

804. *To James Power*

Rice University

Jan^r 11th 1829

My dear Sir.

I think the present order of the Legends will do very well, only putting perhaps 'the Voice' instead of 'the Stranger', the former being a more elegant & taking air (at least, in my opinion) than the other.[1] But, if there is any inconvenience in this change, they may stay as they are. I find people are pleased very much with all the designs, except that of 'the Leaf & the Fountain',[2] in which the figure of the female & particularly the unaccountable change the engraver made in her *eyes* by opening them so unmeaningly, offends every one— Couldn't he manage to *restore* the downward look that the eyes had before? if he could, it would be a material improvement.

We thought it not safe to take Anastasia to the Annual Dance at Bowood (though there were beds & every facility for our whole establishment there) but Tom & Master Russell went & made, I assure you, a great sensation. I wish your Bessy had been with us to be of the party— they would have been most glad to have had her.

I have not drawn yet, because the people have withheld their Bills longer than usual, but as, on the eighteenth, I shall have to send my mother her half-year's rent, I must not delay it much beyond that time.

Y^{rs} ever
T. Moore.

Mr Hughes bid me thank you very much for the fish— I ought to have given you his right direction, which is 'Buckhill, Calne'— it, however, reached him safely.

The Camphor Loaf is to be had at Gray's 97, New Bond St.

805. *To Mary Shelley*

Abinger Collection

Bowood
Feb^r 1, 1829

You see what it is to be so amiable—there is nothing more true than that it is by their bad qualities women *rule* us. If you had been a cross or exigeante person, you would have heard from me long

[1] *Legendary Ballads* (*Poetry*, pp. 296–302). Power made the revision in the order of the songs as Moore requested.
[2] *Poetry*, p. 298.

before—but then I should have written to you, and disliked you, and now I like you & don't write to you, which is surely far better.

I have not been at all happy since I saw you. Not only my Anastasia has made but slow, if any, progress, but the long nursing & anxiety have at length begun to tell upon the (still more precious, I own) health of her mother, whose wan looks & sleepless nights make me, at times, very miserable. My poor old, excellent mother, too, has been so very ill that I was for some days in readiness to start for Ireland to see her.— She is now, however, much better.

Did I ever write this note, word for word, to you before? If not, I must have *dreamt* that I did—every syllable of it. How often this happens! Continually, I have said to myself in society—have I not passed this very day & said & heard these same things *before?* All this must be the glimmerings of our pre-existent state, and there must have been some *very* nice person in that state to whom I wrote *exactly* such a scrawl of a note as this is.

I shall soon go to press with Byron, & you shall see what I say of Shelley and what I *don't* say of yourself. Indeed, I shall give but a *petit mot* to any one.

Y^{rs} ever,
T. Moore

806. *To Elizabeth Pigot*

Pforzheimer Misc. MS. 299

Sloperton Cottage
Feb^r 7th 1829

My dear Miss Pigot— Having caught a Bishop flying yesterday, I secured a frank from him and hasten (though, I fear, in obedience to the old Latin adage, with rather 'slow haste') to acknowledge your welcome letter & present, the latter of which has given great delight at the Cottage, where, I am glad to say, 'Moore's eye' however *passe* elsewhere, has not lost one tittle of its value—[1] Your letter was the more welcome to me, as I was beginning to feel a little anxious about your mother—the illness of my own mother making me think of all those I knew who had still kind, amiable & [in]telligent mothers left to them. Mine is, thank God, [m]uch better & from your saying nothing of yours, I [ta]ke for granted she is as well as you could wish her.

Our poor little girl still continues ill, and every day naturally increases our anxiety by weakening (I grieve to say) our hope about her. Mrs Moore's health, too, by long watchings & cares over her

---

[1] See letter No. 777, to Elizabeth Pigot, 12 Apr. 1828.

poor invalid begins to suffer but too visibly, and altogether,—I am far from happy. Under these circumstances, you will not wonder that my Byron task has forwarded but slowly & interruptedly. I am however, going to press immediately & hope to be out before town separates for the summer.

There were some queries which I wished to put to you, but have not time now to refer to the memorandums I made of them. One, however, I recollect was, to ask of you whether you remembered the way Byron used to *dress* at your evening parties at Southwell— whether he wore *breeches*, showing the leg & foot as all men did at that time, or long trowsers to hide his lame foot as he did afterwards.

I forgot, in replying to your letter before the last, to explain to you that I had no other share in Murray's rejection of Fletcher's materials than what arose from the opinion I gave, at Murray's request, of the *value* they would be to us. With all my desire that Fletcher should get something by them, I could not, of course, when asked my opinion, give a false estimate of them, and I answered that I did not think it likely I should be induced to quote more than a dozen lines, if so much, of the answer to Dr Mayo [?], and all the cream of his *other* paper (the narrative of Lord B^s last moments) had already appeared in the Westminster Review.[1] I added, however, that though the Poem was of so little value to *us*, it would be a great object to keep it from falling into the hands of *others*.[2] You may conclude something, yourself, with regard to the comparative value of the Poem in Fletcher's hands, when I tell you that out of the five or six hundred lines altogether (I believe) which you were so kind as to give me, I doubt if I have retained much more than a hundred.

Pray, write to me soon again, & with my best remembrances to Mrs Pigot, and my little oculist, believe me most truly y^{rs}

Thomas Moore

807. *To Miss Corsham*

Nottingham Public Libraries

Sloperton*
Feb^r 24th 1829*

My dear Miss Corsham— Notwithstanding the wretched state of mind in which I have been kept, for some time, by the dangerous

---

[1] 'Lord Byron in Greece', *Westminster Review*, II, no. iii (July 1824), 225–62. Fletcher's well-known account of Byron's illness and death is printed in this article (pp. 253 ff.).

[2] Elizabeth Pigot placed a number of letters and poems at Moore's disposal (see Russell, v. 249). The poem to which he refers here was probably among them.

illness of our daughter, I should have answered your letter immediately had I been here to receive it—but at the time it arrived
I was in town and am but just returned. It will give me great
pleasure to do what I can for your Volume, & if you will take the
trouble of forwarding it to Mr Power's, 34, Strand, I shall be sure
to receive it.

Yours very truly
Thomas Moore

808. *To Arthur Tegart*

Pennsylvania Historical Society

Sloperton Cottage
March 1st 1829.

My dear friend— Two or three times, during the few days I was
in town last week I meant to call & enquire about you, and to tell
you (what I know will give your heart pain) that our other poor
girl—she who, you know, alone was left to us after her whom you
attended with such kindness—is in a state which gives us but little
hope, if any, of her recovery.[1] Mrs Moore, in whose mind you have
always been connected with that first born & first lost of all her
little ones, often thinks & speaks of you now while watching over
our poor dying girl, and it is as much from her wish as my own that
I write you these few lines. Pray do not think it necessary to
answer me—indeed in the present state of my mind I had much
rather you didn't.

Yours very cordially
Thomas Moore

809. *To John Murray III*

Sir John Murray

March 4th 1829

Dear John— I am most anxious to know whether my first batch of
Proofs which I sent by Coach on Sunday, directed 'Whitefriars'
without the 'Lombard Street' has arrived safe. I dispatched the
remainder of the Slips yesterday, with this latter part of the
address added; but what makes me a little apprehensive about
the first is that, in the note which accompanied it, I begged of
Davison to desire you to forward to me *immediately* the Book of
Byron's Letters I left behind (from 1811 to 14) and it has not made

---

[1] See letter No. 814, to Mary Shelley, 24 Mar. 1829.

its appearance. Do pray look to this *instanter*—I cannot (as the Duke of W. says of Emancipation) '*get on* without it.'

Yours very truly
Thomas Moore.

Give my best remembrances to your mother & sisters & tell them I have not had such good breakfasts since— I would inclose this to your neighbour Mr Benett, but am not quite sure that he is in town. Pray enquire, & any letters you may have for me, leave them with him (19) & he will frank them.

810. *To Owen Rees*

Rice University

March 16th 1829.*

I had a letter from Sir James more than a week since, and answered it immediately. I told him he might make any use of my name in his application to Scott that he thought proper, and that if *they* both undertook the task I should be most proud to join them.[1]

Y^rs ever most truly
T. Moore.

811. *To John Murray*

Sir John Murray

Sloperton
March 20th 1829

My dear Sir— The parcel *was* at Devizes and my servant brought it with him last night— I have read the MS all over (having been at it so early as seven o'clock in bed this morning) and am of opinion that it would be, in every respect, worth your while to get possession of it. In the first place it contains a good deal that would be of the greatest interest in our work, and, in the next place, *after* our having thus turned it to account, it would be available and,

---

[1] The Longmans first approached Moore with a proposal that he and Scott collaborate on a history of Ireland and Scotland, each of them writing a volume. They offered Moore £500 for his part in the work. When he refused, the publishers proposed a three-way collaboration, in which Moore would contribute one volume on Ireland, Scott one on Scotland, and Sir James Mackintosh three on England. The offer was raised to £1,000 for each volume. This was the beginning of the *Lardner's Cabinet Cyclopedia* project, which included Scott's *History of Scotland*, 2 vols. (1829–30); Mackintosh's *History of England*, 3 vols. (1830–2); and Moore's *History of Ireland*, 4 vols. (1835–46). See Russell, vi. 16–17.

I have no doubt, popular (from its connexion with Byron) as a *religious Book.*[1] Mrs Kennedy would not be, I dare say, exorbitant as to terms—indeed in her note to you she said that the credit & fame of Dr Kennedy was her chief object, and this could not be consulted in any way so effectually as in that which I propose. Looking at it as a mere *advertisement,* the sort of notice I should take of the work would be the most rapid & far-spreading she could desire; and I could conscientiously speak of it in a way that would, I think, *ensure* its popularity. The conversations are creditable both to the good-humour, candour & love of truth of the poet, & the simplicity, earnestness & piety of the *proser*—(as he must have been by his own account to a considerable degree, but this you need not tell Mrs Kennedy.) It might be so arranged, if she wished it, that her husband's book should come out at the same time with mine, in order that the impression I shall be *sure* to produce in its favour may tell on the *instant.* You may, I think, collect from all this that you would not be likely at least to *lose* in any moderate speculation you might enter into about it.

Mrs Leigh is an odd person, and if she were not Byron's sister I should be disposed to say something worse of her—but she *is* a very odd person. What you report Hobhouse to have said is very handsome— but, as the old proverb goes, 'handsome is that handsome *does.*' and he has not come to *that* pitch of handsomeness yet. As however, you seem to have more communication with him now than when I left, I think it right to *repeat* my warning against your letting out any thing, either to him or to any one else, of the tone, manner or substance of our work. For, though I have little fear of their being approved, when the *whole* is before people's eyes, I know well that partial glimpses, here & there, would only expose me to be misunderstood & thwarted & worried.

I see Dr Kennedy says it was Byron's right foot that was lame, and I rather think that, under the pressure of the Printers query, I put the *left.*[2] *Which* was it? pray, ascertain this—and, by the same token, do not forget what I said to you about *tipping* Fletcher. I am very willing to go halves in any such politic donation.

Yours very truly
Thomas Moore.

Let me have by the next parcel the *Foreign Quarterly* for Sep^t 1828—Spence's Anecdotes of Pope, and, if possible, the Life of Cowper from the Edinburgh Encyclopedia—the Longmans have

---

[1] Murray was negotiating with the widow of James Kennedy for the publication rights to *Conversations on Religion with Lord Byron,* which appeared in 1830.

[2] Byron's lameness was in the right foot (see Marchand, *Byron,* p. 25).

sometimes sent me the *sheets* in these voluminous cases—[1] I need the few sheets containing what I wanted, & if they are publishers of this work, you can send to them.

812. *To John Murray*

Sir John Murray

March 22nd 1829

My dear Sir— I have written to Mr Davison a letter about the printing, to which I refer you.

May I give you the trouble, in some of your visits to the Athenaeum, to disburse for me six guineas—my subscription for the present year—which, if not paid this week, I shall cease to exist at least on their *list*. And as soon as I get money, I shall pay you.

By the bye, talking of getting money, it just occurs to me that you could do me a most seasonable service, without, I should think, the least inconveniencing yourself—and that is, by allowing me to draw upon you at my Banker's here, for £250, at *three months*, at the *end* of which time I shall give you a draft at the same or shorter date for that sum upon the Longmans on the credit of your *Twelve-month Bill*, which I mean to put into their hands. Let me know as soon as possible whether you have any objection to this—as if so, I must only *open* a *vein* somewhere else. My expenses, these last few sad months, have been enormous.

Yours very truly
Thomas Moore

I shall be anxious to hear how you have arranged with Widow Kennedy.[2]

813. *To John Murray*

Sir John Murray

Private

March 24th 1829

My Dear Sir— Since I received your letter I have been hard at work extracting as much *raw material* as I could out of Mrs Ks papers, in case she should change her mind & not publish the work.[3] Not having time for all I wanted (though 3 or 4 hours of it) perhaps you could get *Byron's two letters* at the end & Gamba's copies for me before you return the MS.— *Not* that we could make use of them

---

[1] Joseph Spence, *Observations, and Characters of Books and Men, Collected from the Conversations of Mr. Pope and Other Eminent Persons of His Time,* edited by S. W. Singer (1820).
[2] See letter No. 811, to John Murray, 20 Mar. 1829.
[3] *Ibid.*

without M^rs K^s permission, but they would serve me as memoranda of dates, facts, &c. &c.

I would not recommend your *binding* yourself to publish at the same time with our work, as there are some points respecting B^s character in which we should clash a little, but soon after would do no harm to either.

Many thanks for your kind compliance with my wish as to the draft. I think £20 would be abundant for Fletcher—as to what his communications are *worth*, twenty *pence* would more than cover it. But I think it as well to buy up his stupid tongue. If you chuse to make the verses he brought the *basis* of your gift—but no—on second thought they are worth little, and he would not think it a gift if he gave ever so little in return.[1]

> Y^rs very truly
> Thomas Moore

I shall write to Dr Ewing, if you please, but the thing is such a monstrosity as not to be presentable—unless it was made something *quite different*, while it is as easy to do *without* the original as *with it*— The inclosed is to enquire about the foot—what is *your* recollection of it?[2]

814. *To Mary Shelley*

Abinger Collection

March 24th 1829*

From the sad news you must have learned you will not wonder that I have not written to you before,[3] and now that I *do* write, it is about 'business'—a word I fear you will hate from my lips, as I have so often plagued you with it, and as indeed (ever since I have known you) 'my lyre is given to that alone'. It was, however, a blessing for me that I *had* business (as a sort of prop to buckle my mind to) during these last sad months—for all the resolution & philosophy in the world would not have been of half such service to me. Mrs Moore has been so ill since as to alarm me for *her* life also, but she is now better, and as to myself, I could not have believed that I could have survived any thing I so loved so calmly—but the preparation was long & gradual, and the last moments (or rather weeks) were so free from pain, so quiet and even cheerful that the impression left behind was any thing but

---

[1] See letter No. 806, to Elizabeth Pigot, 7 Feb. 1829.
[2] See letter No. 811, to John Murray, 20 Mar. 1829.
[3] Anastasia Moore died on Sunday, 8 Mar. 1829, after a long illness (see Russell, vi. 20–21).

gloomy or fearful. However—but to my business. I have got into
a puzzle about my hero's lame foot. I had put '*one* of his feet',
but when the proof came there was one of those dry queries of the
'Reader'— 'Qui? right or left?' which set me thinking, and
between my own recollections & Hunt's book I ventured to insert
'left foot'. I have just, however, been reading a MS. of Doctor
Kennedy's, in which he says it was 'the right foot', so that I am
left 'with one foot on sea & one *ashore*' till you can set me right
(or rather, as *I* think, *left*) again. Riddle me, riddle me-ree, I beg of
you, and as soon as possible.[1]

Ever yours most truly
Tho⁵ Moore

815. *To John Murray*

Sir John Murray

March 27 1829

My dear Sir. I have just looked over Mr Hoppner's recollections,
which are full of interest. I could not take upon myself to appraise
them, as a matter of *business*, but shall only say that I would not,
for a *good deal*, be *without* them. He mentions some other letters
of B⁵ besides those he has given—pray, ask about them.

Yours very truly
T. Moore

I am all impatience to know the result of your application to M^rs
Leigh.

816. *To John Murray*

Sir John Murray

March 30th 1829

My dear Sir. Have the goodness to let Mr Davison know that I shall
send him, by tomorrow's coach, some more copy. I have, however,
made a very provoking mistake. In working upon the year 1812,
which I have now got through, I looked forward to Lord B's London Journal, which I had taken it into my head began at the end
of 1812, to give me a long sweep of pages (for it will fill 40 or 50)
before I should come to 1813. I now find, however, that it is not till
the end of the latter year that the Journal begins, so that I have
still some time to work to get at it. Otherwise, it is rather lucky
than otherwise, as our materials are unfailing through 1812 & 1813,
and the journal will come with a freshened interest afterwards.

---

[1] See letter No. 811, to John Murray, 20 Mar. 1829.

I am not anxious to put the early sheets out of my hands till I see whether there is a hope of something coming from Mrs Leigh & Co.

In about 3 weeks I hope to be able to come to town. Lord Lansdowne has been kind enough to offer us his villa at Richmond— would that be too far for our printing operations? Let me know what you think. I wish you would ask some one (of authority) as to Byron's manner, voice, &c. in the House of Lords. I never heard him speak myself. Lord Holland, by the bye, will perhaps give me some notions on the subject.[1]

I have not yet had time to go into Devizes to make my *pull* on you—but must in a day or two. The copy I send up will be but about 30 or 40 pages, instead of (as I expected, with the Journal) more than double that quantity.

Yours very truly
Thomas Moore

817. *To the Marquess of Lansdowne*

Bowood

April 1st 1829

My dear Lord Lansdowne— There is no end to my thanking you— but if the charm of obligations is their sitting easy upon one (like a well-made ascot) you certainly have the art of fitting the shape of the mind so as not to let them *pinch* any where—which obligations sometimes do, as I have more than once experienced. Pray, tell Lady Lansdowne that I had to reject reading her last kind note to Mrs Moore, as it affected her more (*outwardly*) than any thing had done yet. I believe, however, it did her good, as the vent of tears had been for some time wanting, and kindness was the best thing to draw them out. As soon as the matter is definitely arranged between Starkey & my Landlord, Mrs Moore will begin to dismantle, and I shall betake myself (according to your very kind permission) to Bowood, where I hope to be inspired with a Ten-muse power to dispatch as much as possible of my Byron before I come to town.[2]

---

[1] Lord Holland recorded his impressions of Byron's speech in his diary, saying that he thought it clever and full of wit, but also full of invective. He concluded that Byron's over-irritable temper would have 'prevented him from ever excelling in Parliament'. He did concede that the 'construction of some of [Byron's] periods are very like *Burke's*' (Marchand, *Byron*, pp. 321–2).

[2] John Starkey's interest in helping Moore in the renovation of Sloperton was solely in keeping the poet in the neighbourhood. He offered to take the house and grounds into his own hands, giving Moore 'such a lease of it' as would either furnish him the opportunity of building or letting Dr. Starkey do the remodelling, for which rent would be paid accordingly (Russell, vi. 24).

Should Richmond be wholly vacant and undestined to any worthier occupants when Mrs Moore joins me, I shall be most delighted to avail myself of its quiet for the completion of my work—but it must be only on the condition that any body's claim upon such a privilege must take precedence of ours, and that we must be only used as *airers* for other people's coming.

The sort of arrangement Starkey is making will I fear interfere with my accepting the accommodation you offer as to materials— for it is not by *me* but by *him* that the house is to rebuilt [*sic*]—at least, so it appears at present—but if it should be found necessary that I take the building on myself, of course it will be of the greatest service & saving to have recourse to what you offer.

I rejoice to find you so confident as to the ultimate success of the measure.[1] If the King holds out stoutly against the Ultras, I shall have a better opinion of him, and say, 'The King's a bawcock (not a *shy* one) and a heart of gold'.[2]

Yours ever most truly
T. Moore.

818. *To John Murray*

Sir John Murray

April 3rd 1829

My dear Sir—

Pray let me have any particulars you can recollect relative to the Giaour & Bride of Abydos—I mean as to the printing & the additions he made to each new edition, which, in the case of the Giaour were I know considerable. I wish particularly to know whether the whole passage 'Tis Greece—but living Greece no more' was not introduced subsequently to the First Edition.[3] Pray, answer all this as soon as possible.

Y^rs ever
T. M.

---

[1] Moore is probably referring to the question of Catholic Emancipation, which was championed by Lord John Russell, Lord Lansdowne, and other Whigs.

[2] *King Henry V*, IV. i. 44.

[3] The passage appeared in the first edition. In the 1832 edition of Byron's works, Moore adds the following note to this line: 'In Dallaway's Constantinople, a book which Lord Byron is not unlikely to have consulted, I find a passage quoted from Gillies's History of Greece, which contains, perhaps, the first seed of the thought thus expanded into full perfection by genius:— "The present state of Greece compared to the ancient, is the silent obscurity of the grave contrasted with the vivid lustre of active life."'

819. *To John Murray*

Sir John Murray

April 3, 1829*

I fear I have destroyed the letter your son speaks of— I shall however make a search.

What of Mrs Leigh? Shall I proceed with my final corrections, or is there a hope of something more?

R. S. V. P.

Y^rs

T. M.

820. *To John Murray*

Sir John Murray

Sloperton Cottage
April 8th 1829

My dear Sir—

I cannot help hoping (from your silence and the pause in Davison's operations) that there is something important towards our joint object going on, and that your next letter may tell me of the *adhesion* of the malcontents. What I write about now, however, is to beg you will direct henceforward to me at *Bowood, Calne,* as I am about to betake myself thither during the dismantlement of our cottage, which (as I believe I have already told you) is to be pulled down immediately for the purpose of being rebuilt & made comfortable— I shall be entirely alone at Bowood, and hope to get on rapidly during the fortnight or three weeks I shall stay there— You will have the goodness to let Davison know my change of direction, that he may forward my future proofs to Calne.

Yours very truly
Thomas Moore

821. *To John Murray*

Sir John Murray

Sloperton
April 9th 1829

My dear Sir— Though in all the agonies of déménagement, I *must* write a line to thank you for your kind letter— Mrs Leigh is a most provoking person, and I fear I should have still less chance with her than yourself. The person you mention as having influence with her I know nothing of—I should be afraid to come to town till I shall have put myself beyond the reach of the *devils* sufficiently not to be too closely hunted by them, and a fortnight or so at Bowood will, I have great hopes, do wonders in the way of expedition for me. Mrs Moore has changed her mind as to accompanying me to London, immediately, so that I shall get somewhere in lodgings near you and by a strict 'self-venging ordinance' try & keep off morning visitors. We are most thankful, I assure you, for the great kindness of Mrs Murray & yourself in offering such a set of troublesome animals house-room & had Mrs Moore persevered in her intention of going so soon to town, we should have most joyfully accepted your offer. As it is, she means to visit about with some friends in this neighbourhood, before she joins me in London—

You shall hear from me from Bowood more fully,

Yours very truly
Thomas Moore

822. *To the Marquess of Lansdowne*

Bowood

Sloperton Cottage
April 9th 1829.

My dear Lord Lansdowne— The 'course' of business (like that of love) 'never does run smooth', and so I find it in the case of our intended building— Starkey has taken fright at the plan which the architect (chosen by himself) suggests, and seems inclined to propose a patching expedient instead which would but very little improve our comforts.[1] The fact is I do not think he has a disposable shilling in the world, and the folly of his removal to Spye Park, circumstanced as he is, seems altogether unaccountable. The plan which the architect has proposed will cost (Starkey says) between 4 & 5 hundred pounds, and I *never* expected that anything comfortable could be effected under that sum. I have therefore returned to what was originally my own desire & proposed that he should (conjointly with his son John) give us a lease of three [*illegible*] of the ground, and leave us to build the cottage, according to our own tastes & means ourselves. This arrangement he seems much inclined to come into and writes today to his son (on whom it must chiefly depend) for his concurrence. I thought it right to let you know this change in the aspect of affairs immediately, as if such an arrangement should take place your most kind offer of help in the way of *Hyle* (if Aristotle will forgive the degradation of the word) would be most welcome & seasonable. I have had likewise a proposal from another *worthy* Landlord (Angel), to throw down old

---

[1] See letter No. 817, to Lord Lansdowne, 1 Apr. 1829.

Ramsey House on the hill & build it up for me on whatever plan I chuse— The neighbourhood to Bowood would be the great charm of this.

I am in the very crisis of déménagement for my solitude, and the tilted cart has already taken Batch the First of my movables.

What an admirable display the Lords have made, both materially & numerically! I must own I never expected that I should live to see this day, and (as far as politics is concerned) shall sing my 'nunc dimittis' very willingly.[1]

My best remembrances to Lady L. & believe me

Ever truly yours
Thomas Moore.

823. *To Alicia Lefanu*

Pennsylvania Historical Society

Bowood
April 13th 1829

My dear Miss Lefanu—

Having run away from home to this retreat, desiring that nothing in the shape of letters should be sent after me, it was but yesterday that your letter, which has been all this time sleeping unknown & unheard of, found its way to me with a large batch of equally neglected companions. I need not, I know, ask your forgiveness, though I regret that a delay, which in your case may be of some consequence, should from this unavoidable arrangement of mine have taken place. I hope to be in town in about a fortnight, if that time will be early enough to take the steps towards your object which you desire, and which can be most effectually taken when I am myself on the spot. If, however, you should prefer my writing immediately to the Longmans on the subject (for Murray is, I know, hopeless) you have but to say so & I shall lose no time in obeying your instructions. What makes me say that Murray is 'hopeless,' is the experience I have had lately of his unwillingness to publish novels in more than one experiment which (under the most recommendatory circumstances) I made upon him. In one of these cases he consented, after a great struggle, and in the other (though the fair novelist's application was backed by a sum at her banker's to defray expenses) he decidedly refused, & the lady is now publishing with Colbourn.[2] You will direct to me 'Bowood, Calne'.

---

[1] A reference to the Catholic Emancipation Act, which Parliament passed in April 1829.

[2] See letter No. 767, to Mary Shelley, February or March 1828.

It is very odd, I never have been able to find the passage in Clarke, neither in the Quarto nor in the Octavo Edition—at least, in the former, I am sure it is not to be found

Yours most truly
T. Moore.

824. *To John Murray*

Sir John Murray

Bowood
April 17th 1829

My dear Sir.

I am delighted to find that Hobhouse is so favourable (or rather so much less *un*favourable than I feared) to our project. Had we not better rest a *little* longer on our oars, (in the way of printing) to give a chance of something favourable turning up for us? Croker's book will be delightful, and I felt quite sorry that there was only one sheet of it— I shall be very glad to find something *extractable* in the new matter of it.

You know Mitchell, I think—the Aristophanes Mitchell— He was one of our party the day Lord B. & I dined with Hunt in prison, & I wish you particularly to get from him all he recollects of that dinner *in quod*—above all, ask him whether Scott (the *shot* Scott) was not one of those who dropped in in the evening.[1]

About Sunday or Monday I shall send up near 100 pages more of copy—Mrs Kennedy's MS. will *keep* till I come to town.[2] I think 25 guineas may be sufficient for Mr H.—[3]

How peaceable you are all in town after this destructive Bill![4] I little thought I should ever live to see the *end* of my politics—but so it is—the Duke has had the merit of exorcising the devil of rebellion out of me & I am now (at your service) as loyal & well-behaved an author as you could desire. In this feeling, too, I rather think I am the representative of the great mass (or rather mass-*goers*) of my countrymen. All we wanted was fair treatment, and

---

[1] Thomas Mitchell began a series of articles on Aristophanes and Athenian manners in the *Quarterly Review* in 1813. He later made verse translations of some of Aristophanes's comedies. John Scott, a journalist and editor, was killed in a duel with C. H. Christie. For further details about these two men, see the Glossary of Proper Names. For an account of the dinner, which took place in June 1813, see Moore, *Byron's Works*, ii. 206–7.

[2] See letter No. 811, to John Murray, 20 Mar. 1829.

[3] Probably Richard Belgrave Hoppner, who had furnished some material for the biography of Byron.

[4] The Catholic Emancipation Bill.

God forgive you & your Quarterly Reviewers who so long grudged
it to us.

Ever yours truly
Thomas Moore

825. *To John Murray*

Sir John Murray

Bowood
April 21st 1829

My dear Sir— I fear you will be alarmed for the size of our Volume
by the sight of what I now send up—the whole of it (near 100 pages)
being occupied about the year 1813 alone. However, after the two
next years (14 & 15) I shall have little to do myself but in the way
of notes, and shall most willingly give the *pas* to my Maestro
through the remainder of the Volume. At least, this is my intention
at present, but there always rises something in one's path that
requires diffusion & explanation. I have omitted some remarks on
his projected travels at the beginning of 1813, till I come to the
printing, meaning, when in town, to *pump* my friends, the Lady
Harleys, on that & other points— As I consent, on *my* side, to leave
out all the *paw-paw* particulars the least they can do on theirs is
to furnish me with *decent* ones. The same consideration ought to
influence some other people I could mention—but it *doesn't.*

You must not think of publishing Mrs Kennedy's book till ours
has had a fair start. There are some little particulars in which she
would *take the shine out* of us, if she appeared first.[1]

Yours very truly
Thomas Moore.

I hope the printers will make no mistake with what I send—but not
being near any of the stitching sex, I have been obliged to leave all
loose & abroad—

826. *To Lord John Russell*

Early Correspondence of Lord John Russell, i. 292

Bowood, Calne
April 22, 1829.

My dear Lord John,—I have so long owed you an acknowledgement for your kind letter written months ago that you might well
think I forgot it—[2] but I have not nor ever shall—words of kindness
at that moment sink deep and have associated themselves with

---

[1] See letter No. 811, to John Murray, 20 Mar. 1829.
[2] Russell had probably written a letter of sympathy upon the death of Moore's
daughter Anastasia.

thoughts never to be forgotten. Mrs. Moore is not well—as long as the bustle of leaving our cottage continued she kept up pretty well in spirits, though wretched in health—but, now that's over, her spirits seem again to give way. She is going to Cheltenham as soon as I start for town (in about ten days) and I look to its doing a good deal to restore her.

I hope you will be able to get up some question or other to keep the House together a little longer than they now threaten. My book will otherwise be a *vox clamantis in deserto*.[1] It looks as if you all had not a single thing to think of at home or abroad now that the Paddies are made happy—[2] and for a Paddy like me this is a very natural feeling so much so that I consider my own politics entirely at an end—nothing in the world can ever again conjure up a spirit in me like that which the Duke has now laid, and for anything of a secondary class—anything short of seven millions of people—it is beneath my notice. Even the millions of the Debt are but a poor substitute. For you Englishmen however it should be otherwise at least I hope it will be otherwise this Session for the sake of my book which is now my only politics—as the Jew said when asked what religion he was—'I'se a marchant.'

I am getting on slowly as usual and the devils already 'gall my kibes.' I have still, I fear, two or three good months of working before me in town, and where I am to lodge myself for the purpose I know not.[3] Lady Holland when I was printing 'Sheridan' offered me Holland House as a workshop—and my reason for declining it was (which I shall tell her some time) that I *knew* what I was employed upon would some of it displease Lord H. and therefore felt it to be a sort of treachery to do it under his roof.

If you think I deserve a letter, I should like much to hear from you, but I have no right to ask it.

Yours ever most faithfully
Thomas Moore.

827. *To Sir Walter Scott*

N.L.S. MS. 3908, f. 237

Bowood, Calne
April 25, 1829

My dear Scott— It goes to my heart to *bother* you, knowing how busily & gloriously you are employed for that task-mistress,

---

[1] Evidently a reference to *Odes upon Cash, Corn, Catholics, and Other Matters*, which appeared in 1828.

[2] The Catholic Emancipation Bill passed in 1829.

[3] Moore was at work on the biography of Byron.

Posterity— But you may thank your stars that I have let you off so long. All that you promised me about Mrs Gordon and Gight and a variety of other things is remitted to you—'Ego te absolvo'— but I positively *must* have something from you of your recollections, personally, of Byron, and that, as soon as possible; for I am just coming to the period of your acquaintance with him, which was, I think, in the year 1814?— Tell me all the particulars of the presents you exchanged with each other, and if his letters to you are really *all* lost (which I will still hope is not the case) try as much as possible with your memory 'to lure the tassel-gentles back again'.[1]

You will have seen by the newspapers the sad loss my little circle of home has experienced—a loss never to be made up to us in this world, whatever it may be the will of God it shall be, in another.[2] Mrs Moore's own health is much broken, and she is about to try what Cheltenham can do for her, while *I* proceed to finish my printing in town. It would be far better for me to remain in my present quiet retreat (where I am working quite alone) but the devils beckon me nearer them, and I must obey in a few days.

Direct to me under cover to *Croker* (you see I take for granted you will have a *packet* to send) and he will always know where to find me.

My kindest remembrances to Miss Scott, and believe me ever, my very dear friend,

Yours truly & affectionately
Thomas Moore

828. *To Owen Rees*

Rice University

Bowood
April 26th 1829

Sir.

I have had the pleasure of receiving your two letters, & rejoice to find that you have succeeded in securing the valuable assistance of Sir Walter Scott, with whom & Sir James Macintosh I consider it a high honour to be associated—[3] As I expect to be in town about the end of this week, it will not perhaps inconvenience you to leave the arrangements your letter alludes to till my arrival— I shall then be

---

[1] *Romeo and Juliet*, ii. ii. 160. Moore included several letters from Byron to Scott in his *Life of Byron* (see Moore, *Byron's Works*, ii. 155; v. 298, 330). He also quoted Scott's account of his meeting with Byron at John Murray's in the spring of 1815 (Moore, *Byron's Works*, iii. 160–7).

[2] The death of his daughter Anastasia.

[3] See letter No. 810, to Owen Rees, 16 Mar. 1829.

better able to understand at what interval *after* Sir James Macintosh's Volumes you would wish mine to be published, and thus have it in my power to return you a more satisfactory answer.

I have the honour to be, Sir,

your obliged Servt

Thomas Moore

829. *To John Murray*

Sir John Murray

Bowood

May 1st 1829

My dear Sir— Something either very good or very bad seems portended by your long silence— It may, however, be nothing more than your expectation of my arrival in town, which *was* to have taken place to-day, but will not be till Tuesday next, in consequence of some arrangements about the rebuilding of my Cottage which have delayed me. It is with much reluctance I go up, as I dread the distractions of town, and nothing must now obstruct my finishing our work as well as I have begun it. It is true what remains is independent of me—for, only think what materials! His letters from abroad, his Journal at Ravenna, Mad^e Guiccioli's Memoir, Mrs Shelley's recollections of him in Switzerland, Hoppner's & my own at Venice &c. &c.—but the weaving all these together judiciously, though little more than mechanical, will require more thought than I fear I can command at N° 19 Bury St.— We shall, however, see—if worried, I shall fly back here.

Who is the person that sustains so admirably the character of Sir Simon *Grumbleton* in the new Quarterly ? It is a remarkable Article —As Fox once said 'I suppose no one was ever so wise as Thurlow *looks*' so I should say 'no one was ever so informed as the writer *seems*.' But there is far more than *seeming*— I should like to know who he is.

Yours very truly

Thomas Moore.

830. *To John Murray*

Sir John Murray

Bowood

May 3rd 1829

My dear Sir—

In order that you may know where to send anything you have for me, it is right to tell you that my domicile will be—*not* in Bury St—but at 15 Duke St, where I hope to be on Tuesday evening—

To John Murray

I have just received a very curious letter written by *Matthews* to his sister from Newstead in 1808, giving an account of the place, mode of life &c. &c.—[1] You will, of course, have decided by the time I come, whether I am to proceed with my *final* corrections of the early part, or still keep it open.

Yours very truly
Thomas Moore.

831. *To John Murray*

Sir John Murray

Friday—May 7, 1829*

My dear Sir—

Six o'clock will suit me perfectly & I shall let my friend Corry know in time. As to music—I fear it is out of the question, as far as I am concerned. I but *once* ventured to sing for any one, since our poor child's death, and the *scene* that I then inflicted on my audience was such as I should not like to risk again for some time.

Yours very truly
Thomas Moore

Pray do not give the above as my *reason* to any one but Mrs Murray. She will understand it.

832. *To Richard Sharpe*

National Library of Ireland

May 19th 1829.*

My dear Sharpe— I have been in search of you for the very purpose your note proposes, and on Thursday morning (as soon after ten as Almack's the night before will admit of) I shall be with you. I want you to put me at 'mine ease in mine inn' as soon as possible.

I left Mrs Moore at Cheltenham.

Ever yours most truly
Thomas Moore

833. *To Mary Shelley*

Abinger Collection

15 Duke St
Wednesday [postmark May 20, 1829]

If you could manage to be here at *three* o'clock to-day, 'I'm your man'—for a *minute*. Don't be angry at this unsentimental note.

Y^rs ever
T. M.

[1] This is the letter written by Byron's friend Charles Matthews to his sister on 22 May 1809 (not 1808), in which the writer gives an account of life at Newstead during his visit there with Hobhouse and others (*LJ*, i. 153–5 n.).

834. *To Mary Shelley*

Abinger Collection

Athenaeum
Friday [postmark May 30, 1829]

Came up yesterday and found both my luncheon (at Lady Lynd-
hursts [*sic*]) and my dinner at Agar Ellis's knocked in the head by
his Majesty—which *tried* my loyalty exceedingly, being thrown
thereby luncheonless & dinnerless on the world.

It is impossible to say at this moment, when or where we can
meet—but I hope some-where & soon.

Yʳˢ ever
T. M.

835. *To Richard Sharpe*

National Library of Ireland

19 Bury St., St. James's*
May 31ˢᵗ 1829*

My dear Sir— I have a favour to ask of you. Our friend Rogers told
me the other day of his having met in company, where I believe you
were present, a Mʳ Cowell (if I remember the name correctly) who
described himself as an intimate friend of Lord Byron's, and said
that he had some of Byron's letters in his possession. Rogers added
that this gentleman was well acquainted with the family of Mʳ
Marshall, whom you last week did me the favour to ask me to meet.
Now, if you could manage,—and as soon as possible, for my stay
in town is rather limited—to open a communication between Mʳ
Cowell & me, you will do, what I know you delight in doing, a very
useful & friendly service.[1]

Ever very truly yʳˢ
Thomas Moore

836. *To Mary Shelley*

Abinger Collection

15 Duke St., St. James's
[May 1829 ?]

Here I am, arrived the day before yesterday, and already thinking
of taking flight again, so beset with all sorts of devilments do I find

[1] Moore met John Cowell at breakfast on 11 June 1828, at which time
Cowell gave him some of Byron's letters, two of which are printed in *Byron's
Works*, ii. 119 and iii. 123. Several anecdotes concerning Byron which Cowell
related to Moore are recorded in the diary (Russell, v. 302-3).

myself in this most distracting & destructive place. Where am I to
see you, for a *minute*, some day? Nothing less than minuting
everybody will leave me a single second for myself—

Ever yours (but, like a French
cutlet, 'à la minute')

T. M.

837. *To Mary Shelley*

Abinger Collection

[May or June 1829]

This is the only bit of paper I can find. As far as *I* am concerned I
say 'yes' most heartily; but to-night I shall be in other people's
hands. However, I shall do my best.

To morrow morning I can *not* say 'yes'—for my breakfast time is
always occupied with my proofs. Like the pudding, the *proof* is in
the eating of it.

Yʳˢ ever
T. Moore.

Kiss Julia's white shoulder for me.

838. *To Mary Shelley*

Abinger Collection

Thursday* [postmark June 4, 1829]

Time flies & so shall I soon—and we do not see each other, which,
believe me, is no fault of mine— Though Murray lives so near me &
I have been these 2 or 3 days anxious to talk with him on business, I
have not found a moment, being whisked away in so many various
directions— Yesterday I was on my way to you when a request
from my employer (*Historical*) Dʳ Lardner[1] that I would help him
to receive some fine Ladies at the London University carried me off
to the outskirts of London & I was with difficulty back in time to
dress for dinner & Ancient Music— But to-day I *do* think I shall be
allowed to reach Somerset St. between 3 & 4.

Yours most truly
T. M.

[1] See letter No. 810, to Owen Rees, 16 Mar. 1829.

839. *To J. H. Merivale*

National Library of Ireland

Richmond
June 19th 1829

My dear Sir— I received safely both your packets, but had not time, in the racket of town, to acknowledge either. A thousand thanks for your attention to my request— Being but just arrived here, I have not yet had time to look beyond the first leaf of your recollections, but feel quite sure that they cannot be otherwise than useful & interesting.[1] I shall be occasionally in town during the summer, & look with hope to the prospect of our sometimes meeting.

With best remembrances to Mrs Merivale, believe me very truly y^rs

Thomas Moore

840. *To John Murray*

Sir John Murray

Richmond
[June 28, 1829, *not in Moore's hand*]
[*Expresses regret at not being able to dine with Murray on Tuesday.*]

841. *To John Murray*

Sir John Murray

June 29 1829

My dear Sir—
You have, I fear, made rather an embarrassing mistake (if there was any thing of importance, besides Lawrence's letter in your cover) by enclosing *my own* note back to me, instead of, I *apprehend* one written by *yourself*— If this is the case you can put your note in the Post before eight this evening, & I shall receive it at nine tomorrow morning, when, if it should be any thing of importance, I shall answer it in person in an hour or two. I feel quite overwhelmed by the compliment you pay me in thinking my head worth the costly 'Pencil' of Sir Thomas,[2] and I must try and furbish it up into its least *potatoe looks* for the occasion.

[1] Moore printed one letter from Byron to Merivale (*Byron's Works*, ii. 337), in which Byron congratulates him on his *Roncesvalles* (1814).
[2] Murray commissioned Sir Thomas Lawrence to paint Moore's portrait.

I was on the point of writing you a long business letter on the subject of my Ways and Means—but may as well, as I have the opportunity, dispatch it briefly here. Last night, in looking over my Banker's book ('a beggarly account')[1] I was startled by seeing that we are in a day or two of the resurrection of that awful Bill, that ghost of Specie, which has been 'doomed for a certain time to walk the earth'[2] before it returned to plague us, & which, without your assistance, it is wholly out of my power to *lay*. Now, what I want to know briefly *is*—whether, taking into consideration the unexpected delay that has occurred in our work, and the dependance which I had placed (vainly as it now appears) on my power of bringing it to a conclusion about this time, so as to give me a claim upon the sum still remaining in your hands—whether, taking all this into your merciful consideration you would think it too *hard upon* you, or too *soft of* you, to advance me forthwith the twelve-month Bill, and let me raise the supplies on it.

I have not left myself a minute more even to read over what I have written, but committing it to your night-cap's consideration (and merely adding that even 14 months would be acceptable) am ever most truly yours

Thomas Moore

842. *To John Murray*

Sir John Murray

Richmond
Friday Morning [postmark June 29, 1829]

My dear Sir— I forgot to send you Ashe's letter before I left town, & cannot find it among the papers I have brought down—you had better, therefore, call in Duke St. & desire Mrs Soane, my landlady, to show you the letters &c. &c. I left loose about the room, & bid her collect—The sooner you write to Ashe for his letters the better, as we are just at the period when they are wanted.

I have had but a chilly reception from the weather—but this place is delicious, and quiet to my heart's content.[3]

Y^{rs} very truly
Thomas Moore

[1] *Romeo and Juliet*, v. i. 45.
[2] *Hamlet*, i. v. 9–10.
[3] Lord Lansdowne's villa at Richmond Hill, where Moore spent the summer of 1829.

843. *To Mary Shelley*

Abinger Collection

[June 1829]

I shall not be able to stir out all this day—at least not till too late for what you propose—but I hope time enough to be able to call in Somerset St. when we shall settle something. I am worked like one of the devils themselves.

Ever yours
T. M.

On Saturday I think it is most likely I shall go & see my little Tom.— it is a shame I have not been there yet, and it is a shame I have not seen you, and—but there is no end to my shames.

844. *To John Murray*

Sir John Murray

Richmond
July 2nd 1829

My dear Sir—

I inclose a letter which I shall be much obliged by your franking & forwarding for me. The Steam-Packet (as this Dutch correspondent of mine says) is the best conveyance, but I rather think our Post-office must be the surest. I have told him that as soon as our first sheets are printed off I shall let him know whether you can comply with his request—which is, that you would let the House of Vander Meer & Ver Bruggen have an early copy (or even an early sheet) of the Life for the purpose of securing the right of having it rendered into *Dutch!*[1]

Yours very truly
Thomas Moore

You quite charmed my wife yesterday.

845. *To John Murray*

Sir John Murray

Richmond
July 13th 1829

My dear Sir— Pray send the inclosed proofs & copy immediately to Davison—first looking, as a curiosity, into the latter proofs to see the additions I have made. I flatter myself I have cobbled it up into something not a little piquant.

[1] Moore's *Life of Byron* was not translated into Dutch.

In a day or two I shall be at you with queries, & shall then give the draft on the Longmans—you should have had it before, but I was not sure that a common draft would do.

Yours very truly
Thos Moore.

846. *To Richard Milliken*

Rice University

Richmond Hill
July 21st 1829

My dear Milliken— Having been in town for a couple of days I did not receive my sister's letter concerning your affairs till yesterday evening. Believe me I sympathize most sincerely in all your grief & annoyances & most happy would it make me could I be of the least service to you—but Huskisson I was never personally acquainted with and (between ourselves) some misdeeds of mine, in the way of rhymes, towards him, with which, (puny as were the attacks, [*sic*] he is, I fear, but too well acquainted, would make me the unfittest person in the world to appeal to his good services in any way. It just occurs to me, however, that, through Lady Cowper, who is a great friend & I believe relative of his, I might be able, without putting forward my own name, to incline his heart a little towards the object you desire;[1] and I shall lose no time in trying this channel, if I should find, on going to town tomorrow, that Lady Cowper is still in London.

I have hardly a minute before post-time.

Yours, my dear Milliken, very truly
Thomas Moore.

847. *To John Wilson Croker*

Rice University

Richmond Hill
Thursday Evening [July or August 1829]

My dear Croker— Your note was, I believe, at Murray's before I left town yesterday evening, but by some mistake did not reach me till now. I had already half promised to dine with Denman on Sunday to meet Mackintosh & Brougham, which would, of itself, be sufficient to deprive me of the pleasure of coming to you; but I doubt whether, if ever so free, I could have been able to manage it,

---

[1] Moore recorded a call on Lady Cowper in his diary for 24 July 1829 (Russell, vi. 58) but made no mention of interceding on Milliken's behalf.

from the difficulty of getting back at night. I shall, however, make enquiries on this point, in case you should be tempted to try me again, as it would delight me to be able to avail myself of your neighbourhood, without the necessity of sleeping from home.

With best remembrances to Mrs Croker & thanks from Mrs Moore, I am, my dear Croker

Most truly yours
Thomas Moore.

848. *To Mary Shelley*

Abinger Collection

Brooks's
Thursday [July or August 1829]

If you were any thing else than what you *are* I should despair of your ever forgiving me. To have received such a proof of real kindness from you, and never to have been at your door since! But I am not so bad as all this seems— The sort of whirligig life I am leading here leaves scarcely an instant at my own disposal, and what with Printers' devils pulling at me, on one side, and you and other such angels attracting me on the other, Don Juan in his last scene was nothing to me. I have this moment however got rid of the *former* set of followers, and shall be henceforward *all* for *the angels.*

Ever y^rs
T. M.

849. *To John Murray*

Sir John Murray

Richmond Hill
August 2nd 1829

My dear Sir— There are two or three queries you must answer me, if you please (and *can*) immediately. What was the precise sum you sent Lord B. on Novr 14th 1815, and which he acknowledges & declines in the letter beginning 'I return you your bills not accepted &c. &c.'?[1]

What did the Vase contain which he gave to Sir Walter Scott? Attic hemlock wasn't it? and was the Vase silver? Did not Scott

---

[1] Byron returned 1000 guineas, which Murray, knowing that the poet was having financial difficulties, had sent as advance on the publication of the *Siege of Corinth* and *Parisina* (see Marchand, *Byron*, p. 556).

give him some sort of Scotch dagger in return ?[1] As Sir Walter will not send me the promised communication you must tell me as much as you can of what passed between them; it would not be amiss if you would forward these queries to Lockhart, as they might be the means of drawing out from Scott something more. Now don't delay this, I pray you.

There is a letter of B[s] to me about Sir Walter's 'Lord of the Isles', which I am sadly puzzled about,—as to whether I should insert it or not.[2] If Scott himself was the only person to be considered, I know he is above minding such things—he can well afford to have *one* of the feathers of his mighty wing a little ruffled, particularly by Byron who abounds with so many testimonies of enthusiasm for him—but whether others would understand my retaining the passage I know not. What makes me anxious to do so is that the criticism is mixed up with so much real kindness to Scott, and (what was much rarer in Byron) *fairness* to Southey—altogether it would be a loss—but I should prefer any thing to the being suspected of *lèse-majesté* towards Scott.

Yours very truly
Thomas Moore

850. *To Mary Shelley*

Abinger Collection

Richmond Hill
Monday [postmark August 3, 1829]

I was most unlucky in my attempts to see you the two last times I was in town— The last time I rather suspected that you were at home, but *frightened* by the carriage-full I had with me. Tomorrow, if the weather does not put an 'estoppel' to it, I shall try your door again. My only consolation for not finding you at home was its proving to me that you were well enough to be out.

Ever cordially y[rs]
T. M.

---

[1] Moore did not mention an exchange of gifts between Scott and Byron in his biography, and there is no reference to it in Marchand's *Byron*. If such an exchange did occur, the facts are now obscure.

[2] Byron alludes to Scott's *Lord of the Isles* in several letters to Moore (*LJ*, iii. 150, 153, 169, and 184). The essence of his remarks is that Moore should not fear Sir Walter's success but push on with his work on *Lalla Rookh*.

851. *To the Marquess of Lansdowne*

Bowood

Athenaeum
August 4 1829

My dear Lord Lansdowne— I should have answered your last immediately but that I was waiting to see the end of the negocia-tion about the 3 acres, which had been put into an *apparent train* of settlement since I last wrote, the old gentleman having, at length, produced his papers. I lost no time in putting them into the hands of a solicitor, and it turned out that one of the deeds on which the Title is founded has been mutilated both of seals & signatures and is worth no more than so much waste paper. There is also some other defect relative to the claims of two female relatives, and altogether the case they make out is of so very ricketty a nature as to render it a bad foundation even for Poetry to build upon—accustomed as it is to 'give to airy nothing a local habitation and a *name*'[1] (N.B. *not* Slopperton). The man of law (whom I have just called upon) said he would *see* whether they could produce a better title—but I know what this seeing means—they have evidently done their best in the way of title, and any thing more I could do would be only in the way of expence. I, therefore, told him to stop all further pro-ceedings, and to guard against his forgetfulness, shall repeat the same mandate by letter.[2]

With respect to the other 'angelus' I mentioned the particulars I can give you amount but to this—and on enquiry will be found, perhaps, to amount to nothing at all. While we were at Sloperton, & known to be acre-hunting, our maid Hannah was told by old Wilkins (a carpenter who lives in one of the cottages near us) that there was a spot of ground, half an acre or three quarters in extent, on the Sloperton side of the way, and a little farther towards Melksham than his cottage, which was, as he understood, to be disposed of. Hannah, knowing that we had then other views, and not thinking this spot would suit us, kept the matter to herself till just before I last wrote to you. Whether there is any thing in it more than idle talk, I know not—but if you would (I ought to be ashamed of this 'if' to *you*) take the trouble of sending some one to 'know the rights' of the matter from Wilkins, it would at least prevent the indulgence of false hopes, which is after all perhaps one of the

---

[1] *A Midsummer Night's Dream*, v. i. 17.

[2] Moore was consulting Lord Lansdowne on whether to renovate Sloperton Cottage or to lease property and build a new home. See letters Nos. 817 and 822, to Lord Lansdowne, 1 Apr. and 9 Apr. 1829. For Moore's decision con-cerning the three acres, see letter No. 852, to Samuel Clark, 4 Aug. 1829.

best results of knowledge—there being more time lost in hoping than in any thing else I know of.

I have not time to write more now, having an abundance of queries to solve & commissions to execute—besides the prospect of a first sitting to Lawrence, which, however, I shall fight off as long as I can.

My best & kindest remembrances to Lady Lansdowne—

Ever most truly yours
Thomas Moore

A Cambridge man has just been giving me a very good account of Kerry—that he has 'a clear mathematical head &c. &c.'

852. *To Samuel Clark*

Rice University

Brooks's
August 4th 1829.

Dear Sir— As I am quite sure that the old Lord of the Three Acres has done his best in the way of title, it would be but a waste of hope & time to pursue the matter any further.[1] You will, therefore, have the goodness to act upon the opinion you expressed to me today of the insecurity of the Title and let the other party know that I have abandoned all idea of the purchase.

Your obliged & faithful &c
Thomas Moore.

853. *To Mary Shelley*

Abinger Collection

Curzon St.
Tuesday [postmark August 11, 1829]

I am just arrived here to join my wife, who is come up for a day or two to visit our friend the Dowager, and will be with you (God & you willing) to breakfast tomorrow morning— I shall not be much beyond 10, as I have afterwards to go with Mrs Moore to see our young Carthusian.[2]

Yrs ever
T. Moore

[1] See letter No. 851, to Lord Lansdowne, 4 Aug. 1829.
[2] Moore's son Tom was in school at the Charter House.

854. *To the Marquess of Lansdowne*

Bowood

Richmond Hill
August 14, 1829.

My dear Lord Lansdowne— 'Light after light goes out till all is dark.'[1] So it is with our hopes of a house. We knew of the acres you mention before, and they are, I believe, *not* Mrs Goddard's but Sir Henry Bayatums, and consist of five acres & half, instead of 3 or 4—but, if they are those I mean, they are half on the hill & half in the valley, without a single tree on the whole space,—the ground in the valley is quite wet & if we built on the brow, we should be so exposed to wind that (as I remember Mrs Moore telling Lady Lansdowne in talking of these same acres) we should some fine morning or other, be found in the nettle-bed below. Since I wrote to you, encouraged by Fielding's plan and an estimate he got from his Laycock Palladio (which confined the expenses of re-building Sloperton within 150) I tried back to the old spot again & wrote Doctor Starkey on the subject—but his answer informed me that in consequence of not being able to agree upon terms, his negociation with Goddard was entirely broken off; and all he could offer us was the use of the Lodge till something better turned up. 'To this complexion (a very bleak one) we must (I suppose) come at last.'[2]

Mrs Moore's trip into Wiltshire will not be solely on account of the house; but the fact is, as soon as I leave this, she will be better there than any where else, and if Lennard's House is to be had, she will move our furniture thither & settle there— the hope of being able to take her & the children to Ireland this year being (I fear) wholly out of the question, though I shall defer telling my mother that she must be contented with a short visit from me as long as I can. I have but just now finished the 1st Volume of my Work, and though the second will consist chiefly of Correspondence, the delays & difficulties that spring up *en route* are such as I find I have never made sufficient allowance for.

The painters have been these two or three days at our outskirts, the lower grounds, green house &c. &c. and do not talk of reaching the house itself till the end of the month, when Mrs Moore will be ready to take her flight into Wiltshire, leaving Richmond Hill 'poetis & pritoribus'—for I do not think that I, myself, shall

---

[1] Probably an adaptation of Pope's line 'Art after Art goes out and all is Night', *The Dunciad*, iv. 640.
[2] David Garrick, 'Epitaph on Quinn' (Murray, *Life of Garrick*, ii. 38).

mind them for a week or so, if I may so far lengthen my un-conscionable visit as to stay on for that time longer. It has been a most delicious séjour tous, & it is in vain to *think* of saying what we both feel for the kindness and seasonableness of it. For myself, I find that the *elastic spring* within me is gone,—or, at least going fast—but I shall always have enough left for gratitude to you.[1]

Talking of the Times, I wonder whether you took any notice of some verses in it a week or two since and whether you had any calumnious notions that they were mine.[2] In execution & neatness I could not have done better, or so well—but in that rather indis-pensable article, *meaning*, neither I nor any one I have talked to about them have been able to make out what on earth could be their object. They were, between ourselves, C. Sheridan's & sent by him through me.

What a letter I've written! but you encourage me to such things —long letters—long visits &c. &c.

Ever faithfully y^{rs}
T. Moore.

855. *To Lady Holland*

Pforzheimer Misc. MS. 310

Duke St.
Sunday [August 1829]

Dear Lady Holland— I have just been informed that the person with whom I am negociating for an acre or two of ground in the neighbourhood of *Slop*-perton (or Hog-wash Cottage, as, I think, you re-christened it the other day) has fixed to meet me on the subject tomorrow morning at ten o'clock—so that it will not be in my power to accept your kind offer of a bed to-night & I must trust to your interest for prevailing on some of your guests to bring me to town.

Very faithfully your Ladyship's Serv.
Thomas Moore.

---

[1] Moore lived at Lord Lansdowne's villa at Richmond during the summer of 1829.

[2] Moore is probably referring to a piece of doggerel entitled 'The Sow, the Eagle, and the Polecat', which appeared in *The Times* on Tuesday, 4 Aug. 1829. The subject of this inept satire is the separation of Church and State.

856. *To his Mother*

Russell, ii. 120, no. 374

[August 1829]

My dearest Mother,

We are in expectation of some visitors here. Bessy's brother-in-law is arrived from Edinburgh, and we mean to have him out for a day or two: and Barbara Godfrey, Lady Donegal's niece, comes to pass a few days with us next week—our neighbourhood to town imposes a little of this upon us. Our most welcome visitor, however, comes to-day, meaning no less a person than that gentleman of the gown and breeches, Master Tom (you know, I suppose, that a gown and short breeches form part of his costume). Sir Francis Burdett's brother, who lives in our neighbourhood, brings him to us from the Charter House, with his own two sons, and takes him back again on Monday. God bless you both. Your own,[1]

Tom.

857. *To Mary Shelley*

Abinger Collection

Saturday [August 1829]

One is sure of nothing in this world— The moment after I wrote to you I received a letter from Mrs Moore inclosing one from the Doctor of the C. H. to say that our little Tom was seriously ill. I went off to him, of course, immediately—it being most unlucky I had not gone before, as Mrs M. would have been spared the pain of that letter. I found the dear fellow much weakened by the bleeding & blistering necessary to subdue the inflamation, but cheerful & doing as well as could be expected.

The breakfast tomorrow, I need not add, is out of the question— I am just setting off to the C. H. now.

What with his illness & the effect it may have on Mrs Moore (who is already ill herself) and the lingering state of weakness of my poor mother, I am in a state of mind by no means enviable, with all my honours.

Y^{rs} &c
T. M.

Pray, don't write to me any more till after you have seen me.

[1] This letter is incorrectly dated 'Hornsey, June, 1817' in Russell's edition. Thomas Lansdowne Parr Moore was born on 24 Oct. 1818, and was in the Charter House school in 1829. On 5 Aug. 1829 Moore recorded in his diary: 'Barbara Godfrey brought by her aunt Philly to pass a few days with us. . . . Murray (Bessy's brother-in-law) came out to dine accompanied by his sister, Mrs. Henry Siddons, to pay a visit' (Russell, vi. 67).

858. *To Mary Shelley*

Abinger Collection

[August 1829]

My poor little man gets better but (owing to this sharp weather) much slower than I could wish, and part of the time since I saw you I have been rather wondering about him—[1] However, he is certainly better— To-day I dine with Poodle Byng & too late to accompany you to the opera, but if I can I'll meet you there.

Y^rs ever
T. M.

859. *To Lord Sandon*

Rice University

Richmond Hill
Wednesday Night [August 1829]

My dear Lord Sandon— I shall have great pleasure in accepting Lady Bute's invitation for Friday.

Yours very truly
Thomas Moore

You have not mentioned the hour, but I shall take for granted *six*— as a good rural medium. If you should be at home, however, when this arrives, you can say by the messenger.

860. *To Mary Shelley*

Abinger Collection

Saturday [postmark September 2, 1829]

I shall not, I fear, be able to see you till I have got rid of my Household Deities— Even my 'Book' has been forced to lie by during this week of sight-seeing, and I have been delivered up to Wild-beasts all the mornings and to *mummers* all the evenings.

What you tell me about your melancholy grieves me, though I can well understand it.

On Monday, I rather think, my people take their departure & soon after we shall meet.

Y^rs ever
T. M.

[1] See letter No. 857, to Mary Shelley, August 1829.

861. *To Mary Shelley*

Richmond
Septr 3rd 1829

I have, since I saw you, made two (or, I rather fear *three*) runs up
to town without being able to reach you—though I went last time
around with a list of queries for you that would, of itself, have
reached Somerset St.— I am now deep in the Lake of Geneva, and
only hope I shan't meet with the same fate I once invented for
William Bankes, who in a memorable speech of his, stopt short at
a simile about the Lake of Geneva & sat down— Have you heard
(said I, in my rhymes)

> How this wisest of young gentle*men*,
> Fell, one night, by mistake,
> In Geneva's deep lake,
> And never was heard of again,
> Master Bankes
> And never was &c. &c.

I find Shelly [*sic*] not so easily dealt with as I expected—such men
are not to be dispatched in a sentence. But you must leave me to
manage it my own way—I must do with him, as with Byron—blink
nothing (that is, nothing but what is ineffable)—bring what I
think *shadows* fairly forward, but in such close juxtaposition with
the *lights*, that the latter will carry the day. This is the way to do
such men real service. I have been reading a good deal of Shelley's
poetry, but it is, I confess (always excepting some of the minor
gems) *beyond* me, in every sense of the word. As Dante says (and,
by the bye, the quotation [might] not be a bad one to apply to him)
'Con suo lume medesimo cela'.[1]

On Saturday (this is to give notice) I leave Richmond for good
and for—19 Bury St. Mrs Moore & her little et-ceter[a] will stay a
week at Lady Donegall's [*sic*] & then set off for Wiltshire, l[eaving]
me in the hands of the Printers Devils for God knows how long.
S[o] prepare for a surfeit of me.

Yours ever most truly
Thos Moore

I wish Hunt had not quoted your pretty passage about Shelley in
your Preface to the Poems—but it will bear repetition.[2]

[1] Moore did not quote the passage correctly. It should read, 'E col suo lume
se medesmo cela', *Purgatorio*, canto XVII, l. 57.

[2] In *Lord Byron and Some of His Contemporaries* (London, 1828), 2nd
edition, vol. i, pp. 298–9, Leigh Hunt quotes a lengthy passage from the Preface
to Mary Shelley's edition of Shelley's *Posthumous Poems* (1824). The passage
deals with the extent of Shelley's observations on natural objects and the fact
that his greatest concern was the happiness of those about him.

862. *To John Murray*

Sir John Murray

Saturday Sep 20 1829

My dear Sir— You will be glad to hear that I have succeeded in getting Lady Holland to look for Byron's letters to Lord H. & that she has just given me seven or eight, which are most valuable to us, not only for their own interest, but as enabling us to add the name of another distinguished friend of Byron's to our list and to put to shame (if that were possible) those *soi-disant* friends of his who have treated us so unhandsomely—[1] I must on Monday go to Davison's & arrange about the insertion of this new matter.

Yours very truly
T. Moore

863. *To Sir Thomas Lawrence*

University of Texas

19 Bury St., St. James's
Monday* [postmark September 29, 1829]

My dear Sir Thomas— I have deferred my trip to Wiltshire till Monday, and therefore either Friday or Saturday (or *both*, if you will) I am at your service.

Not to give you the trouble of writing, I shall take for granted, if I do not hear from you, that I may come on Friday at 11.

Yours very truly
Thomas Moore

864. *To Mary Shelley*

Abinger Collection

Brooks's
Tuesday [postmark September 30, 1829]

I was on my way to you, but the letter-hour brought me back here. Tomorrow evening I am to meet my little Tom at the Coach office & take him to the Charter-House. Should I dine *before* I meet him you will see me, chez vous, pretty early—if *after*, I shall be late (ten or so) but at all events, shall come.

I had a long letter in *English* from the Guiccioli yesterday—all anxiety about the Life.

Yrs ever
T. Moore

[1] Moore received little help from Hobhouse and none from Kinnaird. See letters Nos. 682, 689, 690, and 740, to John Cam Hobhouse, 21 Dec. 1825, 17 and 26 Jan. 1826, and 24 Oct. 1827. For his unsuccessful application to Kinnaird see letter No. 764, February 1828.

865. *To the Marquess of Lansdowne*

Bowood

19 Bury St., St. James
October 1st 1829

My dear Lord Lansdowne— I have heard of all your kind doings &
counsellings relative to our poor *Stray* Cottage as well as your
heroic patience under Mrs Moore's questionings &c. &c. which she
has reported to me with all due praise & gratitude. It is delightful
to think that I am still to hang upon your skirts. I should be indeed
(to use Sydney Smith's version of a *fish* out *of* water) 'like a
mackerel in a gravel-walk' any where else. Mrs Moore (or rather
Tom, who boasts of being by at the conversation) tells me that you
have said it would not be inconvenient to you to receive me at
Bowood for a few days; but, as I know you very wisely object to
being broken in upon when *alone* I shall wait till I hear from yourself how soon I might venture to invade you. I have been staying
a good deal at Holland House and should have been more there
could I have found it possible to work among so many pleasant
distractions. Indeed, even at this season I find engagements rather
too rife & am inclined to think September is coming into fashion.
Lord Dudley & Lord Essex find materials for dinners daily, and
I met your friend Bailey (who I am told is cellaring his own wine
& hanging his own pictures from a fear of trusting either upholsterers
or wine-merchants) at his namesake's in Seymour St. on Monday
last. I hope he doesn't mean to be as suspicious about the lady as
about the cellar.

There does not seem to be any more Eastern news to-day—but
the general impression is that there is *Peace*. What else, in fact, *can*
there be, when there is no one to 'show fight?'[1]

With my very best regards to Lady Lansdowne believe me ever
faithfully yrs

Thomas Moore.

I shall be glad to hear how Kerry is.

[1] The *Morning Chronicle* for 1 Oct. 1829 contains a paragraph copied from
the French newspaper *Constitutionnel* which clarifies Moore's comment and to
which he evidently alludes. The excerpt discussed the uncertainties of the
position of the Russian commander since he entered Adrianople. He was faced
with the alternatives of marching on Constantinople or of negotiating, and the
writer conjectured that he favoured negotiation, 'which accounts for the slow-
ness of his operations'.

866. *To the Marquess of Lansdowne*

Bowood

Brooks's
October 5th 1829

My dear Lord Lansdowne—I take you at your word that I shall not be a trouble to you and on Thursday morning mean to leave town.[1] You will not think of me as a *diner* that day, for I shall stop at Barkhill and have a few moments of conjugal converse before I come to you. The same day I got your last letter Mrs Moore forwarded to me yours to her, which was most kind & satisfactory. There is a letter, by the bye, in one of the Tatlers (No. 169, I think) which I have often thought of pointing out to you as a pretty faithful description of the relations in which I stand (and shall now, I trust, long stand) as a neighbour to Bowood—with the exception of turning the streams into my domains (as a delicate mode of supplying me with fish) you are as close a resemblance of the noble neighbour there described as need be.[2] I hope I have remembered the number rightly—but pray, at all events, turn to it.

Lord Clifden just tells me he has heard from very good authority that in Kent, Lincolnshire & other places the tenants are in great numbers throwing up their leases. A tenant (one of the most respectable) of Lord Brownlow's has just done so.[3]

Ever yours most truly
Thos Moore

Lady Holland told me I should 'bring a bad name' on Holland House by saying I could not work there.[4] I mean to try the experiment (with Lady Lansdowne's leave) at Bowood, & all I ask towards it is a somewhat larger bed-room—as I am in the habit of pacing about all day, while I work—and therefore too the more out of the way I am of disturbing others by my peripateticism the better.

---

[1] See letter No. 865, to Lord Lansdowne, 1 Oct. 1829.

[2] A letter from 'Frank Bickerstaff' in the *Tatler*, no. 169, extols the virtues of the 'Noble Lord' who is his neighbour. Among other benevolent acts mentioned was that of 'altering the course of canals and rivulets, in which he has an eye to his neighbour's satisfaction, as well as his own'.

[3] For an account of the difficulties in Kent, which broke into full-scale riots in the autumn of 1830, see letter No. 945, to Lord Lansdowne, 7 Dec. 1830.

[4] See letter No. 865, to Lord Lansdowne, 1 Oct. 1829.

867. *To John Murray*

Sir John Murray

Brooks's
Octr 6th 1829

My dear Sir— The moment I heard, at your house, of the anger you had expressed against Simmons I set off to Davison's, thinking the delay might have been caused by the sheet they sent me to show the effect of the new Title. I did not see Simmons himself, but from the account his brother workman gave me, I am convinced he was not to blame. The note from your house, it appears, did not arrive till after he had left the Printing-office, and, as soon as he received it this morning, he set off to you (I understand) himself with the sheet. I trust you will not follow up your threat of taking away the printing from him. We have got into such a good understanding on the subject, that it would be a material derangement to me should you resolve to turn me over to another printer.

What an agreeable day we had yesterday!

Y^{rs} ever
T. M.

868. *To John Murray*

Sir John Murray

Bowood, Calne
October 13th 1829

My dear Sir— I have been, ever since I came down, in brisk communication with Simmons, but am stopt short (or at least, disconcerted) by the misdating of your letters, some of which I *know* (and God knows how many that I don't know) to be of 1819 which are dated 1818. My host won't let me go till next week, but in the mean time, I shall not be idle, and hope to find your son arrived & ready to assist me on my return.

Remember me most kindly to Mrs Murray & your daughters. I have found Mrs Moore a good deal better.

Yours very truly
Thomas Moore.

Yesterday our poor old Cottage was pulled down & the reedification is to begin forthwith. If you can get enough for me out of the French & American bibliopolists to pay for it, you shall have my benediction, such as it is.

869. *To John Murray*

Sir John Murray

Bowood
October 19th 1829

My dear Sir— You will tell the Printer not to forward any more proofs after tomorrow as I mean to start for town on Thursday morning—not very well pleased, as you may suppose, to exchange this Paradise for the back shop in Bury St. But 'needs must when the *devils* drive.'[1]

I hope Irving will not have left town, as he is our main hope for the American market. Whoever you deal with in Paris, Made Belloc must not be forgotten as transla*tor* (or rather *trix*) we having both bound ourselves to her apron-string, and it is time she had some of the sheets too—isn't it? but this we shall settle when we meet.

In the mean time,

Ever truly yrs
T. Moore

870. *To Mary Shelley*

Abinger Collection

Bowood
Tuesday—Octr 20 [postmark October 21, 1829]

Near Post-hour—just came in to dress & have only time to say that on Thursday I leave this for town and as soon after that as is practicable or *walkable* shall find myself at 33 Somerset St.

A sad change for me from an Italian Terrace full of Dahlias to my back room in Bury—*you* however must be 'my *Dalia*' as Sir Lucius O'Trigger has it.[2]

Ever yours
T. M.

871. *To Mary Shelley*

Abinger Collection

Tuesday [29 October 1829]

A further embargo was laid upon me at Bowood & I did not reach town till Saturday night—[3] Sunday I went to my little Tom, who

---

[1] Proverbial. See John Heywood, *Proverbs*, part ii, chap. v. See also *All's Well that Ends Well*, i. iii. 32.

[2] *The Rivals*, ii. ii. 6–7.

[3] Moore visited Bowood in October 1829 and on the 24th recorded that his host pressed him to remain longer than he intended. He arrived in London on the evening of the 26th (see Russell, vi. 88–89).

had been confined with a hurt on his ankle & all yesterday I was
Byronizing— but we shall soon meet.

Y^rs ever
T. Moore

872. *To Sir Walter Scott*

N.L.S. MS. 3910, f. 307

Brooks's
October 31st 1829

My dear Scott.— I ought to blush 'terrestrial rosy red, *shame's
proper hue*' for not sooner acknowledging your precious notes
about Byron.[1] *One* conclusion however you might have drawn from
my silence, namely, that I was satisfied & had all that I asked for.
Your few pages indeed will be the best ornament of my Book.

Murray wished me to write to you (immediately on the receipt of
the last things you sent me) to press your asking Hobhouse for the
letter of your own (in 1812) that produced Byron's reply—[2] But
I was doubtful whether you would like to authorize the publication
of this letter, & besides, it would be now too late as the Devils are
in full hue & cry after my heels—

Health & prosperity to you, my dear friend, & believe me ever
yours most truly

Thomas Moore

873. *To John Murray*

Sir John Murray

[October 1829]

My dear Sir—

Taking for granted from your silence that you have (as I suggested) stopped the further progress of the *printing off* beyond the
first five sheets, I have made some alterations of importance in the

---

[1] See letter No. 827, to Sir Walter Scott, 25 Apr. 1829, and No. 849, to John
Murray, 2 Aug. 1829. The quotation has not been identified.

[2] The correspondence to which Moore alludes concerned Byron's strictures
on Scott in *English Bards*, ll. 171–4, and a meeting between Byron and the
Prince Regent, who praised Scott as the greatest living poet. Byron had
accused Scott, in the lines cited, of writing *Marmion* solely for the sake of
'half-a-crown per line'. On 3 July 1812 Scott wrote to Byron, saying that he
was not under contract when he composed the poem but that he had to publish
it in 'a very unfinished state' in order to extricate himself from difficulties
resulting from the misfortune of a very near relative. He thanked Byron for
sending, through Murray, the Prince's remarks about him. On 6 July 1812
Byron replied, apologizing for his lines and giving a more complete account of
his meeting with the Prince. For this exchange of letters see *LJ*, ii. 131–5.
Moore printed Byron's reply (*Byron's Works*, ii. 155), but not Scott's letter to
Byron.

sheets that follow. It is possible that I may be in town on Monday, as Lord L. has offered to take me, and if I can manage to be ready, I shall accept his offer.

> Yours most truly
> Thomas Moore.

An Irish paper says that you have made it an express condition with every purchaser of the 1st Volume that they must buy the second at the same high price! ! !

Tell the Printer not to forward any thing more to me here—but to send every thing after Monday to 31 Sackville St.

874. *To Mary Shelley*

Abinger Collection

> Brooks's
> Friday Evn [postmark November 7, 1829]

I meant to have come last night, but Lord Essex (my *eternal* Amphytrion) dined so late that there was no chance of reaching you before your assembly time. Lawrence has put me off from to-morrow, sine die—at least till we meet & arrange at Crobin on Sunday.

> Yrs ever
> T. M.

The verses are beautiful—but thrown away, on such a subject.

> Il n'y a qu'un tems pour les aimables vers,
> Il n'y a qu'un tems pour les douces folies.[1]

875. *To S. C. Hall (fragment)*

Abinger Collection

> 19 Bury St., St. James's
> Novr 13th 1829

Dear Hall—

The sheets arrived quite safe & I feel a little ashamed of having made such a fuss about them. The wise thing would have been to have told you all my anxieties on the subject & to have

---

[1] Not identified.

876. *To The Countess of Blessington*
Lady Blessington, *Memoirs*, ii. 270

> Sloperton Cottage, Devizes
> November 18th, 1829.

My Dear Lady Blessington,—It is now six months since (after a conversation with Lord John Russell about you) I exclaimed, 'Well, I shall positively write to Lady Blessington to-morrow!' Whether I have kept my word, you and the postman know but too well. The fact is, I live, as usual, in such a perpetual struggle between what I like to do and what I ought to do (though communing with you would come under both these heads), between junketing abroad and scribbling at home, that for any thing but the desk and the dinner-table I am not left a single instant of time.

In addition to our neighbors at Bowood, we have got, lately, their relatives the Fieldings, who have settled themselves near us; and having some very pretty girls for daughters (things I have not yet lost my taste for), they contrive, with music, visits, &c., to disturb me not a little.

I have had but one short glimpse of Mrs. Purves for the last year, as she has taken flight to some distant and outlandish place (called Fulham, I believe), to which a thorough *town* man (such as I always am for the few weeks I stay there) could never, even with the help of the 'march of intellect,'[1] think of arriving. I wish she would return into the civilized world, for I miss her very, very much, I assure you. To talk of *you* and old times—of those two dazzling faces I saw popped out of the hotel windows in Sackville Street— of the dance to the piper at Richmond, &c., &c. All this is delightful to remember and to talk about, and if ever 'we three meet again,' we shall have a regular *cause* of it.

Lord John Russell told me (and this, I own, was one of the reasons of my above-mentioned fruitless ejaculations) that you saw a good deal of Lord Byron during his last days in Italy, and that you mentioned some anecdotes of him (his bursting into tears as he lay on the sofa, &c.), which he (Lord John) thought might be very interestingly introduced into my life of him. He also told me that you had some verses addressed to yourself by Lord Byron, which were very pretty and graceful—in short, in every way worthy of the subject.[2]

[1] The *Oxford Dictionary* notes that 'march of intellect' or 'march of mind' was a common expression (especially in an ironical allusion) between 1827 (the date of the founding of the Society for the Diffusion of Useful Knowledge) and 1850. The quotation is found in the *Gentleman's Magazine*, xcvii (1827), ii. ii; Robert Southey, *Colloquies on the Progress and Prospects of Society* (1829), ii. 360; and Richard Froude, *Remains* (1838), i. 309.

[2] For the verses to Lady Blessington see Moore, *Life of Byron*, vi. 16 and 17.

Now, my dear Lady Blessington, if you have any thing like the same cordial remembrances of old times that I have—if ever the poet (or the piper) found favor in your ears, sit down instantly and record for me, as only a woman *can* record, every particular of your acquaintance with Byron, from first to last. You may depend upon what you write never meeting any eye but my own, and you will oblige me more than I have time at this moment to tell you.

Above all, too, do not forget the verses, which will be doubly precious, as written *by him* and *on* you.

Lord Lansdowne told me, some time ago, that he had had a letter from Lord Blessington, which gave, I was sorry to hear, but little hopes of seeing either him or you in England. My most sincere and cordial regards to him, and believe me ever, my dear Lady Blessington, faithfully yours,

Thomas Moore.

I hope to hear that you liked my last *pious* story; it has been very successful.[1]

877. *To John Wilson Croker*

Rice University

Sloperton Cottage, Devizes
Nov[r] 30th 1829

My dear Croker— Pray forward the inclosed, per Twopenny, as soon as possible, to the Printer, & let one of your Mercuries leave the letter at the Foreign Office for me, to go off tomorrow.

I find there is nothing in Walker's Bards about O'Kane,[2] but the source I expected something from is that great 'Universal Cambist', Doctor Kelly,[3] who is deeply learned in Irish Minstrelsy, and particularly I believe, in that sonorous branch of it—the bagpipes. As soon as I hear from him I shall commune with you.

Ever y[rs] truly
Thomas Moore

878. *Addressee unknown*

National Library of Ireland

Sloperton Cottage
Nov[r] 30 1829.

Sir. I know not how or what to plead in excuse of my long neglect of your kindness—though neglect it certainly was not, as your book

---

[1] Moore is probably referring to *The Epicurean* (1827).

[2] Probably Joseph Walker's *Historical Memoirs of the Irish Bards* (Dublin, 1786).

[3] Probably Joseph Kelly, brother of Michael, the composer and singer. Both of these men were 'deeply learned' in Irish lore.

lay before me every day to remind & reproach me for my delay in acknowledging it. But, in town, I never have a minute to myself, and the first use I make of my leisure here is to thank you very sincerely for your welcome present, to which I see your own pen has contributed some of the most valuable ornaments.

Your obliged & faithful sv^t

Thomas Moore

879. *To Mary Shelley*

Abinger Collection

[November 1829]

I am to sit *to-day* & shall be *trouvable* there about ½ past 12.

Y^{rs}

T. M.

880. *To Mary Shelley*

Abinger Collection

[November 1829]

Many thanks for the wine— I can answer (just now) for nothing but Saturday when you will find me at Lawrence's, but you need not bring the carriage as I should not have time for the C. House.

Yours most truly

T. M.

About ½ past 12 on Saturday.

881. *To Mary Shelley*

Abinger Collection

[November 1829]

I *did* receive your note last night, and will see you as soon as I can, though after what I told you in my note of yesterday it appears to me a *little* unreasonable that you should complain—you are the only person who does, though numbers of friends ten times your standing (you will hate, I am afraid, this prosaic word) are left equally unseen & unvisited. To Irving I mentioned 2 or 3 times your wish for us to pass an evening together with you, but he always put it off with some excuse or other.[1] I shall try & come to-day— if you were but in the *beat*— But there is no use in complaining

Y^{rs} ever

T. M.

[1] Moore and Irving were often together in November 1829 (see, for example, Russell, vi. 91). This letter was probably written at that time.

882. *To Mary Shelley*

Abinger Collection

[November 1829]

From my not having heard any thing more from Lawrence I take for granted that *tomorrow* is the day—but you shall know when I hear. If it is not tomorrow, my countenance must remain fixed as it is for some weeks as on Thursday, I think, Lord L. takes me into Wiltshire. But you shall know all, when I know, myself.

Ever y^{rs}

Ever y^rs
T. M.

883. *Addressee unknown*

N.L.S. MS. 582, no. 634

Brooks's
Friday [November 1829]

My dear Sir— I regret exceedingly that I cannot join your party tomorrow, but it is the only day I shall have to take my young Carthusian out, and I must give him some treat or other—I *did*, indeed, meditate hooking you in both for a dinner and your company afterwards to some theatre, but this your party puts out of the question. You will, however, be able perhaps to give Tom a bed, as he must be at Chapel at the Charter-House before *nine* on Sunday. I have been at home each of my two days at work till about four, so have not had time to call upon you.

Pray send the inclosed to Tom for me as soon as you can.

Yours ever
T. Moore

884. *To John Murray*

Sir John Murray

I have been scribbling all day & am too tired to write legibly.

Decr 8th 1829

My dear Sir— I have been wondering & wondering at hearing nothing of either you or the Printer—but the last marvel has been solved by the arrival only this morning of a packet of proofs sent off on the 3rd & kept therefore, I suppose, at Devizes ever since. I shall be *at* them about this, which is but a bad beginning of my country operations in the way of printing. Otherwise, however, I am getting on very well, having satisfied myself with respect to the Italian Loves, by omitting the whole of the letter about

Angelice [*sic*] (making a love the less) and transferring the long account of Margarita from the place of its date, (where it jars with our Guiccioli Romance) to an earlier period where it chimes in with his dissolute course of life, and this keeps the character of each epoch more consistently.[1]

What is all this about Mad^e Belloc? She has written me a long letter (sending *duplicates*, to guard against the dangers of privateers & storms between town & Devizes) about your taking away the sheets from her, your refusing to negociate with her &c. &c.[2] Pray let me have some inkling of what all this means, either from self or John, & believe me ever yours truly

Thomas Moore

885. *To John Murray*

Sir John Murray

Decr 10 1829

My dear Sir— Many thanks for your attention in letting me know the particulars of your transaction with our transla*trix* (*tricks* being a most apt termination both of her name & task) who whatever may be her talent for turning a version is certainly no bad hand at turning a penny. If you have any more communication with her it will be best to say that the whole matter, as far as regards France, is now placed in Mr Galignani's hands, and that he is, according to promise, (the only promise *I* ever promised to procure for her) ready to negociate with her for the translation— I mean to write to him to-day to that effect.[3] I must own I feel rather sorry now that there has been (at least, at so late a period) any attempt at an arrangement of this kind with France, as I fear it will only end in

---

[1] 'Angelici' is probably the eighteen-year-old Angelina, whom Byron met in the spring of 1819 (see *LJ*, iv. 302–3, and Marchand, *Byron*, p. 772). For the story of Margarita Cogni see *LJ*, iv. 328–36. Moore quoted part of the letter of 1 Aug. 1819, in which Byron told Murray of the Cogni affair. He altered it in places and omitted certain passages but left the essentials intact. The part concerning Margarita was removed from its context and placed in the portion of Moore's text which deals with Byron's life in 1818, about the time the liaison was formed. Moore also concealed the identity of the addressee, saying simply that 'A portrait of this handsome virago, drawn by Harlowe when at Venice, having fallen into the hands of one of Byron's friends after the death of the artist, the noble poet, on being applied to for some particulars of his heroine, wrote a long letter on the subject' (Moore, *Byron's Works*, iv. 112–21).

[2] See letters No. 869 and 885, to John Murray, 19 Oct. and 10 Dec. 1829.

[3] Louise Swanton Belloc was planning to translate Moore's biography of Byron, but the author waited for a commitment from the publisher Galignani before coming to terms with her (see Russell, vi. 95).

fuss & worry to *you* as well as to *me*. The Madame's French-Irish Dead is to be sure a notable document—[1]

One is seldom allowed to go on smoothly in this world— We yesterday morning received an account of our little Carthusian having shown symptoms of Scarletina—and this, just as we are expecting him down here for the Christmas Holidays. Mrs Moore has, in consequence, set off this morning for town, & will stay with him till he is pronounced well enough to venture on the journey.— And so goes on this world.

Yours, my dear Sir, very truly
Thomas Moore

I send you a letter from Hall,[2] in which, you will see, he again praises away in the most bare-faced manner— What I wish you particularly to look at is what he says about Lord Cochrane—

886. *To F. W. Burney*

National Library of Ireland

Sloperton Cottage, Devizes
Decr 11th 1829

My dear Sir— You must have thought me a very neglectful person in not sooner answering your letter; but I delayed in expectation of being able to get at some papers in which it struck me that there was a note or two of Burke's—not otherwise worth sending than as a proof that I had *done* my *best* for you— I find however that I was mistaken & that what I took for a note of Burke's (and which turns out *not* to be his) has been already used in my Life of Sheridan. I am very happy to hear that we are to have the Correspondence you speak of. Lord Holland, as you perhaps know, has some curious letters of Burke's, but he reserves them, I rather think, for some purpose of his own.

Yours very truly
Thomas Moore.

Lord & Lady Lansdowne are very well, and Kerry, I think, better since he came home.

[1] There is no evidence that Louise Belloc completed a book about the 'French-Irish Dead'.

[2] Probably Samuel Carter Hall, editor and writer.

887. To John Murray

Sir John Murray

Sloperton
Decr 13th 1829

My dear Sir— I have all along dreaded, as I told you in my last, that this attempt of ours (which has been like that of Swift's philosopher 'to extract sunbeams from cucumbers')[1] could end in nothing but worry & disappointment to us both. I foresaw, as you will recollect, from the first (at least from the moment I knew how little Scott got for his Napoleon)[2] that the sum we should obtain from Paris would be hardly worth taking. Still, as you were kind enough to appropriate whatever little it might be to my use, I was resolved not to incur the charge of being *above* making the most of it, and therefore (for the first time in my life I believe) set myself seriously about *bargaining*. It was of course not to be expected that Galignani would give *any thing* unless, by a previous possession of the sheets he was enabled to bring out the volume soon after its appearance in London;[3] and this I saw was your own view of the case when you permitted, and indeed advised my sending over the sheets to Captain Hall. Little as was the time left for negociation (from the late period at which you notified your intention of transferring to me these profits) even this short interval was abridged by your determination to publish the 1st Vol. immediately—so much so, that had I been left to myself at that time, I should have given up all thoughts of pursuing the thing any further. But when I found that you *still* talked of my chances of deriving something from Paris— (aware as I knew you must be that it was only by making it worth Galignani's while that we *could* have such chances)—I most assuredly could conclude nothing else than that it was your intention that the sheets then in Paris, by your permission & for that purpose, should be immediately given to Galignani. Under this impression I certainly did write to Hall desiring that they should be so given, in order that G. might be enabled (as I understood all along to be your wish) to have the work out at a reasonable time after yours, and taking my chance for whatever pittance might accrue to myself out of the concern. Being left too in utter ignorance till yesterday of your having received any communication from Galignani for me, I at the same time wrote to *him*, expressing my surprise & displeasure at his never having taken any notice of my letters

[1] *Gulliver's Travels*, part iii, chapter v, the voyage to Laputa.
[2] Sir Walter Scott, *The Life of Napoleon Buonaparte* (Edinburgh, 1827), 9 vols. Translated into French, 1827.
[3] See letter No. 885, to John Murray, 10 Dec. 1829.

& impressing upon him in the very strongest terms that (though a sum of money would of course not be unwelcome to me) my *first* & *greatest* object was that nothing should be done prematurely on his side, so as to endanger by any *possible* chance, so precious a property.

The sum he offers is, I agree with you, paltry, but not much more so than I expected—nor should I ever have appeared in the shape of [Cozzener ?] for such a trifle, but from my unwillingness to appear to make light of your very kind offer & my horror of the charge so often dinned into my ears of being unmindful of my own interests.

Pray, do whatever you think best towards repairing this false step (putting me & my hundred pounds completely out of your mind)—I inclose a *carte blanche* (as far as my consent is required) for any thing you may think proper to write to Hall—though I fear the best & only measure you now can take is to publish the volume immediately.

Hall's address is under cover to Hamilton Hamilton Esqr through the Foreign Office.

Yours in a hurry
T. M.

I shall send you the Preface & dedication tomorrow—the former will be little more than a page & I shall want but one proof of it so that you may publish, I should suppose, on Monday next. Why have the Printers sent me no proofs lately?

My little boy is come down with Mrs M. & pretty well.

888. *To Locke, Hughes, and Company*

John Rylands Library

Wyatt's
Decr 17th 1829

I shall be obliged by your sending me, by the bearer, the amount of the inclosed cheque—half in your own notes & half in Bank of England, or sovereigns.

If a stamp should be necessary for a draft (like this) at sight, have the goodness to send me one & I shall return it signed by the Post.

Yours &c
Thomas Moore.

3/5 [*illegible*]	15	
2/5	10	
4 over	4	10
Silver	8	
Stamps	2	
	£30	

889. *To John Murray*

Sir John Murray

Sloperton Cottage, Devizes
Decr 17th 1829

My dear Sir— It was this morning I was congratulating myself on having got rid of, at least, the First Vol. of our work, when, on my return from Bowood where I slept, I find your *plaguing* letter. There is no use in complaining of what's past & gone, but I can't help remembering how often I entreated your attention to those verses to Lady Jersey (which I rather doubted about, myself & were, in the first slips, too, printed in all the plenitude of their abomination) and how confidently I relied on the promise you gave me that either you or Mr Lockhart would, in the quarto sheets, look to these matters.[1] How we are to fill up the chasm I know not, nor would it be possible at this distance without access to the rejected materials of the First Vol. some of which I returned to you & others I have locked up, at my lodgings. I must therefore only run up to town for a day or two & see what I can do. We might retain surely a few *innocuous* lines out of those to Lady J. for the sake of his note to her, and it strikes me that there is a poem of his among those that I returned to you which (though I did not think it of interest enough to insert) may do in our present distress, and stand in the gap for us. I should have determined on starting tomorrow morning, but that being in the practical condition of having but a few shillings in my pocket, and too late for the Devizes Bank to-day, I must wait over tomorrow for money and (Sunday being a blank day) should but throw away a day by starting on Saturday. I shall therefore send & take a place for Sunday morning, and whatever time may be thus lost I shall make up by being on the spot.

When you came to the conclusion that the last dying words of the Volume should be consigned to a note I wish you had, at the same time, contrived for me some graceful way of announcing his departure, which certainly can *not* be done in a note. I had great hesitation in quoting those verses to Mrs Leigh at all & doubt very much whether I ought to give them the importance of closing the Volume with them.[2] However all this we can decide upon on Monday—or

---

[1] 'Condolatory Address to Sarah Countess of Jersey, on the Prince Regent's Returning Her Picture to Mrs. Mee' (Byron, *Poetry*, vii. 37 and note).

[2] Byron sent the 'Epistle to Augusta' and 'Stanzas to Augusta' to Murray in 1816, giving him permission to publish them if Mrs. Leigh should agree. She decided, after some hesitation, that the '*least objectionable* line will be *to let them be published*'. The 'Epistle' did not appear until 1830, however (see Byron, *Poetry*, iv. 54 and 57).

(if you should be at home) on Sunday evening, when I shall call
upon you for that purpose—not however till latish, as I may not
leave Calne till *nine* in the morning.

With respect to the assignment, I am ashamed to say I had
totally forgot it, but shall not fail to bring it up with me on Sunday.
It is as well that we did not proceed with it as I perceive by a note
of your son's inclosed with the draft that your intention was to
introduce a clause making over to me the foreign copyrights—
a step which in your present view of the matter you most probably
would have repented.

Pray, *pray* watch me a little better through the Second Volume
so that we may have no more of these after-claps. No later than
yesterday I expunged a passage which you told me Mr Lockhart
objected to, and I am, I assure you, always docile with those who,
I see, mean me well & fairly.

Yours very truly
Thomas Moore

As I shall stay but two whole days in town, you will have the goodness to try & accommodate whatever business you have for me to
that period. I find I omitted sending back the Proofs of the Contents
—but there was nothing, as far as I saw, to alter in it.

890. *To John Murray*

Sir John Murray

Sloperton
Thursday [postmark December 25, 1829]

My dear Sir— It has occurred to me on the way that we had better
perhaps leave out the Preface altogether—[1] I had no other object
in writing one but the point relating to myself which we have so
wisely omitted, and, as the Puff for the Second Volume the best &
only puff will be their liking the first. Think of this— *I* am all for
leaving it out—because in fact there is nothing in it.

The Coachman summons us.

Y^rs ever
T. M.

891. *To John Murray*

Sir John Murray

Decr 27th 1829

My dear Sir— As *you* seem to care nothing, one way or the other, I
think the Preface had better be out. It is but a meagre & unmeaning

---

[1] See letter No. 891, to John Murray, 27 Dec. 1829

sign hung up before (what I flatter myself will be found) a good &
well-frequented inn.

'For why you not speak, Mr Maddocks?' said the Princess of
Wales to old Joe (having got him jammed into Falstaff's buck-
basket with her at a private Theatre)— 'Because, Madam' answered Joe, bowing reverently—'I have nothing to say'. This is
exactly our case, as to Preface, and we could not do better, therefore, than imitate the Hero of the Buck-basket.[1]

I hope you have not forgot the Errata, about Lord Hartington,[2]
(vice Huntington) as well as about a full stop which Hall detected.
If you have, however, it is no great matter—a Duke & a comma are
things that can *wait*.

Yours very truly
Thomas Moore.

I forgot whether I marked Barnes's copy as one from myself—
if not, it had better be so— I write to him by this post.

892. *To John Murray*

Sir John Murray

Sloperton
Decr 29th 1829

My dear Sir— I feel inclined, like the noble subject of our labours,
to fall to *damning* every body—*except* yourself. The last words of
your note this morning seem to imply to my horrified imagination,
that the proofs which I corrected on *Wednesday night last* (the night
before I started) and which the Printer was to have called for the
next morning, have been lying in that infernal den of mine ever
since! Whether this is the Printer's fault or that of the Boeotian
boobies of my lodgings, I know not—but pray, row *some* of them,
or *all*, for fear of making a mistake. I cannot tell you how this vexes
me on your account—so much time has been lost—nor can I sufficiently admire your gentleness & good-humour (if the case *has* been
as I have stated) in not taking me to task for withholding the
revises at such a crisis. What makes me almost sure it has been so is

---

[1] The 'Preface' appeared in the first volume. In it Moore promises that the
greater part of the second volume will be composed of 'all those interesting
letters' written while Byron was in Italy, and that they 'will be found equal,
if not superior, in point of vigour, variety and liveliness, to any that have yet
adorned this branch of our literature'.

[2] The following erratum appears at the end of the 'Preface': 'Page 114,
line 3, *for* Huntingdon, read Hartington.' The line on page 114 reads, 'The
opposition muster strong here now, and Lord Huntington, the Duke of Leinster,
&c. &c. are to join us in October, so every thing will be *splendid*' (letter of
5 July 1807).

that I left at the same time a small packet of fruit sent by our little boy to Lady Donegall's [*sic*], with a request that *you* would forward it for me, and a letter to Mrs Moore this morning says that the fruit has never been sent.

You will, of course, send to my lodgings immediately, and I shall be most anxious to hear that it will not make much derangement in your plans of publication. I have been expecting every day to see us announced in the paper. This certainly makes me feel that it is a material injury, sometimes, not to be in town—but when I *am* there, nobody will let me alone. So what am I to do? [*illegible*] 'Basket' you! Not for the wealth of Ind.[1] Seriously—if the Preface is likely to be the *least* help to our Second Volume, keep it by all means,[2] and I should hope by setting them to work tomorrow, you *still* will be able to publish on Monday.

Yours very truly
Thomas Moore.

In addition to my list of Presentations, I must mention (my mother), 'Mrs Moore, 96 Abbey St Dublin' (this can go through Milliken)—Dr Brabant, Devizes (the physician who attended my poor child) and 'The Surgeon General, Dublin,' (also through Milliken).

The assignment (which I also filled up the blanks of that night before I went to bed) has I suppose been lying equally neglected.

Mind, the Preface—*in* or *not*—is wholly with yourself. It is a matter merely of taste—and one *grain* of *utility* is sufficient to weigh down the balance.

893. *To John Murray*

Sir John Murray

Bowood
Decr 31st 1829

My dear Sir—There seems a fatality to hang over every thing connected with this most disturbing cancel—and I must again entreat of you to let us take every possible precaution against the recurrence of such perplexity in our Second Volume. Up to this point I had proceeded (slowly enough, God knows) but with perfect regularity, not omitting any thing that I wished to insert nor inserting any thing that I have (as yet at least) repented.

---

[1] 'A Spanish proverb says, "He who would bring home the wealth of the Indies, must carry the wealth of the Indies with him"' (Boswell, *Life of Johnson*, iii, 283).

[2] See letter No. 891, to John Murray, 27 Dec. 1829.

I *did not*—and indeed *could* not—tell Davison that I must take the cancels with me to the country, the fact being that it was for the sole purpose of dispatching them *then* and *there* that I went to town. But I *did* tell Simmons that I must bring away four pages of the slips of Vol. 2, for the purpose of new insertions, and it was this that Davison confounded with the thrice-confounded cancels.

With respect to the revises of the cancel sheets, if *they* were not in the packet I left behind at my lodgings, this must have been wholly *my* fault—and having, late on Wednesday night, to refund into my box all the heap of papers I had rooted out to find some substitute for the cancelled matter, it is not very wonderful that I should by mistake have tossed these revises in with them. Should this have been the case, all you have to do is to print the new sheets as they are, without any further reference to me—though I re-collect two or three alterations I made which I should like to be preserved & which I shall write on a slip of paper for you to send to *Simmons*.

Yours very truly
Thomas Moore

894. *Addressee unknown*

Rice University

[*c.* 1829]

My dear Sir— I am overwhelmed with devilish letters—one of the inclosed is to the Artists Proprietors of the National Gallery who have applied to me (on account of that 'taste which flows almost exclusively from my pen') to write the Dedication of their Work to the King. I have just dispatched off another answer to an appli-cation from York for me to write the inscription on a monument they are erecting there to the seven young people who were drowned! There is no end to these applications— I inclose a note I wrote you to go by my last letter but which slipped out.

You will I know take care of little Tom in coming & returning through the streets.

Yours ever
T. M.

Thanks for the permission to draw the Bill.

895. *To Mary Shelley*

Abinger Collection

[*c.* 1829]

Thanks for your *very* nice note. I shall be engaged the greater part of to-day with the concerns of my little Tom, whom Lord Grey has been good enough to put on the foundations of the Charter-House for me—but I think towards four I shall be free for a few minutes (working at home seems now quite out of the question) to call at Hookham's and shall be most truly happy to see you.

Y^rs
T. M.

896. *To Mary Shelley*

Abinger Collection

Brooks's
Monday [postmark 1829, dim]

I have flown up to town, at a beck of the illustrious John's, and am flying back again the day after tomorrow— So *pray* don't stir out *all* tomorrow. You have, indeed, no temptation to stir out in these snow-showers, unless you want to make yourself really what Barry Cornwall calls you all—'white creatures'— I shall be delighted to have a glimpse of you.

Y^rs ever
T. M.

897. *To Mary Shelley*

Abinger Collection

[*c.* 1829]

I hope to be able to come tomorrow, but, if I shouldn't, *don't you be angry*— I shall always enjoy seeing you the more for your taking me, as all my other friends do, when *they* can & *I* can. If it wasn't for such tolerance, I never should be able to get on at all.

Yours most truly
T. M.

I have a *task* to set you, when we meet.

898. *To Mary Shelley*

Abinger Collection

[*c.* 1829]

I am so wretchedly ill with cold as to be unfit for any gay party— so that Mrs Stanhope's is hopeless for me. I shall be at Longman's (if you do not dislike coming there) till 4 o'clock, when I start for this end of the town on various errands. At all events, I must not miss seeing you.

Y^rs ever
T. M.

Neither pen, ink, sealing-wax or wafer!

899. *To Mary Shelley*

Abinger Collection

[*c.* 1829]

I shall be engaged, I fear, all day, but if you should be able to come, upon the chance, between 4 & 5, you may be sure that I shall be here, if possible.

I was tired to death yesterday, and have had but four hours of sleep to make me alive again.

Ever y^{rs}
T. M.

900. *To Mary Shelley*

Abinger Collection

[*c.* 1829]

I can neither stir *out* to-day nor let any body (even you) *in*, being all in a chaos—but I *think* I could answer for meeting you here at three.

Yours ever
T. M.

901. *To Mary Shelley*

Abinger Collection

[*c.* 1829]

Between rain & racket I have not been able to reach you— What *did* you say about to-day? I have sent to take my place in the Coach for Barnes Terrace, but this shall not interfere with any thing you may have set your mind upon. I only think—however, I have not time to say my thinking just now—therefore tell me your will & pleasure per bearer, believing me

Ever yours & truly
T. M.

902. *To Mary Shelley*

Abinger Collection

[*c.* 1829]

My poor friends in Curzon St (whom I have at last persuaded with much difficulty to receive Tom) are to perform the office of fetching from [*sic*] the C. H. tomorrow, but, if I should keep him *over* to-morrow night (and you shall know in the course of the day) he & I will come breakfast with you on Sunday morning. I don't despair, (in spite of what you say) of reaching Somerset St. to-day.

Y^{rs} ever
T. M.

903. *To Mary Shelley*

Abinger Collection

[*c.* 1829]

The inclosed was on the very point of being despatched to you when your note came. There's no use in my 'thinking' any more, therefore, at [¼ before four *deleted*]—on second (or rather 3rd) thoughts, I shall come to you at ½ past one or thereabouts, as I should like to call at Holland House on my way to Barnes, if you will let me—

Yours &c.
T. M.

4th thought.—you had better come here at *two*, as it is more in the way & will give me more time.

904. *To Mary Shelley*

Abinger Collection

Athenaeum
Thursday, 20 minutes past three [*c.* 1829]

There has been some fatal mistake between us. Taking for granted that *two* was the hour we fixed to meet at Miss Linwood's, I found myself there (from my watch being too fast) at twenty minutes *before* two & from that time continued to pace up & down those disreputable flags (to the great risk of my moral character) till a quarter past three—in a state of double distress, both at being there so fruitlessly, and not being somewhere else, where I was *due*. How has this mistake arisen? I left a card, with a little memorandum on it, at the confectioner's, to be given to a lady 'in a hackney-coach, when she should arrive'—though with very little expectation that such lady would arrive.

Tomorrow & Saturday I shall be, I fear, out of town, and therefore must endeavour to get to Kentish Town some time on Sunday.

Yrs ever
T. M.

905. *To John Murray*

Sir John Murray

Janr 1st 1830

My dear Sir—

Keep the Preface by all means.—[1] I trust I have now done with the First Volume,—at least, till the criticisms & the hole-pickings

---

[1] See letter No. 891, to John Murray, 27 Dec. 1829.

begin. I find that I *had* already seen & corrected the Cancels, so that there was nothing more to do with them. I suppose I omitted to say this, and 'hinc illae lacrumae'[1] after them. It shows that I have a pretty good memory, as all the alterations I sent yesterday had been already made in the Revise.

On Sunday I shall send a *large* batch of copy for the second Volume.

Yours most truly
Thomas Moore

You see we have lost our kind friend Lady Donegall [*sic*]—the best & kindest & most unvarying I have ever known.[2]

906. *To James Power*

Rice University

Bessy bids me remind you of some copies of your engravings which you promised her.

Jan^r 2 1830.

My dear Sir— You perceive we have lost our dear friend Lady Donegall [*sic*]—one of the truest & most unchanging, during a space of seven & twenty years, that it has ever been my lot to know.[3] I now begin to feel great alarm about my mother in this most trying weather.

Bessy wishes you to send her in *writing* the particulars about the Mants Bible,[4] as my verbal report does not satisfy her friend.

Pray, try & get me in the Arcade a pair of *carpet slippers* that will fit me. I had fixed with the man (who lives on the same side with Salter, about a dozen doors above him) to bring me a pair to Bury St. the evening I came away, but he neglected doing so. I shall send the size of my foot herewith. I hope your cough does not increase, & that you & all yours are as well as we wish you.

Ever y^{rs}
T. Moore

Bessy says you are likely to get the *carpet* slippers cheaper in the Strand—I should like them of the *darker* colour. She trusts you will find the goose good & regrets not having been able to get a turkey.

---

[1] Terence, *Andria*, I. i. 99.
[2] Lady Donegal died in the autumn of 1829.
[3] See letter No. 905, to John Murray, 1 Jan. 1830.
[4] Probably Richard Mants, *Book of Psalms, in an English Metrical Version* (1824).

907. *To John Murray*

Sir John Murray

Sloperton Cottage
Jan^r 15 1830.

My dear Sir— Mrs Moore has been expecting her copy this week past, while *I* have been keeping a sharp look-out a-head for my critics. I take for granted this additional delay has been for the purpose of waiting for the Portrait, and shall be glad to find that I am not mistaken.— On second thought, I fear that we cannot well be off sending a copy to the Aberdeen School-master (Mr David Grant) particularly as you *won't* publish his Battle & Murder-Pieces.[1]

What I now chiefly write for is to say that, as I find there have not yet been any of the sheets of the 2nd Vol. printed off, it might be as well to let me have one *more final* revision of them before that operation commences. I shall not keep them more than a single day.

Barnes's publication of the Preface has already drawn down upon me a proposal to write the Life of Petrarch.

Yours most truly
Thomas Moore

Has Irving no tidings yet from America?[2]
If there should be any very choice *praise* of us, I should like to have it—but the abuse may always stay where it is.

908. *To John Murray*

Sir John Murray

Sloperton
Jan^r 17th 1830

Thank you, my dear Sir, for your account, so far, of our Book. I certainly hope that a part, at least (I never expected the *whole*) of your sanguine anticipations with respect to it may be realized.

Miss Pigot's direction is *Southwell, Notts*— I regret very much that I did not leave a memorandum of this, as she deserved one of the *very first* copies, and it is the more awkward as her neighbour Mr Becher (to whom I take for granted you have dispatched a copy) will have received his so long before her. I have written to her by this day's post to explain the mistake & to say that you will forward the volume to her tomorrow—so pray don't forget.

---

[1] There is no evidence that Grant's manuscript was ever published.
[2] Irving was assisting Moore in the American distribution and sale of the *Life of Byron*.

Madame Guiccioli's copy Byng promised to forward for me through the Foreign Office—so pray send it under cover to him directed for the *Contessa Guiccioli, Ravenna.* Dr Glennie, who gave me information is dead, but Mrs Glennie (if you think it right) is the person to receive his copy & both this & the one for Hancock will be directed properly for you by the Longmans, who know the residences of both.

Yours very truly
Thomas Moore

909. *To John Murray*

Sir John Murray

Bowood
Jan^r 18th 1830.

My dear Sir— I wish you to take the trouble, with as little delay as possible, of forwarding a copy of the Byron to Paris for Lord Lansdowne, directed to the 'Duchesse de Cesarini.' Her address Lord L. does not know, but it may be ascertained at Madame de Bourke's, Rue du Fanbourg St. Honoré, and perhaps the best way would be to forward the Book either by Estafette (if there is any such extra-official conveyance) to the care of Madame de Bourke with the words 'to be forwarded to the Duchesse Cesarini immediately' or to get Byng (whom I shall write to) to undertake the sending it through the Foreign office by tomorrow's post. As Lord Lansdowne is very anxious that the Volume should reach Paris before any other arrives (at least to *this* lady) I shall take it as a great favour if you will look to it without any delay.

I find Lord Lansdowne's own copy has not come to him yet,— perhaps through some mistake of his Porter in town.

Yours very truly
Thomas Moore

Your best way will be to send that Volume *at once* with my note to Byng, who will be prepared for it, I think, by a letter from Lord L. himself; and if Byng is not able to manage it for us, you can then dispatch it in the ordinary way.

910. *To John Murray*

Sir John Murray

Jan^r 22nd 1830

My dear Sir— Having been busy to the last moment correcting &c. I have not time for more than to acknowledge your welcome packet of to-day & thank you most cordially for it— People are all, indeed,

(679)

very kind, and I *begin* to think myself that 'the book's a good book'—

I am getting on as fast as I can with our second Volume, and am just now dispatching the last *difficulty* I shall have to encounter before the Catastrophe—as soon as I have placed my task beyond the danger of interruption &c. &c. I shall come up to town.

You shall have a longer letter by Sunday's Post.

Yʳˢ most truly
Thomas Moore

911. *To John Murray*

Sir John Murray

I hope you sent Miss Pigot's book—as I have had no acknowledgement of it from herself.[1]

Janʳ 24ᵗʰ 1830

My dear Sir— I expected to have had some revises or proofs from the Printer, but (though there is plenty in his hands to work at, both in slip revises & copy) none has come these two days— This, coupled with the haste you expressed in your last letter, puzzles me a little. I was half inclined, indeed, to beg you to call a 'Halt' in the way of *printing* off till I can come up, as some of my qualms respecting the plagy Italian loves have returned & I should like much that you & Lockhart & myself should lay our heads together thereon. There does not seem (as far as I can learn) to have been any objection to what is said in Vol. 1 about his Newstead 'strumpets' (as he calls them page 333)[2]—and this approaches the nearest to the sort of offence that might be given by his details of the Fornarina &c. &c.—[3] It is a most puzzling case as of the *attraction* & *amusement* of this part of our 2ⁿᵈ Vol. there can be no doubt— and yet, having made so favourable an impression in the First, particularly with respect to Byron's character, one trembles at the idea of effacing or disturbing it. What say you? In about a week I shall be, I think, sufficiently *en train* to come up, and we shall then post away at the printing as fast as your devils can spur. I mean to come to Fielding's in Sackville St. where I shall be quite alone & more quiet than in Bury St.

---

[1] See letter No. 908, to John Murray, 17 Jan. 1830.

[2] 'The women are gone to their relatives, after many attempts to explain what was already too clear. However, I have quite recovered *that* also, and only wonder at my folly in excepting my own strumpets from the general corruption,— albeit a two months' weakness is better than ten years' (Moore, *Byron's Works*, ii. 118; letter to Hodgson, 16 Feb. 1812).

[3] See letter No. 884, to John Murray, 8 Dec. 1829.

Do not, I pray, say any thing about our hesitation on the subject of his Italian adventures—it would be *sure* to be misrepresented. I have received abundance of the most gratifying letters about the 1st Vol.

Ever yours most truly—
T. Moore

From Mr Irving's letter I fear there is but little to be looked for from America.[1]

912. *To Mary Shelley*

Abinger Collection

Sloperton
Jan^r 24th 1830.

You really are a most unlucky *female*—considering, too, how truly you deserve to be otherwise. It is, however, not half so bad as I thought at first,—for, in my utter ignorance (thank God) of law processes, I fancied, at the first glimpse, that it was on *you in propria persona*, that the execution was to be executed—[2] I did not answer your letter about Lawrence because though feeling our loss (the *general* loss) most sincerely, I knew I must fall far short of your emotion on the subject & therefore did not like to disappoint you. I had already, too, a little before, been deprived of one of my oldest & most real friends, who though but a simple & unpretending-minded woman had more value in my eyes than all the geniuses with whom I am acquainted.[3]

I am glad you like the Byron—but shall not answer your criticisms, for fear you should give me more of them; for you know (or at least *ought* to know) that there is nothing so fidgetting to me as these little nibbling details after the whole thing's dispatched & 'the fool's bolt shot' irrevocably. It is bad enough to run the gauntlet of the *public* criticism without having also little smug *private* ones. It is like a man being scolded by his wife at home besides being bullied abroad. I will only say that with respect to the religious part I had a very difficult part to play & in my own opinion, have so managed it that there is not a thought or judgment

---

[1] See letter No. 907, to John Murray, 15 Jan. 1830.

[2] It would be interesting to know what legal difficulties Mary was involved in at this time. There is no indication in F. L. Jones's edition of her letters, and although Grylls quotes part of this letter in his *Life of Mary Shelley* (p. 202), he carefully omits the section about 'law processes' and makes no mention of it in his own text.

[3] Sir Thomas Lawrence died on 7 Jan. 1830. The 'simple & unpretending-minded woman' was Lady Donegal, who died late in 1829.

expressed there that is not sincerely & thoroughly my own. I pro-
fess no creed in it nor do I blame any man for not having one; but
I dwell on what I think the *dangers* of being without a religion
& condemn (not half so strongly as I feel) the worse than larceny &
felony, as I consider it, of those who try to filch away the beliefs
& hopes of others.[1] In this, too, I am at least consistent, as the
letter which I told you Shelley wrote to H. Smith near ten years
ago will prove. Alluding to some expostulations of mine to Byron
on the subject, he says 'I do not agree with Moore that the Christian
Religion is an advantage (or useful, or some such phrase) to mankind.'[2]

There are, by the bye, some things on the subject (connected
with the education of Allegra) in B's letters to Hoppner, which
though important, in the world's view of such matters, to Byron,
I don't think you would like to appear. We shall, however, consult
about it.[3]

I shall stay down here as long as I can, but as *the* Murray is
impatient for the 2nd Vol. I fear I shall be obliged to come up in
a week or so. Pray take of yourself [*sic*]—keep clear of the law—
don't wet your feet—and *don't* write criticisms.

Yours most truly
T. Moore.

By all accounts, my book is doing very well—but I am (as you will
divine from the foregoing) still in a twitter about it.

---

[1] The 'religious part' of the *Life of Byron* is contained in Moore's letters to
Byron, dated 9, 19 Feb. and 16 Mar. 1822 (letters Nos. 618, 619, and 620).

[2] Moore is referring to the letter which Shelley wrote to Horace Smith on
11 Apr. 1822 (see letter No. 619, to Lord Byron, 19 Feb. 1822).

[3] On 22 Apr. 1820 Byron wrote to Hoppner expressing his disapproval of the
manner in which Allegra had been treated while she was living with Claire
Clairmont and the Shelleys. He stated his determination either to send her to
England or put her in a convent for education and continued with the following condemnation of the mode of life at the Shelley home: 'But the child shall
not quit me again to perish of starvation, and green fruit, or be taught that
there is no Deity.' Claire objected to the decision, saying that she would be
willing to 'undergo any affliction rather than her whole life should be spoilt by
a convent education'. Shelley replied to Byron's letter, agreeing with Byron's
decision to separate the mother and child, but condemning Byron's harsh tone
(see *LJ*, v. 14–15).

913. *To John Murray*

Sir John Murray

Croker's letter shall go another day— I want to show it to Lord L.

Jan^r 25th 1830

My dear Sir.

I return you Croker's letter which is most gratifying— Praise from such a head as there shows itself (if one even knew nothing else of what it could do) would be a sufficient reward. I have had an equally flattering tribute from Lord Holland & your *favourite*, Matthews,[1] is in the skies. Altogether, between public & private opinions my mind is somewhat *easy*—though still prepared for the reaction to all this which, in some shape or other (I never knew it to fail) will come.

What I write now for is to prevent you from thinking, in consequence of my yesterday's letter, that it is either my wish or intention to throw overboard *all* his Italian loves. I rather think, indeed, that the suppression of some of the details in his long letter about the Fornarina will be sufficient for our purpose.[2]

You simply *must* let me see, in some way or other, his original letters to you. You cannot conceive how clumsily the castrator of the copy has cut & slashed away every thing. I found this in looking over the originals of 1819, where there were many things of the greatest importance to me in the story of the Guiccioli most needlessly & indeed unaccountably cut out. You shall stand over me if you please while I read them, and act flugleman—'eyes right— eyes left' whenever I come to the objectionables, but see them I ought and—I was going to say, *must*.[3] No time for more.

Ever y^{rs}

T. Moore

---

[1] Probably the Reverend Arthur Matthews, son of John Matthews and brother of Byron's friends Charles Skinner and Henry Matthews. At the time Moore published his biography Arthur was Prebendary of Hereford and the only surviving member of the family.

[2] See letter No. 884, to John Murray, 8 Dec. 1829.

[3] Murray decided to leave the Byron papers which were in his possession as a legacy to his children. See letter No. 715, to John Cam Hobhouse, 28 Feb. 1827.

914. *To John Murray*

Sir John Murray

Bowood
Jan^r 28th 1830

My dear Sir— As I have no idea how you are going on in the way of sale I merely write *par précaution* to say that you must let me know in time when you see any prospect of a Second Edition as there are two or three little things I should like to retract— I see the verses he wrote in Miss Chaworth's book were not his own, but some Lady Tuite's—this is curious, if fact![1]

I had no less than eight letters yesterday morning all 'about it, Goddess, and about it'—[2] The fidget it keeps me in (praise though it be) almost incapacitates me for my Second Volume.

Mr Irving's financial report from America is a good deal below the mark I expected—but you need not say so to him, as he did his best for me.[3] Tell him, however, I shall acknowledge his letter tomorrow.

I have queries for you in abundance.

Ever Y^rs
T. Moore

915. *To John Murray*

Sir John Murray

[January 1830]

I was in hopes the packet you sent me last night was the missing fragment.[4] Pray, look for it. I should be in despair about it but that you *must* have the original. My copy must have got among some of the MS returned from the Printer & been thrown into the fire as done with. But it is among the most valuable parts of his letters— therefore pray search, or let me have the original letters of 1817 18 & 19 to look through myself as soon as possible.

Y^rs
T. M.

I do not think you are likely to get much by either the French or American market.

[1] See letter No. 922, to Lady Tuite, 1 Mar. 1830, and Moore, *Byron's Works*, i. 85 n., 2nd edition.
[2] *The Dunciad*, iv. 252.
[3] See letter No. 907, to John Murray, 15 Jan. 1830.
[4] See letter No. 893, to John Murray, 31 Dec. 1829.

916. *To Mary Shelley*

Abinger Collection

Brooks's
Feb^r 5. 1830

I was very sorry for having written you that cross letter,[1] but if it is any consolation to you to know that I am always crossest to those I like best, there is nothing more true. I am more busy now than ever, and, in order to escape visitors, am only nominally at Bury St.— However, to *you* I rather think I shall reveal the *Real Presence*—that is, if you promise *not* to criticise—though, on second thoughts, you *may* now, as I at last feel myself out of danger, and can stand it.

As soon after Sunday as possible I shall *appear* to you.

Yours ever
T. M.

917. *To Mary Shelley*

Abinger Collection

31. Sackville St.
Tuesday Ev^n [postmark February 10, 1830]

I sallied out to-day for the first time in broad day-light & thought to have reached you—but the gravitation was all in the opposite direction, city-ward. I however live in hopes. Only think, I have not been able to see even my dear little Tom yet!

You will be surprized at *one* result of my book. —Lady Byron is very much pleased with it![2]

Ever yours.
T. M.

918. *To John Murray*

Sir John Murray

Sackville St
Feb^r 16th 1830

My dear Sir— I send back the letter I brought away— I am at a standstill for those of 1820 and 21. If you really don't like me to have them, the best way will be for you or John to take the

---

[1] Probably letter No. 912, to Mary Shelley, 24 Jan. 1830.
[2] Lady Byron refused to give Moore any information for his biography and, after the appearance of the first volume, wrote a pamphlet entitled 'Remarks occasioned by Mr. Moore's Notices of Lord Byron's Life', in which she declared that 'Mr. Moore has promulgated his own impressions of private events in which I was most nearly concerned, as if he possesses a competent knowledge of the subject' (quoted from Jones, *The Harp that Once—*, p. 273).

collation & correction of this part into your hands—as somebody *must* do it, & that speedily.[1]

My old ill-luck about money-matters sticks to me. I have often said that if the rewards of heaven were to be in *cash*, I should have but little hope. Irving told me yesterday that, by some mistake committed in the exportation of the sheets after I left town, an hiatus of 120 pages were [*sic*] discovered by the American publishers, who had just written to him in dismay about it, but were of course only relieved from their difficulty by the arrival of the published Book—if even that reached them, as soon as it did others.

I found exactly what I wanted in the Richardson you sent me— My little boy is much better, at least *was* when I saw him yesterday.

Yours very truly
Thomas Moore.

919. *To John Murray*

Sir John Murray

Feb. 23. 1830*

My dear Sir—

'Last time of asking'—*am* I to have the originals or no?[2]

I wrote you a note from Davison's yesterday, which I trust has quickened your mandates to the Printer.

Pray, let me know Finden's address, that I may go & see what *he* is about.

Yours most truly
T. Moore

920. *To Sir Cuthbert Sharp*

N.L.S. MS. 1810, f. 118

31 Sackville St.
Febr 25th 1830

Mr Moore presents his best compliments to Sir Cuthbert Sharp, and returns him very sincere thanks both for the interesting letter of Lord Byron's which he has had the goodness to furnish him with and the flattering terms in which the communication has been conveyed.

---

[1] See letter No. 715, to John Cam Hobhouse, 28 Feb. 1827, and No. 913, to John Murray, 25 Jan. 1830.

[2] See letter No. 913, to John Murray, 25 Jan. 1830. A note on the manuscript reads, 'sent the originals'.

921. *To Mary Shelley*

Abinger Collection

Thursday [postmark February 26, 1830]

I am now, in *my* turn, a little alarmed at not hearing from you—particularly in answer to my last, where I informed you of my unsuccessful search after you at the Opera. Can it be possible that you *were* in that last box I looked into, & out of which a gentleman jumped to make room for me? The women all looked towards me, but *none* spoke a word, and the gentleman resumed his seat—all which convinced me *you* were not of the party. I even waited a few minutes after the door was shut, lest through my short-sightedness I might possibly have been mistaken—but no signs of life were given, and I immediately left the Opera-House.

Do write me a line, as I know nothing would give me more pain than your being offended with me.

I am just about to give my poor little fellow an airing for the *first* time— I have been in sad anxiety about him & continually at the C. H.

Yours ever
T. M.

922. *To Lady Tuite*

Trinity College, Dublin

Brooks's
March 1st 1830.

Dear Lady Tuite— As I have not time, at the moment, to explain the reasons of my delay in answering your letter, I shall content myself with asking your pardon for the apparent neglect, and saying how happy I feel at such an agreeable opportunity of renewing my old acquaintance with your Ladyship. I had been already informed, through the medium of the newspapers, of the mistake made in assigning your pretty verses to Lord Byron, and I had, indeed, more than once suspected, from their style being so much more formed than any thing he had yet written at that early age, that they might possibly not be his. It is curious enough, too, that he should have allowed Miss Chaworth to consider him as the author of them (which she certainly did) when he transcribed them in her book— You may depend upon my restoring them to their rightful owner in the second Edition of my work, and with every thanks for the kindness with which you express yourself towards me, I am, my dear Lady Tuite,[1]

Very truly yours
Thomas Moore

[1] In the first edition of the *Life of Byron* Moore published the poem beginning

923. *Addressee unknown*

Rice University

Sloperton Cottage
March 7th 1830

My dear Sir— Had I the advantage of being more intimately known to you I might have hoped, perhaps, to persuade you into forgiving me for the very shameful delay that has intervened in my answer to your letter—but, as it is, I can only beg pardon & trust to your general good-nature. At the time, indeed, when I heard from you, I was overwhelmed with a heap of correspondence, and the best proof you could have of my not intending any neglect to *you*, is that I was myself most selfishly interested in answering you as soon as possible, in order to avail myself of your kind offer to communicate some materials to my Work, which offer (if I have not disqualified myself for it by my silence) I now beg to say I shall be most happy & thankful to accept.

There was nothing in the blank marked by asterisks that related to your brother, and I grieve much (from what I hear of the annoyance you felt at other parts of the extract) that I had not strewed those stars (much as they are complained of) more plentifully over that page— But I had no clue in this case to guide me, nor was even aware that the gentleman to whom I had been introduced by Charles Sheridan was in any degree connected with the interesting friend of Lord Byron. I had so much, therefore, in other places to leave out that would, I *knew*, be essentially hurtful to living people, that I was sometimes tempted to retain what was only *doubtful*— particularly when, as in this case, it added so much to the true interest of the work. Upon the whole I am happy to say that the instances have been *very* few in which I have left any thing calculated to wound feelings that were at all to be respected, and I much regret that this little annoyance to the surviving family of your brother should be among the number.[1]

I shall be delighted to hear that you forgive me all my

'Oh Memory, torture me no more', attributing it to Byron. In the second edition he added the following note, correcting his mistake: 'These stanzas, I have since found, are not Lord Byron's, but the production of Lady Tuite, and are contained in a volume published by her Ladyship in the year 1795' (Moore, *Byron's Works*, i. 85 n).

[1] There is no clue in this letter or in Moore's diary as to the identity of the addressee. Many pages in Moore's *Life of Byron* are marked with asterisks, in order to conceal the names of people Byron mentioned in his journal. See, for example, the entry for 17 and 18 Dec. 1813 (Moore, *Byron's Works*, ii. 304).

delinquencies, and trusting to your kindness for supplying me with the papers you speak of towards our Second Edition, I am, my dear
Sir, very truly yours
Thomas Moore

924. *To Mary Shelley*

Abinger Collection

Bury St
April 3rd 1830

It comes to *my* turn now to complain of not being minded &c. &c.—I have not been able to ascertain any thing about Lady C. Rawdon, but am almost sure she is in Paris and *not*, as far as I can learn, expected here. I meant fully to have joined you at your friends on Thursday, but having dined at H. House, I was forced to wait for a cast in a cabriolet, & got so drenched therein, the wind driving the rain right in our faces, that I was inadmissible any where but in bed.

What a trick Dr Bowring has played me after all! I could have *sworn* (such are my innocent notions of such persons) that I was for evermore safe from abuse in his hands—and then asking me so kindly to his party! Bad as my 'aristocratic' acquaintants are, the worst of them would hardly have put a man in the situation of accepting their hospitality, while they had a horse-pistol in the house ready to fire after him down stairs. This is not the way to make me regret the sphere of society I have chosen for myself.[1]

Campbell too!—my revenge *ought* to be, perhaps, to restore all I have suppressed about him—'cankered carle' &c. &c.—but I won't—he has done fine things and I forgive him.[2]

[1] Sir John Bowring, editor of the *Westminster Review*, furnished copies of Byron's correspondence for Moore's use in the biography (see letter No. 779, to Mary Shelley, 15 Apr. 1828). The letters were published in *Byron's Works*, vi, *passim*. The *Life of Byron* was reviewed in the *Westminster*, xii. 269–304. The reviewer accused Moore of having scraped an acquaintance with Byron, of hiding behind the curtains of the *Edinburgh Review*, of being unable to produce a figure of speech that would stand analysis, and called attention to the 'farcical nature' of his politics. He concluded by saying that it was impossible for Moore to do justice either to the dead or to the living.

[2] In the *New Monthly Magazine*, xxviii. 377–82, Thomas Campbell published a letter which he had received from Lady Byron and informed the public that she was a much injured woman. He declared on the one hand that Moore was his friend, and on the other that he was thankful that he (Campbell) did not have to answer for 'the tact of Moore's conduct in this affair', i.e. in such matters as presenting Byron's inconsistencies on the subject of his wife and of showing 'gallant indifference' toward Lady Byron's acquittal. Moore's biography was reviewed in the *New Monthly*, xxx. 94–95. The reviewer expressed his admiration for Byron's genius, his friendship for Moore,

Do let me hear something of you, as I have called twice unsuccessfully—the only double call I have made, except in Sackville St.
where they have *all* been ill— Shall we meet at the Speaker's on
Saturday next?— I am going down to Cashiobury with Ld Essex
on Tuesday, but shall be up for that day.

Y^rs ever
T. Moore

925. *To John Murray*

Sir John Murray

Send the inclosed scraps to Simmons & bid him reserve space for
them according to their date July 1822—with space also for two
or three lines of introduction.

Sloperton Cottage, Devizes
April 14th 1830

My dear Sir— I am much disappointed & inconvenienced by not
having received a copy of *Count Gamba's narrative*, having left a
note for you with Sir H. Bunbury's servant the day that I started
to say that I wanted the book by next day's coach— The fellow,
I suppose, never took the note, but *pray* let me have a copy immediately— Send me also at the same time all the sheets of M^rs
Kennedy's book printed since the last you gave me.[1] You still, I
trust, persevere in your intention of keeping her volume back till
ours is ready.

Yours very truly
Thomas Moore

I send back the sheets you gave me with your Deles—to almost all
of which I have attended. Every thing that is either *tiresome* or
too *personal* I am most willing to get rid of—but those parts

and concluded with an open letter from Campbell to the author, which said in
part, 'Ah! my dear Moore, if we had him back again, how easily could we settle
these matters!'

The second volume of the *Life* was reviewed in the *New Monthly*, xxxi.
159–64. This article, which was evidently not by Campbell, accused Moore of
presenting the worst side of Byron's nature by 'dwelling upon his most vicious
actions . . . and assuming that pseudo-tone of apology, which only revolts the
sense of right it affects to blind. . . '.

On 1 Apr. 1830 (Russell, vi. 113) Moore recorded in his diary that Lord
Melbourne showed him a letter from Lady Byron, in which she expressed
regret at Campbell's 'injudiciousness', although it was 'good-naturedly' meant.
For further details see Ethyl C. Mayne, *The Life and Letters of Lady Noel
Byron* (London, 1929), pp. 319 ff. See also letter No. 1242, to Edward Moxon,
12 Oct. 1845, for Moore's allusion to Campbell's 'over-vehement' attack.

[1] Pietro Gamba, *A Narrative of Lord Byron's Last Journey to Greece* (London,
1825). James Kennedy, *Conversations on Religion with Lord Byron* (London,
1830).

relating to his liaison with Mad^e Guiccioli (a circumstance not to be blinked) which tend rather to his vindication than otherwise (as is the case with some of those you have marked in these sheets) I see no reason whatever for omitting. Indeed, I think you could hardly have read some of the passages you have marked with pencil, for by showing how much all the relatives of the lady were *for* Byron & *against* the husband these passages are as good as a speech for Defendant in a Crim-Con case, and would certainly lessen the amount of Damages. Stick to what you think surplusage & dulness—don't spare that. I am myself too superstitiously fond of every line of his to do justice in this way—therefore cut away. I have added, you see, to Lockhart's 'quite absurd'.[1]

Recollect that I am to have sheets 393 to 408 which I left with you back again.

[*Note on the address side of the letter:*]
Pray don't detain the sheets, sent herewith from the Press— I have myself kept them too long.

926. *To The Countess of Blessington*

Lady Blessington, *Memoirs*, ii. 272

Sloperton Cottage, Devizes
April 15th, 1830.

My Dear Lady Blessington,—I received a most kind letter from you the other day, through our pretty *spirituelle* young friend in Palace Yard; so kind that, hurried as I am with all sorts of distractions, I can not resist the impulse of dispatching a hasty line to thank you for it.

I am also glad of the opportunity to tell you that *it was* all *owing* to a mistake (or rather a difficulty in the way of business) that you did not receive from the author himself one of the first copies of 'The Life of Byron.'

It is too long a story for a man in a hurry to relate, but you will understand enough when I tell you that the dispensation of the presentation copies was a joint concern between Hurry and me,

---

[1] Moore is evidently referring to some passages in the biography which Murray had deleted. Thus 'Lockhart's "quite absurd"' refers to a comment made by Lockhart on Murray's unaccountable cancellations.

Byron's letters and journals for the period confirm Moore's statement that her relatives sided with Byron rather than with the Count. See, for example, *Byron's Works*, v. 43, where he recorded Teresa's own words about the first meeting and subsequent friendship of Byron and her brother. Moore made use of much material which Teresa sent him, and apparently little of the liaison was 'blinked'.

and that, having by mistake exceeded my number, I was unwilling to embarrass my account by going further.

But mind, whatever copy you may have *read* me in, the one that you must go to *sleep upon* (when inclined for a doze) must be a portable octavo presented by myself.

You deserve ten times more than this, not only for our old friendship, but for the use you have been to the said volume, by the very interesting and (in the present state of the patrimonial question) apropos contributions you have furnished.

I was sorry, some time ago, to see that the pretty verses to you had found their way into some French periodicals, and from them into ours; but I trust most sincerely that the same accident will not occur to the lines about Lady Byron.

They gave me some hope at the speaker's that we might soon see you in England. Is there any chance?

> Ever yours most truly,
> Thomas Moore.

927. *To Mary Shelley*

Abinger Collection

> Athenaeum
> April 29th [1830]

I came up on Sunday, and am off again without seeing you—only for 2 or 3 days though. On my arrival I found your notes, which were then, alas (though far from weary 'in state') unprofitable. I am now running down to an Inn somewhere for quiet, which is an impossible thing in town, at this season—for *me*, at *any* season.[1] I heard of your well-being & well-*looking* (which in a woman includes the former) from Mrs *Parleuse* yesterday—

> Ever y^rs
> [*unsigned*]

928. *To Lord Dudley*[2]

University of Edinburgh

> May 10th 1830.

My dear Lord Dudley

I send you at last Movris's verses, which for a muse of eighty five or six are at least envious. I should be glad indeed if any one

---

[1] On 29 Apr. 1830, Moore noted in his diary that he was going to Richmond 'to the Castle' for a little quiet (Russell, vi. 116).

[2] This is a copy of a letter from Moore to Lord Dudley, which the latter forwarded to a friend with the following explanation: a short time before the letter was written, Sir William Scott (Lord Stowell) and 'old Charles Movrice (the Captain)' were at dinner together. Both men were about eighty-five or

would ensure to me, the being able, in thirty five years hence to write even a thirty fifth part as well. The present name of the fair Molly is I understand Clarke (Lady Clarke)[1]

Your's [sic] very truly
Thomas Moore.

eighty-six years of age. During the course of their conversation Movrice told of his youthful love for a young lady, a 'recollection which had shed warmth and cheerfulness over his whole life'. As their discussion continued it became apparent that Scott had also been in love with the young lady, whose name was Molly Dacre. Neither had married the girl, who had become the wife of a man in her native county. Upon later inquiry they found that she was also still living, after a lapse of about seventy years. This discovery drew from Movrice the verses which are quoted in note No. 1 below.

Lord Dudley concluded his account of the dinner meeting in the following manner:

> It was Moore that told me the story one day as we were dining with poor Lord & Lady Charlemont.— I expressed a strong wish to have them, and as he is the best natured, most obliging as well as the cleverest creature in the world, he transcribed them himself and gave them to me. You may copy— but I must have Moore's—which I prize very much. I could not refuse you the pleasure of reading them in his beautiful handwriting—

D.—

[1] The following poem, in the same hand as the letter and explanatory note, is attached to the letter:

By Captain Movrice

Though years have spread around my head
    The sober veil of Reason
To close in night sweet Fancy's light
    My heart rejects as treason.
A spark there his [sic] still fann'd by sighs
    Ordain'd by Beauty's Maker;
And fir'd by fate, burns yet, tho' late,
    For lovely Molly Dacre.

Oh while I miss the days of bliss
    I pass'd in raptur'd gazing,
The dream impress'd still charms my breast
    Which Fancy's ever raising.
Tho' much I meet in life thats [sic] sweet
    My soul can ne'er forsake her,
And all I feel still bears the seal
    Of lovely Molly Dacre.

I've often thought the happy lot
    Of health and spirits lent me
Is deem'd as due to faith so true
    And thus by Fate is sent me.
While here lives she, there's life for me
    But when high Heaven shall take her
A like last breath I'll ask of death
    To follow Molly Dacre.—

929. *Addressee unknown*

Rice University

Brooks's
June 14th 1830

I got a frank from Lord Durham, in order to write to you yesterday, but was whisked away to the House of Commons, to hear Brougham on the Niggers[1] & so lost my frank— Now, too, this must go merely as a remembrance, which is all I have time to give it as. But I *do* remember you, be assured, very cordially. I called at your house after you had taken flight & was disappointed.

My Book is finished,[2] but Murray is in the doubts about it— fearing that if he throws it into this torrent of Dissolution, it will be dissolved also,— I am just now dispatching the last proofs & on Saturday shall be off home.

Yours most truly
T. Moore

930. *To Mary Shelley*

Abinger Collection

June 17th [postmark June 18, 1830]

I should have written to you yesterday but that I thought (vain thought) to reach you. You do not say for how long you are to be absent, or where— if at the Cottage I shall hope to be able to propose myself to the little nest of beauties some day next week. That is, if Mrs Moore changes her mind about coming up.

I was by no means tired of your party, but as nobody (out of your own fairy circle) seemed to care much about hearing me, I thought I might as well be off—particularly, as I wished to look in at Lady Jersey's before it was too late.

Ever yrs
T. M.

[1] On 13 July 1830, Brougham delivered a speech on 'Slavery in the Colonies' in the House of Commons and moved that 'this House resolve, at the earliest practicable period of the next Session, to take into its serious consideration the state of the Slaves in the Colonies of Great Britain in order to the mitigation and final abolition of their Slavery, and more especially in order to the Amendment of the Administration of Justice within the same'. The motion was seconded by Lord Morpeth but failed by a vote of 56–27. (Hansard, *Parliamentary Debates*, xxv. 1171–1214.)

[2] The biography of Byron.

931. *Addressee unknown*

Rice University

[June 1830]

I *do* go out of town tomorrow—not to return till Wednesday evening, so that our Exhibition together (Live & Liveness [*sic*]) cannot be till afterwards. Monday the 7ᵗʰ of June will do very well.

Yours ever
T. M.

I *again* fell in love with Mʳˢ N.¹ last night at Almack's. Only think of her young sister being [*sic*] to *be* a Duchess— The blood of old Brinsley! his three grand-daughters Peeresses.

932. *To John Murray*

Sir John Murray

Sloperton
August 6ᵗʰ 1830

My dear Sir— As I think it possible you may be on the wing, with all the rest of the world, out of town, and, taking for granted that you have finally resolved upon deferring our publication till November, I must no longer defer saying one or two things respecting it— particularly as I shall be myself flying off, in about a week, for Ireland. In the first place—what shall I do about the Edinburgh Review? As it would be a great object to have Jeffrey to undertake the article, and this is about the time he could best spare leisure for it, it might be worth considering how *soon* you would think it prudent to entrust him with a copy for that purpose.² I should like much, too, to have asked you some questions respecting the intentions of the Quarterly—but this, delicate a point as it would be even in conversation, is still more so in a letter & I shall therefore no further enter upon it.³

¹ Caroline Elizabeth Sarah Norton, *née* Sheridan, the wife of George Chapple Norton. One of her sisters was Helen Selina, who married Commander Blackwood, Baron Dufferin and Clandeboye in the peerage of Ireland. The other was Jane Georgiana, the wife of Edward Adolphus Seymour, later twelfth Duke of Somerset. They were the daughters of Sheridan's son Thomas. Jane married Seymour on 10 June 1830, and this letter was evidently written either shortly before or after the wedding.

² Macaulay reviewed Moore's *Life of Byron* in the *Edinburgh Review*, liii (June 1831), 544–72.

³ Lockhart reviewed the biography in the *Quarterly Review*, xliv (January 1831), 168–226. Since Murray was the publisher of the *Quarterly*, Moore was reluctant to ask him about the intentions of the reviewer.

There is also another circumstance which gives me no small uneasiness—and that is, the scrape I have brought you into by accepting the Bill of £500 for me, when (according to your new arrangement) the funds from America, with which I had hoped to have covered the greater part of the sum, cannot possibly arrive till some months after it has become due. I say this, taking for granted that you have not thought it prudent (as it certainly would *not* have been) to send any more sheets out *there* till we approach the period of publication *here;* and, of course, till they have received the whole book, I cannot possibly expect to be paid. What is to be done about this? It would grieve me very much if you were to suffer any inconvenience by it, and yet, so wholly have I been, this year past, anticipating all my own sources of supply, that I could as soon think of placing old Charles Capet[1] upon his seat again, as of helping you with a single Item of the sum.

I meant, when I began this letter, to take the opportunity of doing—what I could not do so well, face to face, when we parted,—and that is expressing to you my warm acknowledgements for the kindness, courtesy, and tractableness which I have so invariably experienced from you during the whole of a task, trying enough to the temper & courage of us both, and surrounded both by risk & difficulty; but throughout which, it is delightful to me to think & to be able to say (as I do to every body) that in no one instance have I found you otherwise than considerate, good-tempered, liberal, and (what includes in it, or *ought* to include, every thing else) perfectly gentleman-like. This I meant to say more at large—but perhaps could not have expressed more had I talked till doomsday, and, at all events, cannot *now* add more than that I am, ever

Most truly yours
Thomas Moore.

My best regards to Mrs Murray & your family

933. *To C. Fitzsimon*

Lieut.-Col. M. O'C. Fitz-Simon

Septr 6 1830

Dear Sir— I ought to have written to you long before this, but I am scarcely left a single minute to myself. It would be, indeed, difficult for me to find a moment for the task you have so flatteringly required of me, even were there no other reasons against my undertaking it. But it appears to me that an address is by no means

---

[1] Charles IV, King of France, 1322–8. He was notorious for oppressive taxation and heavy fines.

the best mode of proceeding. The usual method by Resolutions has not only the advantage of being the common course, but affords an excuse and a topic for speakers which (in England at least where the orators are apt to be rather shy) is of no inconsiderable convenience. An address, too, would I rather fear bring back to some peoples' minds—what is but too apt to recur already—the example of the first French Revolution and the addresses from corresponding Societies &c. &c. with which it was hailed. In addition to these general objections to such a mode of proceeding, I should also, on my own part, object to being made the mouth-piece of a meeting where, if I expressed myself as strongly as I feel, there would be many to whom I should appear to have gone too far, while, on the contrary, if I endeavoured to assume a moderate tone, I should both do injustice to my own sentiments & disappoint those of others.

I shall be very glad to hear by return of post what arrangements you may have made and what success has attended your applications, being quite sure you will agree with me that unless we can assemble a very *good* meeting, we had better have none at all.[1]

With best compliments to Mrs Fitzsimon, I am, Dear Sir,

Y^rs Truly

Thomas Moore

934. *To Sir Charles Morgan*

Lady Morgan, *Memoirs* (Leipzig, 1863), iii. 90

September 20th 1830

My dear Morgan,

I need not say to you how much I feel both the honour and kindness of the invitation which you propose to me, but the fact is, my mind is now wholly set upon getting away as soon and as safely as these equinoctial breezes will let me. Having the nervous task of transporting women and children, at this time of the year, either by Bristol or Liverpool, I am preparing to take advantage of the very first appearance of more settled weather, and, therefore, could not form any engagement that would be likely to interfere with this purpose, nor, indeed, enjoy it at all as I ought, if I *did* form it. It is my intention, however, to be here again before the end of next spring, and then (if my kind friends of the Dawson Street Club continue still in the same disposition towards me) it will give me the most sincere pleasure to accept their invitation. I write in

---

[1] 'Heard from Mr. Fitzsimon (O'Connell's son-in-law), on the subject of the French meeting. Wants me to write an address for them to the French nation, but declined' (Russell, vi. 135).

a hurry, but you will, I know, have the kindness to convey all this to them in a way that will best do justice to my feelings, and believe me,

Ever, my dear Morgan,
most truly yours,
Thomas Moore.

935. *To John Murray III*

Sir John Murray

Sloperton
October 5, 1830

My dear John— I returned from Ireland but the day before yesterday, after such an enthusiastic reception from the warm-hearted Paddies as has sent me home sublimated to the seventh Heaven of self-satisfaction— I found your packet lying here in a dormant state since the beginning of September—had you written I should have received your letter in Dublin. I have, however, lost no time in complying with your request, having dispatched a letter to Miss Pigot, entreating not only a loan of the first Quarto Edition (which I know she has not herself but may procure from Mʳ Becher)¹ but also her permission for me to give you those MS. poems which she placed at my disposal but of which I have published only some fragments. As soon as I receive her answer I shall let you know.

You ask me what I think of Galt's Byron ?— What do *you* think, I should like to know, of 'alarming Intelligence' ?— The gentleman is, I suspect, damaged for life.²

Best remembrances to all chez vous & believe me truly yours
Thomas Moore

936. *To John Murray III*

Sir John Murray

October 10ᵗʰ 1830*

Dear John— I think the portrait very good, indeed, and so you may tell Mʳ Fendin [*sic*]— The likeness is even an improvement on the picture³— I wish you to send for your father's criticism a proof

¹ Although Byron's *Fugitive Pieces* (1806) was withdrawn from circulation at the suggestion of the Reverend John Thomas Becher, and nearly every copy burned by Byron himself, the copy which he presented to the clergyman was preserved (see the bibliographical note in the facsimile edition of *Fugitive Pieces*, New York, 1933). Moore is evidently referring to this volume.

² John Galt, *Life of Byron* (London, 1830). In the preface to the second volume of his biography Moore quoted a letter from Barry, Byron's banker in Genoa, which disproved Galt's 'insinuations, calling into question the disinterestedness of the lady whose fate was connected with that of Lord Byron during his latter years' (Moore, *Byron's Works*, I. xiv).

³ W. Finden's engraving of the portrait of Moore by Lawrence was published in the *Illustrations of the Works of Byron* (1836).

of the Preface which I now forward to Davison— It was quite necessary to account for what, at first blush, I find startles every body—namely, that Lord Byron should address letters upon matters so little connected with literature, to his publisher. It was also my wish to enhance the value of the letters we give by showing that he wrote but little (which is a fact) to any one else. These two points I think I have gained & without saying any thing, I should hope, on the *first*, that your father will dislike. It is a constant remark (which neither you nor he, of course, are likely to hear) 'How strange that a nobleman should write such letters to his bookseller!' —and I have given what I think the true as well as most polite solution of it.[1]

Ever y^{rs}
T. Moore

The framed print will be very welcome.

937. *To Sir John Doyle, Bart.*

Huntington Library

Sloperton Cottage, Devizes
October 15 1830

My dear Sir John— I am about to ask of you (as an old & kind friend) a very great favour; and it was my hope that I should have been able, after my late visit to Ireland, to run up to town & ask it of you face to face—the most agreeable way of managing such matters, whether with man or woman. Circumstances, however (*reduced* circumstances, they may be called, from the expenditure of my Irish trip) force me to remain quiet at home for some time, and I must therefore trust my petition to the hasty & unsatisfactory medium of a letter. Some papers, —indeed, a large mass, —relative to poor Lord Edward Fitzgerald have been lately put into my hands by different members of his family, and it appears to me that a sufficient time has now elapsed since his death to take away any political objection there might have been hitherto to paying some tribute to his memory.[2] Lady Campbell, Ogilvie, De Roos are all, to their utmost assisting me. Now, as I know you served with Lord Edward in America, it would be doing me the most essential service if you would rally together all your recollections of that very interesting period of his life and let me have, as soon as you can *possibly* manage it, the result. As it may not only put you in possession of the points on which I most immediately want to be informed, but

---

[1] See letter No. 939, to John Murray, 27 Oct. 1830.
[2] Moore's *Life and Death of Lord Edward Fitzgerald* appeared in 1831.

may in some degree *give* a *jog* to your memory, I shall set down a list of Queries, to which your answers (with whatever overflowings the spring of memory, once let loose, may furnish) will be most precious & acceptable and most gratefully received.

Did not Lord Edward first arrive at Charleston as a Lieutenant in one of those three Regiments from Ireland, in June 1781, which by joining Lord Rawdon enabled him to releive [*sic*] the garrison of Ninety-Six? Of those three Regiments, as far as I can learn, the 19th & 3rd formed a part— In *which* of these two Regiments was Lord Edward? and who commanded his Regiment? Had Lord Edward first been in the 3rd & then changed into the 19th?

It is stated in some accounts that Colonel Doyle joined Lord Rawdon on his way to Ninety-Six, with the troops that had been left at Monk's Corner—is this correct? (I should like much to have a convenient niche for the commemoration of an old & gallant friend, such as I suspect this same Colonel Doyle, from *Monk's Corner*, to be.)

Was it not in some of the skirmishes connected with this movement of Lord Rawdon that Lord Edward was wounded? —as he mentions in one of his letters being ill of a wound at Charleston.— It is said somewhere that 'an unsuccessful attempt was made by the Americans upon the 19th Regt. at Monk's Corner'—was it in this affair Lord Edward was wounded?[1]

I have only left myself time to repeat that whatever communications you can find leisure to favour me with on these & all other points connected with Lord Edward, will most truly oblige

Yours, my dear Sir John, cordially & faithfully

Thomas Moore.

938. *To John Murray III*

Sir John Murray

October 21st 1830

My dear John— It has just occurred to me that you may *possibly* (though I don't think it likely) have forgot to dispatch the remaining part of the 2nd Volume to America. At all events, it is as well to remind you about it, as I look to the receipt of the monies therefrom accruing to enable your father to meet the Bill I have drawn upon him, falling due in December next.

Miss Pigot has given her permission, and you shall have the unpublished verses of Byron, which will give a novelty to your Edition. I must rout them up from among my papers as soon as

---

[1] Fitzgerald was wounded at Eutaw Springs.

possible, & any that I know may have lost the copies of [*sic*] she promises to re-transcribe for me. Mr Becher will not trust the copy of B^s first Edition out of his hands, but has promised to collate it with the subsequent ones & send you copies of any that the latter do not contain.[1]

Y^{rs} very truly
Thomas Moore

939. *To John Murray*

Sir John Murray

Sloperton
October 27th 1830

My dear Sir— I am delighted to find you have all got well & safe back again. What you say about your claims on Byron's friendship & consideration (in *every way*) is perfectly just, and if I did not fear that it would look like a eulogy got up between us I should most willingly incorporate the whole of it with our Preface—but I also think that the view I have taken of Byron's *leading* motive for such a voluminous correspondence with you is no less true & just, & ought, in *some manner or other*, be noticed, not only as illustrative of his character, but as meeting, in limine, the objection which I *know* will be started on the grounds mentioned in my letter to John.—[2] It has been a remark made to me over & over—not by foolish fine people, but by sensible men of the world, and I thought it was but doing justice to your own manly good sense to, at least, put it before you in the shape I have done & let yourself decide as to whether it should thus meet the world. Having done so, however, I am now quite ready to alter, omit or modify whatever part of the Preface you object to, and, if you will send me down a proof with a line drawn through such passages as you dislike I will endeavour to retain what may appear to me of importance towards *impressing* on the Public the value of his letters to you, and at the same time get rid of all that you think derogatory to the nature of your inter-course with him.

---

[1] See letter No. 935, to John Murray III, 5 Oct. 1830.

[2] See letter No. 936, to John Murray III, 10 Oct. 1830. In the preface to the second edition of his *Life of Byron*, Moore suggested that the reason for Byron's large correspondence with Murray was that he wanted to keep his name before the English public, and knowing that Murray's drawing-room was a centre of literary society, he transmitted to the publisher whatever he wanted to circulate in society. Moore also noted that 'It was on this presumption that he but rarely, as we shall find him more than once stating, corresponded with any others of his friends at home' (Moore, *Byron's Works*, I. xiii).

I shall not be able to come to London for a long time. My building & my Irish journey together, coming at the end of my long unproductive labour on the Second Volume, have again left me—as ruined as you found me—et c'est beaucoup dire.

My best remembrances to Mrs Murray

Ever y^rs
T. Moore

940. *To James Power*

Huntington Library

Sloperton
October 27 1830

My dear Sir— I send you some more of the Summer Fete, which will still spread out to two or three hundred lines more—all good for your letter-press book.[1] I inclose also Lady Headfort's letter which you will return to me some time or other. You had already seen the mention of poor Stevenson's paralytic attack in the newspapers.

It will not be necessary for you to make provision for the Bill which (having found your stray letter) I see will come due the 26th of November—as I had already apprized the Longmans of my intention to renew it—but I shall perhaps have to ask you to let me *increase* the sum, as my resources are at present in a most deplorable state.

I have been passing three days with the Duchess of Kent & our little future Queen at Erle-State Park & we had a great deal of music. The Duchess sang some of my Melodies with me better than I ever heard them performed—I promised to send her some of the songs of mine she most liked, and I should be glad if you would get them bound together (not *too* expensively) for me to present to her. They are as follows.

Meeting of the Ships—Indian Boat—The Evening Gun—Say, What shall be our sport— (Can you detach this from the Nationals ?) —Keep your tears for me—The Watchman—I love but thee— (beginning 'If after all'—) Reason & Folly & Beauty.[2]

She has promised me copies of some very pretty German things she sang.

Yours very truly
Thomas Moore

I should be glad to have my hamper of wine down as soon as you conveniently can send it.

[1] *Poetry*, pp. 266–77.
[2] *Poetry*, pp. 306, 301, 308, 242, 317, 307, 318, and 236.

Bessy will be obliged to you to buy her a slop-bason, and another bason a size smaller, of the same pattern as the egg-cup inclosed— and they can come with some things which are to be sent to your house for me.

FOR
   Mr Power

The letter to Sir James Cockbourn must be put in to-morrow—it need not be paid for.—nor Mrs Branigan's either

941. *To Samuel Rogers*

H. O. Mackey[1]

[October 1830]

My dear Rogers— I send you (as being more worthy of it) a present of fruit I found on my table yesterday evening—together with the note that accompanied it, which is, at least, as good as the fruit and which, after having read it, you may put it in the fire.

   I am hard at work prefacing, and have promised to go to an early dinner at Mathew's to see his gallery etc—but if you will call here, when you come, I shall have a glimpse of you.

Yours etc.
T. Moore

Samuel Rogers Esq.

942. *To Lord John Russell*

Early Correspondence of Lord John Russell, i. 315

S. Wolverton
November 24, 1830.

My dear Lord John,—It is a long, long time since we have taken any notice of each other, and, if you did not know me *not* to be a Courtier, my choosing *this* moment to put you in mind of me, when you are just become a man in office, might look somewhat suspicious.[2] But, if ever I did expect any thing from any body, in the way of Place, that dream is long gone by, and it is far more with fear for them than with hopes for myself that I contemplate the accession of so many friends to office. For myself, my 'crust of bread and liberty' is all I have or want, and while a Whig Administration is not likely to butter the former for me, it may but too much embarrass the latter by making me silent (for friendship's sake) when a good

---

[1] Transcript provided by Dr. H. O. Mackey.
[2] In November 1830 Russell was appointed Paymaster-General.

grumble would be a relief to me. I shall, however, try hard not to abuse you, though that you'll all want it before long I have very little doubt. The serious fact is, that we are come to a pass where nobody can do any good. The country is going too fast *down* and people's minds too fast *up* for ever a Whig Ministry to reconcile these two opposite movements, and though you may delay the crash you cannot prevent it. At all events, 'them's my sentiments,' as some of our Irish orators say.

I wish you would tell me (though that's another calamity of one's friends being *in*, that you all get so official and diplomatic) what were the real facts connected with Lord Lansdowne's demur to office—if he really *did* demur, which I have no other authority for than rumour, backed by the circumstance of his having taken a situation so avowedly invaliding himself for active service.[1]

God bless you, my dear Lord John—there are few in this world that wish you more heartily every earthly blessing than I do, and the only place I desire of you or ever shall is the little corner in that honest heart of yours, which is, I believe, now mine, and which (though I treat it so like a *sinecure* by never writing to you) you cannot doubt that I value.

Mrs. Moore (who luckily does not trouble herself so much with the reverse of the medal as I do) is all delight at your official elevation.

Ever yours most truly,
Thomas Moore.

943. *To John Murray*

Sir John Murray

Devizes
Dec[r] 1st 1830

My dear Sir— I came in here immediately on receiving your letter, —fearful, I own, that I should be but little successful with my bankers, who have always made it a *favour* to discount for me *at all* at three months, and unfortunately my fears have been (as their letter to you will show) but too much realized— I should have written to you on the subject before, but, having no means myself of meeting the Bill I was in hopes that the interval between your paying it & the arrival of the money from America would be so short as to render your taking it up a matter of no great inconvenience— All I can offer now is that you should draw upon *me* for the sum at as long a date as you can possibly allow me, and I shall on your sending me down the Bill accept it.

---

[1] Lansdowne was appointed President of the Council.

As there are things in the Preface I think it important to preserve, pray send me down as soon as possible a proof of it, and I shall omit *all* the parts relating to yourself.

Yours very truly
Thomas Moore

From what I can understand from the bankers they are just now selling exchequer Bills at a *loss* to meet their own exigencies— This of course, is *private*.

944. *To John Murray*

Sir John Murray

Sloperton Cottage
Decr 3rd 1830

My dear Sir— I thought to have heard to-day how you meant to manage about the Bill—but take for granted you have written to Devizes.[1] One thing I forgot to mention in my last which is that, from the *first*, my bankers knew it was as a matter of accommodation to me, and not for any debt, that you allowed me to draw for this sum. Indeed, Locke, who is an intimate friend of mine has all along known every thing connected with the transaction— I think it right to tell you this, as you might otherwise feel uncomfortable at the idea of their supposing that you were in any way bound by *business* to take up this Bill. I grieve, I assure you, to be the cause of the least inconvenience to you.

Yours ever
Th^{os} Moore

I shall expect a proof of the Preface—all that I want to keep may be thrown under the head of *errata*.

945. *To the Marquess of Lansdowne*

Bowood

Sloperton
Decr 7th 1830

My dear Lord Lansdowne— I did not like to pester you with letters, knowing how much you must have had to do & to think of, & besides not liking to say the ungenerous truth that I was most sorry the turn of affairs had made it necessary for you & my other friends to come into office.[2] You know well what has long been my

---

[1] See letter No. 943, to John Murray 1 Dec. 1830.
[2] The Whigs came into office in the autumn of 1830.

opinion of the state of the country and have often smiled at my predictions of the fatal crisis I thought them hurrying to. The only difference I find in the event from what I expected is that the crash is coming at somewhat a quicker rate than I counted upon, and that there is an unlucky concurrence of circumstances from all quarters to accelerate it. So far, too, from being a *Radical*, just now, I think that the Reform which the whole country is so blindly urging you to (and which must, at all hazards, come) is nothing more or less than the 'commencement de la fin', and that whatever transient satisfaction or calm it may produce will be but what the poet describes

> ad praeceps immane ruinae
> Laevior en facies fit properantis aquae

(the original, by the bye, of 'The Torrent's smoothness ere it dash below' in Campbell).[1]

As to my own poor poetical politics they are the same, God help them, as they have been ever since I can remember them. At the time of our Catholic triumph,[2] I thought their task, like that of the 'tricking Ariel' was done & that I should have no more occasion

---

[1] The trouble to which Moore refers arose in the rural areas of Kent in the autumn of 1830 and rapidly spread to Sussex, Hampshire, and Wiltshire. Farmers, attempting to cut expenses, hired Irish labour and began using more farm machinery. The English workers, fearing total unemployment, sought to drive out the Irish and sabotaged machinery (see Elie Halévy, *History of the English People in the Nineteenth Century*, iii. 7). Such widespread disorders inevitably raised the question of 'reform', which was of primary importance on the 1830–1 agenda for Parliament. The first Reform Bill was introduced by Lord John Russell in 1831 and passed in 1832. It deprived fifty-six English boroughs (the 'rotten boroughs') with less than 2,000 inhabitants each of all representation and took one or more seats from thirty others with a population of less than 4,000. These seats went to larger unrepresented towns. In this redistribution Ireland gained five new representatives and Scotland eight. Suffrage was extended to any householder who paid a yearly rental of £10 in boroughs or who owned rental property. In counties all leaseholders voted who could meet the £10 rental qualification. Sixty year tenants-at-will who paid £50 yearly could also vote.

Moore recorded his attitude toward the Reform Bill in his diary for 6 May 1831 (Russell, vi. 191), noting that he had given his views on the question to two lords and in March had written a letter to Lord Lansdowne, setting forth his ideas. In a note to this passage in the diary, Russell remarked that 'There must be some mistake here, as the plan was opened on the 1st of March' (Russell, vi. 192 n.). The mistake was Moore's, since his letter was written on 7 Dec. 1830, rather than the following March.

The lines from Campbell are:

> But mortal pleasure, what in sooth art thou?
> The torrent's smoothness ere it dash below.

[2] The Catholic Emancipation Bill passed the House of Commons on 30 Mar., the House of Lords on 10 Apr., and became law on 13 Apr. 1829.

for them. These late events, however, in the world have affected me, as they have other people, and have given a new shake to the bottle which has brought up all the Irish spirit (or sediment, if you please) again into ferment. The author of the Green Flag & Captain Rock would prove himself to have been but a firebrand of the moment *then* if he did not go on burning a little *now*. The union I always detested the very thought of, and though I resent most deeply the introduction of the question now, & under auspices that would disgrace a far better cause, I never could bring myself so far to sanction the principle, origin or mode of carrying that measure as to oppose myself to any steps taken for its repeal.[1]

Never was there, I believe, before such an open avowal of heterodoxy made by a poor penniless poet to a great statesman in office, —but if it does but little credit to him who makes the confession it is at least honourable to the liberality and tolerance of him who will, I know, good-humouredly receive it.

I suspect that rogue Corry is one of those who have been taking away my fair fame in this way—which was very ungrateful of him, as I actually forced him up to town to look for a place for himself in the scramble, & would have been most heartily rejoiced had he got it.

I had some thoughts at first of going to town for the winter, not liking to encounter the 'sovereignty of the people' in the disagreeable shape it has assumed down here—but the measures taken have, I think, produced a subsidence of the mischief & the landlords & parsons must only see that it does not return.[2]

It is possible I may run up to town on Thursday or Friday for two or three days (at the utmost) to put the first half of my 'Life & Death of Lord E. F.' in the hands of the printer. I am keeping it as cool as the subject will let me.

Yours, my dear * Lord Lansdowne

most truly

Thos Moore

*You'd say I was indeed turned Radical if I had left this as it was, by mistake, written at first.

[1] On 29 Nov. 1830 the *Morning Chronicle* reported that a Mr. Clarke of Waterford attended the Council of the Birmingham Political Union and asked them to co-operate with the cause of repealing the Act of Union of 1800. The question was referred to a committee, which rejected the appeal. The Act gave the Irish thirty-two members in the House of Lords and one hundred in the House of Commons, allowed Ireland free trade, provided for the continuance of the Anglican Church in Ireland, and abolished the Irish Parliament. Moore objected to the measure because it did not provide for Catholic emancipation.

[2] The 'measures taken' were severe indeed. In December a 'special commission' was given to a number of justices, empowering them to try summarily

946. *To John Murray*

Sir John Murray

Sloperton
Decr 8 1830

My dear Sir— Finding, by enquiring of Simmons, that you had not, so late as yesterday, sent my directions about the Preface, it occurs to me that my request of a proof of it, for the purpose of making the necessary omissions, may be the cause of embarrassment & delay to you. I therefore write to say that I most freely give up the Preface altogether, retaining only the Errata (in their *present* state) which are quite indispensable & which Simmons will see to having properly placed.[1]

Yours very truly
Thomas Moore.

947. *To John Murray*

Sir John Murray

Sloperton Cottage
Decr 12th 1830

My dear Sir— Your long silence on this transaction made me begin to hope—I know not what. Here's the Bill, however, accepted, though I tremble at the prospect. If the American money should fail, what's to become of me? I trust nothing has been omitted in the way of transmission of sheets to diminish my chance of it.[2] I mean to run up to town tomorrow, chiefly for the purpose of seeing Irving on the subject, and shall be at 19 Bury St.—

Yours truly
Thomas Moore

948. *Addressee unknown*

Rice University

Sloperton
Decr 12th 1830

My dear Sir— I have but time to acknowledge the receipt of your letter (taking advantage of a frank of Lord F. Gower's) and to say that when I return from London for which place I am on the wing,

cases of people accused of violence, and death sentences began to be issued. In spite of the fact that the sentences were usually commuted, three persons were actually executed and 457 were transported. The riots ceased (see Halévy, iii. 15).

[1] See letter No. 939, to John Murray, 27 Oct. 1830.
[2] See letters Nos. 943 and 944, to John Murray, 1 and 3 Dec. 1830.

I shall have the pleasure of answering you. You find me again deep dipt in Printer's ink, as my mission to town is to put the MS. of a new work ('Life & Death of Lord Fitzgerald') to press—but this I shall soon despatch & then hope to be at your service.

Ever most truly yours
Thomas Moore

949. *To John Murray*

Sir John Murray

Decr 19th 1830

My dear Sir. Little as I am versed in bill-work, it struck me that I ought to have made this payable to some 'local habitation';[1] but as you had merely bid me put my name on it, I ventured no farther. I now return it in proper form. It was odd enough that on the night of Werner I went to the Theatre merely to see 'Turning the Tables', without having an idea that there had been even an intention of acting Byron's tragedy, and arrived in time for the 5th act. The applause at the end was most gratifyingly enthusiastic, and, from what I saw of the acting, struck me as almost entirely arising from a warm feeling for the *author*—nothing could be more cordial.[2]

I hope you have got a list of my *Presentees*—but, if not, let your son apprize me in time & I shall furnish the best I can from memory. I have heard nothing of Lady B^s publication, nor do I think it probable.

Four Cabinet Ministers did not quite reconcile me to the loss of your dinner on Friday.

Ever yours most truly
Thomas Moore

I had written the 'Payable &c' before I saw your pencilling of the right place for it—but I trust the bunglement doesn't matter.

950. *To Lady Morgan*

National Library of Ireland

Sloperton Cottage
December 22, 1830

My dear Lady Morgan— As you seemed to think it better that I should commune *direct* with the Publishers, and I had a prospect of being shortly in town, when I could deliver my answer in person,

---

[1] *Midsummer Night's Dream*, v. i. 17.
[2] Although *Werner* was produced at the Park Theatre in New York in 1826, it was not put on at Drury Lane until 15 Dec. 1830 (see Byron, *Poetry*, v. 324).

I deferred writing to either you or them till that opportunity should occur. I have now seen your Messrs—at least, one of them—as very grave, respectable bibliopolist as I should wish to meet with, and have given him my answer (as I feared, all along, I should) in the *negative*. I was glad, however, to see that he had not much set his heart upon the plan, and I shall hope that neither have *you* been very desirous of it, as I hate to refuse any thing that *any body* (how much, therefore, such a luminous body as yourself) wishes me to do. The fact is, it would not be worth a publisher's while to give me such a sum as would *alone* make it worth *my* while to put myself so much out of my way. I was once offered at the rate of £100 a month to conduct the Times for a certain period, and at another time had a proposal from Constable to edit the Edinburgh Review at £1000 a year—but neither tempted me.[1] Talking of the Times, I have no conception who was the *author* of that malignant attack upon you, but meant to have asked the Editor, had I seen him when I was in town.[2] That great Machine & I have long parted company,—their politics under the Duke of Wellington (as I took care to tell them) being every thing that I most detested. I shall be always glad, however, when they are in the ways of orthodoxy (as they seem to be just now) to put a helping hand to the lever—for such it is of the most massy kind.

Mrs Moore begs to be most kindly remembered to you & Sir Charles, who is, I trust, by this time quite himself again.

Ever yours most truly
Thomas Moore

People express a little alarm about my 'Life & Death of Lord Edward', and I get hints from all sides that it would be prudent to defer its publication—but I shall not mind them.

---

[1] This letter was published in *Lady Morgan's Memoirs: Autobiography, Diaries and Correspondence* [edited by W. H. Dixon] (London, 1862), ii. 316–17. There is a curious discrepancy in the two versions, however. Where the original reads 'and at another time had a proposal from Constable to edit the Edinburgh Review at £1000 a year', the printed version reads 'and at another time had a proposal from Croker to edit the *Quarterly Review*, at a thousand pounds a year. . .'. The printed text also gives 'massive' for 'massy' in the last line of the first paragraph, and 'publishing' for 'publication' in the postscript. Except for these differences the texts are identical. For Moore's account of the offer see Russell, iv. 89.

[2] The review of Lady Morgan's *France in 1829–30*, which appeared in *The Times* for 15 Nov. 1830, p. 5, was unfavourable throughout, maintaining that the book was primarily concerned with her Ladyship's own '"volitions," "sensations," "opinions" and "organizations,"' rather than with France.

951. *To John Murray*

Sir John Murray

Decr 31st 1830

My dear Sir— I must lose no time in thanking you, in Mrs Moore's name for the beautifully framed print you have sent her. It comes most seasonably to take its place beside some others we have just hung up—(among the rest Jeffrey) though it will put them all out of countenance by the better taste of its frame.

Barnes has, I see, at last, put [in] a little costive paragraph which is almost word for word what I said in my letter to him on the subject—so that it did not cost him much trouble. He will, however, I dare say, do something better for us. Mr Hoppner's letters (I rejoice to hear of his appointment) shall be sent up in a day or two,[1] together with a few scraps of yours which have turned up since I sent back your papers.

Barry's address is— 'C. Barry, Banker, Genoa'. I don't know how I came to omit him before. It would be as well to inclose Mad^e Guiccioli's Second Vol. *with* his, inclosing a note to say that Mr Moore requested he would have the goodness to forward it to her.

Yours very very truly
Thomas Moore

I must get you some time or other down here to see how well the Print looks.

952. *To John Murray*

Sir John Murray

Monday Night* [1830, *not in Moore's hand*]

My dear Sir.

Unless you send me either Frelings [*sic*] answer about the packet or the packet itself tomorrow morning I shall be obliged to *shell out* the [*illegible*] to the Postman when he comes, which will be highly incommodious

Y^{rs} ever
T. Moore

---

[1] Moore was returning material which Hoppner had loaned him for his *Life of Byron.*

953. *Addressee unknown*

Sloperton Cottage
Jan^r 13th 1831.

Dear Sir— I have but just time to avail myself of a cover to town & return you my best thanks for your kind & flattering letter. I trust the next time I come to London I may be luckier in my attempts to reach your part of the town.

Yours very truly
Thomas Moore.

954. *To John Murray*

Devizes
Jan^r 31st 1831

My dear Sir—

Pray, have the goodness to forward the inclosed, as soon as possible, to Irving—it is about the American monies which are just now to me of the most vital importance—(as my friends the Jacobins say of the Liberty of the Press) 'like the air I breathe—*without them I die.*'

I hope you are as well pleased with the success of the 2nd Volume as I am— Though I fight off *printed* critiques, I can't keep out *written ones*, and every day's post brings me tributes, both from friends & strangers, which are not a little gratifying. I am also, I must say, very well satisfied with the article in your Quarterly— it is evidently *meant* well towards all the parties concerned and the author (whoever he may be) is as generous towards myself as his nature would admit of. In short, I feel about it as Dogberry did about the gift of beauty i.e. 'give God thanks and make no boast of it.'[1] And in this too I imitate the piety of my Reviewer, whose 'Let us pray' at the end is worth any money in these wicked days.[2]

I see you are going to be furieusement Tory, and to die in the last ditch of ultra-ism. Perhaps you are right—as the man said to Jupiter, 'your turn may come again'—but I don't think it very likely.

Pray remember me very kindly to Mrs Murray and your very nice daughters & believe me most truly

Yours
Thomas Moore

[1] *Much Ado about Nothing*, III. iii. 19.
[2] Moore's *Life of Byron* was reviewed in the *Quarterly Review*, xliv (1831), 168–226. At the close the writer quoted Jeremy Taylor's nightly prayer for himself and his friends, and 'for God's merciful deliverance and preservation'.

955. *To John Murray*

Sir John Murray

Sloperton Cottage
Feb^r 6th 1831

My dear Sir— I was as much astounded & puzzled as yourself to think what could induce my friends of Printing-House Square to admit such an article against us, till I recollected the attack upon Barnes in your last Quarterly, making him out as the most profligate of God's editors. This, at once, solved the whole matter to me, and I must say his revenge has been most spitefully ingenious.[1] To notice directly your attack upon him would have shown that he winced, but a damaging shot at your Seventy Four, the Byron, was a piece of vengeance that came just apropos and which even his friendship for me (Printing-House Square friendship) was not able to resist. Never you mind, however,—these little hitches on the *stocks*, at launching, were to be expected, but once fairly out at sea, your gallant vessel is sure of a *trade*-wind to posterity. A man of *all time* like Byron has nothing to fear from the *Times* of yesterday.

I have so little to alter (having done my best at it) that it will not be necessary to send me an inter-leaved copy—but if you have any damaged or *returned* copy (Sir Roger Gresley's, for instance) you can let me have it for the purpose, and say, at the same time, what omissions or alterations you yourself wish to have made in either volume.

I am glad you don't patronize the article upon us in the Quarterly —it is done in a poor spirit— I shall look at the list of Places you send tomorrow. It is provoking but I found, only yesterday, the copy of Byron's verses to the Oak, which you ought to have had for his Juvenile Poems. I shall send it, at all costs.

Yours very truly
Thomas Moore

---

[1] On Wednesday, 2 Feb. 1831, *The Times* published a review of the *Life of Byron*. The reviewer objected primarily to the fact that Moore chose to reproduce Byron's correspondence, since there are, he maintained, few men whose reputations would not suffer under such circumstances.

The attack on Barnes to which Moore alludes occurred in an article entitled 'Moral and Political State of the British Empire', *Quarterly Review*, xliv (1831), 295–6. The writer criticized *The Times* for its editorial policy concerning the war with France and concluded with this denunciation: 'such were the sentiments expressed, and such the advice given, by the most influential, though, at the same time, the most notoriously profligate of the London newspapers, and the most impudently inconsistent in every thing, except in malice and mischief.' See also Russell, vi. 167.

956. *To W. M. Robinson*[1]

American Art Association, Sale Catalogue, 6 December 1928

Feby. 9ᵗʰ 1831

Your letter, which had been delayed some time at Mʳ Murray's, has just reached me. I fear you will not find the decision of your wager a very easy matter, as Lord Byron, at different periods of his life, pronounced his name differently, and therefore may be said to have adopted both the modes of pronunciation to which I take for granted you allude. During all the first part of my acquaintance with him he called himself Bȳron, with the y long, but it was, I believe, at the time of his marriage, that he changed it to Bўron, with a short y, and in this manner I rather think he pronounced his name ever after—though, singularly enough, he taught some of his Italian friends, to whom this latter mode would have been so much more convenient, to call him according to his first manner of pronunciation Bȳron.

I cannot sufficiently thank you for the very kind and flattering manner in which you have addressed me. Such language is gratifying from any quarter, but from America—a country which I have long learned to value as I ought—it is, I assure you, peculiarly welcome.

957. *To Arthur O'Connor*

B. Y. McPeake

Sloperton Cottage, Devizes
March 10ᵗʰ 1831.

Private

Sir— For the liberty which I thus take in writing to you, without any previous introduction, I shall not attempt to apologize, feeling assured that the nature of the subject on which I address you will, of itself, sufficiently account and atone for such intrusion. It had been my wish, indeed, long since, to call your attention to the request I am now about to make; but, doubtful how far you might like to have your privacy broken in upon or your attention again called to events & scenes with some of which no very agreeable thoughts must be associated, I forebore (notwithstanding the interest I myself felt in opening such a communication) to intrude upon a retirement which so many circumstances combine to render sacred.

Having seen, however, in a late Irish paper, a letter with your

---

[1] Address: W. M. Robinson / William and Mary College / Williamsburg.

signature, which shows that your interest about the affairs of your country remains unabated by either time or sufferings, I feel emboldened to resume the intention which I had abandoned, and to state briefly the object on which it has been so long my wish to address you.

To come at once to the point— I am now far advanced, as the English newspapers may have told you, in an account of the Life and Death of your friend Lord Edward Fitzgerald. The particular circumstances (besides the interest I have always felt in his story) that have induced me at this moment, to undertake such a work, I have not at present time to detail. It may be sufficient towards the purpose of satisfying you with respect to the qualifications I bring to the task to state that, by the kindness of some members of his Lordship's family I have been furnished with papers & letters, both of his own & of other persons, throwing light on all the most interesting circumstances of his life and death.[1]

Now, the question is can you, without inconvenience, or violence to your own feelings, communicate any materials towards the object of my work? As I mean rarely to give the names of my authorities, the source of any information you may favour me with shall be kept sacredly secret, and with respect to any papers you may be disposed to entrust to me, though I must allowed [sic] my own discretion as to whether I shall make use of them at all, you may depend on my not making such use of them as will give you any reason to regret your confidence in me.

The work has been some time in the Press, and is now, I am sorry to say very nearly printed. If you do not therefore answer this letter with a promptness which I feel I have no right whatever to ask of you, any communication you may be inclined to favour me with will come too late for me to avail myself of it. I shall, however, suspend the operations of the Press till I hear from you, & trusting that, at all events, you will forgive both the liberty I have taken in addressing you and the abrupt & hurried terms in which my application, I fear, is couched, I have the honour to be, Sir,

Your humble & faithful servant
Thomas Moore

In order to give you some idea of the points on which your information would be of service to me, I shall mention a difficulty, with respect to yourself, which has, within this day or two, occurred to me, and on which, at least, you will perhaps have the kindness to satisfy me in your answer. It is generally understood that you

[1] In April 1830 Henry de Ros gave Moore some family papers which threw light on the capture and death of Lord Edward Fitzgerald.

accompanied Lord Edward when he went to concert with Hoche the plan of invasion in 1796—but, in apparent contradiction to this, I find the following statements in your published answers before the Secret Committee:—

Q. 'When did you become a United Irishman?'
A. 'About *November 1796*.
Q. 'When was it agreed to accept the offer of assistance from France?'
A. 'I *understood* it was accepted at a meeting of the Executive in summer 1796. I was *apprized* of the offer and acceptance by my brother members of the Executive *after* I became a member of it, and before the arrival of the French in Bantry Bay'.[1]

I shall take it as a very great favour, indeed, if you will as soon as possible, set me right upon this material point, and if you will also at the same time say at what period you think Lord Edward himself became a United Irishman.

Any packet you may wish to send me, if directed under cover to Messrs Longman & Co. Paternoster Row, London, will reach me.

958. *To Arthur O'Connor*

B. Y. McPeake

Sloperton Cottage, Devizes
March 21st 1831.

Dear Sir— Your letter (for the promptness & courtesy of which I beg you to accept my best thanks) only shows how important it would have been to me to have had the aid of your information, somewhat earlier in my task.[2] Unluckily, many of the points on which I should have wished to consult you are such as could be only come at satisfactorily through the medium of conversation, some, on account, of the delicacy & confidential nature of their bearings, others, as being mere anecdote; and therefore always difficult to give otherwise than orally. Of this latter kind, for instance, I should like much to have heard your own account of the scene at the Curragh when Lord Edward was rode after by the dragoon officers, in consequence of the green handkerchief he wore,

[1] Fitzgerald and O'Connor went to France in 1796 in an attempt to negotiate for a French invasion of Ireland. The invading army was to be under Hoche. The expedition of 1796 failed; the French lost a ship on the rocks in their own harbour; and after they had finally arrived in Bantry Bay (the place chosen for a landing), they did nothing until it was too late and a storm had swept them out to sea.

[2] See letter No. 957, to Arthur O'Connor, 10 Mar. 1831.

and which I have given, as well as I could make it out, from the various versions that are afloat. His habits of life too, while at the Lodge of Kildare (though much of this comes out most amiably in his letters) could have been far better presented by you than by any one I have had access to. As it is, I will just hastily put down a few points, merely to set your memory going, and if you will but (as hastily & without any regard whatever to style) scribble down all that occurs to you connected with them, I cannot tell you how truly I shall feel obliged to you.

1. At what period he became *actually* connected with the United Irishmen?— This question, I rather think, I troubled you with in my last. *I* make it about the beginning of 1796.

What are the particulars of Lord Edward's interview with a French Agent in London, in 1797, thus stated by one of the Secret Committees. 'A conference was held in the same summer (1797) in London between Lord Edward Fitzgerald & a French agent who came from Hamburgh, in which further arrangements were made for the intended invasion.'

How far did Lord Edward *personally* assist in the military training of the people? did he attend their night meetings frequently? and by what other military persons (as far as this question can be answered, without breach of confidence) was he assisted in his plans for disciplining the force of the Union?

This is all I have time to inflict upon you now, in the way of queries, and from your good-nature in answering my last so promptly, I venture to look to the same kindness now. When I mentioned that you should direct to Longman's, it was under the hope that you might possibly have some letters of Lord E^d or some Memorandums of your own relative to those transactions which you would do me the honour to entrust to me, and which would come most safely, I thought, in a packet to that House—but your *letters* will reach me more quickly by being directed to me here. Believe me

Your obliged & faithful servant
Thomas Moore

One of the delicate points which I should have put to you in conversation, and which I shall here, in perfect confidence hint at (leaving to yourself whether you will even notice it in your answer) is with regard to the degree of knowledge which the *opposition* in England and Ireland had of the plans & objects of the United Irish leaders. I ought to add that any wish I have to ascertain this point arises much more from a desire to satisfy my own mind on the subject than from any intention of availing myself of the facts—either on this occasion, or any other; and, indeed, on second thoughts

I feel that I ought hardly have put the question to you—but I have not time to withdraw it, and so—let it take its chance.[1]

959. *To Mary Shelley*

Abinger Collection

Sloperton
March 25th 1831

You are a great deal more amiable to me than I deserve,—at least, judging by the outward & visible signs of desert, which you are, however, far too spiritual a person to do, and which I, of all people, am most interested in your *not* doing. I am a sad fellow, that's the truth of it, but I *know* you will forgive me. By your saying nothing about it I conclude you did not know of my short transit through London some three or four weeks since, in my way from Ireland whither I had been called in a hurry by an alarm of my mother's illness— Indeed, I but little expected to find her alive on my arrival. She had however rallied most wonderfully & is now going on very well. I staid in Dublin five days, on one of which I dined with Lady Morgan (who got up a very good show of beauties for me at a short notice) and on another with Lord Anglesey. I was obliged to come back by London, on account of some papers I wanted to see about, & having caught cold on the way by night-travelling was 'sans eyes, sans voice, sans every thing' during the three days I staid.[2] One attempt I *did* make to try if I had eyes enough to find my way to Somerset St.—but I found that Friendship was as blind as love, & was obliged to turn back.

Such is 'the story of my wandering life'—at least wandering for that fortnight of it. When I can again come to town I know not— but think, possibly, about the middle of April, when I hope to find you in all your best good looks & good-humour.

Ever yours most truly
Thomas Moore

---

[1] Moore's reluctance to put this question is understandable. A statement from O'Connor asserting that the Opposition was aware of the invasion plans would be tantamount to an accusation of treason.

[2] For Moore's detailed record of his journey to Dublin see Russell, vi. 168–77. On 17 Feb. 1831 Lady Morgan noted in her diary (*Memoirs*, ii. 321): 'I had a little dinner got up in a hurry for Moore, yesterday; it was got up thus. I threw up my windows, and asked the inmates of the cabs and carriages of my friends as they passed the windows, and sent out some penny porters, and lighted up my rooms.' Moore dined with Lord Anglesey on 18 Feb.
The papers which Moore returned to see turned out to be 'all on the subject of the attainder, and not very interesting' (Russell, vi. 177).
For the quotation see *As you Like It*, ii. vii. 166.

I know nothing for a long time that has given me so much pleasure as your saying that you were not dissatisfied with what I had written about Shelley. Horace Smith, in writing (very kindly) to me about it, talks of my 'courage in doing justice, though *not full* justice to the &c. &c. '— To be sure not—how *could* I do full justice to a man whom I knew but through others?— Mind & *don't you* say any thing more on this subject, lest you should spoil the pleasure you gave me.

960. *To Arthur O'Connor*

B. Y. McPeake

Sloperton Cottage
April 15. 1831

My dear Sir— I inclose you the result of my first application, and sincerely regret that it is not more favourable— I mean, however, to be in town in the course of the following week, and shall then try some other publishers with, I hope, more success.[1]

The last lines of the letter allude to my own progress through the Press, which has been delayed by various causes much longer than I expected. As soon as the book is out I shall have the pleasure of sending you a copy, & I shall take it very kind of you if you will mark whatever is wrong in it that I may, in a future edition, avail myself of your corrections.

Yours in great haste
T. Moore

961. *To Colonel Houlton*

B.M. Add. MS. 27425A, f. 7

April 19th 1831

My dear Houlton— I'll read any thing—even tragedies—that you recommend, though I am sinner enough, I own, to prefer *your* daughters to any of Herodias's— My best remembrances to said daughters, not forgetting their mother, & believe me ever yours truly

Thomas Moore

I am about to start for town on Thursday and am to be heard of at 19 Bury St. if Wilson (with whom I *take* for granted your Eliza is) should take a fancy to have me. You see what a taking mood I am in, but I haven't time to correct—so you must *take* it as it is.

---

[1] See letter No. 958, to Arthur O'Connor, 21 Mar. 1831.

962. *To John Murray III*

Sir John Murray

April 21st 1831

Dear John— I send you the 2nd Vol. corrected— I thought it such a pity to spoil the *set* (though I am afraid you are still pretty well provided with them) that I have made the corrections here in penciling, though whether that will save it, I know not. There is still an extract I want to insert from the cancelled Preface to the Second Volume, if you should happen to have preserved a copy of it.

On Saturday I hope to see you in town & am to be heard of at my old den in Bury St.

Yours truly
Thos Moore

963. *Addressee unknown*[1]

Huntington Library

May 2nd 1831

My dear Sir— I thought to have been able to call & answer your note in person, but have been so *uncomfortably* ill since I came to town that it has not been in my power to reach you. To any one else but yourself I should not hesitate as to the sort of answer I ought to give (being, indeed, pretty well practiced in it) on the subject of your note— But to you a '*no*' does not come so readily to my tongue, and as far as a sincere wish to oblige you goes, my *will* is with you, however the *deed* may turn out. It is odd enough that the two things I have least confidence in my own power to do— even tolerably—are what I am oftenest asked for, and these are an Epilogue and a Review. Accordingly, of *both* tasks I have an especial horror. However, I shall (when I get to my quiet Cottage, which will be in a few days) turn the thought over in my mind, and if I see but the least chance of succeeding, shall be most happy to let you have the advantage of it.

Yours, my dear Sir, most truly
Thomas Moore

---

[1] It is possible that this letter was addressed to Macvey Napier, who was at this time editor of the *Edinburgh Review*.

964. *To James Crissy*

Pennsylvania Historical Society

Sloperton Cottage, Devizes
May 8th 1831

Dear Sir— Your letter of October 21st, 1830, accompanied by a very acceptable present, reached me but last week in London, and it was some alloy to the great pleasure I felt in receiving it to think that during so long an interval I must have appeared insensible to your kindness;—as you, no doubt, must have taken for granted that the packet had been long since in my hands.

It cannot be otherwise than most gratifying to me to find that my works are thought worthy of being put into such a permanent form in America, & begging you to accept my best thanks for the kind feeling towards me that prompted both your letter & your gift, I am, dear Sir, your obliged & faithful servant

Thomas Moore

965. *To John Murray*

Sir John Murray

Sloperton Cottage, Devizes
May 19th 1831

My dear Sir— I think it right to tell you in time (lest you should know so little of my situation as to *depend* upon me) that it will not be in my power, by any contrivance, to meet your Bill in the ensuing month. I did hope that the work I am employed upon would have been, by that time, in sufficient career of sale to authorize me to draw upon the Longmans for sufficient to cover at least *half* the amount, but it will be still at least a month before I can get my book out, and I have therefore no possible source from which I can raise the supply.[1]

And now that this sum has, I fear, assumed the shape of a debt from *me* to *you*, I must own (as I hate not to hold the same language to a man himself that I do of him to others) I *did* hope it would be in your power to let the whole or at least a part of it go (in addition to the £100 on account of France) as some compensation for the time, labour, and ultimate embarassment [*sic*] which the extension of my task so unexpectedly brought upon me. I do not, you see, reckon the £300 from America, because though God knows how convenient it was, & though it was very kind of you to allow me to accept it, *you* could not have had it if *I* hadn't, and therefore it was a God-send to me from another quarter, and not from your pocket.

[1] *The Life of Lord Edward Fitzgerald*, which appeared in September 1831.

Mind, I do not think (as some of my friends—Rogers, & others—do) that you were at all *bound*, by any further than a liberal and generous interpretation of our agreement, to add any thing to your first fair and, I will say, munificent price— To no such *claim* do I make the least pretensions, but I *do* think that, if either the present success or future property in the work had been such as to enable you to *afford* such a step (and on this all depends) it would have been a kindness worthy of you to have cancelled this Bill and let me hear no more of it— Whatever hope I had that such would have been the result was, I must say, considerably increased by the expressions you used in sending me back the first Bill you drew upon me (to be made payable somewhere)—'the inclosed Bill (you said) which I was in hopes you would never have again seen,' or 'never been again troubled with,' I forget which.[1]

I have now disburdened my mind—as I said before, I cannot bear that, in any thing of importance, a *friend* (and such I consider you to be) should not know all that I say of and about him to others. And I shall only add, in the same spirit of truth, that never have I spoken on the subject without doing justice, as warmly as I have done in your own presence, to the cordiality, courtesy & liberality which I have at all times and invariably experienced from you.

As this is the last time I shall ever pester you on this past & gone hope of mine, I will take the opportunity just of saying that if you could at least relieve me of the prospect of having the Bill impending over me by taking my acknowledgement for the debt (to be paid, you may depend upon it, without any unnecessary delay) it would free me from an incubus I am little accustomed to & would be a great kindness to me. You need not trouble yourself to answer this— We shall meet over a bottle of your good Port in a week or two, I hope, and then—we shall either talk or *not* talk upon the subject, just as you chuse.

I inclose a note upon *little* business matters for my friend John, and am,

Very truly and cordially yours

Thomas Moore

---

[1] Murray allowed Moore to take advantage of whatever he could obtain from America and France for the publication of the *Life of Byron*. Moore agreed on £333 from the American publisher, and Murray advanced him £500, which he was to pay back when the money from America arrived. Delays occurred, his bankers in Devizes refused to renew the bill a second time, and Moore was forced to propose that Murray draw upon him (Russell, vi. 194).

966. *To John Murray*

Sir John Murray

May 20th 1831

My dear Sir— It is odd enough that our two letters on the same business should have crossed each other; but I trust we shall have no further *cross*-work on the subject. With your view of the matter my hopes, with respect to this sum, must have appeared somewhat of the most extravagant—but never mind—they were not so much my own as those of some of my friends, and it was the wish of one person (Mrs Moore) that I should never even mention them to you— but as it has often been the discussion *behind your back* (as they say) I felt it would leave our future intercourse (which I trust may long continue) on a better footing of mutual understanding to let you know all that had occurred, both to others and myself, upon the subject.

To come now to the matter of business— What I told you, in my yesterday's letter, is unfortunately but too true—that the delay of the publication of my present work has deprived us of the only means to which I looked for the command of money for this Bill, and there is but one way (my drawing upon you through the Long-mans) by which the Bill can be paid when presented & the disagree-able circumstance you mention with your banker avoided.[1] You will not, I trust, feel any fears (after the clear understanding we now have of our relations to each other on the subject) that I can take any unfair advantage of this arrangement. You may be assured, —and I am ready to be bound legally, as I am bound honourably, to it—that the means shall be put in your hands of meeting the Bill before the end of the three months.

Yours very truly
Thomas Moore.

967. *To John Murray*

Sir John Murray

May 27th 1831

Thanks, my dear Sir, for the statement you have taken the trouble to make. I am most ready to own that you have done most mag-nificently by me, and the only provoking thing is that so many thousands should have run *clane* through me (as we say in Ireland) without doing me any good—You may depend upon my showing (or, at least, telling) your statement to those friends of mine who might not have remembered all the particulars of the transaction when, in their kind zeal for me, they thought you ought to have done more.

[1] See letter No. 965, to John Murray, 19 May 1831.

I will even let the little American item of £300 remain in its place—though really and truly it has no business there—as I have it from the best authority (the American market itself) that *you* couldn't have had the sum if *I* hadn't. You have but to make the experiment yourself & you'll find whether I am right or not. However, this is nothing—the money has gone into my pocket—and *out* again, fast enough.[1]

I never could have expected that this book would turn out any great source of profit to you, and, indeed, considering the honour & glory it must redound to your name, in saecula saeculorum, I think you may consider yourself well off if, in a pecuniary point of view, you do not *lose* by it—and this I am much encouraged by the particulars which your letter states to hope.

As for myself I assure you that, convenient as money is to me, no sum of money could give me half such real pleasure as the consciousness that I have by this book done a service to poor Byron's memory. This was my great object, and all I have heard and read upon the subject (reviewing letters as I do from all Quarters—almost of the globe—about it) convinces me that the result of the work has been to raise considerably the average estimate of our friend's personal character— In this I am convinced you will rejoice as much as I do.

Next week I hope to see you in town.

Ever yours truly
Tho⁵ Moore

968. *To John Murray III*

Sir John Murray

[May, 1831, *not in Moore's hand*]

My dear John— I shall take it very kind if you will again lend me Bland's Anthology—[2] I shall not keep it long & shall take every care of it.

In the second Volume there are two other corrections I must trouble you to make. Page 406— I wish the sentence about Campbell (beginning 'The secret of Tom Campbell's &c. &c.' and ending 'to stumble upon it') omitted.[3]

---

[1] See letter No. 965, to John Murray, 19 May 1831.

[2] Moore could be referring to John Bland, *The Gentleman's Collection of Catches* (1787), *The Ladies Collection of Catches* (1787?), or to *Translations Chiefly from the Greek Anthology*, edited by John H. Merivale and Robert Bland (1806).

[3] The sentence was not omitted (see Moore, *Byron's Works*, v. 70): 'The secret of Tom Campbell's defence of *inaccuracy* in costume and description is, that his Gertrude, &c. has no more locality in common with Pennsylvania

Page 700—the name *Kutoffski* to be altered into Jonkoffsky* &
the following note appended.[1]

*One of the most celebrated of the living poets of Russia, who
fought at Borodino & has commemorated that battle in a Poem of
much celebrity among his countrymen.

Yours ever
T. Moore

969. *To Mary Shelley*

Abinger Collection

Brooks's
June 25th 1831

Diary

Friday week—*could* have come to you, and was on the point of
writing a note to say so when I received yours.
Sunday—set off to Tunbridge Wells to see the Godfreys.
Monday—Tuesday— Received your note, which had been sent to
Bury St (instead of Lord John's) and was sent after me.
Wednesday Ev— Returned from Tunbridge Wells.
To-day—was on my way to Somerset St.—seized with a fit of
hunger mid-way, and turned into a friend's to lunch where I was
embargoed till too late.

Look with hope to seeing you at Speaker's this evening.

Ev y^{rs}
T. M.

970. *To D. F. Ryan*[2]

National Library of Ireland

Sloperton Cottage, Devizes
July 8th 1831.

Sir.

I lament that it was not my good fortune to hear of you somewhat earlier—as the part of my work where you could be of use to
me has been some time finished. I was lucky enough to learn the

than with Penmanmaur. It is notoriously full of grossly false scenery, as all
Americans declare, though they praise parts of the poem. It is thus that self-
love for ever creeps out, like a snake, to sting any thing which happens, even
accidentally, to stumble upon it.'
The close quotation mark after 'to stumble upon it' in the text was supplied
by the editor.
[1] The French spelling of Zhukovski (see the Glossary of Proper Names). He
is mentioned in a letter from Byron to Moore, dated 27 Dec. 1823 (Moore,
Byron's Works, vi. 110).
[2] Daniel Frederick Ryan was the son of the Ryan who was killed by Lord

particulars of the encounter not only from Major Sirr, but also from Murphy in whose house it took place and who was present part of the time. The assistance, however, of your recollections would have been a great satisfaction to me; & if you would still be so obliging as to put hastily on paper the particulars you remember respecting your father's share in the conflict I might avail myself of any new circumstance you recollect either in a note or in some future Edition of the Work, should such be called for.

With many thanks for the kindness of your offer,

I am, Sir, your obedient Servt

Thomas Moore

971. *To Lord Brougham*[1]

University College, London

Sloperton, Devizes
July 19th 1831.

My dear Lord Chancellor.

As the inclosed is rather a precious piece of paper (being an autograph letter of Byron's which our friend Mrs Meynell asked me for) I venture to send it through your hands.

Though you are never at a loss for an apt quotation, I think the following which I hit upon the other day might, with such *setting* as you could give it, come in apropos, some time or other, against the borough-mongers.

'Tum vero isti quos paverat per aliquot annos publicus peculatus, *velut bonis* spoliotis? *ereptis, non furto eorum manibus erepto, insensi* et *irati*, Romanos in Annibalem instigabant.' Livy.[2]

Yours very truly
Thomas Moore.

Mrs Meynell mentioned something of your having been so kind as to ask me to dinner for the 3rd of last month; but I had never heard any thing of it, having left town some days before.

Edward Fitzgerald on 19 May 1798, when Fitzgerald was captured. For Moore's summary account of the incident see Russell, vi. 134, and his *Life of Fitzgerald*.
    [1] Lord Brougham was Chancellor under Grey from 1830 until 1834.
    [2] Livy, *Historiarum ab Urbe Condita*, lib. xxxiii, cap. xlvii. The 'Spoliotis?' is Moore's interlineation. See also letter No. 972, to Lord Brougham, 20 July 1831.

972. *To Lord Brougham*

University College, London

Sloperton
July 20th 1831

Dear Lord Chancellor— I find, from trusting too much to memory I made a mistake in my passage from Livy yesterday—and then attempted bunglingly to mend it by a query.—the words are thus 'velut bonis ereptis, non furto eorum manibus *extorto*'—as, no doubt, *your* better memory told you.[1]

Pardon the stupidity that has brought me to inflict a second note on you, and believe me, with all truth, admiringly & sincerely y^{rs}

Thomas Moore.

973. *To D. F. Ryan*

National Library of Ireland

Sloperton
July 25th 1831.

Sir— I have had the pleasure of receiving your packet & regret that you should have taken the trouble of paying the postage. Any further communications you may favour me with if sent under cover to C. C. T. Greville Esqr, Council Office, Whitehall, will be forwarded to me by that gentleman.

I am happy to find from the documents you have sent that the only mistake I have made in my account of the conflict is in asserting that your father was armed with nothing but a sword-cane—[2] From the statement you have been so kind as to send it appears that he had also a pistol. Of the circumstances that took place between your father & Lord Edward, before Major Sirr came upstairs, I have said nothing whatever, in my account, not having any evidence on the subject that I could depend upon. I shall, however, avail myself of the particulars you mention in a future edition.

In telling you the sources from which I derived my information I forgot to say that my friend Mr Watson Taylor *was* one of the persons who kindly told me all that their memories retained of the transaction— Again begging you to accept my best thanks for the trouble you have taken, I am, Sir, your obliged & faithful servant

Thomas Moore

---

[1] See letter No. 971, to Lord Brougham, 19 July 1831. 'Extorto' is correct.

[2] Before his death Ryan gave an account of his struggle with Fitzgerald, which was described as 'unequal' because Ryan was armed with 'no more formidable weapon than a sword-cane, which bent harmlessly against him' (*DNB*).

974. *To Macvey Napier*

B.M. Add. MS. 34615, f. 140

Sloperton
August 19th 1831

My dear Sir— From some difficulty I have found in procuring the necessary books I have been rather doubtful whether it would be in my power to furnish you with the intended article for this number— but I think I may now say that it will be ready for you, and I only hope that the subject I have chosen may not have been anticipated by any one else. My *victim* is Professor Lee, the author of an attack on the German Theologian Gesenius, and as he affords a good opportunity for some remarks on the Rationalists & Neologists of Germany, I hope to be able to make out ten or a dozen readable pages on this subject for your next number.[1]

Yours very truly
Thomas Moore.

975. *To Macvey Napier*

B.M. Add. MS. 34615, f. 162

Farley Castle
September 1st 1831

My dear Sir— Your letter has found me here, *idling*. One of those engagements which I am but too subject to has called me away from home and obliged me to leave the article I was preparing for you unfinished.[2] I shall however be back again on Saturday, and, as soon after as I can manage it, shall forward my paper through my friend Greville, of the Council office— I think you may *depend* upon its reaching you next week, &, as you expressed an anxiety to hear from me, as soon as possible, on the subject I dispatch this letter by post rather than incur the delay of a frank through London. I know not whether, after all, you will think my Theology worth printing, but it shall, at all events, take its chance.

Yours, my dear Napier (if you will so
far agree to waive form) very truly
Thomas Moore.

---

[1] Article X in the *Edinburgh Review*, liv (1831), 238–55, was a composite review of four books: Hugh James Rose, *The State of Protestantism in Germany* (1829); E. B. Pusey, *An Historical Enquiry into the Probable Causes of the Rationalist Character* (1828); Pusey, *An Historical Enquiry, Part the Second* (1830); and S. Lee, *Six Sermons on the Study of the Holy Scriptures* (1830).

[2] See letter No. 974, to Macvey Napier, 19 Aug. 1831.

976. *To Colonel Houlton*

B.M. Add. MS. 27425BC, f. 25

Septr 19th 1831

My dear Houlton— as Mrs Napier is going into that enviable neighbourhood of yours in the morning, I scribble this to go *with* her
(as I should like to do myself) for the purpose of telling you about
Merewether, as you desired— I saw him two days ago, and he was
then walking about his grounds, without either pain or difficulty,
but had the leg still bandaged.[1]

Lady Lansdowne is come down much recovered— I have not
seen her yet.

Best regards to all yours, & believe
me ever faithfully
Th^{os} Moore

977. *To John Murray*

Sir John Murray

September 23rd 1831

My dear Sir— Mrs Moore, I found, had lent the Second Volume of
her Life of Byron to one of our neighbours, and it is but within this
half hour I have got it back— I have therefore not had time to look
through it very carefully, but as I take for granted your first object
is to have my opinion respecting the subjects you have chosen for
the three *first* Volumes of your projected work I hasten to say that
I do not think you could have better—though as the vignette of
Dr Glennie's school is more appropriate to the earlier part of the
work, it would be better, perhaps, to let it change places with the
vignette of Newstead which will suit either volume equally.

I have just hastily run through the pages 81–333 of the 2 vol
Quarto, and the only subject that met my eyes was one of which
a very pretty drawing could, I think, be made—namely, Byron in
the Campo Santo at Bologna, comparing the skulls around with the
blooming face of the Sexton's daughter.[2] This is in page 243. There
is also the moonlight scene at Venice, pp. 271, 2, to which the only

---

[1] According to A. Houlton's note attached to this letter, Serjeant Henry
Aldworth Merewether had injured his achilles tendon while drawing a bow at
an archery meeting in Melksham.

[2] 'I afterwards went to the beautiful cemetry of Bologna . . . and found . . .
an original of a custode, who reminded one of the grave-digger in Hamlet. He
has a collection of capuchins' skulls, labelled on the forehead, and taking down
one of them, said, "This was Brother Desiderio Berro, who died at forty—one
of my best friends"' (Moore, *Byron's Works*, iv. 161).

objection is that the wicked artist might be tempted to make *me* look rather too like *Sancho*, in depicting me seated beside the great poetical Quixote, in the moonshine.

I shall look again more carefully, and answer with respect to Vols 4 & 5 on Sunday— Your subjects for the last are beautiful— particularly 'Head of Editor'!

Ever yours
T. Moore

978. *To Macvey Napier*

B.M. Add. MS. 34615, f. 198

September 24th 1831

My dear Napier— By return of Post I send the Proofs, not having had time to add any 'more last words' as you desired. I am glad you like the article[1]—there is no subject to me so piquant as that of Theology, and I am now about a little work on that scent. It is right to tell you that for the two pages containing the very clear & well written exposition of the principles of the Rationalists I am indebted to a medical neighbour of mine.[2] He also pointed out to me (being no German scholar myself) the mistakes of Professor Lee respecting Gesenius.

Pray, attend to my corrections— I have written most of them in pencil at the bottom of the page to avoid mistakes.

Ever yours truly
T. Moore

I have just had a letter from Ireland containing an opinion respecting my Lord Edward from our Chief Justice Bushe, which I should be glad your reviewer could have seen while he was sitting in judgment on me.— 'I did not think it possible that so much truth could have been told with so little mischief.'[3]

979. *To John Murray*

Sir John Murray

September 30th 1831

My dear Sir.

I have been in hopes of a letter from you to say whether the hints I suggested in my last met your taste.[4] As to the portion which is to form the Fifth Volume I have been looking over it and

---

[1] See letter No. 974, to Macvey Napier, 19 Aug. 1831.

[2] Dr. Brabant.

[3] *The Life and Death of Lord Edward Fitzgerald* was reviewed in the *Edinburgh Review*, liv (September 1831), 114–46. The writer laments Moore's choice of subject but admits the brilliancy of his treatment.

[4] Suggestions for illustrations to *Byron's Works*. See letter No. 977, to John Murray, 23 Sept. 1831.

PLATE 7

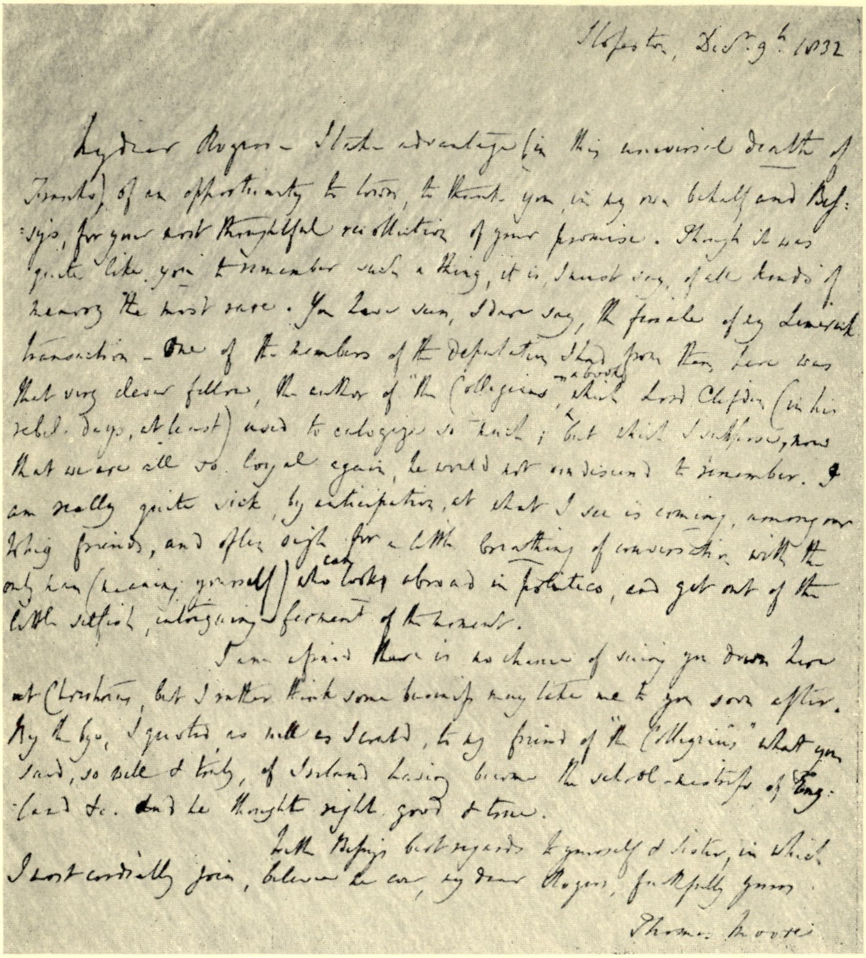

Sloperton, Decr. 9th 1832

My dear Rogers — I take advantage (in this universal dearth of franks) of an opportunity to London, to thank you, in my own behalf and Bessy's, for your most thoughtful recollection of your promise. Though it was quite like you to remember such a thing, it is, I must say, of all kinds of memory the most rare. You have seen, I dare say, the finale of my Limerick transaction — One of the members of the deputation I had from thence here was that very clever fellow, the author of the "Collegians", which Lord Clifden (in his rebel days, at least) used to eulogize so much; but which I suppose, now that we are all so loyal again, he would not condescend to remember. I am really quite sick, by anticipation, at what I see is coming, among our Whig friends, and often sigh for a little breathing of conversation with the only man (meaning yourself) who can look abroad in politics, and get out of the little selfish, intriguing ferment of the moment.

I am afraid there is no chance of seeing you down here at Christmas, but I rather think some business may take me to you soon after. By the bye, I quoted as well as I could, to my friend of the "Collegians" what you said, so well & truly, of Ireland having become the school-mistress of England &c. And he thought it right good & true.

Both Bessy's best regards to yourself & sister, in which I most cordially join, believe me ever, my dear Rogers, faithfully yours

Thomas Moore

LETTER TO SAMUEL ROGERS, 9 December 1832

cannot find any thing that would at all *se prêter* to the pencil. Byron before the fountain in the garden at Bologna would be a pretty subject—but, since I wrote last, I see, by your list that it is not your wish to have subjects of this nature, but rather views of houses & places where he had been. Why not Petrarch's Tomb or Dante's, at Ravenna? if there is any drawing of it. Do, let me have a line on the subject, at your leisure.

Yours very truly
Thomas Moore

980. *To John Murray*

Sir John Murray

October 6th 1831

My dear Sir. Our last letters crossed each other on the road, & I do not exactly recollect what I said in mine relative to the Illustrations. You have puzzled me a little too by the variance there is between your two lists. In the First List the two opening Volumes stood thus.

Vol. 1.	Frontispiece—	Head after Phillips
	Vignette—	Newstead
Vol. 2.	Frontispiece	Lynn of Dee
	Vignette—	Glennie's School

This I perfectly approved of, only suggesting that the two vignettes should be exchanged—Newstead to come in the 2nd Vol. & Glennie's School in the first.

| Vol. 3. | Frontispiece— | Margaretta [*sic*] Cogni |
| | Vignette— | House at Venice |

So the 3rd Volume stood in your first list, but in the second you have put a Query for the Frontispiece, and instead of 'House at Venice' substituted 'Pisa'.

All this puzzles me, and untill I hear further from you I do not like to venture on any further suggestions.[1]

A thousand thanks for your offer of a bed and if I can manage to come up, it will give me great pleasure to accept to it [*sic*].

Yours ever
T. Moore

[1] The illustrations in the first three volumes are not as Moore described them in this letter. Volume I has as its frontispiece a full-length portrait of Byron at 19, engraved by Finden, and the 'vignette' is a picture of Cadiz. The frontispiece of volume II is a view of the palace of Ali Pasha at Tepaleen, while the 'vignette' is a view of Constantinople. Volume III has a view of Marathon as the frontispiece, with a picture of a street in Athens as the 'vignette'. An engraving of Newstead serves as the frontispiece of volume VI.

981. *To John Murray*

Sir John Murray

October 7th 1831

My dear Sir.

My letter through Lord Mahon which you have received to day will have reminded you of your *first* arrangement of the Illustrations for the 1st & 2nd Volumes, from which I see your last (received to-day) also deviates by the omission of the Lynn of the Dee as a Frontispiece, & by making Newstead Abbey a Frontispiece instead of a Vignette, as it was at first.[1] However, as we may soon meet, it will be well to leave all this till then. My position at present is as follows. I had entirely given up the thought of going to town, and had fixed to keep an engagement (to which I have for some months pledged myself) to Sydney Smith at his pretty place Coombe Flory. I meant, indeed, to have written to him to-day to say I could be with him on Tuesday next—but your letter has made me withhold my pen, and I shall accordingly wait till I receive your answer to this, by return of post, letting me know whether, if I come up on Tuesday or Wednesday next (at the farthest) I shall be still in time enough to have a few days chance of seeing Sir Walter. This will decide me. My own wish to see him (though very strong & sincere) would not perhaps have led me to come up, because one never knows whether such a thing might be welcome or not—but, as you now tell me that he has also expressed a wish to see me, I shall most certainly run up as soon after receipt of your answer as I can manage.

With respect to your question as to the best means of giving interest and novelty to your new Edition, I should certainly say that for the *works* a running Commentary, in the manner of Warburton on Pope,[2] would be the thing most likely, if well done, to be attractive—but it would be a task of great responsibility to the critic who would undertake it, and still greater if it was a *rhymer* who undertook to criticize such a *poet*. As to the Life—the raking up of all the refuse of the Hunts, Medwins &c. (as your friend suggests) would be any thing but creditable. All this, however, we can talk of (if we meet) over *just* such a supper as you gave me the night before I last started from London.

Ever yours truly
Thomas Moore

[1] See letter No. 980, to John Murray, 6 Oct. 1831.
[2] William Warburton, *A Commentary on Mr. Pope's Essay on Man* (1739).

982. *To John Murray*

Sir John Murray

October 9th 1831

My dear Sir— In order to inflict as little postage as possible I shall write a scrap of a note to Lockhart on the other leaf which you will have the goodness to inclose to him. On Wednesday evening I shall be in town, but too late (as I have told him) for his six o'clock dinner. I have also some business to do on that evening which will prevent me from being *your* guest. But *Thursday* or Friday (according as Lockhart may make his selection) or *Sunday* I shall be at your disposal and you can so arrange with him. I will name even *Monday*,—but *beyond* that day I cannot answer for my stay in town.

I have some misgivings as to the inconvenience I may put you to by occupying your bed-room so long as I have here stated—but you must treat me as a moveable and turn me out when *de trop.*

Is town *safe* now for a country-gentleman?

Ever yours most truly
Thomas Moore

Let me have one line by return of post, to name the days.

983. *To J. G. Lockhart*

(*Attached to the letter to John Murray, same date*)

Sir John Murray

Sloperton Cottage
Octr 9th 1831

My dear Mr Lockhart.

It will give me great pleasure to have a day with my dear friend Sir Walter, and I am, I assure you, most thankful to you for so kindly proposing it. As, however, I am not likely to be up in town early enough for a dinner on Wednesday, I trust it will make no difference to you to name some other day in the week—*Thursday, Friday*, or *Sunday*— I have promised to keep Saturday for my little Charter-House boy, to take him to some theatre.

Ever yours truly
Thomas Moore.

984. *To Mary Shelley*

Abinger Collection

[17 October 1831]

I meant to have come to you this morning, but am summoned off to meet Bishop at Power's, where I shall remain *busily* for two or three hours. I should like to know Fletcher's address.

Tomorrow, though I have given up Harrow, I cannot come to you—for reasons you shall know when we meet.

Y^{rs} ever
T. M.

985. *To John Murray*

Sir John Murray

Sloperton
October 25 1831

My dear Sir. I hope you will soon be able to send me down the blank-leaved Byron— I should also like to add a little note on the 4th or 5th Vol. of the Life, on the subject of 'Mariners' Tonga Islands',[1] having promised the poor author of that book to do so in my 1st Edition, but forgot it.

I see that what I took for a mere joke of yours is true and that you *are at* me in this number of the Quarterly.[2] I have desired Power to send you back my copy when it comes, not liking to read it just now, for *reasons*. In the mean time, here's some *good-*humoured doggerel for you.

Thoughts on Editors
Editur et edit

No—editors don't care a button
    What false and fruitless things they do;
They'll let you come and cut their mutton
    And then, they'll have a cut at *you*.
With Barnes I oft my dinner took,
    Nay, met ev'n Horace Twiss, to please him!
Yet, Mister Barnes traduc'd my Book,
    For which may his own devils seize him!
With Doctor Bowring I drank tea,
    Nor of his cakes consum'd a particle,

---

[1] William Mariner, *Of the Tonga Islands* (London, 1817).
[2] Moore's *Life of Lord Edward Fitzgerald* was reviewed by Southey in the *Quarterly Review*, xlvi (1831), 213–63.

And yet, th' ungrateful L. L. D.
  Let fly at me, next week, an article!
To sup with Wilson was my lot,
  Mong Bards of fame, like Hogg and Packwood,
A dose of blackstrap then I got,
  And next a dose, still worse, of Blackwood.[1]

I've stopped short here, for the ending does not please me—but, some time or other, you shall have the whole. Should you again see that great & noble Scott before he goes, remember me most affectionately to him.

Ever yours truly
Thomas Moore

986. *To E. R. Moran*

Bodleian MS. Eng. misc. d. 279, f. 37

Sloperton Cottage
Novr 5th 1831

Dear Sir. I take, in haste, the opportunity of a cover to a friend to thank you for your very kind note which I, some days since, received. I congratulate you sincerely on your having been able to establish yourself so respectably, and [soon?]

Your obliged & faithful Servt
Thomas Moore

987. *To John Murray*

Sir John Murray

Private & confidential

Sloperton
November 9th 1831

My dear Sir— I shall be glad to hear that you have succeeded in finding the MS. you were in search of. In turning over my memorandum book yesterday I was horrified to see that our Bill becomes due this very next month, which was a most startling discovery to me, as I had somehow got it into my head that it was in July it was drawn whereas it turns out to have been in June. I have been for these two or three month's past employed upon a work which I looked forward to having ready in January (the month when I thought the Bill would become due) or at least so far ready as to justify me in asking the Longmans for an advance of £250 on it to

---

[1] There is an incomplete and incoherent fragment of approximately three lines of a conclusion to this poem in Sir John Murray's collection. Lockhart is mentioned, but otherwise no meaning can be read from the lines.

discharge a part of the Bill, suspending the remainder by another
Bill to that amount till I should be able to pay it— As it is, I have
no possible means of meeting the debt this next month, and must
only renew the whole Bill, unless some other means can be devised
of getting me through it. If you are still set upon the plan of
employing me as Editor & Commentator in this new Edition,[1] some
arrangement might surely be made by which, without distressing
you at present, any remuneration you might think due for my name
& cooperation in the scheme might be made available towards my
future release from a debt so embarassing [*sic*] to both of us. Do,
my dear Sir, think of this, both as a man of business & friend, and
let me know as speedily as you can your determination. I have had
a letter written these few days from Lardner urging me strongly
for my History—but till I know how you intend to proceed, or to
what extent my labour for you is likely to go, I cannot of course
arrange my plans.[2]

I communicated all the circumstances of the position in which
we stand to Mr Rogers, when I was last in town, and have now
written to him fully on the subject, so that perhaps whatever is to
be done had better be arranged through him. With two persons
so much my friends as both you & he are I have no doubt of finding
that consideration which my circumstances just at this moment
so very much require—a little time and I have no doubt of being
able to work through all my difficulties.

Ever yours most truly
Thomas Moore

988. *To John Murray*

Sir John Murray

Sloperton
Novr 13th 1831

My dear Sir. I give you full credit (as I have every right to do) for
your good-natured intentions towards me, and though our connexion in matters of business is, from this out, to cease, I sincerely
trust we shall always continue on the same friendly terms.

There is only one passage of your letter against which I must
most strongly protest, as doing me a great injustice. It is the
following— 'Surely, after your promise you cannot think of turning a piece of good which I have done you into an evil to myself.'—

---

[1] After the appearance of the biography, Murray asked Moore to edit Byron's
works. Although the first six volumes are taken up with the *Life* and the entire
seventeen-volume set is commonly called 'Moore's edition', he had little or
nothing to do with editing the poetry.

[2] Moore had been requested to write a *History of Ireland* for Lardner's
Cabinet Cyclopaedia.

This intimation of suspicion that I could have meant to *shrink* from my engagement to pay this Bill is (to say the least of it) unfair.[1] Whatever difficulty I might have felt in so doing you would never again have been troubled by me on the subject but for this new plan (which you yourself proposed to me) of cooperating with you in your new Edition of Byron. Taking for granted that you meant I should have some reasonable remuneration for my assistance, I thought that my debt to you might, in a way convenient to both of us, be thus cancelled or at least reduced. This you well know is the state of the case and it is more for your sake than my own that I beg to recommend you *never* again to hint such a suspicion as the words I have quoted would seem to imply. For myself, I have little to fear that any one who knows me would for an instant credit the imputation.

As to your agreement with Mr Harness & how far it may have proceeded at the time you accepted of my proposal to be Editor, I shall not say a single word. I wish him & you success in your undertaking & there's an end on't.[2]

I have no doubt of being able, either through the Longmans or Mr Rogers (both of which parties know the *whole* of the transaction between us) to provide for the Bill when it becomes due; and you may therefore dismiss all anxiety upon that point from your mind.

With sincere thankfulness for all the kindness I have experienced from you, & my very best regards to Mrs Murray, I am yours very truly

Thomas Moore

989. *To Thomas Spring Rice*

Harvard College Library

Bowood
Decr 12th 1831

My dear Rice— I venture to add to your million & one applications (on all possible subjects) by calling your attention to the case of a poor friend & neighbour of mine, Robert Hughes, once Fellow of King's, afterwards Captain in the East-India service, then *Farmer*,

---

[1] See letter No. 987, to John Murray, 9 Nov. 1831.

[2] On 14 Oct. 1831 Moore recorded in his diary: 'Spottiswoode and Harness to breakfast at Murray's, for the purpose of consulting about the new edition of Byron. I have not myself come to any decisive explanation with him as to what *my* part or share in the business is to be.' He also noted that he tried to impress upon Murray the fact that as editor he must work alone, without interference (Russell, vi. 225). Murray evidently agreed to the request (see letter No. 995, to John Murray, 1 Mar. 1832).

(and, as might be expected from the antecedents, *ruined*) and now & for some years past, Seller of Licenses to Hawkers & Pedlars. On the first rumour of the breaking up of this latter corps, Lord Lansdowne, who takes a great interest in the poor fellow's family, undertook to see what could be done for him, and, as it was supposed that *all* would not be dismissed meant to employ his interest towards having Hughes among the *retained*. It now appears, however, that the whole body are to be sent to the right about (or rather wrong about, as poor Hughes thinks) and the sole thing to ascertain is whether the Hawkers come under Mr Bankes's Act for the remuneration of discharged officers, and whether through that, or any other means, some pittance may be found to keep the Ex-Fellow of King's, Ex-Captain, Ex-Farmer, and now Ex-Licenser from starving. He really and but too seriously has no other resource left. His *official* claims are that he has, since his appointment, wrung more money out of the Hawkers than ever was thought possible—having remitted from that source, in ten years & a half near £8000—

I think I need say no more (even if I had time to do so) to excite your interest in this case—and should you not be able to give *hope*, it will be some relief to know the *worst*. He dreams of something in the Woods & Forests—but I fear you will say 'that's Poetry, God knows!'— However, do your best for him, for *my* sake, & believe me, my dear Rice,

Very truly yours
Thomas Moore.

Be kind enough to send the enclosed to the Twopenny for me— All well here and, as usual, *charming*.

990. *To John Murray III*

Sir John Murray

Sloperton
Jan^r 9th 1832

My dear John— I have only time for a word by a parcel I am sending to Power. Nothing was ever more strong upon my mind than the impression that it was from a MS. (and one of the MSS. I had from your father) that I printed the portions of the letter to Blackwood. Therefore, pray make a still further search.

I must also ask you to do a favour for me, in the same line—which is to see that those papers (the material of my Lord Edward) which I left in your father's care are safe & to let me know, as I must give you the trouble of sending them for me to

Mrs Beauclerck, when she comes to town. They are not directed by myself, as I begged that one of your clerks do it for me.

Best regards to all your family

Very truly y^rs

T. Moore

I am rejoiced at what you say of the new Edition.

991. *To John Murray*

Sir John Murray

Sloperton

Feb^r 5th 1832

My dear Sir— When I began your letter I was in hopes you were about to tell me that you had, at last, found the lost letter to Blackwood.[1] As to the assignment I remember your once asking me about it in town, and saying at the same time (if I recollect right) that the drawing it up had cost you £40.—but further than this I have no remembrance of any thing connected with it. It is possible, however, that in a Diary of matters of business which I have kept for several years past I may find some notice of it, and, as soon as I am well enough to look for the Volume (having been for some days ill with a most incapacitating influenza) I shall make a search & let you know the result.

I receive constant evidence by the Post of the circulation of the Byron—it has reached evidently quite a new class of readers. One man, in a letter I received to-day, says that till he found and purchased the Volume at Chelmsford, he 'did not even know that I was at work on the subject'. The same innocent gentleman (who is an author himself but has lived, it appears, very much out of England) asks whether I can 'let him know who the Mr *Thomas Brown* is to whom a Poem on Mont Blanc (in the Fables for the Holy Alliance) is attributed'. It is quite delightful to meet with such *fresh* readers.

Best regards to all around you.

Ever yours truly

Thomas Moore

I find that all the people who write fancy *me* to be the Editor— which is perhaps as well.[2]

---

[1] See letter No. 990, to John Murray III, 9 Jan. 1832.

[2] That is, the editor of the *Works of Byron*, which Murray was publishing.

992. *To James Power*[1]

Pforzheimer Misc. MS. 306

Feb^r 19th 1832.

My dear Sir. I am very nearly well of my Influenza, and hope you & yours keep free of all aches & alarms, in these alarming times. Tom is all agog about the Cholera, and looking for you daily to bring him away—but there is no necessity for this just now. I depend upon you for keeping a good lookout, as to the approach of the foe, which does not seem to be very formidable as yet.

Yours ever truly
Thomas Moore

Many thanks for your kindness about the Bill. I shall be anxious to hear how your Lease affair turns out.

Pray let the Printer have the inclosed speedily.

993. *To John Murray*

Sir John Murray

Feb^r 19th 1832

My dear Sir— A note which I sent to Lady Elisabeth Fielding the other day, under cover with one to you, having, I find, never reached her, I fear the same fate may have befallen yours, & therefore send these few hasty lines through Power. The object of the note was to tell you that I had not been able to ascertain any thing about the assignment, nor indeed to find any document at all connected with the transaction. Another object was to ask you, on the part of a friend, whether you would be willing to accept an article (as a sort of Companion-picture to one in the last Quarterly) on the origin of the *Greek* language.[2] If you will send your answer to this, as briefly as you please, directed to me at N⁰ 31 Sackville St. it will reach me.

Yours ever
T. Moore

---

[1] No name appears on the original of this letter; the addressee has been supplied from the context by the editor.

[2] No article on the origin of the Greek language appeared in the *Quarterly* at this time. The article to which Moore refers is evidently a review of Ernst Jäkel, *Der germanische Ursprung der lateinischen Sprache und des römischen Volkes* (Breslau, 1831), which appeared in the *Quarterly Review*, xlvi (1832), 336–49.

994. *To John Murray*

Sir John Murray

Feb^r 26th 1832

My dear Sir— Having an opportunity by a parcel to Simmons (who is printing a Third Edition of my Lord Edward) I can only say, in haste, that it would be impossible for me now (however willing I was once for such a profit) to accomplish what you desire. The *form*, indeed, is such as I should have always objected to—an Essay being nothing more than a Review (of which there has been, God knows, enough) and even if *I* could bring myself to write such a 'crambe repleta' of the Edinburgh & Quarterly, few, I suspect, would be brought to read it. A light commentary on the works, running throughout, and admitting of anecdotes, quotations from other writers, and all such touch-and-go things as are unmanageable in an Essay, is what I originally proposed and what is now unluckily too late to think of.[1]

Yours ever truly
Thomas Moore

I inclose you a letter which I know not whether you will think worth attending to—but I believe the young man is not undeserving.

995. *To John Murray*

Sir John Murray

Sloperton
March 1st 1832

My dear Sir. I regret very sincerely that, situated as I am, it is utterly impossible for me to accede to your proposal.[2] This, I repeat, gives me very sincere regret, as I should have liked the task and the terms are, to the utmost of what I myself ever contemplated. Should my inability to do what you desire be any natural disappointment to you (which I trust it will *not* be) I can only say, without wishing to call up any disagreeable recollections, that it is

---

[1] Murray asked Moore to furnish him an essay on Byron's poetical character as an introduction to the new edition of Byron's works. Moore, who had agreed to write a history of Ireland for the Longmans, first wrote to them seeking their advice. When they told him that they would like him to finish the history as quickly as possible, he wrote this letter to Murray. The publisher replied indicating that he believed Moore could do what Murray desired and offered 500 guineas for the task (Russell, vi. 246–8). For Moore's refusal to comply with the second request see letter No. 995, to John Murray, 1 Mar. 1832.

[2] See letter No. 994, to John Murray, 26 Feb. 1832.

not my fault. After those few sentences which passed between us, outside your drawing-room door, when I told you that if I undertook the Edition, no one else was to have any concern with it (to which you answered 'oh certainly not',) and still more after the conversation we had the same day, in going to Sir Walter Scott's, when I told you I had made up my mind to undertake the Edition and you might as soon as you please *announce* me, (at which you expressed yourself much gratified)—after these two circumstances I certainly did consider myself as *sure* of being the Editor of the work as I am now of eating my dinner this first day of March. When, however, I learned from you that this idea had been given up, I naturally turned my thoughts to other subjects, and undertook much more than I fear it will be in my power to accomplish. You may have some notion of the little *extra* time I have left myself, when I tell you in confidence (for I should not like for every one to know that I am such a 'maid of all work') that, besides having bound myself to furnish Lardner with the long-promised Irish History at a certain time I am endeavouring to finish a work which has long been a favourite hobby of my own,[1] and, at the same time, am engaged upon *two* musical works for Power, preparatory to a settlement of my accounts with him. You will say this is like the items of Betty Blackberry's dress—'then, over that—and then again, over that'—but so it is, and I should neither do justice to you, myself, nor my other publishers, if I were to undertake such a responsible task as writing Commentaries on Byron's Poetry under such circumstances.

This is all I have now time to say— I never leave myself more than the last fag-end half hour for letter-writing, and my Epistles show it but too plainly—about five letters in ten minutes being my *stint.* I must again, however, say how sorry I am not to be able to do what you wish, and how truly I am

Your obliged & faithful
Thomas Moore

996. *To Mary Shelley*

Abinger Collection

Sloperton
March 3rd 1832

I see you have entirely given me up, which is rather too hard a punishment for *not* writing—particularly on a man who writes more than enough to all the world beside. Much as I feel the withdrawal of your light from me I doubt whether, even now, I could

---

[1] Probably *Travels of an Irish Gentleman in Search of Religion* (1833).

have brought myself to *this* sort of effort to lure it back again ('tassel-gentle'[1] as you are) but for the nature of the subject on which I write & which is, as briefly as possible, this. I have just heard from a friend who has been to Bath that there is some subscription going on there for Leigh Hunt, who (he added, to my very sincere regret) was represented to him as in a state of great distress. Now, if this be true (which is one of the things I want you to tell me) it would be a very great satisfaction to me to contribute my mite, if you think my doing so would not be offensive to *him* or appear ostentatious to *others*. I have not time to go farther into the subject, but do *you* think & feel *for* me, as my proxy, and say whether, by giving my name & five guineas or so to the subscription, you think I should serve him, *without* at the same time *wounding* him.[2] I wish I had time to make myself intelligible—but you are not among the slow ones of this world, and can well eke out what is wanting.

Good bye—Ever yours
T. Moore

997. *To William Lisle Bowles*[3]

Rice University

March 24th 1832

My dear Bowles—

I deferred writing for a day or two from my plans being so uncertain— but it is now fixed that I go to London on Monday, which puts an end to all our vision of Music, Psalmody, Salisbury girls, &c, &c. I do not quite like being routed from home just now (except indeed, for you & such articles as the above-mentioned) but business makes it necessary for me to visit 'the City of the Plague,' where I shall stay, for all reasons, as short a time as possible.

With best regards to Mrs Bowles,

Yours ever most sincerely
Thomas Moore.

998. *To the Countess of Blessington*

Lady Blessington, *Memoirs*, ii. 273

Sloperton Cottage
April 15th, 1832.

Dear Lady Blessington,—You were one of the very first persons, during my late short and busy visit to London, whom it was my intention, as soon as I discovered you were in town, to call upon;

---

[1] *Romeo and Juliet*, II. ii. 160.
[2] Moore probably refers to the 1832 subscription edition of Hunt's poems.
[3] This letter was published in Greever, *A Wiltshire Parson*, p. 87.

but just as I was about to have that pleasure, your letter, forwarded from home, reached me; and the tone of it, I confess, so much surprised and pained me, that I had not courage to run the risk of such a reception as it seemed to threaten. I can only say that, had I the least idea that the very harmless allusions in Byron's letter to the very harmless pursuits of Lord Blessington's youth could have given him (had he been alive) or yourself the slightest uneasiness, I most certainly would not have suffered those passages to remain; nor can I now understand, with all allowance for the sensitiveness which affliction generates, either the annoyance or displeasure which (you will, at least, believe more from wrong judgment than any intention) I have been so unfortunate as to excite in you.[1]

I have lost no time in searching both for the letters and MS. book which you wished for, but, as yet, have been unable to find only the latter, and rather think that the letters of Lord Blessington, to which you allude, shared the fate of many others on the same subject, which I tore up when done with them. Again expressing my sincere regret for the pain I have given, I am, dear Lady Blessington, very truly yours,

Thomas Moore.

999. *To John Murray III*

Sir John Murray

April 19th 1832

My dear John— As I fear my frankers in town may have fled for the recess, and this letter is already delayed too long by my absence from home, I write direct to say that the two books reviewed by Byron were, to the best of my recollection, Wordsworth's Poems and Sir W. Gell's Argolis (as I think the book was called.)[2]

I have received intelligence of the safety of the Fitzgerald Papers and thank your father for his punctuality in sending them.

Yours very truly
Thomas Moore

---

[1] Moore is probably referring to the following passage in a letter from Byron to Moore (*Byron's Works*, vi. 13): 'M * * [Mountjoy, the Earl of Blessington] seems very good-natured, but is much tamed, since I recollect him in all the glory of gems and snuff-boxes, and uniforms, and theatricals, and speeches in our house . . . and sitting to Stroeling, the painter, . . . to be depicted as one of the heroes of Agincourt. . . .'

[2] Byron reviewed Wordsworth's *Poems* (1807) for the *Monthly Literary Recreation* in July 1807, and Sir William Gell's *Geography of Ithaca* (1807) for the *Monthly Review* in August 1811.

It ought to be chronicled, I think, as account in these bad times that I had a visit from a publisher, the other day, who came down by the mail express for the purpose to offer me 1000 guineas for a Poem (to be illustrated) a third of the length of Lalla Rookh. Brave man, you will say.[1]

1000. *To E. R. Moran*

Bodleian MS. Eng. misc. d. 279, f. 21
Private

Sloperton
May 4th 1832

Dear Sir—

I received the note you favoured me with through Lord Lansdowne, for which I thank you very much.

It is probable there may be some verses in the Times tomorrow which if you are inclined to copy (though I rather think they will take up too much space for your columns) I shall feel much obliged by your making the following correction of a foolish mistake that occurred in the transcribing.

For '*a thousand parsons* to every soul' read 'a *score of* parsons &c.[2]

Yours very truly
Thomas Moore

1001. *To Lady Morgan*

Lady Morgan, *Memoirs* (Leipzig, 1863), iii. 116

May 24th, 1832.

My dear Lady Morgan,

At the time I received your letter, I was not very well able to answer it, and, indeed, till within these two days, have felt by no means well, or like myself. I am, however, now much better. I have been in correspondence, during part of the time, with your friend of the *Metropolitan*, Captain Marryatt, and if the most cautious and flattering liberality, on his part, added to your kind persuasions, could have made a contributor or editor of me, I should have been

[1] A bookseller named Harding from Cornhill called on Moore on 12 Apr. and proposed that the poet write a poem a third the length of *Lalla Rookh*, which he would publish in an illustrated form like Rogers's *Italy*. Moore told the man that he would consider the proposition but obviously had no thought of undertaking the task (Russell, vi. 268–9).

[2] Evidently written for one of the anti-Episcopal squibs but not used. (See, for example, *Poetry*, pp. 626 and 647.)

one at this moment.[1] But I hate to be *tied;* it is this, far more than what you call my aristocratic (God help me) prejudices, which makes me reject so often the golden bait flung at me. If I were to judge, indeed, of the state of literature from my own experience, I should say it never was more prosperous, as I have actually turned away from my *door* (as the shop-keepers say) fifteen hundred guineas and a thousand pounds a year within the last three months; all the time, too, wanting money most pinchingly. From what you said in your letter I took for granted that Campbell had intimated some intention of abdicating the editorship; but this I find not to be the case, and if I were ever so disposed to accept of the chair, I should shrink from the slightest step, on my part, that could be construed into a wish to supplant him. I lament to hear of his present state, but he *has* been a noble fellow.[2] You will think it looks very like contributorship when you come to see some verses of mine announced for the next number of the *Metropolitan;* but, besides my wish to show, by some trifling mark, how much I felt the kindness both of Captain Marryatt and Dr. Saunders, these verses were of a kind that would not *keep*, being a good deal circulated, or, at least, shown about by those who are interested in them, and, therefore, likely to get into print. All I have told you about *shop* business here is for your private self alone; for, though vain enough, God knows, at being praised so much higher than I am worth, I think it, in general, not right to proclaim the particulars of my negociations with the bibliopolists.

Give my best regards to Morgan,

And believe me, very truly yours,

Thomas Moore.

1002. *To Captain Marryat*

University of Texas

Sloperton
June 6th 1832

My dear Sir— I should have answered you by yesterday's post but that I happened to be from home. Your letter has removed all fears from my mind as to any such attack on Mr Rogers occurring again, and we are now therefore *in statu quo ante*—[3]

[1] See letters No. 1003, to Captain Marryat, 12 June, and No. 1010, to Mary Shelley, 23 July 1832.

[2] Moore is referring to difficulties which faced Campbell after the death of his wife (1828), which included a generally unsuccessful period as editor of the *Metropolitan* (1831-2).

[3] Moore recorded in his diary for 1-16 June that he was disgusted at seeing some 'ribald attacks' upon Rogers and some 'vulgar trash' about himself in

Every succeeding day brings such changes in men & things that if I attempt anything to Lord Gray, it must not be till the *last* moment you can give me previous to publication—and, in the mean time, I shall prepare something else, in case of non-performance or failure on this topic.

I omitted saying (though I assure you it had been ready enough in my thoughts) how happy I should be to see you in this very humble Cottage, whenever you can make it convenient to come. I meditate a visit to Sydney Smith, one of these coming weeks, and towards the end of July shall be obliged to take a run to Dublin to fetch my sister, who I hope will take up her abode with us for some time—but any time, in the intervals between these short flights, that you will do me the honour to come, Mrs Moore & myself will be most happy to receive you.

Yours, my dear Sir, very truly
Thomas Moore

1003. *To Captain Marryat*

Huntington Library

June 12th 1832

My dear Sir— I am trying to get up a little Eastern tale for your prose & verse, but cannot yet tell how long it will be.[1] I fear longer however than I can often afford to give you, for I am ashamed to say how much time it takes me to write even the shortest trifle. I hope to let you have it the beginning of next week, Monday, perhaps,—as I shall want to see proofs. Will that be time enough? It was a very kind *galanterie* to Lady Valletort to put her in such distinguished type as you did, in the last number, but trust that you will now let *me* subside into the same uniform with your other contributors.[2]

I have no right to put in any plea for Lord Grey. Fair criticism, whether of men's actions or writings, nobody can object to. It has always, I own, however, made one of my difficulties in giving my

a recent issue of the *Metropolitan*. He wrote to Captain Marryat, saying that he must 'ask leave to be off [his] bargain' (see letter No. 1010, to Mary Shelley, 23 July 1832) if there 'could be the slightest risk of any repetition of such disreputable attacks'. Moore received a reply from Marryat, saying that he was also shocked at the passages and assuring the poet that there would be no recurrence of such incidents (Russell, vi. 275–6).

[1] Moore published 'Ali's Bride. A Tale, from the Persian' in The *Metropolitan*, iv (1832), 209–18.

[2] Moore's lines 'To Viscountess Valletort' appeared in the *Metropolitan*, iv (1832), 105. Marryat paid him £100, which Moore returned, saying that he could not pledge himself to any more contributions.

name to periodical publications that one seems thereby made responsible for the misdeeds of all one's *collaborateurs*—and to me, who have enough of my own to answer for, this is rather too much.

We shall be most happy to see you at the time you mention.

Yours, my dear Sir, very truly

Thomas Moore.

I should think the Tale would be 3 or 4 pages, but you had better allow for 5 or 6, as I almost always underrate the quantity of my MS.

1004. *To Louis McLane*

New York Public

Sloperton Cottage
June 13ᵗʰ 1832

My dear Mʳ McClean— I have been requested by a young countryman of mine, Mʳ Maturin (the son of a man of much genius, the author of Bertram) to assist him with some letters of introduction in a very praiseworthy attempt he is about to make to try his fortune by industry in your great country ;[1] and it is not without a feeling of pleasure that, in the present instance, I comply with his request as it affords me an opportunity of recalling myself to your recollection and expressing the interest I can never cease to take in yours & Mʳˢ McClean's happiness.

Mʳ Maturin is a graduate of Trinity College Dublin, and any thing you can do towards assisting him in bettering his fortune will be very thankfully acknowledged by

Yours most sincerely
Thomas Moore

McClane Esqʳ [2]

1005. *To Washington Irving*

Pennsylvania Historical Society

Sloperton Cottage
June 14ᵗʰ 1832

My dear Irving— I trust the gentleman who is to be the bearer of this note will be lucky enough to meet you in America, as I have no doubt that you will have both the power & will to serve him in

---

[1] See letter No. 1005, to Washington Irving, 14 June 1832.

[2] Note the difference in the spelling of the name. Moore probably addressed the letter to Louis McLane (1786–1857), who was minister to England from 1829 to 1831, when Moore became acquainted with him.

the trial of his fortune he is about to make in your Land of Adventure. His father's name* will be, among all lovers of literature, a pass-port for him, and his own good dispositions will, I trust, show him not unworthy of such an introduction.[1]

I hope you received the letter, inclosing a scrap of Byron's writing for Mr Van Buren, which I sent you through Byng.

Yours, my dear Irving, most truly
Thomas Moore

Washington Irving Esqr.

* Maturin [*probably Irving's note*]

1006. *To E. R. Moran*

Bodleian MS. Eng. misc. d. 279, f. 23

Private.

Devizes
June 28th 1832

Dear Sir. I feel very much the kind interest you take in my prospects at Limerick.[2] I have had proposals also from Cashel & Waterford, but from none of the three places has any thing definite or of a *public* nature reached me.

Many thanks for the Globe of Tuesday.

Yours faithfully
Thomas Moore.

1007. *To E. R. Moran*

Bodleian MS. Eng. misc. d. 279, f. 28

July 18th 1832

Dear Sir

Having but just returned home from Bath, I shall not have time before Post hour to answer your letter as I could wish. But you shall hear from me by tomorrow's post. I had, indeed, already had thoughts of begging you to be my medium of communication with Limerick, as hitherto [I] have had no direct means of conveying my sentiments to my friends there.

Yours very truly
Thomas Moore

[1] See letter No. 1004, to Louis McLane, 13 June 1832.
[2] See letter No. 1008, to E. R. Moran, 19 July 1832.

1008. *To E. R. Moran*

Bodleian MS. Eng. misc. d. 279, f. 31

Sloperton Cottage
July 19th 1832

Dear Sir.

I have unluckily left myself but little more time for answering your letter to-day than I could command yesterday. Your Limerick friend's remarks are sensible & kind—but he labours under a few mistakes respecting me, some of which are natural, while others are of a kind that not a little surprise me. Pray, assure him from me that should I make up my mind to accept the honour of a seat in Parliament,[1] I shall go in an unfettered & independent Irishman —thinking but of Ireland & her interests and not bound to any man or *party* whatsoever. My whole life ought to have been an assurance that this would be the case. I have, it is true, formed friendships in England, high & honourable ones; but none that have ever interfered for a moment, or *can* interfere, with either my right of thinking for myself, or of speaking with perfect freedom what I think. With respect to Lord Lansdowne (who knows far better than I see your friend does the part I should take in Irish politics) I very much doubt whether, with all his good-will to me, he would even *think* of offering me his interest in Limerick, and most undoubtedly I (from the same cause) should never think of asking him for it.[2]

[1] In 1832 Moore was asked to stand for Parliament for Limerick. The request was transmitted through Dr. Gerald Griffin, who told Moore that he had little doubt of success. When Moore declined on the grounds that giving up his writing for a seat in Parliament would be financial ruin for him, Griffin replied that his Limerick friends had started a subscription in order to buy Moore an estate of £400 per year. Later he wrote for a decision, saying that they could not proceed with negotiations for the estate until they were certain of the poet's intention to stand for election. Moore refused again, this time on the grounds that he could not accept such a gift *before* he had served in Parliament, since it would place him under obligation to the Limerick Union, which was backing him. For further details see letter No. 1020, to the Limerick Union, 8 Nov., No. 1021, to E. R. Moran, 26 Nov., and No. 1024, to Samuel Rogers, 9 Dec. 1832.

[2] A copy of this letter, probably in Moran's hand, is in the collection of material now in the British Museum (B.M. Eg. MS. 2149), which the editor of the *Globe* made in anticipation of a life of Moore. Moran also copied out a part of Dr. Griffin's letter, in which the writer expresses a fear that Moore's association with Lord Lansdowne would be detrimental to his interests in Ireland. He would like to know whether Moore would be completely independent of Lord Lansdowne and not be under obligation to support him in such matters as the Tithe Bill. Moore is here replying to this expression of doubt about his political freedom.

When Dr Griffin talks of my being placed in the *old* affection of my Irish friends, *can* he mean that I have done any thing since to chill their affections? but no—I will not do either him or them the injustice to think the phrase was so meant. They who have cast their eyes over the last work I published may accuse me of imprudence—violence—or even (as some in England do) of *treason*, but certainly not of any abatement of my zeal for Ireland & her liberties.[1]

Whether I shall make up my mind to stand for Limerick or not is a point (to *me*), of far less consequence than those I have above adverted to, and I the less therefore regret my not having time now [to] allude to it. But I shall be glad that you would communicate what I have here hastily said to Dr Griffin, and that, through him, it should reach such persons in Limerick as do me the honour to think it a matter of any interest. All I ask is that my letter may not get into print.

Yours, my dear Sir, very truly

Thomas Moore

1009. *To George Crabbe (the Younger)*

Harvard College Library

Sloperton Cottage

July 21st 1832

My dear Sir— I am about to publish some verses which I was tempted to write on receiving your very welcome & flattering present of your father's ink-stand,[2] verses, not worthy of their subject, but still sufficient to show my feeling of the gift—and it has just occurred to me that the opportunity might be taken of preparing the Public for the appearance of your book[3] by annexing a note to say briefly that you had such a work in contemplation. Pray, let me have a line (by return of post, if possible) to say whether such an announcement would appear to you unseasonable.

I should like, too, to know whether you would feel any objection to my quoting in a note a few sentences from the letter which you wrote me in sending the inkstand. As you may have forgotten what you said, I shall here transcribe the words.

'My brother & I, desirous of honouring these writing implements of my Father, wish to place them in your hands. Were they

---

[1] Probably *The Life and Death of Lord Edward Fitzgerald* (1831). Moore was accused of sanctioning rebellion in this work (see letter No. 985, to John Murray, 25 Oct. 1831).

[2] See 'Verses to the Poet Crabbe's Inkstand', *Poetry*, p. 533.

[3] *The Life of the Rev. George Crabbe*, by his son, in *The Collected Works of George Crabbe* (1834). vol. I.

of any intrinsic worth, we might not think ourselves authorized to offer them to you, but their value arising wholly from their connexion with his memory, we do not hesitate to beg you will accept them.'

Yours, my dear Sir, very truly
Thomas Moore.

The verses are to appear in the Metropolitan—a Magazine to which I have been induced to become, for a short time, a contributor.[1]

1010. *To Mary Shelley*

Abinger Collection

Sloperton
July 23rd 1832.

You may be sure I felt for you on the occasion you allude to, not that the matter was of any real importance, but knowing how sensitive you are, and how femininely you shrink even from publicity that every one else would be so proud of. I was sorry for the poor little girl herself, from the circumstances brought to light about her father &c., and principally, indeed, because she is your friend. You have lost nothing of *me* by not being in London, as I have not been there myself since we last met. At this moment, I am in a good deal of anxiety about my poor little sister who is coming to pass some time with us, and never having been on the salt sea, is I dare say trembling at every blast of wind on the other side of the water while I am equally trembling *for* her here. I go to Bristol tomorrow evening to meet her.[2]

You see I have been at last drawn in to the detestable vortex of Periodicalism.[3] I resisted as long as I could, but when they came to talk of five hundred a year for writing (or *not* writing, such being nearly the terms) twelve scraps of any *thing* for them in the year, why—I know I should be laughed at if I refused; and though

---

[1] See letter No. 1010, to Mary Shelley, 23 July 1832.

[2] Moore met his sister at Bristol on 25 July 1832 (see Russell, vi. 280).

[3] On 23 June 1832 Captain Marryat offered Moore £1,000 a year to become editor of the *Metropolitan*. The terms were flattering, since there was to be a 'sub-editor' who would look to all details, thereby relieving Moore of the necessity of living in town. Upon learning that Campbell, the incumbent editor, would continue with the journal, Moore replied that although he 'should consider it an honour to *succeed* Campbell, [he] could not possibly think of *supplanting* him'. Thereupon Marryat offered him £500 a year 'for contributions as often as it might suit [him] to give them, and only stipulating that for each of the three next numbers [he] should give them something'. On 30 June after some hesitation, Moore accepted the second offer (see Russell, vi. 274–5).

I know I shall be equally laughed at for accepting, it is at least the best side of the joke for me, and accordingly I gave in. My only comfort is that it is a work nobody reads, so that I shall have the pleasure of writing *incog.* and in a year (which I have made the limit of my engagement) it will be, with *my* help, consigned to its grave. You never tell me what you're doing.

Ever most truly yours

Thomas Moore

1011. *To Peter Legh*

Rice University

Sloperton
August 3rd 1832

My dear *Peter*— (You see how I presume upon old times—my old times, alas) I desired Ellen before she left Dublin to ask you to come to us here, and though she gives me but very little hope of your doing so, I shall not easily surrender the prospect of such a pleasure. Another thing which I bid her do (and which she did *not* do) was to draw upon me for sufficient money to pay the debt I owe you— a debt far more easily discharged than that of the gratitude connected with it for your truly kind & delicate performance of the sad duties you took upon yourself.[1] I was about to inclose the sum in this letter, but I had much rather you would come for it, and in the hope that I shall receive an answer to say you *will*, shall remain a little longer your debtor.

Our dearest Nell bore her voyage very well, and is, I think, looking better since she came to us.

Yours most truly

Thomas Moore

1012. *To Alicia Lefanu*

Rice University

Sloperton
August 7th 1832

My dear Miss Lefanu.— I have this moment received your *very* pretty verses by which I feel not only much flattered but (what is better) cordially gratified at finding that you still bear me so

---

[1] Peter Legh assumed much of the responsibility for the funeral arrangements at the death of Moore's father in December 1825 (Russell, v. 22–23). Since it is unlikely that Moore would have left this debt unpaid for seven years, he is probably paying Legh for financial assistance at the time of his mother's death in May 1832 although there is no mention of such aid in the diary or in other letters.

kindly in remembrance. Should you have any objection to their
being in the Metropolitan?—that is, if I *can* get them *to give* you
something *worth* your acceptance for them. I have no other connexion with the work myself than as contributor of scraps, for
a short period.[1]

Happening at this moment to be sending some inclosures to our
County Member who is at Leamington, I shall pop this in with
them.

Yours most truly
Thomas Moore.

M[r] Benett will forward any communication you may have for me.

1013. *To James Corry*

Oscar E. Lancaster

Sloperton
August 21st 1832

My dear Corry— You are summoned to attend here, without fail,
on Monday next 27th for three special purposes— 1st & foremost, to
see your old friend Ellen[2] (who, I am sorry to say, will not stay long
with us)— 2[ndly] to attend an archery meeting which takes place on
Tuesday, and 3[rdly] to dance at a Ball which M[rs] Phipps gives on
Wednesday.— Now, if there's a single hop, step or jump left in
you, all this you will do without a word more about it.

I don't think I have ever answered your sensible letter about my
Parliamentarianism[3] (what a long word for a short M. P. !)—but
I agreed with every word of it, and mean to act accordingly. I hope
you saw the paragraph from Waterford, where they are now all in
a stir about me, I find.

We have just returned from a most delightful visit to our friends
the Houltons.

Most affectionate regards to M[rs] C. from hers & yours ever

T. Moore

---

[1] Alicia Lefanu's poem entitled 'Lines Suggested by Mr. Moore's "Verses
to the Poet Crabbe's Inkstand"'' appeared in the *Metropolitan*, v (August 1832),
231. The theme of this supercilious tribute is that Moore is not to consider
himself 'alone a child of earth'.

[2] Moore's sister Ellen. See letter No. 1010, to Mary Shelley, 23 July 1832.

[3] See letter No. 1008, to E. R. Moran, 19 July 1832.

1014. *To James Murray III*

Sir John Murray

Sloperton Cottage
August 21st 1832

My dear John— As I know your father is always too much occupied to attend to the *Romance* concerns of the establishment, I think it better to put poor Bani[m's][1] case (whose letter to me I inclose) in *your* hands, and it will give me great pleasure if it would suit your purpose to undertake the publication of his novel for him. Though he did not authorize me to lay his letter before you, yet it is so much more a compendious mode of putting you in possession of the poor fellow's position at this moment, that I venture to do so, and you can return it to me when you answer this, which I beg may be speedily.

It is so long since I have been in town that I fear you will all forget me—but pray remind your mother & sisters of me & believe me very truly yours

Thomas Moore

In your answer to me, you had better perhaps not say that you had read the inclosed.

1015. *To John Gibson Lockhart*

N.L.S. MS. 924, No. 38

Sloperton Cottage
September 27th 1832

My dear Mr Lockhart— I felt it to be *very* kind of you to think of me at such a moment. I assure you I often thought of you & poor Mrs Lockhart and all you must have suffered, nor could I have supposed that news so melancholy could ever have been welcomed by me as this was.[2] When such great & good men are to go, the more quickly they are released from their sufferings the better, and the thoughts of the pain *he* was enduring haunted me day & night. With my kindest regards to Mrs Lockhart & Miss Scott, believe me

Ever most truly yours
Thomas Moore

---

[1] The name is partially illegible, but Moore could be referring to Michael Banim, whose *Ghost Hunter and His Family* (attributed to his brother John but actually written by Michael) appeared in 1833.

[2] Scott died at Abbotsford on 21 Sept. 1832.

1016. *To Mrs. Mereweather*

Rice University

Sloperton
October 7th 1832

My dear Mrs Merreweather—[1] There seems to be some fatality over my engagements to you & sergeant Merreweather which forever defeats your kind intentions towards me and my own wishes. I have just had letters from town which oblige me to lose not a day in hastening thither, upon business which unluckily will *not* wait, and am thus again baffled in my very anxious desire to find myself at your hospitable table. Pray, do not give me up as a lost case, nor treat as a fault what is only a misfortune, but believe me, with sincere regret for my disappointment,

Yours very truly
Thomas Moore.

1017. *To Mrs. Smith*

National Library of Ireland

Sloperton
October 18th 1832.

My dear Mrs Smith— You, who know what the little bearer of this letter is, will easily understand how grieved we are to lose her. Indeed, to Mrs Moore it is a privation which she will not speedily get over, as her loves & likings are few, but when she *does* take to people, she (as Shakespeare says) 'grapples them to her heart with hooks of steel',[2] and Ellen is among those the most strongly *hooked on*.[3] Our only hope is that her recollection of her time here will be agreeable enough (in spite of you and one or two other rivals) to [*the remainder of the letter is missing*].

1018. *To E. R. Moran*

Bodleian MS. Eng. misc. d. 279, f. 35

Sloperton
October 18th 1832

My dear Sir—

I came away in a great hurry from town, but left such directions respecting your tickets as I trust secured their safe delivery to your messenger. We were, by an unexpected accident, deprived of the

---

[1] Moore spelled the name with two r's in the salutation; Russell spells it 'Mereweather' in the index to his edition of Moore's *Memoirs and Correspondence.*   [2] *Hamlet,* i. iii. 63.
[3] Moore's sister Ellen visited Sloperton during the summer of 1832, leaving on 19 Oct. (see Russell, vi, 297).

power of availing ourselves of your Kindness that night, but my young Carthusian did not the less feel the interest you took in his pleasures.

Mrs Moore receives, with pride & thankfulness, the flattering profer [*sic*] of your dedication.

Very truly yours
Thomas Moore.

1019. *To E. R. Moran*

Rice University
Private

Sloperton
Novr 6th 1832

My dear Sir— Our dear friends, the Gursyone boys, are running away with this affair of my election most sadly,[1]—or rather, as usual, too merrily. Twice have I expressly & decidedly declared to them the impossibility of my becoming their representative—first to that letter which I believe you knew of, from your friend Dr Griffin, in which I told him that, however warmly it had been the ambition of my whole life to sit in Parliament for Ireland, the precarious as well as limited state of my pecuniary circumstances rendered it wholly impracticable. In this letter, by the bye, I volunteered an opinion respecting the Repeal of the Union as follows.— 'For myself I will say with Grattan, in 1810 "I was an enemy to the extinguishment of the Irish P^t and must be a friend to its restoration"—but I will also add with Grattan that "such a proposition in Parl^t to be either prudent or useful must be called for & backed by the Irish nation".'

Of this declaration of mine they published the *first* clause, sinking altogether the qualifying condition appended to it, and have ever since enrolled me among the *Pledged* on the Repeal!

Some time after this letter I received a confidential one from Dr Griffin informing me that my generous friends in Limerick were resolved to remove the obstacle that lay in the way of my representing them, and were actually then in negociation for the purchase of an estate in Limerick for that purpose. When pressed to give a definite answer to this very flattering proposal I wrote to Dr Griffin that this plan would undoubtedly remove, to a great degree, my objections on the score of limited circumstances, but that it was attended with another difficulty still more insurmountable. Such a reward from the people for parliamentary services actually performed would be a tribute as honourable to

---

[1] See letter No. 1008, to E. R. Moran, 19 July 1832. Although the addressee of this letter is unknown, he is conjecturally Moran.

him who accepted as to them who gave it—but to receive such a gift before-hand, to be sent into Parliament as a feed Counsel, with the suspicion that I derived my inspiration from my rent-roll—this, I said, was a situation in which, neither for my own sake nor for theirs, ought I to consent to [*sic*] put myself.

Such was in substance, at least, but not less decisive—the purport of my letter—notwithstanding which, you see, my friend Tom Shete and the rest 'keep never minding,' and I greatly fear that, between warm-heartedness & warm-*headed*ness, they may make my position at last not a little embarassing [*sic*].

I tell you all this, because you have, from the first, taken so kind an interest in my parliamentary proceedings—*not* wishing you to notice publicly any thing I have here said, but in order that you may be in possession of the whole circumstances should any thing occur to induce me to require your aid.

Yours faithfully
Thomas Moore

1020. *To the Limerick Union*

Russell, vi. 305

Sloperton Cottage
November 8th, 1832.

Gentlemen,

I have to acknowledge, with every feeling of respect and gratitude, the requisition so numerously signed, which I have this day had the honour of receiving from you. Already had I been in a great degree prepared for such a call by a correspondence in which I have been engaged with one of your fellow-citizens, and which, though but preliminary to the decisive step which has now been taken, had put me fully in possession of the kind feelings entertained towards me by the greater portion of the enlightened electors of your city.

To know that even a thought of selecting me as their representative had once entered into the contemplation of persons like yourselves, so well qualified by a zealous sense of the value of liberty to judge of the requisites of those to whom such a trust should be confided, would in itself have been a source of pride and gratification to my mind; you may judge therefore what are my feelings on receiving so signal a proof, both in the cordial and unsought requisition which has this morning reached me, and in those further proceedings which I understand you meditate, that the honour you did me in selecting my name from among the many offered to you was no light or transient compliment, but that you deliberately think me worthy of being the representative of your interests in the great crisis, as well for England as for Ireland, which is now approaching.

But, Gentlemen, rarely in this life can so high and bright a position as that in which your offer now places me be enjoyed without its opposing shadow; and in proportion to the pleasure, the triumph, which I cannot but feel at this manifestation of your opinion,—placing as it does within my reach a post of honour which I have so often in the ambition of my young days sighed for,—in proportion to my deep and thorough sense of the distinction you would thus confer upon me, is the pain with which I am compelled reluctantly to declare that I cannot accept it. The truth, plainly told, is, that my circumstances render such an appropriation of my time impossible; not even for a single session could I devote myself to the duties of Parliament without incurring considerable embarrassment. To the labour of the day, in short, am I indebted for my daily support; and though it is by being content with this lot that I have been able to preserve that independence of mind which has now so honourably, and I may be allowed to boast in so many quarters, won for me the confidence of my fellow-countrymen, it is not the less an insuperable impediment to the acceptance of the high honour you offer me.

I am not unaware, as I have already intimated, that, in your strong and generous desire to remove this only obstacle which you know opposed itself to my compliance with your wishes, you have set on foot a national subscription for the purpose, as you yourselves express it, of providing me with the qualification necessary for a member of the House of Commons. This proof of your earnestness in the cause I feel, both on public and private grounds, most sensibly. But, however honourable I might deem such a gift after the performance of services in Parliament, I see objections to it which to me are insurmountable. Were I obliged to choose which should be my direct paymaster, the Government or the People, I should say without hesitation the People; but I prefer holding on my free course, humble as it is, unpurchased by either: nor shall I the less continue, as far as my limited sphere of action extends, to devote such powers as God has gifted me with to that cause which has always been uppermost in my heart, which was my first inspiration and shall be my last,—the cause of Irish freedom.

I have the honour to be, Gentlemen,
Your faithful and devoted Servant,
Thomas Moore.[1]

---

[1] See letter No. 1008, to E. R. Moran, 19 July 1832.

1021. *To E. R. Moran*

Bodleian MS. Eng. misc. d. 279, f. 39

Sloperton
Novr 26th 1832

My dear Sir—

I have time, at this moment, but to thank you for your kind letter, and to tell you that it is *not* my *fault* there being no public notice from me of the proceedings at Limerick, as my Definitive answer to the Requisition addressed to me has been in the hands of Members of the Limerick Union this fortnight past.[1] I have, indeed, declined the proposal in every shape in which my kind-hearted friends there have put it, nor did the estate of four hundred a year which they were in negociation for tempt me to change my mind. My letter was on the point of being laid before the Union & published, when O'Connell, arriving in Limerick, desired that they should still withhold it and that he himself would write to me on the subject. I have not since heard from him, but have written to Dr Griffin to say that if the Letter does not appear speedily in the Limerick papers, I shall be obliged, in my own defence to publish it here— It is a shame to inflict postage upon you for all these nothings about myself, but I have no opportunity at this moment, of sending through a Member.

Yours, my dear Sir, very truly
Thomas Moore.

By the bye, if the letter should appear in the Limerick papers before my last letter reaches Dr Griffin, there is, I rather think, a word omitted in it which you will replace for me in copying it. Instead of 'without considerable embarassment' read 'without incurring considerable embarassment'

1022. *To Mr. Stanley*

Rice University

Sloperton Cottage
Novr 29th 1832

My dear Mr Stanley— I am well aware how little right I have to apply to you either on my own behalf or that of others; but having been entreated by Mr William Power, of Dublin (the original publisher of the Irish Melodies) to use my interest with you for some of those situations which he tells me you have now in your gift I have assented so far to his request as to trouble you with this

---

[1] See letter No. 1020, to the Limerick Union, 8 Nov. 1832.

letter, and shall be most agreeably surprised (as well as gratified) to find that, in doing so, I shall have been the means of rendering him any service.

Trusting that, at all events, you will forgive the liberty which I thus take, I am, my dear Mr Stanley, very faithfully yours

Thomas Moore

1023. *To E. R. Moran*

Bodleian MS. Eng. misc. d. 279, f. 41

Sloperton
Decr 2nd 1832.

My dear Sir— Thanks for your kindness in sending the Globe, which I am now about to treat myself to, for a spell, as I always do when matters begin to be interesting. Your printer, however, has made a devil of a mistake in one of my sentences. Thinking it must be the fault of the Irish typographer, I referred anxiously to the Limerick Edition, but it is there all right. May I ask you to correct it in your next paper, in some such manner as the following.

Erratum.— In the Letter of Mr Moore to the Electors of Limerick, which we copied in our last, we perceive that the meaning of one of the sentences has been rendered imperfect by the omission of a few words. The passage, according to its correct rendering, is as follows: 'However honourable I might deem such a gift, *after* the performance of services in Parliament, I see objections to it, as a prospective tribute, which to me are insurmountable'.[1]

You perceive what havoc the omission of the words 'as a prospective tribute' has made in my poor sentence.

Pray, forgive all this trouble & believe me

Most truly yours
Thomas Moore

I was about to write to the Times on this same subject—but it will be *very* kind of you if you will undertake to see your paragraph (whatever it may be) copied into their paper. You may make use of my name, if necessary, in doing so.

1024. *To Samuel Rogers*

Rice University

Sloperton
Decr 9th 1832

My dear Rogers— I take advantage (in this universal *death* of Franks) of an opportunity to town, to thank you, in my own behalf and Bessy's, for your most thoughtful recollection of your promise.

[1] See letter No. 1020, to the Limerick Union, 8 Nov. 1832.

Though it was quite like *you* to remember such a thing, it is, I must say, of all kinds of memory the most rare. You have seen, I dare say, the finale of my Limerick transaction—[1] One of the members of the deputation I had from them here was that very clever fellow, the author of 'The Collegians',[2] a book which Lord Clifden (in his rebel days, at least) used to eulogize so much; but which I suppose, now that we are all so loyal again, he would not condescend to remember. I am really quite sick, by anticipation, at what I see is *coming*, among our Whig friends, and often sigh for a little *breathing* of conversation with the only man (meaning yourself) who can look abroad in politics, and get out of the little selfish, intriguing ferment of the moment.

I am afraid there is no chance of seeing you down here at Christmas, but I rather think some business may take me to you soon after. By the bye, I quoted, as well as I could, to my friend of 'the Collegians' what you said, so well & truly, of Ireland having become the school-mistress of England &c. and he thought right good & true.

With Bessy's best regards to yourself & Sister, in which I most cordially join, believe me ever, my dear Rogers, faithfully yours

Thomas Moore.

1025. *To James Hews Bransby*[3]
Harvard College Library

[*c.* 1832]

You have here all that at this moment occurs to me in the way either of recollection or remark, on the subject of our able & venerated friend. The delightful day which Mr Rogers & myself passed with him at Sydenham, you have already I believe an account of from my friend Mr Campbell, who was our host on the occasion. Mr Lockhart has I take for granted, communicated to you the amusing anecdote of Crabbe's interview with the Two Scotch Lairds;—an anecdote which I cherish the more freshly & fondly in my memory, from its having been told me with his own peculiar humour, by Sir Walter Scott at Abbotsford.[4] I have therefore nothing further left than to assure you how much and truly I am

Yours

Thomas Moore.

[1] See letter No. 1020, to the Limerick Union, 8 Nov. 1832.

[2] Gerald Griffin published the *Collegians* in 1829. For Griffin's account of his visit to Sloperton see Strong, *Minstrel Boy*, pp. 182–4.

[3] This letter was probably addressed to James Hews Bransby, who published 'Brief Notices of the Late George Crabbe' in a letter to the editor of the *Carnarvon Herald* in 1832.

[4] See letter No. 1044, to John Murray, 29 Dec. 1833.

1026. *To Macvey Napier*

B.M. Add. MS. 34616, f. 32

Sloperton
Feb^r 15th 1833

My dear Sir— I was very agreeably surprized by your letter & its contents, nor will I deny that, though conscious of how little real worth was the article I sent you (the subject not being of a kind to attract many readers) I still looked for some return of *substance* for my *shadow*.[1] You have however made full amends for any disappointment I may have felt, and the seasonableness of the contents would have sweetened a far less satisfactory explanation than yours.

As to writing something else for you, I should be by no means disinclined to do so were I not now plunged into my Irish History over head & ears in rebellions, massacres, &c. and having therefore little leisure for any thing else.

I am sorry I was so unlucky as to miss you during your last visit to London, as I do not forget the agreeable day we had together at the Longmans—but I shall hope some time or other for the renewal of that pleasure, and am, my dear Mr Napier, very truly yours
Thomas Moore

1027. *Addressee unknown*

Huntington Library

Sloperton
April 23rd 33

Dear Sir— I feel much obliged by the kind offer which you have made; but, on considering the matter more maturely, I do not think that there can be much more, on the subject of the Round Towers, than is to be found in those works to which every one has access, and shall therefore not spoil your secret for others by asking any disclosure of it to myself.[2]

I am your obliged & faithful Servt
Thomas Moore.

---

[1] This may be a reference to Moore's article on German rationalism, which appeared in September 1831 (see letter No. 974, to Macvey Napier, 19 Aug. 1831), although it is quite possible that he later wrote another review of the same type. See, for example, the *Edinburgh Review*, lvi (October 1832), 221–44, which is an article on Robert Vaughan's *Life of Wycliffe* (1831) and Charles Webb Le Bas's *Life of Wycliffe* (1832).

[2] On 26 Apr. Moore recorded in his diary that he had received a letter from a man who offered to reveal to him the 'whole secret history' of the Round

1028. *To the Earl of Shrewsbury*

National Library of Ireland

Sloperton Cottage, Devizes
April 26th 1833

My dear Lord Shrewsbury— I ought, long before now, to have acknowledged your kind letter—but a mass of correspondence grew upon me while in town, and this, added to the other demands upon my pen, must plead my excuse for such silence.

I assure you, you were one of the first persons I enquired after, on my arrival in London; and it annoyed me exceedingly to hear that you would not be in town till after Easter, as I was thus deprived of my only chance (for a long time, perhaps) of seeing you.

Your letter about my book came most seasonably to inspire a little courage in me, respecting its success. I have no idea whether it sells or not— I could ill afford the time I spent in writing it, and if I do not lose money as well as time by it, it is the utmost I expect. I had counted a good deal upon our fellow Catholics for the sale, though my publishers told me I must not expect much from that quarter.[1]

A friend has just quoted to me some journal which says, in speaking of the work, 'These two little volumes will, we predict, be the parents of two thousand others.' If this be the case I must depute to able pens like your Lordship's the task of answering my opponents— 'literavi animam meam'.

Trusting that, if any chance should take me to town during the season, I may be lucky enough to enjoy the long-wished pleasure of meeting Lady Shrewsbury & yourself, I am most truly yours

Thomas Moore.

1029. *To William Lisle Bowles*[2]

Rice University

May 7th 1833

My dear Bowles—

I was most sorry to have missed you on Saturday and, provokingly, I arrived at home about ten minutes after you were gone. I want much to see & hear how you are and how you have been

Towers. A second letter from the gentleman contained an 'offer' of a visit to Moore, during which the man would, for a hundred guineas, reveal the secret of the Towers (Russell, vi. 327). See also letter No. 1050, to Macvey Napier, 18 Feb. 1834.

[1] Moore is referring to *Travels of an Irish Gentleman*, which appeared in two volumes in 1833.

[2] This letter was published in Greever, *A Wiltshire Parson*, p. 89.

& fared since we last met. Would that Sloperton and Bremhill could be thrown beside each other,—by any means but a convulsion of nature, which, God knows, we don't want just now, having plenty of convulsion, in the political way, preparing for us. But it is a sad thing that you & I, Arcades ambo, should be so far separated. My foot still prevents any effort of pedestrianism, but I should like a day with you at Bath prodigiously.

Best regards to Mrs Bowles,

Ever yours truly
Thomas Moore

1030. *To Macvey Napier*

B.M. Add. MS. 34616, f. 92

Sloperton, Devizes
May 30th 1833

My dear Sir— If any thing could make me regret leaving town & its bustle for my quiet little cottage it would be the loss I have had in not meeting with you and enjoying a day together such as we once had with our friends in Paternoster Row. I liked town less, this time, than ever I did, and one of the few treats I had, while there, was the seeing your excellent predecessor, Jeffrey, one evening, and having a little quiet talk with him. I fear it is wholly impossible for me to do any thing for the Review—my last work[1] was so purely the indulgence of a *Hobby* and my canter on it is so little likely to be profitable, that I must now work hard to arrive at the produce of my Irish History or rather replace, I am sorry to say, the produce already but too much anticipated. It flatters me that you should so much wish me to write for you, and if any thing should turn up, in the way of subject, that could be at once easily & effectively turned to account, I shall not fail to take advantage of it—but I cannot make any promise.

It will not be in your power, I fear, to notice my Theology ;— for I flatter myself it would go against the grain with you to abuse me, and you could hardly do otherwise. If I could get my Rationalist neighbour here to review me for you, it would be rather good fun—only that I fear he would be equally objectionable on the opposite tack. I find I am called in Ireland 'Defender of the Faith' and 'Father of the Hibernian Church'!

Yours most truly
Thomas Moore

---

[1] *Travels of an Irish Gentleman in Search of Religion* (1833).

1031. *To William Lisle Bowles*[1]

Rice University

[May or June 1833]

My dear Bowles— I am still too much of an invalid to come to Bath,[2] and have been obliged to let Bessy go without me to-day. I hope she will be lucky enough to meet you & Mrs Bowles.

I desired the Longmans to do what you wished, and also mentioned the offer of publication at their House, but they have not answered me. I take for granted, however, that the announcement has appeared, as they seldom are inattentive to any thing I request of them. What are you doing with respect to this?

You see Blackwood has laid on hard, but it is very well done—by far the cleverest thing yet written on the subject.

Yours ever,
T. Moore.

1032. *Addressee unknown*

Rice University

Sloperton Cottage Devizes
Sunday June 2nd 1833

Sir.

I shall be obliged by your securing for me an inside place in the York House Coach on Wednesday morning next (the 5th) for town, to take up at the Black Dog, Studley, near Calne.

An an[swer wi]th particulars will oblige

Yours &c
Thomas Moore

1033. *To Lord Kerry*

Rice University

Sloperton
June 12th 1833[3]

My dear Kerry— You see you have brought an inclosure on yourself by your *little* note, which must have astonished the Great Post, I think exceedingly. Both myself & my Irish History are most

---

[1] This letter was published in Greever, *A Wiltshire Parson*, p. 88.
[2] See letter No. 1029, to William Lisle Bowles, 7 May 1833.
[3] This letter is postmarked June 13, 1833. Moore either made a mistake in the date or formed the '2' of 'June 12th' to look like his usual '9'. Evidence that he was confused lies in the fact that the first digit of the '19th' is heavily inked over a '2'.

thankful for your enquiries, but as to the forth-coming of *either* in London any time within this year, it is more than I am able to answer for. It is, indeed, not at all probable that I shall visit London again this season.

Dennis Bulgruddery, you recollect, thought that one of the kindest things he could do by a friend was to advise him not to drink any of his (Bulgruddery's) beer, and in the same manner, I counsel you, as a friend, *not* to read my last book.[1] It is an advice, I must say the world seems much inclined to act upon.

Pray don't mislay the inclosed.

Ever yours, my dear Lord Kerry
(I must begin to give you your due,
now you are a Senator) most truly
Thomas Moore

1034. *To Mrs. Lockhart*

Abbotsford[2]

Sloperton, Devizes
July 3rd 1833

My dear Mrs Lockhart— Though fearful that I may, even now, be too early in intruding upon your sorrow, I cannot forbear any longer telling you how sincerely & deeply I feel for you. I know not when, indeed, I was so shocked as on reading the account in the newspapers (not having been in the least degree prepared for it by hearing of her previous illness) and coming so soon after, and no doubt occasioned by, our great and general loss, it affected me, I assure you, more than I could have conceived possible out of my own immediate circle of interests. Most truly do I pity you, & trusting that you will forgive whatever there may be of unseasonable or intrusive [*sic*] in this letter, am, my dear Mrs Lockhart

most faithfully yours
Thomas Moore.

1035. *Addressee unknown*

Harvard College Library

Sloperton
August 22nd 1833.

Sir— I have had much pleasure in receiving the kind note with which you have favoured me, as well as the very pretty and gracefully composed song, which accompanied it. You do not say whether

---

[1] *Travels of an Irish Gentleman in Search of Religion* (1833).
[2] Transcript provided by Dr. James C. Corson, University of Edinburgh Library.

it is your intention to pursue music as a profession, but, if so, it will give me great pleasure to lend any assistance that may be in my power towards forwarding your views.

Your very obliged & faithful Servt
Thomas Moore

1036. *To Mary Shelley*

Abinger Collection

Tuesday—3 o'clock* [postmark August 23, 1833]

I have, indeed, been wishing much to see you—but, if you knew all the disagreeable demands I have on my time, you would not wonder at my being so often unable to do what I wish. Tomorrow, I am sorry to say, I cannot breakfast with you, as I shall be engaged upon business the whole of the morning and on Thursday I go to the country for some days—On my return, however, I shall be sure to call upon you, and with many, many thanks for your kindness in thinking of me, believe me

Faithfully yours
[*Signature effaced*]

I hope this will reach you in time, but I did not receive your note till just now.

1037. *To Macvey Napier*

B.M. Add. MS. 34616, f. 134

Sloperton, Devizes
August 31, 1833

My dear Mr Napier— I have made the best I can of this dull Reverend for you.[1] If you think the thing altogether too long, you may throw overboard the introductory tirade against poetry (vineta mea caedo) and begin where I have placed a pencil mark at the bottom of page 3.— I shall be glad to see a proof, as I never can get my sentences into any decent order till I have them before me in print.

Whatever you may think it worth while to give me for this skimble-skamble will come very welcomely *just now*, as I am collecting all the odds and ends of my small supplies for a short tour in

---

[1] Moore's review of Charles Overton's *Ecclesia Anglicana, a Poem; Containing an Historic Portraiture of the British Church* (1833), appeared in the *Edinburgh Review*, lviii (1833), 31–40. See letter No. 1039, to Macvey Napier, 12 Sept. 1833.

Ireland with Lord John Russell— or, should you even send me *more* than this stuff is worth it shall be placed to your credit towards some future & better article which I shall, in that case, feel myself bound to furnish. I hate reviewing, you *know*—but money makes the author, as well as the mare, to 'go'.

Ever yours truly
Thomas Moore.

1038. *To Dr. Dionysius Lardner*[1]

Quaker Collection, Haverford College

Sloperton
September 1st 1833

My dear Dr Lardner—

It was a grievous disappointment to me not to find you in town, as one of my chief objects in going there was to have some conversation with you. Ever since our last correspondence I have been employed in reducing the scale of the sketch I had made of the early history & antiquities of Ireland, and it has given me no small trouble. With the narrative, however, I shall get on more glibly. I expect by Christmas to have my manuscript so far advanced as fully to justify me (on my own old plan) of going to press with the Volume—but I question whether, on our agreed scheme of waiting till the whole is finished, I can be ready so soon.[2]

With respect to the extent of the work, I cannot even yet say how far I shall be able to bring my Introduction within limits; as the speculation & research into which it invites me is infinite, and, if indulged in, would easily fill the First Volume. I shall in a short time, however, see my way more clearly and shall then let you know.

I have been asked by Lord John Russell through whom I send this letter, to join him in a fortnight's trip to Dublin, and, as there are some things there I should like much to enquire into, I rather think I shall agree to his proposal.[3]

Yours ever truly
Thomas Moore.

---

[1] Dr. Lardner was the general editor of the *Cabinet Cyclopaedia*, for which Moore wrote the *History of Ireland*.

[2] The first volume was not published until 1835.

[3] See letter No. 1039, to Macvey Napier, 12 Sept. 1833.

1039. *To Macvey Napier*

B.M. Add. MS. 34616, f. 146

September 12th 1833

My dear Mr Napier— I am glad you thought the enclosed worth any thing. Between us, we shall immortalize Mr Overton, as I mean, on the appearance of the article, to address a Series of Odes to him.[1]

I have been so far getting money from you under false pretences that (with merit & long reluctance) I have given up my intended trip to Ireland. From the route and time of Lord John's journey, I must have left out Dublin in my course (the only place where I had *real* business)—and this would have made it so *merely* a tour of pleasure that I could not, in conscience, indulge myself in it— otherwise, to have been with him and my neighbours, the Lansdownes, who were also gone for a short spell, would have been very agreeable.

If you should ever be tempted to diverge so far in your courses to town, Mrs Moore & myself would be most happy to see you here.

Yours most truly
Thomas Moore

1040. *To James Power*

Rice University

Brooks's
Novr 13th 1833

Dear Sir— I have sent the Draft to Serjeant Merreweather with a request that he would forward it to you without delay.[2]

Tomorrow I shall be ready to sign at any hour you may appoint, and it had better be done *here*, as I shall the more easily get someone to witness my signature.

I have the pleasure to send a cheque for the amount of my debt to you.

Yours truly
Thomas Moore

I think of starting for home at the end of this week. It does not appear to me that anything can arise to require my presence before

---

[1] Charles Overton, *Ecclesia Anglicana, a Poem; Containing an Historic Portraiture of the British Church* (1833). Moore evidently sent Napier a review of this work in letter No. 1037, 31 Aug. 1833, and is now returning the proofs. The review appeared in the *Edinburgh Review*, lviii (October 1833), 31–40. For Moore's satiric verse on Overton see *Poetry*, p. 643. The poem was first printed in *The Times* for Wednesday, 6 Nov. 1833.

[2] By 1832 Moore's accounts with Power were hopelessly muddled, and Serjeant Mereweather served as an arbiter between poet and publisher (see Russell, vii. 4 ff.).

the abstractors; but, if there should, I can come up again without much loss of time.

1041. *To Isabella Houlton*

B.M. Add. MS. 27425BC, f. 29

Sloperton
Decr 10th 1833

My dear Isabella Houlton—for so I am resolved to have the pleasure of calling you, for the last time,—it was on my return this morning from the agreeable operation of helping *one* fair friend to marry that I was greeted with your welcome announcement of *another* being so near the same happy fate.[1] Happy may it be, say I, from my 'heart of hearts,'[2] and there is a lady beside me who joins most cordially and devoutly in the same aspirations. Really, with all this marrying, it makes me feel as if I was married over again, myself— How does your mother feel? something the same way, I hope. Best regards to her & all from yours & theirs truly and affectionately

Thomas Moore

Mrs Moore is all agog about *when* and *where* and a variety of other such adverbs.

1042. *To Macvey Napier*

B.M. Add. MS. 34616, f. 237

Sloperton, Devizes
Decr 20th 1833

My dear Mr Napier— I returned but last night from town, whither I had been called, for the second time, within a very short interval, to the no small disturbance, as you may suppose, of my comfort & studies, and upon business by no means agreeable.[3] The business, luckily, has terminated in a manner more satisfactory than I had anticipated, but the loss of time, money & other such valuables has been most serious to me, and will take a great deal both of time and money to repair. Among other derangements, the task I undertook for *you* has been interrupted just at the moment when (from your requiring it at a particular period) the delay was most

---

[1] On 12 Jan. 1834 Isabella Houlton married Captain Quintus Vivian, of the Eighth Hussars.

[2] *Hamlet*, III. ii. 78.

[3] Although Moore recorded his visit to London in his diary (Russell, vii. 18–20), his object in making the journey is not clear.

inconvenient, if not fatal. I had deferred answering your letter—not being able to say whether I could write for you, or not, untill I had found that somewhat necessary part of the business (at least, with matter-of-fact authors like myself) something to write about, and I had just hit upon this sine-qua-non, when I was summoned to town. The work I thought of was one that not a soul, I believe, but myself has ever read—namely, Nimrod—written by a brother of the late Lord Caernarvon's,[1] and full of 'all such reading as was never read;'[2] but affording, in its eccentricity & odd, learned whims not a bad subject, I think, for fun. I had but just begun to read the book before I left home, and have this morning returned to it, with the intention of trying my hand at something for you, though I fear too late for the next number— At all events, I shall go on, and you will, perhaps, let me have an immediate answer to this direct, to say whether in a week or ten days from hence will be time enough.

Yours ever truly
Thomas Moore

I should not like my name to be mentioned, in connexion with this article, as it was the late Lord Caernarvon who gave me the Volumes, and though I mean to give due praise to the learning of his brother, the quizzing might be thought treacherous. The author himself I know nothing about.

1043. *To Macvey Napier*

B.M. Add. MS. 34616, f. 239

Sloperton
Dec[r] 21, 1833

My dear M[r] Napier— I find I was most rashly premature in my letter of yesterday— On looking a little more considerately at my task, I see it is wholly impossible for me to accomplish it in any thing like the time that I am limited to—or that I could, under any circumstances, spare at the present moment.[3] Even to read the work through, so as not to commit myself in criticizing it, would take almost the whole of the time I could now afford,—there being three closely printed Octavo Volumes, counting, in pages, as follows—Vol. 1, 512, Vol. 2, 666, Vol. 3, 570 !— I actually trembled

---

[1] Algernon Herbert, *Nimrod, a Discourse upon Certain Passages of History and Fable* (1826). Moore gave up the idea of reviewing this book (see letter No. 1043, to Macvey Napier, 21 Dec. 1833).

[2] *The Dunciad,* iv. 250.

[3] See letter No. 1042, to Macvey Napier, 20 Dec. 1833.

at my own rashness when I came to look at them, and all that can be said is that it, at least, shows how anxious I was to consult your wishes, when I could, even for a moment, think of facing such a mass of mad learning. Whether I could, at any time, turn such a book to account in the way of amusement, I very much doubt— but at present, it is wholly out of the question, and I have only to express my regret, as well as ask your pardon, for the false expectations to which my last letter will have given rise.

Yours very truly
Thomas Moore.

1044. *To John Murray*

Sir John Murray

Sloperton
Decr 29th 1833

My dear Sir— I had not the least notion that you were so far advanced in the part of the work where our Epistolary notices were to be inserted, having taken for granted that they were to form a sort of supplement to the Volumes containing the Life;[1] and, ever since I came from town, the little time I could manage to steal from the distractions of society (this being our high flood-time of festivity here) has been employed in poring over some books about Ireland which I was lucky enough to borrow while in town, but am only allowed to use for a very limited time. As I find, however, that your printing is so far advanced and that whatever I give must be given quickly, you may depend upon my not losing a moment in putting together the few particulars I can recollect, and in a day or two, at the farthest, shall furnish you with manuscript.

It surprises me as much as it delights me to find that your materials are so abundant. If I understoood you rightly, it is in form of a familiar letter to yourself that the communications, already given in, have been connected. Of course, Lockhart has not forgotten, in *his* notices, the amusing scene between Crabbe, as a French Abbé, and the two Scottish Lairds.[2]

Yours most truly
Thomas Moore

[1] Moore is referring to the *Life of George Crabbe*, by his son (London, 1834). See letter No. 1047, to John Murray, 1 Jan. 1834.

[2] In his review of the *Life and Poetical Works of George Crabbe*, which appeared in the *Quarterly Review*, L (1833–4), 502, Lockhart related a story of Crabbe's meeting two Scotch Lairds, whom he mistook for foreigners since he was familiar with neither their dress nor language. They in turn mistook him for a French clergyman, and the trio was trying desperately to converse in terrible French when Sir Walter Scott entered the room and spoke to them in English.

1045. *To Colonel Houlton*

B.M. Add. MS. 27425BC, f. 27

Saturday [December 1833]

My dear Houlton— I received your kind, comfortable, *Christmas* note on my return from town the day before yesterday, and avail myself of Arthur's[1] transit to send this answer to it. We shall be, of course, delighted to come to Farleigh, and Mrs Moore bids me say she will settle every thing 'about it, Goddess, and about it', when she meets *your* Goddesses at the Chippenham Ball.

Ever yours most truly
Thos Moore.

1046. *To John Murray*

Sir John Murray

Bowood
Jan^r 1st 1834

My dear Sir— I walked home from this to-day for the express purpose of having a quiet moment to copy out the letter I have written to you, on the subject of Crabbe;[2] and now, on my return here to dinner I find I have most carelessly left the copy behind. This is too provoking—and the more so if you should happen to be *waiting* for my communication. I write this line, however, to say that you may *depend* on the manuscript by tomorrow's post.

You will be able, I trust, to let me have a *proof* of my Notices, as they have been written so hastily that correction will be wanted, not a little.

Yours ever truly
Thos Moore.

1047. *To John Murray*

Life of Crabbe, by his son (London, 1947), p. 231

Sloperton Cottage
January 1, 1834.

My dear Mr. Murray,— Had I been aware that your time of publication was so near,[3] the few scattered notices and recollections of Mr. Crabbe, which it is in my power to furnish for his son's memoir,

---

[1] That is, Arthur Houlton, Colonel Houlton's son. It was he who made the notes to several letters now in the British Museum.

[2] Moore promised Murray a letter about Crabbe, which the publisher could use in the *Life of the Reverend George Crabbe*, by the poet's son. The work appeared in 1834. See letter No. 1047 to John Murray, 1 Jan. 1834.

[3] *The Life of George Crabbe*, by his son (London, 1834).

should have been presented in a somewhat less crude and careless shape than, in this hasty reply to your letter, I shall be able to give them.

It was in the year 1817, if I recollect right that, during a visit of a few weeks to London, I first became acquainted with Mr. Crabbe; and my opportunities of seeing him during that period, at Mr. Rogers's and Holland House, were frequent. The circumstance connected with him at that time, which most dwelt upon my memory, was one in which you yourself were concerned; as it occurred in the course of the negotiations which led to your purchase of the copyright of his poems. Though to Crabbe himself, who had up to this period received but little for his writings, the liberal sum which you offered, namely, 3000£., appeared a mine of wealth, the two friends whom he had employed to negotiate for him, and who, both exquisite judges of literary merit, measured the marketable value of his works by their own admiration of them, thought that a bargain more advantageous might be made, and (as you, probably, now for the first time learn) applied to another eminent house on the subject. Taking but too just a measure of the state of public taste at that moment, the respectable publishers to whom I allude named, as the utmost which they could afford to give, but a third of the sum which you had the day before offered. In this predicament the situation of poor Crabbe was most critical. He had seen within his reach a prize far beyond his most sanguine hopes, and was now, by the over-sanguineness of friends, put in danger of losing it. Change of mind, or a feeling of umbrage at this reference to other publishers, might, not unnaturally, it was feared, induce you to decline all further negotiation; and that such was likely to be the result there appeared every reason to apprehend, as a letter which Crabbe had addressed to you, saying that he had made up his mind to accept your offer, had not yet received any answer.

In this crisis it was that Mr. Rogers and myself, anxious to relieve our poor friend from his suspense, called upon you, as you must well remember, in Albemarle-Street; and seldom have I watched a countenance with more solicitude, or heard words that gave me much more pleasure, than when, on the subject being mentioned, you said, 'Oh yes—I have heard from Mr. Crabbe, and look upon the matter as all settled.' I was rather pressed, I recollect, for time that morning, having an appointment on some business of my own; but Mr. Rogers insisted that I should accompany him to Crabbe's lodgings, and enjoy the pleasure of seeing him relieved from his suspense. We found him sitting in his room, alone, and expecting the worst; but soon dissipated all his fears by the agreeable intelligence which we brought.

When he received the bills for 3000£., we earnestly advised that he should, without delay, deposit them in some safe hands; but no —he must 'take them with him to Trowbridge, and show them to his son John. They would hardly believe in his good luck, at home, if they did not see the bills.' On his way down to Trowbridge, a friend at Salisbury, at whose house he rested (Mr. Everett, the banker), seeing that he carried these bills loosely in his waistcoat pocket, requested to be allowed to take charge of them for him, but with equal ill-success. 'There was no fear,' he said, 'of his losing them, and must show them to his son John.'

It was during the same visit of Mr. Crabbe to London that we enjoyed a very agreeable day together at Mr. Horace Twiss's;—a day remarkable, not only for the presence of this great poet, but for the amusing assemblage of other remarkable characters who were there collected; the dinner guests being, besides the Dowager Countess of Cork and the present Lord and Lady Clarendon, Mr. William Spencer, Kean the actor, Colonel Berkeley, and Lord Petersham. Between these two last-mentioned gentlemen Mr. Crabbe got seated at dinner; and though I was not near enough to hear distinctly their conversation, I could see that he was alternately edified and surprised by the information they were giving him.

In that same year I had the good luck to be present with him at a dinner in celebration of the memory of Burns, where he was one of a large party (yourself among the number), whom I was the means of collecting for the occasion; and who, by the way, subscribed liberally towards a monument to the Scottish bard, of which we have heard nothing ever since. Another public festival to which I accompanied him was the anniversary of the Wiltshire Society; where, on his health being proposed from the chair by Lord Lansdowne, he returned thanks in a short speech, simply, but collectedly, and with the manner of a man not deficient in the nerve necessary for such displays. In looking over an old newspaper report of that dinner, I find, in a speech by one of the guests, the following passage, which, more for its truth than its eloquence, I here venture to cite: 'Of Mr. Crabbe, the speaker would say, that the *Musa severior* which he worships has had no influence whatever on the kindly dispositions of his heart: but that, while, with the eye of a sage and a poet, he looks penetratingly into the darker region of human nature, he stands surrounded by its most genial light himself.'

In the summer of the year 1824, I passed a few days in his company at Longleat, the noble seat of the Marquis of Bath; and it was there, as we walked about those delicious gardens, that he, for the first time, told me of an unpublished poem which he had by him, entitled, as I think he then said, the 'Departure and the Return,' and the same, doubtless, which you are now about to give to the world.[1] Among the visitors at Longleat, at that time, was the beautiful Madame ——, a Genoese lady, whose knowledge and love of English literature rendered her admiration of Crabbe's genius doubly flattering. Nor was either the beauty or the praises of the fair Italian thrown away upon the venerable poet; among whose many amiable attributes a due appreciation of the charms of female society was not the least conspicuous. There was, indeed, in his manner to women, a sweetness bordering rather too much upon what the French call *doucereux*, and I remember hearing Miss ——, a lady known as the writer of some of the happiest *jeux d'esprit* of our day, say once of him, in allusion to this excessive courtesy— 'the cake is no doubt very good, but there is too much sugar to cut through in getting at it.'

In reference to his early intercourse with Mr. Burke, Sir James Mackintosh had, more than once, said to me, 'It is incumbent on you, Moore, who are Crabbe's neighbour,[2] not to allow him to leave this world without putting on record, in some shape or other, all that he remembers of Burke.'[3] On mentioning this to Mr. Rogers, when he came down to Bowood, one summer, to meet Mr. Crabbe, it was agreed between us that we should use our united efforts to sift him upon this subject, and endeavour to collect whatever traces of Beaconsfield might still have remained in his memory. But, beyond a few vague generalities, we could extract nothing from him whatever, and it was plain that, in his memory at least, the conversational powers of the great orator had left but little vestige. The range of subjects, indeed, in which Mr. Crabbe took any interest was, at all times of his life, very limited; and, at the early period, when he became acquainted with Mr. Burke, when the power of poetry was but newly awakening within him, it may easily be conceived that whatever was unconnected with his own absorbing art, or even with his own peculiar province of that art, would leave but a feeble and transient impression upon his mind.

This indifference to most of the general topics, whether of learning or politics, which diversify the conversation of men of the world, Mr. Crabbe retained through life; and in this peculiarity, I think,

---

[1] 'Farewell and Return', *Posthumous Tales. Poetical Works of George Crabbe* (London, 1834), viii. 121.

[2] Crabbe was vicar of Trowbridge, Wiltshire, from 1814 until his death in 1832.

[3] Crabbe was a friend of Burke and on his advice and encouragement published *The Library* in 1781.

lay one of the causes of his comparative inefficiency, as a member of society,—of that impression, so disproportionate to the real powers of his mind, which he produced in ordinary life. Another cause, no doubt, of the inferiority of his conversation to his writings is to be found in that fate which threw him, early in life, into a state of dependent intercourse with persons far superior to him in rank, but immeasurably beneath him in intellect. The courteous policy which would then lead him to keep his conversation down to the level of those he lived with, afterwards grew into a habit which, in the commerce of the world, did injustice to his great powers.

You have here all that, at this moment, occurs to me, in the way either of recollection or remark, on the subject of our able and venerated friend. The delightful day which Mr. Rogers and myself passed with him, at Sydenham, you have already, I believe, an account of from my friend, Mr. Campbell, who was our host on the occasion. Mr. Lockhart has, I take for granted, communicated to you the amusing anecdote of Crabbe's interview with the two Scotch lairds—an anecdote which I cherish the more freshly and fondly in my memory, from its having been told me, with his own peculiar humour, by Sir Walter Scott, at Abbotsford.[1] I have, therefore, nothing further left than to assure you how much and truly I am, yours,

Thomas Moore.

1048. *To Lord Kerry*

Rice University

Jan^r 6th 1834

My dear Kerry— The inclosed is the only scrap of Byron's I have been able to come at— I was going to cut off his writing from the rest, but thought it better to leave all as it is—the copy of the Sacred Song being, I rather think, in Lady Byron's hand-writing and, though they themselves did not much like having their *hands joined*, I thought *you* would have no objection to it.

I shall have another search for something of Scott's—

Ever yours
T. Moore

We have just been released from our visit to Farley in consequence of the marriage being likely to take place this week.[2]

---

[1] See letter No. 1044, to John Murray, 29 Dec. 1833.
[2] See letter No. 1045, to Colonel Houlton, December 1833.

1049. *To John Murray*

Sir John Murray

Lacock Abbey
Jan^r 9th 1834

My dear Sir— I was not able to write you a word with the Proof yesterday— Indeed, it found me here in the midst of Private Theatricals (my *respectable* part being Sam, in Raising the Wind)[1] and I had hardly time to correct it properly, or to beg, as I intended by yesterday's post, that you would, if possible, let me have a Revise. Should this not be convenient, I have only to ask you to correct 'Longle*e*t,' which ought to be 'Longle*a*t'—pray, do not forget this—for, to misspell a marquis's place is a sort of *Lèze-seigneurie* that would never be forgiven. I should be better pleased to have the Revise—but if that is not feasible, it can't be helped. I return home to-day, so, if you should have anything to send me, let it be to Sloperton.

I am afraid the Prologue is among the impossible things—it would be *sure* to be a failure, and the less of that sort of thing a man commits the better.

Ever yours truly
Thomas Moore

1050. *To Macvey Napier*

B.M. Add. MS. 34616, f. 292

Sloperton, Devizes
Feb^r 18th 1834

My dear Napier—(for I don't see why you and I should continue formalists toward each other) I certainly consider myself under a sort of pledge to write something for this next number, but it must be something I can manage more easily, in the little time I have to spare, than the three massy and learned volumes of Nimrod.[2] My three visits to town—for I have been again on the same cursed business to London—have completely thrown me out of all my reckonings, both as to money & time, and how I shall be able to pull up either, God only knows. The work I *now* think of doing for you—in fact, I *can* do nothing else—is O'Brien's Round Towers of Ireland, a most precious piece of foolery, which I shall be most grieved to hear that any one has set hands upon before me.[3] In

---

[1] A play by James Kenney, first produced in 1803.
[2] See letter No. 1042, to Macvey Napier, 20 Dec. 1833.
[3] A review of Henry O'Brien's *Round Towers of Ireland* appeared in the *Edinburgh Review*, lix (April 1834), 143–54. There is a letter in the Moran

order to lose no time in your letting me know, I send this letter direct by post, and if you have no member on the spot, you had better do the same in return. There is really no other work I know or can think of for the purpose.

I gave the passage of your letter about Napier to one of his daughters who was here with us, and bid her tell him to answer me on the subject immediately.[1] I have strong doubts, however, as to his doing any thing for you—his recollections, I know, of what he *did* do for the Edinburgh, in former times, are not very agreeable, and he is now preparing the last sheets of his new Volume for the Press.

Yours very truly
Thomas Moore

1051. *To Macvey Napier*

B.M. Add. MS. 34616, f. 294

Sloperton
Febr 24th 1834

My dear Napier— I have just heard from your namesake & hasten to acquaint you with his answer. He had before told me that his reviewing the book or not would depend upon the tone in which he found it written— He has now read it, and his ire is raised to such a pitch by its contents, that he will not only review it for you, but demolish it *in saecula saeculorum*. You may depend upon it never was such a sacrifice offered up in the Review as he will make of the said Carrick Moore, and, from some things he tells me, I would say never was one so deserved. He makes some stipulations, however, on which he insists peremptorily—in the first place (which shows he has wit in his anger & is therefore more like a Scotchman than

Collection (B.M. Add. MS. 34616, ff. 321–4) from O'Brien to Macvey Napier, in which the writer objects to the manner in which the book was reviewed. The reviewer attacks O'Brien's contention that the Round Towers are 'Phallic Nimrodian Towers', saying that this was a well-known fact, which had been stated previously in a book entitled *Nimrod*. O'Brien maintains that no one had offered 'Buddhist proofs' before and says that he was unable to find a passage in *Nimrod* in which the Towers were even mentioned. He therefore accuses the reviewer of 'forgery'. In spite of Moore's remark in the postscript to the letter of 24 Feb. 1834 (No. 1051), evidence points to him as the author of this review.

[1] William Napier's review of James Carrick Moore's *Life of Sir John Moore* was published in the *Edinburgh Review*, lix (April 1834), 1–29. In a letter to Macvey Napier (B.M. Add. MS. 34616, f. 309), the author of the article states that he will be glad to reconsider any part of the review if the editor feels that it is injurious, but he will not alter any essential facts. He thinks the book is bad in principle and will not treat it in any other manner.

an Irishman) he demands to be well paid for his task—'50 or it is no go' are his own words. In the next place, he requires, on honour, that not a word of his article shall be altered or suppressed.[1] What he says of time is as follows— 'I must also have some time, as I am now publishing my 2nd Vol.[2] but I should think a month will do.'

I thought it better to dispatch you his answer, at once, that no time may be lost in securing him. It is, I think, well worth your while to fix him.

Yours very truly
Thomas Moore

From my not having received answer yet to my last, I take for granted somebody else attack'd the Irish Towers, which I am not at all sorry for.[3] I can still less afford to write for small sums than Napier. Do you know that my few lines in the Times to Overton[4] brought me very nearly as much as the article on him, though the one cost me six days & the other not six hours.

1052. *To Henry Bishop*

Rice University

Sloperton Cottage, Devizes
Febr 26th 1834

Dear Mr Bishop— In sending back your MSS on which I have taken the liberty (knowing how tolerant you are of my unlearned criticisms) to make a few remarks, I cannot resist the temptation of adding also a few lines, to say that, during my late visits to town, it was my wish & intention to call upon you, but, owing to my ignorance of your address, I was unable to have that pleasure. I was anxious to remove any impressions (if any such had been made upon you) that, during my late differences with Mr Power,[5] there was the least intention on my part to depreciate your musical services, or in any manner to belie the high opinion which I have always entertained of your talents as a composer. I write this

---

[1] See letter No. 1050, to Macvey Napier, 18 Feb. 1834.
[2] The second volume of Napier's *History of the Peninsular War* (1828–40), 6 vols.
[3] See letter No. 1050, to Macvey Napier, 18 Feb. 1834.
[4] The satire on Charles Overton, *Poetry*, p. 643 (see letter No. 1039, to Macvey Napier, 12 Sept. 1833).
[5] In 1832 and 1833 Moore's financial accounting with James Power became so hopelessly entangled that arbitration was necessary in order to arrive at a satisfactory settlement. Power later spoke of Moore as one of the few honest men he had ever known, but these negotiations put a strain on their friendship which lasted for many years (see Russell, vi. 319–21).

without in the least knowing, or, indeed, having the least grounds to suspect that any such misrepresentation of my feelings towards you has reached your ears; but, conscious that there were opinions expressed by me, (respecting *prices* &c.) which might bear such a construction, I think it due both to myself & you to guard against any such unjust impression, and to assure you both of my continued admiration of the clever and beautiful things you *have* done, and of my hope of seeing much more from you, of the same kind. I write in a hurry, but trust to your making out what I have so hastily expressed, and am

Very truly yours
Thomas Moore

1053. *To Philip Crampton*

Russell, viii. 270

March 25. 1834.

My dear Philip,

How the time flies! and how you and I keep never minding each other, till at last, some fine day, one or other, or both—but 'away with *melancholy*,' as the song saith, we shall have, with the blessing of God, a merry day or two together yet. Did you know that I was very near paying you a visit at the time of Lord John Russell's excursion to Ireland last autumn? He asked me to go with him, and for two or three days my wings were ready spread for flight. I had invitations from Bessborough and Lord Ebrington, and the Lansdownes offered to bring me back; but, all at once, my heart failed, and I gave it up. *One* of my reasons for doing so *you* were a good deal concerned in, as I found I could not have devoted more than a day or two to Dublin, and that being my principal object (on account of you and poor little Nell), I thought the rest hardly worth the time and expense. However, *next* autumn, I am resolved to invade you, and this bright sudden thought is very much the cause of this sudden, but *not* bright letter, which will, however, I know, give you pleasure.

We are all well, except that *I* am rather plagued of late with weak eyes, which to a poor 'working-day' author is rather inconvenient. We hear of *you* sometimes and of your still blooming looks, which we pray heartily for the continuance of; being ever, my dear good fellow,

Most heartily yours,
Thomas Moore.

Meant *dually* to include Bessy also, though we never were more *one* in our lives, which is saying a good deal, this being the anniversary of our marriage—the twenty-third year!

1054. *To Mary Shelley*

Abinger Collection

April 10th 1834

I do not dare to look back upon the long period of time that has elapsed since you have had a single line of mine, ungrateful reprobate as I am. But, in addition to my other excuses, I have been teased for some time by weakness in my eyes, which makes me even a greater niggard of my writing (to *friends*) than usual. Sometimes, indeed, the fear of their getting worse makes me rather low-spirited—for, as I often say, I know not which are the more precious things, a pretty woman's eyes or a poor author's. *You*, who have tried them in *both* capacities, can best decide. Who could have told you our little Russell was beautiful? He is, on the contrary, a little ugly dog, like his father—or, at least, *was*, for of late he improves.

I am wading through my Irish History slowly & sadly—for it *is* sad work, and ever will be. It makes me feel lighter in my traces, however, to know that *you* are harnessed in the Dionysian Drag along with me.[1]

The next time chance takes me to town I am *determined* to pay you a visit— Show that you forgive past injuries by letting me hear soon from you & believe me

Ever most truly yours
Thomas Moore

1055. *Addressee unknown*

National Library of Ireland

Sloperton
May 6th 1834

Dear Sir— I plead guilty to the correspondence, but to none of the other charges. Mr O'Brien ought, I think, to make sure of his man, before he commences his attack—however, sure or not, he is heartily welcome to *me* as a victim, if he can find no other. All I deprecate is the being obliged to *read* his attack. One of the great blessings of my secluded life is that I am out of the way of seeing any thing that is said of me, good or bad, by such writers as Mr O'Brien. In saying this, I mean no disrespect to him—but I certainly did look over his book on the Round Towers (having been lent a copy by a friend of mine) and the impression was *not* such as

---

[1] Mary Shelley was at work on her novel *Lodore*, which appeared in 1835.

to make me desirous of reading any thing he may write in future.[1]
With many thanks, therefore, for your kind offer, I have thus
hastened to beg you will not put it in execution and am, Dear Sir,

yours very truly

Thomas Moore

1056. *To the Marchioness of Headfort*

National Library of Ireland

Sloperton Cottage*

May, 1834*

It is with a pleasure, not unmixed with melancholy, that I dedicate
the last Number of the Irish Melodies to your Ladyship; nor can
I have any doubt that the feeling with which you receive the tribute will be of the same mingled and saddened tone. To you who
though but little beyond the season of childhood, when the earlier
numbers of this work appeared, lent the aid of your beautiful
voice, &, then even, exquisite feeling for music to the happy circle
who met, to sing them together, under your father's roof, the
gratification, whatever it may be, which this humble offering brings,
cannot be otherwise than darkened by the mournful reflection,
how many of the voices, which then joined with ours, are now
silent in death.

I am not without hope that, as far as regards the various beauty
of the Melodies, you will find this closing portion of the work not
unworthy of what has preceded it. The Sixteen airs of which the
number and supplement consist, have been selected from the
immense mass of Irish music which has for years past been accumu-
lating in my hands; and it was from a desire to include all that
appeared most worthy of preservation that the four supplementary
songs which follow the Tenth Number have been added.

Trusting that I may yet again, in remembrance of old times,
hear our voices together in some of the harmonized airs of this
Volume, I have the honour to subscribe myself

Your Ladyship's faithful friend and servant,

Thomas Moore.[2]

---

[1] See letter No. 1050, to Macvey Napier, 18 Feb. 1834. On 5 May Moore made
the following entry in his diary: 'A column of extract in "The Times," from
my article on the "Round Towers," given as from "an able and lively article
in the last "Edinburgh!"' (Russell, vii. 31).

[2] This is the letter of dedication to the tenth number of the *Irish Melodies*
(1834).

1057. *To Lady Blessington*

Sloperton
June 12th 1834

My dear Lady Blessington— The time *has* indeed come very quickly upon me—dreadfully quick. It is unluckily the *latter* days of life that fly the fastest, as you will find, yourself, some thirty years hence. I am much flattered by your attaching such importance to my scribblings, and it is indeed only such over-rating of them by others that has ever made me think any thing of them myself. You may depend upon having some lines from me in time (that is, if you let me *know* the time) but they will be few and, I fear worthless. The only merit they will have is that they will be sure to bring me into as many scrapes as there are lines—from my ungallant refusals in other quarters which are, if not Books of Beauty, at least *Beauties* of books.[1]

Ever yours truly
Thomas Moore.

You will have literature enough, at your dinner, God knows, without me. I should, at a hazard, prefer your *non*-literary man (Lord D.) to all the rest.

1058. *To Sir Robert Peel*

B.M. Add. MS. 40404, f. 150

Sloperton
June 12th 1834

My dear Sir Robert Peel— Though I had made other arrangements for my little boy during the interval between this & next year, I feel that I ought not to hesitate for an instant in availing myself of your kind & thoughtful proposal. Most gladly therefore do I agree to the plan, and shall write by this post to Mr Saunders to know in what manner I am to proceed so as to give you the least possible trouble in the forms of appointment.

Of my *own* thankfulness for this great service I need say, I trust, no more; but I cannot help adding—what is worth far more than even mine, both in depth and warmth—the *mother's* thanks.

Ever most truly yours
Thomas Moore

I think I have told you already that the little fellow's Christian names are John Russell.[2]

---

[1] Lady Blessington edited *The Book of Beauty* in 1834.
[2] A note on the reverse side of the letter reads:
'I gave him one of my presentations at the Charter House for his Son'
RP.
Moore recorded the appointment in his diary on 13 June (Russell, vii. 33).

1059. *To Cornelius Lyne*[1]

Russell, vii. 57

[26 September 1834]

I will confess to you . . . that much as I have always been in the
habit of speaking freely of public men, this is the first time it has
ever cost me a pang to do so. The cause, the man (for I have ever
personally liked O'Connell), the risk I ran and still run of losing by
this step that popularity among my countrymen, which is the
only reward that remains to me for some personal self-sacrifice;
all this, I own, made it a painful and a bitter effort; but I should
not have stood so well with my own conscience or self-respect, had
I shrunk from it. The feeling began, as I have already told you, as
far back as the visit of George the Fourth to Ireland, when I was
living in Paris, and when Byron sent me those truly Irish verses of
his, which I got printed at a French press, and distributed among
the faithful. It was curious enough that while *he* vented his Italian
feelings on the Irish, I discharged at the same time my Irish rage
on the Neapolitans, in verses which you may perhaps have seen:
'Aye, down to the dust with them, slaves as they are.'[2] With
respect to what O'Connell says of my lukewarmness in the cause of
Ireland, since the grant of Emancipation, he seems to have forgotten already the praises which he himself, under his own hand,
bestowed upon me for the 'courage' of my 'Life of Lord Edward,'
and the 'treasonous truths,' which he said that work contained.
He little knew the extent of the courage he thus praised. It is easy
to brave a *public;* but it was in defiance of the representations and
requests of some of my own most valued friends that I published
that justification of the men of '98—the *ultimi Romanorum* of our

---

[1] This letter (only a part of which was recorded by Moore in his diary) was
written in reply to one from Lyne, who informed Moore that he had shown certain of the poet's letters about the Irish cause to O'Connell. Lyne noted that
O'Connell did not see anything in Moore's letters which would lead him to
regret the 'course of management he has adopted in advocating the cause of
Ireland'; that he used the 'present of the garland to George IV' as a means of
enlisting the king's feelings on Catholic Emancipation; and that he regretted
Moore's apathy for the cause since the Emancipation Bill was passed.

Moore paraphrased the first part of his letter: he was relieved that O'Connell
had seen his letters, since the Irish patriot could determine from them that 'it
was not without reflection I differed; nor without a deep and due sense of his
great talents and services in our common cause'.

[2] Byron sent Moore the manuscript of *The Irish Avatar* in a letter dated
17 Sept. 1821. The poem is concerned chiefly with an attack on George IV at
the time of his visit to Dublin in August 1821, within ten days of the death of
Queen Caroline (see Byron, *Poetry*, iv. 555). Moore's poem is entitled 'Lines on
the Entry of the Austrians into Naples, 1821', *Poetry*, p. 535.

country.[1] He appears also to have forgotten my last work,[2] which, though as regards the rest of the world theological, is in its bearings on the popular cause of Ireland deeply political, and so was viewed by enemies who understood me, as it appears, far better than O'Connell. No, I have little fear that the historian (if he ever meddles with such 'small deer'[3] as myself) will say that, hitherto, at least, I have shown any apathy in the cause of Ireland. How far the chill of years, increasing hopelessness as to the result, and such instances of injustice to my humble efforts as O'Connell has here set the example of; how far these combined causes may palsy me in years to come, I know not. But we must only hope for the best; and in the meantime, wishing you, my dear Lyne, among other blessings, less prosy correspondents than myself, I am, &c. &c.

1060. *To Albany Fonblanque*

Huntington Library

Sloperton, Devizes
Private   Sept[r] 30th 1834

My dear Sir.— I send you a squib of mine which it is but fair to tell you has been declined in the usual 'whereabout' of my squibbery, on account, I suppose, of the too erotic nature of the song which I have parodied.[4] If you should not see the same objection to its being published, I should be glad of its insertion in the Examiner, and you will have the goodness, should it appear, to desire your newsman to send me the paper in which it is inserted.

At all events, I rejoice in the opportunity thus afforded me of saying how lucky I consider myself in being introduced to your acqu[aintance] during my last visit to town, and how [*remainder, including signature, effaced*].

1061. *To E. R. Moran*

National Library of Ireland

Sloperton
Nov[r] 6 1834

My dear Sir— I have the pleasure to inclose a letter which arrived here from M[r] Power during my absence, lately, on a visit to some neighbors. You will learn from what he says the cause of the delay

---

[1] Lords Lansdowne and Russell advised against the publication of the biography of Fitzgerald (see Jones, *The Harp that Once—*, p. 282).

[2] *Travels of an Irish Gentleman in Search of Religion* (1833).

[3] *King Lear*, iii. iv. 144.

[4] 'The Numbering of the Clergy' (*Poetry*, p. 626) appeared in the *Examiner* on Sunday, 5 Oct. 1834, p. 628. The song which it parodied was Sir Charles Williams's ode 'Come, Cloe, and Give Me Sweet Kisses'.

that has occurred and will lose no time, I trust, in availing yourself
of his proposal.

Y[ours] faithfully
Thomas Moore

1062. *To J. Crookes*

Rice University

Decr 9th 1834

Dear Sir— The very day after I received your letter I returned an
answer saying how much gratified I should feel by the honour which
you intended me. What could have become of my note I cannot
conceive. Regretting that you should have been, all this time, under
the impression that I had neglected answering you, I am,

Your faithful & obedient servant
Thomas Moore

1063. *To John Murray III*

Sir John Murray

Sloperton
Decr 11th 1834

My dear John— If (as I rather think) you are the publisher of
Sir ——— Palgrave on the British Commonwealth (a quarto) you
will perhaps be kind enough to lend me a copy of it for a few days.[1]
I had already made some notes from a copy in the Library of
Bowood, and thought myself sure of having access again to it—but
I find it has been sent to be bound and may not return for some time.

Best regards to all around you—you must feel it rather snug,
this cold weather, to be all *in*.

Ever yours truly
Thomas Moore

1064. *To James Power*

Rice University

[*c.* 1834]

I find I have not left myself time to copy out the words (or
rather the first verse of the words) which I meant for Thalberg's
air—[2] It is very difficult to manage—but just say whether you
think this sort of subject will suit for it.

T. M.

---

[1] Sir Francis Palgrave, *The Rise and Progress of the English Commonwealth*
(1832).

[2] There is no indication that Moore used one of Thalberg's airs for a song,
but he may have thought of including one in the first number of the *Vocal
Miscellany* (1834).

1065. *To Richard Sharpe*

National Library of Ireland

Bowood
Jan[r] 16th 1835

My dear Sharpe— I am glad of any occasion that gives me an opportunity of recalling myself to your recollection, and have therefore very willingly complied with the request of a friend and neighbour of mine, M[r] Robert Hughes, once a Fellow of King's, who has a son just entered at Cambridge, and not being very well able to support him there is anxious to pick up some of those exhibitions which are in the gift, it seems, of the different City Companies. On talking over the matter here, the other evening, Lord Lansdowne suggested that *you* were the most likely person he knew to have interest in that line, and at the same time gave me permission to join his name with my own in an application to you, on behalf of our neighbour. In order to put you in possession of the different holders of this patronage, two lists are enclosed, and should you have influence over any of these persons or companies, you really could not exert it for an object more in want of such assistance.

This house wants but you and one or two more like you (in addition to those already here) to make it in the highest possible degree agreeable. Hallam, Lord Lansdowne & myself had a walk together to-day not far short of seven or eight miles, and you & your state of health, about which we are all most anxious, was by no means the least interesting subject of our conversation.

Ever, my dear Sharpe, very truly yours
Thomas Moore

1066. *To Mary Shelley*

Abinger Collection

Brooks's
Thursday Ev[n] [postmark February 27, 1835]

I was meditating (in *my* way) a note to you when yours reached me. We must meet *some* how or another, for I am really most anxious to see you. M[rs] Stanhope I know very little and M[rs] Manners Sutton I have not yet seen, not knowing that they were still at the Speaker's House, and having actually turned away from the door under that impression. I shall however, manage to see her as soon as possible. My mornings are all passed in Paternoster Row, working hard to fill the insatiable swallow of Lardner's devils, who devour a greater quantity of verbosity than I, at least, can afford. My copy has run short (as I find yours did also) and another monthly gentleman has been substituted for me, this time, but I am bound to muster up my quantity against the 1st of April.

I sleep in Bury St. 19, pass the mornings till about four among the devils, and am then ready for—angels all the rest of the evening.

Ever yours most truly

T. Moore

1067. *To John Murray*

Sir John Murray

Brooks's

Friday [Feb. 27, 1835, *not in Moore's hand*]

My dear Murray— I grieve to say that for Saturday I have been *booked* these ten days past—and yet I should not say that I *grieve,* for the incomparable Sydney is to be of the party. Your kindness to Tom, on all occasions I feel most sensibly, and had I been able to come to you, he most certainly should have profited by your invitation.

Pray, present my best wishes & hearty congratulations on his deserved success to Lieut Barnes, and believe me ever

Yrs truly

Thomas Moore.

1068. *To Peter Cunningham*

Rice University

Sloperton

March 8th 1835

Sir— I have many apologies to make for the long delay of my answer to your request, but amidst the distractions of my late visit to town, between business in the East and society in the West, I had not a minute to attend to any thing else. As far as *my* power extends over my Songs, you have full permission to insert the six or eight you speak of, but those I have written for Mr Power of the Strand, are I take for granted his property, and to him of course your application, on the subject, must be addressed.[1]

With many thanks for the kind terms in which you do me the honour to speak of me, I am, Sir,

Yours faithfully

Thomas Moore.

[1] Peter Cunningham had evidently applied to Moore for permission to publish some of his songs in one of Cunningham's collections, probably *Songs of England and Scotland*, which he edited for the Percy Society.

1069. *To Miss Windsor*
Rice University

March 17th 1835

My dear Miss Windsor— Again I am doomed to disappointment and again from the same weary cause, my plaguy Irish history, which you & I will join to curse in Chorus, when next we meet. I was almost sure I should have been able to attend your concert on Thursday, and Mrs Moore had set her heart on accompanying me, should you have been able to find room for her, in any corner, but I am still fixedly and cruelly under the fangs of the Printers' Devils, and shall not be free till the very end of the week.[1]

I gave Lord Lansdowne your note when I was in town, and I am afraid, as I deprived *him* of his chance of coming to you when he so much wished it, he will not be *much* grieved that I am now disappointed myself. He looks forward, however, to summer (he bid me tell you) for better success.

> Yours, in most furious haste, but most
> truly & cordially
>   Thomas Moore.

1070. *To A. Hayward*
Rice University

Duke St.
March 21 [1835]

Sir— I had the pleasure of receiving your book on my return from a dinner-party where it had been very favourably mentioned, and was therefore prepared to welcome it the more confidently.[2] Having not a moment, however, to give the perusal of it here, I intend to reserve that pleasure for my cottage, where I hope to be in a few days. With many thanks, I am, Dear Sir, yours faithfully

>   Thomas Moore

1071. *To the Marquess of Lansdowne*
Bowood

Sloperton
April 23, 1835

Thanks, my dear Lord Lansdowne, for your kindness in answering my note to Lady Lansdowne, from whom I have since heard, and to the same very agreeable purport, respecting Lady Louise.

---

[1] The context of this paragraph indicates that this is the 'Miss Winsor' whose singing Moore praised in his diary (Russell, v. 57).

[2] Moore could be referring either to Hayward's prose translation of Goethe's *Faust* (1833) or to his *Account of a Journey Across the Alps* (1834).

The inclosed paper, drawn up by one of the most famous of the Christian Infidels of Germany (Professor Paulus), has been sent by Brabant from Heidelberg, with the expressed wish that it should be laid before either you or Lord John. The Professor, it appears, takes a great interest in the question respecting the surplus, and, as Brabant represents it, is all on the side of Lord John, though his concluding illustration from the case of Henry 8th would be rather a dangerous one, I think, to venture upon. However, I am afraid you must take the trouble of at least noticing the receipt of the paper, as Brabant, in his Germanic zeal attributes evidently much importance to it, and would never forget it to you should you treat Shenkt,[1] Brockman and the Decretum Gratiae with disrespect.[2]

I can well understand and feel for the reluctance with which you must have entered upon your present hopeless task—but Post-hour cuts me short, luckily for you just now, when even Shenkt must be more agreeable to you than any thing in the shape of politics.

> Yours ever most truly,
> Thomas Moore.

1072. *To Lord John Russell*

Russell, vii. 87

[9 May 1835]

My first feelings on receiving your letter yesterday were those of surprise, joy, and thankfulness.[3] I had long, indeed, given up those dreams which may in former days have haunted me with respect to my chances of being ever thought of by my great friends in the way of place or office; partly because time and other circumstances have made me a different person to serve, and partly because I began to suspect that what Swift says in one of his letters might possibly be the truth. 'I never,' he says, 'knew a Ministry do anything for those whom they had made the companions of their pleasures.' You have shown, however, that this is not the case; and I feel most gratefully, I assure you, your kindness in thinking of my poor wants in the midst of so many cares and distractions of your own. With respect to the manner in which you propose to

---

[1] Moore spelled this name 'Shenkt' here and 'Schenkt' in his diary (Russell, vii. 90), but he must have been referring to the German theologian Maurus Schenkl (see the Glossary of Proper Names).

[2] For Lord Lansdowne's reply, in which he expressed doubt that either the English High Churchmen or the Tory Lords would be impressed by Professor Paulus's arguments concerning the Irish Church surplus, see Russell, vii. 90–91.

[3] See Lord John Russell's letter to Moore (Russell, vii. 87).

serve me, by procuring pensions for my two boys, you have perhaps chosen the only mode of affording me pecuniary help which
I should not instantly decline. I do not know whether I have told
you, that when my father died, Lord Wellesley, then Lord Lieutenant of Ireland, sent very kindly to me to offer a pension for my
mother.[1] This, however, coming as it did from a party adverse to
my own political opinions, I thought it right to decline, and the
Landsdownes, among others, were of opinion that my doing so was
foolish. That I want help is but too true. I live from hand to mouth,
and not always very sure that there will be anything in the *former*
for the *latter*. You may have some notion of my means of my
going on when I tell you that for my last published volume I received 750£., and that I was two years and a half employed upon
it.[2] You should not have been annoyed at this View of the Interior,
but for your own kind consideration of my wants; so you see what
you have brought upon yourself. But to come to the point; to *be*, or
not to be a pensioner, that is the question. If only myself, or even my
other self into the bargain, were concerned, I think I should not
hesitate as to the answer I would give; but I confess the responsibility of refusing such timely aid for my two poor boys is more than
I can take upon myself to encounter. All I can say, therefore, at
present is, that I leave the matter entirely in your hands, begging
you to think, feel, and act for me in that capacity which you have
always shown yourself so worthy to fill, of a sincere, warm friend. You
may even, I think, call Lord Melbourne also into council, as I have
known him at least long enough to count a little upon his goodwill.
Whatever you and he think I *may* do, I *will* do. Ever, &c. &c.

1073. *To Mary Shelley*

Abinger Collection

Sloperton
May 15th 1835

You could not have been more disappointed that day than I was,
and in addition to the *not* being with you was the infernal gloom
of the place where I *was*—but the next time I come, I hope devils
will not be my *only* society. My movements townward depend all,
you know, upon chance, or rather upon a more matter-of-fact
thing, business, and I know of none that will carry me there this
season. The abominable hurry in which I was forced, at last, to print

---

[1] Lord Wellesley offered to continue John Moore's half-pay as a pension to
the poet's sister, not his mother (see Russell, v. 24). The proposal was refused.
[2] His *History of Ireland*, the first volume of which appeared in 1835.

my book gave me a distaste to it in its very birth—but I find it is doing very prosperously. So at least say those best authorities on such subjects, my publishers. I should think the same must be the case with *your* last offspring, to judge by what I see in the public oracles.[1]

Mind, whenever you see Lady Canterbury to remember me to her most cordially. We are just now very happy at the Cottage, having got our two dear boys at home.

Ever most truly yours
Thomas Moore.

Whenever you meet or hear of any thing amusing, in the way of politics, scandal or—I was going to say literature, but that's *shop*— it would be very kind of you to make me a sharer in the fun.

1074. *Addressee unknown*

Rice University

May 23, 1835

Have the goodness to settle my account & send the balance by bearer— £5 Devizes Bank note & the rest sovereigns.

Yours &c
T. Moore.

1075. *To Locke, Hughes, and Saunders*

Rice University

Sloperton
May [29th *deleted*] 30 1835

Be so good as to place the inclosed to my credit.

Yrs &c
Thomas Moore

Longman £25

1076. *To E. R. Moran (copy)*

B.M. Eg. MS. 2153, f. 33

Sloperton
May 31st 1835

Dear Mr. Moran— You cannot doubt my feeling both flattered & gratified by the sort of notice with which you have favoured me. I should like to have seen the paragraph to which you refer & should it be in your power to procure for me the Standard in which it

---

[1] The first volume of Moore's *History of Ireland* appeared in 1835. Mary Shelley's *Lodore* was published the same year.

appeared I should feel very much obliged by it.[1] I am delighted to see by your appearance as a *leader* that you have attained that station in the paper which has long been due to your talents & industry,[2] and wishing you a continuance & increase of such deserved success I am very truly yours

Thomas Moore

Edwd Moran, Esq
127 Globe Office Strand

1077. *Addressee unknown*

John Rylands Library

Captain Fielding, one of the subscribers whose name I gave, is expected soon home from Nice.

Sloperton
June 8th 1835

Dear Sir— I have been in expectation of being able to send my subscription money (for Miss Costello's Poems)[3] by a parcel— but, no such opportunity having occurred, I must trouble you with a cheque upon Messrs Longman, instead.

I regretted very much not having been lucky enough to meet with you during my last visit to town. I owe you a presentation copy, if you recollect, of one of my works, and shall not neglect to perform the promise when I next come to London.

Yours very truly
Thomas Moore

1078. *To Colonel Houlton*

Rice University

Sloperton
Tuesday [June 1835][4]

My dear Houlton— I want you to trust me for a day or two with that book in which you have collected such a formidable array of my *squibbery*—as I think you have got some that I have neglected to keep & I want them just now for a particular purpose.

[1] A note on the original of the letter reads: 'I sent him the standard by that night's Post.'
[2] Moran was made an editor of the *Globe* in 1835.
[3] Probably Louisa Stuart Costello's *Specimens of the Early Poetry of France* (1835), which was dedicated to Moore.
[4] A note at the bottom of the page reads 'Sent accordingly 1st July 1835 JHn.'

I shall be in Bath on Thursday (to stay, I dare say, the night) and if you could get the book to Crawford's on that day, I shall receive it there in my own hands, and keep it sacred and safe, till I find some equally good means of returning it.

Yours ever
T. Moore

1079. *To John Murray III*

Sir John Murray

July 10th 1835

Many thanks, my dear John, for the trouble you have taken, and, as a reward, I am about to give you a little more, which is to send to Hookham's in Bond St. for the Address of Mr Clarkson, who is a friend of Hookham's and lives at —— House, Kentish Town— I *believe*, as to the latter, and *know not*, as to the former, but you will hear all in Bond St. & pray let it be done as soon as you conveniently can—much time having passed since the manuscript was sent to me.

I have *not* been very *gravely* employed lately, as a coming advertisement will show,[1] and in about a fortnight I mean to take wing for Ireland—

Yours very truly
Thomas Moore

1080. *To Mary Shelley*

Abinger Collection

Sloperton
Septr 23rd 1835

Your letter found me here scarcely recovered from the intoxication of my reception in Ireland which was really *almost* beyond what poet could describe and *certainly* far beyond what any poet ever deserved.[2] In order to give you some idea of the honours & glories showered on me I shall send a newspaper by post which will reach you before this, and which you may keep till we meet.

On reading what you said about your boy, it struck me that there was a friend of ours, in this neighbourhood, who would exactly suit the purpose you require, having just now turned a young fellow out of his hands (the son of our neighbour Colonel Houlton) whom he has prepared for the University under no ordinary difficulties.[3]

[1] An ironical reference to *The Fudge Family in England*, which appeared in 1835.

[2] Moore was in Ireland from 8 Aug. to 8 Sept. 1835. For an account of his triumphant visit see Russell, vii. 97–123.

[3] The tutor was probably Dr. Brabant.

But as his own sons have also entered college & he is not likely, I fear, to have any more pupils, the want both of society & of competition would render it perhaps *not* so eligible a position for your boy. You can, however, turn it over in your mind, and he would at all events, have the advantage of whatever attention it would be in *my* power (being within four miles) to show him. I write, as usual, in a hurry, but you will be able to translate me into meaning; and, at all events, believe me

Ever yours
Thos Moore

1081. *To Samuel Rogers*

Russell, viii. 271

Sloperton
Oct. 6. 1835.

My dear Rogers,

I should have written to you sooner after my return from Ireland, but that I thought you must have left London, and did not like to send a letter yelping at your heels. But having heard from some one that you were seen in an omnibus lately, which sounds very like the *neighbourhood*, at least, of London, I take my chance of this catching you in that not *over*-fast conveyance. I don't know whether you have heard anything of my honours and glories in Ireland;[1] but I assure you I thought very often of *you* when I was among my Muses at Bannow; one of which (my Chief Muse) was a remarkably pretty girl of about seventeen, and when I turned round to her, as she accompanied my triumphal car (which went at a very slow pace), and said, 'This is a long journey for you,' she answered, with a smile that would have done your heart good, 'Oh, I only wish, sir, it was three hundred miles.' There's for you ! What was Petrarch in the Capitol to that?

But to come to prosaic matters. You have at least heard, with all the world, that while the People were crowning me at Bannow the King was pensioning me at St. James's (a concurrence of circumstances, I flatter myself, not common in history);[2] and never, I must add, did golden shower descend upon a gentleman nearer what is called his 'last legs' than I was at the moment when this unasked-for favour lighted upon me. With a little time and a good deal of work I have now, you will be glad to hear, every prospect of surmounting my difficulties. With the Longmans I am

[1] See letter No. 1080, to Mary Shelley, 23 Sept. 1835.
[2] See letter No. 1072, to Lord John Russell, 9 May 1835, and Russell, vii. 108 ff.

deeply dipped—or rather, an aggregate of sums which I had in their hands, bestowed by different friends upon the children (viz. Lord John, Admiral Douglas, and Byron), stands confronted in their books by *another* aggregate, equal, I fear, in amount, of the sums which, at different times, I have been obliged to *anticipate* on my labours. All this I shall now be enabled in time to make straight, for it will be in my power to devote the greater part of the sums coming from the next two volumes of my 'History' to this very desirable object.

So much for *one* of my creditors. I now come to my *second*—for I have, thank God, but *two*—no *other* human creature having a demand (beyond the common tradesmen's credit) upon my purse. That *other* creditor, I need not tell you, my dear, kind-hearted Rogers, is yourself; and I blush, even in this matter-of-fact statement, to have connected my obligations to *you* with any in which the mere *quid pro quo* barter of this world is concerned. But I do not the less feel the difference in *sentiment* for having thus mixed them up together in sober *matter of fact;* and that fact being that I owe you, my best of good friends, two hundred pounds: it has been some little relief to my mind to write this letter to assure you that, as soon as I possibly can, I will discharge that debt. This, I know, I need not have told *you;* but, as I have just said, it is a relief to my mind to give the assurance, and I have not the least doubt that you will understand and enter into all that I feel about it.

I leave myself always so little time to write letters, that I much doubt whether I have expressed anything here that I *meant* to express. But you understand me enough by this time (a more than thirty years' experience, isn't it?) not to translate me *wrongly*, however confused may be the text; and, trusting to this for your version of the above, I am, my dear Rogers,

Most truly yours,
Thomas Moore.

1082. *To Thomas Hume*

Rice University

October 18th 1835

My dear Hume.

I write now merely to give you the trouble of putting the inclosed in the Twopenny for me.

We are expecting the Lansdownes daily. Yesterday I received an invitation to meet Lord John at the Dinner the Bristolians are about to give him—10th of next month— Shall certainly go, D. V.

Am hard at work, but have occasional dinners with Luttrell &
Nugent at Devizes— Tomorrow Bessy goes with me to meet these
Adelphi.

Ever most truly yours
Thomas Moore.

1083. *To Mr. Elby*

Yale

Bowood
January 2nd 1836.

My dear Mr Elby— If I could be angry with a *Barrow*-man for any
thing it would be for calling such an acquaintance as ours 'an
imperfect acquaintance'—formed as it was under such auspices
and with the sunshine of two such days to *ripen* it. *My* feeling of
the matter is, I assure you, quite different; for I look upon the few
hours I passed under your hospitable roof as a further advance
towards friendship than could be achieved in *years*, under less social
and less animating circumstances.

It will give me great pleasure to be of any use to your friend Mr
Loftus who had himself already interested me in his behalf; but
unfortunately my chief channel of influence with the London Press
is now closed up by the *Un-Whigging* of the Times. I have, however, some little interest with the Morning Chronicle, and shall be
most happy to exert it *all* in favour of Mr Loftus, if he will only
point out in what manner it is likely to be made most effective.
Does he wish a letter of introduction to the Editor?

Yours, my dear Sir, most truly
Thomas Moore

Pray, Tell [*sic*] our friend Boyse, when you see him, that I *marvel*
he does not write to me.

1084. *To Samuel Rogers*

Russell, viii. 273

Sloperton
Jan. 6. 1836.

My dear Rogers,
This note will be delivered to you by a very deserving young Irish
artist, who is now here on his way to London, with a portrait of
my unworthy self, which he is about to have engraved immediately,
and which, according to the opinion of all who have seen it, comes
nearest to the sublime and lofty original of any version that has

ever been made of him. It is, I believe seriously, and judging from the opinions of all my friends, a most excellent likeness; and as you are an encourager both of art and of me, I venture to introduce my young countryman to you, with the hope that you will see both him and the picture, and, if you approve of the latter, speak a good word for it among your friends. Lord Lansdowne liked it so much that he allows the print to be dedicated to him.[1]

I should not so patiently have forborne from inquiring about you lately, had I not received from many quarters most prosperous accounts of you.

Yours, ever most truly,
Thomas Moore.

My friend's name is *Mulvany*.

1085. *To Thomas Drummond*
National Library of Ireland

Sloperton, Devizes
Feb^r 21st 1836.

My dear Mr Drummond— I have more than once sent you a packet, in this way, for my sister, making a stepping-stone, between you & her, of my old friend the Teller. But it just strikes me that you will have no objection perhaps to save me the additional cover & delay by allowing me (as long as the Irish members are away from Dublin) to send you occasionally, and *only* occasionally, a letter to my sister direct, which you take the trouble of forwarding to her by the 2^d Post.

Pray, give my best remembrances to Mrs Drummond, who, I flatter myself (if for nothing but Music's sake alone) will acknowledge me as an old friend.

Yours very truly
Thomas Moore.

1086. *To John Rogers*
Pennsylvania Historical Society

Sloperton
Feb^r 22nd 1836.

My dear Rogers— I find so many various little businesses have accumulated which require my presence in London that, notwithstanding the bitter recollection I have of the March winds in town

---

[1] The portrait was painted while Moore was in Ireland during August and September 1835. On 2 Sept. he recorded in his diary: 'A last sitting to ——; he has had, indeed, but two before, and in all three I had a sculptor (——) working at me on the other side, chisel and pencil both labouring away' (Russell, vii. 122).

last year, I cannot any longer put off the operation, and you are accordingly likely to see me at your door in a day or two. It is indeed *warming* to me, even in this weather, to think of so soon meeting you—for, only think, it is now a year (a whole feather dropped from the moulting wing of *each*) since we last met.

Trusting, my dear friend, that I shall find you as well as most heartily I wish you, I am

Ever yours
Thomas Moore

1087. *To Lady Cork*

N.L.S. MS. 1003, f. 36

Sloperton Cottage, Devizes
April 30, 1836

My dear Lady Cork— I had very sincere pleasure in receiving your note, which reached me here but yesterday. It gratified me the more from my feeling that (in *appearance*, at least) I have not been worthy of such kindness from you; but when I tell you that, for the last thirteen months I have passed only three hurried weeks in London, you will not wonder that, with so much business and so many engagements to crowd into that short space of time, I have been obliged to leave many friends *unseen* and much work *undone*. This is the actual truth, and I know both your good sense and considerateness too well to doubt that you will make full allowance for my apparent neglect. The next time I come, however, you may depend upon my presenting myself at your door immediately after my arrival.

Mrs Moore, who has never forgotten her few agreeable moments in your society, begs to be kindly remembered by *you* in return.

Ever, my dear Lady Cork, very truly yours
Thomas Moore

I should have been delighted to meet Lord Foley, whom I claim as an old acquaintance.

1088. *To Thomas Drummond*

National Library of Ireland

Sloperton, Devizes
June 1st 1836

My dear Mr Drummond— I wish very much that Lord Mulgrave should see the inclosed letter and shall feel greatly obliged by your sending or giving it to him. I should have sent it direct to him myself, but that I feared to transgress some of those forms which I know 'hedge' a Lord Lieutenant, as well as a King, and though *he*, I am well aware, would readily forgive me such slips, others would not be so tolerant. The poor fellow who pleads so pitifully for himself in this letter is really deserving of what he asks, and I should rejoice to be, however remotely, the means of serving him.[1]

Lord Brougham (to whom I recommended him) is little aware of one obligation which he owes to me, and that is preventing this person from publishing a long pamphlet which he had written in his (Lord B[s]) *defence*. It was almost all that B. wanted at the time to ruin him.

Ever yours most truly
Thomas Moore

1089. *To Thomas Drummond*

National Library of Ireland

June 9th 1836.

Many thanks, my dear M[r] Drummond, for your kind attention to my request.[2] Should you remember, or be able to refer to the letter I sent you for Cradock's address (which I myself forget) pray take the trouble of writing it on the back of the letter to my sister.

On second thoughts, I *withdraw* what I have said about *referring* to poor Cradock's letter, as it is quite inhuman to think of giving you so much trouble; but write the address if you *remember* it.

Yours ever truly
Thomas Moore

1090. *To E. R. Moran*

National Library of Ireland

Sloperton
July 31, 1836.

Dear M[r] Moran— We were not a little disappointed on receiving your letter this morning, as we were led by a notice from Hume yesterday to expect your company at breakfast. The Longmans have been for some time thinking of the plan which M[r] Macrone proposes, and there are few things I am more anxious for than that there should be a General Edition of my works while I am myself yet extant to revise and superintend it.[3] The difficulty lies with

---

[1] See letter No. 1089, to Thomas Drummond, 9 June 1836.

[2] See letter No. 1088, to Thomas Drummond, 1 June 1836.

[3] On 31 July Moran notified Moore of Macrone's proposal to edit the poet's works. Moore was to receive £1,000 ; 8,000 copies were to be printed 'in monthly numbers, commencing with the ensuing year'; the author would receive 2,000

Power, and I am afraid that the Longmans are too much occupied with their multifarious concerns to admit of their exerting themselves sufficiently to surmount it. The plan Mr Macrone suggests, and the hope he seems to entertain of my being able to remove all such obstacles are certainly highly encouraging, nor should I hesitate for a moment to place myself in his hands, should the Longmans, on my again urging the matter upon them, show any hesitation in prosecuting it, or express any doubts as to our success. Enterprize is every thing in these cases; and as to the chances of success, my vanity of course would be more inclined to agree with Mr Macrone's sanguine views, on that head, than with those of more hesitating speculators. There is one cool-headed bibliopolist, however (Cuming, of Dublin, whom I dare say you know) who has been long urging the plan upon me with most flattering anticipations as to the result.

You shall hear from me again on the subject, and in the mean time, believe me

Very truly yours
Thomas Moore.

1091. *To Mrs. Bowles*[1]

Rice University

Tuesday [July or August 1836]
My dear Mrs Bowles— We should like (if you have no objection) to put off our visit to you, which Bowles fixed for Tuesday next, till some later period, when we might be able to combine with the pleasure of dining with you that of also hearing Bowles preach, which my sister has set her heart upon as one of the recollections she should like to carry back with her to Ireland. If I do not hear from you soon in answer to this, I shall take for granted that our engagement for Tuesday is given up.

Ever yours most truly
Thomas Moore.

1092. *To Mary Shelley*

Abinger Collection

Sloperton
August 2nd 1836
I have been kept from writing to you by various interruptions and businesses—too many of them of a loco-motive kind;—in punishment of which I am now rendered scarcely able to write by being

guineas if the set went to fifteen volumes; and Turner was to do the illustrations. It was decided that the project would not be attempted until Moore had his Irish history out of the way (see Russell, vii. 163–4).

[1] This letter was published by Greever, *A Wiltshire Parson*, p. 88.

too *stationary*, having been kept for these four or five days past recumbent on a sofa, in consequence of a severe bruise I got (in *one* of my loco-motions) at an Archery Meeting! This sounds gay, doesn't it? I don't mean the recumbent part which is certainly any thing but agreeable. The damage I received is on the foot, and I have been applying leeches &c.—but, as yet, with very little reduction of the inflammation. It is always most generous & kind of you to write to me, seeing how very little I am able to give you in return. We have been passing some time at a very agreeable house you have often heard me speak of, which is full of beauty, both within and without doors,—Farleigh Castle—and there I sang & listened to singing, and fluted away the time as carelessly as any elderly Anacreon could wish to do.[1] The beauties of the family however, are all marrying off most provokingly, and now a cursed young fellow of three & twenty *years*, and I don't know how many thousands *per* year, is going to whip off the prettiest remaining of all these sweet singers and lookers.

One of the *lesser* pleasant things I have been doing—but still very agreeable—was an excursion which *young* Tom (as he is now insultingly styled) and myself took to Clifton with Bowles, who is, in himself always a treat and would, I am sure, please & amuse you exceedingly—

As I write with some difficulty, I cannot add any thing more than that I am

Ever yours most truly
Thomas Moore

1093. *To Mrs. Sanders*

National Library of Ireland

Sloperton, Devizes
August 31st [1836]

My dear Mrs Sanders— You have always been so very kind to me and mine that I do not hesitate in asking your good offices for a little sister of mine, who left us for Bristol yesterday to sail from thence for Dublin this morning; but, I most anxiously hope, has *not* sailed in this very stormy weather. You have been once before made the *confidante* of my domestic alarms, and I most anxiously hope *this* alarm may prove as unnecessary & groundless as the other was. What I want you or Mr Sanders to do for me is to see my sister, if she have luckily *not* sailed by this morning's packet, and to repeat the advice I all along gave her to go to Liverpool and sail from

---

[1] Moore was visiting his friend Colonel Houlton at Farleigh (or Farley) Castle.

thence. Lest she should not be sufficiently provided with money for that longer course, I shall subjoin a cheque for a few pounds which I know Mr Sanders will be good enough to give her for me. He will find her at the place we usually go to—the Gloucester. Should she have sailed, it will still be very kind of either you or Mr Sanders to let me have a little note saying what sort of passage it is thought the packet may have made.

I know you well enough to feel quite sure you will forgive all this trouble and am most truly yours

Thomas Moore.

1094. *To J. W. Wright*

New York Public

Sloperton
October 18th 1836.

Sir— On my return home from London, where I have been for the last three weeks, I find a letter from you dated October 9th to which you must have been, all this time, vainly expecting an answer.

I have only time to explain to you the cause of my silence, and to say that, if you will take the trouble of presenting this note to the Messrs Longman it will be a sufficient assurance to them that I wish well to your literary undertaking, and shall be happy should they find it worthy of their notice.

I am, Sir, yours faithfully
Thomas Moore

1095. *To George Raphail Ward*

Rice University

Sloperton
October 21st 1836

Dear Sir— Owing to my departure from town, and the delay of your letter, in being sent through the hands of Mr Benett, I had not the pleasure of receiving it till this morning, which will account for your not having more speedily heard from me on the subject of it. I shall be most gratified by the visit of which you give me a prospect, but should be glad if you could, (without deranging your plans respecting the Print) defer coming down till after this next week; as Mrs Moore & I have some engagements hanging over us which are but too likely to take us from home during that period. Should it, however, be inconvenient to you, in the way of business, to defer your visit so long, have the goodness to tell me so frankly and I shall endeavour to arrange matters so as to meet your convenience.

I am, Dear Sir, yours very truly
Thomas Moore

1096. *To E. R. Moran*

National Library of Ireland

Sloperton
Novr 14th 1836.

My dear Mr Moran. I am, I assure you, most sincerely grateful for all the kind interest you take in my poor concerns—though *poor* they certainly would *not* be, were I able to accept all such splendid offers as you have been the means of conveying to me from Mr Bentley. Pray tell him how thankfully I feel this very substantial proof of his good opinion of me—but I should ill deserve that good opinion were I (with the heavy task that is now on my hands) to give him the least hope of my being able to accomplish, within any reasonable time, the work to which he so agreeably tempts me. Were it in my power, indeed, to reverse the present order of my operations,—to write Romance now, while there are some few gleams of sunlight still left me, and take to History when the night of old age sets in, it would be all very well; but bound as I am to my present task, I could not conscientiously pledge myself to any other—at least one *de longue halaine*—till that is finished—I shall trust to your explaining all this, with my compliments and thanks, to Mr Bentley, and am

Yours very truly
Thomas Moore

1097. *To William Lisle Bowles*

Greever, *A Wiltshire Parson*, p. 91

Thursday [*November*, 1836].[1]

My dear Bowles—

I sent to [*illegible*] immediately on receiving your note, and finding that he goes to Bremhill on Monday and will take me and Tom, we shall both be most happy to come to you.

I never was much more pressed for time than just now, having had visitors in the house during the last fortnight who have played the very deuce with my lucubrations. The pleasure of meeting Southey however (and in *your house*) is not to be resisted.

Ever yours most truly,
Thomas Moore.

[1] Greever's date.

1098. *To John Easthope*

Huntington Library

Sloperton
Dec[r] 8th 1836

Private

My dear Sir— Lest you should think that I am gone dead or, at least, dumb, I dispatch a line merely to say that I have not forgotten I still owe *one* shot of the *volley* last agreed for— But the truth is, I am just now very busy—(as busy at least as kind neighbours will allow me to be)—having gone to Press with the Second Volume of my History; and as I cannot, I fear, enter into another arrangement with you for some time to come, it is my wish to make the last of this batch as good as the Apollo of Doggrel can inspire me with. I shall, therefore, be on the look-out for a good subject (which, in squib warfare, makes half the battle) and then let fly my parting shaft.

Yours, my dear Sir, very truly
Thomas Moore.

My best remembrances to Black.

1099. *Addressee unknown*

Pennsylvania Historical Society

Sloperton
Dec[r] 23rd 1836

Sir— Having been absent, for some days, from home it was but yesterday evening that I had the pleasure of receiving your letter. It would gratify me much to undertake so agreeable [a] task as that which you propose to me, but I happen to be just now so busily engaged as to render it quite impossible.

I am, Sir, your obliged Servant
Thomas Moore.

1100. *To William Lisle Bowles*

Harvard College Library

Sloperton
Feb[r] 13th 1837

My dear Bowles— I was delighted to learn that you and M[rs] Bowles had escaped this minor pestilence that has being [*sic*] going about. I have not myself been so lucky, having had a short but sharp attack of the disease, which still obliges me to be careful, at least as long as this ungenial weather continues. Such being the case, my dear Bowles, it is quite out of the question my being able to face the air of Salisbury Downs tomorrow, where I should be sure to meet the *Grippe-Fiend* before I got half-way, and come in for a second scratch of the monster's claw. In a letter I had from Dionysius the Tyrant (alias Dr Lardner) the day before yesterday he tells me that he has had no less than four different attacks of the influenza, *two* of them very severe.

Mrs Moore's maid and myself have been the only sufferers, I am glad to say, at Sloperton.

Yours, with best regards to Mrs Bowles,
most truly

Thomas Moore.

Fielding, who has just been here, tells us that Lord Lansdowne has got completely well since he went to town both in health & spirits.

1101. *To Thomas Longman*

Huntington Library

March 24th 1837

Dear Tom— Your intelligence from the printer has half pleased & half disconcerted me. I am glad not to be obliged to *write* any more new matter now, but still we shall not get enough into this volume for the fair division of my subject. There are still about 10 pages of copy (nearly ready) which *must* be added, and you shall have them in a day or two. I shall most probably run up myself sooner than I at first intended to expedite your final operations. My head quarters will be in Sackville St. but I suppose my '*Row*—brothers, row'[1] will give me, for a few nights lodging, in order to be near the Devils.

Y^rs ever

Thomas Moore.

1102. *To E. R. Moran*

National Library of Ireland

Brooks's
Monday [11 Apr. 1837, *not in Moore's hand*]

My Dear Mr Moran— I have just seen a note of yours to Rogers, and lose not a moment in entreating of you to defer to some other time the kind tribute which you are about to propose for me. I have

[1] A pun on his own 'Canadian Boat Song' (*Poetry*, p. 124) and his publisher friends of Paternoster Row.

not a minute now to write, being engaged to a very early dinner, and therefore must reserve till we meet (which I trust will be soon) my reasons for wishing just now to decline your very friendly and warmhearted proposal.[1]

> Yours most truly
> Thomas Moore

1103. *To Mr. Ward*[2]

Rice University

> Sloperton
> May 3rd 1837

My dear Mr Ward— I received your note just as I was on the point of leaving town, and in the last agonies of the bustle that always attends my visits there. It would give me sincere pleasure, at all times, to be able to comply with any wish of yours; but in addition to my general repugnance to the task of writing upon given subjects, I am just now so busily engaged in preparing a new Edition of one of my works which is about to be published that I could not venture to engage in any thing else.[3]

I beg my best remembrances to Mrs Ward, & am most truly yours

> Thomas Moore.

1104. *To John Murray*

Pforzheimer Misc. Shelleyana 44

> Sloperton
> July 10th 1837

My dear Mr Murray— I returned home, via Southampton, on Saturday last, and shall lose no time in communicating to Lockhart whatever vestiges of Scott may be found among my recollections or my papers.[4] But I must ask of you to send me immediately the portions of the work already published, that I may see the nature of the communications he most wishes to receive. I shall expect at the same time the Volume of Byron you so kindly intended for me, or rather (as I am inclined to flatter myself) your daughter,

[1] Moran proposed that a dinner honouring Moore be given by the poet's friends and admirers and sent notes to several of them, including Rogers and Lord Holland, in order to solicit their interest (see Russell, vii. 178).

[2] There is no clue in the diary or in other letters as to the identity of the addressee. He could have been Robert Ward (later Plumer Ward), who published *Pictures of the World at Home and Abroad* in 1839.

[3] Moore published *The Epicurean* together with the unfinished poetic fragment *Alciphron* in 1839.

[4] See letter No. 1111, to John Gibson Lockhart, 2 Oct. 1837.

whose good-natured mindfulness on the subject I shall not easily
(tell her) forget. I have been lucky enough to place your friend,
Tom, in the house of a very eminent professor at Caen, and under
auspices which, as far as one can judge of the future, promise every
thing I could most wish.[1]

Yours very truly
Thomas Moore.

If Lockhart should not yet have returned from Scotland, you
will of course forward the inclosed to him *without delay*—pray do
not fail to do this.

On second thoughts, I have determined to direct Lockhart's
letter to Scotland—

<h2 align="center">1105. To Samuel Rogers</h2>

Russell, viii. 276

Sloperton
July 13. 1837.

My dear Rogers,

On Saturday last I returned home from my very agreeable
excursion;[2] the only drawback on the pleasure of which was my
being obliged to return by Havre, and so losing my promised visit
to you. My voyage down the Seine to Caen (where I deposited Tom
with an eminent Greek professor)[3] was delightful; the boat, each
day, being filled with gay company, having a good band of music
aboard, and passing every hour through new and beautiful scenes.
The weather, I need not tell you, was a long course of sunshine;
and altogether it was a very pleasant and unexpected dream. Pray
tell Lord Holland that his hint about Caen (which I had never
before thought of) was the rudiment of all this. The Duc de Broglie,
on my making inquiries of *him*, suggested also Caen; and on my
coming to investigate further, I found that one of my early college
friends, who was forced to leave Ireland in 'the time of the troubles,'
and entered into the French service, is now (having attained the
rank of General) commanding the district at Caen.[4] The few days
I passed there with this good Irishman, talking over old rebellious
times, was not the least interesting part of my trip; and his good

---

[1] Tom was placed under the tutelage of Professor Bertrand, a classicist who
translated some of Moore's *Irish Melodies* into French (Russell, vii. 187).

[2] Moore went to Paris with his son Tom on 10 June and returned to Sloperton
on 7 July 1837 (see Russell, vii. 183–93).

[3] See letter No. 1104, to John Murray, 10 July 1837.

[4] General Corbet (see the Glossary of Proper Names and Russell, vii. 189–92).

sense and military knowledge will render his society, I trust, a source of no small advantage to Tom.

We attended the ball at the Hotel de Ville; and, on the night of the fireworks, Tom was saved, perhaps, from being among the *asphyxiés* in the Champ de Mars, by being seated on the roof of the Tuileries, looking at bouquets and fire-balloons.[1]

My love to the Lady of the Park; and believe me ever, my dear Rogers,

Most truly yours,
Thomas Moore.

1106. *To E. R. Moran*

National Library of Ireland

Sloperton
August 16th 1837

My dear Mr Moran— I meant most fixedly to have called upon you during my short stay in town, but an unexpected pressure of business during my two last days put that & many other *fixtures* entirely to rout. I had not, as you supposed, come then directly from France, having returned home by Southampton about a fortnight before, leaving my son at Caen, where a leave for absence for six months will enable him to remain, I hope, sufficiently long to imbue his tongue with a little French. I was lucky enough to be able to place him under the care of a very eminent professor.[2]

I saw poor Macrone the day of his departure, and was grieved to find so much cause for *real* alarm in the state of his health. Looking to a speedy opportunity of being able to visit you in your new house, I am,

dear Mr Moran, very truly yours
Thomas Moore

If you have any influence with the Literary Fund (to which I am myself I believe a subscriber) I should be glad of your aid in directing a little of their Pactolus into the pockets of a poor fellow, at Paris, named Lake, to whom they once before, at my request, afforded some assistance, and who is now very much, I fear, in want of similar aid.[3]

---

[1] Moore and his friend James Corry watched the fireworks display at the Tuileries on 14 June from the garden of the Château, while Tom had a better view from the roof (Russell, vii. 183–4).

[2] See letter No. 1105, to Samuel Rogers, 13 July 1837.

[3] For the outcome of Moore's application on Lake's behalf see letters Nos. 1107 and 1108, to E. R. Moran, 23 and 28 Aug. 1837.

1107. *To E. R. Moran*

National Library of Ireland

Bowood
August 23rd 1837

My dear Mr Moran— Your letter has but just been sent over to me here from Sloperton, and not having access to Lake's papers, I cannot just now give you all the particulars of his case.[1] But I can safely answer for his having been some years past & being still in a very distrest condition—owing principally to severe illness which has prevented him from working for his support. I myself did as much as I could for him (to the amount, as he reminded me the other day in Paris, of five or six Napoleons) and being the only stationary representative, poor devil, of English literature in France, it would be for the credit, I think, of the Literary Fund to do some thing for him.

I feel, I assure you, very thankful for the promptness with which you attended to my request, and am

Most truly yours
Thomas Moore

1108. *To E. R. Moran*

National Library of Ireland

Sloperton
August 28 1837.

My dear Mr Moran— I have again, by absence from home missed receiving your letter in time. I am delighted at your success in procuring the relief for poor Lake, to whom I write by this post informing him of the vote of the Fund, and stating that a friend of mine would take some mode of remitting to him the money.[2] May I ask you to do so in whatever way may appear to you the best and *quickest*—for the 'cito dat' is every thing in such pressing want as I fear his is. This I say from a further reference to the papers which he sent me. His address is G. [*sic*] W. Lake Esqr No 69 Rue de Seine Neuilly-sur-Seine.

Ever yours truly
Thomas Moore.

Mrs Moore will have very little trust in your intentions of visiting us here till you are actually caught in the fact.

---

[1] See letter No. 1106, to E. R. Moran, 16 Aug. 1837.
[2] *Ibid.*

1109. *To E. R. Moran*

National Library of Ireland

Sloperton
Septr 16 1837.

My dear Mr Moran— I send back Mrs Moran's beautiful book (which was a long time on its way to me, having come by canal, together with the pondrous volumes of the Record Commission) and you will find the lines I have written in it old acquaintances of yours & I flatter myself of hers also.[1] If I *ever* wrote any thing new and express for an Album, it would be on the present occasion—but, for obvious reasons, I am obliged to adhere closely to my long observed rule on the subject.

Poor Macrone!— I have been tried severely lately by the loss of one of my best & dearest friends, Admiral Fielding, whose remains I followed yesterday to the grave at Lacock Abbey.[2]

Yours very truly
Thomas Moore

Mrs Moore hopes to be able, before long, to send you a lithograph of Sloperton for the Album.

1110. *To E. R. Moran*

National Library of Ireland

September 20, 1837

My dear Mr Moran—
I inclose you a note and advertisement which were folded in a newspaper you sent Mrs Moore, and which it may save you some trouble to have—
I trust the Album arrived safe.[3]

Ever yours truly
Thomas Moore.

[1] Moran transcribed the lines in his collection for 'Mooreiana', which is now in the British Museum. The poem begins 'When thro' life unblest we rove' (*Poetry*, p. 194).
[2] Fielding died on 2 Sept. and Moore recorded Macrone's death in his diary for 15 Sept. 1837 (see Russell, vii. 199–200).
[3] See letter No. 1109, to E. R. Moran, 16 Sept. 1837.

1111. *To John Gibson Lockhart*

N.L.S. MS. 924, No. 39

Sloperton, Devizes
October 2nd 1837

My dear Lockhart— With some little degree of nervousness (recollecting the fate of Sir William Scott's notices of Johnson)[1] I venture to send you the original MSS. of my precious letters. I should have had them copied but that there occur words here & there which I cannot make out, and not liking to lose (or muddy) a single 'drop of the immortal man', I leave them to you who are so well read in his 'arabian pot-works'

With respect to my recollections of Abbotsford, I hardly know how to set about the task—for admiration is a thing much more easily expressed than the sort of cordial and in some degree homely feeling which that visit left behind and the three plain words a *thorough good fellow* would best do justice to the impression of him I carried away. As I remember, however, having kept a little diary of my time there, I shall see what points I can collect out of it, and let you have them before the end of this week.[2] Meanwhile I wish you would, in answer to this, refer me to some similar communication in the already published Volumes which you would like me to follow as a model—or even like me to *avoid*, which (though rather an Irish sort of model) is often not the least useful of the two—and then I shall better know what to do for you. I am ashamed to say that between my out-of-door distractions, and in-door work (or rather efforts to work) I have not had time yet to read your Volumes.

Should you be able to answer this tomorrow, your letter will find me at Bowood and may be sent under cover to Lord Lansdowne.

Ever yours truly
Thomas Moore

The first of these letters was in answer to one I wrote to him on

---

[1] Sir William Scott published his *Life of Johnson* in 1821.

[2] Moore sent Lockhart several of Scott's letters and a portion of a diary which Moore had kept while on his visit to Abbotsford in 1825 (see letter No. 1104, to John Murray, 10 July 1837). This part of the diary, evidently a copy of one written at Abbotsford, is now in the National Library of Scotland. In its essentials it is the same as that published by Russell, iv. 330–43. There are, however, significant differences in details, which indicate that Russell edited the journal considerably (see, for example, note 2 on p. 815).

Scott's letters to Moore were published in *The Letters of Sir Walter Scott*, edited by Sir Herbert Grierson (London, 1932–7), 12 vols. See vol. ix. 198, 227, 268, 328 and vol. x. 132.

his going to Ireland, expressing my regret at not being there to attend him and saying how much I envied those who would have the honour and glory of showing him and the Lake of Killarney to each other.[1] The paper containing the particulars of Mrs Byron I never, I think, made use of.[2]

1112. *To Richard Bentley*

National Library of Ireland

Sloperton
Tuesday [postmark October 4, 1837]

My dear Mr Bentley—Though we heard of the arrival of your friendly package, some days since at Devizes, it was not till this morning that it reached Sloperton, and I cannot delay (though hurrying off at this moment with Mrs Moore to dine at Bowood) returning you our joint thanks for your most splendid present. The *Pell* Work will, I think (from a glimpse I have just taken of it) be useful to me, and I am most thankful to you for your thoughtfulness in procuring it for me. I have not time for a word more, but shall take this scrawl on with me to Bowood, to take the chance of getting a frank.

Yours very truly
Thomas Moore

Mrs Moore has just scolded me for omitting her thanks for the Seltzer water.

1113. *To Richard Bentley*

National Library of Ireland

Sloperton
October 6th 1837.

My dear Mr Bentley— I find by a letter which I received this morning from our friend Moran that you have lost no time in putting into practice the wish you expressed respecting an Edition of my Works. There is certainly nothing that I myself would more

---

[1] See letter No. 671, to Sir Walter Scott, 24 July 1825.

[2] Moore is referring to a statement concerning Lady Byron which Scott made during Moore's visit, and which Russell printed in the following form: 'Talking of the report of Lady Byron being about to marry Cunningham, said he would not believe it. "No, no, she must never let another man bear the name of husband to her"' (Russell, iv. 332). The remark is recorded somewhat differently in the excerpt of the diary which Moore sent to Lockhart: 'In talking of the report of Lady Byron being about to marry Cunningham he said he "*would* not believe it— No, no! she must never let another man bear the name of husband to her. Being even a W—— would be perhaps better than that."'

desire, even though I were not to gain a penny by it. But as I have already told you (and as you yourself, indeed, fully approved) I would never take a step, in any matter of publication, without previous reference to the Longmans, who (putting private friendship out of the question) have always treated me in a manner which deserves this deference to their wishes.[1] I think therefore that, *before* you proceed another step in your negociation with Mrs Power, you had better see Mr Longman and ascertain how far he would be disposed to sanction or perhaps join with you in such a plan; as otherwise, any steps taken by you towards getting possession of my outstanding works might materially embarrass the project so long contemplated between the Longmans and myself,[2] and place still farther off the object I have so much at heart; and this I know from your kind feelings towards me would be the very opposite of what you wish.

Believe me very truly yours

Thomas Moore.

1114. *To Richard Bentley*

National Library of Ireland

Sloperton

October 8th 1837.

My dear Mr Bentley—

It is really with difficulty I can express to you how very much I regret having been (however innocently) the cause of your being exposed to so very disagreeable a repulse; and had I been in town, or had there been time for a more gradual breaking of the proposition, I feel almost sure that no such unnecessary harshness could have occurred.[3] As it is, I can only lament that your *over* appreciation of my value as an author should have been the means of leading you into such an embarras [*sic*]; and be assured that I feel, as it deserves, your kind offer respecting the copy-right you have purchased.[4]

---

[1] See letter No. 1090, to E. R. Moran, 31 July 1836, and No. 1114, to Richard Bentley, 8 Oct. 1837.

[2] Moore and the Longmans contemplated bringing out a complete edition of his works. It was published in 1841.

[3] See letter No. 1113, to Richard Bentley, 6 Oct. 1837. Moore told Bentley that the copyright to *Lalla Rookh* belonged to the Longmans and that of the *Irish Melodies* to Power. The rest were in Moore's hands, having returned to him from Carpenter. He attempted to persuade Bentley of the difficulty of procuring permission from the 'men of business', but the publisher persisted in his optimism until he received the 'disagreeable repulse' (see Russell, vii. 202).

[4] Bentley had purchased the right of publishing Moore's works in Ireland (see letter No. 1122, to Richard Bentley, 23 Nov. 1837).

The Messrs Longman have no other hold of me than that very legitimate one which old connexion, long habits of friendly intercourse, and (I trust) *mutual* services have established.

Yours, my dear Sir, most truly
Thomas Moore.

1115. *To John Gibson Lockhart*

N.L.S. MS. 924, No. 40

Sloperton
October 10th 1837

My dear Lockhart— I tried my hand at the plan you suggested, but (though I squandered two whole days upon it) without any success, and I have just thrown my abortion into the fire. Had I left your volumes still unread, I might perhaps have been better satisfied with my own tribute—but on looking to one of them for some date, I was tempted to run rapidly through the 2nd 3rd & 4th Volumes (not having yet received the 5th) and was actually overwhelmed with wonder at the career there portrayed.[1] Such a monument of genius, labour & power was never before presented to the world. Trifling as any memorandum or tribute of mine must have been, at *any* period of the work, it would now come with particularly weak effect after so full and able a *ransacking* of all the treasures of your great subject. Lest you should think, however, that it was from any backwardness or want of zeal (which God knows, it *could* not be, where Scott, the mere man Scott—without any reference to his genius— is concerned) that I decline contributing any thing to you, I send the raw material of my Diary to be worked up—as much or little of it as you think right—in your own language.[2] This was what Milman advised at first when we talked on the subject, and whether of any use or not, it is all, I feel, that I can do. There can be little of novelty to *you*, in what I send, but some of it may have escaped your memory, and to me, I need hardly tell you, it was all of it precious.

With respect to my impressions of Scott, I give you *carte blanche* for expressing in my humble name all the admiration and affection which his great, as well as his good and manly qualities, deserved. The whole civilized world admire him in his works, but to *love* him, they ought to have seen him, as you and I have done, at Abbotsford.

Yours, my dear Lockhart, most truly
Thomas Moore

[1] Lockhart's seven-volume *Life of Scott* appeared in 1837–8.
[2] See letter No. 1111, to John Gibson Lockhart, 2 Oct. 1837.

1116. *To E. R. Moran*

National Library of Ireland

[12 Oct '37, *not in Moore's hand*]

My dear Mr Moran— Mrs Moore many days since commissioned me or (in proper matrimonial language) *ordered* me to write and thank you for your great kindness towards her friend Miss Hughes, to whose project you and Mr Bentley have brought not only aid but good luck, as it has prospered thirty fold, in every respect, since you & he lent your countenance to it. I was most seriously grieved to find that the result of his application to the Longmans was so far from agreeable to him—and trust that whatever share I had in bringing him into that scrape will not damp the feeling of cordiality which I was so pleased to see I had inspired in him.[1] A repetition of the visit to Sloperton (on *both* your parts) is the only thing that can convince Mrs Moore you've not had enough of us.

[*Unsigned*]

1117. *To E. R. Moran*

National Library of Ireland

October 25, 1837

Thanks, my dear Mr Moran, for your attention to the paragraph. I thought it was right the world should know that the formidable 'Conclave' (as the Spectator called it) was not wholly political.[2] Indeed, good fare, good music and good-fellowship were far more rife among us than politics.

You will convey the inclosed for me to Mr Bentley as soon as you can conveniently.

Yours very truly
Thomas Moore.

I am not sure whether, in my last note to you, I delivered Mrs Moore's message respecting the Tea—but it was (as far as I can recollect) that you were to have the goodness to send it, directed for us, to the Bear Inn, Devizes.

---

[1] See letter No. 1114, to Richard Bentley, 8 Oct. 1837.

[2] On Saturday, 14 Oct. 1837, the *Spectator* recorded that 'Lord Melbourne and Lord John Russell are gone to visit the Marquis of Lansdowne at Bowood, there to be joined by other members of the Cabinet,—most likely to settle the minimum of business for the next session of Parliament' (No. 485, p. 1; see also Russell, vii. 203).

1118. *To Richard Bentley*

National Library of Ireland

Sloperton
October 26th 1837

My dear Mr Bentley— I have been requested by a lady to employ my interest with you in at least drawing your attention to a manuscript Novel which she tells me is in your hands, called —alas, the name has escaped my memory, & I find that I have torn her letter— but the lady's own name is Ormsby (the wife of Colonel Ormsby)[1] and her residence in London is 33 Gloucester Place, New Road.

It is very possible that what I have written above may be all the very reverse of what I ought to have done, and that the Lady's wish was to have her own name concealed, and the name of her novel, of course, told. But this comes of being a blundering Irishman, and you must only help me out of the scrape as well as you can.

Yours very truly
Thomas Moore

1119. *To James Carpenter*

Pennsylvania Historical Society

Sloperton
Novr 7th 1837

Dear Mr Carpenter— Owing to an accident, I did not receive your letter as soon as I ought, which deprived me of the opportunity of applying personally, on the subject, to Lord Lansdowne. I have, however, forwarded to him your letter and shall be very glad if it produces any good effect. I am afraid however that the supposed profitable results of Mrs Carpenter's talents (to whom I beg my best compliments) will stand very much in the way of any success that might otherwise attend your applications.

Yours truly
Thomas Moore.

1120. *To Macvey Napier*

B.M. Add. MS. 34618, f. 358

Sloperton
November 12th 1837

My dear Mr Napier— I take the opportunity of an accidental frank to acknowledge your kind letter which, I assure you, I was most

---

[1] The husband wrote *Colonel Ormsby: or the Genuine History of an Irish Nobleman in the French Service* (Dublin, 1781). Anne Ormsby published *The Soldier's Family: or Guardian Genii*, a romance, in 1807. The novel to which Moore refers here has not been identified.

glad to receive—having taken it into my head that you had given me up, as an entirely hopeless concern, in all ways. Nor could I have much wondered if you had, after all the efforts you made to galvanize me into a little exertion for you and the *semianimate* results you had for your pains. At this moment I am working double tides at my historical task in order to make up for long idleness caused by the gay 'Conclave'[1] (as the Spectator newspaper called it) at Bowood, during some weeks past. It is therefore I fear quite impossible for me to think of any *extra* work till I have satisfied my conscience as to the recovery of the time lost. In the mean while you may be on the look out for some fit subject for the dissecting knife.

What you tell me about Jeffrey I had heard before from all quarters, and with the sincerest pleasure.

Yours, my dear Mr Napier, most truly
Thomas Moore.

1121. *To E. R. Moran*

National Library of Ireland

Novr 20th [1837, *not in Moore's hand*]

My dear Mr Moran— I have barely time to catch the post for a *feuille volante* to you in answer to your letter of this morning— The *second* format is what the ladies have decided for—emolument being (as I believe we before mentioned to you) the main object of the publication, nor can I tell you half of what is felt to *you* for your hearty cooperation towards this object.[2]

I shall be very glad to have a copy of Charles's letter, of which I can make use even in my next Volume, as a pendant to a similar deceit practised upon the Irish at an earlier period.

Pray tell Mr Bentley how very much we feel the kindness of his welcome packet received this morning.

Yours very truly
Thomas Moore

Many thanks for the army lists.

1122. *To Richard Bentley*

National Library of Ireland

November 23rd 1837*

My dear Mr Bentley— as there appears at last, I am glad to say, some prospect of the Edition of my works being put in train (M^rs

---

[1] See letter No. 1117, to E. R. Moran, 25 Oct. 1837. Moore was at work on his *History of Ireland* (1835–46).

[2] See letter No. 1116, to E. R. Moran, 12 Oct. 1837. Moore is evidently referring to the work by Miss Hughes, which Moran and Bentley were bringing out.

Power having given in *her* demand) I shall take it as a favour if you will let me know, as soon as possible, the amount of the sum you paid our friend Cuming for the right of publishing in Ireland, in order that I may make arrangements to avail myself of your kind offer on the subject.[1]

We are, I assure you, most grateful (Mrs Moore and myself) for the new and valuable addition you have made to our respective Libraries.

Yours very truly
Thomas Moore.

1123. *To Thomas Longman*

Russell, viii. 277

Nov. 23. 1837.

Dear Tom,

With respect to what you say about 'Lalla Rookh' being the 'cream of the copyrights,' perhaps it may, in a *property* sense; but I am strongly inclined to think that, in a race into future times (if *any* thing of mine could pretend to such a run), those little ponies, the 'Melodies,' will beat the mare, Lalla, hollow. As to the other things being 'unproductive,' why, it is to *make* them productive that the edition is contemplated.[2] What have 'Madoc,' 'Joan of Arc,' &c.,[3] been *producing* all this time?

Yours, my dear Tom, very truly,
Thomas Moore.

1124. *To Richard Bentley*

National Library of Ireland

Sloperton
Decr 1st 1837

My dear Mr Bentley—

You may be assured I feel as it deserves both the kindness & liberality of your conduct on this occasion; and, though *used* to generous acts from friends, I am not the less alive to every new instance of friendship that occurs. Most willingly too would I accept the present you offer me, were I *alone* concerned in the publication for which it is destined. But, as there are *others*, I *must for every reason decline* it. When I see you, which I trust is not far off, I shall explain myself more fully.

---

[1] See letter No. 1114, to Richard Bentley, 8 Oct. 1837.

[2] Moore's *Complete Works*, edited by himself, was to appear in 1841. Longman held the copyright to *Lalla Rookh* and Power that to the *Irish Melodies*.

[3] Southey's *Joan of Arc* appeared in 1796 and *Madoc* in 1805.

I have not yet had any communication, on the subject, with the Longmans (having been prevented, by weak eyes from writing more than was absolutely necessary) but I take for granted I have your permission to mention to them the very liberal terms upon which you *meant* me to have this copyright.[1]

Yours, my dear Sir, most truly
Thomas Moore.

1125. *To Richard Bentley*

National Library of Ireland

Sloperton
Decr 7th 1837

My dear Mr Bentley— I trust it will not be inconvenient to you to call, in the course of your City walks, at Sir John Lubbock's where you will find the sum I am in your debt—£52: 10—awaiting you. It is the only way I can ever manage to have my payments in town effected—at least by my *Devizes* Bankers—and will not, I trust, inflict upon you too much trouble.

I have never since heard from my friend Col. Napier (though Mrs Moore has had an announcement from Mrs Napier of the approaching marriage of their daughter) and am therefore ignorant whether he succeeded in his application to you.

Yours, my dear Sir, most truly
Thomas Moore

1126. *To John Murray*

Sir John Murray

Sloperton
Decr 11th 1837

My dear Sir— I have sent up by Captain Fielding the Journal of Lewis's you were so kind as to trust me with, and which no other eye but my own has perused; the only liberty I took with it being one I know *you* will forgive, namely, the reading of the greater part of it out to Mrs Moore after dinner. I hardly know what to do about Crabbe.[2] There certainly never was a man of his *calibre* of whose conversation so little remained in my mind. I remembered having

---

[1] See letters Nos. 1114 and 1122, to Richard Bentley, 8 Oct. and 23 Nov. 1837. Bentley had offered Moore the Irish publication rights to the poet's works, which the publisher had purchased with the intention of bringing out a complete edition.

[2] Murray brought out a *Complete and Uniform Edition of the Poetical Works of the Reverend George Crabbe*, with his letters, journals, and a life by his son

met him, for a few days, at Longleat, some years since, and instantly turned to a sort of Journal I kept at that time to see if any 'drop of the immortal man' had by accident trickled into it. But, no—I found that he had been, as usual, as dry as any *land*-Crab that ever crawled. When shall you want my communication? Though I write to you now, I shall most probably see you almost as soon as you can receive this letter, and therefore you need not take the trouble of answering till we meet. There are two little incidents, in one of which *you* are concerned, which I may possibly be able to make something of—but the Post-hour cuts me short (which you will say is a process not very necessary) and I have only time to say

Yours ever truly
Thomas Moore

1127. *To John Dalby*

Mrs. Mercia Dalby

Sloperton
Decr 11th 1837

My dear Dalby— I have deferred all this time answering your kind letter in order to give myself a better chance of seeing how the land lay before me, and determining accordingly as to the likelihood of my being able to accomplish the visit you propose to me. That I should like it above all things is certain—but then the how? and the when? As to my loco-motive capacities during the time since I received your letter you may guess of their extent when told that for more than five weeks I have not stirred beyond the limits of my own small garden—this owing partly to pen-and-ink work, and partly to an inflammation in the toe joint which I have been obliged to nurse. Well, next week comes my younger boy from the Charter-House and shortly after my elder (the Ensign) from Normandy (where he has been staying for the last six months)[1] and, as it is the last Christmas possibly we may all pass together, Ensigns being rovers, and none of us, God help us, very stationary, I feel myself bound within the magic circle of home, till the beginning of the next year, and then—but I will not speculate farther into the future

(1834), 8 vols., and C. Daly published another edition with an 'Essay on His Genius and Writings' in 1837. Murray may have been contemplating a new edition, which did not appear at this time.

[1] Russell was at the Charter House School and Tom had become an ensign in the army. Moore arranged for the latter to be placed under the tutelage of Professor Bertrand at Caen, in order to learn French (see letter No. 1104, to John Murray, 10 July 1837).

at present, as what they call 'a month's mind' (which is exactly what I feel towards going to Donington) has no right I presume to extend itself beyond the period its name limits it to. You may be sure that, if I *can* come, I *will*.

It delights me, my dear Dalby, to see from the tone of your letters that the years which have passed since you & I first met have done nothing towards chilling the freshness of your heart and mind, but that both are as warm & elastic as ever. Long may they continue so! I myself (if it were not for baldness and wrinkles) have little to complain of. I suspect that Lady Hastings (whom it has never been my good fortune to see) is exactly the sort of person to whom once upon a time I should have been most willing (I will not say *worthy*) to sing my best. But now— I have no time for more,

Y^{rs} ever affectionately
Thomas Moore

1128. *To Mary Shelley*

Abinger Collection

Sloperton
Decr 12th 1837

As I had some prospect of being called to town before Christmas, I had deferred writing to you in hope of the *far* more agreeable operation of *seeing* you. It was Diderot, I believe, who used to leave his mistress in order to have the pleasure of writing to her. But as I am a good Catholic, the Real Presence is what, in all such cases, I greatly prefer. I shall be delighted (for Lord Lansdowne's own sake) to introduce you to each other—but this again is one of the agreeable things that cannot be done well by pen-and-ink work, for though not exactly what the Italians call a 'quattr' occhi' proceeding (as you must be troubled with *my* additional pair of eyes, as introducer) yet eyes to eyes, where a person like yourself is concerned, makes all the difference, and therefore I think that if the object you have in view is not very pressing it will be better to wait till I come to town in February when we can arrange some mode of bringing you both together.[1]

I am hard at work trying to make up for a long & very agreeable idleness, during the autumn— For near five weeks I have not been beyond the limits of our little garden.

Yours ever most truly
Thomas Moore.

[1] Moore did not record in his diary or mention in other letters the reason for Mary's desire to meet Lord Lansdowne, and there is no indication that he introduced them. See letter No. 1144, to Mary Shelley, 10 May 1838.

1129. *To Thomas Drummond*

National Library of Ireland

Sloperton, Devizes
Decr 19th 1837.

My dear Mr Drummond— I want you to do me a little favour in the *historical* line—and, as you have so much business on your hands with the present time, a little airing into the past will perhaps be wholesome for you. The Record Commission here have, as in duty bound, sent me all their massy Volumes—but there is one work which, from my not finding it among them, must belong, I take for granted, to a Dublin publication—its title being, as well as I can recollect, 'Inquisitionum in Officio Rotulorum Cancellariae Hiberniae asservalarum Refertorium'. The copy I saw of it is in the British Museum. Would you kindly make some enquiries for me, on the subject, and by your official interposition, procure me a copy of the work, pleading, if necessary, the example of the Record Commission here. My best remembrances to Mrs Drummond, and tell her that one of her many admirers (Rogers) was here with us in the autumn as gay & blooming as ever.

Yours very truly
Thomas Moore

1130. *To William Lisle Bowles*

Rice University

Bowood
Wednesday [*c.* 1837]

My dear Bowles— I am delighted to learn from our friends here that you are *yourself* (and you could not be any thing much better) once more again. Now that your mind is at ease about Bishops & Archbishops I hope I shall find you in sufficiently good humour with them to oblige *me* (who am always you know in good humour with them) by subscribing *only* a guinea to a History of the Archbishops of Dublin which a friend of mine is about publishing.[1] He is a Protestant and a man well acquainted with the subject, so that you may, I think, *depend* upon the work being well worthy of your patronage. Lord Lansdowne has already given me his name for it.

Ever yours most truly
Thomas Moore

---

[1] John D'Alton, *Memoirs of the Archbishops of Dublin* (Dublin, 1838). The names of Bowles, Moore, and Lord Lansdowne appear on the list of subscribers.

1131. *To Thomas Drummond*

National Library of Ireland

Sloperton
Jan^r 22, 1838

My dear Mr Drummond— So far have I been from reproaching *you* that, had you but waited a little, you would have had a penitential letter from *me* expressing my shame at not having immediately (both as a duty of business and of gratitude) acknowledged the receipt of the two packets you were so good as to send me.[1] The last ponderous *billets*, before these, which I received by the post were the Volumes of the Irish Education Inquiry, which Frankland Lewis, to the astonishment of our Village Post-Office, sent me some years ago.

You will be glad to hear that our friends at Bowood are all much more promising, in the way of health, than they have been for some time. I am, however, a little in fear of the consequences of the young Lord's attending Parliament, which he is now about to venture upon, for a few weeks.[2]

With sincere thanks for your kindness and for Mrs Drummond's flattering remembrance of me, I am most truly yours

Thomas Moore

1132. *To John Easthope*

Huntington Library

Private
Jan^r 26th 1838

My dear Mr Easthope— I do not know whether *you* will think it worth your while to begin a new score with me (either on the former terms or any others, more to your taste that you may suggest) but the foregoing will show that *I* at least am well inclined thereto.[3]

I never sent you (as I ought to have done) the list of the things written under our last agreement; but I have it noted down, and will forward it another time.

Yours very truly
Thomas Moore.

---

[1] See letter No. 1129, to Thomas Drummond, 19 Dec. 1837.

[2] The 'young Lord' was Henry Thomas Petty-Fitzmaurice (1816–66), who succeeded his father as fourth Marquess of Lansdowne in 1863. The son was Under-Secretary of State for Foreign Affairs (1856–8).

[3] Moore contributed satires to the *Morning Chronicle* during most of his career and in March 1836 entered into a new formal agreement with Easthope to furnish 'occasional contributions of Squibs'. He seemed satisfied with the terms, having received £100 in advance (Russell, vii. 151).

My friend Black will I know look carefully to the printing of this trifle.[1] If he wishes to disavow concurrence with the opinion expressed in it, he may concoct, if he likes, a little article on the subject.

I do not wish you, this time, to pay (that is, if you care about the thing at all) till *after* I have completed my number.

1133. *To Macvey Napier*

B.M. Add. MS. 34618, f. 583

Sloperton
Feb[r] 23rd 1838

My dear M[r] Napier— Your letter reached me in town whither I had gone with my eldest son to provide his out-fit for his regiment— Bellona having possessed more charms for him than Alma Mater.[2] I was seized however with so severe a cold in that unexampled weather, that I found myself obliged to fly from business, engagements,—every thing almost that I went up for,—and to make good my retreat for Sloperton—where, however, I had hardly time to find myself comfortably *niché*, when I was again obliged to set off with my young soldier for Bristol, from which port he sailed for Cork the day before yesterday. Under all these interrupting circumstances, and thrown back as I had already been in my appointed task-work, it is wholly out of the question that I should be able either now, or for a long time to come, to extravagate into any other undertaking. I must only wish you better success with other and better men, till an interval of leisure (if ever that arrives) shall allow me to be of use to you.

In great haste, but most cordially
Yours
Thomas Moore

1134. *To John Easthope*

Huntington Library

Sloperton
Tuesday [February 1838]

My dear M[r] Easthope— It is odd enough that I was on the very point of writing to you on Saturday (by parcel) to suggest your deferring the insertion of the 'Box',[3] not for the very good reason

[1] Moore enclosed 'The Song of the Box' (*Poetry*, p. 656) in this letter (see letter No. 1134, to John Easthope, February 1838).

[2] Bellona was the Roman Goddess of War. Moore means that his son Russell had left school at the Charter House in order to enter training for the military service. He enrolled in a preparatory school run by a Dr. Firminger.

[3] 'The Song of the Box' (*Poetry*, p. 656).

you have suggested, but merely because I thought that while the present Canadian fever continued to rage, nothing else would be attended to. *Squibs* versus *Cannon* have but little chance of being heard.[1]

Tomorrow morning I start for town, and shall call upon you in the course of the week. My son's outfit for the army is the business that takes me up.

May I ask of you to send the inclosed to the 2ᵈ post for me

> Yrs. ever truly
> Thomas Moore

1135. *To John Easthope*

Huntington Library

> Private
> Sloperton
> Febʳ [1838]

My dear Mʳ Easthope— I have been fairly driven from town by influenza—blown out in an explosion of sneezing,—the day before yesterday, a whole week before the time I had fixed for my departure, and now write to you from a sofa where I am laid up in ordinary—luckily a very *extra*ordinary thing with me.

I meant to have called before I came away to have a few last touches at the 'Box'—but, as they were mere verbal alterations, I shall not trouble you with them.[2] I should be glad, however, to have the following note appended,—on the words 'Hugo Grotius'

[A namesake of Grote's *deleted*]
where they first occur
    Hugo Grotius*
  * *Groot*, or *Grote*, latinized into Grotius.

> Ever yours truly
> Thomas Moore

1136. *To John Easthope*

Huntington Library

> March 19ᵗʰ 1838.

My dear Mʳ Easthope— The inclosed *ought* to be good, for it cost me some trouble. If bad, it is at least *bitter* bad. I have no idea how

[1] Moore alludes to the French-Canadian rebellion, led by Louis Papineau, in November 1837. Although the revolt was suppressed in December, the question of Canadian home rule was pressing at the time Moore wrote this letter.

[2] 'The Song of the Box', signed by 'a radical reformer, but no friend to the Ballot', appeared in the *Morning Chronicle* for Monday, 19 Feb. 1838. Easthope added the note which Moore requested.

the Box was liked.[1] To me it appeared to fall still-born, and the only quarter where I heard of its having any success, was at our friend Paul's (Methuen) whose lady sent some copies of it about the neighbourhood, and said it 'had done great good in London!' I need not say any thing about attention to the printing of the inclosed—for your people never have failed me, in this respect. Quere—whether 'John of Tuam' had not better have the mark he himself puts before his signature? something this way+[2]

Yours ever very truly

T. M.

1137. *To Richard Bentley*

National Library of Ireland

Sloperton

March 21st 1838

My dear Mr Bentley— I am ashamed not to have sooner acknowledged your welcome packet—but when I tell you that Mrs Moore has been, for this fortnight past, *seriously* ill I know you will not wonder at my forgetting every thing else. She is now, I am happy to say, better, but still very weak—her illness having been an exhausting discharge of blood from the stomach. Pray tell our friend Moran this, as I have long been his debtor in the way of writing.

Miss Hughes, who is now with Mrs Moore, was much gratified & obliged by your account of her lithographical affairs.[3] The little book has succeeded wonderfully & she begs you will be so good as to have a *hundred more* struck off for her. She also bids me say that you shall hear from her very soon on the *business* part of the transaction.

I was delighted to have Prescott's book, some extracts from which I had read with great admiration.[4]

Yours very truly

Thomas Moore.

[1] See letter No. 1135, to John Easthope, February 1838.

[2] 'Sketch of the First Act of a New Romantic Drama' (*Poetry*, p. 653). The poem was first published in the *Morning Chronicle* on Thursday, 22 Mar. 1838. The mark which Moore indicated as the symbol before Tuam's name was placed in the sixteenth line of the last stanza.

[3] See letter No. 1121, to E. R. Moran, 20 Nov. 1837.

[4] Probably William Hickling Prescott, *History of the Reign of Ferdinand and Isabella the Catholic* (London, 1838), 3 vols. Although no publisher is indicated on this edition, Bentley brought out the third and published other works by Prescott.

1138. *To E. R. Moran*

National Library of Ireland

Sloperton
[Postmark March 31, 1838]

My dear Mr Moran— I merely despatch you this line lest you should be wondering at my long silence—but Mrs Moore's serious illness (of which you have heard no doubt from our friend Mr Bentley)[1] has so occupied all my time & thoughts that I could spare but little of either to any thing else. She is now, I rejoice to say, somewhat better, but still very, very weak.

Miss Hughes who has been her chief nurse through her illness is most highly pleased at the manner in which you & Mr Bentley have managed her little work for her.[2]

Yours most truly
Thomas Moore.

I am sorry to see an announcement of the poetic *ébauche* of the Epicurean as a separate work.[3] This is a most inconsiderate plan, and quite remote from my original intention. It cannot prove otherwise, I am convinced, than an abortion and a failure.

1139. *To Mr. O'Dwyer*

National Library of Ireland

Sloperton, Chippenham
[March 1838]

My dear Sir— I have to apologize for not sooner attending to the question which you addressed to me; but the alarm in which I have been kept for some weeks past by the dangerous illness of Mrs Moore has prevented me from attending to any thing else.[4] The portrait of me which you enquire about *was* painted by Jackson at Rome, and I believe in the year 1818.—I am much flattered to find that so good a countryman of mine as yourself should think my portrait worth possessing.

Yours very truly
Thomas Moore

[1] See letter No. 1137, to Richard Bentley, 21 Mar. 1838.
[2] *Ibid.*
[3] *The Epicurean* was published with *Alciphron*, Moore's fragmentary poetic version of the story, in 1839. Illustrations were done by Turner.
[4] See letter No. 1137, to Richard Bentley, 21 Mar. 1838.

1140. *To E. R. Moran*

National Library of Ireland

Sloperton
April 8ᵗʰ 1838

My dear Mʳ Moran—I shall very willingly accept the honour of acting as Steward at the Lit. Fund dinner—but should not like to do it *under* the mark (pecuniarily speaking) of others who have held the office. Neither should I, on the other hand, think it prudent to pay too dearly for my honour and glory. This being the dilemma I shall (unless there is time previously for another communication between us on the subject) leave it to yourself to strike the balance between purse & pride for me.

I should be most glad that it were possible for Bentley to have the bringing out of the Epicurean—but I take for granted it is in the hands of the Creditors.[1]

Yours very truly
Thomas Moore.

1141. *To John Richards*

Rice University

Sloperton
April 22ⁿᵈ 1838

Sir— I have to apologize for not sooner answering your enquiry. If *passing through* Berkshire could entitle me to the honour of your notice, I should be abundantly qualified; but unluckily I never was a resident in that county.

Your obedient Servᵗ
Thomas Moore.

1142. *To Dr. Black*

Rice University

Sloperton
April 22ⁿᵈ 1838

My dear Doctor Black—I am rather in a puzzlement with respect to the fate of an Anti-Episcopal squib which I sent up the beginning of last week, and which I suspect you (from your love of Bishops) must have suppressed, as I have neither heard or seen any thing of

[1] See letter No. 1138, to E. R. Moran, 31 Mar. 1838.

it since.[1] I ought first to have mentioned that Thursday's Chronicle (in which possibly it may have been) has never reached me, owing to the mistake of your people having sent me two Chronicles of the same date successively, in consequence of which Thursday's paper did not come at all. Should this have been the case, the only answer you need not [*sic*] take the trouble of sending me is a copy of Thursday's paper should you have one. One of my fears was (and indeed still is) that Mr Easthope may have been out of town and that my squib may have been sent *fizzing* after him.

Ever yours truly
Thomas Moore

[1] Moore is probably referring to the following lines, sent in an undated note to Dr. John Black, the original of which is in the Harvard College Library:

Sir

    As I perceive that the late achievements of a certain bustling bishop have already been noticed as they deserve by some of your poetical correspondents, I should have hesitated in troubling you with the following trifle had I not recollected that, in the good task of exposing such priestly mountebankism, 'every little helps'; and that, as Luther truly says '*R*eligio maxime periclitatur inter *R*everendissimos.'

Yours &c.

Some account of a new genus of Churchman called the Phill-pot.

As that old married pair, *M*other *C*hurch and the *S*tate,
Have giv'n birth to a new sort of offspring, of late,
Call'd by *savans* the Phill-Pot,—a race, which unite
All that's wrong in both parents, with none of the right;
And, as no one can doubt such a nicely mix'd breed
Will be sure both with sinners and saints to succeed,
We shall soon have the land blackening over with swarms
Of newly-spawn'd *P*hill-*P*ots, in all sorts of forms;—
Not a spot of our isle but will soon be o'er-run with 'em,
'Lordships' and 'Graces' each black mother's-son of 'em.

This being the case, and a breed, now so curious,
Being likely, if multiplied thus, to grow spurious,
Some test is much wanted,—and that, too, no slight one—
To tell if a *P*hill-*P*ot's the wrong breed, or right one;
And, anxious from all such impostures to screen us,
The present *R*ight *R*everend head of the *genus*
Has drawn up some *Q*uestions, so framed as to show
If one's *P*hill-*P*ot is really a *P*hill-*P*ot, or no;
Nor could Irving himself, with his famed *P*olyglottism,
Evade, it is thought, this strict *T*est of *P*hill-*P*ottism.

We subjoin, just to show how they baffle evasion,
The *Q*uestions and *A*nswers drawn up for th' occasion.
1.—What's the *C*hurch?— A large money-establishment, giv'n
    To pamper up priests for the honour of heav'n;
    And inspiring a zeal in each reverend man,
    Just proportion'd to what he gets *by* it per ann.

1143. *To Benjamin Robert Haydon*

Willard B. Pope

Sloperton, Devizes
May 10th 1838

My dear Sir— Of *any* communication from *you* I am most ready to say 'better late than never'. It was exceedingly kind of you to take so much trouble for me, in the first instance, and not at all surprising that you should forget it all afterwards. As to Sheridan, I have really almost forgot every thing about him myself; so many other and different subjects have since occupied my thoughts— As somebody says of the waves of the sea,

> 2.—Name the *O*rders.— *F*irst, *C*urates, the lowest in larder;
> Then *R*ectors, improv'd much in fat and in ardour;
> And so on through *B*ishops, the fervour increases,
> Extending its glow ev'n to nephews and nieces;
> Till,—waxing yet warmer, as upward its motion,—
> In *P*rimates it bursts with a blaze of devotion
> Of which hungry curates have not the least notion!
> 3.—Do you hold that all Christians, who differ from you,
> Are idolaters, heathens, and so forth?— I do.
> 4.—Are you ready, with St. Athanasius,* to damn
> Every man, woman, child, of the Greek *C*hurch?— I am.
> 5.—Can you prove, if required, that the great Irish Dan
> Is the 'lion's whelp' mention'd *Deut.* 20?—I can.
> 6.—Through the whole book of *N*umbers I'll thank you to run,
> And say, *which* the parson loves best?— Number *O*ne.
>
> So far, we've the youth in *Theology* tried:—
> We shall now see how well he's with Ethics supplied.
>
> 1.—What's your pretext for now taking orders?— Devotion.
> 2.—And what your sole object henceforward?— Promotion.
> 3.—Do you think it much matters, when good things are got,
> By what *methods* we get them?— No, certainly not.
> [4].—Have you any slight twinge of those scruples we call
> 'Self-denial', 'humility', 'shame'?— Not at all.
> That will do.—
>   Here th' Examiner closes his task;
>
> A more promising pupil no bishop need ask
> And the *C*hurch gladly welcomes to feed on her clover
> A youth who has proved himself *Phill-P*ot all over.

* See a defence of the Athanasian Creed in a letter addressed to Mr Canning by Rev. Henry Philpotts. [*Moore's note.*]

'And of Dan he said, Dan is a lion's whelp.' Deuteron. 33, 22. [*Moore's note.*]
These lines, which were not included in the 1840 edition of Moore's works, are a lampoon on Bishop Henry Phillpotts, who was under frequent attack by the Whigs because he opposed such measures as Catholic Emancipation, the Ecclesiastical Commission Act, the Reform Bill, and the Ecclesiastical Discipline Bill of 1838.

'And one no sooner kiss'd the shore and died,
    Than a new follower rose'
Even so has it been with my works—the dying, I fear, included.
    Trusting that I may be more lucky in meeting you than I have
been now, I am sorry to say, for many years, I am

my dear Sir, very truly yours
Thomas Moore.

1144. *To Mary Shelley*

Abinger Collection

May 10ᵗʰ 1838

I was away from home (for a wonder) when your letter arrived, or
you should have had an immediate answer. I am dispatching by
this post a letter to Lord Lansdowne, in aid of your request, and
(though not very sanguine about it) hope most sincerely that we
shall succeed.[1]

    I take for granted, as you have not alluded to it, that nobody told
you of the sad alarm I had about Mʳˢ Moore nearly two months
since, when she was seized with a vomiting of blood from the
stomach that threatened for some time serious consequences.[2]
There was however no return of it, and she has ever since been
getting better—slowly, but I trust surely. Her spirit and heart *never*
fail.

    Should all go on right with me (and that all means only *one*) you
will see me in town about the 20ᵗʰ or so.

Yours ever most truly
Thomas Moore.

How *could* you trust to a poet's memory, and not put your address?
I know it has some letter of the alphabet appended to it, but as I
forget which, I must, for fear of accidents, direct this to Hookham's.

1145. *To Smith and Elder, Publishers*

Pforzheimer Misc. MS. 1394

Brookes's
May 22ⁿᵈ 1838.

Gentlemen— I thank you very much for your kindness in sending
me the plates of your projected work and am sorry to be obliged to
repeat what I said, when I had the pleasure of calling upon you,

---

[1] See letter No. 1128, to Mary Shelley, 12 Dec. 1837.
[2] See letter No. 1137, to Richard Bentley, 21 Mar. 1838.

that is [*sic*] *impossible* for me to undertake the task which you propose.

Your very obliged servant
Thomas Moore.

1146. *To John Richardson*

Rice University

Sloperton, Devizes
July 8th 1838

Sir— The inclosed answer to a letter which I received a long time since from Captain Richardson of Calcutta I shall be much obliged by your taking the *very earliest* opportunity of transmitting to that gentleman. It was his own wish that I should send my letter through your hands.

I am, Sir,
your obedient servant
Thomas Moore.

1147. *To the Reverend George Newenham Wright*

N.L.S. MS. 3071, No. 143

Sloperton
July 16th 1838

Dear Sir— I shall have much pleasure in making your acquaintance during my next visit to town, and should have answered your letter more speedily, had it not been unluckily mislaid.

I cannot of course return any answer to your friend the publisher's proposition till I am more acquainted with the nature of it.

I am, dear Sir, your obliged servant
Thomas Moore.

1148. *To Edward Moxon*

Rice University

July* [1838]

My dear Mr Moxon— I again want your friendly aid— I think it was you who borrowed for me Wright's Letters published not very long since—(*Historical* Letters)—and I want them much again— and, if you would otherwise borrow for me, without much delay 'History of Q. Elizabeth' (in Kennet's England Vol. 2)¹ which I see

---

¹ Thomas Wright (ed.), *Queen Elizabeth and Her Times. A Series of Original Letters, Selected from the Inedited Private Correspondence of Lord Burghley, the Earl of Leicester* . . . (1838), 2 vols., and White Kennet, *A Complete History of England* (1706), 3 vols. The quotation mark after 'Elizabeth' has been added by the editor.

in the Catalogue of your London Library, I can promise that it will
be the last trouble that (in *this* way) I shall give you—

Yours most truly
Thomas Moore

1149. *To the Marquess of Lansdowne*

Bowood

Sloperton
August 12th 1838

[*Moore asks Lord Lansdowne to bring another volume of State Papers,
since he is beginning to work on the period of Henry VIII for his*
History of Ireland.]

1150. *To H. D. Scott*

Huntington Library

August 19th 1838

My dear Mr Scott— I hope I shall be lucky enough to get a peep at
you (and who knows but at Mrs Scott also?) during the two or three
days I shall pass in town on my way to Ireland with our Doctor.

I do not know whether you recollect my troubling you with a
copy of our young friend's Lithographs (besides that which you did
Mrs Moore the favour to accept) nearly three months since. It was
directed to Miss Power 22 Buckingham St. Strand, and from a letter
of hers to Mrs Moore lately we find she never received it. If there is
any Limbo to which you consign the troublesome packages of your
Lady correspondents, it is just possible this may be found in it—
but if not, you need not give it a second thought, as the book will
be easily replaced.

Ever yours truly
Thomas Moore

1151. *To E. R. Moran*

National Library of Ireland

October 18th 1838

My dear Mr Moran
The inclosed arrived here two or three days since, and we both
flattered ourselves that it was but a Precursor (not an *Irish* one) of
yourself. Having kept it in pledge, however, so long, without your
coming to redeem it, I now take advantage of an official frank to
forward it to you.

I wish you *had* been in Dublin during my visit, though, as it was, nothing could be more agreeable or more truly gratifying.[1]

Yours very truly
Thomas Moore.

I broke the seal, thinking the letter was for myself, but discovered the mistake before I opened a fold of it.

1152. *To Richard Bentley*

National Library of Ireland

Sloperton
Nov[r] 11th 1838

My dear M[r] Bentley— After an *imbroglio* of difficulties which I little foresaw at the time when you & I talked over the plan of an Edition of my Works, we are at last, I think, come in sight of land, and there remains nothing more, I believe, to complete the Irish part of our business than the affixing of your signature to the assignment you made me of the copy-rights for Ireland, which (on their sending you the paper) you will oblige me much by doing.[2]

I expect to be obliged to run up to town, on this business, in a week or so, and should you then feel any inclination for our long-projected dinner together, I shall be most gladly & heartily at your service.

Yours, my dear Sir, most truly
Thomas Moore

1153. *To Edward Bulwer*

National Library of Ireland

Bowood
Nov[r] 14, 1838

My dear M[r] Bulwer— I have been from home these two days which has prevented my sooner answering your letter. I assure it [*sic*] is most welcome & flattering to me to be remembered by you, and if M[rs] Bulwer (to whom I beg *my* best remembrances) had but joined in the recollection, I should have been still more pleased. As to my contributing to the new Monthly, I fear it is out of the question.[3] The three things I have chiefly written for through life have been for love, for money and for fun. The first and last of these impulses are somewhat abated, and of the other it would not be worth M[r]

---

[1] Moore was in Ireland from 12 to 22 Sept. 1838 (see Russell, vii. 232–7).

[2] See letters Nos. 1114 and 1122, to Richard Bentley, 8 Oct. and 23 Nov. 1837.

[3] Bulwer had asked Moore for contributions to the *Monthly Chronicle*, which was published from March 1838 to June 1841. Moore's reference to Mrs. Bulwer was a *faux pas*, since Bulwer and his wife were legally separated in 1836.

Colbourn's while to give me the quantum that would inspire me. The Times, to do it justice was a mine in this respect, and those things you notice so kindly might be well called (in the same sense in which the words were applied to Virgil's verses on Marcellus) 'verē aurea carmina'.

I shall, however, think over the matter, and the next time I come to town (which may be soon) shall, at least, have the pleasure of talking with you about it, which will be something—to *me* at least—These last words are written in the dark so I must take my chance for their legibility.

Very truly yours
Thomas Moore

1154. *To John Murray*

Sir John Murray

Sloperton
Novr 26th 1838

Dear Murray— I have looked over, I think, the whole of Morris's Vols.—[1] To those songs which I already knew—(and which indeed all the world knows, or *ought* to know)—I have prefixed the mark ⊗ —while to those which were quite new to me but which I thought good, I have affixed the mark X. —The rest is 'all but leather and prunello [*sic*].'[2] A Volume containing just what I have pointed out would be sure of success, as they are, in my opinion, models of English song-writing—but the great mass of the collection is sad shift. —Mind, this mustn't be told to the widow.

Ever yours most truly
T. Moore

Have the goodness to send the inclosed for me.

1155. *To Mary Shelley*

Abinger Collection

Sloperton
Decr 13th 1838

It is very kind of you, as well as *like yourself*, to think that Shelley *must* have sent me a copy of his original Queen Mab. But, alas, he never did, —and the fact is (whatever people who knew no better may have sometimes thought of me) none of the great guns of our

---

[1] Charles Morris, *Lyra Urbanica*, a collection of songs published in 1840. Moore recorded some passages from Morris's songs in his diary (Russell, vii. 248–9).
[2] *Essay on Man*, iv. 204.

modern Parnassus, Shelley, Wordsworth, Southey, and so forth, have ever acknowledged or admitted *me* as a legitimate brother— and in this I have a strong suspicion they were not much mistaken. However, I must only sing, like Audrey, 'the Gods give us joy for our sluttishness' & make the best I can of it. I am, however, very very sorry that I have not the book to send you.[1]

Eight days I staid in town, the whole of which was devoted to Paternoster Row and Co.—it was my intention, after having dispatched that region, to devote a few more days to seeing friends, and you among others. But the fiend, Influenza, laid hold of me (the first time I have ever really felt what it is) and I was but able to get down here and get to bed; and it was not till within these two or three days that I have been allowed to go out for a little air. The still depressing effects of the malady must account for this stupid letter, but I am not the less,

Yours truly & cordially
Thomas Moore.

1156. *To Philip Crampton*

Russell, viii. 278

Dec. 23. 1838.

My dear Crampton,

In my hurry yesterday I forgot to mention what was certainly *next* to Tom's case in my mind,[2] and that was your Discourse or

[1] Moore quotes part of Mary's 'very kind and flattering reply' in his diary for 18 and 19 Jan. 1839:

'I cannot help writing one word to say how mistaken you are. Shelley was too true a poet not to feel your unrivalled merits, especially in the department of poetry peculiarly your own,—songs and short poems instinct with the intense principle of life and love. Such, your unspeakably beautiful poems to Nea; such, how many others! One of the first things I remember with Shelley was his repeating to me one of your *gems* with enthusiasm. In short, be assured that as genius is the best judge of genius, those poems of yours which you yourself would value most, were admired by *none* so much as Shelley. You know me far too well not to know I speak the exact truth' (Russell, vii. 251–2).

For the quotation see *As You Like It*, III. iii. 47.

[2] Moore's son Tom entered the service in March 1838 and in May was stationed in Dublin. He was also in Belfast at some time during the spring and was reported to have insulted a young lady on the street. The accounts of the incident are contradictory, one being that the girl's mother appealed to the colonel of the boy's regiment, and the other that Tom was ill in bed at the time. On 19 Sept. 1838 he published a note in the *United Service Gazette*, denying the accusation.

This incident called Moore to Dublin, where he saw his son, who was 'looking very pale and ill' (Russell, vii. 232). The best account of the affair is found in E. R. Moran's collection of Mooreiana, now in the British Museum.

Lecture, which I read a few days since in one of the Irish papers, and was truly charmed with it. I take for granted, however, that that was but a sketch or abstract of what you said, and that we shall have it *in extenso*. I saw also a clever Letter, by a brother Papist of mine, in reply to some of your observations. I rather think that must have been the work of a little priest belonging to Marlborough Street, who wrote a very good article about Galileo (much in the same spirit) in the 'Dublin Review'.[1]

What I marvel at in *you*, Master Philip, is your finding time for such lucubrations. Go on and prosper, my fine fellow; you have my hearty good wishes and admiration in *all* lines.

Yours affectionately,
T. Moore.

1157. *To Lord John Russell*

Public Records Office

Lacock Abbey
December 27th 1838

My dearest friend— I have frequently sat down to write to you and as frequently thrown away the pen again, feeling that you would understand my *silence* far better than any thing I could say. Even now I can only express my sincere pleasure at hearing that you are again returning to your habits of business and work which is, after all, the only resource against painful thoughts.

I have been ill lately (a rare thing, thank God, with me) having had an attack of that very weakening sort of malady, called Influenza. A course of Bowood & Lacock, however, is gradually setting me to rights again— Three days with the Hollands, at Bowood, was my first reviving dose, and on Saturday Mrs Moore and I go there from this for a day or two— She sends her affectionate regards with mine.

---

[1] An article entitled 'Galileo—The Roman Inquisition' appeared in the *Dublin Review*, v (July 1838), 72–116. It was a composite review of Reverend William Whewell, *History of the Inductive Sciences from the Earliest to the Present Times* (London, 1837); John Eliot Drinkwater, *Life of Galileo* (London, 1833); and Reverend Baden Powell, *History of Philosophy* (London, 1837). The article defends the Church but admits the injustices of the Inquisition, saying that the latter 'had its rise in the wars of the Albigenses,—that is, just 1300 years too late for *us* to feel any very vital interest in it'. Thus, writers who condemn the Church for the unjust accusation of Galileo are mistaken, since in actuality the injustice was perpetrated by a body that was 'local and accidental'.

Do not think it at all necessary to answer this—I *hear* about you & that's enough.

> Yours ever
> Thomas Moore.

1158. *To James Corry*

National Library of Ireland

> Sloperton
> Feb^r 8th 1839

My dear Corry—Though the sages say '*no* news is *good* news', I cannot any longer remain satisfied with this negative proof of your well doing, but must have it [in] your own hand, as soon as you can manage to fly us a line. I believe you know already that I brought an influenza (and a most influential one) from town with me which did a good deal of damage for the time it lasted and has 'thinned my flowing hair' considerably—but, as soon as I was able to shift my quarters, I went to Bowood for a few days (where we had the Hollands &c) and the change did wonders for me— Bessy & I and Russ went there afterwards, for three days, to meet Charles & Lady Mary Fox, and had Charades acted two successive nights by Charles Fox and the juniors, in which Russell joined. I believe we told you that Russell has for some time set his heart upon going to India, as a soldier— It is very hard upon the mother, but she has generously given way to his wish— Hobhouse has given me a Cadetship[1] [*MS. damaged*] he is now at school at Edmonton (having cut the Charter-[*MS. damaged*] him for the military College, Addiscombe.

What a mess is mixing up for mankind [*MS. damaged*] of poor womankind) in all directions! After all war, is [*MS. damaged*] than is rangling [*sic*] and railing and if it but puts an end [*MS. damaged*] strife of tongues, it will so far do good. What a sublim[e] [*MS. damaged*] Shrews O'Connell and Brougham are![2]

My kindest regards to Mrs Corry, in [*MS. damaged*] good wishes to both Bessy joins me.

> Ever yours most trul[y]
> Thomas [Moore]

Bessy continues wonderfully well.

[1] Russell, Moore's second son, decided upon a military career and was first placed in Dr. Firminger's school, later transferring to Addiscombe Military College. After receiving his commission he was sent to India, where he contracted tuberculosis. He died on 23 Nov. 1842 (Russell, vii. 337; see also letter No. 1201, to E. R. Moran, 21 Jan. 1841).

[2] At this time O'Connell was agitating for abolition of the tithe system and Brougham for complete and immediate abolition of slavery.

1159. *To Thomas Longman*

Rice University

Sloperton
Feb^r 20th 1839.

Dear Tom— I take for granted, from not hearing any thing upon the subject, that my suggestions as to the Portrait, designs &c. have fallen to the ground. [I write now to beg of you to have the goodness to pay the inclosed Bill for me (Russy's last) at the Charter House— *deleted.*] By the bye, talking of cash a friend of mine to whom I mentioned the terms of our agreement about the Edition seemed to be of opinion that, if any thing *mortal* happened to me before the publication of the First Volume, you would have the whole of my copyrights, labour &c. for nothing, as it seemed to him to make all payment whatever dependent upon that contingency.[1] This surely *cannot* be the case—but I thought it as well to mention it, not having as yet time to refer to the agreement itself.

I have completed the correction of the Anacreon (which cost some trouble) and the castration of young Mr Little which was done in no time. My intention is (as this portion of the Volume will be headed 'Juvenile Poems') to fill up the vacancies made by the aforesaid operation with other juvenilities from the Odes & Epistles —but I shall want your help, when I send up the *Vellutified* Little, to calculate how many more lines that portion of the volume will admit of— I *should like* to get *in as* much *under that head* as *is practicable.*

I find I shall be able to manage Russell's bill at the Charter-House without troubling you. But I inclose the cash for a small bill of his to a shoemaker which you will be so good as to pay & get a receipt. How does your young lady stand this trying weather? My kindest regards to her.

Yours very truly
Thomas Moore.

1160. *To Richard Bentley*

National Library of Ireland

Private
Sloperton
Feb^r 22nd 1839

My dear Mr Bentley— I sent you off by this morning's post (direct) the promised *squib*, which has grown so large as to be rather a

---

[1] The reference is to the 1841 edition of his works, which was to be published by Longman.

fusee—[1] There is still some more of it which you shall have if you like, though it would take me far more time (as this did) than I can well spare, to lick it into shape. If the merit of my things were at all proportioned to the pains I take with them, they would be good indeed.

If you are inclined to help me to one of those 'draughts' (at sight) of inspiration',[2] which I speak in these verses, it would come very seasonably just now.

Ever yours truly
Thomas Moore

1161. *To Richard Bentley*

National Library of Ireland

Should you decide for keeping the inclosed, I should like to have a *Revise* of it for its present state rather alarms me.

Private
Sloperton
Febr 24th 1839

My dear Mr Bentley—

I am much afraid from the contents of your letter that you supposed the contribution I sent to be a free offering at your shrine—[3] But alas, I cannot afford such romantic dealings particularly just now, when I am trying to scrape together every possible (and in some instances, I fear, *im*possible) pound to prepare my second son for his Indian expedition.[4] No, I meant, in the ordinary way, and as a prelude perhaps to future dealings between us, that you should give me as much as you could afford to give for the long-laboured trifle I sent you, and which little as I myself think of it, is (I cannot but know) moneysworth in the market. Indeed, I have been rather spoiled in the way of prices. Captain Marryat, as I daresay you know, gave me very handsomely of his own free will and pleasure £250 for six contributions to the Metro-

[1] Moore published 'Thoughts on Patrons, Puffs, and Other Matters' in *Bentley's Miscellany*, v (1839), 326–8.
[2] The allusion is to the following lines:

The Muse now, taking to the till,
Has opened shop on Ludgate Hill,

. . . . .

And swallowing there without cessation
Large draughts (*at sight*) of inspiration,
Touches the *notes* for each new theme.
[3] See letter No. 1160, to Richard Bentley, 22 Feb. 1839.
[4] See letter No. 1158, to James Corry, 8 Feb. 1839.

politan[1] and M[r] Reynolds offered me more than twice as much for *one* contribution to the first Keepsake—which I moreover refused.[2] That you may not be frightened, however, by those or many more such instances I could adduce, I will come down to the moderate, and tell you that D[r] Lardner for the only thing I gave to the M Chronicle (two or three months since) sent me twenty guineas. This I mention to save you any difficulty or delicacy. It is curious enough, I never in my life set a price upon any of my own things but once, and then didn't get it. I shall only add that if it is the least inconvenience to you to accept the inclosed, at *any* price, I shall be obliged by your *cancelling it immediately* and sending me *back* the MS—letting me know, at the same time, what has been the expence of setting it up. But I must beg you to let all be decided tomorrow, so that I may have your answer on Tuesday morning— for on that day M[rs] Moore & I leave home on a short visit to Colonel Napiers [*sic*].

Yours ever most truly
Tho[s] Moore

1162. *Addressee unknown*

Huntington Library

March 1st 1839.

Thanks for your kind attention to my literary matters. Three of the inclosed refer to *other* people's literary matters, which I wish to God they wouldn't trouble *me* with. The 'M. P. Cavanagh'[3] I suspect to be a Miss instead of an Esquire—however the *sex* of an author doesn't matter much now-a-days.

Y[rs] ever most truly
T. M.

Should you meet with the work of Thirling Moile (one of the inclosed personages) read his Preface—it is excellent. I praised *that* to him (as it deserved) but pretended not to have read further. The name of his book is 'State Trials'.[4]

---

[1] See letter No. 1010, to Mary Shelley, 23 July 1832. Marryat actually offered £500 per year 'for contributions as often as it would suit' Moore to make them.

[2] In February 1828 Moore was asked to become editor of the *Keepsake*, and in June he was offered successively £100, £500, and £600 for one contribution to the first number. He refused all offers (see Russell, v. 272 and 314–15).

[3] *The Reign of Lockrin, a Poem*, by M. P. K[avanagh] was published in 1839. Morgan Peter Kavanagh (or Cavanagh) brought out a number of lengthy narrative poems during the second quarter of the nineteenth century.

[4] Nicholas Thirning Moile (Henry Bliss), *State Trials* (1838).

1163. *To Samuel Rogers*

Russell, viii. 278

Sloperton
April 18. 1839.

My dear Rogers,

Only think, two such wonders as that *you* should have taken the initiative in writing to me, and that *I* should have been so long in answering you. It was not, I need hardly tell you, from want of thankfulness for the pleasure your note gave me; but I have been busy beyond even my usual stress of business, and at three or four different tasks, too, driving four-in-hand daily; so that they all, I think, run a fair chance of being bungled. I have also had a more than usual pressure of correspondence, and lately on no very agreeable subject—the illness of our boy, Tom, who has been obliged, by rather a severe nervous attack, to get leave of absence from his regiment;[1] while the other little fellow (as I believe you know) has also determined upon being a soldier,—an Indian one,—and is now preparing hard and fast for Addiscombe, Hobhouse having very kindly given him a cadetship.[2]

I did not expect you would have seen my late 'Epistle,'[3] the channel through which it appeared lying so much out of your way, your 'solar track.' Did you at all remember the circumstance in which it originated? It was your saying to me, the last time you were at Sloperton, on seeing the prints we have hung round our dining-room, 'Why, you have all your *patrons* here!' The twelve first lines were written the day after that visit and never thought of again till very lately, when I added the remainder.

Your friend Bessy, who 'does all things but *forget*,' sends her warmest regards and remembrances, along with mine. We trace you now and then among the shining dinner-names (in our *after*-dinner lucubrations), and always wish you a long continuance of such gay doings.

Best regards to your sister; and believe me,

Ever most truly yours,
Thomas Moore.

---

[1] See letter No. 1156, to Philip Crampton, 23 Dec. 1838, and Russell, vii. 232.

[2] See letter No. 1158, to James Corry, 8 Feb. 1839.

[3] 'Thoughts on Patrons, Puffs, and Other Matters' (*Poetry*, p. 683), which appeared in *Bentley's Miscellany*, v (1839), 326–8. See letter No. 1160, to Richard Bentley, 22 Feb. 1839.

1164. *To Mary Shelley*

Abinger Collection

Sloperton
April 26th 1839

From some mistakes I made, in my hurry, the other day, I fear that a letter which was intended for you has gone irrevocably astray. It was merely to thank you for most welcome present [*sic*], and to ask you what you were doing, besides this launch [*sic*] of your boat, side by side with Shelley, into the Future.[1] It is a shame that Shelley and I should never have met. I am sure I should have liked *him* whatever he might have thought of my ordinary ways of going on. He was clearly a noble fellow.

Ever Yrs
T. Moore.

1165. *To Mary Shelley*

Abinger Collection

[Postmark May 9, 1839]

You must not come in the morning— I have made an oath not to see man (or 'woman, good my Lord')[2] before two or three in the day, and if I once depart from it, I'm ruined. Indeed, I have given warning to *all friends* (and I know you will not object to being counted among the *nearest*) that, if they wish to keep me among them, they must let me alone during the day.

Ever yours most truly
T. M.

1166. *To Mary Shelley*

Abinger Collection

Paternoster Row
Monday [postmark June 10, 1839]

I am in utter despair about Putney—for what with engagements of business, in this region, and of pleasure (as it calls itself) in the other, I have not a single moment to myself. *Why* did you disappear just as I was coming?

I meant to have written more (though it would have been only a repetition of my sorrow at not seeing you) but the business I am

[1] Shelley's *Poetical Works*, edited with notes by Mary Shelley, appeared in four volumes in 1839.

[2] Probably an adaptation of *Hamlet*, II. ii. 312.

upon here to-day, namely, the computation of the number of
rhymes I have been guilty of (bad & good) will not leave me time
for another word.[1]

Ever yours most truly
Thomas Moore

1167. *To Doctor Firminger*

B.M. Ashley 5768, f. 80

Sloperton, Devizes
July 31st 1839

My dear Doctor Firminger— Though I fear from my not having
heard from you again on the subject, that there is but little hope of
your having a vacancy for Russell, I take the chance of at least
enquiring of you, before I send him any where else, and shall be
much obliged by your letting me have your answer direct by post,
as every moment is now of the utmost importance to him.[2]

With my best compliments to Mrs Firminger, believe me
Very truly yours
Thomas Moore

1168. *To Locke, Hughes, and Company*[3]

Morgan Library

Sloperton
August 27th 1839

Gentlemen— My friend Mr Kenney, the bearer of this letter, having
some little business to transact at your Bank, I shall feel much
obliged by your affording him all the attention and facility in your
power.

I have the honour to be
Your obedient Servt
Thomas Moore

---

[1] An allusion to the 1841 edition of his works, which he was at this time
preparing for Longmans.

[2] Russell was admitted to Dr. Firminger's school at Edmonton, where he
was to prepare for a cadetship, which Hobhouse promised to obtain for him
(see Russell, vii. 252).

[3] Although not designated, the addressees were Moore's bankers in Devizes.

1169. *Addressee unknown*

Rice University

Sloperton
September 12th 1839

Dear Sir— I have only time to put up the inclosed, which have cost me some trouble, and which I hope you will like. Bellini's air strikes me as too monotonous ;[1] and I rather flatter myself the words I have written to it are deserving of some yoke-fellow of more depth & tenderness.

Yrs in haste
Ths Moore

1170. *To Thomas Longman*

Russell, viii. 280

October 8. 1839.

Dear Tom,

I have received intelligence this morning of a most unexpected turn of good luck from your namesake Tom. By a rapid succession of circumstances he has arrived at his point of *purchase* for a Lieutenancy—an event many wait long years for. But this demands an *instant* outlay, and the sum of 250£. must be placed *without delay* in the hands of Messrs. Cox and Greenwood. Though I have little doubt you would advance me this sum on the edition or the fourth volume of the 'History,' I have, on consideration, preferred the plan of using Russell's money for it, and making all straight to him when convenient. You will therefore have the goodness, *in the course of to-morrow* (as delay might risk the loss of this most fortunate *turn-up*), to deposit the above-mentioned sum in the hands of Cox and Greenwood, specifying to them for what purpose it is so deposited.[2]

Yours in great haste (having returned from a visit to a neighbour, but *just* in time to catch the Post),

Thomas Moore.

I think the sum is 250£.—but I have annexed the scrap from Tom's scrawl for you. I was sending this note by the parcel, but fearing you might delay in opening *that*, despatch it by post.

---

[1] Probably an air by Vincenzo Bellini (1801–35), an Italian opera composer.

[2] After Moore had purchased this commission for his son, the boy decided, early in 1842, to sell it. Later he joined the French Foreign Legion and was stationed in Algiers, where he died in March 1846 (see Russell, vii. 306–7, and Jones, *The Harp that Once—*, pp. 316–18).

1171. *To John Black*[1]

Harvard College Library

Pray see that this is correctly put in—I had not time to transcribe it again T. M.

Sloperton
Octr 20th 1839

Sir.

The writer of an article, in yesterday's Spectator, on the forthcoming edition of the Epicurean, has fallen into a mistake respecting the Poems subjoined in that volume which I think it due to myself to correct. Not having read, I presume, the preliminary Notice which accompanies the edition, he represents these Poems as being a 'versification' of part of the prose story, and also as recently written. The very contrary of this statement happens to be the fact; —the poems now published having been written nearly twenty years since, and then laid aside on my adopting the plan of converting the verse narrative into prose.[2] As some of the conclusions built by the critic on his own error are, to say the least of them, not very charitable, he will himself, I doubt not, rejoice to be thus set right.

I am, Sir, your obedient serv^t
Thomas Moore

1172. *To Thomas Longman*

Russell, viii. 281

Bowood
Nov. 7. 1839.

Dear Tom,

I sent you off from this last night Jones's drawing from the Dismal Swamp, which (as being very precious to Mrs. Moore) you will take good care of for her. I think you would have been pleased to see my noble host, when I told him that I had advised your calling in the alliance of Jones in our edition. He said instantly, and

---

[1] Address: To the / Editor of the Morning Chronicle / Morning Chronicle / Strand / London.

[2] Moore first conceived of *The Epicurean* as a poetical narrative, and some fragments, which now bear the title *Alciphron*, were written while he was in Paris in 1820–1. *The Epicurean* was published in 1827 and reissued in 1839 with these fragments forming an appendix. For details of the bibliographical problems connected with the novel and fragmentary poem see M. J. McManus, *A Bibliographical Handlist of the First Editions of Thomas Moore* (Dublin, 1934).

Lady L. joined most cordially in the opinion, that we *could not* have selected any one *so* fit for the task. This I rejoiced at, for my own sake as well as Jones's, having taken upon myself (ignoramus as I am in art) the responsibility of the selection.

I have set some friends of mine here on the hunt for good subjects from 'Lalla Rookh.' As to the 'Melodies,' I have already mentioned to you, I think, all that struck *me* as capable of being illustrated.

I shall send you by the next packet our third volume corrected.

Yours ever,
T. Moore.

1173. *To E. R. Moran*

National Library of Ireland

Decr 1st 1839

Many thanks, dear Mr Moran, for your kindness to Mrs D. though we were astonished, and a little alarmed at her taking such a frisk out of that nook in which she has chosen to *nicher* herself. I hope, however, that she will in future be more prudent.

It will give me great pleasure to pay my respects to Mrs Moran when I come to town.

Yours ever truly
Thomas Moore

Mrs Moore, with a thousand thanks for your kind & thoughtful supply of the papers, bids me tell you that she unluckily has no further occasion for them at present—the Shop-keeper having become a bankrupt who used to take them from her.

1174. *To E. R. Moran*

National Library of Ireland

Sloperton
Decr 3rd 1839.

Dear Mr Moran— I did not think when I last wrote that I should so soon again have to trouble you. There is a poor Italian gentleman in London of whom I know nothing more than that his name is Flechia and that he has given the world a '*Profeta Velato*'[1] and other translations, from my unworthy self. He is, however, (as you will see by the inclosed note) known to Panizzi, who speaks favourably of him. The poor man is wind-bound in London, being most anxious to get back to Turin, but not able to raise enough of that loco-motive power to waft him thither. Could his case, by any

---

[1] 'The Veiled Prophet of Khorassan', one of the tales in *Lalla Rookh*.

possible interpretation, be brought within the sphere of the Literary
Fund Charity ? The power of sending literary men out of the country
might, in some cases I could name, be most usefully applied—but
that would be from motives of charity to others, not to themselves,
and therefore I suppose not contemplated in your plan. Seriously,
if you could contrive to make out a few pounds, by using my name
in M. Flechia's behalf, and showing Panizzi's note you will do what
I know you like doing—a very kind thing.

Y^{rs} very truly
Thomas Moore

1175. *Addressee unknown*

Harvard College Library

Sloperton
Decr 9th 1839

My dear Sir— It would give me great pleasure, I assure you, to be
your *collaborateur* in some musical work—but just now I have two
important tasks (important to *me*, at least) on the anvil, and until
they are despatched I shall have no time for any other.

I am not sure whether the Airs I enclose are *all* that you were so
kind as to send me, but should any be missing, let me know and
I shall make another search.

Yours, my dear Sir, very truly
Thomas Moore

1176. *To Thomas Longman*

Russell, viii. 281

Sloperton
Dec. 23. 1839.

Dear Tom,

I feel really and truly obliged to my friends Co. for their prompt
and kind compliance with my request. I recollect an old woman in
Dublin, Mrs. Mackavino (how *such* a Mac got there, I don't know);
but she was a pensioner of my mother's, together with her daughter;
and the usual form of their petition used to be 'a couple of shillings
for a couple of grateful hearts.' Now a couple of hundreds deserves
a proportionate amount of gratitude, and I hereby remit you the
same.

Yours ever truly,
Thomas Moore.

1177. *To Thomas Longman*

Huntington Library

Sloperton
Jan^r 23, 1840

I forgot yesterday to notice and thank you for the Query in page 291.— If you will look again at the passage you will find that the change of rashly 'overrunning the bounds &c' does not refer to the Pope's first measures but to those which followed, namely 'the depriving the English king of his crown—dissolving all leagues &c. &c.'[1]

There was a very unfortunate error (had it escaped my attention) in page 305, where, instead of 'preaching in *defence* of the Pope' the printer had made it 'in *defiance* of the Pope'—[2] quite reversing the sense. Though I corrected this in the sheets sent yesterday, I think it as well to mention again

Thomas Moore.

1178. *To E. R. Moran*

National Library of Ireland

Sloperton
Feb^r 5th 1840

My dear Mr Moran

Thank you for thinking of my historical task. You will see in the Dublin Evening Post of *tomorrow* (I should think) a correction of an Erratum in the Third Volume (merely as to a date) which I should like you to copy into the Globe, if not inconvenient, quoting the Dublin Evening Post for it— As to the Volume of Proclamations, what I should like you to do for me (the purchase of the books being, I fear, out of the question, and, indeed, an 'impetus in Tenebris,' ignorant as I am of their value) would be to try and find out for me who are the purchasers, so as to give me a chance of having access to them.

My dinner-bell summons me.

Y^{rs} most truly
Thomas Moore

---

¹ *The History of Ireland* (London, 1835–46), iii. 291. As Moore says, the passage refers to the fact that Pope Paul III was 'rashly overrunning the bounds of his spiritual dominion' in attempting to deprive the King of England of temporal power. The end quotation mark was supplied by the editor.

² *The History of Ireland*, iii. 305. '. . . when [the unreformed clergy of the Pale] found that by preaching in defence of the Pope, they would incur the penalty of praemunire, [they] refrained from preaching altogether, and gladly took refuge in the safe, though inglorious, policy of silence.'

1179. *To Thomas Noon Talfourd*

Huntington Library

Sloperton
March 3rd 1840

Dear Serjeant Talfourd— I was delighted to receive from your own hand a volume which, under any circumstances must have been precious to me, but which as a gift from yourself will take its place among the Chosen of my Library.[1] During the earlier part of the proceedings on this question I was often tempted to beg you would take some opportunity of stating the resolution I had, from the first, formed not to avail myself of those retrospective enactments which were contained in the first form of the Bill, but of which, as it appeared to me, I could not honestly take advantage. All this, however, you were probably made acquainted with by Milnes and others to whom I mentioned it at the time—and, at all events the moment for such an explanation (except thus privately to yourself) is now long gone by.

Wishing you every success in all your various pursuits, I am very truly yrs

Thomas Moore

1180. *To R. R. Madden*

Lady Blessington, *Memoirs*, ii. 274

Sloperton
March 8th, 1840.

Dear Mr. Madden,— I have but time to acknowledge and thank you for the very interesting paper on slavery which you were so kind as to send me through the hands of my sister. I am not surprised that you should have returned bursting with indignation, more especially against those fellow-countrymen of ours (and fellow-Catholics), who, by their advocacy of slavery, bring so much disgrace both upon their country and creed.

Wishing you every success in your benevolent efforts, I am very truly yours,

Thomas Moore.

[1] Talfourd sent Moore a copy of his collected speeches on the Copyright Bill. Moore resolved not to avail himself of retroactive interests to which he was entitled under the terms of the Bill, and Lord John Russell alluded to Moore's determination in one of his speeches on the measure. (Russell, vii. 273–4. The dating of Moore's diary is confusing at this point. Russell dated this entry 14 Feb. but it was evidently made on 14 Mar.)

1181. *To Mary Shelley*

Abinger Collection

Sloperton
April 7ᵗʰ 1840.

Your letter found me in all the uncomfortable bustle of preparing for Mʳˢ Moore's departure with our boy,[1] for London, in order to complete his out-fit, and I shall myself, in a few days join them there, as he is to sail, poor fellow, next week. It will be a sad operation both for her and me—but my thoughts about my own loss are all merged in my feeling for her.

I had already seen the accounts of poor Ratcliffe[2] in the newspaper—and they at once explained to me the change of manner I had observed in him. Indeed I had been so unjust to my own dear country as to think he had been spoiled in Ireland. Your account of him interested us all very much.

Mʳˢ Moore and myself are most thankful for the letters of introduction, and the kind terms in which they are expressed. His destination has been since changed to Bengal—but he will take the letters with him notwithstanding—I fear I have but little chance of seeing any one of my West End end [*sic*] friends during the few days I shall now pass in London—but in June next!

Ever yours most truly
Thomas Moore

1182. *To Thomas Longman*

Russell, viii. 282

Sloperton
April 18. 1840.

Dear Tom,

I send you the inclosed *only*, because it will be necessary for me to have a revise of it, which will not, I trust, be the case with what follows. Prose always gives me a hundred times as much trouble in correcting as poetry does. Besides, the printer, you will see, has made a mistake about my 'Greek Ode.'[3]

We have had a line from Russell by the pilot, and he was then only *giddy*—not yet sick. Mrs. Moore is still very depressed in spirits, and it will be some time, I fear, before she gets over her loss.

---

[1] Russell, who was preparing to enter the military service.

[2] On 5 Mar. 1840 Mary recorded in her journal: 'Ratcliffe taken ill.' See F. L. Jones, ed., *Mary Shelley's Journal* (Norman, 1947), p. 208.

[3] Probably 'Ode to the Goddess Ceres' (*Poetry*, p. 570), one of the satirical poems.

Pray say to your lady how very much we felt her kind service and kind note.

Yours very truly,
T. Moore.

In looking over some old diaries and memorandums, I find that, however of late years I may have seen reason to grumble a little with Co. and Co., it was in former years all sunshine between us. Indeed, I will venture to say, that there are few tributes from authors to publishers on record more honourable (or, I will fairly say, more deserved) than those that will be found among my papers, relative to the transactions for many years between myself and my friends of the Row.

1183. *To Richard Bentley*

National Library of Ireland

Sloperton
May 18th 1840

My dear Mr Bentley— I trust nothing has happened to an MS. which an MISS. (named King) sent you through my hands some time since, as, taking for granted you do not mean to publish it, she wants it back most importunately. Have the goodness therefore to despatch it to her directed

Miss King
D. Ingliss Esqr
23 Hans Place
Sloane St.

I hope to see you in town in June.

y^{rs} ever truly
Thomas Moore

1184. *To the Marquess of Lansdowne*

Bowood

Sloperton
July 21, 1840

My dear Lord Lansdowne— I have been for some time anxious to consult with you respecting a scruple I have had on the subject of my dedication to you—a scruple, on *your* account, of course, not on my own—and the time is now gone on so far, and the printing so advanced that we shall be but barely soon enough to catch the *devils* by your answering me directly on the subject of this note. To come to the point at once—have you ever thought of the large portion of my versicles which is devoted to political satire, and the number of persons with names merely gutted of their vowels that must accordingly figure in my pages? I myself think that a Dedicatee can by no means be thought responsible for the progeny of the Dedicator throughout ten whole volumes—but I thought it right to lay the case before you, and am only sorry that my delay in doing so should make the matter now so inconveniently pressing.[1] I was in hopes I should be able to run up to town before the dispersion—but my leg still says 'no.'

Y^{rs} ever most truly
Thomas Moore

1185. *To Samuel Rogers*

Rice University

Friday July 24th 1840

My dear Rogers— I have been so doubtful as to my time of coming up that I deferred answering your kind note till I could do so satisfactorily. I have now decided upon going to town on Sunday next, so that, if you are still *able* (I take the *willingness* for granted) to have me to dinner on Monday, I am then & ever

Yours
T. Moore

I shall perhaps *try* you at breakfast on Monday.

1186. *To John Easthope*

Huntington Library

Private
Brookes's
August 1st 1840

My dear Mr Easthope— I am afraid we shall not be able to arrange our dinner affair *this* time—for my time of departure is fast approaching, and my dinner-list has filled even more rapidly & multifariously than usual.— Either Tuesday or Wednesday next I could manage, if I heard from you *soon* on the subject.

Inclosed is a list of things for which I should *like* something in return *as soon* as is convenient. I want to put some questions to

---

[1] The 1840–1 edition of Moore's *Works* was dedicated 'To the Marquis of Lansdowne, in grateful remembrance of nearly forty years of mutual acquaintance and friendship'.

you, on this particular subject, before I leave town, if we could
manage to meet.

Y^{rs} ever

T. Moore.

Thoughts on Mischief— May 2nd
Religion & Trade—   June 1st
Account of Extrdⁿ Dream   June 15th
Retreat of the Scorpion—July 16.[1]

£60: 0: 0

I still think I am in your debt £15 on the last account, but shall not
be quite certain till I see the last memorandum I sent you

1187. *To John Easthope*

Huntington Library

Private

Brookes's

Saturday Night [August 8, 1840, *not in Moore's hand*]

My dear Mr Easthope— I trust you will be able to tell my friend
Mr Eastlake, who will either transmit or present to you this letter
the number of the £50 note which I received from you a day or two
since. I have not time to explain to you the reason of this request
further than that I have lost the note and have every reason to
think I have been *robbed* of it.[2]

Yours truly

T. Moore.

1188. *Addressee unknown*

Rice University

Sloperton

August 10th 1840

Sir— I have to apologize for not sooner answering your letter—the
delay being chiefly owing to my absence from home. During my
stay in Dublin, at the time you mention, Messrs Smith & Hodges
employed a copyist to make some extracts for me from a MS.

---

[1] 'Thoughts on Mischief' (*Poetry*, p. 684), appeared in the *Morning Chronicle*
on Saturday, 2 May 1840, and 'Religion and Trade' (*Poetry*, p. 675), in the
Morning Chronicle on Monday, 1 June 1840. 'An Account of an Extraordinary
Dream', and 'The Retreat of the Scorpion', which appeared in the same newspaper on 15 June and 16 July respectively, were not included in the 1841
edition of Moore's works and hence are not in the *Poetical Works* edited by
Godley.

[2] See letter No. 1190, to John Easthope, 12 Aug. 1840. See also letter No.
1237, to the Governors of the Bank of England, 15 Feb. 1845.

translation of the Annals of Inisfallen ;[1] and this is doubtless the person to whom you refer, though of his name I was before ignorant. The work he did for me was very fairly and correctly done, and I have little doubt, from the character of his employers, that you will find him useful & trustworthy.

Y^r obedient Servt
Thomas Moore.

1189. *To John Easthope*

Huntington Library

Bowood
August 11 1840

My dear Mr Easthope— You have received, I doubt not, my note respecting the tragic accident that has happened to me.[2] I trust you will be able to furnish me with the number of the note, that being my only chance of ever recovering it.

I have but this moment arrived here, and am almost too late for the post—so no more at present from

Yours ever most truly
Thomas Moore

1190. *To John Easthope*

Huntington Library

Bowood

[August 12, 1840, *not in Moore's hand*]

My dear Mr Easthope— Be assured I shall not easily forget the kind promptitude with which you have offered to come to my relief on this occasion. Though all my life too careless about money, I never was robbed (probably from the very little I have ever had to be robbed of) before.[3] The worst of it is, too, that I see very little chance of ever recovering the note,— the chance of its being stopped at the Bank, being I am told a very poor one. All I have for it is to work double tides at the *pen;* and if you *really* do not think I tax your purse too much and too often, a well-sustained course of

---

[1] While Moore was in Dublin in September 1838 he went through the 'Annals of Clomnaenoise' and the 'Annals of Inisfallen' (Russell, vii. 238).

[2] See letter No. 1187, to John Easthope, 8 Aug. 1840.

[3] *Ibid.*

squibs may soon bring *shot* enough to the *locker* to make me forget
my loss.

Yours most truly & thankfully
Thomas Moore

We are here (Mrs M. & myself) in the midst of racket and company.

1191. *To John Easthope*

Huntington Library

Sloperton
August 25th 1840

My dear Mr Easthope— In the dearth of all more stirring subjects
I have directed to the Chronicle office today a skit about M^rs
Nethercoat, whose name alone deserves a squib to her honour.[1]

I shall so far anticipate my shot in the locker (*your* shot for *my*
shot) as to ask you to send me £30 *as soon* as you *conveniently* can.

Most truly yours
T. Moore

No tidings of my lost note![2]

1192. *To E. R. Moran*

National Library of Ireland

Sloperton
October 9th 1840.

Dear Mr Moran— Your notice of our first Volume was very friendly
and very well done—[3] I already know all about the Sentimental
Magazine, having got a copy of it in my own library—But the
system of 'touch and go', was what I looked to, in my notices of
those very Juvenile things, and I think *you* too had better leave
them still in their swaddling-clothes. The one you allude to (something about Myrtilla and Maria) is not mine at all.[4] I shall be however most thankful to be entrusted for a few days with your

---

[1] 'Musings Suggested by the Late Promotion of Mrs. Nethercoat' (*Poetry*,
p. 676), which appeared in the *Morning Chronicle* on Thursday, 27 Aug. 1840.

[2] See letter No. 1187, to John Easthope, 8 Aug. 1840.

[3] The first volume of Moore's *Complete Works . . . Collected by Himself*
(1840–1), 10 vols., was reviewed in the *Globe* on Thursday evening, 8 Oct. 1840.

[4] The reviewer attributed 'Myrtilla to the Unfortunate Maria. A Pastoral
Ballad' to Moore. The poem appeared in the *Sentimental and Masonic Magazine*
in August 1795.

Moorish scraps[1] which I know are multifarious, and must therefore contain a good deal of the sort of matter I chiefly want. But the sooner you can let me have them, the better.

Yours most truly
Thomas Moore

1193. *To James Carpenter*

Huntington Library

Sloperton
October 12 1840

My dear Carpenter— I think of being in town in the course of this week, in which case we shall settle the Dinner and Debt together; but, should any thing prevent my coming, you shall hear again from me. In the mean time, it would be a great relief to me to know what is the longest time you could conveniently give me for the Bills— 'A long day, my Lord!' as the Old Bailey culprits say.

My best regards to M^rs C.
Yours very truly
Thomas Moore

1194. *To Miss Murray*

Harvard College Library

Bowood
October 22nd 1840

My dear young friend— Your letter has but just reached me here, and I have but a minute to answer it. Most willingly shall I read over your Manuscript, and give my opinion of its merits as honestly as a strong wish to think of it as you would *have* me think, will let me. I shall, at least, come fresh to the task as it will be the first novel I have read for—I'm ashamed to say how long.[2] Should you be writing to Lady Virginia, pray mention to her that I have acknowledged your letter, and will answer hers in a day or two,—

---

[1] Moore is probably referring to a collection of miscellaneous material made by Moran in preparation for a biography of the poet. Five volumes of this collection, which consists mainly of newspaper clippings, are in the British Museum; two volumes are in the Bodleian Library.

[2] Moore sent a manuscript by a Miss Murray to Moran for approval (see letter No. 1204, to E. R. Moran, 21 Feb. 1841). This letter was probably addressed to her.

A French translation of this letter, written in another hand, is also in the Harvard College Library.

giving her at the same my affectionate remembrances and regards [*sic*].

> Ever truly yours
> Thomas Moore

1195. *To John Easthope*

Huntington Library   Private

> Sloperton
> Novr 1st 1840

Many thanks, my dear Sir, for your kind promptness in sending me the cheque for £45 in advance which I received this morning. The following is the present state of our Accounts—

Received	Furnished
£15 too much on a former account. (This you will recollect my mentioning at the time.)	'Mrs Nethercoat'

Received	Furnished
Thirty pounds, by cheque about the 1st I think of September last.	'Triumphs of Farce' 'Latest Accounts from Olympus.'[1]

I must repeat, my dear Mr Easthope, the request I have more than once made, which is that you will not hesitate to cry 'halt,' should you find my communications too frequent, which I rather begin to fear they are. I shall try and make this last advance you have sent last for somewhat a longer period.

> Y^{rs} very truly
> Thomas Moore

1196. *To Mr. Money*

Rice University

> Sloperton
> Novr 14th 1840

My dear Mr Money. On my return from Laycock yesterday (unluckily too late for the Post) I found your letter & the Dean of Hereford's, both of which I fear arrived the day before. Trusting that no great inconvenience will arise from this delay, I return your paper signed by myself in pencilling, and giving you full authority to invest it with the sanction of *ink*, should you find, under the

---

[1] See *Poetry*, pp. 676, 682, and 680.

circumstances, that my testimony can be of any use to you. The chief of these circumstances is, I fear, a fatal one, namely that I am not (as far as I can collect or *re*collect) a member of the Society of Antiquaries. But as it is just possible I may be, and also possible that (even if I am not) my testimony, as that of one who cultivates general literature, though not science, may be of some use to you, I think it best to send my signature, at all events, leaving you the power of preserving or effacing it, as you may think proper.

Pray, say to the Dean of Hereford how much I was gratified by his kind recollection of me, and believe me

Yours very truly
Thomas Moore

1197. *To E. R. Moran*

National Library of Ireland

Novr 21st 1840

My dear Mr Moran— I feel, you may be sure, most thankful for your kind thoughtfulness respecting this unfortunate affair—but I fear it is past all power of hushing or concealing, and must even take its course.[1] I am myself totally ignorant of the circumstances of the case—but above all things should dislike (be they what they may) the bringing down upon myself any suspicion of wishing to conceal the truth. Should any statements that I know to be *false* make their appearance, I shall then most gratefully avail myself of your intervention. I have but time for these few words and likewise to beg that you will forward the enclosed letter for me *without delay.*

Yours most truly
Thomas Moore

[I trust you think it advisable to say that (*illegible*) it would be wrong *deleted*]

1198. *To E. R. Moran*

National Library of Ireland

['Rec'd . . . Nov. 27. 1840']*

My dear Mr Moran I fear you will think I am keeping your Moorish scraps an unconscionable time but you shall have them early next

---

[1] There is no clue to this allusion in Moore's diary for this period, but it is possible that he is referring to difficulties with his son Tom, who was causing his father and mother considerable trouble by drawing bills on Moore which the poet was unable to pay (see Jones, *The Harp that Once—*, p. 315).

PLATE 8

Brooks's
. Wednesday

My dear Lady Holland — I was in great hopes that I should have been able to release myself from an engagement I had formed for to-day, but I found that it would be taken unkindly — the dinner being all but a tête-a-tête, and with a friend who is suffering a good deal in mind. As soon as I am free from this week's engagements I shall give myself a chance of being allowed to come to Holland House by letting you know.

Yours most truly

Thomas Moore

LETTER TO LADY HOLLAND

week.[1] Your devils played the devil rather too much with some of the extracts from me the other day—putting 'memory had clouded' instead of 'morning had clouded', and one or two other such diabolic readings. I meant to have written yesterday about them—but was prevented, and as I now forget the others, you need trouble your head no more about them—only give them a hint in future.

Y^{rs} most truly
T. Moore

1199. *To Benjamin Robert Haydon*

Willard B. Pope

Sloperton
Decr 1st 1840

Dear Mr Haydon— I am delighted to find myself so kindly remembered by you and trust that some good chance may, before long, bring us together. I am not surprised at your success, whether as lecturer or painter, and if you inspire the Broad-brims with a love for the Arts you will indeed do wonders.

Mrs Moore was much pleased by your remembrance of her.

Ever, my dear Sir, truly y^{rs}
Thomas Moore

1200. *To Benjamin Robert Haydon*

Willard B. Pope

Sloperton
Jan^r 2. 1841

My dear Mr Haydon— I have been away from home, which must account for my not having sooner acknowledged your kind letters &c. &c.— I am ashamed to say I do not very well recollect whether I ever came to any decision as to which of the great Italian painters I should venture to pronounce the best. What is of far more consequence, however, than my opinion (or even the great Duke's) on such a subject, is the fact that both Jackson & Chauntrey, to the best of my recollection, preferred Tintoretto, on the whole, to all

---

[1] Moran's collection of material for his projected life of Moore (see letter No. 1192, to E. R. Moran, 9 Oct. 1840).

other Italian painters.[1] Thanks for the reports of your Lectures, with which I was delighted—but praise for [*sic*] an ignoramus on the subject, like myself, is of very little value.

Yours very truly
Thomas Moore.

1201. *To E. R. Moran*

National Library of Ireland

Sloperton
Jan^r 21st 1841

My dear Mr Moran— I have left your letter a most unconscionable time unanswered—but as I am just now writing to *all the world*, it may be some excuse for not writing to any one in particular. Do you think you could prevail on our friend Bentley to pay some attention to the case of a young would-be authoress (the relative of some very dear friends of mine) so far at least as to have her novel read over by some of his minor Rhadamanthuses, and either damned or saved, at once, as it may deserve.[2] This would be a most signal relief, as well to her friends as herself, and I should take it as a great favour— I have not had time to read her MS. myself, but am most anxious that she should be put out of suspense one way or the other. I suppose the rush there is now into the literary market must be overwhelming.

We have been in no small alarm about our boy Russell, who had a severe attack of illness soon after his landing—but when he last wrote, he had quite recovered again.[3]

Many thanks for your notices of the Edition, which seems to be doing very well.

Yours very truly
Thomas Moore.

[1] Professor Pope called the editor's attention to an unpublished entry in Haydon's diary, made shortly before 16 Jan. 1841, which helps to clarify this allusion: 'The Duke [of Wellington] told me he liked Tintoretto better than any other, & so Moore said to Jackson & Chantrey. I said so in my lectures, & wrote Moore. The two letters here are his replies.' See letter No. 1202, to Benjamin Robert Haydon, January 1841.

[2] A novel by a Miss Murray (see letter No. 1194, to Miss Murray, 22 Oct. 1840, and No. 1204, to E. R. Moran, 21 Feb. 1841).

[3] Russell, Moore's second son, was in the army in India. He became ill soon after his arrival there and was befriended by Lord Aukland at Government House. Aukland informed Moore of Russell's illness and partial recovery in a letter dated 19 Oct. 1840, which Moore recorded in his diary (Russell, vii. 286–7). It soon became apparent that the boy had tuberculosis and he was invalided home, where he died on 23 Nov. 1842 (see Russell, vii. 285–7 and 338–9).

1202. *To Benjamin Robert Haydon*

Willard B. Pope

Sloperton
[January 1841]

My dear Mr Haydon— I think, from what you say, as well as from what I myself know of the influences under which my taste was formed, that the anecdote is correct—therefore, pray do not disturb it.[1]

Y^rs ever truly
Thomas Moore.

1203. *To E. R. Moran*

B.M. Eg. MS. 2152, f. 105 (copy)

Sloperton
Feb^r 3, 1841

My dear Mr Moran— Your notice of the volume was all most kind, & the allusion to Sloperton just what it should be.[2] I wish I had had some conversation with you about the Irish Melodies, as I cannot make out what sort of particulars you expected, concerning them besides such as I have given. In your own Volumes of Scraps (interesting as they are to me) the only single thing I found for my purpose was that proof of celebrity which such swarms of parodies afforded, and I intended to mention there having been sixteen (I think) parodies of the Last Rose of Summer. But, on a little reflection, I thought I could dispense with the mention of this tribute.

I shall take the earliest opportunity of sending up your volume through the Longmans.

Yours very truly
Thomas Moore

Should Bentley look unfavourably on my young protegee's volume, pray, try & do something for her in some other quarter.[3]

1204. *To E. R. Moran*

National Library of Ireland

Sloperton
Feb^r 21, 1841.

My dear Mr Moran— My poor young lady cannot wait any longer, having been summoned by her aunt, Lady Virginia, to return to Paris—you must therefore *immediately* get her MS. from Mr Bentley

---

[1] See letter No. 1200, to Benjamin Robert Haydon, 2 Jan. 1841.
[2] Moore is referring to a review of the second volume of his *Complete Works*.
[3] See letter No. 1204, to E. R. Moran, 21 Feb. 1841.

& forward it to her directed 'Miss Murray 46, Manchester St.
Manchester Square—' Now, pray do not delay this and pray also
forgive my having inflicted upon you so much trouble.[1]

Yours very truly

Thomas Moore

1205. *To Mary Shelley*

Abinger Collection

Sloperton

Feb[r] 21st 1841

I am rejoiced to hear something again of you, having been puzzled
by your long silence, and even now am left in the dark as to where
you have been— As to me, I have been to that region which
Rabelais calls Oudamothi or No-where (Percy will put the word in
Greek characters for you.)[2] but I think of sporting my hoary locks
in London about the beginning of March, and hope I shall be lucky
enough to find *you* there.

We had a good deal of alarm about our boy Russell (to whom
you were so kind) as he was seized soon after his landing with the
fever of the country—but our last accounts left him quite well
again.[3] The Auklands, immediately on his landing, made him their
guest at Government House, so that he was, luckily for himself in
good quarters.

Yours ever most truly

Thomas Moore

1206. *To Lord John Russell*

Public Records Office

Sloperton

April 6, 1841.

My dear Lord John— I think of running up to town at the latter
end of this week and shall consider myself lucky if I catch even
a glimpse of your parting footsteps—though it is just possible that
business may still keep you there, and then I shall profit, according

---

[1] See letter No. 1194, to Miss Murray, 22 Oct. 1840. On 16 Feb., in answer to
repeated inquiries from Moran, Bentley wrote that the novel had been judged
unsuitable for publication. He quoted part of the criticism, which described
the work as 'prosey', and not very clear or interesting in its attempts to
demonstrate the error of those who 'live under the guidance of intellect without
reference to *heart*'. On the basis of these remarks, Bentley rejected the work.

[2] The reference to Rabelais is not correct. In *Quart Livre*, chapters 2 and 4,
Rabelais mentions 'Medamothi', meaning 'no-where' (see *Œuvres de François
Rabelais*, tome vi: *Le Quart Livre* (Geneva, 1955), 84, 104, 105).

[3] See letter No. 1201, to E. R. Moran, 21 Jan. 1841.

to the ways of this world, by your misfortune. I want to ask you a little question. You know I have already *once* mentioned our trip to Milan together,[1] in my Life of Byron, and I shall now again have occasion to notice it in reference to my Poem to you, in this next volume—[2] that Poem which I *hope* you know is constantly referred to as a *pendant* to my Prophetic Lyric respecting the Duke of Wellington.[3]

April 9th

The above was written, you will perceive, a few days since—but having some hopes of being able to start for London immediately, I preferred talking with you to writing. The point I wish to refer to you on is this. In speaking (briefly of course and passingly) of our fortnight at Paris, on the way I mention, as one of your objects there, your having a wish to consult Barillion's papers for a new Edition of your Life of Lord Russell[4] which was then preparing. This shining little bit of literary anecdote is (as connected with you and that work) invaluable, and I trust I am correct about it.

Direct your answer to this to Brooks's, where I shall find it in the course of Monday, meaning to be in town on that day. Lady Elisabeth's house is going through a course of painting, so that I don't know where I shall be lodged. But, if you are in an *accessible* place out of town, I shall run down some day for a glimpse at you.

Ever most truly yrs
Thomas Moore

1207. *To John Easthope*

Huntington Library

Salisbury St.
Saturday [April 24, 1841, *not in Moore's hand*]

Dear Easthope— I called here with the hope of meeting you and proposing the only day I find open for the next week (Tuesday) to

---

[1] Lord John Russell accompanied Moore on his tour of the Continent in 1819, when the latter was forced to leave England because of the difficulty over his Bermuda deputy's defalcation.

[2] Moore's poem to Russell is entitled 'Remonstrances after a Conversation with Lord John Russell' (*Poetry*, p. 530). There is no mention of the visit to Milan in it, however.

[3] Moore is probably referring to 'The Wellington Spa' (*Poetry*, p. 662), in which he satirizes the Duke of Wellington's stand on Catholic Emancipation. The irony of the poem lies in the fact that, even though the Duke opposed the measure during his term as Prime Minister (1828–30), he became convinced that the only means of avoiding civil war in Ireland was to force the Emancipation Act through Parliament. It was passed in 1829.

[4] Russell published his *Life of William Lord Russell* in 1819.

dine with you—but learning from your servant that you will not be back till Monday, I must at once give up the notion, and reserve myself for the chance of the week after next should I stay in town so long.

Y^{rs} ever truly
Thomas Moore

1208. *To John Easthope*

Huntington Library

Brooks's
April 26th 1841.

My dear Easthope— Your letter inclosing a cheque for £150 reached me here, and I lose no time in acknowledging the receipt of it with many, many thanks.

Yours most truly
Thomas Moore

1209. *To John Easthope*

Huntington Library

Private
Sloperton
[April *deleted*] May 10th 1841

My dear Easthope— I am happy to see by the papers to-day that you are promoted from the bed (in which you were confined when I left town) to the *Chair*—rather a better position.

I omitted to tell you before I left town that the task of correcting and prefacing my eighth Volume (in which I am hunted at present by the Devils) would prevent me from doing any thing for you during the next ten days or fortnight—but you need not fear my forgetting the squibbery, which will be soon wanted more than ever.

Poor Barnes! I confess I am sincerely sorry for him—no person with whom I have ever been connected having left on my mind a more satisfactory impression of unvarying courtesy, liberality and serviceableness. I dined with him in Soho Square yesterday fortnight and, though then suffering from the effects of his fall, he sate through a long dinner and music in the evening with apparent strength and cheerfulness.[1]

Yours ever truly
Thomas Moore

[1] Thomas Barnes, editor of *The Times*, died in 1841.

1210. *Addressee unknown*

National Library of Ireland

Sloperton
August 6th 1841

My dear Sir   You did yourself but justice in considering my silence as a proof of the ready & thankful assent I could not but give to the kind compliment you proposed to pay me in connecting my name with your new work. I only regret that such an adjunct to your pages should carry with it so little real value. [*Remainder of the letter missing.*]

1211. *To Lord John Russell*

Rice University

Cheltenham
September 11th 1841

My dear Lord John— The kind *command* from Woburn was sent after me to Ireland,[1] and in sufficient time (had other circumstances turned out more favorably) to enable me to avail myself of so very welcome an invitation. But, after a very sickening passage to Liverpool, the vessel I came in arrived just too late to allow me to avail myself of the train to Leighton (which would have compassed for me every object I had in view) and I was thus deprived of the very great pleasure of joining the Duchess's party— Could I have waited for the next day's train in that direction, I should still have been in time to find you together; but other circumstances prevented this; and I should be in despair at having missed such an opportunity of refreshing my recollections of Woburn did I not trust to the Duchess's good-nature for giving me another such chance, some time or other.

Yours, my dear Lord John, most truly
Thomas Moore.

[1] Moore was in Ireland from 25 Aug. to 9 Sept. 1841 (Russell, vii. 298–301). The dating of the diary is confusing here. He recorded his passage to Ireland on 25 Aug. (Russell, vii. 298), but a later entry concerning a dinner with the Cramptons and a visit to the opera is dated 7 Aug. (Russell, vii. 301), which was either a mistake by Moore or the editor of the *Journal*. The date probably should be 7 Sept.

1212. *To John Easthope*

Huntington Library

Private.
Sloperton
Septr 13th 1841

My dear Easthope— Here I am once more, after a most gratifying visit to Dublin;[1] and lose not a moment in congratulating you on your late well-deserved honours.[2] Our friend Black, I dare say, communicated to you the fears and scruples, respecting my further squib-operations, which I expressed to him, during the short conversation we had together, in Salisbury St.— I find it every day, indeed, more difficult to satisfy *myself* (whatever I may do with *others*) on subjects so trite and hacknied as those which now engage public attention. The same men, committing the same follies, and in almost the same way as has been their wont for more than 30 years past furnishes matter more fit for yawning than for laughter. As the latter operation, however, is far the pleasanter of the two, I shall not without an effort give it up, and you shall soon hear from me in that strain.

Ever yours
Thomas Moore

You may, of course, in *any* case, depend on my balancing correctly our account. [*On address side of the letter.*]

1213. *To Edward Moxon*

Rice University

Sloperton
Jan^r 2, 1842

Best thanks, my dear Mr Moxon, for your kind letter and promised presents. Your thoughtfulness about our two young soldiers we feel with pleasure & thankfulness.

I have been long meditating a little talk about *business* with *you* —but whether the intention will ever take any tellable or talkable shape, I know not. In the mean time, I must again thank you for your kindness and am

Very truly yours
Thomas Moore

[1] See letter No. 1211, to Lord John Russell, 11 Sept. 1841.
[2] On 24 Aug. 1841 Easthope was created a baronet by Lord Melbourne.

1214. *To Edward Moxon*

Harvard College Library

Sloperton, Devizes
Feb^r 11, 1842

My dear Mr Moxon— Mrs Moore has frequently reminded me of the *duty* (for it is no less) of thanking you for your very kind presents to her, and still more for your thoughtfulness about our two Indian boys. Poor fellows—they are both coming home on sick leave and your gifts must await them here. It is not a little hard upon me— I have hardly had time to devise the means of paying their expences *out*, when I am suddenly called to meet the difficulties of paying the cost of their *return*. It is only to penniless men these things happen.

Yours most truly
Thomas Moore.

I wish you had some light task to employ me in—something that would require little more than a Preface and 'the whistling of a name' and would bring us both a little money.

1215. *To Lord John Russell*

Rice University

Sloperton
April 17, 1842

My dear Lord John— You have heard, I dare say that our poor Russell has returned to us in a state of health which gives us serious alarm.[1] I should have written to you—*you* to whom he owes so much—immediately on his arrival here, had I not hoped that after a week or two I should have had a less painful account to give you of him. But though better than when he first came to us, I can hardly hope that he is yet out of danger.

I wish I had any occupation so stirring as yours to keep my mind from dwelling on what is painful. Pray, tell Lady John that there are few things I find so pleasant to recal [*sic*] as those two or three mornings which I passed in Chesham Place, when last in town. I hope the portrait has turned out better than it then promised.

Yours ever truly
Thomas Moore

[1] See letter No. 1201, to E. R. Moran, 21 Jan. 1841. Russell returned to Sloperton on 6 Apr. 1842.

1216. *To John Hancock*

Rice University

Sloperton
April 20ᵗʰ 1842

My dear Sir— I have written, according to your request, to Doctor Madden, and send herein the papers which you wish back.

Yours truly
Thomas Moore

On second thoughts, not knowing the direction of Dʳ Madden, I think I had better trouble *you* with the conveyance of my letter to him.

1217. *To Friedrich C. F. v. Pechlin*

Royal Library, Copenhagen[1]

Sloperton, Devizes
May 8ᵗʰ 1842.

Monsieur le Baron— I have to apologize for not sooner acknowledging the receipt of the welcome present which you have done me the honour to send me—but your beautiful Volume and its kind inscription reached me at a time when the alarming illness of my younger son, just returned from India, engrossed all my thoughts.[2] I am now however sufficiently relieved from my alarm to attend to correspondence, and take the first opportunity of thanking you for very [*sic*] flattering gift. Allow me to hope that, should you ever visit England, you will give me a chance of forming your acquaintance, and thanking you in person for the honour you have conferred on my work.

Your obliged and faithful servᵗ
Thomas Moore

[1] Transcript provided by Professor Nils Erik Enkvist, Åbo Akademi, Åbo, Finland.

[2] Baron von Pechlin had evidently sent Moore a copy of his *Gedichte, Altere und Neuere* (Stuttgart and Tübingen, 1842). Moore's son Russell, fatally ill, had returned from India.

1218. *To Mrs. S. C. Hall*

Rice University

I shall be anxious to hear that your precious book arrived safe

Sloperton
May 31st 1842

My dear Mrs Hall— My short and, I fear, unintelligible scrawl of Sunday (or Saturday last?) was I trust in time to prevent your being kept any longer in suspense as to our acceptance of your kind offer. It was, indeed, to the last, so tempting in almost every point of view that I felt unwilling to utter 'no', when 'yes' would have been, in so many respects more agreeable. But the fact is that, in one sad instance (one always present to my memory) we had reason to think that the removal of a beloved child from home, when in a state of suffering, was a wrong and fatal step;[1] and this feeling, however unfounded it may have been, a good deal influenced me in the resolution which I have come to. Pray, believe however how deeply we feel your Kindness—it was indeed true friendship; and familiar as I am, thank God, with arts of Kindness, I know few that have ever touched me more sensibly than this— With best regards to yourself & Mr Hall, in which Mrs Moore most cordially joins, I am, my dear Mrs Hall

Very truly yours
Thomas Moore

[*On reverse side*]
Our dear boy, you will be glad, I know, to hear, becomes more *himself* every day.

1219. *To Locke, Hughes, and Company*

National Library of Ireland

Friday, June 17th [1842]

Mr Moore will be obliged by Messrs Hughes & Locke sending him a thirty pound Bank of England note by tomorrow's post

---

[1] Moore is probably referring to their decision to take Anastasia to Bath for treatment at a time when her suffering must have been severe. Mrs. Hall had evidently offered her assistance in the care of Russell, who was ill with tuberculosis.

1220. *To John Easthope*

Private

Inclosed Bank of England Note £20 N⁰ 30058
Do. - - - - - - -   10   21250

Sloperton, Devizes
June 19, 1842

Dear Sir John Easthope

You will recollect, I doubt not, that when in February last, you were so kind as to make me an advance of £75, I said that I should be able, I hoped, to repay part of the sum in the prosaic form of *cash*. This I have now the pleasure of doing, and begging that you will take the trouble of merely acknowledging the receipt of the inclosed thirty pounds, I remain

Yours truly
Thomas Moore.

Feb^r 1842— 'Threnody on the approaching &c.—   £15
April 7th 'Sayings and Doings of ancient Nicholas'—15
May 12— 'More Sayings and Doings—   15[1]
Remittance to Sir J. Easthope by post June 19.   3—0
                                                  _____
                                                  75:0:0

1221. *To Lady Kerry*

Saturday, July [1842][2]

My dear Lady Kerry— Thanks for the book from Bowood which is one I very much wanted. Good-natured people, like yourself, are sure to be made to pay for it. I had a present some time since of some pencils from London—but they are not at all what I wanted, being the softest of all possible pencils, and I wanted hard ones to write with. If you think they would change them at Morell's for me, it would be very kind of you at least to try.

I am very sorry I cannot run away with you to London as I proposed—but shall look to some other time for that pleasant *escapade*

Yours ever truly
Thomas Moore

[1] 'A Threnody on the Approaching Demise of Old Mother Corn-Law' appeared in the *Morning Chronicle* on 23 Feb. 1842. The other two poems were published on the dates indicated. None of the three was included in the 1841 edition of the works.

[2] In January 1842 Moore noted in his diary that Lady Kerry had 'now become a constant inhabitant of Bowood' (Russell, vii. 306). This letter must have been written after that date.

1222. *To Mrs. Villamil*

Public Records Office[1]

Sloperton, Chippenham
October 24, 1842

My dear Mrs Villamil.— You see I address you by your old English title—it was that by which I first knew you and I cling to it fondly. The intelligence, my dear friend, your letter conveys, would have been hailed by me with the sincerest delight, if so many difficulties do not stand in the way of such a union as my poor sanguine boy proposes. To Tom himself an alliance with your family and with such a young person as I am quite sure a daughter of yours *must* be would be absolute salvation. For Tom wants steadying, and the gentle control of an affectionate and sensible wife would be the best as well as most agreeable sort of discipline for him. But, alas, my dear friend, *money* is, in this strange world the thing upon which every thing turns, and my son, so far from being able to support *others* has thrown away the only chance I was able to give him for supporting himself. However, as the very prospect of such a union may stimulate him to try and *deserve* it, I say 'yes' to the proposed marriage most willingly; and, though I have already made myself bankrupt for him no effort shall be wanting to further so desirable an object.[2]

You ask me in confidence about his temper. Owing to the absurd practice in England of sending Boys away from home at so early an age, Fathers and Mothers are in general those who know least about their own children. But, I should say, from all I *do* know, that Tom's is, on the whole, a very good temper. I happened to be from home when your letter arrived which must account for the few days delay of my answer.

With kindest regards to my excellent friend Villamil I am ever yours most truly

Thomas Moore

1223. *Addressee unknown*

Huntington Library

Bowood
October, 1842.

Dear Sir— Your kind note and very welcome inclosure was forwarded to me here, and was therefore a means of giving pleasure

[1] This letter is printed in Jones, *The Harp that Once—*, pp. 317–18, which served as the source of the present text.

[2] Jones suggests (p. 317) that Tom's enlistment in the French Foreign Legion was motivated by his desire to marry Mrs. Villamil's daughter.

to more than myself. I have delivered your message to Lord Lansdowne, who returns through me his kindest regards. There is likewise another friend of yours here, that Prince of Wits, Sydney, who
begs also to be cordially remembered to you.

Yours, my dear Sir, very truly

Thomas Moore

1224. *Addressee unknown*

Huntington Library

Sloperton

Novr 7th 1842

Sir

Having been absent from home, it was not till this morning that
I received your letter. You will find no difficulty, I think, in gaining
access to all such *books* as you may want at the Museum, but I am
not so sure about *Manuscripts*, having had facilities, I rather think,
afforded to me, which it required some little interest to obtain.

Regretting that it is not in my power to give you more explicit
information, I am, Sir,

Your obedient Servant

Thomas Moore

1225. *To E. R. Moran*

B.M. Add. MS. Eg. 2150, f. 191

Sloperton

Decr 12 1842

My dear Mr Moran— I am quite ashamed of having been so long
without writing to you to say how much I feel your great kindness
(not the first time experienced by me) in attending to the melancholy commission with which you were troubled on our account.
Pray, let me know how much I am in your debt, besides very
sincere thanks which both Mrs Moore and myself owe you.

It will be long, I fear, before she recovers this very trying affliction, and it has shaken even *me* far more than I could have anticipated.[1]

yours very truly

Thomas Moore

I shall not trouble you to send me the critique you mention—both
praise and blame have somewhat lost their flavour for me.— My
poor friend Brown *was* the man.[2]

---

[1] Russell died on 23 Nov. 1842.

[2] The only clue to this allusion is a clipping from the *British Register* for

1226. *Addressee unknown*

Morgan Library

Decr 21st 1842

Sir

I have been prevented by painful circumstances from acknowledging sooner your letter. I have no very clear recollection of the
lines of mine to which you allude but think it very probable that
the reading which you suggest may be the right one—

Your obedient Servt

Thomas Moore

1227. *To the Reverend Joseph Fitzgerald*

National Library of Ireland

Bowood

January 17th 1843

Dear and Reverend Sir— Your kind and affecting letter has but
just reached me here which must account & apologize for the delay
there has been in acknowledging it. Be assured that both Mrs Moore
and myself feel with reverential gratitude both the sympathy you
express in our late severe loss and the solemn mode in which you
have employed your ministry for our consolation. It will give me
great pleasure should any good fortune give me an opportunity of
thanking you in person for this great kindness.

Believe me very truly yours

Thomas Moore

August 1808, now in Moran's collection in the British Museum. The short
article concerns the death of John Brown, who, says Moore in a note to 'The
Young May Moon', translated from the Irish a poem entitled 'Steals Silently
to Morna's Grove', which was included in Bunting's collection of Irish songs.
Moore describes Brown as 'one of my earliest college companions and friends,
whose death was as singularly melancholy and unfortunate as his life had been
amiable' (*Poetry*, p. 202 n). The clipping reads as follows:

John Brown, a merchant in Dublin, was aboard a ship from Antigua to
another island when she was captured by the French, who later decided to
capitulate. They released Brown, who was sent to negotiate with the British.
He neglected, however, to take a flag of truce and was shot by a 'black
centinel' in the service of his country.

1228. *To Thomas Longman*

Rice University

Brooks's
Monday [postmark April 3, 1843]

Dear Longman— I forgot to give you a message which I have had from my friend, Corry, this morning, begging that I would order for him Drury's book Arundines Cami[1]—to be sent to him to Cheltenham, together with a bill of the price which he will remit to you immediately.

Yours for the present
T. Moore

1229. *To Mr. Addison*

Rice University

Sloperton, Chippenham
May 14th 1843

Dear Mr Addison— I am sorry to find that the negociation between you and Mrs Power which I had hoped was likely to lead to something satisfactory remains still unconcluded. May I ask you to take the trouble of letting me know the present state of the matter and what chances there are of its being settled?[2]

Yours very truly
Thomas Moore

1230. *To Thomas Longman*

Huntington Library

October 30th 1843

Many thanks, my dear Longman, for your kind & acceptable present. Mrs Moore who delights in being a distributor of gifts, is quite charmed at the agreeable task you have given her. Meanwhile she bids me beg of you to send copies to my sister Ellen, Doctor Hume (Hanwell) and the Honble H. Pierrepont, at Lord Manvers's, Portman Square, a young Beau of hers.

[1] A collection of Cambridge Latin verse, edited in 1841 by Henry Drury, Archdeacon of Wilts.

[2] Addison had evidently been negotiating with the widow of James Power (the publisher died on 26 Aug. 1836) for the copyrights to some of Moore's songs. On 5 June 1842 Moore recorded in his diary: 'Heard rather bad accounts of the conference yesterday between Addison and Mrs. Power' (Russell, vii. 347).

You ask about my History— 'Prodigious bold request!' as the man in Tom Thumb says.[1] It yet wants nearly a year of the time when I told you it *might* be ready.[2] All I need add to this is that I am working incessantly, though (as usual) slowly at it, and that you may be assured I shall shake the incubus off me as soon as I *possibly* can. Meanwhile, I should like to send you a portion, if you will tell me what is the safest way of conveying it.

As to my portrait, I am glad it is liked, but there is one person (I need hardly say who) in whose eyes it is the very worst of all the monstra horrenda that have ever been made of me![3]

Talking of monstra horrenda, I beg to send my kindest regards to that very ugly person, Mrs Tom Longman.

Yours very truly
Thomas Moore

I see you can tell Irish stories quite *pat.*

1231. *To Edward Moxon*

Morgan Library

Decr 17 1843

My dear Mr Moxon— You were good enough to say that you could get for me the loan of any books I wished from the London Library — The following, either together, or successively, I should very much like to borrow and you shall have them back without much delay.

Miss Aikin's Memoirs of the Court of James I

Secret History of the Court of James I by Osborne, Weldon &c.[4]

If you would take the trouble of sending them to the Longmans', with orders to forward them *immediately*, together with any parcels there may be there for Mrs Moore you'll double and treble the obligation.

Yours most truly
Thomas Moore.

[1] Fielding, *Tom Thumb*, i. iii. 63.

[2] The fourth volume of Moore's *History of Ireland* appeared in 1846.

[3] An engraving of the portrait by Sir Thomas Lawrence was used as the frontispiece of volume I of Moore's *Complete Works*. Other portraits were painted by Thomas Phillips, Maclise, Shee, and Jackson.

[4] Lucy Aikin, *Memoirs of the Court of King James the First* (1822), 2 vols. Sir Anthony Weldon, *et al.*, *Secret History of the Court of James the First* (1811), 2 vols.

1232. *Addressee unknown*

Rice University

January 5th 1844

Dear Sir— On my return home, after an absence of some days, I find the letter with which you have favoured me and regret that it should have remained so long unanswered. I really could not conscientiously advise you to adopt poetry as a probable source of either fame or emolument. You will forgive me, I trust, for being thus sincere, and wishing you all success in your other pursuits, I am, Dear Sir,

Your very obedient serv^t
Thomas Moore

1233. *To Mr. Wright*

Rice University

Sloperton
April 29th 1844

My dear Mr Wright— I was away from home when your letter arrived here, which must partly account and apologize for the delay of my answer. The remaining part of the interval has been employed by me in endeavouring to recollect for you the small squib (or *squiblet*) to which you allude. I also called in the aid of a friend of mine here, a *lay* theologian, who I remembered was pleased to be pleased with the lines—but between us, all we could call to mind was (what I take for granted was the cream of the joke)

'When asked his name, in heaven
His answer will be John v. 7.'

I am sorry, for my own sake, that I cannot call the whole to mind, as I should like exceedingly to be honoured with a *niche*, even so small in your work.[1]

Yours, my dear Mr Wright, very truly
Thos Moore

[1] On 1 and 2 May 1844 Moore recorded that he had 'Received a letter from my old Paris friend Wright, on a subject which we used often to converse upon; namely the much-agitated text of 1 John v. 7, which he is employed in writing a history of for the Encyclopaedia of Biblical Literature; detailing everything of any interest respecting it from Erasmus to Scholz, the last critical editor of the New Testament' (Russell, vii. 369). The squib from which the couplet was taken has not been identified.

1234. *Addressee unknown*

Pennsylvania Historical Society

Sloperton
July 10th 1844

Sir— I have to apologize for so long delaying my answer to your letter. I have (unluckily for myself) no power over my works, and the object you seek can only be obtained by application to the Messrs Longman, Pater-Noster Row.

Your ob^t Servant
Thomas Moore

1235. *To Mrs. Guthrie*

N.L.S. MS. 3925, f. 107

Sloperton
August 21st 1844

My dear Mrs Guthrie

Though I dare say you have forgotten all about our 'hair-breadth scrapes' the other evening, I assure you *I* shall long remember your great good-humour (as well as Mrs Moore's) in all our getting-ups and getting-downs in that long series of gates we had to pass through. As to Thebes, it was nothing compared to Spye Park for gates. I shall be very glad to hear that you were not the worse for the trouble I gave you. It was very lucky that I did not return (as at one time I intended) to Sloperton; for I should have lost a most agreeable evening—

Yours very truly
Thomas Moore

1236. *To John Cam Hobhouse*

Sir John Murray

September, 1844

[*Congratulating Hobhouse on his efforts for the Byron statue.*]

1237. *To the Governors of the Bank of England*

Pforzheimer Misc. MS. 307

Sloperton, Chippenham
February 15th 1845*

Gentlemen

I beg respectfully to submit to your consideration, the following case.

On the eighth of August 1840 I lost a Bank of England note,

value fifty pounds, No. 91,174, which note, I understand, has never been presented for payment; and I venture to ask whether you will now grant me the favour of having another note, on the usual securities being given.[1]

I have the honour to be, gentlemen,
your obedient Servt
Thomas Moore.

1238. *To Thomas Longman*

N.L.S. MS. 581, No. 540

March 24th 1845

My dear Longman— In the old receipt for dressing a hare, the first step is 'Catch your hare' and so my proceeding this morning was to *catch my magistrate*, not always an easy thing where the gentry are so widely separated as here. I have however succeeded, & dispatch you the result.

By the bye, I sent away my Gesgehegan (I never can spell that infernal name) and want him again—I mean the French History of Ireland—so pray, when there is any thing to come, send Gehog with it.[2]

Yours most truly
Thomas Moore

1239. *To Kirkman D. Hodgson*

Russell, viii. 284

Sloperton
March 30. 1845.

My dear Sir,

I could much better *tell* you than I can *write* to you, the very warm and grateful acknowledgments I feel, not so much for the *matter* (though to a poor poet fifty pounds is no trifling matter), as for the *manner* of the kind service which you have been enabled to render me. It will give you pleasure too, I think, to hear that, welcome as the restored note is to myself, it is fifty-fold more welcome in another and better quarter; as I had been lucky enough to be able to conceal the loss from Mrs. Moore, so that it came to her as a gift fresh from the skies.[3]

[1] See letter No. 1187, to John Easthope, 8 Aug. 1840. On the security of Kirkman Hodgson and Thomas Longman, the bank issued Moore another note for £50 (see letter No. 1239, to Kirkman Hodgson, 30 Mar. 1845).

[2] James MacGeoghegan, *Histoire de l'Irlande ancienne et moderne* (Paris, 1758–63).

[3] ['This letter alludes to a Bank of England note for 50*l*. which had been lost

Trusting that our friend Longman may, sometime or other, give me an opportunity of thanking you in person,

> I am, dear Sir,
> Yours very truly,
> Thomas Moore.

1240. *To John Dalby*

Mrs. Mercia Dalby

April 8th 1845

My very dear old friend—(though I feel my pen checked in calling you '*old*,' for your letter is as brisk and buoyant as in your best days of penmanship) I am quite ashamed of having left you so long unanswered, but the incessant calls upon me, in the way of correspondence, (and almost all with entire strangers) leaves [*sic*] me scarce a moment to give to friends. Washington Irving says of me 'you'll far more easily get a *book* from Moore than a *letter*'—and it is nearly true. Nothing now would have wrung this scrawl from me but the duty (as well as pleasure) of acknowledging your friend's very interesting volume, and begging of you to let me know how much (besides pleasure) I am in his debt for it. Your old & never-forgetting Bessy sends kindest regards to you & all yours.

> Ever, my dear friend, your attached
> Thos Moore

[*On reverse side*]

This hurried scrawl I have carried about in my waistcoat pocket hoping to find a spare minute for a few additional words. But the post-hour presses and I must stop.

1241. *To the Reverend Dr. George Croly*

Rice University

Sloperton: Chippenham
July 11, 1845

My dear Dr. Croly,

May I trouble you to say in which volume & of which edition of Byron's works the misrepresentation you mention occurs—[1] You may depend on my noticing it to Murray

> Yours very truly
> Thomas Moore

by Mr. Moore in 1840. On the security of Mr. Kirkman Hodgson and Mr. Longman, the Bank gave Mr. Moore another note for 50*l*. The lost note was never presented for payment.' *Russell's note*.] See letter No. 1237, to the Governors of the Bank of England, 15 Feb. 1845.

[1] See *Don Juan*, xi. lvii–lviii, where Byron satirizes Dr. Croly as 'the very Reverend Rowley Powley'.

I trust I may nail *you* as a brother member of the Irish Society or Club— I have been so national as to take my name out of Brookes's to belong to it—

Rev Dr Croly
   Lansdowne Crescent
     Bath

1242. *To Edward Moxon*

New York Public, Berg Collection

Private
October 12 1845

My dear Mr Moxon— At this time of the year when, as the old song says 'London all is out of town,' I am not left a minute to myself, and this must account and apologize for the delay of my promised contribution to your work. This morning afforded the very first opportunity I have had of looking through my papers, and I grieve to say that the letter which I now enclose is the only one I could find worth sending to you. I was in hopes that I should find also some letter or paper that would throw light on the particular occasion which drew from him this very creditable letter. But I have failed in my search. The 'over-vehement attack' on me to which he alludes took place in the course of the excitement which the destruction of Lord Byron's Memoirs produced, and in which Campbell stood forth as a champion of Lady Byron.[1]

I have only time to refer you to another result of this event which his biographer may think worthy of notice. Campbell on receiving my ready assent to his amicable advance proposed that a dinner at his house should be the scene of our reconciliation, and this took place under auspices very worthy of such an occasion, Crabbe and Rogers being the two other guests— I have alluded to this dinner and its origin in some verses which you will find in the Metropolitan.[2]

Yours very truly
Thomas Moore

---

[1] In 1849 Edward Moxon published the three-volume *Life and Letters of Thomas Campbell*, by William Beattie. He evidently asked Moore to contribute information for the work. For an explanation of the allusion to Campbell as the 'champion of Lady Byron' see letter No. 924, to Mary Shelley, 3 Apr. 1830.

[2] Campbell wrote to Moore on 2 Jan. 1831, expressing regret at the 'over-vehemence of manner' in which he addressed Moore on the 'unfortunate subject which divided our opinions'. He invited Moore to dinner with 'a select company who would be but too proud to dine with so honoured a guest'. See William Beattie, *Life and Letters of Thomas Campbell* (London, 1850), iii. 74, where a portion of Moore's poem on the occasion is quoted in a note.

1243. *Addressee unknown*

Rice University

February 27th 1846

My dear Sir Roderick—

I must throw myself on your forgiveness— I had delayed too long acknowledging the Kind letter with which you had favoured me and then, alas, came that heavy affliction upon me,[1] which you doubtless have heard of and which of course put every thing else out of my head. It will be long indeed before I can hope to recover the effects of so sad and sudden a calamity.

Yours most truly
Thomas Moore

1244. *To Mrs. Holland*

Rice University

June 15 1846

My dear Mrs Holland— If you knew the remorse I feel at not having *once* called upon you during my late short visit to town you would, I am sure, in your Christian spirit forgive me. One thing is certain (however paradoxical it may appear) that I *thought* of you all the more for not having ever called upon you. As the lover says in some play of his mistress 'I vowed so often not to think of her that in fact I thought of nothing else', and such was very much the case with my often vowed visit to you.— Seriously speaking, I was placed in difficulties both of business and society (two ingredients which I never again shall endeavour to mix) that did not leave me master of myself or time.

Mrs Moore has just desired me to remember her most kindly to yourself & Dr Holland.

Ever yours most truly,
Thomas Moore

1245. *To Andrew Doyle*

Huntington Library

Sloperton, Chippenham
June 15th 1846

My dear Mr Doyle— We Irishmen are bound in honour to stick by Lalla Rookh, if not for her poet's sake at least for the affinity to her claimed by our countryman who insists that the true way of

---

[1] The death of Moore's sister Ellen, who died in February 1846. He was also aware of the illness of his son Tom, although he did not learn of the boy's death until March.

writing her name is Larry Rourke. Seriously, I wish you to oblige me by putting before the English public a circumstance connected with that poem which few if any of them know any thing about.

To go at once into *medias res*—on the occasion of a state visit paid to the Court of Berlin, in the year, 1822, by the Grand Duke Nicholas and the Grand Duchess, among the festivities prepared to welcome them was a Grand Divertissement founded upon the poem of Lalla Rookh and got up with all the taste and splendour which so princely an occasion demanded. The Grand Duke acted Feramorz, while to his Duchess fell of course the part of the heroine, Lalla Rookh. The various groups that under the titles of Dames de Cachemire, Dames de Bucharie &c attended the Grand Duchess, and among these attendants are found the names of the Duchess of Cumberland, the Princess Louise Radziville, the Princess Alexandrine &c. &c.

The splendid volume containing the account of this Royal pageant was published at Berlin in the year 1822, and contains twenty-three coloured engravings of the most remarkable costumes worn on the occasion. The different scenes and events of the Poem were represented in tableaux vivans and the effect of all was heightened by appropriate and touching music— 'Le romantique' says the editor of the Berlin account 'qui regne dans ce recit, tel que nous le lisons dans l'original anglois, acquit un nouveau degré de vie, d'expression et de vivacité par la musique et la pantomime de cette representation théatrale.'[1]

The above, I fear, my dear Sir, will too much intrude both on your pages & your patience—but I hope to make up for it some other day— You may put what I have said in whatever shape you please—indeed I have written it with that view.

Yours Ever
T. M.

1246. *To Andrew Doyle*

Huntington Library

June 23rd 1846

My dear Mr Doyle—

I have been prevented from sooner acknowledging your kindness. What you tell of the Pole is quite new and of course gratifying to

---

[1] The story of the performance is recorded in much simpler form in his diary for 3 Apr. 1821, where he merely states that a gentleman 'accosted' him in a shop and told him that a Princess of Prussia wanted Moore to be informed 'how beautifully the fête in Berlin . . . went off'. The Grand Duchess of Russia acted Lalla Rookh, and the sister of Prince Radzivil, who played the Peri, was 'a most beautiful girl'. He promised to show Moore some drawings of the principals in their costumes (Russell, iii. 217).

me. I have already a Polish relic in my possession which I value of course exceedingly—namely the the [*sic*] proof sheets of a Polish translation of the Fire-Worshippers snatched *from* the fire when the poor Poles, in one of their struggles were routed and flying—[1]

Yours ever truly
Thomas Moore

1247. *To Andrew Doyle*

Huntington Library

July 2nd 1846

My dear Mr Doyle

I rejoice at having got into such safe hands— There was a point or two to which I had intended to draw the reader's attention in a short preface, but being pressed for time was obliged to abandon the prefatory matter to other hands. I meant to have called the readers [*sic*] attention to the new light I had been enabled to throw on Shane O'Neill, who has hitherto been represented as a mere sot and savage, but whom the State Paper officer enabled me to do justice to, and show that that [*sic*] he was surrounded by accomplished advisers and was likewise a special favourite with Elizabeth —[2] Another point on which I was enabled through the S. P. office to shed some new & curious lights was the mysterious flight of Tyrone.[3]

Yours very truly
Thomas Moore

[1] *Lalla Rookh* was translated into Polish in 1826. For a similar account of this incident see Russell, vii. 365–6.

[2] Moore's account of Shane O'Neill is contained in the *History of Ireland*, vol. iv. 24–58. The author recognizes O'Neill's crudeness but is nevertheless sympathetic toward what he terms 'strength of character', by which Shane was able to command the attention, if not the respect, of the English Court. Moore alludes to the Queen's 'friendly bearing' toward O'Neill on page 56.

[3] The 'new light' which Moore claimed to have thrown on the flight of Tyrone is found in vol. iv. 155–7. He quotes from some letters written by Tyrone's contemporary, Sir John Davies. These letters, he maintains, were written at the very time of Tyrone's flight and had since lain, unnoticed by historians, in the repository of State Papers. Davies made several suggestions for the cause of the flight, the main one being depleted funds. He also gave an account of the journey from Slane to Rathmulla, where Tyrone met the Earl of Tyrconnel. The narrative ended with a description of the voyage to Normandy.

1248. *Addressee unknown*

Rice University

Sloperton, Chippenham
Novr 7, 1846*

Dear Sir

With many thanks for your great kindness I lose no time in forwarding to you a list of the articles belonging to my lost son which I wish to have transmitted to me as soon as will suit your convenience[1]

1. The Malette with its key
2. The Purse with its contents
3. The two gold rings
4. The Portfolio, with all letters, books, and other small effects
The *Cabane*, clothes &c to be sold.

Your obliged servant
Thomas Moore.

1249. *To Edward Moxon*

Rice University

Sloperton, Chippenham
Jan^r 26 1847

My dear Mr Moxon— I ought to have, long before this, sent my mite to Poor Campbell's monument, but a severe & indeed dangerous illness under which M^{rs} [*sic*] has been suffering put every other thought out of my head. She is now, however, much better, though still confined to her room, and among the duties which during her illness I neglected was the payment of my mite towards poor Campbell's monument— May I ask you to repair this omission for me by paying in my name to the persons appointed to receive subscriptions £2:2 and I shall send you a post-office order for the amount—

Y^{rs} most truly
Thomas Moore

1250. *To Lord John Russell*

Public Records Office

Sloperton, Chippenham
March, 1847

My dear Lord John— As you have no time to read letters, I will only say that in this *last* glorious burst of yours you have more than fulfilled all that *one* devoted friend of yours (writing then, for *once*,

---

[1] Moore's son Thomas died in March 1846.

with the spirit of a true *vates*) foretold of your future course—of this I am proud—unspeakably proud!¹

No answer to this necessary—

My kindest remembrances to Lady John—how happy she must be!

[*Unsigned*]

1251. *To Samuel Rogers*

Russell, viii. 285

Sloperton
June 23. 1847.

My dear Rogers,

When, when are we again to meet? I was in hopes that those Irish friends of mine who, as you may remember, gave me lodging under their roof these two last summers, in Albemarle Street, would again have been at their post this summer, and again made me their guest. But the state of Ireland compels them to stand to their post; and this is to me a sad disappointment, for I had set my heart, my dear old friend, on having a few more breakfasts with you (to say nothing of dinners) before 'time and the hour has quite run out our day.'²

Yours, my very dear friend, most truly,
Thomas Moore.

I am sinking here into a mere vegetable.

1252. *To Samuel Rogers*

Russell, viii. 286

Sloperton
June 27. 1847.

My dear Rogers,

I show how welcome was your summons by the readiness with which I respond to it. Already Bessy is preparing all for my flight, and as I have some little businesses to despatch in Town, I shall be able to get through them all before you return.

Yours ever most truly,
Thomas Moore.

¹ From 1846–52 Lord John Russell was Prime Minister and First Lord of the Treasury. During this time he quieted agitation in Ireland by a combination of coercive and relief measures. It is probably to one of these triumphs that Moore is referring.

² *Macbeth*, I. iii. 146.

1253. *To Samuel Rogers*

Russell, viii. 286

July 10. 1847.

My dear Rogers,

I am but just settling down into rural quiet after the week of gay doings with which you so kindly greeted me. Long, long, my dear friend, may you be able to keep up this spirit not only in your own buoyant heart, but (as I found while with you) in the hearts of all those whom you draw within your chosen circle.

In this instance, too, I have brought home with me a double stock of pleasure, as your friend Bessy has heard the whole proceedings from me, and in my narrative enjoyed a great part of my pleasure.

Thomas Moore.

UNDATABLE LETTERS

1254. *To William Lisle Bowles*

Sloperton Cottage
Friday

My dear Bowles— I have been sub-poena'd suddenly to town on a trial, and shall not be back, I dare say, for a week— Upon my return, I shall be most happy to meet Grossets or anybody with you—as soon at least as a friend of Mrs Moore's (who comes to her on Saturday) leaves us— If there is any thing I can do in town for you, direct a line to me at Rogers's, & I shall be most happy to be employed by you—or Mrs Bowles—to whom I beg my best remembrances & am

Yours very truly
Thomas Moore

1255. *To Lady Holland*

Brooks's
Wednesday

My dear Lady Holland— I was in great hopes that I should have been able to release myself from an engagement I had formed for to-day, but I found that it would be taken unkindly—the dinner being all but a tête-à-tête and with a friend who is suffering a good deal in mind. As soon as I am free from this week's engagements I shall give myself a chance of being allowed to come to Holland House by letting you know.

Yours most truly
Thomas Moore

1256. *Addressee unknown*

Rice University

I grieve to say that it will not be in my power to dine here on Monday, as my cold has become so bad as to drive me from London altogether. A thousand thanks for the permission to show the gallery to my son, who goes away dazzled & enchanted.

T. Moore

1257. *To Mrs. Starkey*

Rice University

Friday

Thank you, my dear Mrs Starkey, for your kind note. I did not expect that he would be able to come after such an expedition, and must only let the pension rest in *sus*pension till Monday.

I should have liked exceedingly to come to you to dinner, but as I must have returned at night, the walk home would not have been agreeable— Tomorrow, should it be finer, and you *inclinable*, I shall be very happy to come.

Yours very truly
Thomas Moore

1258. *Addressee unknown*

Huntington Library

31 Sackville St.
Friday Evening

My dear Sir— Had I known (which I did not, till Edward Moore told me this Morning) that you lived out of town, I should not have ventured, with the multiplicity of engagements that press upon me, to answer for being able to dine with you—and, from the same ignorance, I have unluckily promised some very old & near friends who had expected me to dinner tomorrow, that I would be with them at *nine* in the evening, having still other engagements to perform afterwards. This being the case, should you not have collected any persons you are particularly anxious for me to meet, it would be the kindest thing in the world of you to absolve me from my engagement, and to allow me to reserve the great pleasure I should have in passing a real *bonâ-fide* day with you till my next visit to town which will be in the course of six weeks or two months. Should you still wish me to come to you tomorrow, the *next* kindest thing would be to dine as early as the convenience of your other guests would admit, as I *must* be back in town as soon after nine as is possible. Trusting you will pardon all this trouble (which you would, if you knew but half the *embarras* of a man 'with *one* fortnight and a thousand friends') I am, my dear Sir, most truly yours

Thomas Moore.

On Monday I mean to be off for Sloperton, and therefore should like to have a few minutes of *business* with you on Sunday.

1259. *To the Reverend Henry Drury*

Rice University

My dear Mr Drury— I need not say how truly I feel for your loss, but I must add how much we *both* feel the justice you have done us in taking for granted that we sympathize with your affliction.

Pray, remember me most kindly to your mother, and with Mrs Moore's sincere condolence and regards, believe that I am truly yrs

T. Moore

You will be glad, I know, to hear that Mrs Moore is better.

1260. *Addressee unknown*

Huntington Library

Friday*

Bessy's days are generally unlucky ones— You must dine without us, but if any symptoms of sunshine appear towards evening, we shall contrive to reach you—childless, of course.

Ever yours
T. Moore

1261. *To Mary Shelley*

Abinger Collection

[Postmark November 30]

If you will put the scrap for Miss Lefanu in the 2d Post, directed to me at Lord Clifden's, Rochampton I shall get it tomorrow time enough to write.

Yrs
T. M.

1262. *To Mr. Spencer*

Rice University

Duke St.*
Monday*

My dear Spencer— I have been reminded since I saw you, that I was under a promise to dine at Lansdowne House to-day, & tomorrow I am engaged to a Play-party, so that our dinner together (which I would not lose for a good deal) must be put off to some other day.

Yours ever faithfully
Thomas Moore

1263. *To Mary Shelley*

Abinger Collection

Your servant had hardly left the door when I received the inclosed, and instantly sent after him, but he had vanished.

As I have not yet heard from Lord Lansdowne, I know no further of my movements.

Y^{rs}
T.

1264. *Addressee unknown*

Rice University

Tuesday
Two o'clock

It looks so like rain, that I think we shall accept your very kind offer, and rob you of your carriage about five o'clock—We are off tonight—Bessy & brats, bag & baggage; & If [*sic*] I had seen more of such friends as you, I should feel sorrier than I own I do now at our departure.

Goodbye—Ever yours
Thomas Moore.

Your carriage will find us at Power's in Westmoreland St.

1265. *To Mary Shelley*

Rice University

I write this in the Porter's Lodge—a thousand thanks, but I am already provided—not time for a word more

Y^{rs} ever
T. M.

1266. *To Sir Gore Ouseley*

Rice University

Monday Morning
Six o'clock

My dear Sir Gore Ouseley— I am just at this moment starting for
the country—to the wonder of all my political friends who cannot
understand a man's leaving town at such a crisis. One of my few
regrets in doing so is the loss I shall have of the very agreeable party
you offer me.

With my best compliments and thanks to Lady Ouseley for
thinking of me, I am, dear Sir Gore, very truly yours

Thomas Moore.

1267. *To John Bennet*

Rice University

My dear Bennet— I am quite ashamed of my forgetfulness in not
having left orders for the Books to be given to your Servant the
other day— Let me know when there is another opportunity & you
may depend upon having them—

Yrs ever
T. Moore

1268. *To A. Hayward*

Rice University

Friday

My dear Sir— I have but time to say that I shall have great pleasure
in joining your party on Thursday next.

Yours very truly
Thomas Moore

1269. *To Dr. Holland*

Rice University

Tuesday

My dear Doctor Holland— I came up to town but for a week, and
am now lingering on through my *third* week, expecting from day to
day the termination of the business which brought me up. I would
be off tomorrow, if I could—but it is highly possible that I shall
be detained *over* Thursday, and if you will allow me to give a *con-
ditional* answer, I can assure you with truth that there is no one

whose society would more fully make me amends for the delay
than your own, and that I shall, in the event of my stay, have
great pleasure in dining with you.

Yours very truly
Thomas Moore

1270. *To Colonel Houlton*

Rice University

Sunday Evening

My dear Houlton— I have just got your note & dispatch an
especial messenger with this to the Post, to say that, as our power
of coming to you on Monday week is very uncertain, we shall make
sure, at least, of Tuesday, & therefore you may expect us on that
day— We shall come pretty early, in order that Mrs Moore may see
the flowers, Mummies &c. &c.

Yours ever truly
T. Moore

1271. *To Mr. Locke*

Rice University

Thursday

My dear Locke. I had a visitor with me yesterday evening when
your note came, or should have answered it then. It would have
given me great pleasure to agree to your proposal for tomorrow;
but I am in expectation of our friend Corry coming to us, and
should not like being out of the way, when he arrives.

Ever yours truly
Thomas Moore

1272. *To James Carpenter*

Rice University

Bessy received your beautiful presents & bids me give you her
best thanks—

I was in hopes from the beginning of your letter that it was my
friend *William* had got some splendid appointment— Many happy
new years to you all, my dear Carpenter

Ever yours most cordially
Thomas Moore

1273. *Addressee unknown*

Yale

Sloperton
Nov^r

Dear Sir— I feel much obliged by your kind thoughtfulness in sending the Volume which I left behind at the State Paper office, and which reached me just as I was leaving town.

Yours truly
Thomas Moore

1274. *To Mrs. Murray*

Pforzheimer Misc. MS. 1998

Brooks's
Friday

My dear Mrs Murray— I was exceedingly sorry to be obliged to desert you so shabbily the other evening—but our *séance* after dinner, though very agreeable, was I must say unusually long; and I had promised my old friends, the Miss Berrys, to come early to their small assembly. Another time I shall hope to retrieve myself in your eyes (as well as in your daughters') by somewhat better behaviour

Yours very truly
Thomas Moore

1275. *To James Carpenter*

Morgan Library

11 Duke St.

My dear Carpenter—

We have come to our old quarters again—the smell of the paint in our friend's new house was too much for Mrs M. I am again tied fast by the leg—

Yours truly
T. Moore

Pray send the inclosed as soon as possible to Woolriche—I don't know his number—

Mrs M. will be very glad of another Novel, if you can get her one—

1276. *To Mrs. Long*

Morgan Library

Sloperton
Thursday

My dear Mrs Long— I was not able to answer your kind note yesterday, being rather in suspense as to some engagements I had formed, and Mrs Moore being at the time from home. But I now can say that *tomorrow* it will be in my power to come to you, should this note reach you in time to enable you to send the carriage for me. *Another time*, it will not be necessary to send the carriage farther than Melksham, as I can meet it there in my pony-carriage [*sic*]. You will see by this that I look forward to more than one opportunity of thus troubling you. Mrs Moore, I am sorry to say will not be able, *this* time, to accompany me.

Y^rs ever truly
Thomas Moore

I open my note again to say something about the hour, which may be, if convenient to you, three o'clock, though I shall be in readiness sooner should the carriage come.

1277. *To Dr. Brabant*

Bodleian Autograph c. 24, f. 354

Thursday E^v

My dear Dr Brabant— Our Captain comes tomorrow evening, & I claim the promise you made to come & meet him at dinner on Saturday at five o'clock, bringing Rufa, as per agreement, with you.

Yours ever
T. Moore.

1278. *Addressee unknown*

Bodleian Autograph b. 10, No. 965

Wednesday *Morning* one o'clock
My dear Sir.

In all the extremities of packing &c. &c. I inclose you the note you require & am ever most truly y^rs

Thomas Moore

1279. *To Thomas Longman*

N.L.S. MS. 3713, f. 416

March 30th

My dear Longman
   Inclosed is my quarterly draft on the Treasury.
   Wishing you and yours all well I am, my dear friend, as usual,
Thomas Moore

1280. *To John Rogers*

Morgan Library

Sunday Morning*

My dear Rogers— If you are forth-coming (as I was told you would be at this time) pray, let me know by the bearer, & if you are passing this way before two, I will tell them to let you up if you call.
   Is there any chance of Highbury being in receipt of visitors to-day?

Yours ever
T. Moore.

1281. *To Mary Shelley*

Abinger Collection

Sloperton
Friday

My dear Mrs Shelley— I should have answered your welcome note—most welcome after so long an interval of silence—by return of post, but that being in expectation of coming to town, I waited till I could tell you the when, where and whereabouts of the matter—which is briefly this. I start by the mid-way train to day—fix my quarters at my accustomed abode, Sackville St, and am to be heard of chiefly at Brookes's. This is all I have time for now, except

that I am truly y^{rs}
Thomas Moore

1282. *To Mrs. Milman*

National Library of Ireland

My dear Mrs Milman— I meant to have had the pleasure of being myself the bearer of my answer this morning, which would not have been so long delayed had I been quite sure of remaining in town till Thursday. I am now however most happy to be able to say 'yes' to your most kind invitation.

Yours very truly
Thomas Moore
Your messenger has just caught me on the threshold.

1283. *To Frederick Byng*

National Library of Ireland

My dear Byng— I have been enabled (by Talbot's changing *his* day for Thursday) to meet your wish and on Friday shall be most happy to come to you.

Yours ever
Thomas Moore

I hope there is some chance of my meeting Charles Greville.

1284. *To Miss Coulson*

National Library of Ireland

Sloperton
September 15

My dear Miss Coulson— I have been flattering myself ever since we met that the Fates would be *this* time propitious to me and allow me to dine with you one of the days which you so kindly propose— but a visit to town, which I fear will detain me there some time puts it again out of my power to have the great pleasure of waiting upon you.

Yours very truly
Thomas Moore

Should the 'Weired sisters' relent and give me a chance of being back in time I shall at least let you know.

1285. *Addressee unknown*

New York Public (fragment)

I hope *you* mean to be at the Artists' Fund Dinner—it was one of my inducements (added to their frequent entreaties) to the consent which I have given to attend.

I have not had my usual robust health during this winter, and you will see me, I think, a good deal thinned & furrowed—but heart & head are as *good as new*, so I need not complain.

Yours ever most truly
Thomas Moore.

1286. *Addressee unknown*

Rice University

27 Bury Street*
Monday*

Sir—

I have to ask your pardon for delaying my answer to the application with which you favoured me, but I was out of town when your letter arrived at my lodgings—

It will give me great pleasure to recommend your very meritorious undertaking & I beg you will add my name to the list of Subscribers— I am, Sir,

Your very obliged Servant
Thomas Moore
Esqr

1287. *To the Editor of the Illustrated London News*

Rice University (facsimile)

Sloperton
Feb^r

Sir—

I think it right even thus late, to acknowledge and thank you for a copy of the Illustrated London News, which I take for granted, came from your office, and in which it was not till yesterday (owing to our attention having been solely occupied by the wood-cuts) that either myself or any of my family discovered the very kind and (I should hope for your *paper's* sake) interesting notice which you have done me the honour to take of our poor old homely cottage at Mayfield. My family circle has been sadly thinned since then, but the few that remain feel and thank you for your kindness.

I have the honour to be
Your obliged Servt
Thomas Moore

1288. *To Mr. Hardman*

Rice University

Sloperton Cottage*
Sunday*

Dear Hardman

The only difficulty that has arisen to prevent our dining with you on Tuesday is that our friend Mrs Branigan (whom you may remember with us last year) has written to say that she will be with us at that time.

Yours very truly
Thomas Moore

1289. *Addressee unknown*

Huntington

My dear Sir— The sooner you can manage to send the inclosed to the Twopenny Post for me the better, as it is to account for my little boy's non-arrival at school tomorrow night, owing to the *plenitude* of the Coaches

Y^{rs} ever
T. M.

1290. *To Locke, Hughes, and Company*[1]

Huntington

16th May*

I had drawn for £5 which I now inclose— It was not my intention to take away the balance in your hands, but I suppose I expressed myself wrongly, having only wished to know what were the cheques given in since my last settlement. However, it is no matter now.

T. M.

1291. *To E. R. Moran*

B.M. Eg. MS. 2149, f. 117 (copy of a passage from a letter)

I had indeed already had thoughts of begging you to be my medium of communication with Limerick as hitherto I have had no direct means of carrying my sentiments to my friends there—

1292. *To the Reverend Mr. Money*

Bodleian MS. Autograph b 3, Vol. I (14b)

Sloperton
Tuesday

My dear Mr Money— Though you have always temptation enough for me within your own circle, yet the party you name in your note is so full of attractions that I regret exceedingly it is not in my power to join it.

Yours very truly
Thomas Moore

---

[1] Although the addressees were not designated, it is assumed that they were Moore's bankers in Devizes.

1293. *To the Marquess of Lansdowne*

[*Moore expresses his regret that Lord Lansdowne has had the gout. He sends 'the Conqueror's papers who seems resolved to make his victories* tell—*on friends as well as enemies.'*]

1294. *To Patrick B. Fitzpatrick*

University of Lund

Jarvis Street*

Wednesday Nov^r* [postmark November 31, *remainder torn away*]

My dear Sir— I thought to have had the pleasure of calling upon you this morning and thanking you in person for the very welcome mark of your recollection you have sent me—but I have left so many things to be done at the last moment, that I fear I shall be prevented, even tomorrow, from waiting upon you— I do not pretend to have *read* the book you were good enough to send me, but I just looked into it, and expect a great deal of pleasure from what that glimpse presented to me.

Yours, my dear Sir, in much haste
but with much truth,
Thomas Moore.

1295. *To Lewis Phipps*[1]

Chester L. Shaver

Sunday*

My dear Phipps— Do not perform the wine part of your dinner at home to-day, but reserve your powers in that way till the evening, when I shall want your assistance— We dine at five, so that you can guess the time for *falling* in, & I really shall be obliged by your doing so.

Ever yours
T. Moore

1296. *To Sydney Owenson*

Rice University

Wednesday morning*

Don't you think you can manage these six tickets for me?

Upon second thoughts, I shall send you *nine*, the number of your own Muses, and you may send me back as many, as you chuse, of them.

Very much yours.
Thomas Moore.

To Miss Owenson

[1] Transcript provided by Professor Chester L. Shaver. Oberlin College.

1297. *To Thomas Longman*

Rice University

August

My dear Longman— I am glad you liked my prefatory morceau,
—but you see I have been at it again with my small tomahawk,
and must therefore ask for *one* peep more at it before you go to
press with it.¹ My second thoughts, I know, are not *always* improvements though in general I am sure they are.

I must now work hard and fast at our 'horrid history'²

Yours ever
T. Moore

1298. *Addressee unknown*

Rice University

My dear Sir—

I am ashamed of [havin]g kept your MS. so long, but I took the
liberty of letting a friend of mine read it, after I had finished it
myself— Your story is *excellent*, and I have no doubt, with some
curtailments and alterations, that the Piece will succeed as well
on the Stage as in the Closet.

Yours, my dear Sir, very truly,
Thomas Moore.

¹ Moore is probably referring to the preface to his collected works, which
Longman published in 1840–1.
² *The History of Ireland* (1835–46).

APPENDIX

THE following letters came to the attention of the editor too late to be included in chronological order in the text.

1299. *Addressee unknown*

Rice University

Duke St., St. James's
Monday* [8 July 1817, *not in Moore's hand*]

I shall be most happy to wait upon your Lordship on Wednesday evening, if I can disengage myself from some Irish friends, whom I expect in town every hour on their way to Paris— Should they not have left London by Wednesday, I fear it will not be in my power to join your party—

Very much your Lordship's
obliged Servt
Thomas Moore

1300. *To Sir James Mackintosh*

Rice University

11 Duke Street, St. James's
Friday* [July 1819]

My dear Sir James— Your very kind letters have been among the most precious of those consolations, which my friends have given me, in such flattering abundance, since this mishap of mine— *Counsellor* Phillips, in a speech he made about me the other day, called me 'a bruised flower' and said I should be 'all the sweeter for it'. Whether the bruising will have the effect of extracting any sweetness from *myself*, I don't know— but it certainly has been the means of drawing forth a kindliness of feeling towards me in all quarters, both among friends & strangers, which cannot but gratify me very deeply— At the same time that I received your last letter, there came one from Allen, inclosing Mr Thomson's (of Edinburgh) answer to his enquiries with respect to Holyrood House—he says there is not a shadow of doubt that the privileges of Holyrood House are all-sufficient to protect me against every

(905)

Court whatever and against the Crown itself—he also adds that
I shall be safe in any part of Scotland, till a *Charge* of *Horning*
(which sounds very like a Crim-Con Action) is brought against me,
and that even then six day's interval would be allowed me before
caption could take place.[1]

I have not yet decided whether I shall go in the first instance,
to Edinburgh or the Continent; but I shall let you know the
moment I determine & mean, if *at all* possible, to take a run down
to Mardocks before I go.

Ever faithfully your obliged
Thomas Moore.

1301. *Addressee unknown*

Carl H. Pforzheimer Library[2]

Tuesday Morning [*c.* 1820]

My dear Sir— I grieve to say that our friends the Branigans will
not be able to wait upon you on Saturday, and Mrs Moore cannot
leave them; so that I am the only one of the party you are to
expect to dinner— I never have before dined away from her on
her birth-day, and you are one of the very few for whom I would
do it—Mrs B. & Bessy mean to call upon your ladies tomorrow—

Ever yours
Thomas Moore.

1302. *To William Lisle Bowles*

Rice University

[Watermark 1820]

My dear Bowles— Phipps is afraid of your roads, and will not
venture, so that the party is given up much to the regret of us all.

Let me see you soon here. I hope the Bath stimulus still continues
to act upon you, & that, when we meet again, I shall find you as
well & gay as I left you.

Best regards to Mrs Bowles—

Yours ever
Thomas Moore.

[1] Moore is referring to the difficulties with his deputy in Bermuda. See
letter No. 535, to Lady Donegal, 2 Apr. 1818.
[2] Quoted by permission of the Carl H. Pforzheimer Library.

1303. *To William Lisle Bowles*

Rice University

Thursday* [watermark 1820]

My dear Bowles— I cannot make up my mind to-day—but *if* I go,
I shall take my own little gig & poney [*sic*], and join you at the
White Hart. This I think better than making any appointment
with you at Chippenham, which either the weather or something
else might incline me to break. I am delighted that your health
enables you to be 'a wandering Clergyman' once more.

Yours ever
Thomas Moore.

1304. *To William Lisle Bowles*

Rice University

[Watermark 1820]

My dear Bowles— You forgot to write the few words for Hughes's
English letter—so, pray do, as soon as possible. I would save you
the trouble but that I know nothing of the forms of English Universities.— The following extract will remind you of the *sort* of thing
it is he wants— 'It is perfectly formal & usual to write to the President beforehand to request to know the needful preparations for
a Candidate, & he is particularly civil in answering these letters'—
A few words to this effect, in the proper form, is all that you have
to write for him.

Yours very truly
Thomas Moore.

1305. *To the Editor of 'The Times'*

The Times, 27 May 1824

May 26, 1824.*

Sir,— In consequence of the many misconceptions that are abroad,
with respect to the share which I have had in the destruction of
Lord Byron's Memoirs, I think it right to state the leading facts
of that transaction to the public.

Without entering into the respective claims of Mr. Murray and
myself to the property in these Memoirs, (a question which, now
that they are destroyed, can be but of little moment to any one),
it is sufficient to say that, believing the manuscript still to be mine,

I placed it at the disposal of Lord Byron's sister, Mrs. Leigh, with the sole reservation of a protest against its total destruction—at least without previous perusal and consultation among the parties. The majority of the persons present disagreed with this opinion, and it was the only point upon which there did exist any difference between us. The manuscript was accordingly torn and burned before our eyes; and I immediately paid to Mr. Murray, in the presence of the gentlemen assembled, 2,000 guineas, with interest, &c., being the amount of what I owed him upon the security of my bond, and for which I now stand indebted to my publishers, Messers. Longman and Co.

Since then the family of Lord Byron have, in a manner highly honourable to themselves, proposed an arrangement, by which the sum thus paid to Mr. Murray might be reimbursed me; but, from feelings and considerations which it is unnecessary here to explain, I have respectfully, but peremptorily, declined their offer. I am, Sir, your's [*sic*], &c.[1]

Thomas Moore

1306. *To William Lisle Bowles*

Rice University

Saturday* [watermark 1824]

My dear Bowles— *I* have also heard from Bain, and his postponement of the day till Friday was entirely in consequence of my announcement of your coming, as *my* time was to be any day between the 17th & 20th. I shall, however, be ready for you on Tuesday morning & we shall then be guided by circumstances.

Yours ever
T. Moore

Bain's note to me is full of delight at the prospect of your coming.

1307. *To William Lisle Bowles*

Rice University

London*
Tuesday* [watermark 1827]

My dear Bowles. I have this instant received your note & have only time to say that, instead of £20 which I mentioned to you as

---

[1] For an excellent account of the destruction of the Memoirs, see Doris Langley Moore, *The Late Lord Byron* (New York, 1961), pp. 12–45. See also letter No. 631, to John Murray, 13 Feb. 1823.

the sum I meant to give I mean to give only £10 & think it will be quite enough for you to contribute also.

When I see you, I will tell you all about the verses &c.

Y^{rs} ever
T. Moore

1308. *To Mary Shelley*

Abinger Collection[1]

[December 1829]

My dear boy is much better—indeed I should hope getting well again—I have been with him every day at the C. House, & have lost ground with my work very much. But I *will* see you to-day between 4 & 5 in Somerset St. I am now scarce up.

Mind between 4 & 5.

Y^{rs} ever
T.

1309. *To Frederick Byng*

Rice University

Tuesday [watermark 1833]

My dear Byng—after all, it is but deserting one old friend for another who is pleasanter—a thing which a good Casuiste relâché like you will easily forgive. Therefore, I shall dine with you to-day most willingly, as will also another relâché friend of mine, Fielding, to whom I gave your message.

Seven, I suppose?

Ever yours
T. Moore

1310. *To William Lisle Bowles*

Rice University

Sloperton
Feb^r 18 1836.

My dear Bowles— I would willingly have deferred answering you for a day or two longer, in order to give myself a chance of being able to accept your tempting invitation—the pleasure of visiting you at Salisbury having been long a favourite speculation of mine.

---

[1] This letter, with others addressed to Mary Shelley formerly in Lord Abinger's collection, is now in the Carl H. Pforzheimer Library.

But the wish you expressed for a *speedy* answer makes me think
it not quite right to delay any longer, and I am sorry to say that,
'as at present advised', I could not venture to engage myself to
come to you next week. We have at present my brother-in-law,
from Ireland, on a visit with us, and how long he means to stay I
have not yet learned from him. In addition to this difficulty I am
in daily expectation of a call upon business to London—so that,
in every respect, it is impossible for me to answer with any certainty; and you must therefore *not calculate upon me*. If, however,
things should turn out so as to leave me free, I will then place
myself (without Mrs Moore) at your disposal, and you may then
have me or not, according to your convenience.

    With best remembrances to Mrs Bowles

Ever yours most truly
Thomas Moore

1311. *To Miss Coutts*

Rice University

Sloperton
March 8, 1840

My dear Miss Coutts— Most happy shall I be at all times to obey
your summons & to dine with you and sing for you as often as
the Fates are propitiously pleased to allow me— I ought to add
also (with regard to the singing) as often as my *voice* is in a propitious mood for such displays—the weather, during my last trip to
town having been most fatal to my feeble powers of song. However,
as the postponement of the sailing of the Reliance till the 10th of
April (though very deranging to us in some ways) will give me
time to recover from my cold before I see you again, I shall hope
by that time to have voice enough at your command and (with
the sole proviso that there shall not be a large audience) will sing
as *much* and as *well* as I can for you. You will perceive from what
I have said that it is not my present intention to be in town so
soon as would admit of my dining with you on the 16th but should
any change take place in our very unfixed plans, I shall inflict
another note upon you to say so.

Yours most truly
Thomas Moore

    Should you happen to meet with Mr Lock it would give me
great pleasure if you would say how much I felt the kind *promptness*
with which he acceded to my request—it was really doing a favour
with a good grace.

(910)

1312. *To William Lisle Bowles*

Rice University

Sloperton
Wednesday [postmark June 17, 1840]

My very dear friend— I have but just a moment to acknowledge your note which it gave me most cordial pleasure to receive; and the next very agreeable thing, both to Mrs Moore and myself, will be to see you at our gate which we have been some time expecting, having heard with great delight that you had spoken of your wish and intention to pay us a visit. I have been myself not very well for some weeks past—otherwise I should have been, about this time, in town—so pray come and see us.

With kindest regards to Mrs Bowles,

ever yours most truly
Thomas Moore

1313. *To Thomas Longman*

Rice University

Sloperton
July 14th 1840

Dear Tom— Mr Shaw was right as to my having *finished* with the 1st Volume.

I do not like to leave the Preface to the tender mercies of the Compositor, who sometimes (I must say, however, *rarely*) makes fatal blunders.—therefore, must, if you please, see the Preface again.

I am now getting on with the Second Preface & hope to let you have it in the course of the week. *Perhaps* (if my leg goes on as well as at present) I may take it up to you myself.

Yours ever
T. Moore

T. Longman Esqr Junr

1314.

Rice University

A copy in Moore's handwriting of a letter from Sydney Smith, followed by Moore's reply:

August 7th 1843

Dear Moore

The following articles have been found in your room and forwarded by the Great Western.—a right-hand glove, an odd stocking—a sheet of music-paper—a missal—several letters, apparently from ladies—an Essay on Phelim ONeill—Thoughts on Rogers, beginning

> 'A devilish good fellow
> Though morbid and yellow'

There is also a bottle of Eau de Cologne.—what a careless mortal you are!

Answer—

Rev. Sir—having duly received, by the post,
Your list of the articles missing and lost,
By a certain small poet, well known on the road,
Who has lately put up at your flowing abode,
We have balanced what Hume calls 'the tottle o' the whole',
(Making all due allowance for what the bard *stole*)
And, hoping th' inclosed will be found quite correct,
Have the honour, Rev. Sir to be
                              yours, with respect.
Left behind—a kid glove that had once made a pair—
An odd stocking, whose fellow is—heaven knows where;
And (to match these odd fellows) a couplet sublime,
Wanting nought to complete it but reason and rhyme.
Such was all that, on diligent search, we could find
That the Bard, so miscalled, in his flight left behind;
While, thief as he is, he brought slyly away
Rich treasurers to last him for many a day;—
Recollections unfading of sunny Combe Florey;
Its cradle of hills where it slumbers in glory;
Its Sydney himself, and the countless bright things
That his tongue or his pen, from the deep-shining springs
Of wisdom and wit, ever flowingly brings!
Such being, on both sides, the 'tottle' amount
We shall leave to your Rev'rence to balance th' account.

[*Unsigned*]

1315. *To Robert Howe Gould*

Rice University

Sloperton, Chippenham
July 1st 1845

My dear Sir. I regret exceedingly that it was not till after your departure I discovered the curious and interesting gift which you so kindly and at the same time so modestly left behind for me. I assure you I shall value it most highly, not only for its own intrinsic worth, but for the graceful, and only too flattering verses which accompany it. Much as I have *written* of English poetry I am ashamed to say how *very* little of it I have ever *read*—prose having been always my favourite line of study. I may therefore plead guilty to being far less versed in *American* poetry than I ought to be. But if your Parnassus can boast many such denizens as the author of the graceful lines you have done me the honour of addressing to me, I shall certainly be tempted, though my own poetical days are over, to refresh my memory of them with a taste of *yours*, and as, in my youth, I drank of the waters of your Niagara, regale myself now with the 'torrentia flumina' of your poetry.[1]

Believe me, dear Sir, yours
very truly
Thomas Moore

1316. *To Robert Howe Gould*

Rice University

Sloperton
June 12th [1846]

My dear Mr Gould— I returned here about five or six days hence, preceded & followed by swarms of letters which I am still employed in endeavouring to answer— You have before this, I dare say, succeeded in making your way to Rogers's Sanctum-Sanctorum, both for yourself and Mr Kirk—

'Else wherefore do you breathe in Christian land?' *Such* men are *made* to meet.

Lest you should *not*, however have succeeded in reaching him I enclose a note, which I think will work the charm for you.

On looking again at your note, I find I have rather confused the affair—but I can hardly, I think, do wrong in committing Mr Kirk's case to *you*, with full authority to say for *me* all that your taste and good-nature would prompt you to say from yourself.

I have not time for a word more.

Yours most truly
Thomas Moore.

[1] For Gould's letter and verses to Moore, see Russell, viii, 22–24.

1317. *To William Lisle Bowles*

Rice University

[*Salutation and first line missing*]

received this morning I find it would be necessary for me to be back here on Saturday evening, and therefore as *you* could not manage that for me I am afraid we must give up our plan. If there are Chaises to be had at the Bustard (which I know nothing about) we could have the advantage of your company and *instruction* as far as Stonehenge, and then return here ourselves, leaving you to proceed unencumbered to Salisbury. But if there are no conveyances to be had at the Bustard, what I mean to do (not to disappoint Tom & his Mamma) is to have a Fly from hence, and return here in the evening. With a thousand thanks from all *three* for your most kind readiness to be our Carrier & Cicerone, I am, my dear Bowles, ever truly yours

Thomas Moore.

1318. *To William Lisle Bowles*

Rice University

Tuesday

My dear Bowles— I send you Pickering's answer, which is all just as it should be. You will see that I was wrong in my guess as to the author and that it is 'a second *Daniel,* come to judgment.'

I hope your 'Navigation' will now come to an *Anchor* without delay.

Yours ever
T. Moore

1319. *To Archbishop John MacHale*

Archbishop John MacHale, *Moore's Melodies* (Dublin, 1871), v.

Sloperton
December 10*th,* 1841.

My Dear Lord,

On my return, but a few days since, to Sloperton, I found a heap of letters awaiting me, many of which being 'de omnibus rebus et quibusdam aliis', I thought might safely be left a few days without answers, and among these (from my not immediately making out the signature) was unfortunately your Lordship's. By the greatest good luck I happened, but a few minutes since, to open this packet, and lose not a moment in acquainting you with the cause of a delay which must have appeared to you so uncourteous and so unaccountable. As the post hour presses upon me, I have time at this moment for no more than to thank you most cordially for your kind and flattering communication, and to subscribe myself

Your Lordship's obliged servant,
Thomas Moore.

To His Grace the Most Rev. John MacHale,
Archbishop of Tuam, Tuam, Ireland.

1320. *To Archbishop John MacHale*

Archbishop John MacHale, *Moore's Melodies* (Dublin, 1871), vi.

Bowood
December, 1841.

My Dear Lord,

I trust that ere this you have received my letter accounting for the long delay of my answer to your very gratifying announcement. That these songs of mine should be translated into what I may call their native language, is in itself a great gratification and triumph to me; but, that such a tribute should come from the pen of your Grace, considerably adds to the pride and pleasure I feel in it.

I need hardly say that any assistance I can lend by making inquiries of publishers, or otherwise facilitating your task, shall be most heartily at your Grace's command.

I am most truly your Grace's
Faithful servant,
Thomas Moore.

To His Grace the Most Rev. John MacHale,
Archbishop of Tuam, Tuam, Ireland.

1321. *To Archbishop John MacHale*

Archbishop John MacHale, *Moore's Melodies* (Dublin, 1871), vi.

Bowood
January, 1842.

My Dear Lord,

Almost ever since I received your last letter, I have been in expectation of being called to town for the purpose of pursuing my labours at the State Paper Office, which will now be a long and frequent task of mine, as I have re-embarked, after a long interruption, in my Irish History. It was my intention, had I gone to town, to make such inquiries on the subject of your translation, as would be more satisfactory than any I can procure through the medium of letters. I know nothing of the state of the *property* of the work in Dublin, but in London it is in the hands of the widow of the late James Power, from whom the Longmans derive the power of publishing it. To her, therefore, any application must be made to authorize the use of either the words or the music for publication in England. I should be most sorry, I assure you, if by any of those difficulties my work were to lose the high honour you intended it by giving your translation to the world.

The letter in the newspaper which you were so kind as to send me, did not want any additional interest to its own power of language and thought; but, if it did, the sight of my own poetry (in what might be almost called its natural language) enshrined thus in the midst of *your* prose, would most abundantly afford it.

I am, my dear Lord,
Your Grace's very faithful servant,
Thomas Moore.

To the Most Rev. John MacHale, Archbishop of Tuam,
Tuam, Ireland.

1322. *To Archbishop John MacHale*

Archbishop John MacHale, *Moore's Melodies* (Dublin, 1871), vii.

Sloperton
April 30th, 1842.

My Dear Lord,

I feel really ashamed of myself for having so long delayed my acknowledgment of your great kindness; but, in addition to the usual pressure of business, I have been, lately, much and painfully occupied by the state of health in which my younger boy has returned from India. He is now, thank God, doing better, but we are still not free from alarm about him.

Your Irish (truly Irish) Melodies are a shame and a reproach to me, and I would willingly give up much of what I know of other languages to have been Irishman enough to accomplish such a work.

Yours, in great haste, but
Most truly,
Thomas Moore.

To His Grace the Most Rev. Doctor MacHale,
Archbishop of Tuam, Tuam, Ireland.

1323. *To Archbishop John MacHale*

Archbishop John MacHale, *Moore's Melodies* (Dublin, 1871), VII.

December 26th, 1845.

My Dear Lord,

I was for two reasons pleased and proud to hear from you. In the first place, to find myself kindly remembered by you, could not be otherwise than a pride and a pleasure to me, and in the next, the sight of another number of *the* Melodies relieved me from a fear which I was beginning to give way to, that you had not met with sufficient sympathy in your national work to induce you to continue it. This would, indeed, have been a pity and a shame, and I hail your new number as a proof that I was mistaken.

I find you have been able to make the metre of the Irish words exactly suit the airs, which must have been no easy achievement. I have a Latin translation of the Melodies, but of course no such *tour de force* is attempted in it.

Believe me, your Lordship's very sincere
And obliged servant,
Thomas Moore.

To the Most Rev. Doctor MacHale, Archbishop of Tuam,
    Tuam, Ireland.

GLOSSARY OF PROPER NAMES

ABERDEEN, Earl of. *See* Gordon, George Hamilton.

ADAMS, Dr. A lawyer whom Byron retained, with Drs. Robinson and Jenner, to represent him in Doctors Commons in his domestic difficulties (*see LJ*, iii. 308, and Marchand, *Byron*, 577 *n*).

ADDINGTON, Henry, first Viscount Sidmouth (1757–1844). Member of Parliament from Devizes; Speaker of the House of Commons (1789–1801); Home Secretary (1812–21); First Lord of the Treasury and Chancellor of the Exchequer (1801–4).

AGRIPPA, Henricus Cornelius (1486–1535). German scholar, theologian, and writer on occult sciences; author of *De Occulta Philosophia, libri tres* (1529), and *De Vanitate Scientiarum* (1530). Said to be the astrologer, Herr Trippa, of Rabelais's Third Book.

ALLAN, Sir William (1782–1850). Scottish historical painter; travelled in Russia (1805–14); known especially for scenes from Russian life and scenes from Scottish history.

ALTHORP, Lord. *See* Spencer, John Charles.

ARCHDALL, Richard. A major in the fortieth (or second Somersetshire) Regiment of Foot. *See* the diary (Russell, ii. 149) where Richard Archdall, a schoolmate of Sheridan, is mentioned as having translated some verses of Pindar.

ARKWRIGHT, Mrs. Robert. A relative of the family of Richard Arkwright (1732–92), the inventor of the spinning frame, and of the Strutts of Derby, whom Moore visited on several occasions. Bradford Booth, *MLN*, lv (1940), 43 n., identifies her as 'a composer and singer of some talent'.

ARNOLD, Samuel James. A producer who brought out Moore's musical comedy *M.P. or the Blue Stocking*.

ASGILL, Lady. Wife of Sir Charles Asgill (1763–1823), general of the army.

ASHE, Andrew. A Dublin flutist, husband of Mrs. Ashe, principal singer at the Bath concerts, of which, after 1810, he was director (see Russell, v. 126.)

ASHE, Mrs. Andrew. The wife of the well-known Dublin flutist Andrew Ashe. She was a singer of note and a pupil of Rauzzini. She and Ashe were married in 1799 and for years were prominent in the Bath concerts, she as the principal singer and he (after Rauzzini's death in 1810) as the director.

ATHOLL, Duchess of (d. 1842). Second wife of John Murray, fourth Duke of Atholl (1755–1830).

ATKINSON, Joseph (1743–1818). An Irish dramatist. Secretary of the Ordnance Board and officer in the army until he attained the rank of captain. He produced a comedy in Dublin entitled *Mutual Deception*, which appeared at the Haymarket under the title *Tit for Tat*. It was he who introduced Moore to Lord Moira.

AUKLAND, Baron. *See* Eden, George.

BAILLIE, Dr. Matthew (1761–1823). Physician; brother of Joanna Baillie.

BAILY. Moore's friend and neighbour in Wiltshire; a frequent visitor with the poet to Bowood, where they engaged in conversation on literature and politics with Lord Lansdowne and his circle.

BAIN, Dr. A friend of Sheridan from whom Moore got information for his biography of the dramatist.

BANIM, Michael (1796–1874). Irish novelist. Author of *Ghost Hunter* (1833); *Clough Fion* (1852); and *Town of the Cascades* (1864). His brother John wrote drama (*Damon and Pythias*, produced at Covent Garden in 1812) and novels (*The Denounced*, 1829, and *The Smuggler. A Tale*, 1831).

BANKES, William (d. 1855). Member of Parliament, traveller in the East, and friend of Byron.

BANNISTER, John (1760–1836). An actor to whom Moore read the libretto of *The Gipsy Prince*. The son of Charles Bannister (1738?–1804), actor and bass singer. John Bannister made his debut as Whiskerandos in Sheridan's *Critic* (1779) at the Haymarket. Other roles included Sir Anthony Absolute and Bob Acres.

BANTI, Georgina Brigida (1757–1806). A famous Italian singer.

BARBAZON, John Ghambre, tenth Earl of Meath (d. 1851).

BARNES, Thomas (1785–1841). Editor of *The Times* (1817–41).

BARRY, Charles F. The Genoa partner of Webb and Company, with whom Byron banked.

BATHURST, Henry, third Earl of (1762–1834). Held several offices under Pitt and successors, including Secretary for War and Colonies (1812–27). He was also Lord President of the Council (1828–30).

BEAUJOLOIS, Count de. *See* d'Orléans, Louis Charles.

BECHER, Reverend John Thomas. Vicar of Rumpton and Midsomer Norton, Nottinghamshire, to whom Byron presented a copy of *Fugitive Pieces*. He advised the poet to recall most of the copies and destroy them, although Becher retained the one presented to him.

BECTIVE, Earl of. *See* Taylor, Sir Thomas.

BEDFORD, Duke of. *See* Russell, Francis and John.

BEECHER, Nick. A member of the circle in Dublin which included Moore, James Corry, and Richard Power. Moore alludes to his 'very sensible speech . . . on the Catholic question' in his diary (Russell, ii. 301). He is referred to in the diary (Russell, iv. 110 and 113).

BELCHER, Mrs. Wife of the Reverend Belcher, vicar at Ashbourne, Derbyshire.

BELLINI, Vincenzo (1801–35). Italian opera composer. Composed, among others, *Adelson e Salvina* (1825); *Bianca e Fernando* (1826); *Il Pirata* (1827); and *Norma* (1831). He also wrote some sacred music.

BELLOC, Louise Swanton (1796–1881). French translator of Moore's *Life of Byron*, *Loves of the Angels*, and a two-volume edition of Byron's works. She was also the author of a two-volume biography of Byron, published in Paris in 1824.

BEMBO, Bernard (1470–1547). A Cardinal who contributed much to the interest in the study of Greek and Latin. His principal works are a *History of Venice, Gli Asolani* (dialogues on the nature of love), and some Italian sonnets.

BENETT, John. Moore's friend at Calne, Wiltshire; Member of Parliament for Calne.

BENNISON. A printer employed by Power to work with him, Moore, and Stevenson on *The Irish Melodies*. Moore sometimes spelled the name with one *n*.

BENTINCK, William Henry Cavendish, third Duke of Portland (1738–1809). Lord Chamberlain (1765); Lord Lieutenant of Ireland (1782); Prime Minister (1783) and again (1807–9).

BENTLEY, Richard (1794–1871). Publisher, who started *Bentley's Miscellany*, with Dickens as the editor, in 1837.

BENTLEY, Mrs. Wife of Richard Bentley, publisher of *Bentley's Miscellany*.

BERESFORD, Sir John Poo (1766–1844). Admiral; served first on board the *Alexander* chiefly on Newfoundland and West Indies stations; on board *Resolution* (1794); sent to West Indies (1798); became commander of a succession of large ships; became Vice-admiral (1825); Admiral (1838); Member of Parliament from Coleraine (1809–12; 1814–23), Berwick (1823–6), Coleraine (1832), and Chatham (1835); junior member of Admiralty (1835).

BERNIS, François Joachim de Pierre de (1715–94). French Cardinal and statesman, who wrote little poems and *bouquets poétiques*, as he called them.

BERRY, Misses. Friends to whom Moore referred often in his diary. It is to one of them that we are indebted for the story (second hand through Moore, it is true) of his first appearance as a singer in London, when he overcame the initial condescension of the audience by singing so beautifully that some people expressed regret that he was studying law, and one venerable lawyer thought it wise to advise him not to let his success turn his head from his profession (*see* Russell, vii. 240–1).

BESSBOROUGH, Earl of. *See* Ponsonby, John William.

BESSBOROUGH, Lady (d. 1821). Wife of Frederick Ponsonby, third Earl of Bessborough (1758–1844). Before her marriage she was Lady Henrietta Frances Spencer, daughter of John, first Earl Spencer.

BEXLEY, Baron. *See* Vansittart, Nicholas.

BEZA, Theodore (1519–1608). A noted Calvinistic theologian, who was associated with Calvin in Geneva and succeeded him as Professor of Theology at the University.

BIGGIN, Mr. The only clue to the identity of this man is found in letters Nos. 20, 21, 22, and 81. He is best described in No. 22, and in No. 81, where Moore recorded his shock after reading an account of Biggin's death.

BIGGS, Miss. An actress at Drury Lane.

BILLINGTON, Elizabeth Weichsel (1768–1818). A famous opera singer, who married James Billington, also a musician, in 1783. She sang with great success at Covent Garden, Drury Lane, and King's Theater.

BIROM, Mrs. A music teacher who instructed Moore in 'thorough bass'.

BISHOP, Sir Henry Rowley (1786–1855). Composer, who worked with Moore and Power on the last three numbers of the *Irish Melodies*. He was noted for his glees and songs, but also wrote operas, burlettas, and incidental music to Shakespeare's plays.

BLACK, John. Editor of the *Morning Chronicle* (1819–43).

BLESSINGTON, Marguerite, Countess of (1789–1849). Writer, who published several novels, and, as a result of an acquaintance established in 1822, the *Conversations with Lord Byron*.

BLOOMFIELD, Hannah. Daughter of Robert Bloomfield, poet.

BLOOMFIELD, Robert (1766–1823). Poet, author of *The Farmer's Boy* (1800); *Rural Tales* (1802); *Good Tidings* (1804); *The Banks of Wye* (1811); and *May Day with the Muses* (1822).

BOILEAU-DESPRÉAUX, Nicolas (1636–1711). French critic and poet, author of *L'Art Poétique* (1674).

BONAPARTE, Jerome (1784–1860). King of Westphalia, youngest brother of Napoleon. He served as a lieutenant in the navy in the West Indies and on a visit to the United States met Elizabeth Patterson (1785–1879), of Baltimore, whom he married in 1803. Napoleon declared the marriage null in 1805, giving as his reason that it took place without the consent of the Emperor.

BOOTH, Mrs. Moore's landlady when he had rooms in Bury Street.

BOOTHBY, Sir Brooke, seventh Baron Boothby (1743–1824). Poet and pamphleteer who published, among other things, *A Letter to the Right Honorable Edmund Burke* (1791, a reply to Burke's *Reflections on the French Revolution*); and *Sorrows Sacred to the Memory of Penelope* (1796), a volume of verse.

BORINGDON, Baron. *See* Parker, John.

BOURBON, Constable (1490–1527). Duc Charles de Bourbon, commonly called Constable Bourbon. Became Duke (1505); created Constable of France (1515); quarrelled with Francis I and concluded private alliance with Emperor Charles V and Henry VIII of England; aided Imperial Army in driving French from Italy and unsuccessfully beseiged Marseilles (1524); made Duke of Milan by Charles V (1526); said to have been mortally wounded by Benvenuto Cellini.

BOURBON, Louis Henri Joseph, Prince de Condé (1756–1830). Last of the Condé princes. Son of Louis Joseph de Bourbon (1736–1818), distinguished soldier in the Seven Years' War. Louis Henri was wounded at Gibraltar (1782) and later served under his father against France. He is supposed to have committed suicide. *See also* Condé, Prince de.

BOWLES, William Lisle (1762–1850). English clergyman and poet; Rector of Bremhill Vicarage, Wiltshire, near Moore's home. Among his important works are *Fourteen Sonnets* (1789), which won the praise of Coleridge, Wordsworth, and Southey; *The Spirit of Discovery, or the Conquest of the Ocean*, a poem in five books (1804); and a ten-volume edition of Pope's works (1806). Bowles's strictures on Pope, which caused the controversy with Byron, are contained in his *Invariable Principles of Poetry* (1819).

BOWRING, Sir John (1792–1872). Honorary Secretary to the Greek Committee; linguist; writer; editor of *Westminster Review*; biographer of Jeremy Bentham; Member of Parliament for Bolton (1841–7); plenipotentiary to China, Japan, and Siam (1854–60).

BRABANT, Dr. R. H. Moore's close friend and neighbour in Wiltshire. He was a tutor and amateur theologian, who assisted Moore with some of his reviews of books on theology. He was a friend of Coleridge during the poet's residence in Calne in 1815 and of George Eliot, who was associated with Brabant's daughter.

BRAHAM, John (1774?–1856). Real surname Abraham. A famous opera, oratorio, and concert tenor. He collaborated with Byron and Isaac Nathan on the *Hebrew Melodies*.

BRANIGAN, Eliza. Niece to Mrs. Ready, a friend of the Moores, and a frequent visitor to Sloperton Cottage.

BROCKMAN, Johann Heinrich (1767–1837). A Catholic theologian, clergyman, and university professor.

BROGLIE, Achille Charles Léonce Victor, Duc de Broglie (1785–1870). Member of Chamber of Peers (1814); Minister of the Interior and Public Worship and Instruction (1830); Minister of Foreign Affairs (1832–4); President of the Council (1835); retired from political life after 1851. Author of four volumes of *Souveniers*.

BROUGHAM, Henry Peter, Baron Brougham and Vaux (1778–1868). Scottish jurist and political leader. Founded *Edinburgh Review* with Sydney Smith and Francis Jeffrey; Member of Parliament (1810); fought against slave trade; defended Queen Caroline (1820); a founder of London University (1828); Lord Chancellor (1830–4); helped pass reform bill (1831); advocated immediate abolition of slavery (1838).

BRYAN. Godfather to Moore's first child, Anne Jane Barbara. After the death of this child, he bequeathed £1,000 to Anastasia, the second daughter, to whom he considered his 'duty as godfather transferred' (*see* Russell, iv. 200).

BULWER, Edward George Earle (1803–73). Politician and novelist. He was created Baron Lytton of Knebworth in 1866. Best known perhaps for *The Last Days of Pompeii* (1834) and *Pelham* (1828). Editor of the *New Monthly Magazine* (1831–2).

BUNTING, Edward (1773–1843). Musician who collected traditional Irish airs. Many of Moore's *Irish Melodies* were probably taken from Bunting's *General Collection of Ancient Irish Music* (1796).

BURDETT, Sir Francis (1770–1844). A Member of Parliament who championed parliamentary reform, prison reform, removal of Catholic disabilities, abolition of flogging in the army, and free speech.

BURSTON, Beresford. Moore's friend and schoolmate at Trinity College. Burston's father, a lawyer, gave Moore encouragement in the writing of poetry. Moore and Beresford Burston entered the Middle Temple at the same time.

BUSHE, Charles Kendall (1767–1843). Chief Justice of the King's Bench of Ireland (1822–41).

BYNG, Sir John (1772–1860). General, who was created Baron Stafford (1835) and Earl of Stafford (1847).

BYRON, George Gordon, sixth Baron Byron (1788–1824). Poet.

CAMBRIDGE, Duke of. Adolphus Frederick, Duke of Cambridge (1774–1850). Tenth child and seventh son of George III and Queen Charlotte.

CAMPBELL, John Frederick, second Baron and first Earl of Cawdor (1790–1860).

CAMPBELL, Thomas (1777–1844). Poet, author of *The Pleasures of Hope* (1799). It was probably he who was one of the first subscribers to Moore's *Anacreon*.

CANNING, George (1770–1827). Statesman. Member of Parliament (1793); Under-secretary for Foreign Affairs (1796–9); Foreign Secretary (1807–10); Prime Minister and Chancellor of the Exchequer (1827); established British independence of Holy Alliance; supported Catholic emancipation.

CANTERBURY, Lady. *See* Mrs. Manners-Sutton.

CAPET, Charles. Charles IV (1294–1328). King of France (1322–8); last in direct line of the Capetian kings; sought to strengthen royal power by increasing taxes, exacting fines and duties, debasing coinage, confiscations, and other tyrannical methods.

CARDON, Anthony (1772–1813). An engraver who was born in Brussels but lived during the latter years of his life in London.

CARNARVON, Earl of. *See* Herbert, Henry John George. (Moore spelled the name 'Caernarvon'.)

CARPENTER, James. Publisher and bookseller. Moore was associated with him throughout the poet's early career. Carpenter published, among several other works, the *Works of Thomas Little* (1801).

CATALANI, Angelica (1780–1849). An Italian operatic soprano.

CAVENDISH, William, fifth Duke of Devonshire and Marquess of Hartington (1748–1811). Moore probably also knew the Duke's son, William George Spencer, sixth Duke of Devonshire (1790–1858).

CAWDOR, Earl of. *See* Campbell, John Frederick.

CAWTHORN, James. Byron's publisher who brought out, among other things, *English Bards*.

CHANTREY, Sir Francis Legatt (1781–1841?). English sculptor and portrait-painter. Moore frequently spelled the name 'Chauntrey'.

CHAWORTH, Mary. *See* Musters.

CHAWORTH, Mrs. Mother of Mary Chaworth, Byron's first love, who married John Musters (*see* Marchand, *Byron*, p. 99).

CHESLYN, Richard. Moore's friend who was owner of Langley Priory.

CHRYSOSTOM, St. John (345–407). One of the Fathers of the Greek Church. Noted for his eloquence.

CHURCHILL, Charles Spencer- (1794–1840). Army officer; second son of fifth Duke of Marlborough. Married Ethelred Catherine Benett (d. 1839).

CLARE, Earl of. *See* Fitzgibbon, John.

CLIFDEN, Viscount. *See* Welbore, Henry.

CLIFTON, Lord Edward, fifth Earl Darnley and Baron Clifton (1795–1835).

CLONCURRY, Baron. Created Baron in Ireland (1789) and Baron in England (1831).

COBBETT, William (1762–1835). A Tory journalist until 1801, but afterwards adopted popular opinions and championed reform movements.

COCHRANE, Archibald, ninth Earl of Dundonald (1749–1831). A naval officer and chemical manufacturer.

COCKBURN, Sir Alexander James Edmund (1802–80). Judge. Member of Parliament (1847); Attorney-general (1851–6); Chief Justice of Common Pleas (1856); Lord Chief Justice of England (1859).

COCKBURN, George. Commanding officer of the *Phaeton*, on which Moore sailed to America. He was subsequently advanced to the rank of Rear-admiral (1812); was involved in the War of 1812; appointed Commander-in-chief at the Cape of Good Hope and the island of St. Helena (1815); promoted to Vice-admiral (1819), and Major-general of the Royal Marines (1821).

CODD, Richard Joyce (d. 1809). Moore's uncle who lived with the family at Aungier Street, Dublin.

CODE, Henry Brereton. An Irish dramatist who collaborated with Sir John Stevenson on three musicals which were produced in Dublin: *The Patriot, or Hermit of Saxellen* (1811); *Spanish Patriots a Thousand Years Ago, an Historical Drama* (1812); and *The Russian Sacrifice, or The Burning of Moscow, an Historical Drama* (1813).

COLLY, Richard, first Marquess Wellesley and second Earl of Mornington (1760–1842). Indian administrator; a Lord of the Treasury (1786). As Governor-general of India (1797–1805), rendered British power in India supreme by replacing French soldiers with British in Hyderabad, replacing Mohammedan dynasty in Mysore with a friendly Hindu dynasty, and by persuading Indian princes to cede territory and contribute to support of British forces. He was ambassador to Spain (1809); Foreign Secretary (1809–12); Lord-lieutenant of Ireland (1821–8; 1833–4); and Lord Chamberlain (1835).

COLMAN, George, the younger (1762–1836). Dramatist and manager of the Haymarket Theatre. His first romantic comedy was *Zukle and Yarico* (1787), and his most famous work was *The Heir-at-Law* (1797).

COLUMELLA, Lucius Junius Moderatus, first century A.D. A Roman writer on agriculture.

COMPTON, Captain William. Commanding officer of *Driver*, on which Moore sailed for Bermuda from Norfolk. It is conjectured that he was the brother of Commander Henry Compton, one of Nelson's officers.

CONDÉ, Prince de. *See* Bourbon, Louis Henri Joseph. Condé was the name of a great family of French nobility bearing the title Prince and forming a branch of the house of Bourbon.

CONINGSBY, George Capel-, fifth Earl of Essex (1757–1839). Member of Parliament for Westminster (1779–80); Lostwithiel (1781–4); and Radnor (1796–9). Military commander. Held various county offices.

CONNER, Edward. Moore's friend in the War Office, Dublin Castle, through whom Moore occasionally received mail that had been franked.

CONSTABLE, Archibald (1774–1827). First publisher of the *Edinburgh Review* (1802). Joint publisher with Longmans of Scott's *Lay of the Last Minstrel* (1805) and *Marmion* (1807). Purchased *Encyclopaedia Britannica* in 1812 and added supplement in six volumes (1816–24). Involved with Scott in the failure of 1826. Began *Constable's Miscellany* in 1827.

CORBET, General. An Irish rebel whom Moore knew at Trinity College, Dublin. He escaped from prison at Kilmainham by hiding in a heap of sand on the recreation area until dark and climbing the wall by a rope ladder prepared by some of his friends on the outside. He fled to France concealed aboard the same ship with Major Sirr, who captured Lord Edward Fitzgerald. Corbet rose to the rank of general after entering the French service.

CORK, Lady, formerly Mary Monckton (1746–1840). Daughter of John Monckton, first Viscount Galway; married Edmund Boyle, seventh Earl of Cork in 1786. She is the original of Mrs. Leo Hunter of *Pickwick Papers*.

CORRY, Isaac (1755–1813). Irish politician.

CORRY, James (1772–1848). Associated with Moore in the 'Kilkenny Theatricals'. He was called to the Bar in Ireland but did not practice law, taking instead a position as Clerk of the Irish Journals in the House of Commons, and Secretary to the Linen Board. In 1810, after the Linen Board was abolished, he moved to Cheltenham, where he lived until his death.

COSTELLO, Louisa Stuart (1799–1870). Painter and writer. She produced books of poems and travel and was one of the first artists to devote considerable time to copying illuminated manuscripts.

COWELL, John. A friend of Lord Byron. Cowell gave Moore several of Byron's letters and related a number of anecdotes about the poet when Moore met Cowell at breakfast on 11 June 1828. See the entry in Moore's diary for that date (Russell, v. 302–3). *See also* letter No. 800.

COWPER, Lord. Peter Leopold Louis Francis, fifth Earl Cowper (d. 1837).

CRABBE, George (1754–1832). Poet, author of *Tales in Verse* (1812) and *Tales of the Hall* (1819).

CRADOCK, Dean. Moore's friend in Dublin, son of the librarian at Marsh's Library. Through the young Cradock, Moore arranged for permission to read in the library during seasons when it was closed (*see* Russell, i. 59).

CRAMPTON, Sir Philip (1777–1858). A prominent Dublin surgeon, who was three times president of the Dublin College of Surgeons.

CREWE, Mrs. An acquaintance of Richard Brinsley Sheridan. *See* Russell, ii. 197 and 295, where she is mentioned in connexion with the dramatist.

CRISSY, James. A publisher in Philadelphia.

CROKER, John Wilson (1780–1857). Tory leader. Born in Galway. Secretary to the Admiralty (1810–30). A frequent contributor to the *Quarterly Review*. In 1800 he received the B.A. degree from Trinity College, Dublin, where Moore first became acquainted with him.

CROLY, George (1780–1860). An Irish author and divine, whose principal poem was *Paris in 1815*. He was also a frequent contributor to the *Literary Gazette* and *Blackwood's Magazine*.

CROOKSHANKS. Irish friends of Moore (*see* Russell, i. 213 and 233, and letter No. 173).

CROTCH, Dr. William (1775–1847). Compiler of a collection of melodies entitled *Specimens of Various Styles of Music* (*c.* 1807), on which Moore drew for some of the tunes in his *Irish Melodies*. Composer; Professor of Music at Oxford (1797–1806); first Principal, Royal Academy of Music (1822–32).

CROWE, William (1745–1829). Writer and orator, of Winchester and New College, Oxford; at one time public orator at Oxford; author of *Lewesdon Hill* (1788), a descriptive poem somewhat in the style of Thomson and Cowper.

CRUMPE, Miss. A friend of Moore from Limerick. Evidently he negotiated with Murray for the publication of a novel which she had written (*see* Russell, v. 34 and 36). Moore sometimes spelled the name 'Crump'.

CUMBERLAND, Richard (1732–1811). Dramatist, author of sentimental comedies of which *The West Indian* and *The Brothers* are the best. Wrote two novels, *Arundel* (1789) and *Henry* (1795). He is perhaps best known for his *Memoirs of Richard Cumberland Written by Himself* (1806–7). Sheridan caricatured him as Sir Fretful Plagiary in *The Critic*.

CUMING. The artist who made the drawings for Moore's translation of *Anacreon*.

CUNNINGHAM, Peter (1816–69). Scholar and editor; author of *Poems upon Several Occasions* (1841); *Inigo Jones. A Life of the Architect* (1848); *A Handbook for London* (1849). Cunningham also edited *Songs of England and Scotland* and other anthologies.

CURRAN, John Philpot (1750–1817). Irish orator and judge. Member of Irish Parliament (1783); a Protestant who championed Catholic emancipation; known chiefly for his defence of the leaders of the insurrection of 1798; acquitted of implication in Robert Emmet's insurrection of 1803.

CURTIS, Sir William (1752–1829). Lord Mayor of London and Member of Parliament. He was a staunch Tory, supporter of Pitt and of the war, which accounts for Moore's ironic allusion in letter No. 344. Curtis was long a subject of ridicule and was satirized by Peter Pindar in 'The Fat Knight and the Petition'.

DACRE, Barbarina Brand, Lady Dacre (1768–1854). Dramatist, author of *Ina* (1815); *Le Canzoni di Petrarca* (1815?); *Frogs and Bulls* (1838); and other dramas. At the time Moore wrote the epilogue for her tragedy *Ina* she was known simply as Mrs. Wilmot.

DALBY, the Reverend John (d. 1852), of Castle Donington, Leicestershire. Moore remained a close friend of Dalby and his sister Mary long after the poet had settled in Wiltshire.

DALBY, Mary. Sister of the Reverend John Dalby of Castle Donington.

DALTON, Edward T. An Irish musician who at one time competed with Sir John Stevenson for the task of arranging some of Moore's compositions. Dalton and Moore were friends of long standing, and Moore recorded in his diary his sorrow at learning of the musician's death (Russell, iii. 164–5).

DARUSMONT, Frances. *See* Wright, Frances.

DAVIES, Scrope Berdmore (1783–1852). Fellow of King's College, Cambridge, and friend of Byron, who once spoke of him as 'one of the cleverest men I ever knew, in conversation . . .'. Davies is supposed to have written his recollections of his friends, but the notes, if indeed they were ever written, have not survived. He was a popular member of fashionable society during the Regency.

DAVISON. A printer whom Murray engaged to print Moore's *Life of Byron*.

DAVY, Sir Humphrey (1778–1829). Professor of chemistry at the Royal Institution. Noted for work in chemistry and for invention of miner's safety-lamp. His collected works, prose and verse, were published, with a memoir by his brother, in 1839–40.

DAWSON. Moore refers frequently to the Dawsons in his diary. A good clue to his identity is in reference to an 'attack' which Dawson made upon one Shiel in a speech at Derry (Russell, v. 35). In other places he mentions George, William, and 'the Reverend' Dawson.

DE BATHE, Colonel William Plunkett. A Lieutenant-colonel on half pay, unattached.

DENNIE, Joseph (1768–1812). American editor. In New Hampshire he became the leader of a group of conservative Federalists and edited the *Farmer's Weekly Museum* (1796–8), for which he wrote *Lay Preacher Essays*. He also contributed satirical prose and poetry to various newspapers, founded the Tuesday Club in Philadelphia, and edited *The Port Folio* (1801–9), for which he wrote other *Lay Preacher Essays*.

DERING, Lady (d. 1830). Wife of Sir Edward, seventh Baron Dering.

DE ROOS. Son of Lord Henry Fitzgerald. His mother assumed the name De Roos in 1806 after the title 'Baron De Roos' had been in abeyance for more than a century.

DEVONSHIRE, Duchess of. Georgina (1757–1806), daughter of first Earl Spencer and wife of the fifth Duke of Devonshire. A reigning queen of London society, and friend of such men as Fox, Sheridan, and Dr. Johnson.

DEVONSHIRE, Duke of. *See* Cavendish, William.

DODD, Mrs. 'An elderly maiden lady' to whom Anastasia Moore sent her young son for instruction in etiquette.

DOLOMIEU, Marquise de. Wife of Marquis de Dolomieu (d. 1834). *Dame d'honneur* to Queen Amélie. She made one of the finest autograph collections in Paris.

DONEGAL, Lady Barbara (d. 1829). The daughter of the Reverend Luke Godfrey, D.D., and third wife of Arthur, first Marquess of Donegal. Moore met Lady Donegal and her sister Mary Godfrey before sailing for Bermuda in 1803, and they remained his life-long friends.

D'ORLÉANS, Louis Charles, Count de Beaujolois (1779–1808). Brother of Louis Philippe.

DOUGLAS, John Erskine. Commanding officer of the *Boston*, on which Moore sailed for England. He became Moore's close friend and in 1815, after he had reached the rank of Rear-admiral and been appointed to the Jamaica post, offered the poet a position as his secretary.

DOUGLAS, Sylvester, Baron Glenbervie (1743–1823). First Chief Commissioner of the United Land and Forest Department.

DOWLING, Matthew. An attorney who was later involved in the tragedy of Lord Edward Fitzgerald.

DOWNSHIRE, Lady, formerly Mary, Baroness Sandys (d. 1836). Wife of Arthur Hill, second Marquess of Downshire.

DOYLE, Andrew. Editor of the *Morning Chronicle*, 1843–8.

DOYLE, Carlo. A close friend of Moore during his early years. Mentioned (Russell, iii. 367) as being a member of the circle of friends which included Lords Forbes, Rancliffe, and Strangford.

DOYLE, Colonel Francis. One of Lady Byron's advisers. Urged the burning of Byron's Memoirs and was present when they were destroyed on 17 May 1824.

DOYLE, Sir John (1750?–1834). An Irish general who was with Lord Rawdon and Lord Fitzgerald in America during the Revolution.

DRAKARD, John (1775–1854). Started the *Stamford News* in 1809, and *Drakard's Paper* in London in 1813. The name of the latter was changed to the *Champion* in 1814 and to the *Investigator* in 1822.

DREW, Lucy. A friend of Moore while he was living in Paris, 1819–22 (*see* Russell, iii. 200, 213, and *passim*).

DRUMMOND, Thomas (1797–1840). Engineer and administrator. Entered Royal Engineers (1815); inventor of the 'Drummond Light', a limelight apparatus; Under-secretary of State for Ireland (1835–40).

DUDLEY, Earl of. *See* Ward, John William.

DUDLEY, Sir Henry Bate (1745–1824). Journalist, editor of the *Morning Post*, the son of Reverend Henry Bate. The son assumed the name Dudley in 1784, in compliance with the will of a relative of that name. After taking orders he succeeded his father as rector of North Tambridge. Most of his time, however, was spent in London where he became well known as a man of pleasure.

DUIGENAN, 'Paddy'. With Fitzgibbon on the tribunal which examined Moore and others concerning liberal activities and meetings at Trinity College. He was author of a number of pamphlets 'sounding the tocsin of persecution against the Catholics', as Moore says (Russell, i. 64).

DUNDONALD, Earl of. *See* Cochrane, Archibald.

DURAZZO, Madame. Descendant of a noble Genoese family.

DUNSANY, Baron. *See* Randall, Edward.

EASTHOPE, Sir John (1784–1865). Owner and publisher of the *Morning Chronicle* (1834–47).

EDEN, George, Baron Eden of Norwood and Earl of Aukland (1784–1849). Master of Mint and Treasurer of Board of Trade (1830); Privy

Councillor (1830); auditor of the Receipt of the Exchequer (1834); First Lord of the Admiralty (1834–5); Governor-general of India (1835–42); First Lord of the Admiralty (1846); President of the Senate, University of London.

ELDON, Earl of. *See* Scott, John.

ELLENBOROUGH, Baron. *See* Law, Edward.

ELLIS, George Agar (1797–1833). Writer and contributor to the *Quarterly Review*.

ERSKINE, Thomas, first Baron Erskine of Restormel (1750–1823). Brother to David Stewart Erskine, eleventh Earl of Buchan (1742–1829) and Henry Erskine (1746–1817). Thomas was a successful attorney, defending Captain Baillie, who was accused of libel. He also successfully defended Admiral Lord Keppel and Lord George Gordon, thereby demolishing the doctrine of constructive treason. Member of Parliament (1783); Attorney-general to Prince of Wales (1783); procured acquittals of Tom Paine, Frost, Hardy, and Horne Tooke; advocated Negro emancipation; defended Queen Caroline (1820); worked for cause of Greek Independence (1822–3).

ESSEX, Earl of. *See* Coningsby, George Capel-.

EWING, Dr. An early acquaintance of Byron when the poet lived in Aberdeen. Moore corresponded with him while he was writing his biography of Byron (*see* Russell, v. 221 and letter No. 762).

FABER, Tanaquil. Latin for Tannequi le Fèvre (1615–72). An eminent French scholar and critic. He published annotated editions of Lucretius, Longinus, Horace, and Virgil, as well as French translations of a number of Greek classics.

FANCOURT, Mrs. A fashionable leader in society. Moore was a frequent visitor in her home.

FELLOWES, Mrs. John. Moore visited the Fellowes family on his trip to Newstead in October, 1827. They had been acquainted with Byron and his mother, and Moore records that Mrs. Fellowes's son had a lameness similar to Byron's (Russell, v. 214; *see also* other entries in volume v).

FIELDING, Captain (later Admiral). Moore's neighbour and friend, who lived at Laycock Abbey. In 1804 he married Elizabeth Theresa, daughter of the second Earl of Ilchester. She was the sister of the Marchioness of Lansdowne.

FINDEN, W. An engraver who did an engraving of Moore after the portrait by Sir Thomas Lawrence.

FIRMINGER, Dr. The proprietor of a school to which Moore sent his son.

FITZGERALD, Augustus Frederick, third Duke of Leinster (1791–1874).

FITZGERALD, Lady Charlotte. Lord Moira's sister, who married Hamilton Fitzgerald in 1814.

FITZGERALD, Lord Edward (1763–98). Fifth son of first Duke of Leinster; served in American Revolution; wounded at Eutaw Springs (1781); Member of Irish Parliament; journeyed through Canada and United States to New Orleans, fraternizing with Indians; cashiered for attending revolutionary banquet in Paris, where he repudiated his own title (1792); joined United Irishmen (1796); accompanied Arthur O'Connor to Continent to negotiate for French invasion; captured and wounded, dying on 4 June 1798.

FITZGERALD, Maurice, Knight of Kerry (1772–1849). Privy Councillor; Member of Parliament for thirty-five years from Kerry; Commissioner of Customs; Lord of Treasury and Admiralty; Vice-treasurer of Ireland.

FITZGIBBON, John, second Earl of Clare (1792–1851). A school-fellow of Byron at Harrow. He succeeded to the earldom in 1802 and was Governor of Bombay (1830–4).

FITZHERBERT, Sir Henry. Probably the son of Alleyne Fitzherbert, Baron St. Helens (1753–1839).

FITZHERBERT, Lady. Wife of Alleyne Fitzherbert, Baron St. Helens (1753–1839). She was formerly Mary Meynell of Bradley, near Ashbourne.

FITZHERBERT, Maria Anne, *née* Smythe (1756–1837). First married Edward Weld (d. 1775); second marriage to Thomas Fitzherbert (d. 1781). She became the mistress of the Prince of Wales, whom she married in 1785. The marriage was declared illegal under the Royal Marriage Act, since the Prince was under age at the time and Mrs. Fitzherbert was a Roman Catholic. She continued to live with the Prince and was recognized by the Royal Family until 1803, and maintained relations with him for a while after his marriage to Princess Caroline of Brunswick.

FITZSIMON, Christopher (1793–1856). Deputy-lieutenant and Justice of the Peace for Counties Dublin and Wicklow; Member of Parliament for County Dublin (1835–7); Clerk of the Crown and Hanaper; Treasurer to the Lord Chancellor's Office. In 1825 he married Ellen Caroline O'Connell, daughter of Daniel O'Connell. Moore was a friend of the Fitzsimons, and stayed at their home on various occasions.

FLECHIA, Giovanni. An Italian writer who had an interest in Oriental subjects; hence his translations of part of Moore's *Lalla Rookh*.

FLETCHER, William. Byron's valet.

FOLEY, Thomas, third Baron Foley (1780–1869).

FONBLANQUE, Albany (1793–1872). Journalist. First contributor to and later editor (1830–47) of the *Examiner*. He was also a statistical officer in the Board of Trade (1847).

FONTENELLE, Bernard Le Bovier de (1657–1757). A French author who wrote *Dialogues of the Dead* (1683) and *Essay on the Geometry of the Infinite* (1727), two of his most famous works.

FORBES, Lady Adelaide (1789–1858). Daughter of George, sixth Earl of Granard and his wife, Lady Selina Rawdon, daughter of the first Earl of Moira. Lady Adelaide died in Dresden, unmarried.

FORBES, George, sixth Earl of Granard in the peerage of Ireland, and first Baron Granard in the United Kingdom (1760–1837).

FOSTER, John Leslie (d. 1842). Irish politician and Member of Parliament whom Moore had first known in Dublin before going to England.

Fox, Sir Charles (1810–74). Engineer. Constructing engineer of the London and Birmingham Railway; introduced the switch into railway use.

Fox, Henry Richard Vassall, third Baron Holland (1773–1840). Whig in the House of Lords; Lord Privy Seal (1806–7); Chancellor of Duchy of Lancaster (1830–4, 1835–40). Throughout his career he championed liberal and humane causes, such as mitigation of the severity of the criminal code, and abolition of the death penalty for stealing. He also supported abolition of the slave trade. Author of biographies of Lope de Vega, and of his uncle, Charles James Fox.

Fox, James (1749–1806). Foreign Secretary at the time Moore's father was appointed Barrack-master in Dublin (May 1806).

Gallois. A Frenchman with whom Moore became acquainted in Paris (1819–22). Gallois liberally opened his library for Moore's use (*see* Russell, iii. *passim*).

Gardiner, William (1770–1853). Musician. Best known for his publications of popular works on music and for the *Sacred Melodies from Haydn, Mozart, and Beethoven . . . Adapted to the Best English Poets* (1812–15). He also published *The Music of Nature* (1832).

Garrow, Sir William (1760–1840). Baron of the Exchequer. Student at Lincoln's Inn (1778); called to the Bar (1783); appointed King's Counsel in Hilary Term (1793); Member of Parliament for Gatton (1805); Solicitor-general (1812); knighted (1812); Attorney-general (1813); Baron of Exchequer (1817–32).

Gifford, William (1756–1826). Critic, poet, and first editor of the *Quarterly Review* (1809–24). Edited the works of Juvenal, Massinger, Jonson, and Ford.

Gillespie, Mr. A business associate of Moore's father.

Gisborne, Thomas (1758–1846). Curate of Barton-under-Needwood, who lived at Yoxall Lodge. Gisborne wrote nature poetry modelled chiefly upon Cowper. He was the elder brother of John Gisborne, poet and husband of Maria.

Gisborne, Thomas (1794–1852). Son of Thomas Gisborne, the poet.

Glenbervie, Baron. *See* Douglas, Sylvester.

Glennie, Dr. In 1799 Byron attended Dr. Glennie's school, which was located in a residential suburb of Dulwich, about seven miles from London.

Godfrey, Mary and Phillipa. Sisters of Lady Barbara Donegal.

Godwin, William (1756–1836). Writer, author of *Caleb Williams, Political Justice*, and other novels and political works. Husband of Mary Wollstonecraft and father of Mary Shelley.

Gordon, George Hamilton, fourth Earl of Aberdeen (1784–1860). Statesman. Succeeded grandfather to title in 1801; British Foreign Secretary (1828–30 and 1841–6); established friendly relations with France and with United States by Ashburton and Oregon treaties; headed coalition ministry (1852); was forced into Crimean War; resigned in 1855 upon vote of censure on mismanagement of war.

Granard, Earl of. *See* Forbes, George.

GRANVILLE, Earl of. *See* Leveson-Gower, Granville.

GRATTAN, Henry (1746–1820). Irish orator. Member of the Irish Parliament (1775–97, and 1800), and of the British Parliament (1805–20). Spoke and worked for Irish independence and Catholic emancipation; opposed union with England (1800).

GRENVILLE, Thomas (1755–1846). Served as a diplomat in America, Austria, and Germany. First Lord of Admiralty. A bibliophile whose bequest to the British Museum contained the first folio of Shakespeare's works. Moore recorded in his diary that he had letters from Sheridan to Grenville but on the advice of Rogers did not intend to print the extracts he had made from them (*see* Russell, ii. 189–96).

GRÉTRY, André Earnest (1741–1813). French composer. In addition to his numerous musical compositions, Grétry left some literary works, among which was *Mémoires ou Essais sur la musique* (1789). The work appeared in three volumes in 1797. In 1802 he published a pretentious three-volume work entitled *De la Verité*, which dealt with his political and social philosophies and how best to express them in music.

GREVILLE, Colonel Harry. Manager of the Argyle Institution. Byron satirized him in *English Bards* (ll. 638–67). A note to the passage refers to the loss of several thousand pounds sustained by one Billy Way in the rooms of the Institution. Greville demanded satisfaction. Byron sent Gould Francis Leckie, Greville's representative, to Moore and wrote to the latter explaining the manner in which he wanted the affair handled (*LJ*, ii. 109). Byron noted that no inference of foul play was made in the passage cited and that 'if the business can be settled amicably Lord B. will do as much as can and ought to be done by a man of honour towards conciliation'.

GREY, Charles, second Earl Grey, Viscount Howick and Baron Grey (1764–1845). Statesman who held the same liberal views as Lords Russell and Lansdowne.

GRIERSONS. The Grierson family were friends whom Moore visited frequently in Dublin. Grierson was the King's Printer in that city.

GUTHERIE, Mr. and Mrs. Moore's friends who lived near Sloperton and Bowood. Gutherie was Lord Kerry's tutor.

HALHED, Nathaniel Brassey (1751–1830). Orientalist in service of the East India Company. Reputedly the first to call attention to the philological affinity between Sanskrit words and words in Persian, Arabic, Greek and Latin. Translated *Aristaenetus* with Sheridan.

HALL, Captain Basil (1788–1844). Writer. Author of travel books, such as *Extracts from a Journal Written on the Coasts of Chili, Peru, and Mexico . . . 1820, 1821, 1822* (Edinburgh, 1823), 2 vols., and *Hall's Voyages* (Edinburgh, 1826–7), 3 vols. He furnished Moore with a statement disputing the accusation that Byron was inhospitable to his own countrymen while abroad (Moore, *Byron*, iv. 129–32).

HALL, Bond. A friend of Moore at Trinity College, Dublin. Moore speaks favourably of the influence which Hall and Beresford Burston exerted on him during their college days (*see* Russell, i. 49).

HALL, John Elihu (1783–1829). Lawyer and editor. Publisher of the *American Law Journal* (1808–17); author of *The Practice and Jurisdiction of the Court of Admiralty* (1809) and *Tracts on Constitutional Law, Containing Mr. Livingston's Answer to Mr. Jefferson* (1813). Editor of Joseph Dennie's *Lay Preacher Essays* (1817).

HALL, Robert (1764–1831). A prominent minister and theologian. Published *Christianity Consistent with the Love of Freedom* (1791); *Apology for the Freedom of the Press with Remarks on Harsley's Sermon, 30 Jan. 1793* (1793); and *Modern Infidelity Considered in Respect to its Influence on Society* (1800). His works were edited by O. Gregory in 6 vols. (1832–8).

HALL, Samuel Carter (1800–89). Editor and writer. Founder and editor of the *Amulet* (1826–37); *Art Union Monthly*, later *Art Journal* (1839–80); published *Book of British Ballads* (1842), and *Gallery of Modern Sculpture* (1849–54). His wife, Anna Maria *née* Fielding (1800–81), collaborated with him and wrote nine novels herself including *Marian, or a Young Maid's Fortune* (1840), and *Midsummer Eve, a Fairy Tale of Love* (1848).

HALLAM, Henry (1777–1859). Historian; for many years Commissioner of Stamps; retired in 1812 to devote time to historical study. Author of *State of Europe during the Middle Ages* (1818); *Constitutional History of England from Henry VII's Accession to the Death of George II* (1827); and *Introduction to the Literature of Europe* (1837–9). His son Arthur (1811–33) is the subject of Tennyson's *In Memoriam*.

HAMILTON, Colonel John. An Irishman who had come to America (1767), fought for six weeks (evidently under compulsion) with the American forces in the Revolution, later saw action with the British, was taken prisoner, and exchanged. At the time Moore knew him he was the British Consul at Norfolk.

HAMMERSLEY. A banker of Moore's acquaintance, with whom he negotiated in several financial matters. Hammersley was also Byron's banker (*see* Russell, iii. 4; v. 251 and *passim*; *see also* Marchand, *Byron*, 246 n).

HANCOCK, Charles. A merchant, with whom Byron was associated while on the expedition to Greece.

HANSON, John. Byron's lawyer and friend.

HARDWICK, Earl of. *See* Yorke, Philip.

HARLEY, Lady Jane and Charlotte, daughters of Lady Oxford. It was to Lady Charlotte Harley, under the name of 'Ianthe', that Byron addressed the five stanzas which prefaced the seventh edition of *Childe Harold*.

HARNESS, Reverend William (1790–1869). A friend of Byron. Harness wrote a biography of Shakespeare (1825), 8 vols., and edited Shakespeare's works.

HARRINGTON, Earl of. *See* Stanhope, Charles.

HARRINGTON, Lady, wife of Charles Stanhope, fourth Earl of Harrington and Viscount Petersham. She was formerly Maria Foote, actress. Acted at Covent Garden as Amanthis in *Child of Nature* (1814), and played at Covent Garden until 1825, when she moved to Drury Lane. Married Stanhope (1831).

HARROWBY, Earl of. *See* Ryder, Dudley.

HASTINGS, Sir Charles. Cousin of Francis Rawdon-Hastings, Earl of Moira.

HASTINGS, Francis Rawdon-, first Marquess of Hastings and (in Irish peerage) second Earl of Moira (1754–1826). Soldier and Governor-general of Bengal. His support of the Prince of Wales in the Regency question earned him the disfavour of his Whig friends and eventually resulted in his being sent to India. He established British supremacy in central India, purchased the island of Singapore (1819), and in 1824 was made Governor of Malta. Moore looked to him for patronage but was disappointed in his hopes.

HASTINGS, Lady. Either the wife of Sir Charles Hastings, Lord Moira's cousin, or of Sir Jacob Henry Astley, fifth Baronet Hastings (1756–1817).

HAYDON, Benjamin Robert (1786–1846). English historical painter. Author of *Lectures on Painting and Design* (1844–6), and an autobiography edited by Tom Taylor (1853). One of the few who recognized that the Elgin Marbles were of first-class merit and was instrumental in getting the government to purchase them.

HAYLEY, William (1745–1820). Poet. Author of *Triumphs of Temper* (1781); *Triumphs of Music* (1804); and *Ballads Founded on Anecdotes of Animals* (1805).

HAYWARD, Abraham (1801–84). Writer. Author of *Faust* (1833), a prose translation of Goethe's poetic drama; *The Statutes Founded on the Common Law Reports* (1832); *Some Accounts of a Journey across the Alps in a Letter to a Friend* (1834); *The Life and Writings of Mrs. Piozzi* (Mrs. Thrale) (1861), 2 vols. Hayward also published several volumes of essays and a book on Goethe (1877).

HEADFORT, Marchioness of (d. 1834). Wife of Thomas Taylor, Marquess of Headfort. She was Olivia, second daughter of Sir John Stevenson.

HELY-HUTCHINSON, John, second Baron Hutchinson, afterwards second Earl of Donoughmore (1757–1832). Army general, who was educated at Eton and Trinity College, Dublin. He was a lieutenant-colonel in the 77th Athole, a regiment of Highlanders which served some years in Ireland and mutinied when ordered to India in 1783. At the outbreak of the French Revolution, Hutchinson was in Strassbourg, gained access to the French army camp, and was with the French when La Fayette was forced to fly from his troops (1792). In 1793 Hutchinson joined the Duke of York's army as a volunteer.

HEMANS, Felicia Dorothea, *née* Browne (1793–1835). Poetess and collector of songs. *The Domestic Affections, and Other Poems* (1812), *Welsh Melodies* (1822), and *Lays of Many Lands* (1825) are among her important works.

HERBERT, Algernon (1792–1855). Antiquary, sixth son of Henry Herbert, Earl of Carnarvon (d. 1811).

HERBERT, Edward, second Earl of Powis (1785–1848). Active in suppression of Chartist Riots of 1839; led in defeat of scheme for creating bishopric of Manchester, winning thereby gratitude of clergy and universities.

HERBERT, Henry George, second Earl of Carnarvon (1772–1833).

HERBERT, Henry John George, third Earl of Carnarvon (1800–49). Traveller in Barbary, Spain, Portugal, and Greece. Author of *Don Pedro*, a tragedy acted by Macready and Ellen Tree (1828).

HERBERT, James D. An actor and friend of the Moore family in Dublin. Author of *Irish Varieties*.

HEYNE, Christian Gottlob (1729–1812). A German classical philologist at Göttingen. Edited the works of Virgil (1767–75), 4 vols.

HILL. A friend with whom Moore was associated during his Paris residence (1820–1).

HOBHOUSE, John Cam, Baron Broughton de Gyfford (1786–1869). Member of Parliament and liberal pamphleteer. Friend of Byron. Secretary of War (1832–3); Chief Secretary for Ireland (1833); President, Board of Control (1835–41; 1846–52); author of *Recollections of a Long Life* (1865).

HODGSON, Francis (1781–1852). Fellow of King's College, Cambridge (1802). For three years a private tutor; for one (1806) a master at Eton; resident tutor at King's (1807); took orders (1812); Archdeacon of Derby (1836); Provost of Eton (1840). Among his published works are *Translations of Juvenal* (1807); *Lady Jane Grey, a Tale; and other Poems* (1809); *Sir Edgar a Tale* (1810); *Leaves of Laurel* (1812); *The Friends, a Poem in Four Books*; and *Mythology for Versification* (1831). With S. Butler he translated Lucien Bonaparte's *Charlemagne* into English. For an account of the relationship between Byron and Hodgson see *LJ*, i. 196.

HOHENLOHE, Alexander Leopold, Prince of Hohenlohe-Waldenburg-Schillingsfürst (1794–1849). A German Roman Catholic priest; born at Kupferzell, near Waldenburg, near Württemburg; ordained (1815); member of the society of 'Fathers of the Sacred Heart'; became known in Munich and Bamberg as a miracle-worker. He was canon of Oradea (1824) and titular Bishop of Sardica (1844).

HOLLAND, Baron. *See* Fox, Henry Richard Vassall.

HOLLAND, Lady (1770–1845). Wife of Henry Fox, third Baron Holland. *Née* Elizabeth Vassall. Born in Jamaica. Was divorced in 1797 by Sir Godfrey Webster for adultery with Lord Holland. Beautiful and vivacious hostess at Holland House, the centre of a brilliant circle of wits and statesmen. Sent messages and books to Napoleon, who bequeathed her a gold snuff-box given him by Pius VI. Satirized by Byron in *English Bards* (l. 1046).

HOLMES, William (d. 1851). 'Billy Holmes' mentioned in the diary (Russell, vi. 332). He was born in County Sligo and in 1795 was graduated from Trinity College, Dublin, where Moore must have known him. Except for a short period (1832–7) he was a Member of Parliament (1808–41) and for many years was the Tory Whip.

HOPE, Thomas (1770?–1831). English antiquarian and writer; collector of marbles and sculptures; patron of Canova, Thorvaldsen, and Flaxman.

Hopkinson, Joseph (1770–1842). Son of Francis Hopkinson. The son practiced law in Philadelphia, was a Member of the House of Representatives (1815–19), and a judge of the U.S. district court of the eastern district of Pennsylvania (1828–42). Moore alludes to Mrs. Hopkinson in the poem 'Alone by the Schuylkill'.

Hopkinson, Mrs. The wife of Joseph Hopkinson. She was formerly Emily Mifflin, daughter of the first governor of Pennsylvania.

Hoppner, Richard Belgrave (1786–1872). Originally intended to be an artist. Published a translation from the German of A. J. von Krusenstern's *Voyage Round the World in the Years 1803–1806* (1805); appointed British Consul in Venice (1814); friend of Byron and Shelley in Italy.

Horner, Francis (1778–1817). Politician. Member of Parliament, 1806 to his death. He contributed articles to the *Edinburgh Review* and was Jeffrey's second in the duel with Moore.

Houghton, Baron. *See* Milnes, Richard Monckton.

Houlton, Colonel. Moore's friend who lived at Farleigh Castle, Wiltshire, near Moore's home.

Houlton, Mrs. Wife of Colonel Houlton of Farleigh Castle.

Howard, Frederick, fifth Earl of Carlisle and Viscount Morpeth (1748–1825). Sent by Lord North to attempt reconciliation with American Colonies (1778); Viceroy of India (1780–2); sided with Prince of Wales on Regency question; grandson of fourth Lord Byron and guardian of Lord Byron the poet, who attacked him in *English Bards* for his refusal to introduce his ward in House of Lords; wrote tragedies *The Father's Revenge* (1783), and *The Stepmother* (1800).

Howard, George, sixth Earl of Carlisle and Viscount Morpeth (1773–1848). Member of Parliament from Cumberland; Commissioner for Affairs of India in All-the-Talents Administration (1806–7); held positions in cabinets of Canning and Grey.

Hudson, Edward (1772–1833). A friend of Moore at Trinity College, Dublin, where they were associated in patriotic meetings and debating societies. Hudson became a member of the 'Emmet conspiracy', was arrested, spent several years in prison, was exiled to Holland, and in 1803 made his way to the United States. In April 1804 he married Maria Bridget Byrne and went into the stationery and bookselling business with her father. Failing in this venture, he returned to his former profession of dentistry. He worked out some techniques which had great influence on dentistry in the early stages of its development.

Hughes, Mary. Probably the daughter of Hughes of Locke and Hughes, bankers in Devizes. She was a frequent visitor at Sloperton and a great help to Bessy Moore on several trying occasions.

Hughes, Polly. A relative of Hughes of Locke and Hughes, bankers in Devizes. She was from Buckhill.

Hughes, Susan. A friend and neighbour in Wiltshire. It was she who brought Moore the news of his sister Ellen's death (*see* Russell, viii. 13).

Hume, Dr. Thomas. Moore's friend in London, who gave him encouragement and aid in the preparation and publication of the *Odes of*

Anacreon. He later represented Moore in the latter's duel with Jeffrey (1806).

HUNT, Henry (1773–1835). A radical politician, who was sometimes called 'Orator Hunt'. He was an unsuccessful candidate for Parliament for Bristol (1812) and was later imprisoned for exciting the populace to riot at the time of the Peterloo Massacre.

HUNT, James Henry Leigh (1784–1859). Essayist and poet. Editor of the *Examiner* (1808 ff.) and the *Reflector* (1810); founder, with Byron and Shelley, of the *Liberal* (1822–3).

HUSKISSON, William (1770–1830). Financier and statesman. Member of Parliament (1796–1802; 1804–30); Secretary of Treasury (1804–5; 1807–9); President of Board of Trade and Treasurer of Navy (1823–7); Colonial Secretary and leader of the House of Commons (1827–8).

INCLEDON, Charles (1763–1826). A singer who made his greatest impression by singing ballads in such musicals as *The Beggar's Opera*.

IRVING, Washington (1783–1859). Well-known American writer. Author of many novels and short stories, including *The Sketch Book* (1820) and *Bracebridge Hall* (1822).

JACKSON, John (1778–1831). English portrait-painter.

JEFFREY, Francis, Lord (1773–1850). Scottish critic and jurist. One of the founders of the *Edinburgh Review* (1802) and its editor (1803–29). Judge of the Court of Sessions (1834–50).

JENKINSON, Robert Banks (1770–1828). Second Earl of Liverpool; M.P. (1790); member of India Board (1794–1801); Master of Mint (1799). As Foreign Secretary under Addington he negotiated the abortive treaty of Amiens with Napoleon. Home Secretary and leader in the House of Lords (1804–6); Prime Minister in the Tory ministry (1812–27). He suffered a stroke in February 1827 and died on 4 December 1828.

JERSEY, Earl of. *See* Villiers, George Child.

JERSEY, Lady. Wife of George Bussy Villiers (1735–1805), fourth Earl of Jersey and seventh Viscount Grandison; the so-called 'Prince of Macaronis' at the court of George III.

JOHNSTONE, John Henry (1749–1828). 'Irish Johnstone', an actor and singer, who had his greatest success as a tenor at Covent Garden from 1783 to 1803. He was particularly gifted in portraying Irish parts; hence his nickname.

JONES, George. The artist who illustrated the 1840–1 edition of Moore's works.

KEAN, Edmund (1787–1833). Actor, noted for his portrayal of Shylock, Hamlet, Iago, Lear, Macbeth, Othello, and Richard III.

KELLY, Michael (1762–1826). Tenor and stage composer, who wrote the music for *The Gipsy Prince*. Although Moore's opinion of him was not very high, Kelly did attain considerable success as a musician. He was engaged to sing at the court theatre in Vienna (no mean achievement), where he was intimately associated with Mozart, who assigned to him (spelling his name 'Occhely') the roles of Basilio and Don Curzio in the first performance of *The Marriage of Figaro*. Kelly's *Reminiscences* (1826), written by Theodore Hook from materials furnished by Kelly, while not always reliable for dates, are important for their personal notices of Mozart.

KEMBLE, Charles (1775–1854). Actor, famous for Shakespearian roles at Covent Garden.

KENNEY, James (1780–1849). Dramatist, author of *Raising the Wind*, *Sweethearts and Wives*, and *False Alarms*. Moore spelled the name 'Kenny'.

KERRY, Knight of. *See* Fitzgerald, Maurice.

KING, Peter, seventh Baron King of Ockham, Surrey (1776–1833). A staunch supporter of liberal measures in the House of Lords. In addition to several pamphlets on political matters, he published *The Life of John Locke* in 1829. In 1804 he married Lady Hester Fortescue, daughter of Hugh, first Earl Fortescue.

KINNAIRD, Charles, eighth Baron Kinnaird (1780–1826). Member of Parliament (1802–5); succeeded his father to baronetcy (1805); lived much of his life on the Continent; after second restoration of Bourbons, was expelled from Paris in 1816.

KINNAIRD, Douglas James William (1788–1830). Fifth son of the seventh Baron Kinnaird. Educated at Eton, Göttingen, and Trinity College, Cambridge. Friend of Hobhouse and Byron. Member of Parliament for Bishop's Castle (1819–20); lost his seat in the general election and did not again enter Parliament; partner in the bank of Ransom and Morland; a member of the committee for managing Drury Lane Theatre; author of the acting version of *The Merchant of Bruges, or Beggar's Bush*, which was performed at Drury Lane on 14 December 1815.

KYLE, Dr. Provost of Trinity College, Dublin, while Moore was in residence there.

LAKE, J. W. A scholar and translator, whose 'Notices of the Life of Lord Byron' prefaced the 1822 Paris edition of Byron's works. He also edited Moore's works in 1827.

LAMB, Lady Caroline (1785–1828). Daughter of Frederick Ponsonby, third Earl of Bessborough, and wife of William Lamb, second Viscount Melbourne. Notorious for her infatuation with Byron. Author of *Glenarvon* (1816); *Graham Hamilton* (1822); and *Ada Reis* (1823).

LAMB, William, second Viscount Melbourne (1779–1848). Statesman. Whig Member of Parliament (1806); supported Catholic emancipation; lost seat in 1812; Irish Secretary (1827, 1828); Home Secretary under Grey (1830–4); Prime Minister for a few months (1834), and again (1835–41). Husband of Lady Caroline Lamb.

LANSDOWNE, Marquess of. *See* Petty-Fitzmaurice, Henry.

LARDNER, Dionysius (1793–1859). Irish writer of science. Wrote scientific treatises on mathematics. Compiled the *Cabinet Cyclopaedia*.

LAUDERDALE, Earl of. *See* Maitland, James.

LAW, Edward, first Baron Ellenborough (1750–1818). Lord Chief Justice of the King's Bench (1802–18). In 1788 he was chosen as leading counsel for Warren Hastings. He accepted a seat in the cabinet of All-the-Talents Administration, retaining Chief Justiceship. He was a forceful speaker but in the House of Lords often used intemperate language.

LAWRENCE, Dr. The classical scholar to whom Moore submitted his translation of Anacreon for an opinion. For Dr. Lawrence's criticism *see* letter No. 21.

LAWRENCE, Miss. A friend of Bessy Moore and a frequent visitor in the Moore household.

LAWRENCE, Sir Thomas (1769–1830). English painter of such portraits as that of the Countess of Derby (1790) and George III (1792). Principal painter to the King in succession to Reynolds. Painted Moore's portrait in 1829 and J. P. Kemble's as Hamlet.

LECKIE, Gould Francis. Writer. Author of *Practice of the British Government* (1812), which was characterized by Jeffrey in the *Edinburgh Review* as 'The most direct attack . . . in England upon the free constitution of England, or rather upon the political liberty in general'. It was satirized by Moore in the second letter of the *Post Bag*, purportedly addressed to the author by the Regent's favourite Colonel McMahon. McMahon, of course, praises Leckie for his book.

LEFANU, Alicia. Poetess and writer. Niece of Richard Brinsley Sheridan. Published *Memoirs of Mrs. Frances Sheridan, with Remarks upon a Late Life of R. B. Sheridan* (1824). (The 'Late Life' was by Watson.)

LEFANU, Mrs. Richard Brinsley Sheridan's sister.

LEFANU, Thomas. The nephew of Richard Brinsley Sheridan.

LEGH, Peter. Moore's friend in Dublin who assumed much of the responsibility for funeral arrangements at the death of Moore's father.

LEINSTER, Duke of. *See* Fitzgerald, Augustus Frederick.

LEITH, Sir John James (1788–1843). Rear-admiral, son of General Alexander Leith-Hay, of Rannes and Leith Hall.

LEVESON-GOWER, George Granville, first Duke of Sutherland (1758–1833).

LEVESON-GOWER, Granville, first Earl Granville (1773–1846).

LEWIS, Frankland. A friend of Moore who was often a visitor at Bowood, where Moore became acquainted with him (*see* Russell, ii. 193–4, and *passim*).

LEWIS, Matthew Gregory (1775–1818). Novelist, dramatist, and poet. Friend of Byron and Moore. Author of *Ambrosio, or the Monk* (1796), and producer of *The Castle Spectre* at Drury Lane (1798). Other works include *The Bravo of Venice, Tales of Terror* (1799); *Tales of Wonder* (1801); and the ballad *Alonzo the Brave and the Fair Imogen*. He was also attaché at The Hague in 1794.

LINLEY, William (1771–1835). The son of the composer Thomas Linley. The son was also an author and composer. His sister, Elizabeth Ann, was Richard Brinsley Sheridan's wife.

LINWOOD, Miss. The only reference which gives a clue to her identity is in the diary (Russell, iv. 85) where Moore says he went to 'Miss Linwood's exhibition'.

LIVERPOOL, Earl of. *See* Jenkinson, Robert Banks.

LOCKHART, John Gibson (1794–1854). Scottish editor and novelist. Son-in-law of Sir Walter Scott, whose biography he wrote and published (1837–8), 7 vols. Among his other works are *Valerius* (1821); *Adam Blair* (1822); and *Reginald Dalton* (1823). Editor of the *Quarterly Review* (1825–53).

LONGMAN, Thomas Norton (1771–1842). Publisher, who brought out works of Wordsworth, Coleridge, Southey, and Scott, as well as those of Moore. He brought Owen Rees into the firm.

LOUDOUN, Lady. Wife of the Earl of Moira. She was before her marriage Lady Flora Mure Campbell, Countess of Loudoun in her own right.

LOWE, Sir Hudson (1769–1844). Lieutenant-general. Governor of St. Helena (1815–21). Although by nature a humane person, his lack of tact and pedantic attention to details created ill-will between him and his exile, Napoleon.

LUTTRELL, Henry (1765?–1851). Writer. Author of *Advice to Julia* (1820); *Letters to Julia in Rhyme* (1822); and *Crockford House, a Rhapsody* (1827). Friend of Byron and Moore.

MACKENZIE, Henry (1745–1831). Scottish novelist. Author of *The Man of Feeling* (1771); *The Man of the World* (1773); and *Julia de Roubigné* (1777).

MACKINTOSH, Sir James (1765–1832). Scottish philosopher and historian. Recorder of Bombay (1804–6); Judge in the Admiralty Court, Bombay (1806–11); M.P. (1813); Professor of Law, Haileybury College (1818–24); Commissioner of Board of Control for India (1830). Author of *Dissertation on the Progress of Ethical Philosophy* (1830); *The History of England* (in Lardner's *Cabinet Cyclopaedia*); and a fragmentary *History of the Revolution in England in 1688* (posthumously published in 1834).

McMAHON. A Dublin apothecary who had come to London before Moore arrived there. Mrs. McMahon offered to lend Moore money to pay his fees at the Middle Temple. He did not accept the offer, but recorded the event in his *Memoirs* (*see* Russell, i. 74).

MACREADY, William Charles (1793–1873). English actor. Gained prominence by his Richard III (1819); associated first with Covent Garden, then Drury Lane; played successfully in America (1826), and Paris (1828); manager of Covent Garden (1837–9); manager of Drury Lane (1841–3). He last performed at Drury Lane as Macbeth (1851). Chief roles Macbeth, Cassius, Lear, Henry IV, and Iago.

MACRONE. A publisher who, in July 1836, proposed that he be allowed to bring out an edition of Moore's works. Moore's reply was that if Macrone could surmount the difficulties of procuring copyright privileges from the Longmans and Power, he would be pleased to attempt such a project. Macrone did not carry out the plan.

MADDEN, Dr. R. R. (1798–1886). Irish historian and biographer of Lady Blessington.

MAHON, Viscount. Courtesy title of the eldest living son of the Earls Stanhope. Moore was probably acquainted with Philip Henry Stanhope (1805–75), fifth Earl, who was better known by the courtesy title.

MAITLAND, James, eighth Earl of Lauderdale (1759–1839). Member of Parliament (1780–9); Scottish Representative Peer (1790); created Baron Lauderdale of Thirlestane, peerage of Great Britain and Ireland (1806); Lord High Keeper of Great Seal of Scotland (1806); shifted to Tory principles (1821); voted against Reform Act (1832); author of *Inquiry into the Nature and Origin of Public Wealth* (1804), and *The Depreciation of the Paper-currency of Great Britain Proved* (1812).

MANNERS, Lord Robert William (1781–1835). Third son of the fourth Duke of Rutland.

MANNERS-SUTTON, Mrs. The wife of Charles Manners-Sutton (1780–1845), who was Speaker of the House of Commons (1817–35). He was later made first Viscount Canterbury.

MARDYN, Mrs. An actress who achieved success on the Dublin stage and who acted first at Drury Lane on 26 September 1815, in *Loves' Vows*.

MARSH. A friend of Lords Lansdowne, Russell, Holland, and Moira. *See* the diary (Russell, vi. 36 and 314), where an account of his being arrested as a spy is given.

MASON, W. (fl. 1810). A printer with whom Moore had some business dealings. Mason wrote *The Printer's Assistant* (1810), and *The Printer's Price Book for Job Work in General* (1816).

MASTERSON, Mr. and Mrs., of Manchester Street, Manchester Square. Not much is known of the Mastersons except that they were friends of the Moore family and hence took an interest in young Tom when he arrived in London.

MASTERSON, Sally. The daughter of Mr. and Mrs. Masterson who befriended Moore on his first trip to London. She was a close friend of Moore's sister Catherine.

MATCHETTS. Friends and neighbours of the Dalbys and Moores at Ashbourne.

MATURIN, Charles (1782–1824). Dramatist and novelist. Author of *The Wild Irish Boy* (1808); *Bertram, a Tragedy* (1816); *Melmoth the Wanderer* (1820); and other works of mystery and terror.

MATURIN, Edward (1812–81). Teacher and writer, the son of Charles Maturin. He settled first in South Carolina and later in New York City.

MEATH, Earl of. *See* Barbazon, John Ghambre.

MELBOURNE, Viscount. *See* Lamb, William.

MEREDITH, Samuel (1741–1817). Financier of Philadelphia. Supported the revolution, serving as an officer in the Revolutionary War; served in Pennsylvania Colonial Assembly (1778–9; 1781–3); elected to the Congress of the Confederation (1781–6); first Treasurer of the

United States. It is conjectured that Moore met him through Joseph Dennie.

MEREWEATHER, Henry Alworth (1780–1864). Serjeant-at-law of Calne, Wiltshire. Called to the Bar (1809); created serjeant-at-law (1827); King's Counsel with patent of precedence (1853); D.C.L., Oxford (1839).

MEREWEATHER, Mrs. Wife of Henry Alworth Mereweather, serjeant-at-law, Calne, Wiltshire.

MERIVALE, John Herman (1779–1844). Poet and translator of poetry. His *Poems Original and Translated* appeared (1828–38) in 2 vols. He furnished Moore with material for the *Life of Byron*.

MERRY, Mr. and Mrs. Anthony. A newly wedded couple, who were on their way to Washington in 1803. Moore met them before sailing, and they became close friends during the voyage. Merry introduced Moore to Jefferson, whom the poet professed not to like. In their dislike of Jefferson's administration, the Merrys opened their drawing room to the Federalists, and when Moore arrived, found a ready listener to their condemnation of 'republicanism'. For an account of the Merry's life in Washington see Henry Adams, *History of the United States during the Administration of Thomas Jefferson*, book ii, chap. xvii.

METHUEN, Paul (1779–1849). Raised to the peerage in 1838 as Baron Methuen of Corsham. He was for many years Moore's neighbour at Calne, Wiltshire, and according to Moore 'the author of all those [squibs] about the Rat Club' in the *Morning Chronicle*. He was the father of Paul Sanfor Methuen, who was later Governor of Natal and Malta.

MILLIKEN, Richard. Moore mentions Milliken only once in the diary (Russell, vii. 98), where he recorded that Milliken had received fifty copies of the *Fudge Family in Paris*, and had already sold them all.

MILLS, Mrs. Probably the wife of Dr. Mills who attended Moore's father (*see* Russell, v. 26, and letter No. 190).

MILMAN, Henry Hart (1791–1868). Poet and historian. Author of the tragedy *Fazio* (1815), the epic poem *Samor* (1818), and hymns and translations from the classics. Professor of Poetry, Oxford (1821–31); Dean of St. Paul's (1829). Wrote historical works: *History of the Jews* (1830); *History of Christianity under the Empire* (1840); and *History of Latin Christianity* (1854–5), 6 vols.

MILMAN, Mrs. The wife of Henry Hart Milman.

MILNES, Richard Monckton, first Baron Houghton (1809–85). Poet and politician. Member of Parliament (1837); created baron (1863); championed oppressed nationalities and slaves. Author of *The Brookside*; *The Beating of My Own Heart*; *Strangers Yet*; and a *Life of Keats* (1848).

MITCHELL, Sir Andrew (1757–1806). Admiral, who at the time of Moore's visit to America was Commander-in-chief on the North American station. He died in Bermuda on 26 February 1806.

MITCHELL, Thomas (1783–1845). A classical scholar who contributed a series of articles to the *Quarterly Review* in 1813 on Aristophanes' comedies.

MOIRA, Earl of. *See* Hastings, Francis Rawdon-.

MONEY, Mr. A friend whom Moore often visited and with whom he was in company at dinner parties (*see* Russell, ii. 174, and *passim*).

MOORE, Charles. A close friend of Moore and Bessy.

MOORE, Sir John (1761–1809). British general; served in America (1779–83), and in the West Indies, Ireland, and Holland. Commander-in-chief in Portugal, ordered to occupy Madrid, found Napoleon's army already there, made retreat, attacked by Soult, defeated the French, but was mortally wounded (16 January 1809). The subject of a biography by his brother James Carrick Moore.

MOORE, Peter (1753–1828). An expert on Indian affairs who was able to supply important material to Burke and Sheridan for their attack on Warren Hastings.

MORAN, E. R. Editor of the *Globe*.

MORGAN, Sir Thomas Charles (1783–1843). Surgeon and writer. Married Sydney Owenson in 1812. Author of *Sketches of the Philosophy of Life* (1818); *Sketches of the Philosophy of Morals* (1822).

MORGAN, Lady. *See* Owenson, Sydney.

MORPETH, Viscounts of, and Carlisle, Earls of. *See* Howard, Frederick and George.

MORRIS, Charles (1745–1838). A song writer of Welsh origin, who served as a soldier in America during the Revolution and wrote political songs for Fox's party. Author of *The Town and the Country*; *A Reason Fair to Fill My Glass*; and *The Triumph of Venus*.

MOSELEY, Benjamin (1742–1819). A physician who was appointed to the Royal Hospital in Chelsea in 1787.

MOUNT-EDGECUMBE, Lady (d. 1806). Wife of Richard Edgecumbe, second Earl of Mount-Edgecumbe.

MOXON, Edward (1801–58). Publisher, best known for his editions of outstanding writers of the age, including Mrs. Shelley's edition of Shelley's Poetry. He published work by Wordsworth, Southey, Lamb, Landor, and Browning. Moxon also brought out *The Prospect and Other Poems* (1826, a collection of his own poetry), and a volume of his sonnets (1837).

MULGRAVE, Barons and Earls of. *See* Phipps, Henry and Sir Constantine Henry.

MURRAY, John (1778–1843). London publisher. Called by Byron, whose works he published, 'the Arak of Publishers'. Also published Moore's *Life of Byron* and the works of other important writers of the day.

MURRAY, John III (1808–92). Son of John Murray, the publisher. Became head of the firm at his father's death. Published the works of Hallam, Gladstone, Lyell, Dean Stanley, Darwin, Livingstone, and others. Projected the series of Murray's *Handbooks for Travellers*.

MURRAY, William. Bessy Moore's brother-in-law, whose home was in Edinburgh.

MUSTERS, Mrs. (d. 1832). Formerly Mary Chaworth, Byron's first love. She married John Musters in 1805.

NAPIER, Macvey (1776–1847). Editor of the *Edinburgh Review* (1830–47).

NAPIER, Sir William Francis Patrick (1785–1860). General who served in Portugal (1809–11); wounded; retired in 1819; Lieutenant-governor of Guernsey (1842–7). Wrote *History of the Peninsular War* (1828–40), 6 vols., and *History of the Conquest of Scinde* (1844–6), a defence of his brother Sir Charles James's decision to annex the Sind.

NEWTON, Gilbert Stuart (1794–1835). British portrait-painter.

NORBURY, Earl of. *See* Toler, John.

NUGENT. An engraver who did a head of Anacreon for Moore.

O'CONNELL, Daniel (1775–1847). Irish national leader. Known as 'the Liberator'; united Irish Catholics into league to urge Irish claims; originated Catholic Association (1823); Member of Parliament (1828), but did not take seat until after Catholic Emancipation Act (1829); led agitation for abolition of tithes and of established church in Ireland; Lord Mayor of Dublin (1841); worked for repeal of Union of Great Britain and Ireland; re-created Catholic Association and held mass meetings (1842–3); arrested for seditious conspiracy (1843), but released (1844); power broken by opposition of revolutionaries of Young Ireland (1845); died at Genoa.

O'CONNOR, Arthur (1763–1852). Irish rebel. Member of the Irish Parliament; joined the 'United Irishmen' (1796); associated with Lord Edward Fitzgerald; went to France (1803); appointed general of a division by Napoleon.

OGLE, George (1742–1814). Irish statesman. Composer of 'Banna's Banks' and 'Shepherds, I Have Lost My Love', two popular songs; elected Irish Parliament (1768); Colonel in Irish Volunteers (1782); consistently and actively asserted the claim of Ireland to legislative independence.

O'NEILL, Eliza, later Lady Becher (1791–1872). One of the most talented actresses of the age. She was the daughter of an Irish actor and first appeared in Dublin in children's parts. Her greatest success was in tragic roles, including Mrs. Belvidera in Otway's *Venice Preserved*. She left the stage, after a brilliant career, in 1819, when she married William Wrixon Becher. On 17 May 1819, Moore recorded in his diary that he called on Miss O'Neill and 'was agreeably surprized by her sitting down to the harp and singing very sweetly and unaffectedly one of my songs' (Russell, ii. 310).

ORIGEN, surnamed Adamantius (185?–254?). One of the Greek Fathers of the Church. Wrote a defence of Christianity, entitled *Contra Celsum*, against attacks by the philosopher Celsus.

OTWAY, Sir Robert Waller (1770–1846). A native of Ireland, who rose to the rank of admiral and was created a baronet in 1831.

OUSELEY, Sir Frederick Arthur Gore (1825–89). Musician and composer. His work includes such pieces as *The Martyrdom of St. Polycarp* (1855), and *Hagar* (1873), two oratorios. He was also the author of three valuable treatises on musical theory: *A Treatise on Harmony* (1868);

A Treatise on Counterpoint, Canon, and Fugue (1869); and *A Treatise on Musical Form and General Composition* (1875).

OWENSON, Sydney, afterwards Lady Morgan (1783–1859). Novelist. Married Sir Thomas Charles Morgan (1812). Author of *St. Clair* (1804); *The Novice of St. Dominick* (1805); *The Wild Irish Girl* (1806). She also published *The Lay of an Irish Harp* in 1807.

PANIZZI, Sir Anthony (1797–1879). Librarian. Implicated in the conspiracy against the Modenese government and escaped to England (1823). Assistant Librarian at the British Museum (1831); Keeper of Printed Books (1837); Chief Librarian (1856–66). Edited Boiardo's *Orlando Innamorato* and Ariosto's *Orlando Furioso*.

PARKER, John, second Baron Boringdon and first Earl of Morley (1772–1840).

PARKINSON, Dr. Godfather to Moore's daughter Anastasia.

PARKYNS, George Augustus Henry Anne, second Baron Rancliffe (1785–1850). He married Elizabeth Mary, Lord Forbes's daughter.

PARR, Samuel (1747–1825). Classicist and one of Sheridan's teachers at Harrow. He was a political writer and strong supporter of the Whigs. Published *Characters of Fox* (1809). He was godfather to Moore's son Thomas, and Moore printed one of Parr's letters in the *Life of Sheridan*, i. 9.

PASTA, Giuditta (1798–1865). An Italian soprano.

PAULUS, Heinrich Eberhard Gottlob (1761–1851). A 'Rationalist' professor of theology at Heidelberg.

PEACH. A friend of Moore who lived at Leicester.

PECHLIN, Friedrich Christian von, Baron (1789–1863). Danish diplomat; envoy to Frankfurt (1825–46).

PEEL, Sir Robert (1788–1850). Statesman. Tory Member of Parliament and Under-secretary of War and Colonies; Chief Secretary for Ireland; First Lord of the Treasury; Chancellor of the Exchequer; Prime Minister (1834–5); Prime Minister again (1841). Among his contributions was the reorganization of the Bank of England, and removal of penal laws against Roman Catholics. Opposed O'Connell and Roman Catholic emancipation until forced by circumstances to propose it himself during his term as House Secretary (1821–7).

PERCEVAL, Spencer (1762–1812). Statesman. Solicitor-general (1801); Attorney-general (1802); opponent of Catholic emancipation; Chancellor of Exchequer (1807); Prime Minister (1809); made banknotes legal tender (1811); assassinated by John Bellingham, a broker.

PERRY, James (1756–1821). Editor and owner of the *Morning Chronicle* (1789–1819).

PERRY, William. An Englishman with whom Moore was associated during his residence in Paris (1820–1).

PETERSHAM, Viscount. *See* Stanhope, Charles.

PETTY-FITZMAURICE, Henry, third Marquess of Lansdowne (1780–1863). His amazing political career was begun at the age of 22, when he became a Member of Parliament from Calne, Wiltshire. He was

Chancellor of the Exchequer under Lord Grenville at 25. In November 1809, when he succeeded his brother as third Marquess of Lansdowne, he terminated his career in the House of Commons, but maintained his influence in the Whig Party in the House of Lords. Throughout his career he championed liberal causes, such as that of Roman Catholic emancipation (an issue which held his attention for several years). He also supported the relief bill for destitute Irish in 1847. In 1817 the Moores moved to Sloperton cottage, three miles from Bowood, the seat of the Marquess of Lansdowne, and a friendship developed which lasted throughout the last thirty-five years of Moore's life.

PHILLIPS, Thomas (1770–1845). English painter of historical scenes and portraits.

PHIPPS. A Fellow at Trinity College, Dublin, and Moore's tutor.

PHIPPS, Sir Constantine Henry, first Marquess of Normanby and second Earl of Mulgrave (1797–1863). Governor of Jamaica (1832–4); Lord Privy Seal (1834); Lord Lieutenant of Ireland (1835–9); Colonial Secretary (1839); Home Secretary (1839–41); Ambassador at Paris (1846–52); Minister at Florence (1854–8).

PHIPPS, Henry, third Baron Mulgrave, first Earl of Mulgrave, and Viscount Normanby (1755–1831). Military commander. Pitt's military adviser; Chancellor of the Duchy of Lancaster (1804); Foreign Secretary (1805–6); First Lord of the Admiralty (1807–10); Master of Ordnance (1810–18); Cabinet Member (1810–20). Patron of the arts.

PHOCION (402 ?–317 B.C.). Athenian general and statesman. Distinguished himself in the naval battles of Noxos (376); opposed anti-Macedonian policy in Athenian assembly; negotiated favourable terms for Athens after her defeat at Chaeronea by Philip of Macedon (338); after Alexander's death became virtual dictator in Athens under Antipater's domination; condemned to death by Democratic party in Athens on false charge of treason; executed (317).

PIGOT, Elizabeth (d. 1866). A friend of Byron while the poet was at Southwell. She has left an interesting account of her first meeting with him (*see LJ*, i. 32–33, and Willis Pratt, *Byron at Southwell*, Austin, 1948).

PLANCHÉ, James Robinson (1796–1880). English playwright and anti-quary of Hugenot descent. Author of *Amoroso, King of Little Britain* (1818); *The Vampyre* (1820); *Maid Marian* (1822); and *Court Favour* (1836). Translated and adapted plays for the English stage. Also well known for his knowledge of costume and heraldry.

PLUNKETT, Captain Edward. Captain in the Coldstream Regiment of Foot Guards.

PONSONBY, George (1755–1817). Brother to first Baron Ponsonby, a Whig leader. Chancellor of Irish Exchequer (1782); Lord Chancellor of Ireland (1806); leader of Whig opposition in House of Commons (1808–17).

PONSONBY, Sir John, Viscount Ponsonby (1770 ?–1855). Diplomat. Ambassador at Constantinople (1832–7), and at Vienna (1846–50).

PONSONBY, John William, fourth Earl of Bessborough and Viscount Duncannon (1781–1847). Whig leader in House of Commons (1805–34); Member of House of Lords (from 1834); Home Secretary (1834–5); Lord-lieutenant of Ireland (1846–7).

PONSONBY, Sir William (1772–1815). Soldier, who was killed leading the charge of the Union Brigade at Waterloo.

PORTLAND, Duke of. *See* Bentinck, William Henry Cavendish.

POWER, James. Music publisher who brought out Moore's *Irish Melodies*, *Sacred Songs*, and *National Airs*.

POWER, Richard. A friend of Moore who lived in Dublin. He was not related to the publishers, William and James Power.

POWER, William. Brother to James Power and a partner in the publishing business.

POWIS, Earl of. *See* Herbert, Edward.

RAIN, Mrs. A friend and neighbour while the Moores lived at Mayfield. Her residence was Wooten Hall.

RANCLIFFE, Baron. *See* Parkyns, George Augustus Henry Anne.

RANDALL, Edward Wadding, fourteenth Baron of Dunsany (1773–1819). Colonel in the Coldstream Guards.

RAWDON, Lady Charlotte. Sister of the Earl of Moira.

READY, Mrs. A friend whom the Moores visited at her home, Oakhanger Hall.

REES, Owen (1770–1837). One of the partners in the Longman publishing firm. He negotiated with Sheridan's son in arranging for the author's share of the profits for the *Life of Sheridan*.

RENOUARD, A. A. Translator. Translated Moore's *Epicurean* into French.

REYNOLDS, F. Mansel. Publisher. Editor of the *Keepsake*.

RICE, Thomas Spring (Lord Monteagle). A Member of Parliament of Moore's acquaintance. At one time he expressed a hope that Moore would stand for Parliament for Limerick (Russell, vi. 276).

RICHARDSON, John (1780–1864). Solicitor. Friend of Cockburn, Jeffrey, Campbell, and Scott. Practiced in Westminster as a parliamentary lawyer.

RIDGWAY. A publisher who attempted to get Sheridan to let him publish *School for Scandal*. Sheridan's reply was 'I have been nineteen years endeavouring to satisfy my own taste in this play, and have not yet succeeded'. Ridgway 'teased him for it no longer' (*see* Russell, ii. 302).

ROBINSON, Henry Crabb (1775–1867). English journalist and diarist. Friend of Lamb, Coleridge, Wordsworth, and Southey. Kept a voluminous diary and journal, part of which has been edited and published. Foreign correspondent and subsequently foreign editor of *The Times*.

ROGERS, Samuel (1763–1855). Poet. Author of *The Pleasures of Hope* (1792). Friend of Byron, Scott, Wordsworth, and Moore.

ROSS, Archibald. A captain in the nineteenth Regiment of Light Dragoons.

RUMBOLD, Lady. The wife of Sir William, third Baronet Rumbold (1788–1833).

RUSSELL, Francis, fifth Duke of Bedford (1765–1802). Attacked by Burke as 'the leviathan among the creatures of the crown'. He razed Bedford House, designed by Inigo Jones, and built Russell and Tavistock Squares in London about 1800.

RUSSELL, John, sixth Duke of Bedford (1766–1839). A Privy Councillor in 1806 and Lord-lieutenant of Ireland (1806–7).

RUSSELL, John, first Earl Russell of Kingston (1792–1878). Statesman, Whig leader, and writer. Editor of Moore's *Memoirs, Journal, and Correspondence* (1853–6); author of *The Life of William Lord Russell* (1819); *Memoirs of Affairs of Europe* (1824–9); and *Recollections and Suggestions* (1875). Prime Minister (1846–52; 1865–6).

RUTLAND, Duke of. *See* Manners, Robert.

RUTLAND, Duchess of, *née* Elizabeth Howard, daughter of the fifth Earl of Carlisle. She was the wife of Henry Manners, fifth Duke of Rutland (1778–1857).

RYAN, Daniel Frederick (1762?–98). Irish royalist killed by Lord Edward Fitzgerald when the latter was captured on 19 May 1798. Ryan was sent with Major Sirr to make the capture.

RYAN, D. F. Son of Daniel Frederick Ryan who was killed by Lord Fitzgerald. The son was a lawyer and an assistant secretary in the excise office, London.

RYDER, Dudley, first Earl of Harrowby and Viscount Saudon; also second Baron Harrowby (1762–1847).

SANDERS, Mr. and Mrs. Two of Moore's friends who lived at Bristol.

SCHENKL, Maurus v. (1749–1816). German Rationalist theologian.

SCOTT, Anne. Daughter of Sir Walter Scott.

SCOTT, John, first Earl of Eldon (1751–1838). Statesman. Member of Parliament (1782); supporter of Pitt; Solicitor-general (1788); Attorney-general (1793); Chief Justice of Common Pleas (1799); Lord High Chancellor of England (1801–6; 1807–27); opponent of Roman Catholic emancipation and parliamentary reform.

SCOTT, John (1783–1821). Journalist. Editor of the *Champion*; famous for his brilliant impressions of Paris in 1814 and 1815. Attacked *Blackwood* for its scurrilous satires. Challenged to a duel by Lockhart, the subsequent settlement of which was bungled so that Scott was accused of cowardice by Lockhart's friend C. H. Christie, whom Scott then challenged. In the duel Scott was mortally wounded and died in February 1821.

SCOTT, Sir Walter (1771–1832). Novelist and poet. Author of the *Waverley Novels*. Collaborated with Moore and Henry Mackenzie to write a *History of Scotland* for the *Cabinet Cyclopaedia*.

SCOTT, Sir William, Baron Stowell (1745–1836). Jurist. Brother of John Scott, first Earl of Eldon; friend of Dr. Johnson; Advocate General for Lord High Admiral (1782); Judge of Consistory Court (1788–1821); Privy Councillor (1798); Judge of the High Court of

Admiralty (1798–1828); authority on maritime and international law.

SCOTT-WARING (1747–1819). An agent of Warren Hastings and at one time major in the Bengal Division of the East India Company. His Blundering defence of Hastings in several pamphlets and in the House of Commons brought to prominence charges which might otherwise have been dropped.

SCULLY, Anne and John. Brother and sister, friends of the Moore family in Dublin. John Scully married Catherine Moore. Moore recorded in his diary (Russell, iv. 127) that Scully wrote a tract entitled 'Penal Laws'. See also Russell, ii. 165, where Moore gives an account of Scully's persuading the Shanavest rebels in Tipperary to turn over their arms to him, promising them that they would not be prosecuted if they did. He threw the arms in the river, for which he was reprimanded by the commander-in-chief, 'Thinking', writes Moore, 'that no one should keep faith with the rebels. Scully, however, differed with him, and he was right.'

SHARP, Sir Cuthbert (1781–1849). Antiquary. Served as cavalry officer in Ireland during rebellion (1799); visited Paris (1803) and was detained for some years as a prisoner of war; collector of customs at Sunderland and Newcastle upon Tyne; published antiquarian works, including *History of Hartlepool* (1816).

SHARPE, Richard (1759–1835). A wealthy hat manufacturer. Consistent Whig; Member of Parliament (1806–12). Because of his gregarious nature and enjoyment of society he became known as 'conversation Sharpe'. He published anonymously *Epistles in Verse* (1828), which was reproduced with additions in his *Letters and Essays*, and published with his name in 1834. Both Byron and Moore spelled the name 'Sharpe', although Prothero in the biographical note omits the final *e* (*LJ*, ii. 341–2).

SHEDDON. London merchant whose nephew was Moore's deputy in the Bermuda position as Registrar of the Naval Prize Court.

SHEE, Sir Martin Archer (1769–1850). Irish portrait-painter.

SHELLEY, Mary (1797–1851). Daughter of William Godwin and Mary Wollstonecraft Godwin. Wife of Percy Shelley. Author of *Frankenstein* (1818) and *The Last Man* (1826).

SHERIDAN, Charles Brinsley. Son of Richard Brinsley Sheridan.

SHERIDAN, Richard Brinsley (1751–1816). Irish dramatist and statesman. Moore's *Memoirs of the Life of . . . Richard Brinsley Sheridan* appeared in two volumes in 1825.

SHERIDAN, Thomas (1775–1817). Son of Richard Brinsley Sheridan. The son, also a dramatist, was the author of *Bonduca*, which was produced at Covent Garden on 3 May 1808. He became Colonial Treasurer at the Cape of Good Hope.

SHIRLEY, Robert Sewallis, Viscount Tamworth (1778–1824).

SHREWSBURY, Earl of. *See* Talbot, John.

SIDDONS, Mrs. Sarah, *née* Kemble (1755–1831). Actress famous for her tragic roles, including Lady Macbeth, Ophelia, and Desdemona.

SIDMOUTH, Viscount. *See* Addington, Henry.

SIMMONS. A printer who worked on Moore's *Life of Byron* for Murray.

SIRR, Major. A royalist who was sent with Daniel F. Ryan to arrest Lord Edward Fitzgerald on 19 May 1798. Sirr shot Fitzgerald in the right arm.

SMITH, Horace (1780–1849). Humorist and writer, best known, perhaps, for the *Rejected Addresses*, satires on addresses submitted to be read at Drury Lane Theatre, which he published with his brother James in 1812.

SMITH, Robert Archibald (1780–1829). Composer. Set some of his own verses to music and made collections such as *Devotional Music, Original and Selected* (1810), which included twenty-four of his own works. Gained renown by his settings of Tannahill's songs, especially 'Jessie, the Flower o' Dumblane' (1816). His *Scottish Minstrel, a Selection from the Vocal Melodies of Scotland Ancient and Modern, was* published in six volumes (1821–4). Among his other works are *Introductions to Singing* (1826); *Select Melodies* (1827); and *The Sacred Harmony of the Church of Scotland* (1820).

SMITH, Sydney (1771–1845). Canon of St. Paul's (1831–45). He started the *Edinburgh Review* with Jeffrey and Brougham. Noted for his sparkling wit, which made him a favourite among the Whigs. Wrote sixty-five articles for the *Edinburgh Review* and produced the *Peter Plymley Letters* in defence of Catholic emancipation (1807).

SMYTHE, Percy Sydney, sixth Viscount Strangford and first Baron Penhurst (1780–1855). Educated at Trinity College, Dublin, where Moore became acquainted with him. He published *Poems from the Portuguese of Camoëns* (1803).

SOMERSET, Lady Edward. Wife of Lord Robert Edward Henry Somerset (1776–1842).

SOUZA, Adèle Marie Émilie Filleul de (1761–1836). Widow of Comte de Flahaut, who was guillotined in 1793. In 1802 she married the Marquês José Maria de Souza Botello (1758–1825), a Portuguese diplomat. She was the author of several novels including *Eugène de Bothelin* (1808); *Eugénie et Mathilde* (1811); *La Comtesse de Fargy* (1822); and *Mademoiselle de Tournon* (1820).

SPENCER, Sir Brent (1760–1828). A major-general in the army.

SPENCER, John Charles, Viscount Althorp (1782–1845). Whig M.P. (1804); Junior Lord of Treasury (1806–7); leader of Whig opposition (1830); Chancellor of Exchequer (1830); helped carry Reform Bill (1832).

SPENCER, William Robert (1769–1834). Poet and wit. Younger son of the third Duke of Marlborough. He was a Whig and friend of Fox and Sheridan. His poetry (*The Year of Sorrow*, 1804; *Poems*, 1811) was admired by Byron, and his ballads, including *Beth Gélert*, were praised by Christopher North. It was probably he who secured the pistols for Moore's duel with Jeffrey (*see* Russell, i. 202 ff).

SPOTTISWODE, A. Publisher. Member of the firm of Spottiswode and Company.

STAËL, Anne Louise Germaine, *née* Necker (1766–1817). Mme de Staël, a French writer, whose salon Byron frequented while in Switzerland. She married Baron de Staël-Holstein, Swedish Minister to Paris; fled from France during the Revolution and was exiled by Napoleon; returned after 1815. Author of *Lettres sur le Caractère . . . de J. J. Rousseau* (1788); *Corinne* (1807); and other novels.

STANHOPE, Charles, fourth Earl of Harrington and Viscount Petersham (1780–1851).

STANHOPE, Mrs. Wife of Colonel Leicester Stanhope, later fifth Earl of Harrington (1784–1862), who was with Byron in Greece.

STANLEY, George Geoffrey Smith, fourteenth Earl of Derby (1799–1869), called Lord Stanley until 1851. Statesman. Member of Parliament (1820); Chief Secretary for Ireland (1830–3); Colonial Secretary (1833–4; 1841–4); Prime Minister (1852; 1858–9; 1866–8). He was also an accomplished classical scholar; translated the *Iliad* into blank verse (1864).

STARKEY, John, D.D. (1770–1834). Vicar of Bromham, near Sloperton Cottage, and close friend of the Moores.

STEVENSON, Sir John Andrew (1761–1833). Vicar-choral at St. Patrick's Cathedral, Dublin, and at Christ's Church. He was a composer of note who collaborated with Moore on the *Irish Melodies*, composed operas, and wrote musical scores for light farces produced on the Dublin stage.

STOWELL, Baron. *See* Scott, Sir William.

STRANGFORD, Viscount. *See* Smythe, Percy Sydney.

STRUTT, Joseph (1765–1844). First mayor of Derby under the Municipal Corporation Act of 1835. His gift of the arboretum to the city is noteworthy since it is an early instance of a gift of land for such a purpose. He was a patron of the arts and counted Maria Edgeworth among his literary friends.

SUETT, Richard (1755–1805). An actor to whom Moore read the libretto of *The Gipsy Prince*.

SUTHERLAND, Duke of. *See* Leveson-Gower, George Granville.

SWAYNE, Hugh. In 1802 Swayne was allowed to retire on full pay as a lieutenant-colonel in the Royal Irish Artillery.

TAAFFE, John. Friend of Byron and Shelley at Pisa; involved with them in the famous 'Pisan affray' with the Italian Serjeant-major Masi. Descendant of an old Irish Catholic family; came to Italy in 1815 after an unfortunate affair with a woman. In addition to his *Comment on the Divine Comedy* (1822), he wrote a poem entitled *Adelais* (1852), 2 vols., and *The History of the Holy, Military, Sovereign Order of St. John of Jerusalem* (1852), 4 vols. Taaffe was a Knight Commander in this Order.

TALBOT, Henry John Chetwynd, eighteenth Earl of Shrewsbury, third Earl and fifth Baron Talbot (1803–68). Admiral; captain of honorary corps of Gentlemen-at-arms.

TALBOT, Lady. Wife of John Chetwynd Talbot, Earl of Shrewsbury.

TALBOT, John, sixteenth Earl of Shrewsbury (1791–1852).

TALFOURD, Sir Thomas Noon (1795–1854). Judge, author, and Member of Parliament. Published Lamb's *Letters* (1837) and *Memorials* (1848); wrote a tragedy entitled *Ion* (1835), conceived in the Greek spirit.

TAMWORTH, Viscount. *See* Shirley, Robert Sewallis.

TAMWORTH, Lady. Wife of Robert Sewallis Shirley, Viscount Tamworth.

TAYLOR, John. Editor of the *Sun*.

TAYLOR, Sir Thomas, first Earl of Bective (1724–95). He was elevated to the peerage as Baron Headfort, of Headfort Meath; created Viscount Headfort in 1762; and advanced to an earldom as the Earl of Bective Castle in 1766. The lineage continued through his son Thomas, the first Marquess of Headfort.

TAYLOR, Watson. At the time Moore was a student at Trinity College, Dublin, Watson Taylor was secretary to Lord Camden and a friend of Moore's political opponents.

TEGART, Arthur. A physician who attended Moore's daughter Barbara before her death in 1817.

TEMPLE, Sir William (1628–99). English diplomat, statesman, and essayist. Among diplomatic triumphs was the bringing about of the triple alliance of England, Holland, and Sweden against France, for protection of Spain. Author of *Essay upon the Present State of Ireland* (1668); three volumes of *Miscellanea* (1680, 1692, 1701), including his best known essay, 'Of Ancient and Modern Learning'.

THALBERG, Sigismund (1812–71). Swiss piano virtuoso. Natural son of Prince von Dietrickstein; professional début (1827); composer of a concerto, a sonata, études, fantasies, and variations on opera themes.

THOMSON, Captain. Private secretary to Lord Moira.

THOMSON, George (1757–1851). A musician and collector of national airs. He issued three separate collections: Scottish airs in 6 vols. (1793–1841); Welsh airs in 3 vols. (1809–14); and Irish airs in 2 vols. (1814–16). In an effort to procure new words for the melodies, he corresponded with Burns, Scott, Hogg, Moore, Byron, Campbell, Joanna Baillie, and others. He wrote to Moore in May 1805 asking him to supply words for a trio of Welsh numbers. Although Moore promised several times to write the words, they were never forthcoming. Burns began to write for Thomson in 1792 and continued until his death in 1796. James Currie collected their correspondence, which can be found in several early editions of Burns's works. For a complete account of Thomson's correspondence with Moore and others *see* J. Cuthbert Hadden, *George Thomson, the Friend of Burns: His Life and Correspondence* (London, 1898).

TIERNEY, George (1761–1830). Political leader. As a Member of Parliament, he opposed Pitt's policies. Treasurer of the Navy in Addington's ministry (1802); President of the Board of Control (1806); Master of the Mint in Canning's ministry (1827–8).

TIGHE, Mary, *née* Blackford (1772–1810). Irish poetess, who married Henry Tighe in 1793. Best known for her poem *Psyche* (1805), which was written in the Spenserian stanza. Moore commemorated her death in 1810 in the fourth of the *Irish Melodies*: 'I saw thy form in youthful prime'.

TOLER, John, first Earl of Norbury (1745–1831). Chief Justice of the Court of Common Pleas.

TOMLINE, Sir George Pretyman (1750–1827). Bishop of Winchester; published the *Refutation of Calvinism* in 1811.

TOWNSHEND, John Thomas, second Viscount Sydney (1764–1831). Under-secretary of State for the Home Department (1783–9); Lord of the Admiralty (1789–93); and a Lord of the Treasury (1793–1800).

TOWNSHEND, John, fourth Marquess Townshend (1798–1863). Rear-admiral.

TRELAWNY, Edward John (1792–1881). Sailor and adventurer. Acquainted with Shelley and Byron in Italy; went with Byron to Greece; author of *Adventures of a Younger Son* (1831), and *Recollections of the Last Days of Shelley and Byron* (1858).

TUITE, Lady. Either the wife of Sir Henry Tuite, eighth Baronet, or Sir George Tuite, ninth Baronet. The former married Elizabeth Cobbe (d. 1850), grand-daughter of Charles Cobbe, Archbishop of Dublin. The latter married Janet Woodall (d. 1845), widow of Major Thomas Woodall, Twelfth Regiment of Foot.

VAN BUREN, Martin (1782–1862). Vice-president of the United States (1833–7); President (1837–41). Moore probably met Van Buren through Irving. On 4 April 1832, Moore recorded that he 'went to look for the American Secretary of Legation, through whom I wished to send a scrap of Byron's writing which I had promised to Van Buren, but could not find him'.

VANSITTART, Nicholas, first Baron Bexley (1766–1851). Chancellor of the Exchequer (1812–23).

VILLAMIL. A Spanish family with whom Moore was associated both in England and France. See the diary for the period 1819–21 for frequent references to visits with the Villamils. He was a guest at their estate at La Butte de Coaslin during the summer months of 1821.

VILLIERS, George Child, fifth Earl of Jersey and eighth Viscount Grandison (1773–1859).

VOITURE, Vincent (1597–1648). French court wit, poet, and man of letters. His *Works* were translated into English in 1736.

WAITHMAN, Sir Robert (1764–1833). A linen draper and a Member of Parliament mentioned in the diary (Russell, ii. 260): 'Talked of Sir R. Wilson's failure in his parliamentary début; and said the representative of the *commercial* talent of the country (meaning Waithman) had been just as promising in his commencement as he of the *military* had been unfortunate'.

WARD, John William, fourth Earl of Dudley and ninth Baron Ward (1781–1833). Byron said of him, 'Ward is one of the best-informed men I know, and in a *tête-à-tête*, is one of the most agreeable companions' (Lady Blessington, *Conversations*; quoted in *LJ*, ii. 82).

WARD, Robert Plumer (1765–1846). Novelist and writer on international law. Kept political diary from 1809. Author of *Tremaine, or The Man of Refinement* (1825); *De Vere, or The Man of Independence* (1827); and *De Clifford, or the Constant Man* (1841).

WARDLE, Gwllym Lloyd (1762–1833). In 1809 he was suspected of collusion with Mary Anne Clarke, who was on trial for accepting bribes to influence her lover, the Duke of York, in political matters.

WARREN, William. Known to the Moore family as 'Billy'. He was Catherine Moore's music teacher.

WELBORE, Henry, second Viscount Clifden (1761–1836).

WELLESLEY, Marquess. *See* Colly, Richard.

WELLINGTON, Duke of (1769–1852). British general and statesman.

WENTWORTH, Sir John (1737–1820). Governor of New Hampshire (1766–75) and of Nova Scotia (1792–1808).

WHITBREAD, Samuel (1758–1815). A Member of Parliament, who took much interest in rebuilding and reorganizing Drury Lane Theatre.

WICKHAM, William (1761–1840). At the time Moore was offered the Irish Laureateship, Wickham was Chief Secretary for Ireland, and it was through him that the offer was made.

WILKIE, Thomas. Printer associated with John Murray in the publication of Moore's *Memoirs of Richard Brinsley Sheridan* and the *Life of Byron*.

WILLIAM, Prince. *See* Ward, John William.

WILMOT, Mrs. Barbarina. *See* Dacre.

WINDHAM, William (1750–1810). Statesman. Friend of Dr. Johnson and Burke; Member of Parliament (1784–1810). On the outbreak of the French Revolution he turned reactionary and joined the cabinet under Pitt as Secretary of War (1794–1801); held Secretaryships of War and Colonial Office (1806–7).

WOLCOT, Dr. John (1738–1819). Writer of satiric verse which he published under the pseudonym 'Peter Pindar'.

WRIGHT, Frances. Married William Phiquepal D'Arusmont (1831), but was better known by her maiden name (1795–1852). Mary Shelley met her in Europe and received from her some interesting letters (see Jones, i. 366 n.). Among Frances Wright's many philanthropic ventures was an attempt in 1824 to settle freed slaves on a farm near Memphis, Tennessee. The scheme failed; the Negroes were sent to Haiti; and after a severe illness, Frances Wright returned to Europe. In 1829 she came back to America and took up residence at New Harmony, Indiana, Robert Dale Owen's colony.

WRIGHT, George Newnham (1790?–1877). Editor of philosophical writings, among which were the works of George Berkeley (1843), and the works of Thomas Reid (1843).

WYNNE, William Watkin Edward (1801–80). Antiquary. Received Hengwart collection of manuscripts as a bequest (1859); published catalogue of its contents in *Archaeologia Cambrensis* (1869–71). Other works include notes to Meyrick's edition of Dwnn's *Heraldic Visitation of Wales* (1846); to Breece's *Kalendars of Gwynedd* (1873); and to *The History of the Gwydr Family* (1878).

YORK, Duke of. Frederick Augustus, Duke of York and Albany (1763–1827), second son of George III and Queen Charlotte.

YORKE, Philip, third Earl of Hardwicke (1757–1834). Lord Lieutenant of Ireland under Addington until 1804, and later under Pitt until 1806.

ZHUKOVSKI, Vasili Andreevich (1783–1852). Russian poet. Tutor to Alexander II (from 1818); friend of Pushkin; noted for innovations in poetical language and for his translations of German and English poetry. Author of the words to the Russian National Anthem, 'God Save the Czar'.

INDEX

Abbotsford, 544, 762, 778, 817.
Aberdeen, Lord, 417.
Ackroyds, 277, 372.
Acres, Bob (*The Rivals*), 170, 378.
Act of Agrarian Protection, riots connected with, 358.
Act of Union of 1800, effort to repeal, 707.
Adams, Dr., 569.
Adams, Mr., 397.
Addington, Henry, 93.
Addison, William, 304.
Agrippa, Cornelius, 310.
Aikin, Lucy, *Memoirs of Court of James I*, 879.
Akenside, Mark, *Pleasures of Imagination* quoted, 71.
Albany, N.Y., 71.
Alexandrine, Princess, 886.
Alfred (Byron's club), 170.
'All the Talents' Administration', 169.
Allan, William, proposed as candidate for Royal Academy, 528, 529.
Althorp, John Charles Spencer, Viscount, 293, 584.
Anacharsis en Grece, 13.
Anacreon, Nugent begins head of, 16.
'Anacreon Moore', mentioned in *Morning Post*, 35.
'Anacreontic dinner', Moore attends with Bowles, 475.
'Ancient Music', concert at King's court, 25.
Angelina, liaison with Byron, 665.
Anglesey, Lord, 718.
Annals of Innisfallen, 858.
Annual Register, The, 457.
Anthologia Hibernica, letter to editor of, sending first published poem, 1.
Antonio, Nicolas, *Bibliotheca Hispana nova*, 37.
Arabian Nights, 334.
Archdall, Major Richard, 18.
Argile, Lady, 131.
Aristaenetus, 456.
Aristotle, 467.
Arkwright, Richard, Moore uses franking privilege, 382.
Arkwright, Mrs. Robert, 583, 594.
Arkwrights (Moore's neighbours in Derbyshire), 263, 286.
Arnold, Samuel James, 157, 160.
Artists' Fund Dinner, 900.
Arundel, 583.
Asgill, Lady, 417.

Ashbourne, Derbyshire: Moore takes cottage near, 259; 260; comparison with Kegworth, 261; public dinner at, 287; 292, 293, 581.
Ashbourne Ball, Moore as steward of, 281.
Ashbourne Hall (Lord Boothby's estate), 263.
Ashe, Andrew, 204.
Ashe, Mrs. Andrew, 236.
Ashe, Thomas, 642.
Ashley, Lady B., 241.
Asmodeus, 300.
Astley, Philip, 366.
Athenaeum, 625.
Athol, Duchess of, 35.
Atkinson, Captain Joseph, 7; Moore sends proposal for *Odes of Anacreon* to, 17; 24, 28, 30; second edition of *Poems of Thomas Little* dedicated to, 34; 38; procures Moore offer of Irish Poet Laureateship, 42; 46, 51, 53, 54, 55, 58, 59, 62; makes arrangements for John Moore's appointment, 98; 106, 111, 114; to write Prologue to Lady Morgan's *First Attempt*, 115; 154, 193, 233, 281–2, 317; visits brother-in-law in Derbyshire, 318; 325, 371, 398, 402, 408; death, 457, 460.
Atkinson, Mr. and Mrs. Joseph, 117, 122.
Auckland, Lord, 570.
Auckland, Lord and Lady, 866.
Audrey (*As You Like It*) quoted, 839.
Aungier Street, 1.
Austen, Jane: *Emma* praised by Moore, 396; Moore requests copy of *Persuasion*, 435.
Austria, 128.
Azores, Moore's visit to, 48.

Bach, Johann Sebastian, 350.
Bagshaw, Sir W., 372.
Bailey, 655.
Baillet, H., *Critique de Savants*, 37.
Baillie, Dr. Matthew, attends Moore in illness, 19; 135.
Bain, Dr., 555.
Ballantyne, James (Scott's associate in printing business), 123, 551.
Ballater, 614.
Banim, Michael, 755.
Bankes, William, Moore's epigram on, 653.

Index

Blessington, Lord, 611; Byron's allusions to, 744.

Blessington, Lady: recollections of Byron, 661-2; Moore's apology to, for not sending *Life of Byron*, 691; contributions to *Life of Byron*, 692; *The Book of Beauty*, 785.

Bloomfield, Hannah, sends father's poems to Moore, 528.

Blücher, G. L. von, 322.

Boileau, 185; works of, 248-9.

Bolingbroke, 150.

Bonaparte, Jerome: Moore sees, in New York, 64; 65; French frigates come to 'steal him away', 69.

Bonaparte, Lucien, Moore asked, to translate his poem *Charlemagne*, 164.

Bonaparte, Napoleon, 91; the 'Grand Thresher', 110; 111, 163, 175; abuse of, in Code's *Spanish Patriots*, 214; 287, 289, 296; defeat of, 311, 366-7, 373; Moore's opinion of, 355; account of meeting with the Royal Army, 356; 358, 600.

Bonaparte, Napoleon II, 366-7.

Booth, Mrs. (landlady), 145.

Boothby, Sir B., 263.

Boringdon, Lord and Lady, 347, 348.

Borodino, battle of, 725.

Boroughes, 154.

'Boston' frigate, 69.

Boswell, James, *Life of Johnson* quoted, 672.

Bottom (*A Midsummer Night's Dream*), quoted, 357-8.

Bourbon, Constable, 209.

Bourbon, Duke of, 155.

Bourbons, 317.

Bourke, Madame de, 679.

Bow Street, Moore and Jeffrey taken to, after duel, 103.

Bowles, William Lisle: objects to Moore's title for *Epistles, Odes, and Other Poems*, 40; visit of, 431; Moore's mixed opinion of, 441-2; 460; pamphlets by, 475; 481; alliance with *Blackwood's*, 507; criticism of Moore's books, 539; attacked by *Quarterly Review*, 540; expresses interest in Moore's *Life of Sheridan*, 546; Hobhouse's verses on, 590 n.; invited to join committee for Byron monument, 606-7; 803; accompanies Moore to Clifton, 804; invites Moore to meet Southey, 806; subscribes to work on Archbishops, 825.

Bowles, Rev., and Mrs. William Lisle, 455.

Bowles, Mrs. William Lisle, 539, 807.

Bowood (estate of the Marquess of Lansdowne), 511, 527, 536, 543, 579, 583, 630, 655-6, 777, 788, 815; gay 'conclave' at, 818, 820; 826, 840-1, 874.

Bowring, Sir John, 492, 604; correspondence with Byron, 606; 608; Moore's compliment to, 610; attacks Moore in *Westminster*, 689.

Boyd, Stuart, *Selected Passages of St. Chrysostom*, 330.

Boyle Farm, Moore's conversation with Hobhouse at, 581-2.

Boyntun, Mrs., 455.

Boyse, 799.

Brabant, Dr. R. H., 599, 611; on list of presentations for book, 672; Moore indebted to, 730; 792; proposed as tutor for Mary Shelley's son, 796-7.

Bradshaw, Lord, 362.

Brady, Captain, 151.

Braham, John: Moore plans to write song for, 137; plays *M.P.* at Bath, 164; Moore writes song for, 208; Moore would collaborate with, on musical drama, 304.

Branigan, Mr., 418, 420, 422, 440.

Branigan, Mrs., 413, 464, 535, 703, 901.

Bremhill (Bowles's vicarage), 489-90, 765, 806.

Brereton, Jane, epigram quoted, 293, 607.

Briareus, 365, 502.

Bride of Abydos, The, 287; anticipates Moore's *Lalla Rookh*, 289.

Briers, Mrs., 114.

Britton, John, 561.

Brochman, Johann Heinrich, 792.

Broglie, Duc de, 810.

Brookes's, 899.

Brougham, Henry Peter, Lord: Byron's dislike of, 498; 499, 507-8, 644, 694, 726; pamphlet in defence of, 802; 841.

Brown, Captain, 12.

Brown, John, 876-7 n.

Brown, Thomas the Younger (Moore's pseudonym), 36, 256-7, 277, 394, 513, 739.

Brownlow, Lord, 656.

Brownrigg, 15.

Brummel, George Bryan, Rogers's joke on, 396; 600.

Bryan, 146, 237-8; Moore's strictures on conduct of, 303; role in Catholic Emancipation question, 307; Moore's visit with, 366; 369.

Index

Index

Gulley and Gregson, 169.
Gulnare (character in *The Corsair*), 305.
Gursyone boys, 757.
Guy's Greece, 542.

Hainault, Countess of, 329.
Halhed, Nathaniel, 462.
Halifax, 68–69, 75, 80.
Hall, 13.
Hall, John E., sends *Lay Preacher* to Bessy Moore, 458.
Hall, Samuel Carter, 666, 667.
Hallam, Henry, 533, 789.
Hamilton, Colonel (consul in Norfolk): hospitality accorded Moore, 50; Moore lodging with, 51; 53, 57, 61, 68, 82, 200, 210, 288.
Hamilton, Mrs., kindness of, 67.
Hammersley, 25, 140, 141.
Hancock, Charles, receives copy of *Life of Byron*, 679.
Handel, George F., 142; arrangement of songs, 432.
Hannah (maid in Moore household), 647.
Hanson, John, projects biography of Byron, 526.
Harden, 7.
Hardwicke, Lord, 120.
Harley, Lady June and Charlotte, 634.
Harness, Mr., 737.
Harrington, Lord, 83.
Harrington, Lady: gave Moore ticket for 'Ancient Music' concert, 25; 27, 91, 131.
Harrington, Lord and Lady, 109, 112, 326, 327.
Harrow, 734.
Harrowby, Lord and Lady, 347, 348.
Harwood, Mrs., 19.
Hastings, Sir Charles, 252; adverse comment on Napoleon, 289.
Hastings, Lady, 417, 824.
Hastings, Lord (Moira), 581.
Hastings, Warren, 462.
Haydn, Joseph, 88, 198, 207.
Haydon, Benjamin Robert: sends Moore pamphlet on Hunt, 597, 602; success as lecturer and painter, 863.
Hayley, William, Moore received letter from, 105.
Haymarket, production at, 486.
Hayward, A., works by, 791.
Headfort, Marchioness of, 702; *Irish Melodies* dedicated to, 784.
Heath (editor of *The Keepsake*), 614.
Heffleton, 557.
Helsham, Fanny, Moore's inquiry about, 439.

Hemans, Mrs., 'Far from My Own Bright Land', 583.
Henry VIII, 792.
Herbert, Algernon, Moore plans review of his *Nimrod*, 772, 779.
Herbert, James D., 10, 155.
Hereford, Dean of, 861.
Heyne, Christian G., edition of Virgil's works, 248–9.
Heywood, John, *Proverbs*, 658.
Hickson, 296.
Highbury, 311, 899.
Highgate, 279.
Hill, Mr., 493.
Hobart: travels with Moore, 13; takes lodging in same house with Moore, 15; 32.
Hobhouse, John Cam: Moore to request information from, 542; Moore offers to collaborate with on *Life of Byron*, 544–5; opposed to Moore's *Life of Byron*, 548–9, 550–3; believes Byron's will to contain information regarding Memoirs, 550; waives claim on papers in Barry's possession, 581; offers little assistance to Moore, 587; sends Moore's letters to Byron, 588; suppressed passage in Moore's letter to Byron, 588; *Imitations and Translations*, 588–9; beneficiary in Byron's will, 595; 598; attitude toward biography of Byron, 606; 607, 633, 659; procures Moore's son cadetship, 841, 845.
Hoche, Louis, 716.
Hodgson, Francis, 165, 166, 167, 594; beneficiary in Byron's will, 595.
Hohenlohe, Prince of (Alexander Leopold), reputation as miracle worker, 548.
Holland House, 105–6, 175–6, 280, 285, 417, 475, 497, 511, 655; Moore's inability to work there, 656; 676, 689, 775, 891.
Holland, Lord, 148, 168, 177, 243, 293; reads *Lalla Rookh*, 421–2; advises Moore concerning Memoirs, 497; 499; Moore requests conversation about Sheridan, 535–6; Moore requests Sheridan's letter to King from, 536; on Byron's manner in the House of Lords, 628 n.; Byron's letters to, 654; 666; praises *Life of Byron*, 683; 810.
Holland, Lady: surmises upon Augusta–Byron relationship, 498; 536, 654, 656.
Holland, Lord and Lady, 840.

Index

Index

(980)

Index

Index

PRINTED IN GREAT BRITAIN
AT THE UNIVERSITY PRESS, OXFORD
BY VIVIAN RIDLER
PRINTER TO THE UNIVERSITY